CORRECTIONS

The Science and the Art

CORRECTIONS
The Science and the Art

LEE H. BOWKER
University of Wisconsin, Milwaukee

Macmillan Publishing Co., Inc.
NEW YORK

Collier Macmillan Publishers
LONDON

Macmillan Publishing Co., Inc.
866 Third Avenue, New York, New York 10022

Collier Macmillan Canada, Ltd.

Library of Congress Cataloging in Publication Data

Bowker, Lee Harrington.
  Corrections, the science and the art.

  Bibliography: p.
  Includes index.
    1. Corrections—United States. 2. Criminal
justice, Administration of—United States.
3. Corrections. 4. Criminal justice, Administration of. I. Title.
HV9304.B68   365'.973   81–6056
  ISBN 0–02–313140–3   AACR2

Printing: 1 2 3 4 5 6 7 8   Year: 2 3 4 5 6 7 8 9

Preface

Corrections: The Science and the Art has been written with three general principles in mind. First, the text is based on the latest scientific research, which is documented in the references for each chapter. The use of technical jargon in presenting research findings has been carefully controlled, in keeping with the educational level of the students who will be using the book. Descriptions of interesting, innovative or typical programs are balanced by evaluations of the programs where possible.

The second principle followed in *Corrections: The Science and the Art* is that contemporary American corrections should be placed in proper perspective along a number of dimensions, the major ones being historical, philosophical, political, ideological, and cross-cultural. There are special chapters on the history of corrections, philosophies of corrections, the setting of corrections in the criminal system and the larger political system, critiques of corrections, and international corrections. In addition, many of these materials are integrated in the other chapters of the text. The introduction of philosophical and humanistic perspectives into various discussions helps to remind us that corrections is an art as well as a science.

The final principle guiding the writing of this text is that there should be solid coverage of a number of contemporary trends in correctional scholarship and practice. For the first time in a corrections text, correctional officers are given "equal billing" with prisoners and administrators. Among the topics given substantial coverage at various points in the text are: women, racial and cultural minorities, unions, advanced correctional programs in other nations, the increasing impact of the public, legislators and state corrections administrators on correctional practice, the development of correctional standards, the accreditation movement, victimization in correctional institutions, scientific evaluations of correctional programs, and critiques of the correctional establishment that are based on nontraditional views of the field. Those materials balance the traditional elements of corrections that are covered in this text, as they are in other treatments of the subject.

I would like to express my appreciation to Leo Carroll and Ron Huff, who read and creatively criticized the entire manuscript, and to Jim Sprowls, Carl Pope, John Conley and Bill Feyerherm, who contributed their ideas to the conception and organization of the manuscript. They caught many of my errors and oversights. The remaining ones are my responsibility alone. I would also like to acknowledge my indebtedness to MaryAnn Riggs, who spent endless hours producing the manuscript on the Wang word processing system, and to Dorothy Brostowicz and Penny Thornton, who helped with the typing on numerous occasions. The ability to produce an organized manuscript directly from tape is, like corrections, an art as well as a science.

Contents

Contents

Part I
Corrections as a Social Institution

Chapter 1

An Overview of Corrections in America

The academic discipline of corrections consists of the study of convicted criminals and their processing in the criminal justice system. There are three major parts in the criminal justice system. The police identify suspects and bring them to the attention of the courts. The courts try suspects and make a determination as to whether or not they are guilty of the crime charged. If suspects are found guilty, they are sentenced to be punished or "treated" for their crimes, whereupon they enter the province of corrections. During most of history, passage through the correctional system was as brief as a trip to the scaffold. Today, a succession of institutional reforms has resulted in a correctional apparatus which is much more complex and certainly more humanitarian. It is this apparatus and its effect on offenders that are the subjects for this book.

The title of this text is *Corrections: The Science and the Art.* Is this a contradiction in terms? It is not, and the reason is partly historical. Art is the use of imagination and talent to produce individualized outcomes. Until the last decade or two, we did not know enough about the bases of human behavior to provide much scientific guidance to correctional workers trying to ameliorate the grinding brutality of correctional systems. Consequently, their work was more of an art than a science. Correctional innovators did not create beautiful vases or symphonies, but they showed an artistic imagination in working with offenders. Each offender, as an individual, was unique; so the architects of innovative correctional programs had to adapt to a wide variety of offender characteristics and situations.

As sociological data about human behavior accumulated, these were brought to bear upon correctional systems. The science of corrections arose when these findings of outside research were combined with the results of research carried out within correctional institutions. Except for a few pioneering studies, this codification did not occur until the 1960s.

3

We now have a burgeoning science of corrections exemplified by myriad research projects, university courses of study, training academies and in-service training sequences for correctional workers, and the day-to-day activities of many correctional administrators and treatment staff. On the other hand, correctional officers (guards), houseparents, and other lower-level correctional workers not requiring a college education are exposed to correctional science only as it is conveyed to them in training and by their supervisors. Their work—which still comprises the largest segment of all correctional work—continues to be carried out primarily as an art. Even at the administrative level, correctional science does not always have the answers to problems that arise in the correctional system. The result is that administrators and ancillary treatment personnel use scientific findings in dealing with some situations, while in others they rely on their "artistic judgment"—which they often call "gut feelings"—to make decisions. Because penal corrections requires the application of abstract theories to concrete individuals in unique situations, there is a sense in which it will always be an art.

THE STRUCTURE OF CORRECTIONS

The Law Enforcement Assistance Administration published the *Dictionary of Criminal Justice Data Terminology*[3] in 1976. This dictionary proposed standard terms and definitions to be used in describing the activities of criminal justice agencies in the United States. The typology of correctional agencies proposed in this dictionary is the clearest and most comprehensive outline available to us, so we have used it as the model for our discussion in this section.

Figure 1.1 presents a typology of public correctional agencies in graphic form. Most diagrams containing arrows refer to the flow of offenders from one agency to another. This is not true in Figure 1.1. The arrows in this figure represent breakdowns in the taxonomy of correctional agencies. That is to say, the four arrows leading from public correctional agencies to probation agencies, parole agencies, correctional facilities, and correctional day programs indicate that these are the four types of public correctional agencies, and the two arrows leading from correctional facilities to confinement facilities and community facilities indicate that these are the two types of correctional facilities that exist. The chart is greatly simplified, since some kinds of facilities—such as camps, ranches, and farms—can be classified under more than one type, depending upon the characteristics of each individual institution. It is not possible to depict these complexities here without adding to the confusion that Figure 1.1 is intended to dispel.

There are three basic types of correctional agencies, all of which are primarily the province of government at the federal, state, and local levels. These are probation, parole, and correctional facilities.

Probation agencies, which are often called probation departments, supervise convicted adults and adjudicated juveniles. An adult who has been found guilty may be sentenced to probation instead of a fine or a stay in a correctional

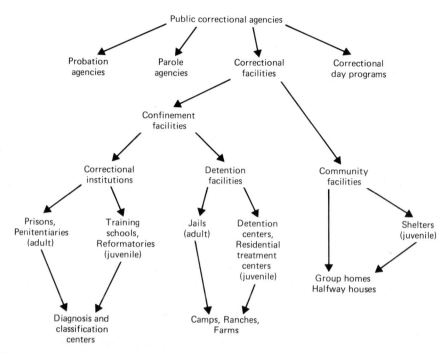

Figure 1.1 A typology of public correction agencies. (Adapted from: Law Enforcement Assistance Administration, *Directory of Criminal Justice Data Terminology*. Washington, D.C.: Government Printing Office, 1976.)

facility. Probation agencies perform a wider variety of functions for juveniles than they do for adults. They perform intake functions for the juvenile court, investigating cases before they are adjudicated as well as supervising juveniles after adjudication.

Parole agencies differ from probation agencies in that they supervise offenders who have already served sentences in correctional facilities, rather than supervising offenders who have been sentenced to probation only. There are two qualifications to this definition. The first is that, in some states, probation and parole functions may both be exercised by the same department. The second qualification is that offenders sentenced to probation may already have served considerable time in jail prior to trial because of inability to post bail. (In unusual cases, they may have accumulated more jail time than offenders who have served institutional sentences and are now released on parole.) Parole agencies are charged with ensuring that parolees conform to the stipulations of their parole agreements, and that they regularly report to the agency so that there can be a continuing record of their conduct.

Both probation and parole are community corrections activities, in that they do not house their clients in residential facilities. Two other types of community corrections programs are the correctional day program and community facilities. Correctional day programs permit offenders to live at home and offer them daily activities administered from a central office. Community facilities house offenders overnight and release them during the day for training or occupational activities.

Community facilities are one of the three broad classifications of correctional facilities. A correctional facility is a building or group of buildings, often enclosed by a wall or fence, in which offenders live. If the offenders regularly depart from the facility during the day for work or education, then it is a community facility. If their work or educational activities occur within the facility, then it is a confinement facility. Community facilities are generally located in cities so that offenders can be close to the education and work programs in which they are involved during the day. Some of the kinds of agencies referred to as community facilities are halfway houses, group homes, and shelters.

Halfway houses are designed for individuals who need more supervision than they can receive on probation, or for those who have just concluded a period of confinement and are not yet ready for complete reintegration into the community. Most halfway houses are privately operated, although funding is largely from government sources. Group homes are similar to halfway houses, except that they are much smaller, and are designed to provide as natural a family experience as possible to adjudicated adults and juveniles. Shelters are community facilities for juveniles, primarily for those who have not yet been adjudicated. Facilities such as shelters, along with the intake functions of probation agencies, are generally thought of as being part of the corrections system, but are really in the province of the courts because they are used prior to adjudication. Residential treatment centers are facilities for juveniles who do not require the strict confinement of a training school or reformatory. Many of these facilities are essentially community facilities, while others have the characteristics of detention facilities.

A detention facility is a correctional facility that confines adults and juveniles prior to adjudication and also houses adults who have been sentenced to a year or less of confinement. In some cases, ajudicated juveniles are also included in detention facilities, a practice which the Office of Juvenile Justice and Delinquency Prevention is making major efforts to eliminate. Adult detention facilities are generally known as jails, but some county farms and work camps are also classified as detention facilities. Detention centers are juvenile detention facilities limited to juveniles who are in custody pending disposition by the courts. In practice, some of these facilities mix preadjudicated with sentenced youth. Road camps, ranches, county farms, and a number of other vaguely defined confinement facilities are hard to classify. They may hold adults whose sentences are a year or less, in which case they are detention facilities; or they may hold adults who have longer sentences, in which case they are correctional institutions. If they hold only committed juveniles, they are classified as juvenile correctional institutions.

Correctional institutions confine adults who are serving sentences of more than one year and juveniles who have been committed to confinement after a juvenile disposition hearing. Most adult correctional institutions are called prisons or penitentiaries. Like detention facilities, they may release a small proportion of prisoners during the day for educational of occupational activities, but the majority of their occupants are restricted to the correctional facility 24 hours a day. A diagnosis or classification center is a specialized correctional institution in which individual evaluations are performed to determine in what facility a person's sentence should be served, or perhaps to what programs a person should be assigned. In many correctional systems, classification centers are units within correctional institutions rather than separate institutions.

Juvenile corrections facilities are primarily used for delinquents who have been committed to confinement after a juvenile disposition hearing. Despite activities to remove status offenders (juvenile delinquents whose offenses would not be crimes if they were committed by adults) from correctional institutions, many still remain in 1980. Sometimes known as training schools, reform schools, reformatories, or by other names, these correctional institutions are not limited to individuals serving more than a year in confinement. The crucial elements in the definition of a juvenile correctional institution are that the young people are rarely released to go into the community even on a temporary basis and that they have already been processed by the courts and received a judicial disposition.

THE SOCIAL THERAPY PROGRAM

One of the most interesting things about being involved in corrections is the possibility of participating in the devising or implementation of innovative correctional programs. One of the questions that this book will try to answer is what students and other citizens not currently employed in the field of corrections can do to help. As an example of this—and to illustrate the possibilities for creative programming in correctional work—this section describes the Social Therapy Program, an experimental program for violent drug abusers in a maximum security prison that was staffed almost entirely by volunteers and directed by the author in the early 1970s.

The program started with approximately 20 community adults and 30 students from Whitman College, co-sponsor of the project with the Washington State Penitentiary. These volunteers were intensively trained in January, 1972, just before the program opened. The core of the training sequence was a 50-hour block of time spread over six days. This training included theoretical material about the structure and culture of the prison, descriptions of other prison programs, didactic sessions on Reality Therapy, lectures by prisoners and staff from the Washington State Penitentiary, and a complete day spent inside the prison. The prison day began with wake-up and ended with lock-up, including some time locked alone in the cells for each volunteer.

There was severe political conflict among prisoners and between prisoners and the Superintendent over assigning a tier to the Social Therapy Program. The harsh realities of the dependence of prisoner political processes on violence soon became obvious to everyone. It was some time before the destructive aspects of prison life became muted on the tier, and they never disappeared entirely.

The program continued to recruit and train volunteers, and soon was delivering approximately 200 hours of service per week to the prisoners. Volunteers performed administrative functions, joined with prisoners in group therapy, and joined in a wide range of other activities on the tier. In a typical week, each prisoner participated in ten hours of group therapy, ten hours of social activities, and additional contact with volunteer administrators such as the director, therapy supervisors, and consultants.

Treatment Model

While most drug programs operate on a medical model that says the addict is sick, Social Therapy utilized a sociological model that did not deny the existence of psychological problems, but concentrated on the acquisition of social skills by drug users. Most drug users in the program were "knick-knack" drug users who were willing to use any drug they could get their hands on in order to "get kicks."

Therapy groups were organized around the model of William Glasser's[2] theory of Reality Therapy.* The past is ignored, and the potential that the future holds is emphasized. Clients are urged to be honest about their conduct and its consequences, and to accept responsibility for their own conduct. They are expected to be realistic about what changes they need to make in their conduct in order to achieve their personal goals. Volunteers participating in the Reality Therapy group sessions with prisoners were as likely to gain self-understanding as were the prisoners themselves. The sessions consisted of an exchange of insights rather than a one-way street. Specially trained prisoner group leaders kept the groups moving and focused on current behavior rather than "war stories" and excuses from the past, two categories of conversation that normally dominate prisoner–volunteer interaction.

In addition to the therapy groups, volunteers participated with prisoners in social activities such as informal discussions, games, and arts and crafts sessions of all kinds. The Social Therapy Program operated on the philosophy that extensive contact with "straight" people would provide highly criminalized drug abusers with both alternative role models to destructive drug use and the opportunity to acquire the social skills with which to play conventional roles, thus increasing their ability to remain law-abiding upon release should they choose to do so.

Because many drug users associate esthetic pleasure with psychoactive drug use, an extensive program of art therapy was designed with funding provided by the Washington State Arts Commission. Arts and crafts materials produced by prisoners were sold at county fairs in order to replenish the initial funding provided by the Arts Commission. Unfortunately, state laws forbade any other type of sales off the prison grounds, and this greatly limited the income potential of the prisoners. Arts and crafts work, participation in therapy groups, basic clean-up and maintenance tasks, educational and vocational classes, and specific program projects such as the renovation of limited areas in the prison were designed to fully occupy the prisoners in the equivalent of a 40- to 60-hour work week.

William Glasser, head of the Institute for Reality Therapy, has observed that volunteers are often more effective than paid staff members because they are not

---

*For an evaluation of Reality Therapy as a therapeutic modality, see Alexander Bassin, Thomas E. Bratter, and Richard L. Rachin: *The Reality Therapy Reader: A Survey of the Work of William Glasser, M.D.* New York: Harper and Row, 1976.

caught in the system. The prisoners know that secrets told to volunteers will not be produced and used against the prisoners at later disciplinary hearings, classification committee meetings, or parole board hearings. As a result, rapport is more easily established, involvement can be deeper, and the therapeutic process has the potential of being more successful than would be likely with paid staff members.[1] Although this conclusion does not do justice to the many excellent paid therapists in prison work who are able to overcome the disadvantages of working in total institutions and to achieve an extremely effective level of help to prisoners, Glasser is correct in pointing out that volunteers have a great deal to offer to correctional programs.

The Decline of the Social Therapy Program

The Social Therapy Program continually sought grant funds from the beginning of its operation. Although three small grants were received, it was never possible to find a source of funds for continuing administrative costs. There was always an ample supply of student volunteers, usually enough nonprofessional community adults, and almost never enough trained professionals to supervise and train them. The result was that those professionals who took on administrative responsibilities in the program became overworked and tended to "burn out." The early success of the program was based on an unrealistically high level of donated professional staff time. In a number of cases, this exceeded 20 hours per week per professional. As professionals began to reduce their commitments to the program so that they could carry on normal activities in other areas of their lives, it was necessary to decrease the number of student volunteers that could be accommodated in the program. It was no longer possible to do extensive work-ups on each prisoner for presentation to the parole board. With fewer professionals spending time on the tier, the conduct of some of the prisoners began to deteriorate. When it became clear that the Washington State Department of Institutions would not provide supportive funding for administrative costs, there was a sharp decline in morale. After 1975, the program was reduced to a prisoner self-help program, with relatively limited input from community professionals, and only several evenings per week of therapy and related activities with college students and community adults.

Evaluation

Approximately 500 volunteers participated in the Social Therapy Program between 1972 and 1975. Nearly 100 were community adults, professors, and mental health professionals, and the other 400 were college students from five different institutions. Approximately 250 of the volunteers stayed with the program for at least 12 months, and each of them delivered a minimum of 100 hours of service to the prisoners. The total number of hours of donated service by all program volunteers exceeded 50,000 in 36 months.

It was impossible to continue to provide 50 hours of training to each new volunteer once the initial cohort of volunteers had begun work. Instead, a training library of books, reprints, audio tapes and videotapes was created to aid in the training of volunteers. Small groups met to be exposed to the tapes and discuss readings with an experienced trainer on a regular basis, and new volunteers were also integrated into the weekly in-service training meetings. While this training sequence was as good as one might hope for in an all-volunteer program, there were difficulties with on-going supervision and screening. There were not always enough trained supervisors to carry on supervisory meetings on a weekly basis, and the screening of volunteers was not done carefully enough until the penitentiary hired a full-time volunteer coordinator.

Because no formal recidivism studies or other post-prison adjustment studies were carried out with program graduates, the only program evaluation attempted was an impressionistic analysis of how the men changed while incarcerated. When the Social Therapy Program began, the residents would get "stoned" every night in order to face the volunteers. Middle-aged men with long records of violence were actually fearful of having friendly discussions with college students. A few of them had not had a conversation with a woman for years. At the same time that the prisoners became more verbally confident and acquainted with the conventions of middle-class deportment, the volunteers were also gaining personal insights as a result of their experiences in the therapy groups. Some of them had initially been as unsure of themselves as the prisoners, and they gradually learned to be more aware of their ideas and reactions and to express these clearly to others without being unnecessarily judgmental. Some volunteers found the experience too threatening and left the program. Only two of the volunteers, both of them professionals, were so severely depressed by their experiences in the prison that they had to terminate their participation in the program for that reason.

This narrative illustrates the point that students can get involved in exciting corrections projects. It also points out that criminal justice agencies must be willing to provide minimal funding for volunteer projects if they are to continue with a high level of performance over a long period of time. The Social Therapy Program was instituted at the Washington State Penitentiary at a time of radical prison reform. It is unlikely that a program such as this could exist, even today, at many maximum security correctional institutions. Community corrections programs are a more likely target for volunteer programs staffed heavily by supervised students.

There are a number of community corrections programs in every city in the United States, most of which would welcome the contribution of services by student volunteers, especially if they were supervised by university professors or other professionals. Interested students should consult their professors as to becoming involved in a correctional agency as a volunteer. There is no better way to find out what is going on in corrections, to understand what crime and delinquency are really all about, and to find out if one really wants to get into corrections as a career.

The example of the Social Therapy Program illustrates some aspects of the current state of American corrections. Training was problematic and could not be maintained at desired levels for new "employees." There was no sound evaluation on which to build better programs in the future. Although a number of social scientists were involved in the design and operation of the program, most of its important accomplishments were the result of the practice of corrections as a humanistic art rather than a science of human behavior.

AN OVERVIEW OF THE TEXT

The text is divided into three parts. The first traces the development of corrections as a social institution; the second looks at the major components of modern correctional institutions; and the third examines alternatives to traditional correctional institutions. After a brief introductory chapter, part one contains a discussion of the interrelationships between the correctional system, the criminal justice system, and the general public (Chapter 2), a brief explanation of competing philosophies in corrections (Chapter 3), and a history of corrections (Chapters 4 and 5). These chapters are designed to enable students to place modern corrections in a proper perspective historically, philosophically, and in relationship to the rest of society.

Part Two focuses on prisons. Chapter 6 discusses correctional clients as individuals and Chapter 7 shows what happens when they are gathered together in correctional institutions and form prisoner subcultures. Chapters 8 and 9 examine the other two major human elements in prison life: correctional officers and administrative personnel. Prison programs and services are described in Chapter 10. These include therapeutic (rehabilitative) programs and maintenance services designed to enable prisoners to live fairly normal lives while incarcerated rather than to necessarily help them to solve their personal problems. Part Two concludes with two chapters on the problems of prison administration and prison life. The discussion includes such problems as prison violence, homosexuality, drug use, court "interference" in the traditional prerogatives of correctional administrators and the introduction of accreditation in corrections. These last two topics are problems for prison administrators even though they have positive long-term consequences for corrections because they often require extensive changes in institutional procedures.

When one thinks of corrections, one thinks of prisons, but the majority of offenders in correctional programs are housed in the community rather than in residential facilities with towers and walls. Jails are discussed in Chapter 13; probation and parole in Chapters 14 and 15; and other community corrections programs, including halfway houses and therapeutic communities, are discussed in Chapter 16. Chapter 17 acquaints students with correctional establishments in industrialized and Third World nations around the world. A number of these countries have developed correctional innovations as alternatives to prison that might be adopted in the United States in the future. It is easy to accept existing ways of doing things as appropriate, but that is not necessarily the case. We need to stand back from existing practices and to be creatively critical from time to time if we are to achieve a balanced view of corrections and to assure ourselves that we are doing the best possible job with the resources at hand. Chapter 18 summarizes the radical (and not so radical) critique of traditional corrections and presents practical as well as theoretical alternatives to existing correctional programs. These include radical nonintervention, amnesty, and deinstitutionalization.

Part Three concludes with a chapter on the future of corrections and a survey of the occupational possibilities that exist for college students in correctional work. This is an important chapter, for it gives our best estimate of what it will be like to work in corrections in the coming decade, the time when current college students will be working in the field (or perhaps working in other occupations but being involved in corrections as volunteers). The text also includes an Appendix on scholarly periodicals containing material on corrections. Students who want to read more about corrections need to know what journals are likely to contain material on correctional topics. The appendix answers this question, and also describes the typical contents of each journal.

SOME INTERESTING QUESTIONS ABOUT CORRECTIONS THAT ARE DISCUSSED IN THIS TEXT

Corrections is a fascinating topic. Newspapers frequently publish articles about violence in prisons, interesting community corrections programs, lawsuits against prison administrators, and many other topics. Here is a list of some of the interesting questions about corrections that are treated in this book, along with an indication of the chapters in which each question is discussed.

1. How did corrections develop—in America and other countries? (See Chapters 4 and 5.)
2. Why do we believe that it is appropriate to spend a large amount of tax money on corrections? (See Chapter 3.)
3. How does corrections in the United States differ from corrections in other industrialized nations and in Third World countries? (See all chapters, particularly Chapter 17.)
4. What opportunities exist for employment in the field of corrections? (See Chapter 19.)
5. In what ways are jails different from prisons? (See Chapter 13.)
6. How much victimization, particularly violent victimization, is there in prisons? (See Chapter 11.)
7. Is it dangerous to work in prisons? (See Chapter 8.)
8. What are prisoners like? (See Chapters 6 and 7.)
9. How were criminals punished before there were prisons? (See Chapter 3.)
10. What are the similarities between prisons and other total institutions such as mental hospitals, concentration camps, and nursing homes? (See Chapter 7.)
11. What is going to happen in American corrections during the 1980s? (See Chapter 19.)
12. What is the new justice model of corrections? (See Chapter 3.)

13. Is it true that nothing works in corrections? (See Chapters 10, 14, 15, and 18.)
14. How do parole and probation officers carry out their duties? (See Chapters14 and 15.)
15. What value is there in all the community corrections programs that came into being during the 1970s? (See Chapter 16.)
16. How are black prisoners and other minority group members treated in correctional agencies? (See all chapters, but particularly Chapters 5, 6, and 7.)
17. What are the major points made by the critics of correctional agencies? (See Chapter 18.)
18. What are the advantages of community corrections and open institutions? (See Chapters 14, 15, 16, and 17.)
19. Where do I go to find out more about corrections? (See the Appendix.)
20. How have judicial decisions in response to lawsuits changed correctional practices? (See all chapters, particularly Chapters 10, 12,and 13.)
21. In what ways are women involved in corrections? (See all chapters, particularly Chapters 6, 7, and 8.)
22. What standards exist in corrections? (See Chapter 12.)
23. How do superintendents administer the prisons of which they are in charge?(See Chapter 9.)
24. What programs and services are generally made available to correctional clients? (See Chapters 10, 12, 13, 14, 15, and 16.)
25. Do the principles of administrative science apply to correctional institutions? (See Chapter 9.)
26. Is it safe to have a halfway house in my neighborhood? (See Chapter 16.)
27. What happens in a prison riot? (See Chapter 11.)
28. What are the conditions under which offenders are allowed to be on probation and parole instead of being institutionalized? (See Chapters 14 and 15.)
29. To what extent are homosexuality and drug abuse found in prison life? (See Chapter 11.)
30. What can I do in corrections *now,* or later if I decide not to choose corrections as a career but still want to help? (See Chapters 8, 12, 13, 14, and 15.)

SUMMARY

There are three major parts in the criminal justice system: the police, the courts, and corrections. *Corrections: The Science and the Art* examines the third of these three parts of the criminal justice system. The title of the text reflects the blend of scientific knowledge and creativity, imagination, and talent that must be used to produce successful outcomes in correctional work. Correctional agencies exist at the federal, state, and local levels. Probation and parole— which involve the supervision of offenders in the community—and correctional facilities are the major components of contemporary corrections in America. Probation agencies supervise convicted adults and adjudicated juveniles as an alternative to imprisonment, while parole agencies supervise offenders who have already served sentences in correctional facilities. Correctional facilities include community facilities such as group homes, shelters, and halfway houses; detention facilities such as jails for adults and detention centers for juveniles; and correctional institutions housing adults in prisons and penitentiaries, and juveniles in training schools and reformatories.

REFERENCES

1. Bowker, Lee H. "Volunteers in Hell: Student Interns and Other Field Placements at the Washington State Penitentiary." Paper presented at the annual meeting of the Midwest Sociological Society, 1975.
2. Glasser, William. *Reality Therapy: A New Approach to Psychiatry*. New York: Harper and Row, 1965.
3. Law Enforcement Assistance Administration. *Dictionary of Criminal Justice Data Termininology*. Washington, D.C.: Government Printing Office, 1976.

Chapter 2

Corrections, the Criminal Justice System, and the Public

The intent of this chapter is to show how corrections relates to other elements of the criminal justice system and to society as a whole. Since we will be talking about systems throughout much of the chapter, we should begin by explaining what we mean when we refer to something as a system.

The *Dictionary of Modern Sociology* defines a system as "any set of interrelated elements which, as they work and change together, may be regarded as a single entity," and then goes on to give the example of "a social system composed of dynamically interactive and interdependent individuals, groups, social structures, and culture traits and patterns."[11:327] The crucial points in this definition are that there must be a number of different elements, that these elements must interrelate, and that they must have enough in common so they can be collectively considered to be a single entity. When we say that elements are interrelating, we mean that they are exchanging information and/or material items. Considering them together as a single entity implies that the elements join together in pursuing superordinate goals in addition to their own individual goals. Taken separately, each element in a system can be considered to be a system itself. This is why we can talk about the corrections system as being a system within the criminal justice system. There is also the implication that both the elements and the system as a whole must have recognizable boundaries and identities. Otherwise, they could not be considered to be entities at all.

Now that we understand what a system is, we can answer the crucial question: "Is the criminal justice system really a system?" The answer is "yes," but this must be qualified in two ways. First, systems need not be physical in nature. They can be analytical, logical models of the operation of complex entities which have been created to help us understand their operation. When we speak of the criminal justice system, we can be referring to our analytic model of an idealized system rather than the physical structures and their personnel as they exist in human society. The second point is that seeing organizations as systems is a

15

perspective—a way of looking at things that is useful—rather than a label that must be rigidly applied. There are no standard criteria for deciding what is a system and what is not. We may even speak of degrees of systemness—the extent to which a given collection of elements approximates an ideal system. With these points in mind, we can look at the criminal justice apparatus as a system because doing so helps us understand how criminal justice is administered in complex societies.

The simplest kind of system is a recursive system with only two elements. An example of a recursive system is "A causes B." In a recursive system, causal effects can only operate in one direction. A can cause B, but B cannot cause A.[3] A much more complex type of system is a nonrecursive (or feedback) system in which changes in A cause changes in B, and then these changes in B have a feedback effect which in turn causes changes in A.[13] All criminal justice systems and subsystems are feedback systems. They are also open systems, in that they are constantly exchanging information and material items with the surrounding environment.

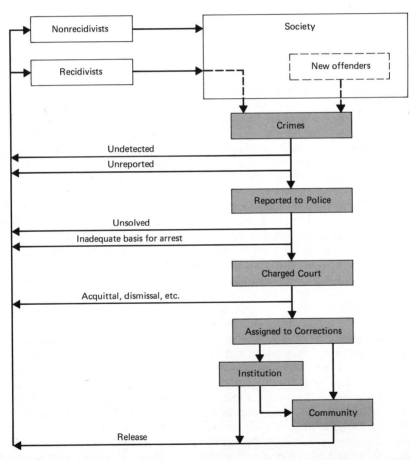

Figure 2.1 Flow diagram of the criminal justice system. (From J. Chaiken et al.: *Criminal Justice Models: An Overview.* Washington, D.C.: Government Printing Office, 1976.)

The kind of model that we develop for a system depends on our purpose. Although criminal justice systems are always open, we may choose to temporarily view them as closed. For example, if we are attempting to improve the flow of communications from police officers to their supervisors, we may want to view the police department as a closed system. On the other hand, if we are interested in knowing how many offenders will be sentenced to a correctional institution in the coming year, we will have to view that system as an open system. The difference is that when we view systems as open, we must identify exchanges of information and material items between the system and its environment. These are known as input and output relationships. In this chapter we begin by examining the criminal justice system as if it were a closed system, and then adopt an open system perspective to summarize the input and output relationships between the criminal justice system and other elements in society as a whole. A general model of the major elements of the criminal justice system and their interrelationships with each other as well as with the external society is presented in Figure 2.1.

Figure 2.1 illustrates the basic flow of offenders from the commission of crimes to the police, the courts, and the correctional system. Crimes arise from the activities of the members of society and are usually external to the criminal justice system. Citizens are also involved in that most crimes come to the attention of the police through citizen reports and the filing of complaints. The basic feedback loop is from corrections back to society through numerous release mechanisms. At the same time, there are other feedbacks from the system into the general society that occur when crimes are undetected, unreported, or unsolved, and when there is an inadequate basis for arrest or when the courts fail to convict offenders.

THE POLICE

Law enforcement agencies exist at the municipal, county, state, and federal levels in American society. In addition, there are numerous private police organizations that aid publicly funded police units in apprehending suspects and keeping order. Not all law enforcement officers are police officers. Sheriffs, Border Patrol offices, U.S. marshals, Postal Service inspectors, and Secret Service agents are examples of law enforcement officers who perform police functions without being members of police departments.

Recent employment statistics for police protection agencies in the United States are summarized in Table 2.1. There were 645,015 full-time equivalent employees in public police protection agencies in 1977. Most of these were at the municipal level, with decreasing numbers at each level up to the federal government. There was a steady growth in the police protection industry from 1971 to 1977. Municipalities grew the least, only 14.8 percent, and counties grew the most, 40.4 percent. Federal police protection employees increased rapidly between 1971 and 1974, and then increased at a much slower rate between 1974 and 1977. The increase in budgets was much greater than the increase in the number of employees, with the average law enforcement agency more than doubling its budget between 1971 and 1977.[16]

Table 2.1. Full-time Equivalent Police Protection Employment, United States, 1971–1977

	Full-time Equivalent Employment			
Governmental Level	1971	1974	1977	Percent Change 1971–1977
Federal	56,528	68,504	71,433	26.4
States	69,372	89,822	93,674	35.0
Counties	68,847	83,068	96,635	40.4
Municipalities	333,844	366,519	383,273	14.8
Total	528,591	607,912	645,015	22.0

Source: Law Enforcement Assistance Administration and Bureau of the Census: *Trends in Expenditure and Employment Data for the Criminal Justice System, 1971–1977*. Washington, D.C.: Government Printing Office, 1980.

Of all criminal justice agencies, the police have the heaviest burden of interacting with the public. Crimes are committed by citizens, generally reported by citizens, and often solved with information provided by citizens. Through all of these activities, police officers must be conscious of public relations considerations as well as the rigorous demands of enacted law and the most recent court decisions. Inefficiency, injustice, and other problems are much more readily observed by the public in police functioning than are similar problems in the courts or correctional institutions. Community corrections programs are the closest to the police in terms of degree of interaction with the public. A final dimension of this broad-based interaction between police officers and citizens is that a great many of the items brought to the attention of police officers are not criminal matters. The poor, particularly the urban poor, use the police for a wide range of social service needs.[6,17] These include many needs that might otherwise be met by social workers, psychologists, lawyers, and clerics.

The primary criminal justice functions performed by police officers are the investigation of crimes reported, witnessed, or suspected, and the arrest and booking of offenders. Many crimes are not reported to the police. Even when crimes are brought to their attention, the investigation process may not result in the identification and arrest of offenders. The FBI reports that 76 percent of all the murders known to the police in 1978 were cleared by arrest. Less serious crimes were considerably less likely to result in an arrest. Comparable statistics for aggravated assault were 62 percent, 50 percent for forcible rape, 26 percent for robbery, 20 percent for larceny, 16 percent for burglary, and 15 percent for motor vehicle theft.[7]

Juveniles may be referred to the police juvenile unit at any time during the investigation or between the arrest and the booking. They then move from the police juvenile unit to the court system through an intake hearing, unless they are released or a station adjustment is made in which the police decide to dismiss or otherwise adjust the case without further processing. Adults may be released without prosecution after the arrest or after the booking. The booking consists of an official record of the arrest. The basic facts of the arrest are entered in the police log, and the offender may also be fingerprinted and photographed.

Police officers do not enforce the law uniformly. When they observe suspicious behavior or receive the report of a crime, they must decide to what extent the incident is worthy of further criminal justice processing. Both legal and extra-legal factors may be taken into account in reaching this decision. Police department policies are also important in establishing crime reporting procedures and priorities. Departments may change these policies according to the political needs of the moment or in response to public pressure or changes in funding and staffing levels. At the level of the individual law enforcement officer, the work load at a given time has a great deal to do with the proportion of aggressive responses that occur when crimes are reported. It is probable that a police department that is straining its resources in a "crackdown" on prostitution and simultaneously devoting extensive staff time to the solving of two murders will decrease its processing of minor crimes until the temporary organizational crisis is over. These adaptations by law enforcement agencies may be seen as homeostatic in that they tend to level out the peaks and valleys in the rate at which offenders enter the criminal justice system. If they did not do so, the delays in court processing and the temporary overloads in local correctional facilities would be worse than they are.

This is an example of a feedback system in which police organizations modify their responses in reaction to changes in the amount and seriousness of crime in the community. Another example of a feedback mechanism in law enforcement work is the way in which the interaction between the police and the community—particularly publicized interaction in handling spectacular crimes—affects the willingness of citizens to report future crimes to the police. Public perception that police officers are willing to cooperate in the reporting of crime and that these officers will accord citizens satisfactory treatment when they report crime tends to increase the proportion of crimes reported to the police.[24] This in turn tends to increase the input of offenders into the criminal justice system. Therefore, better police–community relations can be expected to lead to an increase in official crime rates. This example illustrates the major advantage of employing a systems perspective, which is that interchanges among system units and between the system and the environment are highlighted so that program planning, implementation, and evaluation can be carried out with maximum effectiveness.

THE COURTS

The courts employ many fewer individuals than do law enforcement agencies, but court employment has been increasing at a much more rapid rate than employment in law enforcement agencies. Table 2.2 shows that the total full-time equivalent number of judicial employees in the United States was 150,546 in 1977. The greatest growth in court employees was at the state level, where there was an 88 percent increase in employment over a six-year period. The federal government and local municipalities were at the other end of the scale, with average annual increases of less than two percent. As with law enforcement agencies, judicial budgets have been rising much more rapidly than the full-time equivalent employee count. The cost to taxpayers of supporting the judicial system at the federal, state, county, and municipal levels more than doubled between 1971 and 1977.[16]

We have already mentioned that suspects enter the courts at the point of their initial appearance, which occurs very quickly following arrest. The initial appearance is normally conducted before a commissioner, magistrate, or justice of the peace. The formal notice of the charge is filed, and the suspect is advised of his or her rights. Bail is set where appropriate. If the offense is a minor one, a summary trial may be conducted at this point without further processing in the criminal justice system. The initial appearance is followed by the preliminary hearing, at which the evidence in the case is given its first hearing. The presiding magistrate must decide whether there is probable cause that a crime has been committed based on the evidence presented, and also, if it was committed, whether there is sufficient evidence to assume that it was committed by the suspect. If the evidence does not seem to be sufficient, the charges will either be dismissed or reduced. If the magistrate judges the evidence to be sufficient for continued processing in the criminal justice system, the case then goes either to a grand jury or to the prosecutor's office for the preparation of an information.

An information is a legal document that formally charges the suspect with one or more offenses. If the prosecuting attorney feels that the evidence is not good enough to have a high probability of conviction—or perhaps that the criminal justice system does not have sufficient resources to process the case or that there are technical reasons why the case is unlikely to result in a conviction even if the evidence is strong—then there may be no filing of the information, and this stops all action on the case. Grand juries are an alternative to this process. They consist of panels of citizens who consider the evidence and decide whether or not it is appropriate to return an indictment in the case. In federal cases and in states that use grand juries, the prosecuting attorney may not proceed with a felony prosecution unless the grand jury returns an indictment.

Juveniles enter the judicial system in the intake hearing, at which a probation officer decides upon the desirability of continued criminal justice processing. The youngster may receive a nonadjudicatory disposition at this point, in which case there will be a referral to a social service agency such as the welfare

Table 2.2. Full-time Equivalent Judicial Employment, United States, 1971–1977

Governmental Level	Full-time Equivalent Employment			
	1971	1974	1977	Percent Change 1971–1977
Federal	7,421	6,734	8,165	10.0
States	19,856	23,939	37,337	88.0
Counties	56,421	68,727	78,851	39.8
Municipalities	23,431	25,729	26,193	11.8
Total	107,129	125,129	150,546	40.5

Source: Law Enforcement Assistance Administration and Bureau of the Census: *Trends in Expenditure and Employment Data for the Criminal Justice System, 1971–1977.* Washington, D.C.: Government Printing Office, 1980.

department or a counseling service. If there is an adjudicatory hearing, the case will most likely go directly to the correctional system, as relatively few juveniles are released at this point. All the other steps in the judicial process that protect adult suspects from wrongful punishment are eliminated for juveniles, which is one reason why due process is so weak in the juvenile justice system.

The arraignment is the next step in the criminal justice processing sequence. It is similar to the preliminary hearing in that the suspect is informed of his or her rights,but it differs from the preliminary hearing in that there is no presentation of the evidence and the suspect is asked to make a plea. Should the defendant plead not guilty and the charge not be dismissed at the point of the arraignment, the case will then go to trial. In some cases, the defendant has the option of being tried before a jury or a judge. Extensive plea bargaining between the prosecuting attorney and the defense lawyer results in the reduction of charges in return for guilty pleas in many cases, thus decreasing the cost of criminal justice processing. If every case went to trial, the strain on the court system would be tremendous, and the cost of maintaining the courts would probably triple.

Plea bargaining is the most heavily criticized element in the judicial apparatus of the criminal justice system. The problem is that the plea bargaining mechanism works as well when the defendant is innocent as it does when he or she is guilty. As a result, the use of plea bargaining may result in a leveling of sentences in which the innocent and those guilty of serious crimes end up with the same sentences. Many defendants are too poor to afford their own lawyers, and so they are defended by public defenders who sometimes seem to be more concerned about their relations with the court than with the welfare of their clients. When the only legal counsel available to a defendant advises accepting the plea bargaining offer of the district attorney, and describes in detail the lengthy sentence that the defendant will otherwise suffer, it is not surprising that many defendants accept this advice and give up their right to trial.[29]

Cases which go to trial result in a finding of guilty or not guilty. For those who are found guilty, the next stage in criminal justice processing is the sentencing hearing, at which the judge pronounces the sentence upon the offender. At the point of the pronouncement, the offender departs from the judicial system and enters into the correctional system. This transfer is specified in the sentence and symbolized by the leading away of the offender into captivity or whatever other punishment has been pronounced. Actually, the break is not as clean as this, for offenders have usually spent at least some time in jail awaiting trial, and involvement in the judicial system continues after entrance into the correctional system when appeals are filed.

Trials are predominantly legal dramas, as everyone who has watched trials on television or in the movies is well aware of. At the same time, the trial has symbolic functions that are extra-legal in nature. For example, it is a degradation ceremony, an ordeal through which free citizens are converted to outcasts with much pomp and ceremony.[27] There is also the symbolic value of the trial for society as a whole. The trial reaffirms the values of society by highlighting the evils of the offender. The line between law-abiding and criminal behavior is redrawn and emphasized anew with every trial. To the extent that the operations of the criminal justice system produce a deterrent effect, it may be due as much to the publicity surrounding the trial as to the suffering of the convicted felon.

CORRECTIONS

The number of employees necessary to operate the corrections system in the United States is larger than the number of employees in the judicial system, but much smaller than the number of employees in law enforcement agencies. Correctional agencies in the counties and the federal government have been growing at a more rapid rate than judicial or law enforcement agencies at these governmental levels. They have also been growing at a more rapid rate than correctional agencies in the states and municipalities. Table 2.3 presents full-time equivalent employment data from 1971 to 1977 for the correctional system. The total number of full-time equivalent employees increased by 41.7 percent in just six years, to a total of 255,008. As with the judicial system and law enforcement, the increase in the budget was much steeper than the increase in employees, with total correctional expenditures more than doubling between 1971 and 1977.[16]

Sentenced offenders may be given a fine, placed on probation, sent to a community corrections program of some sort, or incarcerated in a correctional institution such as a jail (for misdemeanors) or penitentiary (for felonies). Probationers who fail to conform to the terms of their sentence may have their probation revoked and be sent to a correctional institution. Felons and juveniles serving time in a correctional institution may be released directly at the termination of their sentence but are more likely to be released on parole. Should they be unable to maintain themselves on parole, they can be remanded to the institution. Only if they maintain good behavior on parole will they finally be discharged from the correctional system. Parole revocation is a major feedback loop through which offenders are returned to the incarceration state of correctional processing.

THE FLOW OF OFFENDERS THROUGH THE CRIMINAL JUSTICE SYSTEM

The number of crimes committed annually in the United States is extremely high. A 1977 National Crime Survey report[15] estimates that 40,315,000 crimes were committed in the United States during that year. More than half of these were crimes against persons, and there were nearly 6,000,000 crimes of violence estimated to have been committed during the year. The existing criminal justice system could not possibly incarcerate this many offenders, or even fine them. As it happens, not all of these crimes are reported to the police, and so most of them remain undetected by law enforcement officials. According to self-report data, three out of every ten crimes committed were reported to the police. The reporting percentage varied according to the nature of the crime. Motor vehicle theft was the most commonly reported crime, at 68 percent, followed by rape (58

Table 2.3. Full-time Equivalent Correctional Employment, United States, 1971–1977

	Full-time Equivalent Employment			
Governmental Level	1971	1974	1977	Percent Change 1971–1977
Federal	7,140	9,967	11,760	64.7
States	106,045	121,160	145,552	37.3
Counties	49,261	62,482	77,682	57.7
Municipalities	17,515	19,588	20,014	14.3
Total	179,961	213,197	255,008	41.7

Source: Law Enforcement Assistance Administration and Bureau of the Census: *Trends in Expenditure and Employment Data for the Criminal Justice System, 1971–1977*. Washington, D.C.: Government Printing Office, 1980.

percent), robbery (56 percent), burglary (49 percent), assault (44 percent), household larceny (25 percent) and crimes of theft (25 percent).[15]

Police officers fail to follow through with many cases of which they become aware. For example, Albert Reiss[28] found that law enforcement officers did not make arrests even in many cases in which they had enough information to establish probable cause that the crime had been committed. In 43 percent of the felonies and 52 percent of the misdemeanors, the officers he studied made no arrests.

Additional cases are lost at the point of the booking, so that the number of offenders is already greatly reduced when the cohort reaches the first point of contact with the judicial system. Figure 2.2 illustrates the filtering effect of criminal justice processing on 19,635 offenders in the urban areas of twelve California counties between 1969 and 1971. The group of offenders was immediately cut to 12,925, of which 54 percent went to the superior court and 46 percent went to lower courts on reduced charges because of plea bargaining. It is for this reason that almost every one of these cases resultd in a conviction. If Figure 2.2 included misdemeanors as well as felonies, there would be a much higher percentage of acquittals and dismissals as a result of legal action in the lower court. It is a testament to the efficiency of prosecuting attorneys that when cases are taken to the superior court, convictions are obtained 83 percent of the time.

The majority of the offenders pleading guilty to a reduced charge in the lower courts received probation, usually of more than three years duration. Of the 5,880 suspects processed by the lower courts, only 2,396 were sentenced to jail, and the number of offenders serving more than 180 days in jail was 553, less than 10 percent of the pool of offenders who pleaded guilty to a reduced charge. Of those offenders convicted in the superior court, less than a quarter were placed on probation and nearly half were sentenced to jail terms, most of which were more than 180 days.

The figures from Carl Pope's[26] study of California felony offenders can be recombined to show the total distribution of offenders from the courts to the different branches of the correctional system. When we do this, we find that 39

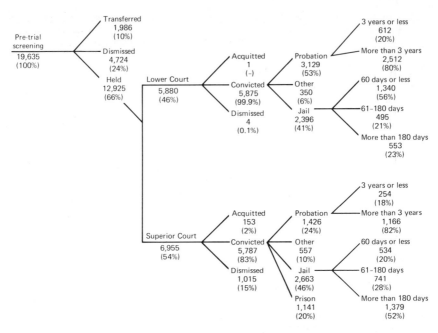

Figure 2.2 Flow of California felony offenders, urban areas. (From Carl E. Pope: *Offender-based Transaction Statistics: New Directions in Data Collecting and Reporting.* Washington, D.C.: Government Printing Office, 1975.)

percent of all the offenders were placed on probation, 43 percent were given jail sentences, 10 percent went to prison, and 8 percent received other penalties. This analysis also shows that 59 percent of the suspects entering the court system are eventually delivered by that system to the correctional system. This proportion is actually much higher than the proportion of crimes reported to the police by citizens or the proportion of crimes known to the police that result in arrests. One may therefore say that the further a suspect goes into the criminal justice system, the greater the probability of moving to the next stage of criminal justice processing. Another implication of this line of reasoning is that the court drama, which is the symbol of justice that most readily comes to the minds of most citizens, is actually the arena in which the smallest amount of decision-making occurs. Most decisions about criminal cases are made at earlier stages of the criminal justice funnel, so that those cases which survive to the point of a trial have already been selected to be those in which the state has a high probability of conviction.

Reality is actually a great deal more complex than the nonrecursive model presented in Figure 2.2. There are numerous feedback loops in the criminal justice system, and these mechanisms make it extremely difficult to estimate the flow of offenders through the system at any given time. Perhaps the most significant of all the feedback loops is recidivism, in which offenders who have been released from the correctional system commit new crimes and reenter the criminal justice system at the point of arrest. A model for estimating projected total arrests from estimates of new arrests and recidivism rates has been developed by social scientists,[1] but is not yet in common use by criminal justice planners. At the local level, it is often difficult to assess the effect of the introduction of a new program or procedure on the total flow of offenders through the system. For example, programs for juveniles designed to be alternatives to secure detention may instead function to bring increased numbers of juveniles into the criminal system. In essence, juvenile justice system personnel are reacting to the availability of certain treatment programs by filling those programs to capacity, in many cases with youngsters who would otherwise not have received further criminal justice system attention.[21]

The Minnesota Department of Corrections[18] found a similar effect in its study of the use of two residential programs that were designed as alternatives to state incarceration. In both of these programs, it was clear that offenders were being received from the courts who would otherwise have received probation. Judges were defeating the original purpose of these two community corrections programs by sending the same kinds of offenders to prison that they had in the past, and at the same time sending the more severe probation cases to the two community corrections programs. The two programs were originally conceived as ways of reducing the amount of social control exercised by the state over relatively minor offenders. Instead, the nature of the feedback reaction by the judicial system resulted in an increase of total social control. The bright spot in this study is that it shows that it is possible to impact feedback mechanisms through education and public relations. The staff at one of the projects went out of its way to communicate the purpose of its project to probation officers and judges, with the result that its project began to be used more as an alternative to institutionalization. We can see from this example that interpersonal relations are important in the functioning of the criminal justice system, and that any realistic model of the operation of the system must take into account the constantly changing conditions caused by multiple feedback loops and reciprocal adjustments made by all of the agencies in the system.

THE IMPACT OF CRIMINAL JUSTICE SYSTEM PROCESSING ON PRISON POPULATIONS

All of the various adjustments, policies, and procedures of the law enforcement and judicial systems impact the correctional system because it is located at the end of the criminal justice processing funnel. The correctional system has very little flexibility in this matter. It must accept those offenders who are assigned to it. The total population of offenders being processed at any given time in correctional agencies has not received much attention from social scientists and planners. State correctional organizations are just beginning to consider extra-correctional factors in projecting needs for manpower, budget, and client housing.

Three examples of this approach are analyses prepared for the Washington, D.C. Department of Corrections, the Florida Department of Corrections, and the National Manpower Survey of the Criminal Justice System.

The Washington, D.C. report[10] was written in late 1976 to give guidance to the Department of Corrections in planning its needs for 1977. It analyzed statistics on the Metropolitan Police Department, Bail Agency, the U.S. Attorney's Office, the courts, parole, and two special topics: Operation Doorstop and the proposed District of Columbia Bail Reform Act. It concluded that arrests for serious offenses would increase slightly in 1977 and other arrests would remain stable; that the Bail Agency appeared to be cooperating in the release of fewer suspects on personal recognizance than it had in the past, which would tend to increase the number of prisoners in preventive detention; and that the number of sentences pronounced on adult offenders by the courts was sharply up. The U.S. Attorney's Office was active in fewer cases during the prior year than previously, but this was as a result of increased attention to each case prosecuted, and led to a higher ratio of convictions to cases taken to court. Therefore, the combined impact of these changes was to increase the flow of offenders in the direction of the correctional system. In addition, the Parole Board showed a trend to decrease releases from correctional institutions. Both Operation Doorstop (a police program aimed at the increased detention of dangerous offenders) and the proposed D.C. Bail Reform Act (which would decrease the number of dangerous offenders released on bail) were estimated to have the impact of increasing the client count in the Washington, D.C. Department of Corrections. The combination of all these considerations allowed the Washington, D.C. Department of Corrections to anticipate a continued increase in the flow of offenders into the correctional system, and gave it enough warning so that it could begin to plan intelligently for this increase in offenders.

The Annual Report of the Florida Department of Corrections for 1977–1978[8] included two pages of charts on population trends affecting corrections to demonstrate that the flow of offenders into the Department was related to factors over which the Department had no control. The factors mentioned in this presentation were not only extra-correctional: they were completely outside of the entire criminal justice system. Because the rate of commitment for the correctional system was highly related to the number of males aged 18–29 in Florida's general population, an increase in this group would be likely to produce an increase in the correctional population in Florida. The Department estimated that there would be 121 new prison admissions for each additional 10,000 males age 18–29 added to Florida's population. It predicted an increase of 31,000 of these men between 1977 and 1978 and an increase of 27,000 between 1978 and 1979. These two increases would be likely to add over 700 prison admissions to Florida's correctional system. A similar projection was made on the basis of the average unemployment rate for the state. In this case, it was estimated that an increase of one percent in the average unemployment rate for Florida would result in an increase of 334 prison admissions. Since the unemployment rate was predicted to decline approximately 2.3 percent in Florida between 1977 and 1979, the corresponding decrease in prison admissions would almost offset the increase from the rise in the number of males age 18 through 29. It is interesting that this report excluded the crime rate based on the FBI's *Uniform Crime Reports* from consideration, commenting that *UCR* data had been historically unrelated to prison admissions in Florida.

A much more elaborate prediction model was developed for the analysis of criminal justice manpower trends by the National Manpower Survey of the

Criminal Justice System.[14] The most important factors in the NMS model are presented in Figure 2.3. This figure shows the crime rate impacting criminal justices expenditures, which in turn impact criminal justice employment. Criminal justice employment has an effect on the probability of arrest and imprisonment, and this probability both influences and is influenced by the crime rate in a complex feedback loop. The brackets in the model contain factors outside of the criminal justice system which impact the operations of the system. Four external factors were seen as impacting the crime rate directly. These were the percentage of the total population between the ages of 15 and 24, per capita income, urbanization, and the unemployment rate. External factors impacting criminal justice expenditures directly include the gross national product, the total state or local budget, and the amount of federal grant money coming into the jurisdiction. Finally, the level of wages paid to criminal justice employees in each major area of the criminal justice system directly impacts the level of employment in that area.

When estimates were inserted for each of these variables, the model predicted average annual growth rates for criminal justice expenditures, employment, and other variables between 1974 and 1985. It was estimated that the crime rate would actually decline very slightly over this period, but that the arrest rate would increase by 12 percent, the number of prisoners in state institutions by 33 percent, the full-time equivalent criminal justice employment by 42 percent, and the budget for criminal justice expenditures by 52 percent. The number of full-time correctional employees was projected to rise 60 percent between 1974 and 1985, which would be higher than the increases in police and judicial full-time equivalent employees. The model showed that increases in arrests and in employment in correctional agencies would be associated with increases in prison populations, while an increase in employment of lawyers for the defense of indigent offenders would result in a decrease in prison populations. The number of prisoners in state institutions for adults was projected to increase from 190,000 in 1974 to 243,000 in 1980, and then less steeply to 252,000 in 1985. Employment in corrections was expected to increase more at the local level (70 percent) and at the state level (53 percent) than at the federal level and to a

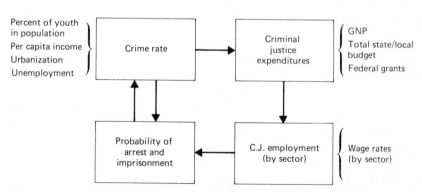

Figure 2.3 Key factors affecting law enforcement and criminal justice employment: The NMS analytical model. (From: Law Enforcement Assistance Administration: *The National Manpower Survey of the Criminal Justice System.* Volume 3: *Criminal Justice Manpower Planning.* Washington, D.C.: Government Printing Office, 1978.)

greater extent in probation and parole services (109 percent) than in adult (58 percent) or juvenile (12 percent) institutions.[14]

Statistical projections made by social scientists in the past have often proved to be inaccurate. It will be interesting for those reading this text in 1985 to check the accuracy of the criminal justice system projections made by the National Manpower Survey.

Influences on Prison Populations

Most of the scholarly research attempting to understand the influence of external factors on correctional systems has focused on prison populations rather than the total number of correctional clients. Some of these have developed models based on general factors, either within or external to the entire criminal justice system, while others have been written in an attempt to predict the prison population effects of changes in correctional policies or enacted law. Among the general external factors found to have an impact on the level of prison populations, we find general conservatism,[20] poverty,[20] the percentage of young males in the population,[4] the percentage of blacks in the population,[4,19,20] and unemployment.[9,12,19,20,32]

As an example of this kind of analysis, Alfred Blumstein and his associates[4] estimated the effect of changes in demographic variables on the prison population in Pennsylvania. They found that the age structure of the population, and to a lesser extent its racial composition, were significant determinants of projected future prison populations in the state. Using a complex estimation model, they predicted that arrests in Pennsylvania would peak in 1980, prison commitments would peak in 1985, and prison populations would peak in 1990. After that time, the decreasing numbers of citizens in the young crime-prone ages would result in subsequent declines in these criminal justice indices. As they correctly point out, this model cannot take into account changes in feedback mechanisms within the criminal justice system that might occur as a response to increasing population pressures. For example, changing policies followed by parole boards, sentencing judges, and prosecuting attorneys could easily mitigate the effects of the temporary increase in criminogenic age groups.

Estimates of the Effects of New Laws and Policies on Prison Populations

When a law creating a new governmental agency comes to the legislature, a cost statement is generally attached estimating the net additional cost to the state of the new program over the ensuing years. The costs to the state involved in passing new criminal legislation or changing administrative procedures in the criminal justice system are less immediately obvious, but no less significant. Unfortunately, it has not been common practice to submit cost statements along with legislative actions such as these. If such cost statements had been automatically appended to all criminal legislation since 1900, it is quite possibly that there would be many fewer criminal laws on the books today than there are.

The recent discussions of the justice model in the criminal justice system and one of the directives in the *Crime Control Act of 1976* have been responsible for recent efforts to predict the effects of proposed new laws or policies on prison populations at the federal and state levels. For example, Joan Petersilia and Peter Greenwood[25] projected the effects of mandatory minimum sentences using data derived from the Denver, Colorado district court. They found that the prison population would have been increased by 450 percent if every person convicted of a felony had been sentenced to a mandatory minimum of five years imprisonment. If the five-year mandatory sentence were applied only to offenders with one prior adult felony conviction, the increase in prison populations would be only 190 percent. Although cost estimates were not provided, these figures make clear that the cost to the State of Colorado of implementing mandatory minimum sentences, just considering staffing and the building of new correctional institutions, would be prohibitive.

The introduction of Senate Bill 995 in Pennsylvania during 1976 stimulated a detailed prison population projection by graduate students under the direction of Alfred Blumstein.[2] This Bill proposed mandatory minimum sentences of one to three years for offenders with at least one previous conviction, with the use of firearms always resulting in a higher mandatory minimum than felonies committed without firearms. Before the population projection could be made, it was necessary to ascertain the current sentencing practices for offenders with previous convictions. It was found that 74 percent of such offenders currently received prison or county jail sentences and that serious felons such as convicted murderers and rapists were more likely to receive state prison sentences (66 percent) than felons convicted of burglary and narcotics violations (13 percent). Prior felony convictions also resulted in a higher proportion of criminals being sentenced to the state prison. For example, 64 percent of convicted burglars with at least three prior felony convictions were sentenced to state prison as compared with only three percent of burglars with no previous convictions. The results of the exercise were that the complete implementation of the Bill would increase prison populations by 50 percent. Furthermore, most of these new commitments would consist of the less serious felons. The annual new commitments to state prisons of burglary and narcotic felons would increase by 1100, while the new commitments of murderers and rapists would only increase by 55 per year. The likely increase in state prison expenditures associated with Senate Bill 995 was 40 percent. As a result of this analysis, the authors recommended that the state should develop alternative ways of improving sentencing practices instead of implementing a law requiring mandatory sentences across the board.

The most comprehensive of all prison population projections was written by a team of experts under the leadership of Andrew Rutherford.[30] This study had been mandated by the legislature as part of the task of the National Institute of Law Enforcement and Criminal Justice, located in the Law Enforcement Assistance Administration. The Rutherford study differs from other prison population projection efforts in that it includes the estimation of populations under eight different policy alternatives using a dynamic modeling approach. A preliminary scan of the data convinced the research team that the adoption of differing policy alternatives was much more important in determining future prison population levels than variables operating outside of the criminal justice system, such as unemployment. Table 2.4 summarizes the eight policy alternatives used in the study. The alternatives used by Rutherford *et al.* range from conservative to liberal, and also differ in the focus of the policy-making activity, the basic motivation for implementing the policies, and the ways in which the policies would be implemented.

Under the dynamic modeling technique, the implications of each policy alternative for all of the elements of the criminal justice system were estimated, with prison population being the joint result of all of the factors in the model. Figure 2.4 illustrates the results of the application of this technique. Here we see

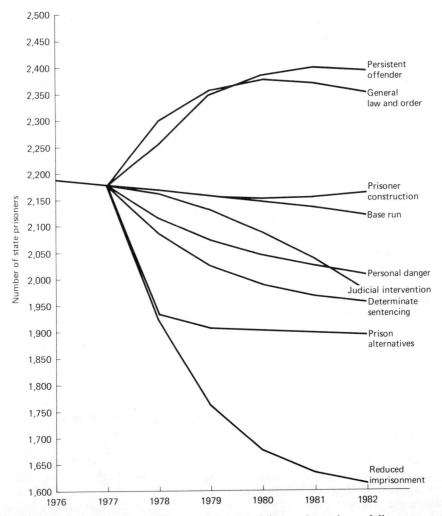

Figure 2.4 Projection of the prison population of Iowa: dynamic modeling approach. (From Andrew Rutherford et al.: *Prison Population and Policy Choices,* Volume 1. Washington, D.C.: Government Printing Office, 1977.

Table 2.4. Summary Chart of Scenarios

Scenario Title	Focus of Activity	Basic Motivation	Policy Application
A. Changes across the board			
1. General law and order	Prosecutors, sentencing judges, and Parole Boards	Tougher policy on all offenses	Higher imprisonment rate (reduced probation rate); longer sentences; stricter parole policy
2. Reduced imprisonment rate	Prosecutors, sentencing judges, and Parole Boards	Relieve prison overcrowding	Increased probation for all offenses; shorter sentences; looser parole policy
B. Mandatory Minimum Policies			
3. Personal danger priority	Prosecutors, sentencing judges, and State legislature	Concentrate imprisonment on violent crime	Two-year mandatory minimum imprisonment for PD convictions; increased probation for others
4. Persistent offender priority	Prosecutors, sentencing judges, and State legislature	Incapacitate repeat felons	Mandatory imprisonment plus sentence enhancement for "two-time losers"
C. Structuring Discretion			
5. Determinate sentencing	State legislature and sentencing judges	Remove time-served disparities; put ceilings on sentences	Legislative preemption of parole system
D. Broader Policies			
6. Judicial intervention	Federal courts	Ensure constitutional prison conditions	Minimum "adequacy of space" standards
7. Federal aid to prison construction	U.S. Congress	Relieve prison overcrowding	Matching federal funds to 50 percent of state requirements
8. Federal aid to prison alternatives	U.S. Congress	Reduce fraction of general population imprisoned	Federal funds for community corrections

Source: Rutherford, Andrew, *et al.: Prison Population and Policy Choices*, Volume I. Washington, D.C.: Government Printing Office, 1977.

that the state prison population in Iowa, which was just under 2200 in 1976, could either increase to approximately 2400 or decline to almost 1600 by 1982, depending upon the policy alternatives adopted. In general, the more conservative the alternative, the greater the prison population projected for 1982. Projections were made for four additional states and the Federal Prison System using the same eight policy alternatives, and three simple flow projections were made for all 50 states.

THE CRIMINAL JUSTICE SYSTEM AND SOCIETY

One property of systems theory that was only briefly alluded to at the beginning of this chapter is the hierarchical arrangement of systems. Each system can be an element in a larger system. At times, such systems may be referred to as subsystems. In this way of looking at things, the correctional system is a subsystem within the criminal justice system, and the criminal justice system is a subsystem within the larger system of the total society. If we focus on the criminal justice system, then we can define societal influences on that system as inputs to the system and influences that the criminal justice system has on the larger society to be outputs of the criminal justice system. The purpose of this section is to step back from our examination of the criminal justice system to think about how it fits into the more general system of the total society.

Talcott Parsons[23] explains that the existence of a society entails some kind of control over a territorial area as well as the economic–technological complex. Much of the formal control exercised over these matters by national governments is administered through the criminal justice system. The criminal justice system operates through the law, which Parsons defines as "The general normative code regulating action of, and defining the situation for, the member units of a society."[23:18] That is to say, the law not only tells people what is right and wrong: it also provides a framework to which they can orient their daily behavior. The law is supplemented by informal social control by which the members of society are motivated to conform to the dominant values embodied in the law.[22] Albert Cohen[5] conceptualizes the criminal justice system as one designed to extirpate deviance. Through this formal structure—as well as through more subtle social pressures—those citizens not conforming to the standards of behavior officially adopted by society are penalized or otherwise induced to acquiesce in the dominant standards of society.

The Legislature

Legislative bodies at the local, state, and national levels are the primary sources of formal input from the larger society to the criminal justice system, and to corrections in particular. There are at least five ways in which legislative bodies influence corrections. These are by passing criminal laws, creating correctional agencies and programs, funding those agencies and programs, investigating correctional agencies, and setting standards for correctional activities (which entails creating and funding agencies to enforce these standards).

Passing Criminal Laws. Criminal laws are enacted by legislative bodies. They cannot be proclaimed by presidents, governors or mayors, nor can they be created by the courts, although court decisions may determine how laws are implemented or whether they can be implemented at all. Enacting criminal laws is not just an abstract exercise in morality by pressure groups or public opinion. The enactment of these laws has the effect of creating overlapping populations of offenders. Each new criminal law that is passed creates a new potential for correctional clients, and each law that is taken off the books reduces that potential. As societies become increasingly complex, they delegate more and more social control to the operation of the criminal justice system, and this delegation invariably increases correctional populations

Creating Agencies and Programs. Correctional units do not arise through their own efforts. They must be authorized by a specific legislative act. The Law Enforcement Assistance Administration (LEAA), which has considerable input to the correctional system as well as the judicial and law enforcement system, was created by a single act of the federal government in 1968. Title I of this act also created the Block Grant Program through which federal funds were funneled to the states with a minimum of federal control and authorized the creation of criminal justice planning agencies in all of the states and certain other American possessions. The ease with which agencies can be modified by the passage of new laws can be seen from the history of the LEAA. It had barely begun to fully institutionalize its own operating procedures before it was significantly altered by the Omnibus Crime Control Act of 1970, and it was subsequently modified at regular intervals by other legislative actions. In the most recent reorganization, LEAA has been targeted for termination in 1982, but three of its offspring, the National Institute of Justice, the Bureau of Justice Statistics, and the Office of Juvenile Justice and Delinquency Prevention, will be strengthened.

Funding Agencies and Programs. Citizens who have fought for the establishment of a specific agency or program may feel that they have won their battle when enabling legislation is passed. Actually, this is an oversimplification of the process, for enabling legislation only makes it possible for an agency or a program to exist: it does not guarantee its existence. The guarantee comes when additional legislation is passed, funding the correctional unit. Correctional units must be funded annually or biannually, according to local custom, and each funding exercise provides an opportunity for state legislatures to influence the shape and scope of correctional activities in their jurisdictions. Correctional administrators must therefore be constantly aware of the political dimensions of their own activities in order to maximize the potential for continued correctional funding at adequate levels.

Legislative Investigations. The political device for focusing public attention on correctional institutions, which also has the function of collecting accurate information for legislative policy-making, is the legislative hearing. If legislators receive a large number of complaints about conditions in a correctional institution—or perhaps that dangerous offenders are being released too early and preying upon citizens—a legislative hearing is a good way to show their constituents that they are interested in the public welfare. On the other hand, these hearings may be engineered in such a way as to give the appearance of action on an issue when no actual change in legislation is contemplated.

Setting Standards. In addition to creating and funding correctional programs, legislative bodies have the power to set standards for the operation of those programs. Realistically, those standards only become important when they are implemented through some sort of enforcement mechanism such as a special agency, which must itself be funded by the legislature. The developer of a new correctional program would be foolish not to consult public health agencies, the fire department inspector, the building inspector, and other government officials charged with the enforcement of minimum standards for correctional institutions as part of their overall responsibilities. Correctional agencies are not permitted to accept offenders until they have received all of the appropriate licenses and passed all of the necessary inspections by regulatory agency personnel.

CITIZENS, ASSOCIATIONS AND PRESSURE GROUPS

Legislators who wish to be reelected cannot afford to ignore the needs and opinions of the electorate. This cumbersome mechanism is one of the ways in which individual citizens influence corrections. Social organization is the most important resource of all but the wealthiest of citizens. Individuals who organize into associations for the advancement of a specific cause are much more likely to be successful than they would be if they operated independently. Associations having a specific political action purpose as their major goal may be considered to be pressure groups. They develop elaborate strategies for influencing legislators, and often hire lobbyists to make the best possible case for their cause directly to legislators in their own offices.

An example of a pressure group impacting corrections is the Kansas Council on Crime and Delinquency. This group has been active in Kansas politics from the time of its organization in 1971, and had a significant influence upon the passage of the *Penal Reform Act of 1973* and the *Community Corrections Act of 1978*.[31] The keys to the success of this group were its use of image manipulation to create an impression of wider public support than was actually the case and its cultivation of ties (or at least the appearance of ties) with numerous other interest groups and prestigious organizations. The image of widespread voter support and interorganizational cooperation allowed the KCCD to have an influence on the Kansas legislature that was far greater than its number and prominence of members could otherwise justify.

There are lobbyists for gun control and for the right to bear arms, for deinstitutionalization and for increasing the severity of criminal penalties, and so on. Legislators are exposed to the best arguments presented on both sides of any important issue, and must then decide what to do based on some combination of what they think is best and what they think is the outcome preferred by their most powerful supporters and most of their constituents.

One of the feedback loops inherent in the legislative process is that agencies created by the legislatures become pressure groups fighting for their own interests. They hire lobbyists, and also take a considerable amount of the time of highly paid administrators to work with legislative committees and individual legislators in order to market their own programs, priorities, and budgetary needs. In some cases, their lobbying efforts may be directly opposed to the lobbying efforts of groups of citizens; but on the whole, the lobbying activities of correctional organizations have tended to be consistent with public opinion.

SUMMARY

A system is "any set of interrelated elements which, as they work and change together, may be regarded as a single entity."[11:327] A system may be physical or it may be analytical. An analytical system is one that is created by scholars and scientists to help us understand the operation of complex entities. Although the criminal justice system might not be a system in a physical sense, it can be regarded as a system in an analytic sense for the purpose of understanding its operation. Systems may be regarded as closed or open. An open system is one that has interchanges with the surrounding environment, while a closed system is isolated. Systems also contain feedback loops in which different elements influence each other reciprocally. The elements of a system may themselves be systems, so that we can speak of the corrections system within the criminal justice system, and we can speak of a prison system within a state corrections system.

Criminals enter the criminal justice system when they are apprehended by police officers. Those offenders who progress past this step are processed by the courts and sentenced to some sort of penalty. The correctional system is responsible for the administration of these penalties, some of which are paradoxically thought of as treatments by many correctional workers. The corrections system is, in a sense, at the mercy of the law enforcement and court systems, for it must take whatever number and composition of offenders are forwarded to it by court orders. At the same time, the courts and law enforcement authorities may adjust to correctional overcrowding by temporarily adjusting their own practices to reduce the flow of offenders into correctional programs. At each stage of the criminal justice system the number of offenders is reduced, as some of them are shunted outside of the system. This can be visualized as a series of filters which progressively modify the characteristics of offenders before turning them over to the correctional system. The filtering process depends on the behavior of many different individuals and the policies of many different criminal justice agencies, and there are numerous points at which biases can creep into the decision-making process. Because of these biases, we cannot assume that any correctional population is representative or typical of criminals in general.

The criminal justice system can be seen as a subsystem of the larger society, just as the correctional system can be seen as a subsystem of the criminal justice system. Much of the formal control exercised by national governments is administered through criminal justice systems. These criminal justice systems function by carrying out (albeit with much discretion) laws that have been passed by legislative bodies. This is the major point at which the larger society exercises control over the criminal justice system. Legislative bodies pass criminal laws, create agencies and programs, fund agencies and programs, carry out legislative investigations of the operation of criminal justice system elements, and set standards for the operation of criminal justice programs. Individual citizens, associations and pressure groups affect the actions of legislative bodies and also impact correctional programs directly.

REFERENCES

1. Belkin, Jacob, Alfred Blumstein, and William Glass. "Recidivism as a Feedback Process: An Analytical Model and Empirical Validation." *Journal of Criminal Justice* 1 (1973):7–26.
2. Bell, Wendy, Deborah Kahn, Ronald Lawson, and Stuart Szydlo. *The Impact of New Sentencing Laws on State Prison Populations in Pennsylvania.* Pittsburgh, PA: Urban Systems Institute, Carnegie-Mellon University, 1979.
3. Blalock, Hubert M., Jr. *Causal Inferences in Nonexperimental Research.* Chapel Hill, NC: University of North Carolina Press, 1961.
4. Blumstein, Alfred, Jacqueline Cohen, and Harold D. Miller. *Demographically Disaggregated Protections of Prison Populations.* Ptttsburgh, PA: Urban Systems Institute, Carnegie-Mellon University, 1978.
5. Cohen, Albert K. *Deviance and Control.* Englewood Cliffs, NJ: Prentice-Hall, 1966.
6. Cumming, Elaine, Ian Cumming, and Laura Edell. "Policeman as Philosopher, Guide and Friend." *Social Problems* 12 (1965):276–286.
7. Federal Bureau of Investigation. *Crime in the United States—1978* (Uniform Crime Reports). Washington, D.C.: Government Printing Office, 1979.
8. Florida Department of Corrections. *Annual Report, 1977–1978.* Tallahassee, FL: 1978.
9. Greenberg, David F. "The Dynamics of Oscillatory Punishment Processes." *Journal of Criminal Law and Criminology* 68 (1977):643–651.
10. Hagstad, Michael A. "Assessment of Recent Criminal Justice Trends in the District of Columbia." Analysis #77-3, Office of Planning and Program Analysis, Washington, D.C.: Department of Corrections, 1976.
11. Hoult, Thomas F. *Dictionary of Modern Sociology.* Totowa, NJ: Littlefield, Adams, 1969.
12. Jankovic, Ivan. "Labor Market and Imprisonment: A Postscript to the Rusche–Kirchheimer Theory of Punishment." Paper presented at the annual meeting of the Pacific Sociological Association, 1977.
13. Kuhn, Alfred. *The Study of Society: A Unified Approach.* Homewood, IL: Dorsey, 1963.
14. Law Enforcement Assistance Administration. *The National Manpower Survey of the Criminal Justice System, Volume 6, Criminal Justice Manpower Planning.* Washington, D.C.: Government Printing Office, 1978.

15. Law Enforcement Assistance Administration. *Criminal Victimization in the United States,* 1977. Washington, D.C.: Government Printing Office, 1979.

16. Law Enforcement Assistance Administration and Bureau of the Census. *Trends in Expenditure and Employment Data for the Criminal Justice System, 1971–1977.* Washington, D.C.: Government Printing Office, 1980.

17. Meyer, John C., Jr. "Patterns of Reporting Noncriminal Incidents to the Police." *Criminology* 12 (1974):70–83.

18. Minnesota. Department of Corrections. Research and Information Systems. *The Effect of the Availability of Community Residential Alternatives to State Incarceration on Sentencing Practices: The Social Control Issue.* St. Paul, MN, 1977.

19. Nagel, Jack H. "Crime and Incarceration: A Reanalysis." Fels Discussion Paper No. 112, School of Public and Urban Policy, University of Pennsylvania, 1977.

20. Nagel, William G. "On Behalf of a Moratorium on Prison Construction." *Crime and Delinquency* 23 (1977):154–172.

21. Pappenfort, Donnell M. and Thomas M. Young. *Use of Secure Detention for Juveniles and Alternatives to its Use.* A report of the National Study of Juvenile Detention, School of Social Service Administration, University of Chicago, 1977.

22. Parsons, Talcott. *Societies, Evolutionary and Comparative Perspectives.* Englewood Cliffs, NJ: Prentice-Hall, 1966.

23. Parsons, Talcott. *The System of Modern Societies.* Englewood Cliffs, NJ: Prentice-Hall, 1971.

24. Pepinsky, Harold E. *Crime Control Strategies: An Introduction to the Study of Crime.* New York: Oxford University Press, 1980.

25. Petersilia, Joan and Peter W. Greenwood. "Mandatory Prison Sentences: Their Projected Effects on Crime and Prison Populations." *Journal of Criminal Law and Criminology* 69 (1978):604–615.

26. Pope, Carl E. *Offender-Based Transaction Statistics: New Directions in Data Collection and Reporting.* Washington, D.C.: Government Printing Office, 1975.

27. Quinney, Richard. *Criminology: Analysis and Critique of Crime in America.* Boston: Little, Brown, 1975.

28. Reiss, Albert J., Jr. *The Police and the Public.* New Haven, CT: Yale University Press, 1971.

29. Rosett, Arthur and Donald R. Cressey. *Justice by Consent: Plea Bargains in the American Courthouse.* Philadelphia: J.B. Lippincott, 1976.

30. Rutherford, Andrew *et al. Prison Population and Policy Choice,* Vol. 1. Washington, D.C.: Government Printing Office, 1977.

31. Stephens, W. Richard, Jr. "Strategic Image Projection and the Production of Social Change: Penal Reform in Kansas, 1966–1979." Paper presented at the annual meeting of the Midwest Sociological Society, 1980.

32. Yeager, Matthew G. "Unemployment and Imprisonment." *Journal of Criminal Law and Criminology* 70 (1979):586–588.

Chapter 3

Competing Philosophies in Corrections

As human beings, we are not content merely to act. We feel the need to rationalize and justify our actions. As members of societies and smaller social groupings, we are similarly motivated to justify actions officially taken on behalf of the group. In modern civilizations, these justifications appear in writings of philosophers, enacted law and court decisions, administrative policy statements, and other documents. Beginning as a justification for the imposition of social control on the individual urge for revenge, correctional philosophies have risen and fallen. As new philosophies were developed, they did not completely replace older ones, so that contemporary correctional systems must cope with competing (and sometimes contradictory) philosophies at the same time. The sections that follow describe the eight major varieties of correctional philosophy that are currently in existence.

RETRIBUTION

The ancient principle of *lex talionis* gained its first written exposition in the Code of Hammurabi, which was written 1750 years before the birth of Christ. The Code specified "an eye for an eye and a tooth for a tooth." Not all eyes were equally valued in Babylon, for the punishments specified in the Code differed according to the social class of the offender. Offenses against members of the upper class carried much more severe punishments than offenses against members of groups that were lower in social status. The Bible also contains many statements about the appropriateness of retribution, particularly in the Old Testament. For example, Malachi tells us to tread down the wicked so that they become ashes under the soles of our feet. It has been theorized that retribution became the property of the government as a way of controlling private feuds that were potentially dangerous to the maintenance of social order, but there is no way to be sure that this was what people had in mind when they constructed the early legal codes.[33] Regardless of what they had in mind, the form of retribution that they espoused was nothing more than naked revenge.

In the 18th century, the philosophy of retribution was given a more sophisticated presentation by Immanuel Kant. Kant[19] argued that the penal law is a categorical imperative. Offenders must be punished because they have broken the law and for no other reason. The state has the right to prescribe appropriate penalties for all criminal acts. In Kant's conception, criminal acts are inherently wrong and therefore have to be punished. Being called for only by the nature of the act itself, criminal punishment could not be imposed to achieve any other end. All retributive theorists have the problem of locating a source of norms for the appropriateness of different levels of revenge. Kant solved this problem by locating authority in the state, but we recognize that all laws are not necessarily just. Some favor certain groups at the expense of others; and in any case, they are the fallible creations of human beings rather than the revelations of a Supreme Being.

The undeniable psychological pleasure that revenge brings to most human beings cannot be turned into a social policy that can be easily defended against critics such as Karl Menninger. Menninger[22] maintains that revenge is inconsistent with the principles of the Judeo-Christian heritage upon which Western civilization is founded and that the focus on revenge diverts us from finding out what kinds of penalties would be most effective in reducing crime. However, as Ernest van den Haag[37] has pointed out, retribution is not necessarily the same as revenge. It is the impersonal expression of social policy, and is devoid of the passion that characterizes revenge.

Philosophical evaluations of the retributive approach to corrections are the only ones that are possible because this approach has no utilitarian goals. It does not claim to reduce crime, nor does it protect society, except to the extent that the imposition of punishment adds to the legitimacy, credibility, and stability of the state. For this reason, belief in the validity of retribution is an act of faith.

RESTITUTION

Restitution has historical orgins that are even older than the Code of Hammurabi. King Ur-Nammu of the ancient Sumerian city of Ur issued a code that eliminated vengeance from criminal procedures 2100 years before the birth of Christ. This code substituted the imposition of fines and restitution for the infliction of mutilation and other savage penalties that had been customary.[22] The principle of restitution holds that offenders should reimburse victims for the value of whatever has been taken from them. In the case of physical injury or death, the reimbursement has to be limited to the financial consequences of the act, since there is no way to completely eliminate the effects of assaults and homicides. Restitution and retribution are similar in that they both attempt to reestablish the state of affairs that existed previous to the commission of the crime. They differ in that retribution proceeds from the victim to the offender while restitution proceeds from the offender to the victim. In retribution, the punishment is designed to lower the well-being of the offender by an amount equivalent to the amount of suffering caused by the crime. In contrast, the goal of restitution is to raise the well-being of the victim back up to the level that existed prior to the commission of the crime. In its purest form, restitution joins retribution in having no goal extending beyond the infliction of the punishment itself. It does not claim that offenders will be rehabilitated or that the threat of restitution will deter others from the commission of similar crimes.

The relative mildness of restitution as compared with retribution has favored its use for the upper classes down through history. Its current use in the United States is more extensive, and restitution is commonly used as a condition for probation for a wide variety of minor crimes.[34] The state assures the appropriateness of the amount of restitution. For example, a Delaware statute provides that the sentencing judge who chooses to impose a fine may conduct a hearing to determine the appropriate amount of money necessary to right the wrong done by the crime. This money, paid in the form of a fine to the state, is then remitted to the victim of the crime.[8]

Restitution to the State

Part of the philosophy behind the creation of criminal law is that offenses harm the state as well as the victims. An extension of this line of reasoning is that offenders may be required to give restitution to the state in addition to giving restitution to their victims. In practice, restitution to the state has often been more common than restitution to individual victims. An offender may be sentenced to give service to the state instead of being incarcerated. Public and charitable service of all kinds has been written into sentencing decrees, especially where juveniles were involved. Prison labor is another form of restitution in that prisoners are almost never paid the minimum wage. The difference between their wage, which is often only a few pennies per hour, and the minimum wage or the appropriate wage for their labor constitutes partial restitution to the state for their crimes. Although it is possible for prison systems to show a profit through the efficient use of prisoner labor, an unsolved problem in the use of prisoner labor is that the amount of the restitution provided by individual prisoners through unpaid labor in prison factories is not judicially set and therefore rarely corresponds to the amount of restitution appropriate for the crimes committed.

MAINTAINING SOCIAL SOLIDARITY

Retribution and restitution are the only two philosophies of punishment that do not see criminal penalty as a means toward an end that is located outside of the punishment apparatus. The use of punishment to maintain and reinforce social solidarity turns punishment from an end itself into a means to achieving the end of the maintenance of social solidarity. In this philosophy of punishment, as in the philosophies that we will discuss later in this chapter, the means–end relationship gives us a yardstick for measuring the effectiveness and appropriateness of the punishment that is imposed. The measurement process is never an easy one, and it does not yield perfect results, but it is at least a theoretical possibility.

The maintenance of social solidarity is not really a legal philosophy of punishment. Instead, it is a sociological theory of punishment. It was given its most extensive treatment by the early sociologist, Émile Durkheim. Durkheim[9] conceived of crime as functional, inevitable, and valuable to society. At the same time, he argued that punishment is necessary in order to maintain social cohesion in the face of criminal acts that would have a divisive effect on society if they were allowed to go unpunished. Durkheim was not referring to a deterrent effect when he talked about maintaining social cohesion. His meaning was closer to what we might call the symbolic function of the law as a representation of the social conscience. The drama of a criminal prosecution symbolizes the commitment of citizens and sovereigns alike to the norms, values, and beliefs that are embodied in the law.

In discussing the social functions of prisons, Johan Galtung[11] mentions two functions that are relevant to the maintenance of social solidarity. These are *social sanitation* and the *reinforcement of the symbols of the power holders in society*. Social sanitation refers to the removal of deviants from society, thus creating the impression that deviance is less common than it actually is. To the extent that social solidarity is based on an impression of moral homogeneity, it can be advanced by the operation of socially sanitizing institutions that lock offenders away from the public view. Reinforcing the symbols of the power holders in society refers to the theory that laws tend to codify the moral

Figure 3.1 The New York House of Refuge, 1832. (Law Enforcement Assistance Administration, U.S. Department of Justice.)

standards of the most powerful members of society. The more they reinforce such symbols, the more they pull the members of society together around common standards of behavior. At the same time, associating certain standards of behavior with high-status individuals has the advantage of making those standards particularly attractive to many other members of society, particularly those who aspire to be upwardly mobile.

GENERAL DETERRENCE

General deterrence refers to the effect of punishment on those who have not been punished. The theory is that we make examples of those who have been found guilty of criminal acts so that other citizens, seeing the suffering undergone by the convicted criminals, will fear that suffering so much that they will refrain from committing similar crimes. Taking this approach requires that we have a theory of human psychology. Jeremy Bentham[1] expressed this theory in a French volume published in 1811, which was translated into English in 1830. He believed that human beings would act so as to maximize their own pleasures and minimize pain and unhappiness. People commit criminal acts when they believe that they will gain a net benefit from having committed them. It follows from this that if punishments can be associated with crimes so that they result in greater pain than pleasure to offenders, then people will find it in their self-interest to confine themselves to law-abiding behavior. Like an earlier legal theorist, Cesare Beccaria, Bentham argued that punishments should never be more severe than what was necessary to deter crime. Excessive severity of punishment constituted oppression.[23]

On the face of it, this is a theory of punishment that seems to make sense. We are all afraid of pain, and few of us would be foolish enough to accept pain for no benefit. As soon as we move beyond the common-sense understanding of general deterrence, problems arise. For example, general deterrence assumes that all people are equally free to make decisions based on the calculus of pain and punishment, that they are equally capable of engaging in such a calculus, that they are equally aware of the existence of punishments for certain acts, and that they are equally fearful of the imposition of these punishments. It is unlikely that any of these assumptions can be supported in human societies.

Deterrence does not work when people are not free to decide on their own behavior, whether this be because of external forces such as poverty or internal compulsions such as those that arise from certain mental illnesses. A full explanation of the punishments that are given for major crimes is not included in the lessons of schoolchildren, nor is it made generally available to adults. Without accurate information about the nature of punishments, it is difficult for even the best-trained minds to weigh the possible consequences of crime against its possible benefits. There is also some evidence that criminals have less fear of punishment than noncriminals,[34] so that deterrence works best on those who probably do not commit the crimes anyway. Many criminals, like noncriminals, make few decisions on a rational basis. That portion of crime which is impulsive is much less likely than predominantly rational crime to be deterred by criminal sanctions.

These difficulties might not be overwhelming if the ideal deterrent systems proposed by Bentham and Beccaria could be put into effect. This has never happened, and probably never will. To do so would require a major reform of the criminal justice system and the expenditure of a huge sum of money. For example, Beccaria requires that punishment should be immediate, but criminal justice processing involves numerous delays. While excessive delays have been eliminated in certain experimental programs, it is not possible to eliminate all delays without violating the constitutional rights of defendants.

Research on General Deterrence

Granted that we cannot implement a perfect deterrence system, the idea of general deterrence still has merit. Furthermore, it can be more easily tested than Durkheim's theory of the maintenance of social solidarity. While the social solidarity theory has never received an adequate empirical test, there have been a great many studies of the effects of general deterrence. These studies are designed to evaluate the hypothesis that as you increase the level of punishment for a crime, you decrease the incidence of that crime. Daniel Nagin[26] has summarized research on the relationship between various measures of punishment and the crime rate. He found that increases in the percentage of crimes solved by the police, the probabilities of arrest, and police expenditures per capita were associated with decreases in crime rates. Increases in the ratio of prison commitments to reported crimes and prison commitments to persons charged were generally associated with decreases in crime, although the evidence was not completely consistent. Finally, the relationship between sentence severity, as measured by length of time served in correctional institutions, and crime rates was inconsistent. This suggests the possibility that the deterrent effects of police activities are greater than the deterrent effects of punishment activities that occur at the end of the criminal justice processing sequence. We can not be sure that this is so, for the deterrence studies cited by Nagin have serious methodological deficiencies. If future research confirms Nagin's conclusion, we will be able to say that the most immediate responses of the criminal justice system are most effective in deterring crime.

Even this general conclusion is undermined by a recent research report on the effects of arrest rates on official crime rates in 98 American cities between 1964 and 1970. David Greenberg and his associates[13] found very little support for the idea that increases in arrest rates depress official crime rates. There was no support at all for the contrasting proposition that increasing crime rates cause increases in arrest rates (or conversely, that decreasing crime rates cause decreases in arrest rates).

Despite the finding of significant correlations in many studies of general deterrence, deterrent effects may be trivial as compared with the effects of other social policies that might be implemented. Differences of only a few percentage points can be statistically significant in large samples. A related problem is that increasing the deterrent effect of penal sanctions just a few percentage points may have an extremely high cost, one that is even greater than the cost of other social policy adjustments that might have the effect of reducing crime. This is the conclusion of a recent study conducted at the Hoover Institution[6] in which crime rates appeared to have greater responsiveness to permanent changes in employment opportunties than to the deterrent effect of increases in either clearance rates or prison sentences. A number of investigators have found a relationship between the unemployment rate and the crime rate.[18,24] Jack Nagel[24] found that unemployment, urbanization, per capita income, and region of the country were much more strongly associated with the crime rate than the incarceration rate. So the ultimate challenge to the theory of deterrence may not be that it is wrong but rather that it is not terribly important and that strategies based on the deterrence philosophy are much more expensive and less efficient than preventive strategies based on unemployment and other economic variables.

Crime and Imprisonment. There is always much debate about the opening of new correctional facilities, and part of that debate centers around their effectiveness as a deterrent to crime. We would expect that if incarceration has a deterrent effect on crime, a rise in the incarceration rate in a jurisdiction would result in a decrease in the crime rate. This decrease would not necessarily be immediate, but might lag one or two years behind the incarceration rate because of the amount of time necessary for criminals to become aware of the increase in the use of imprisonment and to adjust their activities accordingly. This is exactly what we find if we look at the relationship between the F.B.I. crime index rate and the combined incarceration rate for state and federal prisons in the United States between 1958 and 1978. The only significant relationship between these two variables occurs between the crime rate and the incarceration rate two years earlier. This is consistent with the idea that imprisonment deters crime. However, if we perform the same operations with data from the years 1941 through 1957, a completely different pattern emerges. In these years, the dominant effect is that rises in crime are associated with decreases in the imprisonment rate one, two, and three years later. This is completely inconsistent with the deterrence hypothesis, and leaves us with a great deal of uncertainty about the deterrent effectiveness of imprisonment. One way of looking at these findings is to conclude that the crime rate and the incarceration rate operate rather independently of each other.

Since the evidence about the relationship between imprisonment and crime is weak and contradictory, the investing of huge sums of money to build new correctional institutions in the hope that the increased use of incarceration will reduce the crime rate through its deterrent effects is ill-advised. However, there may be other ways in which the use of incarceration and other penal sanctions may depress crime rates. The first of these is special deterrence.

SPECIAL DETERRENCE

Special deterrence refers to the effect of punishment on the future behavior of the criminal rather than on other members of society. Like general deterrence, special deterrence rests upon a conception of humans as rational beings who evaluate benefits and losses to be gained from behavior and then choose that behavior which maximizes the benefit/loss ratio. As applied to special deterrence, this principle means that individuals who have had the unpleasantness of punishment brought home to them by virtue of having suffered it themselves will be deterred from the future commission of the act which led to their punishment. Herbert Packer[29] refers to this as the intimidation theory of punishment.

Special deterrence is more difficult to test than general deterrence. Data on crime and punishment rates for large jurisdictions have been collected for many years, and these have been used to attempt to assess the general deterrent effect of an increase in punishment on crime rates (although methodological problems invariably leave us with a lack of certainty about whether the effects observed really reflect deterrence). The analogous evaluation measure for special deterrence is the criminal career. The question then becomes, "Does the imposition of punishment reduce the number of crimes that the criminal will commit in the future?" We do not as yet have answers to this question.

A simpler measure of the operation of special deterrence is the recidivism rate. Because recidivism rates are generally judged to be "high," legal theorists such as Hyman Gross feel justified in concluding that "The reason that punishment cannot be justified as a means of deterring law breakers from further crime is that it fails to do that."[14:399] This is not a fair test of the special deterrence approach because it ignores all of the other crimes that offenders may commit in their lifetimes other than the crime for which they are labeled recidivists. Although we are unable to evaluate the special deterrence approach at this time, the observation that many prisoners are more comfortable than street people with the idea that they might have to serve a future prison term as a consequence of continuing their lives of crime[36] makes it possible to venture the conjecture that general deterrence is probably more effective then special deterrence.

TREATMENT

The treatment justification for punishment consists of the idea that we can change criminals by involving them in various correctional enterprises, even though that involvement is against their will. Other terms that are sometimes used to express the treatment philosophy include rehabilitation, reeducation, and reintegration. These terms are all misleading in that they imply a return to a former state of law-abiding behavior. There are some criminals who were law-abiding until they committed a crime under great stress or other unusual circumstances, and who could possibly be rehabilitated to their original state. However, most criminals who are subject to correctional treatment programs come from subcultural environments that are conducive to criminal behavior. To restore them to their pre-trial state would be to restore them to a state in which they would be likely to continue their pattern of criminal behavior.

The treatment approach was applied in institutional corrections by the Quakers in the late 17th century, but they never developed an elaborate philosophy of treatment. This philosophical justification for treatment in corrections did not gain a full exposition until Enrico Ferri's work in the early 20th century. Ferri took a social defense approach to criminal behavior instead of a deterrence approach. Questions of guilt became irrelevant in his thinking and were replaced by the application of whatever humane measures were necessary to defend members of society from additional criminal acts. In short, punishments were designed to fit the offenders, not the offences. Ferri proposed many penal substitutes that were preventive rather than corrective in nature, and also included the treatment of offenders in his philosophy. Since Ferri's statement of the philosophy of social defense, that approach has become more and more closely identified with the treatment of offenders and has embodied a corresponding decrease of emphasis on preventive measures. At the same time, the justification of treatment in terms of protecting society became twisted into a justification in terms of its alleged benefits for the offender in a wholesale application of the medical model to criminal justice processing.[28]

Under the medical model, correctional treatment "consists of some course of action directed to transforming individuals into less undesirable, more complete and adequate, better-functioning social beings."[15:130] Because the offender is seen as suffering from some sort of identifiable and correctable disorder, a program of treatment composed of individual or group therapy, educational or vocational training, and other program elements is presumed to be able to change their attitudes and behavior enough to permit them to become law-abiding citizens.[16] The attractiveness of the medical model to correctional practitioners and theorists became so great that they tended to forget there were differences between physical illness and crime. Seeing criminals as sick rather than deviant promoted the illusion that correctional treatment was being forced on offenders for their own good. They were viewed as benefiting from this treatment much as they would benefit from going to a physician for a bad cold, and considerations of justice in assigning sentence length were deemphasized. Indeterminant sentences were imposed which signalled that offenders would be treated until they were cured, however long that might be. In many cases, prisoners ended up serving more time under indeterminant sentences than they would have served under determinant sentences based on the philosophy of deterrence, and this had particularly negative impacts upon juveniles and women.

Much of the thinking about the treatment philosophy has involved a confusion between means and ends. Just because the ends being pursued in correctional programs are humane and positive does not mean that the means employed to reach those ends will be equally acceptable. As experience with treatment programs accumulated, they were increasingly criticized as being inhumane. Excessive zeal in the application of the principles of behavior modification can easily result in programs that substantially brutalize offenders. Lengthy confinement in solitary cells, castration, and even frontal lobotomies administered against the will of the offenders have been justified under the treatment theory of punishment. To the extent that treatment methods dehumanize offenders and leave them less able to cope with the external world than they were before being treated, treatment becomes self-defeating.

The Attack on Treatment

Except for a small number of model programs and experiments, the medical model was never fully implemented in correctional systems. Despite the extensive publicity that was given to correctional changes made under the medical model, the program and staffing modifications made in the average correctional institution or community corrections program were quite modest. Gross[14] comments that the justification for punishment in terms of treatment must be made with reference to treatment in practice rather than treatment in principle. He says that we must look at what is actually being done to prisoners rather than the theory of treatment if we are to see whether it is justifiable. This approach exposes the difference between the theory of treatment and its inadequate application in correctional programs, and leads to the conclusion that treatment is not an adequate justification for punishment. For those offenders who have been imprisoned, Gross thinks that the best that any treatment can hope to do for them is to undo the damage that imprisonment itself has done to them.

A second line of attack on the medical model of punishment came from summaries of evaluation research projects that have been carried out over the years on treatment programs. These summaries generally show that even where treatment programs were fully implemented, they were not terribly effective. Even the best of them were effective only with certain kinds of offenders and under certain conditions.[21] More importantly, these results look particularly shabby when compared with the burgeoning success rates of medical treatments being developed for physical illnesses. The excessive claims that had been made for the treatment of offenders had raised expectations so high that they were bound to fall with a crash, and this occurred in the late 1970s. Theorists were now making statements such as "Not only is it now inconceivable to make a deviant normal, but no one, I submit, really *believes* it conceivable."[31:183] In one of the more innovative studies on the subject, Andrew Hopkins compared offenders sentenced by five different judges, finding that for those offenders incarcerated by a severe judge who would not have been incarcerated by a lenient judge, the probability of recidivism was increased rather than being decreased by institutional treatment.[17] The impression of mounting negative evidence about the effectiveness of treatment (which is not entirely correct, as we shall see in later chapters) has led even the Quakers, who originally developed the justification, to abandon it in the United States[31] and in Australia.[39] Van Groningen quotes a spokesman for the Friends Society in New South Wales as saying that the rehabilitation model is "theoretically faulty, systematically discriminatory in administration, and inconsistent with some of our most basic concepts of justice."[27,39:4]

Rejecting the treatment philosophy of punishment on the basis of its ineffectiveness as measured by recidivism studies is not entirely appropriate. Low recidivism among the graduates of the correctional treatment program requires not only an effective program but also the ability and willingness of law-abiding members of society to welcome the released offenders back into normal life. The long-term failure of many treated offenders may be due more to the inadequacies of the social response to their new identities than to the technical inadequacies of the programs in which they were treated. The criminal justice system has developed elaborate mechanisms for stigmatizing offenders and removing them from society, but there are few parallel mechanisms for the reacceptance of treated offenders back in society. Because correctional programs are entwined with other criminal justice system programs and with elements in the larger society, they cannot hope to be effective where other system elements are not strongly supportive of their efforts. In a sense, the treatment justification for punishment was predestined to be deemphasized by the inability of criminal justice system practitioners to bring about changes in the larger society that were consistent with the philosophy of treatment in corrections.

INCAPACITATION

Even if we concede that we cannot successfully treat a high percentage of offenders, we can still keep them from committing crimes against free people while they are locked up in correctional institutions (except for those free people who work behind the walls, and are therefore subject to an increased probability of victimization). Of course, there is no sense in locking up someone who wouldn't have committed any additional crimes on the streets. So although the incapacitation justification for punishment is not technically concerned with recidivism, it is actually based on the consideration of the relative probabilities of recidivism for different types of offenders. This consideration becomes paramount when correctional systems can only incarcerate a very small percentage of all the offenders who come to their attention.

Estimates of the probability of recidivism are derived from the prior criminal records of offenders, records which document only a small proportion of the total crimes committed by the offenders. The suspicion that the artificiality of official criminal records makes them relatively useless as predictors of candidates for extensive incapacitation has been confirmed in several recent studies which showed that it was not possible to differentiate between offenders who will persistently commit criminal acts if released and those who will commit few criminal acts or none at all.[5,32] This difficulty leads to a second problem: that of false positives. It is estimated that even with the most efficient prediction system available, there will be two or three incorrect predictions for every correct prediction of menace.[30] This means that rational incapacitative policies with the present state of technology would invariably have to violate the principles of justice in that many more "innocent" offenders would be incarcerated for lengthy periods of time not justified by their instant offense than the number who would be appropriately confined for extended sentences. Needless to say, the cost of implementing this policy would be prohibitive.

Two other problems arise with respect to the theory of incapacitation. The first of these is that most of the studies of the effect of incapacitation conclude that any use of incapacitation within reach of current criminal justice systems would be unlikely to reduce the portion of crimes committed by more than a small percentage.[7] For example, a study in Columbus, Ohio found that imposing a mandatory five-year prison term on all felony offenders would reduce known serious crime by only 2.7 percent, while imposing a substantial cost on the local taxpayers.[38] Because estimates of the proportionate reduction in crime that would occur if we greatly increased sentence length vary according to the assumptions made (such as the assumption about the proportion of all future crime that will be committed by current offenders), it is not possible to place a great deal of faith in any of the estimates yet produced.

The other problem is that incapacitation may not actually reduce crime at all. Instead, its major effect may be displacing crime from the streets to the prisons. Felons may commit as many crimes within prisons as they would have had they been on the streets, the only difference being that they now commit them against fellow-prisoners instead of against free people. (See Chapter 11 for more information on criminal victimization.) Statistics about prison victimization are high enough so we cannot dismiss this possibility out of hand. If this is so, then we must ask whether it is legitimate to incarcerate people simply for the reason of displacing their criminal aggressions to other felons.

RETRIBUTION REVISITED: JUST DESERTS AND THE JUSTICE MODEL

Many penal philosophers, social scientists, and correctional practitioners have lost their faith in the philosophies of punishment already discussed. They have increasingly turned to a retooling of the old theory of retribution. If we take the position that the deterrent effect of punishment is rather small and insignificant, that effective incapacitation involves huge costs and the wrongful imprisonment of far too many citizens, and that we cannot treat correctional clients well enough to change them without violating their constitutional rights, then there is little alternative but to return to less complicated theories such as restitution and retribution. This is precisely the position taken by the champions of the recently developed justice or just deserts model of corrections. Under this model, as proposed by Fogel[10], imprisonment and other correctional measures are seen only as punishment for having broken the law. There is no further justification, and correctional administrators following this new model concentrate on fairness in their administration rather than rehabilitation, treatment, deterrence, or anything else. Imprisonment is made decent rather than excessively painful, and accords prisoners as many rights as possible. These include self-governance and ombudsmen to assure the fairness of correctional policies and procedures. In the courts, the justice model requires the elimination of indeterminant sentences and their replacement with determinate sentences in which the penalty for each crime becomes uniform and clear.

The interesting thing about the justice model is that it has been simultaneously embraced by liberals and conservatives. The conservatives find it appealing because it appears to be "tough on crime," and to allow them to argue for longer sentences (which is a distortion of Fogel's intent). The elimination of plea bargaining under the justice model increases the likelihood that offenders will receive the punishment that they appear to deserve on the basis of the evidence. Fewer offenders will escape without punishment. At the same time, liberals find it appealing because it reduces the amount of judicial discretion, which they see as having been associated with a great deal of injustice. Furthermore, they believe that since treatment either does not work or is unlikely to be fully implemented so that it can work in the present correctional system, there is no longer much sense in supporting it as the major justification for punishment.

The difficulty with the justice model is the same as the difficulty with the original theory of retribution. Both these approaches look backward at the crimes that have been committed but make no claim as to the future impact of punishment. As a practical matter, it is difficult to feel completely comfortable with a theory of punishment that promises no diminishing of criminality. There is a strain toward combining the justice model with one or another of the other justifications for punishment. For example, Andrew Von Hirsch[40] argues in his just deserts model that punishments must deter as well as being deserved. The concepts of just deserts and deterrence are intertwined in his argument for a new system of sentencing and correctional treatment.

The fact that the justice model has no reference to outcomes leaves the philosophy with a strange problem. Under the philosophies of general and special deterrence, the severity of punishment could be determined by its effects on general criminality and offender recidivism. With no utilitarian orientation at all, the justice model has difficulty in giving us guidelines for matching appropriate punishments with crimes. Should a robber receive five years or five months in prison? Should the thief be required to pay back the victim with interest or to do public service for a year? The justice model gives us no guidance in these choices, except to refer us to public opinion. Unfortunately, legislators tend to gauge public opinion by those who contact them directly on an issue, so it is difficult for them to judge the extent to which their actions reflect the opinions of the public as a whole.

The advantage of the justice model is presumably that these punishments will be more uniformly administered to offenders than they have been in the past. It is too early to be sure that this will prove true in practice. Granted that the justice model reduces judicial and correctional discretion: there is the possibility that increased prosecutorial discretion will balance decreases in judicial and correctional discretion. In that case, the main effect of the justice model on the criminal justice system will be to shift the focus of discretion rather than to substantially reduce it.

CAVEATS TO THEORIES OF PUNISHMENT

No discussion of competing philosophies of punishment would be complete without mentioning some of the problems common to all theories of punishment. Three of these problems are the relationship between crime and punishment, public opinion about punishment, and the responsiveness of the correctional system to forces other than those included in theories of punishment.

The Relationship Between Crime and Punishment

Mark Kennedy[20] argues that crime and punishment are not analytically separate categories. They only appear to be two independent classes of harms when viewed superficially. He points out that it is the state—which he defines as a community of ruling officials—that creates and sustains the crime–punishment dichotomy. There is nothing inherent in those two classes of harms which differentiates one from the other. Crime is a judicially proven violation of criminal law, while punishment is a harm that is demanded by the law.

When one looks at these two concepts historically, it is evident that revolutions and social movements have the potential for transforming today's punishments into tomorrow's crimes. This is precisely what happened when the recent revolution in Iran resulted in the creation of a new social order in which the previous punishments meted out under the authority of the Shah were redefined as crimes and government officials who had carried out these punishments were labeled as criminals and themselves punished, in many cases by death. Through this same process, civil harms can be transformed into criminal harms and vice versa. After surveying the historical development of crime and punishment in philosophy and practice, Kennedy concludes that "It is power alone which creates and sustains the illusion that crime and punishment are independent, mutually exclusive species of conduct."[20:35] Kennedy's perspective reminds us that (1) crime is arbitrarily defined by governments, (2) few human acts are universally defined as crimes, and (3) it is impossible to separate the definition of a crime from its setting in space and time or from the conditions of its creation.

Public Opinion and Punishment

No philosophy of punishment can ever be fully implemented without the general support of the members of society. It is interesting that the many legal philosophers, legislators, and correctional administrators who develop and implement correctional policies rarely make any attempt to systematically find out what the public thinks about criminal and correctional matters. On the few occasions when social scientists have asked samples of people what they think about criminal punishment, the answers have tended to be less punitive than existing correctional practices. In answer to a question about the most effective ways to reduce crime, only 20 percent of a San Francisco sample and 32 percent of a Portland, Oregon sample favored the conservative methods of heavier sentences and more laws, as compared with 70 percent in San Francisco and 65 percent in Portland who favored better treatment programs in areas such as education, employment, and therapy.[12] These are surprisingly treatment-oriented responses, even given the relatively liberal reputations of Portland and San Francisco. Despite numerous statements by correctional administrators to the effect that conjugal visits (overnight visits between spouses) could not be implemented because of public opposition, samples of citizens drawn in Tennessee and Georgia found the majority of both male and female respondents to be in support of conjugal visits. Furthermore, more than four out of every five respondents in the Georgia sample were in favor of work release for prisoners, and nearly half of them were in favor of furloughs in which prisoners would be permitted to return home to live with their family on weekends.[35] These studies remind us that it is dangerous to make changes in punishment philosophies based partially on assumptions about public opinion without testing those assumptions through scientific opinion polls.

The Stability of Punishment

Starting from Durkheim's observation that there may be an optimum level of crime for each social type, Alfred Blumstein and Jacqueline Cohen[2] developed a theory about the stability of punishment. According to this theory, each society imposes a fairly constant level of punishment and makes adjustments in the criminal justice system in order to maintain that level in the face of increases and declines in the rates of various kinds of crimes. If the level of criminal behavior in a society increases, then the criminal justice system can reduce the severity of punishments for borderline offenses or can redefine the boundaries at which acts become defined as crimes. Both of these strategies will tend to maintain punishment at a fairly constant rate. Similarly, if the level of deviance declines, the severity of punishment can be increased and the boundaries of the official definition of criminality can be expanded. This general model has been shown to be consistent with data on imprisonment from the United States as a whole, Norway,[2] Canada,[3] and 47 individual America states.[4] The rates of imprisonment in all these jurisdictions do not remain exactly constant. They show many ups and downs, but they vary within a reasonable interval around the mean, and therefore may be considered to be essentially homeostatic.

These studies show that punishment rates, at least as indexed by imprisonment rates, have remained generally constant through periods of the application of a number of different punishment philosophies. This leads to the question, "What difference does it make which punishment philosophy we use?" The implication is that forces in the general structure of society may be more important in determining punishment levels than the particular philosophy of punishment that is being used at a given time. An overview of these social forces was presented in Chapter 2, and their historical influence on the development of corrections is described in Chapters 4 and 5. They are also treated in Chapter 12 and Chapter 17.

SUMMARY

Correctional practices are based on a variety of different correctional philosophies. Retribution is the traditional code of an eye for an eye and a tooth for a tooth. Restitution restores to the victim that which has been lost as a consequence of the crime. A third philosophy of corrections says that punishment is necessary in order to maintain social cohesion in the face of criminal acts that would have divisive effects on society if they were allowed to go unpunished. Two related philosophies of corrections are general deterrence, which refers to the effect of punishment on those who have not been punished, and special deterrence, which refers to the effect of punishment on the future behavior of the criminal who has been punished.

The three remaining philosophies of corrections are treatment, incapacitation, and the just deserts or justice model. The treatment philosophy of corrections argues that we can change criminals into law-abiding citizens by involving them in various correction enterprises, even though that involvement is against their will. Incapacitation does not require that we be successful in treating the offenders. Under this philosophy, correctional institutions keep criminals from committing crimes against free people by locking them up. The just deserts or justice model of corrections has its roots in the philosophy of retribution. In this model, imprisonment and other correctional measures are seen only as punishment for having broken the law. There is no further justification, and correctional administrators following this model concentrate on fairness rather than rehabilitation, treatment, or deterrence.

In considering these philosophies of corrections, it would be a mistake to ignore the political nature of crime. The question of which acts will be defined as crimes and subject to punishments is initially decided by legislatures in democratic countries and then subjected to reinterpretation by the courts and to redefinition in practice by law enforcement personnel. Law-abiding behavior becomes crime overnight as a result of legislative action, and entire criminal codes can be changed when there is a major social revolution. Public opinion, acting on all of these elements in the social system, is a major instrument of change in the definition of crime and punishment. There is some evidence that punishment rates at least as indexed by imprisonment rates, have remained generally constant through the application of a number of different correctional philosophies. This leads us to consider the possibility that the general structure of society (including factors such as economic conditions and the demographic structure of the population) may be more important in determining punishment levels than the particular philosophy of punishment used at a given point in time.

REFERENCES

1. Bentham, Jeremy. *The Rationale of Punishment.* London: Robert Heward, 1930. Originally published in 1811.
2. Blumstein, Alfred and Jacqueline Cohen. "A Theory of the Stability of Punishment." *The Journal of Criminal Law and Criminology* 64 (1973): 198–207.
3. Blumstein, Alfred, Jacqueline Cohen, and Daniel Nagin. "The Dynamics of a Homeostatic Punishment Process." *The Journal of Criminal Law and Criminology* 67 (1977):317–334.
4. Blumstein, Alfred and Soumyo Moitra. "An Analysis of the Time Series of the Imprisonment Rate in the States of the United States: A Further Test of the Stability of Punishment Hypothesis." *The Journal of Criminal Law and Criminology* 70 (1979):376–390.
5. Blumstein, Alfred and Soumyo Moitra. "The Identification of 'Career Criminals' from 'Chronic Offenders' in a Cohort." Unpublished paper, Carnegie-Mellon University, 1979.
6. Center for Econometric Studies of the Justice System. The Hoover Institution. *Research Developments.* Stanford University, June 1979.
7. Cohen, Jacqueline. "The Incapacitative Effect of Imprisonment: A Critical Review of the Literature." *In* Alfred Blumstein, Jacqueline Cohen, and Daniel Nagin:

Deterrence and Incapacitation: Estimated the Effects of Criminal Sanctions on Crime Rates. Washington, D.C.: National Academy of Sciences, 1978, pp. 187–243.

8. Delaware Laws, 1969, Chapter 198.

9. Durkheim, Emile. *The Division of Labor in Society.* New York: The Free Press, 1964. Originally published in 1893.

10. Fogel, David. *"...We are the Living Proof..." The Justice Model for Corrections.* Cincinnati: W.H. Anderson, 1975.

11. Galtung, Johan. "The Social Functions of a Prison." *In* Lawrence Hazelrigg: *Prison Within Society.* Garden City, NY: Doubleday, 1968, pp. 27–49.

12. Gibbons, Don C., Joseph F. Jones, and Peter G. Garabedian. "Gauging Public Opinion About the Crime Problem." *Crime and Delinquency* 18 (1972):134–146.

13. Greenberg, David F., Ronald C. Kessler, and Charles H. Logan. " A Panel Model of Crime Rates and Arrest Rates." *American Sociological Review* 44 (1979):843–850.

14. Gross, Hyman. *A Theory of Criminal Justice.* New York: Oxford University Press, 1979.

15. Hartjen, Clayton A. *Crime and Criminalization.* New York: Praeger, 1974.

16. Hawkins, Gordon. *The Prison: Policy and Practice.* Chicago: University of Chicago Press, 1976.

17. Hopkins, Andrew P. *Return to Crime: A Quasi-Experimental Study of the Effects of Imprisonment and Its Alternatives.* Ph.D. dissertation, University of Connecticut, 1973.

18. Jankovic, Ivan. "Labor Market and Imprisonment: A Postscript to the Rusche Kirchheimer Theory of Punishment." Paper presented at the annual meeting of the Pacific Sociological Association, 1977.

19. Kant, Immanuel. *The Philosophy of Law, Part II.* Edinburgh: T.T. Clar, 1887.

20. Kennedy, Mark C. "Beyond Incrimination: Some Neglected Facets of the Theory of Punishment." *Catalyst* 5 (Summer 1970):1–37.

21. Lipton, Douglas, Robert Martinson, and Judith Wilks. *The Effectiveness of Correctional Treatment: A Survey of Treatment Evaluation Studies.* New York: Praeger, 1976.

22. Menninger, Karl. *The Crime of Punishment.* New York: Viking Press, 1968.

23. Monachesi, Elio. "Cesare Beccaria, 1738–1794." *In* Herman Mannheim: *Pioneers in Criminology.* Montclair, N.J.: Patterson Smith, 1973, pp. 36–50.

24. Nagel, Jack H. "Crime and Incarceration: A Reanalysis." Fels discussion paper No. 112, School of Public and Urban Policy, University of Pennsylvania, 1977.

25. Nagel, William G. "On Behalf of a Moratorium on Prison Construction." *Crime and Delinquency* 23 (1977):154–172.

26. Nagin, Daniel. "General Deterrence: A Review of the Empirical Evidence." *In* Alfred Blumstein, Jacqueline Cohen, and Daniel Nagin: *Deterrence and Incapacitation: Estimating the Effects of Criminal Sanctions on Crime Rates.* Washington, D.C.: National Academy of Sciences, 1978, pp. 95–139.

27. Nagle, Justice. *Report on the Royal Commission Into New South Wales Prisons, March 1978.*

28. Newman, Graeme, *The Punishment Response.* New York: J.B. Lippincott, 1978.

29. Packer, Herbert L. *The Limits of the Criminal Sanction.* Stanford: Stanford University Press, 1968.

30. Pease, Ken and Joyce Wolfson. "Incapacitation Studies: A review and Commentary." *The Howard Journal of Penology and Crime Prevention* 18 (1979):160–167.

31. Pepinsky, Harold E. *Crime Control Strategies: An Introduction to the Study of Crime.* New York: Oxford University Press, 1980.

32. Petersilia, Joan, Peter W. Greenwood, and Marvin Lavin. *Criminal Careers of Habitual Felons.* Washington, D.C.: Government Printing Office, 1978.

33. Reid, Sue T. *Crime and Criminology.* Hinsdale, IL: Dryden Press, 1976.

34. Revelle, George H. *Sentencing and Probation.* Reno, NV: National College of the State Judiciary, 1973.

35. Smith, David L. and C.M. Lipsey. "Public Opinion and Penal Policy." *Criminology* 14 (1976):113–124.

36. Sommer, Robert. *The End of Imprisonment.* New York: Oxford University Press, 1976.

37. Van den Haag, Ernest. *Punishing Criminals: Concerning a Very Old and Painful Question.* New York: Basic Books, 1975.

38. Van Dine, Stephen, John P. Conrad, and Simon Dinitz. *Restraining the Wicked: The Incapacitation of the Dangerous Criminal.* Lexington, MA: D.C. Heath, 1979.

39. Van Groningen, John. "Why We Cannot Rehabilitate." *The Bridge* (November 1978):4–5.

40. Von Hirsch, Andrew. *Doing Justice: The Choice of Punishments.* New York: Hill and Wang, 1976.

41. Wilson, James Q. "The Political Feasibility of Punishment." *In* J.B. Cederblom and William L. Blizek: *Justice and Punishment.* Cambridge, MA: Ballinger, 1977, pp. 107–124.

Chapter 4

The Early Development of Correctional Practices

In order to understand contemporary correctional practices, we need to have an appreciation of their historical origins. Chapters 4 and 5 have this function, with this chapter covering the period from the beginning of legal punishment through the 19th century and Chapter 5 discussing American corrections in the 20th century. Material on 20th-century corrections in other nations appears in Chapter 17.

Punishment in a legal sense did not begin until written legal codes were developed. Although punishment by social bodies existed in tribal societies, and although it continues to exist in small groups that are not legally constituted in contemporary society, the definition of punishment used in this book excludes these nonlegal, nonformalized harms. Our definition of punishment follows from the definition of crime as legally prohibited, punishable behavior. Although this definition of crime is an oversimplification—for one may also commit a crime by failing to perform an act that is specifically required by law, and there are also minor legally prohibited, punishable acts such as traffic violations that are not normally considered to be crimes—it is a definition that is useful for our purposes. Following from this definition, correctional punishment as treated in this text consists of legally required harms (or negative sanctions) inflicted upon individuals as a result of judicial determinations that they have committed acts prohibited under the criminal law.

THE BEGINNING OF LEGAL PUNISHMENT

The Code of Hammurabi, which was developed in the 18th century B.C. in Babylon, specified the appropriate level of revenge for each crime in the Code. In doing so, it limited the ruthlessness of revenge that might have been carried out by the extended family of the victim of the crime. This same principle, known as *lex talionis*, is found in such diverse documents as the *Manama Dharma Astra* of India, the *Hermes Trismegitus* of Egypt, and the Mosaic Code.[31] The Mosaic Code went beyond simple revenge to permit offender and victim to reach their own agreement or to have such agreements specified by a legally constituted authority as alternatives to the literal observance of "an eye for an eye and a tooth for a tooth." Although Mosaic Law allowed extreme punishments such as flogging and burning alive, it also specified that offenders could not be tortured and that proof of guilt could not be established without the concurrent testimony of at least two witnesses.[35]

The Greek philosophers stated that criminal punishment should not be retaliatory. It should reform the offender and deter others from committing crimes. In practice, however, reformation was reserved for the citizens of the Greek city-states and deterrence of a most vicious sort was directed toward the resident aliens and slaves. Citizens were likely to be fined for the same crimes that merited flogging when committed by slaves.[23] In criminal justice proceedings, the word of a citizen was guaranteed by oath, but the testimony of slaves could not be admissible unless it was obtained under torture. It was assumed that slaves could not understand the meaning of an oath because they were merely things, not people. Some of the Greek city-states allowed punishment normally reserved for slaves to be administered to a citizen if the citizenship of that offender was first removed in a ceremony of civic degradation.[33]

The punishments inflicted in ancient Greece including stoning, breaking on the wheel, burning alive, strangling, poisoning, banishment, branding, sentencing to penal slavery, and the payment of fines. The bodies of offenders who were fastened to wooden boards by metal bands and then had their bones systematically broken have been excavated in Greece. Although this technique was not always carried out on a wheel, it is known as breaking on the wheel. After the torture was concluded, victims may have been finished off by the torturer or simply left to slowly die from the injuries and the elements.[23] In Sparta, strangulation was carried out by two executioners who pulled at opposite ends of a single rope which was twisted around the victim's neck. Poisoning was a more elite form of capital punishment, and was the method used in the execution of Socrates. At Athens, banishment was decided by vote of the citizens, and resulted in exile for a period of ten years. This was also an elite punishment, and such famous philosophers as Xenophon, Thucydides, and Demosthenes suffered this fate.[35] Thorsten Sellin[33] has shown that imprisonment was used for the purpose of detention in Athens. Those who were waiting for their cases to be heard as well as those awaiting the execution of their sentences were detained in jail. If offenders refused to pay their fines, they could also be remanded to the jail, and this period of incarceration continued until the fine was paid. In this situation, it became the practical, if not legal, equivalent of punishment by fine.

Ancient Rome

Roman criminal law was not fully developed in the early centuries of the Republic because of the philosophy that legal difficulties should be settled between the interested parties as much as possible rather than being dealt with in a court of law. In addition, the tradition of *paterfamilias* gave the husband/father essentially unlim-ited power to punish his slaves and family members as he saw fit. This gradually declined over the centuries as the power of the father was curbed by law.[23]

Punishments that might be suffered by Roman citizens under the law included the paying of fines, the confiscation of goods and property, and the death sentence. As it happened, the death sentence was rarely carried out in the early centuries because citizens were given the choice of voluntary exile instead of execution.[23] A law passed in 509 B.C. prohibited Roman magistrates from flogging or executing citizens unless they received the approval of the Centuriate Assembly.[33] Frederick Wines[35] comments that although citizens could not be flogged under Roman law, it was possible to use the legal fiction that a thief was the slave of the penalty and therefore was no longer a free citizen and could be beaten. It is not clear to what extent this circumvention of legal protection for Roman citizens was practiced.

Two groups of people in Rome suffered much greater public punishment than citizens. These were soldiers and slaves. The discipline required of soldiers was extreme, and even minor offenses could result in severe punishment. The five main punishments that were meted out to soldier offenders were withholding pay, demotion, disgrace (which involved extensive public humiliation), flogging, and death by either beheading or beating. In some cases the beatings were administered by stoning rather than by clubbing.[23]

Slaves suffered even more severe punishments, including whipping, chaining, branding, mutilation, confinement in stocks, and execution by burning, beating, or crucifixion. Stocks were devices which fastened the ankles and perhaps neck and wrists of the offender in uncomfortable positions for long periods of time, perhaps in public places and exposed to the elements. A related torture was the carrying of the *furca,* which was a V-shaped yolk worn around the neck to which the offender's outstretched arms were tied.[33] As in ancient Greece, the testimony of slaves could not be accepted in court unless it was obtained under torture.[35] There were several kinds of prisons for slaves in Rome, one of which was the *ergastulum.* In the *ergastulum,* slaves were forced to do hard labor while attached to their work benches.[33] Another form of imprisonment was the use of underground cisterns entered from above through gratings. These cisterns were used to detain offenders, and in some cases to starve them to death. The Mamertine Prison is an example of this form of construction. It contained two levels, with detained prisoners being on the upper level and those condemned to death being on the lower level where they would starve or perhaps be strangled.[12]

PUNISHMENT IN THE MIDDLE AGES

The period of history known as the Middle Ages stretches from approximately 500 A.D. to 1500 A.D. The Justinian Code of 529 A.D. was the standard law throughout Europe in the Middle Ages. It developed out of the Twelve Tables of Roman law which had originated nearly 1000 years earlier. The Twelve Tables listed every crime then known and specified with precision the penalty to be paid for each offense. For example, criminals guilty of *laesa majestas* (derogating the dignity of the Emperor) were to be punished by flogging to death.[35]

Another early criminal code was the Burgundian Code, which originated around 500 A.D. This Code specified punishments according to the social class of offenders, dividing them into the nobles, middle, and lower classes, and specifying the value of the life of each person in society according to his social status. A murderer had to pay the value set on the victim's life to the victim's family in order to avoid suffering physical penalty. Freemen who committed crimes were usually able to avoid physical punishment by paying indemnities but the value even of a slave was too high for someone from the lower classes to pay the indemnity. Capital punishment was the fate of freemen who could not pay the indemnity for murder, theft, and robbery. Slaves were subject to death for all of these offenses plus manslaughter, assaults on freewomen, sexual relations with freewomen, altering boundary markers, and aiding fugitives to escape. Flogging was not applied to freemen, but it was extensively used as a punishment for minor crimes committed by slaves and serfs. Although judicial torture was never used for freemen, it was habitually applied to slaves, serfs, and strangers to establish their guilt or innocence when accused of a crime. Freeman also avoided punishment through the tradition of compurgation, in which family members and 12 other freemen would swear with the accused that he was free of guilt.[33]

Punishments gradually became more severe throughout the Middle Ages, partially in response to what appeared to be an increase in crime. Mutilating punishments such as amputation of hands, noses, and ears or blinding were reserved for slaves early in the Middle Ages and then gradually came to be applied to freemen. At the same time, the range of acts which called forth mutilating punishments increased. The fragmentation of Europe allowed many of the accused to escape their fate. In some areas, many more offenders escaped and were declared to be outlaws than were mutilated and executed. The intensifying of brutality of punishments heightened the contrast between the classes, with nobles and other high-status individuals continuing to avoid physical punishment in most cases and suffering less brutal punishment in the few cases where physical punishment was unavoidable.[18,33]

Ecclesiastical Punishments

The Church maintained its own criminal justice system throughout the Middle Ages. Except for crimes such as treason, all priests were immune to prosecution in secular courts. Others who were associated with the Church, including acolytes and doorkeepers, could also claim their right to be tried in ecclesiastical courts rather than in secular courts. The benefit of the clergy was eventually extended to anyone who could read. This was clearly a desirable option for offenders, for the ecclesiastical punishments were more lenient than secular punishments in most cases. This was because the focus of the Church was on penance and the salvation of the soul rather than on the administering of physical punishment for the purpose of deterrence or revenge. The ecclesiastical ban on maiming and execution did not extend to flogging, which was liberally applied. One of the most feared punishments was imprisonment in isolation.[18]

The Church also influenced medieval punishments through the substitution of ordeals for legal trials and in the establishment of the sanctuary of the Church. Until 1215 A.D., ordeals were used to establish the guilt or innocence of accused offenders by subjecting them to brutal tests of faith and body.[2] There was a test by immersion, in which those who sank were declared to be innocent, a test in which the innocent had to pick up a stone out of boiling water without being scalded, and a test in which a red-hot iron bar had to be carried without injury.[18] Needless to say, these tests produced a high proportion of findings of guilt. However, it was possible for priests to influence the outcome of tests by, for example, binding up the arm of a person reaching into boiling water so that it would not be scalded, thus affirming innocence.

The use of sanctuary was extended to offenders in the spirit of New Testament compassion. Under this doctrine, offenders could claim refuge in churches for as many as 40 days. This practice, which derived from the ancient Hebrews, ironically excluded Jews. The use of santuary began to decline at the end of the Middle Ages when a 1487 Bull from Pope Innocent VIII allowed offenders to be forcibly removed from sanctuaries if it could be shown that they used them as bases for the commission of crimes. George Ives[18] writes that by 1540, many sanctuaries had been closed and the remaining sanctuaries could no longer be used by offenders accused of crimes such as arson, burglary, rape, and murder.

The Holy Inquisition

The Inquisition is a general label for a succession of Roman Catholic tribunals charged with the detection and punishment of heresy. Although elements of the Inquisition were present throughout the Middle Ages, the Inquisition proper did not begin until the year 1215, when the Lateran Council decided that the use of torture was appropriate. Through the Inquisition, the influence of Church punishment was extended far into secular life at the same time that the harms visited upon the accused became much more brutal. The torture of the accused was supplemented by an extensive system of informers and detailed records kept of every element in the proceedings. Graeme Newman[23] cites the record of one Inquisitor as to the punishments he inflicted during one 15-year period in the early 14th century. Of 636 condemned individuals, 47 percent were imprisoned, 22 percent were condemned to wear crosses, 14 percent were already dead and had their bones exhumed, 6 percent were burned alive, 6 percent escaped punishment by becoming fugitives, and a few of the "guilty" suffered other miscellaneous punishments.

Galley Slavery

Galley slavery existed in ancient Rome and Greece, but was not used as a penal method in those days. It was not until 1348 that this form of slavery was institutionalized as punishment for criminals. Once established, the practice expanded, and did not vanish completely until 1803. In an age in which people witnessed boiling, burning, disembowling, stoning, branding, blinding, castrating, and dozens of other ghastly punishments as perfectly normal, it could be expected that galley slaves would not be well treated. In practice, the mistreatment of criminals consigned to the galleys was so great that by the time they were marched in chains across the countryside to port cities, many of them were unfit to pull an oar. Once chained to their oars in the galleys, their health deteriorated still further. They were chained to their oars for their entire sentences, which in many cases were for life. The only exception was when the galleys put into port to avoid winter weather at sea. By the middle of the 16th century, the branding of galley slaves made certain that even if they escaped from their confinement, they could always be identified and returned. Working long hours throughout the day in the hot sun, the galley slaves slept beside their oars at night in their own excrement, for there were no sanitary facilities provided. One can easily imagine the extent of disease spread by these human cesspools and the short life-expectancy of the average galley slave.[33]

Prisons in Medieval Europe

Castle keeps and dungeons were the only prisons in early medieval times and were still being heavily used for detention, torture, and execution throughout Europe at the end of the Middle Ages.[12] In England, prisons were first mentioned in legal codes in the year 890. The sentence for failing to perform tasks to which one was pledged was a mere 40 days, but these 40 days were to made miserable by punishments of the bishop's choice. The Fleet was the first London structure to have been built specifically as a prison. The date of erection is not known, but it is recorded that it was already in existence in 1130. The use of imprisonment was greatly extended by the Assizes of Clarendon in 1166, which specified that all counties that had not already constructed gaols (local jails) should immediately do so and that their building and maintenance would be paid for by the Crown rather than being taken from local funds. Although some offenders were imprisoned purely for the purpose of punishment, most were either awaiting trial or suffering imprisonment because they were unwilling or unable to pay fines.[4]

The 14th and 15th centuries saw the creation of numerous crimes in English law, many of which specified the use of imprisonment as punishment or as an inducement to pay fines. The most important of these were laws passed with the intent of controlling the labor market. For example, a law passed in 1349 decreed that agricultural day-laborers and workers in manufacturing industries who accepted wages higher than those existing in 1346–1347 or the average of wages existing in the six prior years should be imprisoned. Another law passed in the same year specified that agricultural workers who attempted to change jobs before their agreed-upon term of work was concluded were to suffer imprisonment as punishment. These and other laws were contrived to stabilize the labor market in a time of social change, and to guarantee what was thought to be an adequate level of profits for landowners and merchants.[28]

Conditions in the early gaols were extremely difficult for prisoners unless they were independently wealthy. The gaoler (jailer) extracted fees from prisoners in return for being admitted, being released, being fed, and having better-than-average accommodations. Gaol turnkeys (guards) were paid out of the gaoler's fees. Since staffing was always at a minimum, security in these early gaols was guaranteed by chaining prisoners at the wrists, ankles, and sometimes the neck, and then often attaching these chains to rings in the walls or floor. Again, the payment of a special fee might allow the well-to-do prisoner to avoid being shackled. Beds, blankets, mattresses, firewood, candles, and every other necessary commodity in a gaol were rented or sold to the prisoners by the gaoler at an exorbitant rate. The sexes were mixed together, and both suffered floggings, starvation, and other forms of torture on occasion. Few gaols provided adequate fresh water to drink or sanitary facilities, with the result that gaol fever (probably typhus) was a constant threat to the prisoners.[4]

WINDS OF CHANGE

The 16th through the 19th centuries were characterized by the continuing elaboration of brutal public penalties. At the same time, they saw the development of completely new penal practices such as transportation and a fundamental reconceptualization of the nature and conditions of imprisonment.

Brutal Public Punishments and Executions

Punishments in the 16th, 17th, and 18th centuries were more likely to be administered in local jurisdictions than at the national level. The local jurisdictions differed greatly as to the exact methods of punishment, and reforms that mitigated the brutality of punishment at the national level did not diffuse to the local level until much later in the period. In addition to flogging and branding, mutilation was extensively inflicted on criminals. The nature of the mutilation was often tied to the crime itself. For example, thieves had their hands cut off so that they could no longer steal, liars had their tongues torn out, spies their eyes gouged out, and female adulterers their faces disfigured so as to make them unattractive. Torture methods included the rack, in which the limbs were slowly dislocated, the thumbscrew, and the hooks, in which the prisoner was burned with red-hot pincers.[6]

There were also less severe punishments such as the ducking-stool, the brank, the pillory, and the stocks. Ducking-stools were chairs that could be lowered into a pond until the occupant was half drowned and then lifted up again, whence the act would be repeated. This punishment was used for scolding women, and occasionally for other minor criminals. When repeated often enough, it could, of course, be fatal. The brank, a metal headframe which forced a painful mouthpiece upon offenders so that they could not speak, was another punishment designed to still the tongues of women. Pillories and stocks confined offenders in standing or sitting positions in public places for crimes such as cheating on baked goods, forgery, and selling rotten meat. The ordeal was made much worse if public opinion was strongly against the offender, in which case crowds would throw items such as rotten eggs, dirt from the streets, stones, and even dead cats and rats at the exposed offenders.[3]

To the various punishments of hide and hair that were applied in these centuries, we must add the infliction of capital punishment. By 1760, there were 160 capital crimes in English legislation. Although there is some question as to the actual number of offenders executed, it is clear that the number was very large. The increase in the number of capital crimes was balanced by the decrease in the brutality of the executions. Offenders were less likely to be slowly executed with a variety of horrible tortures applied to their bodies before they expired. This reform movement reached its peak with the use in 1792 of the guillotine in France. This device administered executions cleanly and quickly, and it gave equal treatment to offenders of all classes.[9]

The Beginning of Prison Reform

Descriptions of prisons and prison life during the 16th and 17th centuries are not substantially different from those for earlier times. The beginnings of reform occurred in isolated instances and did not immediately affect most penal institutions. As feudalism disintegrated, more and more people drifted into large cities such as London without either homes or jobs. King Henry VIII tried brutal corporal punishment in 1531, and penal slavery in 1547, and still the vagrants increased. This led to the innovation in 1556 of the Bridewell, a penal institution in which vagrants and prostitutes worked at jobs such as baking and the carding and spinning of wool. The first Bridewell worked out so well that an act of Parliament in 1576 ordered all of the British counties to create Bridewells. These institutions apparently were successful in dealing with minor criminals and unattached laborers until the practice of transportation to the colonies was found to be a more economical and effective solution. By the time John Howard visited the Bridewells in 1775–1776, most of them were nearly empty, and only 7 out of 105 had more than 20 occupants.[33]

Transportation

Banishment was used as a way of ridding society of criminals from the earliest recorded times. The idea of the systematic transportation of large numbers of offenders to colonial lands was a continuation of this tradition. Transportation of convicts in England was authorized at the end of the 16th century, followed by Russia 50 years later and most of the other European countries in the following years.[36] This simultaneously settled the problems of vagrancy in the mother countries and the need for labor in the colonies or other far-flung possessions. The use of transportation in England was so successful that it was extended in 1718 to apply to all criminals who had been sentenced to three or more years of imprisonment. To make sure that transported criminals did not return before their sentences had expired, the penalty for an unauthorized return was set as execution. Because the transporting of the criminals was initially handled by contractors rather than by government agents, they were horribly mistreated, and many died enroute to their new homes. It is estimated that perhaps as many as 2000 prisoners a year were being received in the American colonies by the time of the Revolution, which ended the practice.[6] By that time, the colonists had found that African slaves were more easily brutalized than English convicts, so they were glad to make the change.

The accumulation of sentenced prisoners in English jails was very rapid once transportation to the American colonies was no longer possible. This led to the experiment of using old warships as floating prisons, on which disease and perversion multiplied in the unsanitary crowded conditions. A better solution was the transportation of convicts to Australia, which began in 1787. The total number of convicts transported from England to Australia may have been as many as 135,000 before the practice terminated in 1867.[6]

France did not begin transportation until 1791, but its penal colonies at Devil's Island in French Guiana and other tropical locations were far more brutal than the colonies established by other European countries. As many as 68,000 of the 70,000 prisoners who were sent to Devil's Island before it closed in 1953 perished without reaching the end of their sentences.[34]

The transportation of Russian prisoners to Siberia, which was to expand out of all proportion in the 20th century, began in 1753, at which time death sentences began to be commuted to Siberian exile. Forced colonization with or without hard labor was the fate of perhaps as many as 15,000–18,000 offenders per year in the 19th century and smaller numbers in the 18th century.[35]

Public Works and the Bagnes

The use of convict labor for the profit of the state or wealthy individuals was not limited to the Bridewells and transportation to the colonies. Criminals were also sentenced to labor on fortifications and other public works. In 1660, Saxony reserved the right to convert all sentences of whipping and banishment to forced labor to build fortresses. A similar ordinance was passed in Denmark in 1636. Penal fortress labor in Spain began in 1580, and in the Swiss cities between 1601 and 1661. Countless fortresses were erected all over Europe through the efforts of convicts sentenced to forced labor. The severity of the labor combined with inadequate food and rest led to an extremely high death rate in most of the projects.[33]

The bagnes were a specialized form of penal labor in the dockyards. They developed out of the use of galley slavery when it became necessary to house and extract useful labor from galley slaves during the winter season of bad maritime weather. In Marseilles, prisoner labor was organized into a gigantic state factory which was then leased to a group of merchants in 1701. An agreement signed between the merchants and the state in 1707 specified that they would accept up to 1500 convicts and Turks from the state so long as they were not blind, old, feeble, or manually crippled. Guards, medical services, and the religious needs of prisoners were to be provided by the state and the goods produced by the prisoners would be sold back to the state at fixed prices.[33]

The First Cellular Prison

Many of the abuses suffered by early prisoners were due to their confinement together in large open rooms. It was partially in reaction to this problem and partially due to the religious emphasis on meditation as a way of saving the soul that the first cellular prison was erected at the Hospital of St. Michael in Rome in 1704. The institution had single cells surrounding a congregate work area and arranged so that each prisoner could see the prominent altar in the central aisle, which allowed all the prisoners to join together in religious services while remaining segregated in their cells.[12]

Pope Clement XI, the founder of St. Michael's, placed the following inscription over the door of the institution: "For the correction and instruction of profligate youth, that they who when idle were injurious, may when taught become useful, to the State."[35:121] In the opinion of Frederick Wines,[35] the creation of St. Michael's was an official admission that the penal principles of retribution and repression had failed. With its emphasis on rehabilitation, St. Michael's was the forerunner of the juvenile reformatories of later centuries. Its use of segregation supplemented with silence on those occasions when prisoners were together was later to become the essence of the Auburn system of imprisonment in the United States.

John Howard and Prison Reform

John Howard became the Sheriff of Bedfordshire in 1773, and was greatly distressed by the conditions in English penal institutions. He then traveled to other European countries, visiting hundreds of penal institutions, most of which were crude and brutal. The result of these travels was his book, *State of Prisons*,[16] which was published in 1777. This volume detailed the horrors of the existing penal institutions and made extensive recommendations for their reform, including single cells for sleeping, the segregation of women and youth from other offenders, the provision of facilities for sanitation, and the abolition of the fee system by which jailers obtained money from prisoners in lieu of adequate salaries. He continued his travels and efforts on behalf of prisoners until he died of the plague while visiting a prison in Russia during 1790.[35] Before he died, many of the reforms he had recommended were written into the Penitentiary Act of 1779 and were embodied in the first modern penitentiary, which was erected in Norfolk, England in 1785. His emphasis on reform continues unabated today in active and influential John Howard societies in Great Britain and the United States.

The reforms recommended by Howard were incorporated in the panopticon prison, the plan for which was created by Jeremy Bentham in 1787. This institution was designed to be four stories high with all of the cells constructed around the outside of a perfect circle, their doors to be facing a central chapel and inspection area. The panopticon was to be built of cast iron and brick so as to be fireproof. It included a glass roof, ventilation and heating ducts, and individual sanitation in each cell. Separate accommodations, hard labor, and safe custody were all to be achieved in the panopticon prison. The prison was never built in England, but a similar structure was erected in Virginia in 1797, to be followed by the famous Western Penitentiary at Pittsburgh, Pennsylvania in the 19th century.[12]

CORRECTIONS IN 19TH-CENTURY EUROPE

Beginning about 1780, and continuing through 1830 in England, with similar dates in other European countries, the welfare of the working class was depressed so severely that increasing numbers of previously law-abiding citizens turned to crime. The result was a sharp increase in criminal convictions. In England, the number of convictions by Assizes and Quarter Sessions rose from 2649 in 1805–1806 to 14,408 in 1830–1833 and total convictions in France rose from 35,214 in 1825 to 72,490 in 1842. These increases in crime resulted in a considerable clamor for the reestablishment of a wide variety of brutal punishments that had been abandoned after the Middle Ages. Increasingly harsh laws were reinstituted in Austria, where the penal code of 1803 replaced the previous mild and humane punishments with the heavy use of punishments to hide and hair and execution. The number of offenders sentenced to be executed in England rose from an average of 477 per year in 1806–1812 to 1576 per year in 1827–1833. The number of sentences to imprisonment increased to a similar degree, causing severe overcrowding and deterioration of prison conditions. The increase in prisoners transported to Australia was even greater.[30]

The idea that prison conditions had to be worse than conditions among the poor in the free society meant that the conditions of incarceration had to get worse as economic conditions deteriorated in Europe. This was aggravated by maintaining prison budgets at constant levels while the prison populations skyrocketed. Inadequate nutrition led to little more than starvation in many facilities, and medical attention was completely unavailable in most of them. The result was that prison mortality was three to five times the mortality rate of similar cohorts in the free population.[30]

Ted Gurr[14] points out that the increases in executions in the early 19th century were aberrations in the general decrease of the use of the death penalty. When public order was restored in the 1840s and 1850s, the number of executions resumed its decline. The decline in executions throughout the remainder of the 19th century was paralleled by a decline in the use of corporal punishment. It initially disappeared from public spectacles, and then gradually became less common behind the walls of penal institutions. At the height of the temporary return to corporal punishment, legislation passed in 1830 in New South Wales, Australia allowed as many as 100 lashes and 12 months at hard labor for prisoners found to be drunk, neglectful of their duties, or using foul language. This declined after 1840, and had completely disappeared in New South Wales by the beginning of the 20th century.

As corporal punishment and executions became less common, other ways of making offenders miserable were incorporated into prison systems. These included the treadmill, the crank, and the shot-drill. In the treadmill, prisoners were forced to constantly climb stairs that were so constructed that they ran continuously backward like an escalator in reverse. The severity of this punishment can be gauged from the number of feet climbed per day, which ranged from 7200 to 14,000 feet per day. Considering that a stiff mountain climb is considered to be 3000 to 5000 feet per day, the severity of effort required of the prisoners was very great. In addition, there was the boredom of the routine, which was even worse in the use of the crank. The crank was a handle which had to be cranked round and round for endless hours, perhaps 10,000 revolutions to be done per day. The shot-drill involved carrying heavy cannonballs from one place to another, back and forth again. All of these punishments traded any hope of rehabilitation for pure deterrence.[33] Fears about the fragility of the social order led to a series of laws designed to strengthen the penitentiary system.[17] Prisons became increasingly centralized, with the national control of British prisons being achieved in 1877. At this time, the Prison Commission under Edmund Du Cane extended the use of boring and exhausting labor to the entire nation.[15]

Developments in Russia

Russia added a unique penal system to the workhouses and other penal institutions located in the western provinces. That was the exile of citizens to Siberia, a fate to which over 850,000 offenders were sentenced between 1807 and 1899. The most severe sentences were to hard labor, with forced colonization being much milder. The penal code of 1845 imposed terms of hard labor from four years to life, and added floggings and brandings for those prisoners who were not from the upper classes. If they were lucky, prisoners sentenced to hard labor would go to the factories or fortresses, for sentences to the mines were the most terrible of all. Convoys of prisoners left western Russia and walked between 4700 and 6700 miles to their places of exile, a process which took two to three years. Stockaded depots were located every 15 miles, and the prisoners walked 15 miles on two out of every three days, with the third day being a rest day in the road prisons.[33]

Death rates were extremely high on these extended marches, for the prisoners were heavily chained together and conditions in the rest prisons were verminous and overcrowded. Those sentenced only to forced colonization were more likely to survive, since they were less heavily chained and their families were more likely to follow them into exile, supporting them as best they could on the trek. Once arriving in exile, convicts were subjected to severe discipline and long hours of work. The convicts were easily identified by their heads, which had half of the hair shaved off, and were forced to obey a rule of silence until it was abolished in 1901. If they survived the early years of "probation," they were promoted to a "reform" class and allowed to live under less brutal conditions.[33]

Imprisoned Women in London

The women's prison at Brixton had a capacity of 700–800 in the mid-19th century. New prisoners were subjected to separate confinement for four months and then allowed to work in association with other prisoners under the rule of silence. Continued good behavior eventually resulted in their being permitted to speak to each other, although they continued to retire to their individual cells at the end of the work day. Before 1860, women who gave birth at Brixton were allowed to keep their children until the age of two, and after that year, children were permitted to stay until their mothers were released.[4]

A small proportion of the offenders received at Millbank Prison were women. Female convicts were flogged at Millbank up until 1820, after which solitary confinement in dark cells, loss of privileges, and decreased diet were the major methods of enforcing prison discipline. The darkened cells were so greatly feared by the women that two or three officers were required to remove a prisoner from her normal cell to the darkened punishment cell. The treatment at Millbank was sufficiently bad so that the prisoners would deliberately injure themselves in order to be removed to the infirmary where conditions were better.[4]

Pentonville Prison

Opened in 1842, Pentonville was modeled after the Eastern Penitentiary in Pennsylvania, about which more will be said in the next section. It was three stories high and contained 520 cells arranged along radial spokes that fanned out from a central administration area. This design was rapidly copied all over Europe, with more than 50 similar institutions being constructed in England alone within a ten-year period.[12]

Michael Ignatieff[17] tells us what it was like to be a prisoner at Pentonville. The wake-up bell rang at 5:45 a.m. and the prisoners rapidly dressed for the 6:00 a.m. inspection in their cells. The cells contained a table, chair, cobbler's bench, shelf, bucket, and bed. The initial policy of keeping new prisoners in their cells for 18 months of silence was gradually decreased because of the severe effects of this treatment on mental and physical health. After the prisoners had done an hour and a half of work at the cobbler's bench or some other individual work, cocoa and bread were given to them through a trapdoor in the cell. Then, at 8:00 a.m., the convicts put on masks and silently marched to the chapel, where they sat in box-like compartments so that they could not see each other. At the conclusion of the chapel service, the prisoners were marched to small isolated yards where they exercised without human companionship until 9:00 a.m. This was followed by three hours of labor in their cells before lunch and four more hours after lunch. Dinner was at 6:00 p.m., again served through a trapdoor in their cells. Several hours of silent contemplation or Bible-reading completed the day, with lights out occurring at 9:00 p.m.

CORRECTIONS IN THE AMERICAN COLONIES

Correctional treatment in the early American colonies was extremely primitive. There was neither need nor funding for the establishment of elaborate institutions. The pattern of punishments used in the colonies was directly imported from Europe. Only in the late 18th century did America begin to exercise leadership in the world of international penology.

Early Physical Punishments

The Hempstead Code became law in 1664 on Long Island, having been taken from earlier codes enacted in New Haven, Connecticut. This specified death for 11 crimes, including denying the true God, murder, copulation with animals, homosexuality, kidnapping, rebellion, and striking one's parents. Physical punishments supplemented the use of fines, and included whipping, the pillory and the stocks, and branding.[5,19]

The criminal code passed in Pennsylvania in 1718 punished all felonies except larceny with death. Larceny could be punished by whipping, imprisonment, fine, or restitution to the victim at the pleasure of the court. Offenders committing lesser crimes could be expected to be whipped, branded, or mutilated. The ducking-chair, pillory, and stocks were also in use at this time.[5]

Underground Prisons

The first prison known to exist in the colonies was constructed in 1642 in New Amsterdam (New York). Imprisonment was used as a form of punishment after 1664, but its major use was for those who were awaiting trial and who had refused to pay debts.[19] Lacking funds for the creation of a proper penitentiary, the states of Connecticut and Maine used underground facilities to incarcerate offenders for many years. The Maine State Prison contained cells in the form of pits entered through an iron grate in the ceiling as late as 1828. Connecticut used a copper mine at Simsbury from 1773 to 1827. The prisoners worked during the day and then were fettered by the ankles and necks in the depths of the mine at night.[35]

Model Institutions in Pennsylvania

Due to the influence of the early Quakers, Pennsylvania rapidly became one of the leading innovators in correctional practice in the world. Three model institutions existing in early Pennsylvania were the Walnut Street Jail in Philadelphia, the Western Penitentiary at Pittsburgh, and the Eastern Penitentiary at Cherry Hill.

The Walnut Street Jail. The erection of a set of individual cells in the yard of the Walnut Street Jail in 1790 was the first use of segregated confinement in the colonies. These cells were reserved for the most difficult offenders, with lesser offenders still being confined in the earlier congregate part of the prison. The fee system for prisoners was abolished and adequate food was provided for all regardless of the ability to pay. They also received adequate clothing, bedding, and medical care. The prisoners worked at tasks such as making nails, sawing marble, and cutting stone. All prisoners were forced to remain silent and violators of this and other rules were sentenced to terms in isolation cells.[5]

The Western Penitentiary. The Western Penitentiary was completed in 1826 and received its first convicts in February of the following year. Harry Elmer Barnes called it the "best example that has ever existed of the solitary system carried to the most vicious extreme."[5:157] The architect who built the Western Penitentiary attempted to adapt the panopticon design of Bentham, but was not sensitive to the need for cells that were spacious and well-lit. The prison was constructed with a complete circle of back-to-back cells, one set facing inward and the other facing outward, all built with three-foot-thick stone walls and heavy iron doors. There was very little light in these cells, and prison officers in the central supervision tower were unable to see into any of them.[12] The original policy of total segregation without work was so disastrous that the introduction of forced labor was ordered in 1829. Inspectors also recommended the building of exercise yards for all of the cells. The impossibility of either cell labor or adequate exercise led to the passage of a law requiring the rebuilding of the entire cell block in 1833.[5]

Rather than being a model of prison architecture and programming that was imitated around the world, the Western Penitentiary was significant in that it was hardly imitated at all. It showed the folly of strict segregation beyond any question. Rarely in the history of American corrections have experimental punishments been so quickly abandoned and so thoroughly rejected. The idea of silent and separate prison life continued, and is known as the Pennsylvania System, but the architectural style of its next application was completely different.

The Eastern Penitentiary. The Eastern Penitentiary accepted its first prisoners in 1830. Its architect, having learned from his mistakes in building the Western Penitentiary, created the Eastern Penitentiary as a series of radiating rectangular cell blocks, with all of the hallways visible from a central observation point. The cells were of a generous size, well-lighted, heated, and each provided with a modern toilet. Every cell had its own unroofed exercise yard.[12]

The prisoners, fearing the overwhelming boredom of solitary confinement, worked very hard at their assigned tasks in their cells. In the early years of the system, they produced enough goods to pay for their own upkeep, though not for the salaries of their keepers. Most of them worked at weaving, dyeing, and shoemaking, with a few individuals doing blacksmithing and woodworking.[5] This program was much more salutary than the one tried at the Western Penitentiary, but the excessive solitary confinement must still have left its mark, for Gustave de Beaumont and Alexis de Tocqueville[10] observed that the Pennsylvania system was less healthy for prisoners than the Auburn system, which permitted congregate (though silent) labor. Despite the lack of a good recommendation from de Beaumont and de Tocqueville, the Pennsylvania system was widely admired in Europe, and was adopted in England, Belgium, Sweden, Hungary, France, Prussia, Denmark, Norway, and Holland between 1835 and 1851.[5]

The Auburn System

A new prison at Auburn, New York was authorized in 1816, and began experimenting with solitary confinement in 1819. Tiny cells, no exercise, and no work quickly produced enough suicides and mental breakdowns so that the plan was abandoned in 1824. At this time, the Auburn system of silent congregate work during the day and individual confinement was inaugurated. Any prisoner who dared to break the rule of silence was brutally flogged on the spot, and the liberal use of the whip for other offenses kept the authoritarian regime in order.[21]

Prisoners at Auburn worked all day long in common areas, and then spent their evenings in solitary confinement in their cells. The work routine was standard for six days each week, with only Sundays being rest days. Since no congregate recreation was allowed, the prisoners had to spend every Sunday alone in their cells.[9] Despite the austerity of this regime, with its lock step shuffles amid the silence, there was enough stimulation in the system to keep prisoners from having an excessively high number of mental breakdowns. Two other positive features of the Auburn system were that congregate labor was much more profitable than individual labor, so the net cost of imprisonment to the state was smaller, and that the smaller cells permitted by the Auburn system made Auburn-style prisons cheaper to build than prisons built on the Pennsylvania plan.[12] For these reasons, the Auburn system was widely copied in American corrections during the 19th century.

Punishments at Auburn and Other New York Institutions. Klein[19] has provided us with detailed descriptions of the punishments that were used to enforce discipline on the prisoners at Auburn and other New York State institutions during the 19th century. In Auburn during 1875, there were 1278 floggings, which was reduced to 258 floggings the following year. Sing Sing also used floggings and supplemented these by the deprivation of bedding, food, tobacco, and books; solitary confinement; and the use of the infamous shower bath. The shower bath was a device dropping a column of water on the head of an offender who was locked naked in the stocks. The device was so constructed that the force of the blow of the water on the head was approximately equal to a column of water 72 inches in height. In addition to the pain caused by the water, which was held at 32 degrees, the shock to the body was so extreme that the prisoners rapidly sank into comas from the drop in body temperature.

Punishments such as the shower bath were given wider application after flogging was outlawed in 1847. Klein quotes testimony from an Auburn physician to the effect that prisoners subjected to the shower bath could suffer severe damage in a very short period of time.[19] Others became insane, such as one prisoner who was showered with six pails of water following which he immediately went into convulsions and never regained his sanity. Numerous other punishments were devised to replace flogging; these were similar to the tortures of the Middle Ages. The suffering inflicted on any prisoner who did not exactly follow institutional rules was intense. In addition, the Good Time Law passed in New York State in 1817 and copied by almost every state in the Union

Figure 4.1 The towers and wall of a traditional maximum security prison. (Law Enforcement Assistance Administration.)

by 1900 allowed prison administrators to regulate the length of imprisonment as well as its severity as an additional inducement to hard work and conformity to the rules.[22]

Punishments for Juveniles

Before the beginning of the 19th century, the punishment of juveniles was largely a family affair. In those cases where punishment by agents of the state was called for, juveniles were processed by the same institutions as adults. The harshness of adult punishments combined with the need to find some way to stem the tide of rising juvenile delinquency in the early 19th century led to the development of houses of refuge which served destitute children as well as children convicted of crimes, for both were perceived as an equal threat to the social order. The first of these institutions was the New York House of Refuge, which opened in 1825, followed by similar institutions in Boston and Philadelphia. Hard labor and rigid discipline were the rule in these institutions, with solitary confinement, whipping, and other physical brutalities much in evidence. The boys worked at manufacturing shoes, nails, and chairs, and the girls performed more "feminine" tasks such as spinning cotton and doing laundry.[20]

The many supporters of the reformatory movement were challenged by a new group of reformers known as the Child Savers.[27] In addition to creating new institutions for juveniles, they developed a system of placing out, through which urban juvenile delinquents were removed from their presumably criminogenic families and transported to farm families on the western frontier. The evils of institutional life exposed by these critics also led to the development of the cottage system in existing institutions, whereby young people were broken up into small units for housing and recreational activities.[20]

The Western House of Refuge. Despite the many criticisms of juvenile institutions, the reformatory movement picked up speed in the middle of the 19th century, with 14 juvenile institutions being constructed between 1841 and 1856. The Western House of Refuge is an example of these institutions. The young prisoners in this reformatory worked hard at the making of chairs, shoes, whips, barrels and other items all day, for which they received no payment. They also staffed a 23-acre farm and maintained the institution. Basic education classes and religious training were also part of the institutional regimen. For example, the prisoners memorized and recited a total of 53,160 verses of Scripture during 1857 alone. Punishments included deprivation of food and play, solitary confinement, and corporal punishment.[26]

Female juvenile delinquents were not admitted to the Western House of Refuge until 1876. Once their unit became operational, they were subjected to a program similar to that designed for the boys. One difference is that the work they performed was limited to cooking, cleaning, ironing, washing, and sewing. Although they had probably committed less serious offenses than the boys, the girls were viewed less optimistically, particularly because of their involvement in sexual behavior. Like the boys, they sometimes fought back against the prison officials, escaping, setting fires, and fighting.[26]

The Elmira Reformatory. The Elmira Reformatory, which opened in 1876, moved from punishment and deterrence toward treatment and education more than any other penal institution in the century. Prisoners rose or fell in the institutional status system based on marks assigned for good behavior, work accomplished, and successful studying. In concept, this was the same as modern behavioral modification programs using token economies. The accumulation of marks also impacted the release date of the prisoner, for the use of indeterminant sentences gave the superintendent of the institution great power over sentence length. The early release of successful prisoners was the first use of parole in America. Educational, vocational, and religious programs were provided with the idea of individualizing treatment as much as possible. Only the dungeon-like architecture of the institution kept it from the full implementation of the treatment philosophy as conceived of in those days.[9]

Innovations in Correctional Treatment

Three great innovations in correctional treatment arose in the United States during the 19th century. These were parole, probation, and the abolition of capital punishment. We have already mentioned that American parole practices originated at the Elmira Reformatory. After a 12-month record of good conduct, a prisoner could be considered for parole from Elmira. If the application was approved, the parolee was assigned to a guardian in the community and had to report to that guardian on a monthly basis. After six months, successful parolees were discharged from further supervision. This program was so successful that it was adopted in 26 states by 1900.[1]

Probation was first used in America at an earlier date. John Augustus began bailing out prisoners and helping them to find work and a residence around the middle of the 19th century. If the prisoner did well, Augustus would recommend a sentence other than incarceration to the court, and his recommendations were usually accepted. He eventually helped 2000 offenders, and reported only 10 absconders out of this number. His finances were eventually exhausted but he had made his point so well by that time that others took over his work. The first law authorizing a probation officer was passed in Massachusetts in 1878. However, no other state followed this example until 1898, when Vermont authorized a probation officer for each county in the state.[1]

We can see from these examples that probation and parole had their beginnings at a time when the institutionalization of offenders was on the rise. It was not until the 20th century that these methods of community treatment began to outdistance institutionalization as modes of official punishment. At the time when these practices were increasing, the use of capital punishment had already begun to decline. By the end of the 19th century, the total of all executions in the United States had decreased to approximately 122 cases per year.[7] We can trace this trend back to 1846, when Michigan became the first government in the world to abolish the death penalty.[32]

The Punishment of Racial and Cultural Minorities

We do not know a great deal about the punishment of minority group members in early America. Black delinquents in the North were either segregated from white delinquents or received no treatment at all.[20] A number of authors have observed the high representation of immigrants[29,35] and blacks[10] in American prisons. Alexander Pisciotta[25] has shown that immigrants made up approximately three times the proportion of prisoners that one would expect from their numbers in the general population in the years 1850–1870. He views the use of the penitentiary in those years as an important device for exercising social control over immigrant populations.

The punishment of blacks in the Deep South before the Civil War was largely a private matter. Once blacks had been liberated, Southern elites devised a substantially new set of social control mechanisms. This was made difficult by the destruction of social institutions during the war. Most of these institutions— such as the Ku Klux Klan, were not part of the formal legal machinery of the Southern states. An exception was penal slavery, which was authorized under the Thirteenth Amendment to the Constitution. Penal slavery was implemented in a number of Southern states as early as 1866. With their treasuries exhausted, these states could not afford to construct expensive penal institutions immediately following the war. Their solution was to lease out the convicts to private contractors who either paid for the privilege or were paid a small fee by the state for their efforts. The leasees were interested in profits, not corrections, and they literally worked the prisoners to death in many cases. The death rate of prisoners in Mississippi during 1887 was 16 percent. In Louisiana, it was 20 percent in 1896, and so on. The prisoners labored long hours under horrendous conditions and were not given proper food, shelter, or medical treatment. Between 17 and 19 of every 20 prisoners were black, which indicates the degree to which this device had its historical roots in the recently outlawed practice of slavery. The lease system in Mississippi was replaced by a prison farm system in 1894, but it persisted in Florida until 1917 and in Alabama until 1928.[33]

SOME HISTORICAL TRENDS AND THEIR MEANING

If we look only at individual criminal acts (as most of us do), it is easy to see corrections as no more than a response to those acts. However, when we examine crime statistics internationally and over time, certain trends emerge which show that broad social forces are at work in determining much of the variation in both criminal behavior and the correctional response to such behavior. One way to make sense of these trends is to think of human behavior largely as a coping response to environmental conditions. When social changes in the society as a whole affect people's perceptions of their environment, they may increase (or decrease) their criminal behavior as a way of continuing to live at their accustomed level (which is no more than basic survival for the poor) under changed conditions. At the same time, the changes in the crime rate and other aspects of social conditions affect the responses of governmental officials to crime, and these changed responses are formalized into correctional policy by enacted law, executive proclamation, and administrative regulation.

Many different kinds of factors affect correctional policy. For example, there are perceptions of public disorder, the need for labor, and the role of ideology.

At times when public disorder appears to be high, governmental officials are likely to take a "get tough" attitude toward crime. The disorder (riots, increases in street crime, the adoption of deviant life styles by young people, protests against governmental policies, etc.) is commonly conceptualized by moral leaders as a weakening of the fabric of society, and they cry out that the family is disintegrating or that the streets must be made safe again.

Increases in public disorder are often a response to worsening economic conditions. An alternative source of perceptions of disorder is a strong influx of immigrant groups from outside the society or the community. Immigrant groups tend to come into their new society at the bottom of the class structure and to remain in poverty for a long time. They often have life-styles very different from those of governmental officials, and because of these differences, they are sometimes seen as threatening the social order even when they are as law-abiding as any other group. Regardless of whether the public order is perceived as decaying because of mass riots and increases in street crime or because there is an influx of immigrants with differing life styles, the reaction of governmental officials is usually to increase social controls, and this is certain to increase the number of people in the correctional system.

The need for labor in factories and fields—labor of the sort provided by the relatively poor—at minimum wages is also a determinant of correctional policy. Vagrancy is more likely to be tolerated if there is an excess of workers than if workers are in short supply. Statutes that artificially depress the standard of living of the working class so as to assure a steady supply of cheap labor are broken by some, and these individuals are subject to correctional sanctions if caught.

The need for labor is a fairly concrete concept, and perceptions of disorder also have a basis in the events of the physical world. In contrast, ideology is rather loosely tied to the physical world, and although it is commonly harnessed to the needs of the economic and political systems, it sometimes works contrary to the laws of economics and the needs of political leaders. Reformism, humanitarianism, and utilitarianism are examples of ideological beliefs that have had an impact on corrections in the past. In recent years, the ideology of deinstitutionalization has supported a decrease in correctional activities, while an increase in the adoption of radical ideological positions by minority offenders has tended to increase the level of correctional activities in some cases.

Factors such as these can be used to explain changes in correctional policy in specific political units over a limited time span. The accumulation of these changes in all Western societies since the beginning of recorded history follows four general trends.

First, formal social control by the criminal justice system has tended to increase over the centuries in response to a decrease in both formal and informal social control exercised by the Church.

The increase in social control exercised by the criminal justice system has been associated with the next two general patterns of change. These are increases in criminalization and increases in incarceration as a penal sanction. Criminalization refers to the process of making a legal act illegal by enacting a new criminal law. New penal laws are still being enacted on a regular basis, while few old offenses are removed from the books (decriminalized). There has also been a historical rise in the use of corrections as a penal sanction, starting from zero in early societies and progressing up to the present, when institutional populations are at an all-time high in many nations. Some tentative moves toward decriminalization and strong efforts in the direction of deinstitutionalization in Scandinavia may indicate the future direction of these trends in other parts of the world.

The final general historical trend in international corrections is a decline in corporal punishment and the death penalty. Most nations no longer permit the beating or torturing of prisoners, and many have abolished the death penalty completely. A recent counter-trend is the reestablishment of the death penalty in a number of American states. It is too soon to know whether this is the first step in a return to more barbaric forms of punishment world-wide.

SUMMARY

Crime is legally-prohibited, punishable behavior. Like crime, punishment in a legal sense did not begin until written legal codes were developed. Correctional punishment as treated in this text consists of legally required harms (or negative sanctions) that are inflicted upon individuals as a result of judicial determinations that they have committed acts prohibited under the criminal law. An early criminal code was the Code of Hammurabi, which was developed in the 18th century B.C. in Babylon. By specifying the appropriate level of revenge for each crime, the Code limited the ruthlessness of revenge that might have been carried out against the offender by the extended family of the victim. Although the early punishments inflicted in Assyria, Greece, and Rome were often barbaric, there were also relatively advanced provisions in some of the codes, such as the Mosaic prohibition of torturing offenders and requirements that guilt be based on the concurrent testimony of at least two witnesses. Punishments were not universal, and members of the lower classes, slaves, and aliens received much more severe punishments than free citizens and those from the upper classes.

Punishments gradually became more severe throughout the Middle Ages, and brutal punishments which had once been reserved for slaves came, by degrees, to be applied to free citizens. The ecclesiastical system maintained a separate set of courts from the civil system and also applied its own set of punishments. The 16th through the 19th centuries were characterized by the continuing elaboration of vicious and brutal public punishments. Flogging, branding, mutilation, a variety of torture methods, the ducking-stool, the pillory, and the stocks were part of the arsenal of the correctional system during these centuries. Conditions in correctional institutions were brutal, and there was an extremely high death rate. Overcrowding led to the use of transportation to rid the European countries of large numbers of criminals. Criminals were also used as forced labor for the benefit of the state or for private contractors.

After a brief bout with increased brutality of punishments in the early 19th century, corrections began to slowly move in the direction of humanitarianism and respect for the rights of criminals. This movement also occurred in the American colonies, where early punishments included the death penalty for heresy, copulation with animals, homosexuality, and striking one's parents as well as the usual capital crimes, and prisoners in several states were incarcerated underground because of the lack of funds to build correctional institutions. Two of the most noted American institutions of the 19th century were the prison at Auburn and the Elmira Reformatory, both of them located in New York State. The Auburn system involved silent congregate work during the day and individual confinement at night. Brutal whippings maintained the rule of silence and absolute obedience among the men throughout their daily tasks. The Elmira Reformatory subjected juveniles to a much more benign form of correctional processing. There was an institutional status system based on marks assigned for good behavior, work accomplished, and successful studying. Treatment was individualized as much as possible, and successful prisoners received early release in what was the first use of parole in America.

A number of trends can be discerned in the sweep of correctional practices over time. There has been an increase in the humanization of corrections, and there has been a decrease in the use of corporal punishment, including the death penalty. An increasing number of acts have been declared to be illegal, which has increased the span on control of the criminal justice system. There has also been a historical rise in the use of corrections as a penal sanction, with institutional populations being at an all-time high in many nations. These general trends are sometimes obscured by short-term interruptions of a few years to a few decades in length, during which deteriorating economic conditions have led to increasing public disorder (at least as officially defined), and increases in the use of correctional sanctions. The rapid influx of large numbers of immigrants has also resulted in short-term increases in the use of correctional sanctions to control these populations.

REFERENCES

1. Abadinsky, Howard. *Probation and Parole: Theory and Practice.* Englewood Cliffs, NJ: Prentice-Hall, 1977.
2. Allen, Harry E. and Clifford E. Simonsen. *Corrections in America: An Introduction.* Encino, CA: Glencoe, 1978.
3. Andrews, William. *Old-Time Punishments.* London: Tabard Press, 1890.
4. Babington, Anthony. *The English Bastille: A History of Newgate Gaol and Prison Conditions in Britain 1188–1902.* London: Macdonald, 1971.

5. Barnes, Harry E. *The Evolution of Penology in Pennsylvania.* Montclair, NJ: Patterson Smith, 1968. Originally published in 1927.

6. Barnes, Harry E. *The Story of Punishment.* Boston: Stratford, 1930.

7. Bedau, Hugot A. *The Death Penalty in America.* Garden City, NY: Doubleday, 1964.

8. Bowker, Lee H. "Exile, Banishment and Transportation: A History and a Proposal for Penal Reform." *International Journal of Offender Therapy and Comparative Criminology* 24(1980):67–80.

9. Burns, Henry, Jr. *Corrections: Organization and Administration.* St. Paul, MN: West, 1975.

10. De Beaumont, Gustave and Alexis de Tocqueville. *On the Penitentiary System in the United States and Its Application in France.* Carbondale, IL: Southern Illinois University Press, 1964. Originally published in 1833.

11. Elliott, Mabel A. *Crime in Modern Society.* New York: Harper, 1952.

12. Fairweather, Leslie. "The Evolution of the Prison." In United Nations Social Defense Research Institute: *Prison Architecture.* London: The Architectural Press, 1975, pp. 13–40.

13. Foucault, Michel. *Discipline and Punish: The Birth of the Prison.* New York: Random House, 1979.

14. Gurr, Ted R. *Rogues, Rebels and Reformers.* Beverly Hills, CA: Sage, 1976.

15. Hogg, Russell. "Imprisonment and Society Under Early British Capitalism." *Crime and Social Justice* 12 (1979):4–18.

16. Howard, John. *The State of the Prisons.* London: J.M. Dent, 1929. Originally published in 1777.

17. Ignatieff, Michael. *A Just Measure of Pain.* New York: Pantheon, 1978.

18. Ives, George. *A History of Penal Methods.* Montclair, NJ: Patterson Smith, 1970. Originally published in 1914.

19. Klein, Philip. *Prison Methods in New York State.* New York: AMS Press, 1969. Originally published in 1920.

20. Krisberg, Barry and James Austin. *The Children of Ishmael: Critical Perspectives on Juvenile Justice.* Palo Alto, CA: Mayfield, 1978.

21. McKelvey, Blake. *American Prisons: A History of Good Intentions.* Montclair, NJ: Patterson Smith, 1977.

22. Miller, Martin B. "At Hard Labor: Rediscovering the 19th Century Prison." *Issues in Criminology* 9 (1974):91–114.

23. Newman, Graeme. *The Punishment Response.* Philadelphia: Lippincott, 1978.

24. Pendry, E.D. *Elizabethan Prisons and Prison Scenes,* 2 Vols. Salzburg, Austria: Institute for English Language and Literature, 1974.

25. Pisciotta, Alexander W. "Immigration, Social Control, and the Development of the Penitentiary in the United States." Paper presented at the annual meeting of the Society for the Study of Social Problems, 1978.

26. Pisciotta, Alexander W. "The Theory and Practice of the Western House of Refuge, 1849–1907." Paper presented at the annual meeting of the American Society of Criminology, 1979.

27. Platt, Anthony. *The Child-Savers, The Invention of Delinquency.* Chicago: University of Chicago Press, 1968.

28. Pugh, Ralph B. *Imprisonment in Medieval England.* Cambridge, England: Cambridge University Press, 1968.
29. Rothman, David J. *The Discovery of the Asylum.* Boston: Little, Brown, 1971.
30. Rusche, Georg and Otto Kirchheimer. *Punishment and Social Structure.* New York: Russell and Russell, 1968. Originally published in 1939.
31. Schafer, Stephen. *Introduction to Criminology.* Reston, VA: Reston Publishing Company, 1976.
32. Sellin, Thorsten. *Capital Punishment.* New York: Harper and Row, 1967.
33. Sellin, Thorsten. *Slavery and the Penal System.* New York: Elsevier, 1976.
34. Tappan, Paul W. *Crime, Justice and Correction.* New York: McGraw-Hill, 1960.
35. Wines, Frederick H. *Punishment and Reformation: An Historical Sketch of the Rise of the Penitentiary System.* New York: Benjamin Blom, 1971. Originally printed in 1895.
36. Wood, Arthur E. and John B. Waite. *Crime and Its Treatment.* New York: American Book Company, 1941.

Chapter 5

A 20th-Century History of American Corrections

The story of corrections in 20th-century America really began 30 years earlier in 1870, when the National Prison Association (now the American Correctional Association) held its first national congress in Cincinatti, Ohio. The principles set forth at this meeting provided guidance for American corrections for the next century. Leading prison reformers from all over the country came to the meeting with prepared speeches supporting a humanistic treatment approach to corrections, while the more traditional correctional administrators who were present had not come prepared to defend the status quo as it then existed. This unlikely mixture of reformers and practitioners produced a tremendous amount of enthusiasm for prison reform and a declaration of principles that is remarkable for its farsightedness.[32] The most important principles adopted at Cincinatti are summarized below.

1. The aim of imprisonment is reformation, not the infliction of suffering.
2. Prisons should emphasize rewards more than punishments.
3. Prison administrative posts should no longer be filled through political appointments.
4. All sentences should be indeterminant, with release coming upon proof of reformation.
5. Religion, education, and vocational training should be given high priority in the activities of the prison.
6. Both prisons and prisoners should be classified so that hardened offenders are never mixed with minor offenders.
7. It is the responsibility of the state to provide support services for released prisoners until they are reintegrated into society.
8. Prison sentences should be standardized so that prisoners everywhere receive comparable punishments for comparable crimes.
9. The state is partially responsible for the incidence of crime, and should take all possible actions to ameliorate the conditions that are conducive to crime.

One step in this direction would be to make the education of all children
obligatory.

10. All of the correctional institutions in each state should be unified into one
centrally controlled system. Both women and men may be employed in the
administration of these correctional systems.[25]

MAJOR TYPES OF PRISON ORGANIZATIONS

Five major types of correctional institutions have existed in the United States
during the 20th century, all of which are still in use in one form or another.
These are the Northern industrial prison, the Southern plantation prison, chain
gangs and other decentralized work camps, the custody-oriented prison, and the
treatment-oriented prison.

The Northern Industrial Prison

The Connecticut State Prison at Wethersfield is an example of the Northern
industrial prison. In prisons such as these, there was either no attempt to offer
treatment services, or labor was itself redefined as treatment. The emphasis in
these organizations was to recapture as high a percentage of the cost of running
the institution as possible. One reason that the cost of imprisonment was
uppermost in the minds of the legislatures was that the prison population was
rapidly rising. The number of prisoners in state and federal facilities rose from
53,292 in 1904 to approximately 79,000 in 1909 and then to 126,258 in 1935.[28]
Byers estimates that of the total population of prisoners in 1909, 67 percent were
employed in industrial activities with 22 percent performing institutional
maintenance tasks. The remaining 11 percent of the adult prisoners were in
trade schools, sick and disabled, and idle. He also estimates that the value of
prison-made products in the United States in 1904 was $33,280,940—a
substantial sum of money.[5]

The Oklahoma State Penitentiary at McAlester is a good example of the
industrial emphasis in American prisons in the early 20th century. Using a
careful examination of official records in the State Archives, John Conley[10,11]
was able to reconstruct the events following the erection of the prison in 1910.
Oklahoma officials in those days firmly believed that prisoners should perform
labor for the benefit of the state. This emphasis was so strong that the primary
function of the warden was seen as being to produce profit for the state treasury
from the prison labor operation. The contract, state account, and state-use
systems of prisoner labor were all in use in Oklahoma. In the contract system,
the labor of prisons was sold to citizens or firms for a set fee per day per head.
Contractors in the state account system provided the raw materials and paid the
state a set price for each item produced. The state account system was a more
risky commercial venture, in which the state had to buy all of the raw materials,
construct the factories and market the product. The benefit of this system was
that the state kept any profits earned.

Prisoners at McAlester produced overalls, shirts and brooms in contract industries during the early 1920s. Twine and brick factories were constructed by the state on a state account system. Although official reports overstated the profits earned to these economic endeavors, the Oklahoma prison industries clearly succeeded in offsetting a sizeable proportion of the cost of institutional maintenance. However, prison labor in Oklahoma was inefficient, seasonal, and did not train the prisoners in industrial skills that would be useful to them upon discharge.[10,11]

The Demise of the Industrial Prison. The industrial prison as an ideal type was undermined by the Hawes-Cooper Act of 1929 and the Ashurst-Summers Act of 1935. The Hawes-Cooper Act placed prison products under the laws of whatever state they were shipped to and the Ashurst-Summers Act required that all prison products shipped across state lines had to labeled with the prison's name. A 1940 amendment to the Ashurst-Summers Act prohibited all interstate shipment of prison products. These developments on a federal level were paralleled by the passing of laws in 33 states prohibiting the sale of products of prison labor on the open market.[1] Already handicapped with inefficiency, poor facilities, and often corruption, the industrial prisons could not hope to make a significant profit in the face of these constraints. The proportion of prisoners who were industrially occupied declined, and prisons were compelled to adopt the closed-market system, in which prison goods were sold only to governmental agencies and nonprofit organizations.

The Southern Plantation Prison

Prison labor systems developed out of the economic needs of the surrounding region. The industrial prisons of the North were consistent with the productivity needs of the highly industrialized region. The parallel institution in the South was the plantation, and so Southern prisons placed a greater emphasis on agricultural labor in huge prison plantations. Louis Robinson[40] wrote in 1923 that South Carolina had 4168 acres in prison farms, Louisiana had 15,600 acres, Florida had 17,000 acres, Mississippi had 28,750 acres, and Texas had 73,461 acres in prison agricultural production. We have already described the operation of a Southern plantation prison system in North Carolina at the turn of the century. Now we will say something about the Southern plantation prison system in general.

As the system of leased convict labor was eliminated from Southern states in response to revelations of abuses, state governments absorbed the prisoners into state-owned plantation prison systems. These plantations were inexpensive to operate because their facilities were minimal. At the same time, their high agricultural yield produced income for the states which offset a sizable proportion of the expense of maintaining correctional systems. When the lease system in Louisiana was abandoned in 1901, the 18,000-acre plantation at Angola that had been operated by the leasee, Major James, was bought by the state and business continued as usual. Black and white prisoners were not totally segregated, but the classification system achieved substantial segregation in most correctional facilities. It also assured that blacks would be assigned to the most exhausting and back-breaking labor. The prisoners were seen as productive units, not as human beings. They received no therapeutic treatment at all, and were literally worked half to death. Severe beatings were the fate of any prisoners who failed to produce their quota of work in the fields. Although the heaviest burden of the Southern plantation system fell on black prisoners, it is clear that the system extended the same kind of treatment that had previously existed only under slavery to both black and white prisoners.[44]

The abuses of the plantation system in Louisiana became even greater when the state replaced its paid correctional officers with armed "trusty" convicts, following the practice already used in Mississippi, Arkansas, and Florida. The correctional unit at Angola was still using 239 trusty-guards in 1969. These trusties were typically long-termers, often in for homicide. They were even more brutal with the prisoners working in the fields than the earlier paid prison officers had been. As in the days of slavery, the entire plantation operated only to maximize profits, and no regard was shown for the welfare of the inmate "slaves."[44] Mark Carleton[7] reports that there were 1547 recorded floggings at Angola in 1933 alone, to say nothing of those that were unrecorded.

Things became so bad at Angola that 31 prisoners slashed their heel tendons with razor blades to protest the brutal treatment at the institution. Ten of them subsequently slashed their other tendon as well, completely crippling themselves.[7] What kind of treatment produced such desperate acts? A prisoner in the Arkansas system explains what it was like to work in the fields there.

That evening Capt. Bobby Brinkley loaded us up and took us to the Warren field where the longline was picking cotton. When we stopped we jumped out like a bunch of hogs. There was guns everywhere I looked....

Capt. Brinkley ask me if I could pick him any cotton. I told him I could. He said it is a damn good thing I could. I was just about the biggest in the transfer. I was six-one, I weighed 160 pounds at the time, but I lost that down to 136 in 2 months.... I got 12 licks from Capt. Brinkley because I couldn't keep up. I wasn't the only one out on the turn row, just about all of the short hairs was out there. We was doing our best. But Capt. Brinkley said that was not good enough. There was grown men crying and cursing. They had just about give up.[27:173]

We must agree with Sellin[44] that the change from the lease system to public administration did not greatly improve the condition of prison laborers under the plantation system.

The Southern plantation prison model has developed a negative reputation by virtue of the abuses associated with it throughout its history. However, there is no reason why a plantation system need necessarily be abusive. With many previously pro-treatment corrections personnel now holding the view that treatment is not possible in a correctional system, the attractiveness of heavy labor when combined with fair treatment and adequate supervision has greatly increased. This is precisely the correctional philosophy implemented in the Texas prison system. Approximately half of all the prisoners in the Texas Department of Corrections work in the fields, with 10 percent working in prison industries, 10 percent working on construction and maintenance, and the remaining 30 percent performing institutional upkeep and service tasks. The well-supervised involvement in heavy work is considered by some critics to be abusive, but it tires the prisoners out each day and minimizes many of the vices associated with idlesness in prisons. The productivity of prisoner labor allows Texas to incarcerate offenders at less than a quarter of the cost of incarceration in California, Illinois, and New York.[29] One of the consequences of a low incarceration cost is that the criminal justice system has less of an incentive to minimize the incarceration rate. This may be one of the reasons why incarceration rates in the states using relatively inexpensive plantation prisoners are higher than incarceration rates in most other states.

Road Crews and Other Work Camps

Another solution to the problem of how to gain a benefit for the state from the labor of prisoners is to decentralize and have the prisoners labor on public works throughout the state instead of confining them in the industrial shops of the North or the prison plantations of the South. This system was developed in the Deep South as a response to the economic deterioration brought on by the Civil War. Prisoners in road gangs were chained together to prevent escape, thus coining the term "chain gangs." Whipping, the sweat box (in which prisoners were left in a box in the hot sun as a punishment) and other corporal punishments were used to maximize the work productivity of the prisoners. Conditions were so bad in the early years of the system that J.C. Powell felt justified in labeling it the *American Siberia*. Prisoners in some of the road gangs were locked up in little portable metal cages at night because no better facilities were available.[2]

The chain gangs were originally reserved for black prisoners, with white prisoners not being introduced into the system until later years. For example, white prisoners did not appear in Alabama chain gangs until the 1940s.[44] Those states which operated their road gangs through the local counties exercised little central control, so that conditions and abuses suffered by the prisoners varied greatly from county to county. Some used almost no corporal punishment while others used a great deal.[33] By the 1930s, some North Carolina counties no longer chained their road gangs, others chained only a few of the more dangerous prisoners, and some chained almost all of them.[44]

Chain gangs no longer exist in American corrections. The idea of using prisoners to labor on public works continues in road prisons and corrections camps scattered throughout the nation. Florida organized a system of road prisons under the supervision of the state Division of Corrections. Over 900 prisoners labored in 14 of these institutions in 1971. The road prisons were permanent rather than portable facilities out of which prisoners worked in maintaining roads in their region. Education, counseling, and other treatment programs were provided in these institutions, although the quality and variety of treatment programs was not as great as it was in the larger state correctional facilities.[15] The number of road prisons had decreased to 11 by mid-1978, with some of them having been converted to vocational training centers, but there were still over 800 prisoners involved in road work.[16]

Many Northern and Western states used prisoner labor in public works in corrections camp systems. For example, Michigan was operating 12 corrections camps by the mid-1970s. Like the Florida road prisons, these camps offered basic treatment services as well as labor on public works programs. All of the approximately 1200 prisoners in the camps were rated for minimum security, which is a universal requirement for corrections camps around the nation. Although the major impetus for the development of the camps was to provide a labor force for the Department of Natural Resources, less than 50 percent of the men were involved in conservation work by 1975. The others were enrolled in a broad assortment of work release, vocational training, and educational programs.[34]

Custody-Oriented Prisons

With the decline of the industrial prison, most maximum security facilities decreased their emphasis on maximizing productivity while continuing to emphasize security considerations. The goal was to prevent escapes and riots at all costs. Some institutions, such as the Montana Prison, were custody-oriented from the beginning because they never had an industrial unit as part of the penitentiary complex. While the average number of prisoners under sentence more than doubled between 1923 and 1940, and the average number of prisoners productively employed rose by more than 50 percent, the value of comodities produced through their labor declined from $73,688,879 to $48,995,818.[2]

Donald Clemmer's descriptive book *The Prison Community*[9] details the operation of the custody-oriented institution at Menard, Illinois, and Gresham Sykes has done the same for the Trenton State Prison in his book *The Society of Captives*.[47] We will discuss both of these books in the chapter on prison subcultures. A general description of custody-oriented correctional institutions in America is contained in John Irwin's recent book *Prisons in Turmoil*.[26] He terms these institutions "the Big House."

The Big House contains large cell blocks in which there are stacks of cages running from floor to the ceiling with cat walks being the only source of access to the individual cells. Life in these cell blocks is characterized by the constant clamor and clanking caused by the metal fixtures and the jarring acoustics, combined with visual sensory deprivation due to the monotony of architecture. These conditions, combined with the tedium of scheduling, causes many prisoners to become stupefied, as "they learned to blunt their feelings, turn inward, construct fantasy worlds for themselves, and generally throttle their intellectual, emotional, and physical life."[26:20]

Correctional officers also suffer from the boredom of institutional life in the Big House. They sometimes engage in brutal practices, but more often settle into a pattern of accommodation with the prisoners in which there is a balance of personal satisfaction and maintenance of the status quo. This accommodation is broken by periodic prison riots, in which the prisoners temporarily gain the upper hand over their jailers. Administrators do their best to keep things in balance, walking a tightrope between the demands of prisoners, officers, and the public. The penalty for poor judgment in the balancing of conflicting demands is often a prison riot, although contagion from other institutions recently experiencing riots is also a factor.[26]

Treatment-Oriented Institutions

Treatment and custody-oriented prisons did not exist as mutually exclusive entities. There were treatment elements in almost all of the custody-oriented institutions, and custody was still the supreme commandment in most of the treatment-oriented institutions. Reformers sometimes introduced strong treatment programs in prisons that were previously without any treatment emphasis. In addition to these complexities in adult corrections, the paternalism inherent in the development of institutions for juveniles and women resulted in their being comparatively treatment-oriented.

An example of the rapid development of a treatment program in what was previously a custody-oriented institution is the introduction of the Mutual Welfare League into Sing Sing prison in New York by Thomas Mott Osborne in 1914. Osborne directed the prison officers to become friendly with the prisoners, and introduced a variety of educational and recreational programs. The prisoners were allowed to elect a congress of delegates that became the institution's prisoner government. Osborne routinely delegated prison policy decisions to this prisoner council. Most disciplinary infractions were handled by a prisoner court rather than by the administration.[41] The productivity of prison industries increased and the number of prisoners treated for wounds (an index of prisoner assaults) was cut by more than 50 percent despite an increase in the prisoner population.[51] When Osborne was forced out of office in 1916, his system rapidly deteriorated, a fate that befell all other experiments of this sort until recent years.[41]

Prisoners sometimes lobbied for the implementation of new treatment

Figure 5.1 A pre-employment training session in a halfway house. (Law Enforcement Assistance Administration.)

programs. The leaders in many prison riots presented a list of demands to the administration, often while they held hostages on pain of death. Many of these demands were for increased treatment programs. By and large, these demands were not met after the prisoners had surrendered. Even when reforms were implemented, they usually did not last any longer than the experiments in prisoner self-governments. Reading through the reactions of a number of states to the prison riots of the early 1950s, one is struck by the inflexibility of response demonstrated by most of the prison administrators.[38]

Sellin[44] has argued that many of the punishments previously reserved for slaves were eventually generalized to the population of free prisoners, with a resulting deterioration of the conditions of imprisonment. A similar argument can be made for the more recent innovation and institutionalization of treatment procedures in facilities for juveniles. Once these procedures had considerable public support for use with juveniles, they were then gradually introduced into institutions for men throughout the country. By 1960, treatment had become a major goal in almost all correctional institutions. The percentage of employees devoting a high percentage of their time to treatment activities was always limited, but there were also subtle changes in the roles of nontreatment prison officers and administrators. In addition to the development of complex educational, vocational, and counseling programs within prison walls, there was an expansion of programs such as work release and furloughs, in which prisoners were permitted to spend part of their time in the free community.

All these programs had their origins early in the century. The Huber Law legalized work release in Wisconsin in 1913, and the first furlough program was legislated in Mississippi in 1918. However, few states followed these early examples, with the second work release statute not being passed until 1957 in North Carolina. After the federal prison authorized the use of work release and furloughs in response to the Prisoner Rehabilitation Act of 1965, there was a rapid increase in the number of states offering these programs.[39]

THE RISE OF COMPLEX PRISON SYSTEMS

One of the factors in the spread of treatment progams throughout the United States was the centralization of state prison systems. With this development, prison administrators located in isolated rural regions were able to implement relatively sophisticated programs using information and personnel provided through state corrections agencies. These state central offices exercised considerable control over the local institutions, setting uniform policies for all institutions under their jurisdiction.

This tendency was already evident in Pennsylvania in legislation passed in 1789, 1790, and 1794, which progressively transformed the Walnut Street Jail into the first state prison.[48] States such as New York developed centralized control systems early and relatively successfully, while states such as South Carolina were still centralizing in the 1970s.

The first effort toward centralization in South Carolina occurred in 1866, when the General Assembly transferred the control of felons from the counties to the state and established the state penitentiary. In the political battle that followed, the need to reserve labor for road construction and maintenance at the county level was so great that the state had to give up its control. By 1930, the counties had regained full authority to choose which prisoners they wanted to retain for road work and which ones they wanted to send to the state. Since there were more treatment programs and generally better living conditions available in the state penitentiary than in the local prisons and jails, this resulted in much inequity.[46]

The state gradually built a network of penal facilities, and legislation was passed in 1960 to create a Department of Corrections for the state as a whole. Even these moves did not result in full centralization, and the county facilities continued to handle a heavy proportion of the prisoners in South Carolina. Following an extensive evaluation of the dual prison system, the legislature passed a law giving the state jurisdiction over all adult offenders sentenced to more than three months imprisonment. The transfer of such prisoners from local facilities to state facilities began immediately, but there were still 12 county prisons operating in 1978 (in addition to county jails for detainees and minor offenders).[46]

The Federal Prison System*

We have already noted the practice in which the federal government paid local and state correctional facilities to house its offenders. This system worked fairly efficiently until the years following the Civil War, during which there was a considerable increase in the number of both federal and state prisoners. By 1885, over 1000 federal prisoners were incarcerated in state penitentiaries and ten times that number were being housed in county jails. A decade later, the federal jail population had increased by 50 percent and the population of federal prisoners in state penitentiaries had more than doubled. The result was the passage of a law in 1891 that authorized the construction of three penitentiaries for prisoners.

In the early decades of the 20th century, there was a Federal Prison System in name only. Policies and procedures were individually developed by wardens in their separate institutions. The effect of this was chaotic since all the wardens were political appointees and turnover was very high. The passage of the White Slave Act in 1910 was the beginning of a long series of federal laws which increased the number of crimes under federal jurisdiction and therefore the number of offenders brought into the Federal Prison System. The history of corrections at the federal level is a continuing spiral in which more and more behavior was declared to be illegal, following which an ever increasing number of prison facilities had to be built to accommodate the newly enlarged pool of offenders. New correctional facilities were acquired for federal use in 1926, 1927, 1929, 1930, 1932, 1933, 1934, 1935, 1938, 1939, and so on. 1940 was the first year in which the construction of new institutions caught up with the influx of prisoners so that there was sufficient institutional capacity to house every one

*This section is drawn from an article by Gregory L. Hershberger. "The Development of the Federal Prison System." *Federal Probation* 43 (December, 1979):13–23.

of these federal prisoners sentenced by the courts. New institutions are still being added to the system.

A serious attempt at centralization did not occur until 1930, when the report of the Cooper Committee of the House of Representatives resulted in a law creating the United States Bureau of Prisons within the Department of Justice. This Bureau was designed to centrally administer all of the units in the Federal Prison System from its offices in Washington, D.C. One of the developments made possible by centralization was the creation of a national classification system in which offenders were classified by type of facility, age, offense, and sex to facilitate the delivery of the most effective correctional services for each type of prisoner and to prevent hardened criminals from influencing first-timers.

Other changes made possible by centralization include the creation of a government corporation that oversees all federal prison industries except for farming, road construction, and forestry work, the beginning of a training program for correctional officers, and the moving of correctional employees from a system of political appointments to the civil service system. These changes increased the stability of the system and permitted it to make rational adjustments to changing social conditions and the needs of its correctional clients. In addition to making program changes within institutions, changes are made in all or a group of institutions at once, and new institutions are created to serve special purposes. For example, the two pre-release guidance centers in New York City and Chicago established for youthful offenders in 1961 met the need of youthful offenders for preparation to reenter the community. Expanded in 1965 to include adult offenders as well as juveniles, these centers became the prototype for other community treatment centers developed in the federal system and in many state systems.

When it was decided that co-correctional institutions (in which male and female prisoners have a considerable degree of contact, but do not live together) might be a worthwhile experiment, the flexibility inherent in a large system permitted the conversion of institutions in Texas and Kentucky to co-correctional housing. The development of standard regulations in Washington, D.C. for all federal prison units freed staff members—and permitted the hiring of specialists—to devote more time to research and polishing institutional procedures than would ever be possible in a local facility. An example of this process is the development of the unit management approach in the early 1970s. In this new approach, groups of 50–100 offenders are housed together, work and participate in treatment programs together, and have services provided to them and decisions made about them by a small group of staff members assigned specifically to that unit rather than to the institution as a whole.[8]

LOCAL CORRECTIONAL FACILITIES

The move toward centralization and creation of the statewide correctional systems has had limited impact upon correctional facilities in counties, cities, and towns. These jails generally operate with local control just as they did a century ago. In fact, many of them are still located in the same buildings as they were when they were established. Because jails are geographically based, with at least one in each county, they are more likely to be rural than urban. Some of the large urban jails differ from state penitentiaries only in those aspects of programming and administration necessitated by the shorter sentences served by misdemeanants and the multiple functions that are required of local jails. In contrast, rural jails are likely to be poorly funded, understaffed, and devoid of meaningful programs for the prisoners.

The penal reform efforts of the 19th and early 20th centuries had minimum impact on America's jails. The poor condition and small size of most facilities, together with their remoteness and lack of professional staffing, impeded the implementation of jail reforms.[35] There were still states in which jailers were paid on the basis of fees for services performed instead of by standard salaries as late as the 1940s.[2] When Hastings H.P. Hart[23] surveyed local correctional facilities in 1931, he found that many of them were firetraps, unsanitary, poorly lighted and heated, and with inadequate ventilation. Extensive use of physical punishment was found and there was little provision for the separation of men from women, juveniles from adults, and misdemeanants from those awaiting trial. As an example of the scope of the problem, over 40,000 children were incarcerated in county jails in 1946.[2] Most of these youngsters were not adequately separated from hardened criminals temporarily confined in these facilities, even though few of the youngsters had committed acts that would be designated as crimes if perpetrated by adults.

For most jurisdictions, standardization rather than centralization has been the goal of modern jail reform. The formation of national groups such as the National Jail Association and the Jail Managers Association has helped to raise standards in remote facilities, as has the issuing of jail standards by the federal government. Many states have also been active in attempting to raise jail standards. Three strategies used by different state governments to do this are special training conferences for jail employees, the gathering of information on jail conditions for planning purposes, and the issuing of jail standards that carry the force of law. Corrections officials in Virginia hold an annual management conference for sheriffs and also provide year-round training for jail personnel through their Bureau of Jails Staff Training, which is part of the Virginia Department of Corrections. A careful evaluation system allows state officials to tailor their services to the needs of local jail administrators as well as to developments in other parts of the nation that are relevant to jail administration.[50]

States such as Washington, California, and Wisconsin have published their own jail standards. In the Washington document, the legal authority of the Department of Institutions to inspect jails and require conformity to the standards is explained, and then standards for personnel, the structure of facilities, security, admission procedures, release procedures, the keeping of records, prisoner discipline, health and sanitation, food service, the employment of prisoners, and program activities are presented.[52] These standards are sufficiently detailed so as to provide a comprehensive blueprint for the administration of local jails.

It is difficult to upgrade jails in a state without an adequate information base. Annual jail inspections for the purpose of monitoring compliance with state jail standards do not provide all of the data necessary for state-wide planning. Some states have solved this problem by commissioning special reports on their jails. For example, a comprehensive study of jails in South Dakota was used to develop data on the basis of which 14 recommendations for correctional reform were submitted to the South Dakota State Planning and Advisory Commission on Crime. The study revealed that eight South Dakota jails had been built before 1900, and that only half of the state's jails had been constructed since 1930. Few facilities had undergone extensive renovation of any kind since construction. Three-quarters of the jails had a design capacity of ten or fewer prisoners, and less than half had single cells. Facilities were adequate to separate men from women in 57 percent of the facilities, juveniles from adults in 44 percent, sexual deviates from other prisoners in 39 percent, misdemeanants from felons in 23 percent, and the innocent from the guilty in 15 percent. Only one jail in the entire state provided an educational program, and referral services for the mentally ill, drug addicts, and alcoholics were rarely found. Dozens of findings such as these formed an excellent base for recommending extensive jail reforms. Among the recommendations were that there should be much more use of alternatives to jail incarceration, that the training needs of jail employees should be incorporated in the law enforcement academy currently under development, and that many of the smaller rural jails should be replaced by a series of modern regional jails.[12]

CORRECTIONAL SERVICES TO WOMEN, CHILDREN, AND MINORITY GROUPS

The three basic categories of age, gender, and ethnicity define a number of demographic population groups that have specialized needs for correctional services. Women have specialized needs relating to reproductive functioning. Black Muslims, for example, have special dietary needs; many Hispanic-Americans require bilingual correctional personnel; and young people have psychological and social developmental needs distinct from those of adults. In this section, we see how these groups have fared in American corrections during the 20th century.

Women

By 1900, feminist reformers and correctional administrators had established a series of reformatories for women that were staffed and administered by women.[19] Prisoners in these institutions were taught the same basic domestic skills that made up the largest part of vocational programs in institutions for women 60 years later. The number of these institutions was not large, so that many female offenders were still housed in institutions that also incarcerated men. The pressure to build women's institutions was limited by the relatively small number of female offenders. In 1904, the total number of women in the nation's prisons, jails, workhouses and reformatories was ony 4503, which was

5.5 percent of all incarcerated offenders. The gravity of the offenses committed by these women was rather trivial by modern standards. Most of them had been sentenced for drunkenness, vagrancy, disorderly conduct, or "offenses against chastity." Less then one in every five had committed a crime of violence, and only slightly more had committed a property crime.[3]

Women's institutions changed so slowly in the first half of the 20th century that the description of these institutions published by Harry Barnes and Negley Teeters[2] in 1959 could just as easily have been written in 1900. They described life in all but the few progressive institutions as drab, with a highly regimented daily routine. The furnishings in the institutions were cheap and shoddy, and there were few programs to divert the women from the depressive effects of the environment. Separated from their families and having little to do, many of the women engaged in lesbian practices which the staff members unsuccessfully attempted to curb through extensive repressive measures.

The situation of female offenders in Wisconsin during the 20th century is typical of women's experiences with corrections throughout the nation during this period. Only 11 women were housed in the state penitentiary in 1904, as compared with 566 men. Female offenders were either kept in local jails, released on probation, or sentenced to the maximum security penitentiary. The State Board of Control lobbied for a women's reformatory, arguing not that women needed more humane conditions, but rather that having only the penitentiary as an alternative led to releasing too many women on probation—women who then reverted to their previous "vicious and immoral practices." This institution was finally constructed and opened in 1921. For the first 12 years, it accepted only lesser offenders, with the more serious offenders being incarcerated with the men at the maximum security penitentiary. After the women were removed from the penitentiary, they were still kept separate from the other female offenders in a special building on the grounds of the women's correctional facility. The two groups of women were not combined until 1945.[21]

Many of the women incarcerated in the new women's facility had not committed major crimes. Over half of the women admitted in 1925–1926 were guilty of no more than sexual improprieties; many of them were confined because they had been found to have a venereal disease. At this time, and in later years, the prisoners worked at tasks such as sewing, needlework, embroidery, and rugmaking. Many of the women could not be involved in more complex tasks because they were mentally deficient.[21]

The women's prison in Wisconsin has changed in a great deal since the 1920s. There have been additions to the physical plant, there are many more programs for the prisoners, and there is a thoroughly professional administration. At the same time, there are basic problems that have not yet been resolved. The small percentage of female offenders and their relative lack of publicity assure that funds for innovative programs will more likely be secured by state penal institutions for men rather than by those for women. The number of women incarcerated at the institution has always been small. It was 93 in 1972[21] and 133 in 1979.[53] With numbers as small as these, the variety of programs provided will always be severely limited. A side effect of this is that there are more staff members per prisoner then is usually the case in the men's prisons, which makes per capita operating expenses much higher.

Racial and Cultural Minorities

It has generally been the case that those minority groups overrepresented in the lower third of the American class structure are also overrepresented in correctional populations. We saw in Chapter 4 that immigrants were overrepresented in penal populations in the middle of the 19th century, but that they declined toward the end of the century. This parallels their progress up the class ladder in the mobile society. As immigrant populations became better established, their members were less likely to be processed by the criminal justice system. The pattern for blacks was just the reverse, with blacks being rarely incarcerated in penal institutions while they were slaves, and then greatly increasing their representation in these institutions after slavery was abolished. Hispanic-Americans and American Indians have also been overrepresented in the penal populations of many states.

Commonalities of dialect and culture led to the self-segregation of racial and cultural minorities in many penal institutions. In the case of blacks, this was aggravated by an official policy of segregation in most institutions in the North as well as the South.[2] Physical segregation between the races was reinforced by prejudice and discrimination against black prisoners. Blacks held the least desirable jobs and were subjected to class pressures from both white prisoners and white correctional officers if they asserted themselves in any way.[26] The migration of many blacks from the Deep South to the Northern states resulted in rapid increases in the portion of minority correctional clients in the North. By 1950, there were 17,200 minority individuals in state and federal prisons, and this rose steeply to 28,500 ten years later.[32] Part of the explanation for this increase was the rapid rise in street crime—the type of crime most likely to result in imprisonment. Amazingly, one out of every 26 American black males aged 25–34 was incarcerated on an average day in 1960.[55]

Another area of racial concern is that of the execution of offenders. Blacks were overrepresented among those executed for murder in 1930, and they were the only ones executed for rape in that year. This imbalance has persisted through the years, with blacks being overrepresented among those under sentence of death in the most recent statistics. Hispanic-Americans have usually been counted as white, so they do not appear as a separate group in the statistics on capital punishment, and other racial groups have very rarely been executed or sentenced to death in the years since 1930.[6]

It has generally been accepted correctional practice to deny racial and ethnic minorities any special religious or cultural services while incarcerated. The rise of the Black Muslims in prisons during the 1960s was initially greeted with repression. Spurred by court decisions supporting the freedom of religion for prisoners, correctional administrators have more recently provided for the dietary, cultural, and other needs of minority prisoners that are related to religion. In addition, nonreligious cultural groups have become common in all areas of the country. It is now recognized that minority religious and cultural groups can provide a considerable degree of stability in institutions. Radical individuals and small militant splinter groups are a greater danger to institutional stability than the larger and more religiously oriented groups.

Juveniles

The first juvenile court was established by the Illinois Legislature in 1899. Within the next decade, similar juvenile courts were established in 20 states and the District of Columbia.[20] At the same time, progressive states were passing legislation authorizing the use of probation for juveniles. Twelve states did so between 1900 and 1905, and 11 more had passed similar laws by 1911.[51] Continuing the emphasis pioneered by the early Child Savers, reformers in the early 20th century swayed juvenile courts in the direction of treatment rather than punishment. Informal hearings were held not so much to establish the degree of guilt as to decide upon an appropriate course of treatment. The problem to be treated was seen as a condition in the juveniles rather than in acts that they had committed.

Young women fared less well under this system than young men, for they were considered to be less amenable to change.[42] They were also subject to more rigid behavioral expectations, so that their violations were seen as more serious than comparable acts committed by young men. Therefore, they received more severe treatment for the same offenses than young men. They were less likely to receive probation and more likely to be institutionalized even though their offenses were less serious than those committed by the young men.[42]

The movement to establish child guidance clinics complemented the rise of juvenile courts. The Juvenile Psychopathic Institute was established in 1909 under the leadership of William Healy. He believed that every case had to be intensively studied, and that the causes of juvenile delinquency were mainly found in individual juveniles and their families rather than in the larger society. His ideas were translated into child guidance clinics all over America. They were initially linked directly to the juvenile courts, but many of them eventually drifted to other institutional settings such as hospitals and community agencies. This general trend was given further impetus by the passage of the Social Security Act in 1935, which funded diagnostic and consultative services in all states. Through this act, funds were made available to public welfare agencies wishing to expand services for children in danger of becoming delinquent.[13]

The early hopes of the Child Savers were not confirmed by the results they achieved in their programs. This, combined with the growing awareness of abuses to which juveniles were subject because they lacked the procedural protections of adult courts led to the decision of the United States Supreme Court in *in re Gault* that juveniles were entitled to receive legal counsel, to confront and cross-examine witnesses, to be protected against self-incrimination, to receive formal notice of charges against them, to appeal decisions of the court, and to obtain a transcript of the proceedings of the court.[20] This sweeping decision, which has been further extended by more recent decisions, restored the legal rights that juveniles had lost at the time of the establishment of the juvenile courts, and, in doing so, reactivated a balance between humanitarian concern for the treatment of juveniles and the desire that juveniles be protected by the same procedural safeguards that are available to adults.

PUNISHMENTS OTHER
THAN IMPRISONMENT

Imprisonment has become the central feature of legal punishment in the 20th century. The variety and sadism of tortures has greatly decreased, at least in highly industrialized societies. Capital punishment was used with decreasing frequency throughout the century until it finally disappeared altogether in the United States, only to arise again in 1977. Fines continued to be widely used for minor offenses and even for some major corporate offenses. In addition to these punishments, there was a tremendous rise in the use of community supervision, of which probation and parole are the most important examples. There has more recently been a proliferation of halfway houses, community correction centers, and other types of community corrections programs, but they are so recent that we will postpone their discussion until later in the text.

Capital Punishment

The federal government has kept careful records of state and federal executions since 1930. They show that 3860 offenders were executed between 1930 and 1978. Table 5.1 presents nonmilitary executions in American by race and offense. We can see that the number of executions by five-year periods rose from 1930–1934 to 1935–1939, and then declined steadily to zero in 1970–1974. The killing of a prisoner by a Utah firing squad was the single execution carried out between 1975 and 1978. A second observation that can be made from Table 5.1 is that minority offenders (particularly blacks) are more likely to be executed than whites. Although most murders were committed by whites during this period, most executions for murder were of blacks. The imbalance for rape and other offenses is even greater, with approximately five minority offenders being executed for each white offender. The injustice suggested by these statistics is not just a matter of racial prejudice. It also reflects the extent to which execution (like other serious punishments) has been reserved for the poor throughout American history.

The major methods used to execute prisoners in the United States during the 20th century have been hanging, electrocution, and gassing. Electrocution, in which the offender is strapped into a chair and subjected to an electrical current strong enough to bring about almost instantaneous death, is generally considered to be the method of choice. All of these executions are carried out in private, with only officials of the state and witnesses being present. The last public execution in the United States was the death by hanging of a convicted murderer in Kentucky on August 14, 1936.[2]

The most significant development in the area of capital punishment during this century occurred when the United States Supreme Court ruled in *Furman v. Georgia* (40 U.S.L.W. 4923, June 29, 1972) that the death penalty as applied in the United States was discriminatory and therefore in violation of the "cruel and unusual punishment" clause in the Eighth Amendment. As a result of that decision, all of the 638 offenders then awaiting execution on death rows in the

Table 5.1. Prisoners Executed Under Civil Authority in the United States, by Race and Offense, 1930–1978

Year	White		Black and Other Races		Total
	Murder	Rape and Other Offenses	Murder	Rape and Other Offenses	
1930–34	367	4	350	55	776
1935–39	436	20	361	74	891
1940–44	255	21	281	88	645
1945–49	203	11	325	100	639
1950–54	188	13	160	52	413
1955–59	128	7	125	44	304
1960–64	79	11	66	25	181
1965–69	8	0	2	0	10
1970–74	0	0	0	0	0
1975–78	1	0	0	0	1
TOTAL	1665	87	1670	438	3860

Source: Adapted from Mimi Cantwell. *Capital Punishment 1978.* Washington, D.C.: Government Printing Office, 1980, p. 18.

United States had their sentences commuted to life imprisonment. Many states reacted to this decision by passing new laws that made the death penalty mandatory under certain conditions, thus assuring that it could not be applied in a discriminatory fashion. When the Supreme Court upheld three of these new laws in Florida, Texas, and Georgia in 1976, the execution of offenders again became a legal possibility in the United States. By the end of the year, death penalties had been passed in the legislatures of 35 states, and there were 582 offenders sentenced to death.[18] It should be pointed out that not all of these laws and death sentences occurred after the Supreme Court decision. Most of them occurred before the decision and in anticipation of it.

The debates on capital punishment that occurred in state legislatures, special committees, and public hearings echoed the arguments of the abolitionists and the defenders of capital punishment that had been made throughout the 20th century. We will use arguments presented by the Governor's Study Commission on Capital Punishment in Pennsylvania[22] as an example of these arguments. The Commission was unable to reach a consensus, so it issued a majority report against the death penalty signed by ten members and a minority report in favor of the death penalty signed by seven members. Before reaching its conclusions, the Commission reviewed the literature, commissioned and received original research, held public hearings, and extensively debated the issues within its own body. The majority of the Commission believed that the death penalty should not be reestablished for the following reasons:

1. It is morally wrong for the state to take human life.
2. There is no basis for concluding that the death penalty is a significant deterrent against crime.
3. Prisoners convicted for murder are no more likely to commit violent acts while imprisoned than other types of prisoners.

4. To use the death penalty as a means of plea bargaining for the reason of lessening the backlog of cases in court is not legitimate.
5. It is unlikely that any future application of the death penalty would be nondiscriminatory. It is clear that it has been highly discriminatory in the past.
6. Execution is no more than vengeance, and vengeance is not the aim of justice.
7. Killing by the state diminishes the basic concept of the dignity of the individual, and this dignity is an inalienable right.
8. The loss suffered by the victim's family is a legitimate concern of the state, but it should be dealt with through economic support rather than by perpetrating vengeance.
9. To execute offenders simply because it is cheaper than to imprison them is ethically indefensible.
10. Although public opinion is in favor of capital punishment, it is not in favor of the mandatory imposition of capital punishment necessary to meet the test required by the Supreme Court in *Furman v. Georgia.*
11. There has been a trend toward the abolition of capital punishment since 1796, so that the return to the death penalty would be regressive.
12. No death penalty statute yet seen meets the legal standards acceptable to the Supreme Court of the United States.

The minority report of the Governor's Study Commission on Capital Punishment also contained 12 points, all of which supported the reinstatement of the death penalty:

1. The death penalty is a deterrent to premeditated murder.
2. The experiences of law enforcement officials show that many offenders do not carry weapons because of their fear of the death penalty
3. Statistical studies of the effectiveness of the death penalty have been inconclusive, and are, in any case, unimportant.
4. The public views capital punishment as both a deterrent and a denunciation of those who have committed the most terrible of crimes.
5. Economically compensating the families of victims of murder is important, but this does not obviate the necessity for the carrying out of justice against the murderers.
6. Reinstituting the death penalty will give significant protection to the lives of law enforcement officers.
7. The death penalty is a useful tool in gaining guilty pleas and evidence about co-conspirators from defendants.
8. Although the imposition of capital punishment may have been discriminatory in other states, it has not been discriminatory in Pennsylvania.
9. The Constitutions of both the United States and the State of Pennsylvania permit capital punishment.
10. Existing legal safeguards are sufficient to ensure that the execution of an innocent person would be extremely remote, if not nonexistent.
11. Cost arguments are irrelevant in deciding the issue of the reinstatement of capital punishment.

12. There are religious arguments in support of capital punishment as well as in support of abolition. Therefore, the religious element cannot be a deciding factor in arguments about capital punishment.

We can see from these conflicting arguments that the same statistical data and ethical positions can lead to very different conclusions depending upon the backgrounds and preconceptions of the individuals involved. In the case of the Pennsylvania Commission, all of the members supporting the death penalty were associated with the police or the courts in one way or another. Those favoring the continued abolition of capital punishment included a criminologist, a priest, representatives of several prison reform groups and the National Association for the Advancement of Colored People, and five members associated with the legal system. This is a fair representation of the general split of opinions on capital punishment, with social scientists, religious liberals, and prison reformers being pro-abolition and criminal justice system personnel and political conservatives generally being pro-capital punishment.

Mutilation

One of the most interesting aspects of the historical analysis of correctional punishments is the way in which early punishments that have been largely discarded as barbaric have survived, albeit in changed form, in modern correctional practices. We do not think of mutilation as having been used as a correctional punishment in America during the 20th century, but this is not entirely true. It is fair to say that compulsory sterilization is a type of mutilation. The first law authorizing compulsory sterilization was passed in Indiana during 1907. Other states were quick to follow Indiana's example. Sterilization laws were adopted in Washington, California, and Connecticut in 1909, Iowa in 1911, New York in 1912, and Kansas, Michigan, North Dakota, and Wisconsin in 1913.[54] A total of 1422 sterilizations were performed between 1907 and 1918, mostly on the mentally retarded and the psychotic.[40] The Supreme Court of the United States upheld the practice of sterilization in the case of *Buck v. Bell* in 1927.[39] The procedural safeguards required by the Court apparently did not greatly hamper the supporters of sterilization, for almost every case presented to the Eugenics Board of North Carolina between 1933 and 1942 resulted in the authorization for a sterilization operation. Most of the sterilizations involved the severing of the fallopian tubes in females and vasectomy in males, but one out of every eight male sterilizations was a castration. Thirty states eventually passed sterilization laws[54], and approximately 50,000 sterilizations had been performed by 1956.[2]

Another mutilation in modern dress is psycho-surgery, in which brain surgery is used to permanently tame aggressive mental patients and prisoners. There is some evidence that this has occurred in American prisons on occasion, but there are no available statistics on the practice.[45] It has been infrequently used in the past, and is even less likely to be used in the future. The Social Darwinist argument that those thought to be biologically inferior should be sterilized for "the good of the race" is no longer tenable. The emphasis on the biological causes of social problems that was part of the Eugenics Movement[17] and the confusion between punishment and treatment permitted such practices to occur without consideration for the rights of offenders as individuals.

Mutilation is a fundamental biological alteration inflicted upon the offender. A recent development in American corrections is the application of voluntary biological alterations for the benefit—rather than the punishment—of the prisoners. Some prisoners are concerned about disfigurements or general unattractiveness, and it may be that these factors contributed in some way to their criminal behavior by impeding normal social relationships. To the extent that this is true, the use of plastic surgery to remove disfigurements and improve general facial appearance can be a useful rehabilitative tool. When this was announced as a possibility at the State Industrial Farm for Women at Goochland, Virginia in 1970, 25 percent of the institutional population requested an examination within 48 hours of the announcement. Over the following 18 months, 250 clients were seen (in an institution with an average population of 300) and most of them were approved for surgical procedures. A variety of scars, tatoos, skin tumors, and traumatic hand disabilities were corrected.[14] Unfortunately, the program did not include provision for long-term follow-up of these prisoners to ascertain whether the surgery made a significant difference in their subsequent community adjustment.

Fines

Fines are not even mentioned in many corrections textbooks, and yet they are an important part of the punishment apparatus of society. Louis Robinson[40] points out that more than half of the offenders institutionalized in 1910 were committed for the nonpayment of fines. The same thing was true of those committed to the Philadelphia County Jail in 1960. Fines have been the most common punitive response used in America. Because they have been locally imposed in most cases, and because the punishment is less severe than incarceration or execution, the imposition of fines has never been carefully monitored. As a result, it is impossible to reach a more specific conclusion concerning the trends in fines than that they appear to be less commonly used today than previously.

A major problem with the use of fines as a penal sanction is that the same fine will be a much greater penalty for one with a low income than for one with a high income. In fact, the frequency with which poor offenders serve jail sentences because they are unable to pay relatively small fines raises questions about the appropriateness of their use. Scandinavian countries have solved this problem through the use of the Day Fine, in which the offender is sentenced to pay a fine of the equivalent of so many days work rather than an absolute amount. With this format, fines can be fairly applied across all social classes, and even to corporations of various sizes.

Probation

Only a few states had enacted laws making provision for the supervision of probationers as of 1900. It was then that the rise of the juvenile court movement drastically changed the picture. Probation was associated with the juvenile courts in almost every state. Forty states had introduced probation for juveniles by 1910, with the rest following by 1925. It was not until 1956 that all the states had instituted probation for adults.[37] Although probation has never been limited to juveniles, it made little headway until it became associated with the juvenile courts.[43] It is unlikely that it would ever have reached its fullest development had it not been for that association.

In Massachusetts, where probation originated, 6201 offenders were granted probation in 1900 and this rose to 32,809 in 1929.[49] The President's Commission on Law Enforcement and Administration of Justice[37] reported that there were more offenders in probation in 1965 than in institutions and on parole combined. A major problem in the rapid rise of the use of probation was that the states (and the federal government after 1925) found it difficult to hire enough probation officers to properly supervise the rapidly increasing pool of probationers. Of 2391 courts in 1918, only 1071 had full-time paid probation officers, 337 used part-time officers, and others used truant officers from the schools, police officers and volunteers.[51] The number of salaried probation officers had risen to 2658 by 1924, but there were more than 200,000 offenders being placed on probation each year.[32]

The growth of probation has continued unabated up to the present day. There were 923,064 offenders on probation on September 1, 1976, and these individuals were supervised in agencies staffed by 55,807 paid employees and 20,263 volunteers. Because many offenders are on probation for only a short time, these figures underestimate the total number of Americans on probation at some time during the year. The Law Enforcement Assistance Administration[31] found that there were more than two million Americans on probation at some time in 1975, one-third of them being juveniles. This means that approximately one out of every 100 Americans can be expected to be processed by a probation unit in any given year.

Parole

Twenty states had enacted parole laws by 1900, and 24 more had done so by 1922. Parole decisions are made by parole boards (rather than by judges as in probation) in all states today, but this was not always the case. As late as 1939, there were 16 states without parole boards. In these states, the governor was the paroling authority.[4] The federal parole system was not centralized under a paid parole board until 1930, in which year it paroled 2,644 offenders.[32]

The number of offenders on parole has never been as large as the number on probation. Since parole occurs after institutionalization, and most offenders are not sentenced to incarceration, relatively few of them are ever in a position to be paroled. On the other hand, the proportion of felons released on parole rather than directly without supervision has increased throughout the century.

There were 112,142 adults and 60,483 juveniles released on parole from state and federal correctional institutions in 1965.[37] Data collected by the Law Enforcement Assistance Administration[31] in 1976 combined state parolees with local parolees rather than with federal parolees, so they are not comparable to the 1965 statistics. They show that 234,096 adults and 94,140 juveniles were under parole supervision during 1975. The one-day census of parolees conducted on September 1, 1976 found 156,194 adults and 53,347 juveniles under supervision. It is not clear whether parole populations will continue to rise in the future. This is controlled to some extent by crime and conviction rates, but it can also be modified by changes in social policy as reflected in newly enacted laws. Various versions of the new justice model for the criminal justice system have been enacted in a number of states, beginning in 1976. One version of the justice model eliminates parole completely; others modify it considerably.

Maine was the first state to adopt a justice model; its system includes flat time sentences with time reduced only by a standard amount for good behavior, followed by direct release to the community without parole supervision. California's new law places all offenders on parole supervision for one year with no possibility of extended community supervision. Under Indiana's new laws, released offenders are under parole supervision for one year or until their sentences have expired, whichever is less. Another recent law in Illinois allows the judge to impose a mandatory parole period of one, two, or three years at the time of sentencing.[30] If the trend set by these states continues, the importance of parole supervision as part of the punishment apparatus of the criminal justice system will be considerably reduced in the future.

SOME TRENDS IN 20th-CENTURY AMERICAN CORRECTIONS

It is sometimes difficult to assimilate a large number of historical data and to make sense of them in a coherent framework. In the past 80 years, American corrections has experienced many apparently unconnected changes. At the same time, there are a number of trends discernible in the historical material presented in this chapter.

The first of these is the vast expansion of the correctional industry in nearly all areas of American life. There are many small towns in which the jails are not greatly different from what they were at the beginning of the century, but there is no American city of any size where this is true. There has been a tendency toward an increased use of imprisonment as a penal sanction, although there have been many periods of stagnant or declining prison populations.

The greatest expansion of correctional control has not been in institutions. It has been in the alternatives to institutionalization. Probation and other forms of community corrections have grown tremendously over the years. In some jurisdictions, the span of correctional control has been increased while institutional populations were decreasing because of the simultaneous rapid expansion of community corrections.

Two other complementary trends are the decrease in the use of corporal (including capital) punishment and the increase in the treatment activities of correctional units. The move to a justice model of corrections and the reinstitution of capital punishment are recent indications that both of these trends may soon come to a halt. However, there are, as yet, few states in which capital punishment seems likely to be carried out. Furthermore, treatment programs continue to flourish in systems that have officially adopted a justice model. They may even prove to be more common under justice-oriented administrations than under the treatment-oriented administrations that were in vogue in American corrections until the mid-1970s.

Another trend in American corrections has been a decrease in the level of discrimination against racial and cultural minorities, particularly after the beginning of the Civil Rights Movement. Even in those states where this trend has been pronounced, many of the changes were forced on correctional administrators by the courts rather than being freely adopted as a matter of moral principle or on the basis of the principles of organizational management. The expansion of alternatives to institutionalization has tended to drain off a higher proportion of whites than racial and cultural minorities from correctional institutions, so the percentage of prisoners who are of minority heritage has increased in nearly all jurisdictions.

The mention of the role played by the courts in decreasing racial discrimination reminds us that a number of trends not present in the first half of the 20th century have become important in recent years. These include the increasing willingness of the courts to become involved in correctional matters, the rise of the accreditation movement, and the development of other sets of correctional standards, all of which are discussed in Chapter 12. The trend toward centralization in correctional systems began before 1900, but made only minimal gains in the early decades of this century. This trend has accelerated since 1960, with significant increases in the degree of control of local institutions and programs occurring within states that were officially (but loosely) centralized at an earlier date. The recent countertrend toward regionalization does not necessarily mean a reduction in the degree of central control of state correctional systems, because regional administrators may be limited to carrying out policies set by the state central offices.

SUMMARY

Five major types of correctional institutions have existed in the United States during the 20th century. These have been the Northern industrial prison, the Southern plantation prison, chain gangs and other decentralized work camps, the custody-oriented prison, and the treatment-oriented prison. The 20th century has been characterized by the rise of complex prison systems in which numerous institutions and agencies are combined under a single central administrative office. As the state and federal systems developed, local correctional facilities were ignored and by-passed in most jurisdictions. They continued to exist, but were poorly funded. Their personnel remained unexposed to modern developments in correctional practices. Specialized institutions were developed for women and children. Racial and cultural minorities overrepresented among the poor were also overrepresented in the correctional system. Discrimination against members of these minority groups within the system was the rule.

Mutilation and other corporal punishments declined throughout the 20th century. There were no public executions after 1936, and a steady decline in the number of private executions until none at all were being carried out. The use of the death penalty is now on the rise, but there is little prospect that other forms of corporal punishment will also be reinstituted. In addition to changes in the use of corporal punishment, there have been a number of other trends in 20th-century American corrections. These include a vast expansion of the correctional industry, most particularly in the increased use of imprisonment as a penal sanction in recent years and in the expansion of the alternatives to institutionalization. Other trends include an increase in the use of treatment strategies in correctional institutions (which has recently peaked), a decrease in the level of discrimination against racial and cultural minorities, an increased involvement of the courts in correctional matters, the rise of accreditation and the development of correctional standards, and the trend toward the centralization of correctional systems.

REFERENCES

1. Allen, Harry E. and Clifford E. Simonsen. *Corrections in America: An Introduction,* 2nd edition. Encino, CA: Glencoe, 1978.
2. Barnes, Harry B. and Negley K. Teeters. *New Horizons in Criminology,* 3rd edition. Englewood Cliffs, NJ: Prentice-Hall, 1959.
3. Barrows, Isabel C. "Reformatory Treatment of Women in the United States." *In* Charles R. Henderson (ed.): *Penal and Reformatory Institutions.* Dubuque, IA: Brown Reprints, no date. Originally published in 1910, pp. 129–167.
4. Burns, Henry, Jr. *Corrections: Organization and Administration.* St. Paul, MN: West, 1975.
5. Byers, Joseph. "Prison Labor." *In* Charles R. Henderson (ed.):*Penal and Reformatory Institutions,* pp. 193–216.
6. Cantwell, Mimi. *Capital Punishment 1978.* Washington, D.C.: Government Printing Office, 1980.
7. Carleton, Mark T. *Politics and Punishment: A History of the Louisiana State Penal System.* Baton Rouge, LA: Louisiana State University Press, 1971.
8. Carlson, Norman A. "The Federal Prison System: Forty-five Years of Change." *Federal Probation* 39 (June, 1975): 37–42.
9. Clemmer, Donald. *The Prison Community.* New York: Holt, Rinehart and Winston, 1964. Originally published in 1940.
10. Conley, John A. *A History of the Oklahoma Prison System, 1907–1967.* Ph.D. dissertation, Michigan State University, 1977.
11. Conley, John A. "Prisons, Production and Profit: Reconsidering the Importance of Prison Industries." *Journal of Social History* 14 (1980): 257–275.
12. Dahlin, Donald C. *South Dakota Jails: Current Conditions and Proposed Directions.* Vermillion, SD: Governmental Research Bureau, University of South Dakota, 1971.
13. Eldefonso, Edward. *Law Enforcement and the Youthful Offender,* 3rd edition. New York: Wiley, 1978.
14. Fisher, Jack C. "Plastic Surgery Emphasized as a Resource for Rehabilitation." *American Journal of Correction* 40 (September–October, 1978):11–12.
15. Florida. Division of Corrections. *8th Biennial Report.* Tallahassee, FL, 1972.

16. Florida. Department of Corrections. *Annual Report.* Tallahassee, FL, 1978.
17. Fong, Melanie and Larry O. Johnson. "The Eugenics Movement: Some Insights Into the Institutionalization of Racism." *Issues in Criminology* 9 (Fall, 1974):89–115.
18. Fox, Vernon. *Introduction to Corrections,* 2nd edition. Englewood Cliffs, NJ: Prentice-Hall, 1977.
19. Freedman, Estelle B. "Their Sisters' Keepers: An Historical Perspective on Female Correctional Institutions in the United States: 1870–1900." *Feminist Studies* 2 (1974):77–95.
20. Gibbons, Don. *Delinquent Behavior,* 2nd edition. Englewood Cliffs, NJ: Prentice-Hall, 1976.
21. Gibson, Helen E. "Women's Prisons: Laboratories for Penal Reform." *Wisconsin Law Review,* 1973:210–233.
22. Governor's Study Commission on Capital Punishment. *Report of the Governor's Study Commission on Capital Punishment.* Harrisburg, PA: Commonwealth of Pennsylvania, 1973.
23. Hart, Hastings H. "Police Jails and Village Lockups." In *Report on Penal Institutions, Probation and Parole No. 9.* Washington, D.C.: National Commission on Law Observance and Enforcement, 1931.
24. Hershberger, Gregory L. "The Development of the Federal Prison System." *Federal Probation* 43 (December, 1979):13–23.
25. Henderson, Charles R. *Prison Reform.* Dubuque, IA: Brown Reprints, no date. Originally published in 1910.
26. Irwin, John. *Prisons in Turmoil.* Boston: Little, Brown, 1980.
27. Jackson, Bruce. *Killing Time, Life in the Arkansas Penitentiary.* Ithaca, NY: Cornell University Press, 1977.
28. Killinger, George G., Paul S. Cromwell, Jr., and Bonnie J. Cromwell. *Issues in Corrections and Administration: Selected Readings.* St. Paul, MN: West, 1976.
29. Krajick, Kevin. "'They Keep You In, They Keep You Busy, and They Keep You From Getting Killed.'" *Corrections Magazine* 4 (March, 1978):4–21.
30. Lagoy, Stephen P., Frederick A. Hussey, and John H. Kramer. "A Comparative Assessment of Determinate Sentencing in the Four Pioneer States." *Crime and Delinquency* 24 (1978):385–400.
31. Law Enforcement Assistance Administration. *State and Local Probation and Parole Systems.* Washington, D.C.: Government Printing Office, 1977.
32. McKelvey,Blake. *American Prisons: A History of Good Intentions.* Montclair, NJ: Patterson Smith, 1977.
33. McKelway, A.J. "Three Prison Systems of the Southern States of America." *In* Charles R. Henderson, *Penal and Reformatory Institutions,* pp. 68–88.
34. Michigan. Department of Corrections. *"Dimensions"* Lansing, MI: 1976.
35. Moynahan, J.M. and Earle K. Stewart. "The Origin of the American Jail." *Federal Probation* 42 (December, 1978):41–50.
36. Powell, J.C. *The American Siberia.* Chicago: H.J. Smith, 1891.
37. President's Commission on Law Enforcement and Administration of Justice. *Task Force Report: Corrections.* Washington, D.C.: Government Printing Office, 1967.
38. *Prison Journal* 34 (April, 1954), entire issue.
39. Reid, Sue T. *Crime and Criminology.* Hinsdale, IL: Dryden Press, 1976.
40. Robinson, Louis N. *Penology in the United States.* Philadelphia: John C. Winston, 1923.

41. Scharf, Peter and Joseph Hickey. "Thomas Mott Osborne and the Limits of Democratic Prison Reform." *Prison Journal* 57 (Autumn–Winter, 1977):3–15.
42. Schlossman, Steven and Stephanie Wallach. "The Crime of Precocious Sexuality: Female Juvenile Delinquency in the Progressive Era." *Harvard Educational Review* 48 (1978):65–94.
43. Schultz, J. Lawrence. "The Cycle of Juvenile Court History." *Crime and Delinquency* (1973):457–476.
44. Sellin, J. Thorsten. *Slavery and the Penal System.* New York: Elsevier, 1976.
45. Shapiro, Michael H. "Legislating the Control of Behavior Control: Autonomy and the Coercive Use of Organic Therapies." *Southern California Law Review* 47 (1974):237–356.
46. South Carolina. Department of Corrections. *Annual Report of the Board of Corrections and the Commissioner of the South Carolina Department of Corrections.* Columbia, SC, 1978.
47. Sykes, Gresham M. *The Society of Captives: A Study of a Maximum Security Prison.* New York: Atheneum, 1967. Originally published in 1958.
48. Takagi, Paul. "The Walnut Street Jail: A Penal Reform to Centralize the Powers of the State." *Federal Probation* 39 (December, 1975):18–26.
49. Tannenbaum, Frank. *Crime and the Community.* Boston, MA: Ginn, 1938.
50. Virginia. Department of Corrections. *1978 Sheriffs' Management Conference Evaluation.* Richmond, VA: 1978.
51. Walker, Samuel. *Popular Justice: A History of American Criminal Justice.* New York: Oxford University Press, 1980.
52. Washington. Department of Institutions. *Minimum Jail Standards and Manual of Operating Procedures for Local Jails.* Olympia, WA: 1970.
53. Wisconsin. Division of Corrections. *Fiscal Year Summary Report of Population Movement.* Madison, WI: 1979.
54. Woodside, Moya. *Sterilization in North Carolina.* Chapel Hill, NC: University of North Carolina Press, 1950.
55. Wright, Erik O. *The Politics of Punishment: A Critical Analysis of Prisons in America.* New York: Harper and Row, 1973.

Part II

Prisons

Chapter 6

Correctional Clients as Individuals

Correctional programming needs are partly determined by the composition of correctional populations. This chapter outlines some of the more important characteristics of correctional clients as individuals, and also examines the characteristics of special groups of offenders such as women, juveniles, racial and ethnic minorities, the aged, veterans, and those with developmental, mental, or physical disabilities. The descriptions of correctional clients that follow should not be taken to imply anything about the causes of crime. The fact that a higher percentage of a given group appears among correctional clients than in the general population does not necessarily indicate that that particular group is more prone to crime than any other group. The filtering effect of the criminal justice funnel is so great that it is impossible to make supportable inferences about the causes of crime from any population of correctional clients.

In Chapter 2, we discussed the ways in which criminal justice system processing reduces the population of suspects at each stage until relatively few individuals are sentenced to the correctional system, and fewer still are incarcerated as punishment for their crimes. Two additional examples of the way in which the filtering process operates are (1) variations between major cities in the percentage of crimes reported to the police by victims and (2) variations between states in the total incarceration rate. Table 6.1 displays the percentage of personal crime victimizations reported to the police in 13 American cities during 1973, based on National Crime Survey data. The percentage of personal crimes reported to the police varied from 25 percent in Houston to 42 percent in Washington, D.C. Similar variations were found for crimes of violence reported to the police, which ranged from 39 to 57 percent, and for crimes of theft reported to the police, which ranged from 19 to 36 percent. This means that a minority group heavily represented in a city having a high rate of victimizations reported to the police would tend to appear in larger numbers in the correctional population drawing from that city than would be the case in a city having a

Table 6.1. Percentage of Personal Crime Victimizations Reported to the Police in Thirteen American Cities, 1973

City	All Personal Crimes	Crimes of Violence	Crimes of Theft
Boston	36%	48%	28%
Buffalo	35	43	29
Cincinnati	37	44	32
Houston	25	39	19
Miami	40	57	32
Milwaukee	34	42	29
Minneapolis	33	41	29
New Orleans	31	44	25
Oakland	36	45	31
Pittsburgh	31	44	24
San Diego	30	40	26
San Francisco	32	40	27
Washington, D.C.	42	55	36

Source: Adapted from Law Enforcement Assistance Administration: *Criminal Victimization Surveys in 13 American Cities.* Washington, D.C.: Government Printing Office, 1975.

comparatively low percentage of crimes reported to the police. Even this analysis is oversimplified, for there are compositional effects in which some subgroups within a city have higher crime reporting rates than other subgroups, so criminals victimizing high-reporting subgroups will be more likely to be found in correctional populations than criminals victimizing low-reporting subgroups. This example shows that the criminal justice system filtering effect is based on the behavior of the public as well as criminal justice system employees.

The second example of variations in factors affecting correctional populations is the variation in the incarceration rate that exists from one state to another within the United States. We see in Table 6.2 that Georgia leads the nation with an incarceration rate of 416 per 100,000 residents, followed by Nevada at 396, Florida at 393, South Carolina at 334, and Louisiana at 320. These rates include the state prison population, children in custody, and those incarcerated in local jails. In contrast to the states having very high incarceration rates, we find that North Dakota has an incarceration rate of only 81. Other states with very low incarceration rates include Rhode Island, 89; Hawaii, 99; Massachusetts, 102; and New Hampshire, 114. Since crime rates do not vary nearly as much as

Table 6.2. Total Incarcerated Individuals per 100,000 Residents, by State, 1977–1978

Rank	State	Total Incarceration Rate
1	Georgia	416
2	Nevada	396
3	Florida	393
4	South Carolina	334
5	Louisiana	320
6	Arizona	312
7	North Carolina	311

Table 6.2 Continued

Rank	State	Total Incarceration Rate
8	Maryland	309
9	Texas	307
10	Virginia	276
11	California	276
12	Tennessee	271
13	Delaware	264
14	Alabama	263
15	Alaska	260
16	Michigan	257
17	Oklahoma	256
18	New Mexico	254
19	Oregon	244
20	Washington	238
21	Arkansas	217
22	Ohio	212
23	Missouri	210
24	Colorado	210
25	Mississippi	205
26	New York	204
27	Wyoming	199
28	Kansas	194
29	South Dakota	185
30	Kentucky	185
31	Idaho	183
32	Montana	180
33	Nebraska	175
34	Indiana	172
35	Illinois	166
36	Utah	152
37	New Jersey	151
38	Wisconsin	147
39	Pennsylvania	146
40	West Virginia	142
41	Maine	139
42	Vermont	138
43	Connecticut	133
44	Minnesota	123
45	Iowa	120
46	New Hampshire	114
47	Massachusetts	102
48	Hawaii	99
49	Rhode Island	89
50	North Dakota	81
	Average total incarceration rate for the United States	247

Source: Data compiled by the staff of the National Moratorium on Prison Construction, which is a joint project of the Unitarian Universalist Service Committee and the National Council on Crime and Delinquency.

incarceration rates, these figures imply that differences in policies and procedures in the criminal justice system are responsible for substantial differences in
the number of individuals incarcerated from state to state.

In addition to criminal justice system processing effects, disparities in
incarceration rates between states are also affected by factors external to the
criminal justice system. For example, the age structure of a state is important
because young people commit more crimes than older people. States such as
Nevada and Florida having high populations of tourists tend to be high in the
rankings because tourists are not included in the population base upon which
incarceration rates are calculated.

It is also important to realize that differences between states are purely
comparative. All American states have higher incarceration rates than countries
such as Holland, Spain, Greece, and Portugal, which have incarceration rates of
27, 28, 34, and 39 per 100,000, respectively. Sweden (43), Ireland (48), Norway
(52), and Switzerland (59) are other European countries with extremely low
incarceration rates. No Western European country has an incarceration that is
even half as large as the American rate, and only a few have an incarceration
rate as high as North Dakota, in which offenders are sentenced to incarceration
proportionately less often than in any other American state.[104] There is evidence
that countries outside Europe, such as Japan, Canada, Australia, and New
Zealand, also have much lower incarceration rates than the United States.[108]
Nations incarcerating individuals at an even higher rate than the United States
usually imprison large numbers of political prisoners in addition to prisoners
who would be considered criminals under American law. The latest reports from
the Soviet Union and South Africa suggest that these nations currently have a
higher incarceration rate than the United States.[21]

GENERAL CHARACTERISTICS OF
CORRECTIONAL CLIENTS

In the discussion of the characteristics of correctional clients that we are about
to begin, we rely heavily on prisoner statistics. It should be realized that these
statistics tend to exaggerate differences between correctional clients and the
general population. Offenders on parole will have characteristics that are fairly
similar to those who are in prison, but those on probation or receiving other
community corrections dispositions will tend to be more like the general
population than those who are in prison.

Social Class Origins

The most important characteristic of correctional populations is that they are
predominantly drawn from the lower classes. Most American studies imply class
standing through statements about occupation, income, and education, and
these will be discussed in later sections. One American study used the
Hollingshead scale to rate social class and found that prisoners in Louisiana were

Figure 6.1 An individual cell, Marion Penitentiary. (Law Enforcement Assistance Administration.)

heavily drawn from the lower two of Hollingshead's five classes.[102] A similar study of first-time prisoners in Ontario used a different scale but also found that the prisoners had much lower status ratings than the Ontario population as a whole. In addition, it was found that the prisoners tended to have lower status ratings than their parents.[32] This does not mean that crime is higher among the poor than among the higher social classes. Such a conclusion could only be drawn from a direct study of the incidence of various crimes. All that is shown by the statistics cited in this chapter is the characteristics of the population of offenders who are retained by the criminal justice system after processing by the police and the courts.

Occupation

The Law Enforcement Assistance Adminstration[62] has produced a detailed inmate profile from data collected in the 1974 survey of prisoners in state correctional facilities. Only one-sixth, or 16 percent, of these prisoners had a pre-arrest income of $10,000 or more. Thirty percent of the prisoners had a pre-arrest income of $5000 to $9999, and the other 54 percent had incomes below $5000 per year. Although these figures underestimate the total income available to the prisoners because their illegally obtained incomes are not included, it is clear that these men and women were predominantly from the lower classes and that many of them lived in poverty before their arrests. The low income of these individuals is all the more amazing because 72 percent of them were working at full-time jobs during the month prior to their arrests. Approximately half of the remaining prisoners had been looking for work during the month prior to their arrests and half had not been looking for work at all. The impression of the lower-class origins of American prisoners is given further support by the kinds of occupations they were engaged in before their arrests. Sixty-nine percent of the prisoners had been employed in blue-collar work before arrest, 3 percent on farms, 10 percent in service work, and only 15 percent in white-collar occupations. Other highly industrialized nations report similar occupational distributions among their prisoners. In Denmark, three-quarters of all prisoners are unskilled laborers.[66] Only one in every 100 prisoners in a census carried out in New Zealand correctional facilities held an administrative, executive, managerial, professional, or technical position before arrest. A very high percentage of New Zealand prisoners were either unemployed or had been engaged in blue-collar occupations in the years before incarceration.[76]

Prisoners in Third World countries also have their origins in the lower classes, but it is agricultural work rather than industrial work that predominates. Agricultural work was the most common occupation reported by male convicts admitted to central and district correctional facilities in India in 1971, ten times the number who had been engaged in commerce or who had worked in a white-collar occupation.[47] A study of the prisoners in Central Prison Bareilly by S.P. Srivastava[99] found that almost two-thirds of the prisoners in this long-term facility were poverty-stricken. Nearly all the rest could be considered to be in the middle-income bracket, although they earned less than a street-sweeper. A bare handful of the prisoners considered themselves to be in the upper-income group, but even their salaries were no greater than the income received by an ordinary clerk in an Indian city. It appears that there are even fewer middle- and upper-class prisoners in India than there are in the United States.

Education

The educational level of American prisoners is well below the average in the society as a whole. Most American prisoners claim having completed at least a year of high school, and the median grade completed is 10.3. Fewer than one in every 100 prisoners has completed a college degree.[62] This is rather misleading in that the educational record of a prisoner can indicate a much higher level of academic achievement than is actually the case. For example, admissions to the Florida Department of Corrections in 1977–1978 claimed a tenth-grade education, but had an average tested educational achievement of only 7.2.[28] Since the educational achievement of prisoners is below the average for Americans as a whole, and since education is one of the determinants of intelligence as measured by standard paper and pencil tests, it follows that many prisoners will score below the American average on these intelligence tests. Reports of intelligence testing from a variety of states[5,28,102,105,107] confirm this. However, it should be emphasized that while prisoner intelligence quotients tend to be slightly below the norm, they are well within the range of normal intelligence.

The educational achievement level of prisoners in other countries also tends to be below the national norms for those countries. The average prisoner in Canada has completed approximately one year less schooling than the average prisoner in the United States[32,100] and about the same number of years of education as prisoners in New Zealand.[76] The educational level of prisoners in India is considerably lower, with the majority of the men and three-quarters of the women being functionally illiterate.[47] There is a considerable variation between states in India, some state prison systems having rather few illiterates. Very few prisoners in the correctional facility studied by S.P. Srivastava[99] had completed the equivalent of an American high school education.

Age

Prisoners are considerably younger than the national average in all Western nations. The median age of prisoners in American state correctional facilities is 27, and that does not include any of the prisoners in juvenile facilities. Table 6.3 presents age distributions for five Western nations. Adult prisoners in New Zealand, Denmark, Canada, and the United States are much younger than the national average, while adult prisoners in Sweden are somewhat closer to the national norm. The youth of prisoners in even the most secure adult facilities has implications for correctional administration in that young people have higher rates of drug use, violence, and other problems than older prisoners. Sweden is the only nation in Table 6.3 in which the modal age category of adult prisoners is above 20–24. Statistics from India were not included in the table because the age categories used in Indian reports are very different from the age categories used in the other countries discussed in this section. However, the age distribution of Indian prisoners is similar to the distribution for Sweden. Prisoners over age 30 are found in proportionately larger numbers in Sweden and in India than they are in the United States, Canada, Denmark, and New Zealand.

Family Situation

Prisoners are less likely than free people to be currently married. Just over half of the adult prisoners in American state correctional facilities in 1974 were

Table 6.3. Percentage of Adult Prisoners of Different Age Groups, Select Western Nations

Age Group	New Zealand	Denmark*	Canada*	United States	Sweden*
Under 20	10%	16%	20%	8%	8%
20–24	42	26	27	30	22
25–29	19	25	22	24	23
30–39	17	20	21	23	29
40 and over	12	13	10	15	18

Source: New Zealand. Department of Statistics. "Justice Statistics 1978: Prisons and Prisoners." Wellington, 1979; Lønberg, Arne. *The Penal System of Denmark.* Copenhagen: Ministry of Justice, 1975; Canada. Statistics Canada. *Correctional Institutions Statistics 1977.* Ottawa, 1979; and Law Enforcement Assistance Administration. *Profile of State Prison Inmates: Sociodemographic Findings from the 1974 Survey of Inmates of State Correctional Facilities.* Washington, D.C.: Government Printing Office, 1979; National Prison and Probation Administration. *The Prison and Probation System 1978.* Norrköping, Sweden, 1979.

*The age categories for Denmark, Canada and Sweden differ slightly from the categories for the other categories in that the categories are "Under 21" and "21–24" instead of "Under 20" and "20–24."

married when they were admitted to the institution. By the time of the survey, the proportion of married prisoners had decreased to less than one-quarter.[62] This is roughly comparable to the proportion of married prisoners in other nations for which data are available.[66,76,100] The average prisoner in American state correctional facilities had served slightly more than a year and a half between the time of admission and the time of the survey. The number of prisoners who were divorced increased 66 percent and the number who were separated increased 19 percent during the period between admission and the time of the survey. Prisoners facing longer sentences and those who had already served longer periods of time were more likely to be divorced than the other prisoners.[62] Even if we adjust for the fact that younger people are less likely to be married than older people, we still find that prisoners are "naked nomads" who are much less likely to be married than people in the outside world.[42]

The LEAA survey of state prisoners[62] found that 60 percent of those prisoners who had been self-supporting before arrest had dependents. Unfortunately, this question was not asked of prisoners who were not self-supporting prior to arrest, nor were dependents broken up into adult dependents and children. Nevertheless, we may surmise that most of the dependents were children. Of those prisoners having dependents at the time of arrest, 38 percent were on welfare at the time of the survey. This illustrates the economic effect of imprisonment upon the families of the prisoners, and it also suggests one of the reasons for the high divorce rate experienced by prisoners. The economic, social, and psychological stress of incarceration falls heavily upon the spouses[96,101] and children[35,93] of the prisoners.

Personality

There have been various attempts to understand the personalities of correctional clients. These attempts have been complicated by the fact that most prisoners do not suffer from severe mental illness in a clinical sense. Extreme statements made about psychopathic personalities apply only to a small minority of prisoners. The idea of the "sexual psychopath" is more of a legal fiction than a clinical entity. The general term of the "antisocial personality" is more useful, but still does not describe a high percentage of prisoners. According to James Coleman[16], the antisocial personality consists of five factors: (1) an undeveloped conscience; (2) low frustration tolerance and impulsive behavior; (3) the ability to temporarily behave normally in the service of personal goals; (4) inability to get along well with people over a long period of time; (5) antagonistic feelings toward authority. One of the most common personality dimensions in prisoner populations (and perhaps the poor in general) is the emphasis on short-term payoffs at the expense of long-term efforts.[14] It is often difficult to convince prisoners to participate in activities which will not benefit them in the immediate future because of this emphasis on short-term gains.

The most consistent effort to understand prisoner personalities has been through the use of the Minnesota Multiphasic Personality Inventory. This psychological test is composed of numerous separate personality scales, and has been extensively tested with normal and deviant populations over a long period of time, so that the norms established for the MMPI constitute a ready-made control group for prison studies. As an example of the early use of the MMPI, 300 consecutive male admissions to the Washington State Penitentiary were tested along with a comparison group of college students. The prisoners were found to rate high on the psychopathic deviate scale, but not to have particularly high scores for neurosis or psychosis, two major forms of mental illness. An interesting finding of this study was that prisoners tended to develop neurotic and depressive problems during middle age, which suggests the need for special psychological services in prisons having high proportions of middle-aged residents.[64]

In a more recent MMPI study, James Panton[83] compared samples of male and female admissions to the North Carolina correctional system. He found that the male prisoners had an antisocial sociopathic MMPI profile that included considerable neurotic materials, and that were taken to reflect the male prisoners' heavy alcohol abuse and extensive prior criminality. The female prisoners had more asocial profiles and demonstrated greater emotional sensitivity than the male prisoners. Both groups received high scores on the MMPI psychopathic deviate scale, but they achieved their scores somewhat differently. The women tended to pick items reflecting feelings of isolation and lack of pleasure from social relations while the men picked items reflecting overt conflict with authority. It is difficult to know to what extent the experience of imprisonment contributed to these test scores, or to what extent class biases that have been inadvertently built into psychological tests invalidate these findings.

The most extensive concentrated application of MMPI technology has been in Edwin Megargee's[71,72] research on prisoner types carried out at the Federal Correctional Institution at Tallahassee, Florida. The most important achievement of this research program is his theory of personality controls among offenders. In this theory, both undercontrolled and overcontrolled individuals have tendencies toward violence. The implication is that the best way to guard against violence is to have a more balanced personality that is neither excessively undercontrolled or overcontrolled. This contrasts with the common sense view of aggression, which suggests that the greater one's self-control, the smaller the chances of engaging in antisocial actions. Megargee believes that undercontrolled individuals can easily commit aggressive acts because they have few inhibitions to block an aggressive response to frustration. In contrast, overcontrolled individuals are so rigidly inhibited that they build up huge frustrations over long periods of time, which sometimes erupt into serious assaultive or homicidal behavior. Megargee confirmed his theory with research that showed extremely assaultive offenders to have lower test scores on hostility and aggression than moderately assaultive offenders.

A different way of classifying prisoners was developed by researchers working for the California Youth Authority. This system, which is known as the I-Level Theory, assumes that juvenile delinquents are less mature than conforming youngsters, and classifies them into three main maturity levels within which there are nine subtypes of delinquents. The nine subtypes are (1) asocial, aggressive; (2) asocial, passive; (3) immature conformist; (4) cultural conformist; (5) manipulator; (6) erotic, acting-out; (7) neurotic, anxious; (8) situational emotional reaction; and (9) cultural identifier. Marguerite Warren[109], who played a central role in the development of I-Level Theory, has argued that it is not necessary to see delinquents as unusually immature in order to make use of I-Level Theory. Instead, the types of specified in the theory allow delinquents to be classified according to their personality needs for treatment so that they can receive the delinquency prevention services that are most appropriate for their present state of development.

A major difficulty with typologies of offenders based on personality dimensions is that they ignore the influence of environmental factors on human behavior. Theodore Ferdinand[24] applied I-Level procedures to sample of female delinquents at the Illinois Youth Center in Geneva. He found that the I-Level typology, which was developed for male delinquents, applied fairly well to his sample of incarcerated female delinquents. However, he also found that:

Several of the personality types identified by Warren embrace a rather heterogeneous collection of sociocultural types. A typology of personality patterns that ignores important sociocultural distinctions when classifying an individual for treatment ignores an important aspect of a client's nature.[24:40]

Some of Ferdinand's subjects did not fit any of the I-Level categories because their personalities were entirely normal and their delinquency was related to sociocultural factors. At the same time, a number of the I-Level categories were divided into two or three types in Ferdinand's results, primarily because he added sociocultural variables to the personality variables treated in I-Level Theory.

Drug History

There is considerable evidence that a high percentage of prisoners have a history of heavy or problem use of alcohol and illegal drugs.[86] Recent studies in Wisconsin, Florida, Massachusetts, New York, and Virginia confirm that the problem has not abated in recent years. Forty-two percent of Wisconsin state correctional institution residents admitted to being problem drinkers, and 65 percent admitted having recently used illegal drugs. More than one out of every three prisoners indicated having been addicted to a drug at some time in the past.[114] Fifty-one percent of Florida prisoners[28] and 70 percent of Virginia prisoners[107] were either heavy alcohol users, illegal drug users, or both. Considering only illegal drug use, 48 percent of Massachusetts correctional system residents showed indications of drug problems.[67] While 60 percent of the male commitments and 55 percent of the female commitments to the New York State correctional system in 1978 were users of illegal drugs, just 11 percent of the males and 22 percent of the females were committed for drug law violations. Only one out of every eight users of illegal drugs was incarcerated for a drug offense, so it is clear that one cannot use the presence of a drug law violation as an accurate index of involvement with illegal drugs or presence of drug problems. The New York study[75] also found that while drug users are young, those convicted of drug law violations tend to be much older, with the modal age group being between 45 and 49 years old.

The proportion of prisoners with alcohol and other drug problems seems to be somewhat lower in other countries than in the United States, although that may be an artifact of methodology in some cases. A study of new admittees in Ontario found that 38 percent of the prisoners reported using alcohol regularly and the same percentage reported using illegal drugs.[32] There is no estimate of the overlap between these two groups, so it is impossible to know the total proportion of these prisoners who had either one problem or the other or both. One-third of all Swedish prisoners in 1978 had a history of drug addiction, but statistics from the closed prison of Shogome are much higher, showing 42 percent as drug misusers and 64 percent as alcohol misusers.[73] According to Lønberg,[66] somewhat less than half of Danish prisoners have a history of the abuse of either alcohol or illegal drugs. Drug and alcohol use and abuse appear to be much less problematic in India,[47] but the only precise statistic available shows that only one out of the 30 states and union territories of India incarcerated more than a handful of prisoners under the Opium Act. One nation that appears to have a stronger relationship between alcohol abuse and crime than the United States is the Soviet Union,[17] so it is reasonable to assume that Soviet prisoners are likely to have problems with alcohol use.

Offense and Incarceration History

Approximately half of the prisoners in state correctional facilities are serving time for violent crimes. The most common crime is robbery, for which 23 percent of the prisoners are incarcerated, followed by burglary, 18 percent; homicide, 18 percent; and theft (including auto theft), 9 percent. Table 6.4 presents these figures, and also breaks them down by race of offender. We find relatively few prisoners in state correctional institutions as a result of convictions for public order offenses such as a weapons offense or drunk driving. The percentage incarcerated for drug offenses is also quite low, although we have seen in the preceding section that this is misleading as an index of drug use or drug problems. Property offenses are more common than drug offenses and public order offenses, but still much less common than violent offenses. The reason this is true is that the less serious offenders are siphoned off into community corrections programs instead of being sent to the state correctional institutions. This has implications for the extent of violence and other forms of victimization that may occur within these institutions. When we break down the offense data by race of offender, we see that black prisoners are more likely to be serving time for violent crimes than prisoners of other races. Whites are more likely to be serving sentences for property crimes, and prisoners from racial groups other than black or white are more likely to be serving sentences for public order offenses.

The most important point of differentiation among prisoners by offense is the difference between a violent offense and all other offenses. The American level of prisoners incarcerated for violent acts is extremely high, which is a reflection of America's high violent crime rate. Thirty-three percent of the correctional clients admitted to Canadian penitentiaries in 1977 were incarcerated for violent acts,[100] as were 28 percent of the 1977 population of prisoners in England and Wales,[38] and 52 percent of the prisoners in American state prisons in 1974.[61] The American figure becomes still more unusual when it is compared with other countries from around the world. Comparable percentages of violent prisoners from selected nations are Denmark, 15 percent;[66] India, 14 percent;[47] Sweden, 14 percent;[103] and New Zealand, 17 percent.[79] Even in a nation in which the average percentage of prisoners incarcerated for violent crimes is quite low, these violence-prone prisoners can be concentrated in one or more institutions through a policy of state- or nationwide classification. As an example of this, the Indian correctional facility studied by S.P. Srivastava,[99] contained 52 percent prisoners incarcerated for violent crimes, of which nearly half were for

Table 6.4. Offenses of Sentenced Prisoners in American State Correctional Institutions, 1974, by Race

Offense	All Races	White	Black	Other
Violent offenses				
Homicide	18%	15%	21%	18%
Kidnapping	1%	2%	1%	1%
Sexual assault	5%	5%	6%	4%
Robbery	23%	16%	30%	16%
Assault	5%	5%	5%	14%
Property offenses				
Burglary	18%	21%	15%	17%
Larceny or auto theft	9%	10%	7%	12%
Other	6%	8%	4%	4%
Drug offenses	10%	12%	9%	5%
Public order offenses	5%	6%	4%	10%
Total	100%	100%	102%*	101%*
Number of offenses	184,487	95,000	88,628	3272

Source: Law Enforcement Assistance Administration. *Profile of State Prison Inmates: Sociodemographic Findings from the 1974 Survey of Inmates of State Correctional Facilities.* Washington, D.C.: Government Printing Office, 1979.
*Where percentages do not add to 100, it is due to normal rounding procedures.

homicide. This institution was dedicated for the use of long-term prisoners, mostly those sentenced to life imprisonment, and so prisoners from all over the state of Uttar Pradesh were sent there for confinement.

Another index of the criminality of prisoners is the number of previous sentences they have served in correctional facilities. Approximately one-third of American prisoners are first-timers; a quarter have served one previous sentence; and another quarter have served three or more previous sentences.[62] Since most convictions do not involve sentences to correctional facilities, these figures greatly understate the number of previous criminal convictions in the records of American prisoners. In contrast with American prisoners, Canadian prisoners are more likely to have served no previous sentences and less likely to have served three or more previous sentences.[100] Japanese prisoners are also more likely to be first-timers, but the proportion of Japanese prisoners serving five or more previous sentences is higher than it is in the United States.[52] These differences may to some degree be due to differences in levels of crime between countries, but they are also due to factors such as differences in criminal justice processing policies, alternatives to incarceration that are available, and the seriousness with which certain criminal acts are regarded.

SPECIFIC CATEGORIES OF PRISONERS AND THEIR SPECIAL CORRECTIONAL NEEDS

This section examines nine specific categories of prisoners. These groups of prisoners are briefly described as they exist in the United States, with comparisons drawn from prisoner populations in other nations.

Women

There were 12,736 female prisoners in state and federal correctional institutions at the end of 1978,[61] up from 8850 in 1975[58] and 6272 at the end of 1972.[57] The proportion of female prisoners has stayed around four percent in the United States down through the years. The number of female prisoners has tended to rise and fall in concert with the number of male prisoners. At the moment, both are rising, and the number of female prisoners is rising somewhat more steeply than the number of male prisoners.[10] A much higher proportion of juvenile prisoners than adult prisoners are female. According to the latest available statistics, 30 percent of the incarcerated juveniles in private facilities are female,[59] as are 16 percent of the imprisoned juveniles in public facilities.[60]

Most other nations for which data are available have even smaller percentages of female prisoners than the United States. Sweden,[103] Japan,[52] Canada,[100] and Denmark[66] all have between two and three percent of their incarcerated population being female. India[47] and England and Wales[38] are somewhat higher, with slightly more than three percent females and New Zealand[79] is the highest at six percent. There is no country in the world in which women make up a sizable proportion of the incarcerated offenders.

Female prisoners tend to be less severely criminal than male prisoners. They commit fewer crimes against persons,[1,38,47,79,100] and they are less likely to be recidivists.[62] Table 6.5 illustrates this generalization with statistics on the offenses of men and women admitted to Canadian prisons between 1970 and 1976. We see in this table that although women are more likely to have been convicted of murder, they are much less likely to have been convicted of rape or robbery, so that the total violent crime comparison shows a higher proportion of violent criminals among male prisoners than female prisoners in Canada. Property offenses and drug offenses are even more unevenly distributed, with male prisoners being more than three times as likely to have been convicted of breaking and entering or theft, and female prisoners being more than four times as likely to have been convicted of a drug offense and almost twice as likely to have been convicted of fraud.

Comprehensive data on the characteristics of female prisoners in the United States have been compiled by Ruth Glick and Virginia Neto.[36] They estimate that slightly more than half of the female prisoners are black, and nearly 10 percent are Hispanic. One out of every five women is married, and a similar proportion were living in a nonmarital relationship at the time of arrest. More than a third of the women are separated, divorced, or widowed, and this rises to nearly two-thirds of those women aged 35 and over. Approximately three out of every four women have borne children and the mean number of children per mother is two-and-a-half. Three-quarters of these mothers had children living with them at the time of arrest. Ten percent of these children stayed with their fathers after the mother's arrest, 44 percent lived with their grandparents, 32 percent with other relatives, and 14 percent with other persons or social agencies.

These statistics on the children of imprisoned women suggest that there is a special need for programming to enable the women to continue relating closely

Table 6.5. Offenses of Persons Admitted to Canadian Federal Institutions, 1970–1976, by Gender

Offense	Male	Female
Violent offenses		
Murder/manslaughter	5%	10%
Attempted murder/wounding/assault	5%	4%
Rape/other sexual offenses	6%	0%
Robbery	20%	10%
Property offenses		
Breaking and entering/theft	30%	9%
Fraud	7%	13%
Drug offenses	8%	35%
Other offenses	19%	19%
Total	100%	100%
Prisoners held at the end of 1976	9,136	189

Source: Adams, Susan G. *The Female Offender: A Statistical Perspective.* Ottawa: Solicitor General of Canada, 1978.

to their children while they are incarcerated and a parallel need for support services to be given to the children during this period. A Canadian study shows that only one-third of the mothers living with their children at the time of arrest had seen these children since being incarcerated. Most of the children were forced to change their residence, but the impact of the change of residence was minimized by the fact that the majority of these changes were to a home of another family member. Only 12 percent of these children were placed in foster care as a result of their mothers having been imprisoned.[91] This study, together with a British study that came to similar conclusions,[35] leads to the conclusion that the displacement of the children of imprisoned mothers from their homes may not be as frequent a problem as was peviously thought to be the case.

An exploratory study of the children of imprisoned fathers and mothers in Oregon develops this theme further. This study focuses on antisocial behavior and other problems arising in the children of imprisoned parents as a result of the stigmatizing and traumatizing effects of imprisonment. More than half the children were rated by their parents as having increased on one or more of four negative dimensions: sadness, fearfulness, aggression, and antisocial behavior. Services recommended for these children include short-term family-centered counseling, an outreach effort to involve families of prisoners even if they do not seek help actively, and the active inclusion of family members in any program of rehabilitation for prisoners.[93]

Because female prisoners often have even fewer occupationally salable skills than male prisoners, they have particularly strong needs for programming in the areas of education and vocational training. Providing for the educational and vocational needs of female prisoners has been made difficult by the factors of isolation, sexism and scale. Prisons for women are too small to offer the assortment of programs needed, and they are so isolated that it is difficult to find an adequate number of community placements and part-time employees to make up for the impossibility of implementing a wide range of full-scale programs. The traditional programs that trained women for housekeeping tasks still exist in most women's prisons.[36] Although some of these programs are beneficial in that they increase the household management capabilities of women who are heads of households or in other responsible positions in their homes, they are not an adequate substitute for training in employment skills at a level that is more salable in the economic marketplace.

Juveniles

The number of juveniles who were incarcerated in public and private juvenile correctional facilities on December 31, 1977 was 64,166.[59,60] The characteristics of these young people are summarized in Table 6.6. We see that the average juvenile prisoner is 15 years old, male, white, and being held because he has committed a juvenile delinquency. There are proportionately fewer blacks incarcerated among juveniles than adults, but proportionately more females. One out of every 12 juvenile prisoners is Hispanic. Only a small minority of juvenile prisoners in public facilities are held for reasons other than the commission of juvenile delinquencies. In contrast, two-thirds of the juveniles held in private facilities are not incarcerated as the result of having committed a

Table 6.6. Selected Characteristics of Public and Private Juvenile Prisoners, U.S.A., December 31, 1977

Characteristics of Prisoners	Private Facilities	Public Facilities
Sex		
Male	70%	84%
Female	30%	16%
Average age	14.9	15.3
Race		
White	75%	63%
Black	21%	34%
Other; Not reported	4%	3%
Ethnicity		
Hispanic	7%	9%
Non-Hispanic	93%	91%
Reason held		
Delinquency	33%	86%
Status offense	26%	11%
Dependency, neglect, abuse	18%	2%
Emotional disturbance, retardation	6%	0%
Other	17%	1%
Number of prisoners	29,070	44,096

Source: Law Enforcement Assistance Administration. "Children in Custody: Advance Report on the 1977 Census of Public Juvenile Facilities" and "Children in Custody: Advance Report on the 1977 Census of Private Juvenile Facilities." Washington, D.C.: Department of Justice, 1979.

juvenile delinquency. A substantial number of these young people have committed only status offenses that would not be considered crimes if committed by adults, or were incarcerated because of mistreatment by their parents, emotional disturbance, or mental retardation.

In comparison with other nations, the United States is unusual in its incarceration of many juveniles who have not committed what would be considered to be crimes if perpetrated by adults. Many countries either incarcerate only youngsters who have committed criminal acts, or incarcerate practically no youngsters at all in penal institutions. In Finland, three-quarters of the 15–17-year-olds and one-half of the 18–20-year-olds who are sentenced to imprisonment have been convicted of property offenses. Most of the rest have been convicted of drunken driving, which is considered to be a very serious offense in Finland.[54] Seventy-nine percent of a sample of juvenile New Zealand incarcerates[77] and 75 percent of a sample of incarcerated British juveniles[85] had committed either larceny, burglary, or motor vehicle theft. The remainder had committed a variety of crimes against persons, drug offenses, and only a small proportion of offenses against the public order. Juvenile incarcerates in Japan had committed economic crimes in slightly more than half the cases, violent crimes in approximately one case out of every six, and public order offenses in only a small number of cases. Approximately one in every ten incarcerated juveniles had not broken a law, but had been judged to be pre-delinquent.[51]

There are no longer any long-term youth prisons in Denmark. In 1968, before they were abolished, there were only 385 juveniles incarcerated in these institutions, most of which were open rather than closed prisons. In place of these institutions, there are a number of small youth hostels, and a few of juveniles between the ages of 15 and 17 serve time in adult penal institutions.[66] Only 63 persons were admitted to youth prisons in Sweden during 1978, and the average total population of Swedish juveniles incarcerated in youth prisons during 1978 was 123.[103] Massachusetts followed the lead of nations such as Sweden and Denmark, closing all of its major institutions for juvenile delinquents and decreasing the incarcerated juvenile population from 895 in 1970 to 49 in 1975, a decrease of 94 percent.[112] (See Chapter 18 for more information on juvenile deinstitutionalization in Massachusetts.)

In the United States, there has been a concerted effort spearheaded at the federal level to eliminate status offenders from juvenile institutions. The reasoning is that a young person who has not committed an act which would be a crime for an adult ought not to be placed in a correctional facility. This problem has historically weighed more heavily upon young women than young men. Many young women have suffered extended periods of incarceration for noncriminal acts such as engaging in sexual intercourse with a boyfriend.[13]

It is more difficult to make generalizations about juvenile corrections than adult corrections. One reason is that the variation between states is much greater in juvenile corrections than in adult prison systems, a fact which was demonstrated by the National Survey of Juvenile Correctional Programs carried out by Robert Vinter and Rosemary Sarri.[106] They found that states varied in their juvenile codes, the rates at which they sent young people to correctional institutions, the number and type of community-based correctional programs, the structures for implementing correctional programming, and information and decision systems for controlling juvenile corrections. Another difficulty in making generalizations about juvenile corrections is that so many juveniles are hidden from view, even in a comprehensive national census. It has been estimated that as many as 600,000 young people may serve time in adult jails each year.[112] These juveniles are essentially uncounted and unstudied, and receive practically no services at all.

Even in well-organized correctional facilities intended for juveniles, the average stay is often so brief that it is impossible to provide adequate programming to meet the needs of the prisoners. The most important and general needs of juvenile correctional clients follow from their average age, which is 15. They are in a period of developing gender identity in which incarceration in unisex institutions may have damaging effects. This suggests the need for specialized programs dealing with gender role confusion and development. Relatively few juvenile prisoners have completed high school, and so there is an important need for educational programming. Few youngsters have salable job skills, and vocational programming is therefore particularly desirable in youth institutions having relatively low turnover. Aside from the age-specific needs, the substantial proportion of black and Hispanic juvenile prisoners implies the need for adequate minority staff recruitment patterns and also specialized cultural programs designed to appeal to these prisoners.

Racial and Cultural Minorities

Referring to Table 6.4, we see that nearly half of the prisoners in the United States have an ethnic origin other than European. Blacks and other nonwhite prisoners are more likely to be incarcerated for violent offenses than whites, and less likely to be incarcerated for property crimes. Hispanic prisoners are not represented in Table 6.4, but a separate tabulation by Hispanic origin shows that one out of every 16 American prisoners is Hispanic. Hispanic prisoners are much more likely than other prisoners to have been convicted of a drug offense, and they are less likely to have been convicted of a violent crime or property crime. Black prisoners are more likely than white prisoners to have had a pre-arrest income below the poverty level. They have a somewhat lower average occupational status level than whites, but there are no significant differences in the level of education completed or the percentage employed prior to arrest.[62]

Racial and cultural minority groups overrepresented among the poor in a society are usually overrepresented in its prisons. In the United States, blacks, Hispanics, and American Indians are overrepresented in prison populations, while Japanese-Americans and Jewish-Americans are underrepresented. Blacks are proportionately more likely to be incarcerated than whites in every state except those which have extremely small percentages of blacks living within their borders. In some states, the incarceration rate is ten times as high for blacks as it is for whites.[22] In addition, there is substantial evidence that those states having a higher proportion of blacks in their general populations tend to have higher incarceration rates overall.[74] The United States is not the only nation to have high incarceration rates for minority groups which are overrepresented among the poor. In New Zealand, almost half of the prisoners received in 1977 were Maoris,[77] and 94 percent of all the sentenced prisoners in custody on June 30, 1979 in the prisons of South Africa were Bantu or Colored.[98] (Colored and Bantu prisoners in the South African classification system would both be considered to be black in the United States.)

Although their numbers are much smaller, American Indian groups are significantly overrepresented in correctional institutions in the United States. This is particularly noticeable in those states in which large numbers of American Indians reside. For example, American Indians make up approximately a quarter of the prison population in South Dakota[23] and a tenth of the prisoners in Oklahoma.[82] In Hawaii, nearly three-quarters of the prisoners are ethnic Hawaiians or part-Hawaiians.[63] Native tribal group members are also the largest ethnic minority in Canadian correctional institutions. There are four times as many Amerindian prisoners in Ontario provincial institutions as one would expect from the percentage of Amerindians in the total population of Ontario. Most of the Amerindian prisoners are from rural reservations, unemployed, and with minimal educational achievement and job skills.[48] Canadian penitentiaries as a whole admitted one Amerindian man for every eight non-Amerindian men in 1977, most of them in Alberta, Manitoba, and Saskatchewan.[100]

Minority groups have special cultural needs in correctional institutions. Some groups, such as Hispanics, have many members who do not speak English well enough to communicate with officers who are not bilingual; others have special religious and dietary needs; and representatives of almost all minority groups request permission to develop special culture groups in which minority prisoners regularly meet to enhance their appreciation of their own cultural heritage. In recognition of cultural differences in the needs of prisoners, Japan[50] has a special classification for non-Japanese prisoners who need different treatment. Minority groups in the United States have traditionally been permitted only a minimal participation in their own cultures. A series of court decisions beginning with the Black Muslim religion in the early 1960s[20] and spreading to American Indians and other groups in the following decade[30] have steadily widened the scope of services to incarcerated minority peoples. These cases are given fuller discussion in Chapter 11.

It is generally believed that correctional employees will be more successful in working with their charges if they are from the same racial and cultural heritage. This is an overgeneralization, for many intergroup contacts are extremely effective when handled by correctional employees who are sensitive and adequately trained. In addition, a study of correctional officers in Illinois failed to find the expected differences in the attitudes of black and white guards.[49] However, the weight of practical experience continues to be supportive of the idea that prisoner–staff understanding is seriously undermined in prisons containing a high percentage of minority residents and very few minority staff members. The desirability of having at least a rough matching of the racial-ethnic composition between prisoners and staff members becomes essential when dealing with minority groups containing prisoners who do not speak English. States such as New York, California, Arizona, New Mexico, Texas, and Florida incarcerate substantial numbers of Hispanic men and women, many of whom are not fully conversant with the English language. In these states, the employment of Hispanic staff members is essential.

Veterans

Fewer prisoners have served in the armed forces than citizens in the society as a whole. Even so, more than a quarter of all sentenced prisoners are veterans, and approximately one out of every ten prisoners was in the military during the Vietnam War. Three out of every four imprisoned veterans received an honorable discharge when their military service was terminated. Very little is known about incarcerated veterans, either within the United States or internationally. A Massachusetts study compared Vietnam veterans with other prisoners and found that the veterans were less likely than nonveterans to have prior incarcerations or arrests and more likely to have a history of narcotics abuse. The veterans also tended to be younger and better educated than nonveterans. After examining a number of other factors, the study suggested that the Vietnam veteran population was "a fairly stable group of individuals with a relatively high rehabilitative potential."[56:6]

Aside from the relatively small proportion of veterans who might have special psychiatric needs relating to their military experiences, the major program need for veterans is to make them aware of the veterans benefits to which they are entitled and to ensure that institutional programs conform to eligibility requirements for these benefits wherever possible. A survey of veterans in

Georgia found that fewer than one in every five imprisoned veterans had received any veteran benefits since being incarcerated.[31] One researcher who has worked with imprisoned veterans believes that less than a quarter of America's imprisoned veterans understand that they are entitled to veterans benefits. Many of them have been mistakenly led to believe this by uninformed correctional officers, and the limited outreach practiced in correctional institutions by the Veterans Administration until recent years has not been sufficient to change the situation significantly.[68]

The Mentally Ill

It is difficult to obtain reliable estimates of the prevalence of mental illness in correctional populations, partially because of differences in definitions and partially because most correctional institutions do not have enough psychologists and psychiatrists to monitor mental illness on a regular basis. After surveying the literature on mental illness among criminals, Michael Lillyquist[65] concludes that a minority—and perhaps only a small minority—of criminals are suffering from mental illness. Other scholars have concluded that even if the mental illness levels of criminals are not much higher than normal, the conditions of imprisonment may cause greatly inflated rates of temporary mental illness.[15,40]

One way of ascertaining whether or not higher mental illness rates among correctional populations are due to the effects of incarceration is to look at the pre-institutional mental illness experiences of prisoners. In a sample of prisoners at the Federal Penitentiary at Lewisburg, more than half of the prisoners had a prior psychiatric contact, and nearly one-fifth had spent time in a psychiatric hospital.[92] Eighteen percent of the first incarcerates in a Canadian prison had experienced some form of psychiatric treatment or came from families in which other members had histories of psychiatric problems. Approximately one in every twelve of these prisoners had attempted suicide at least once.[32] These findings suggest that the abnormally high rates of mental illness usually found in correctional populations are not entirely due to the conditions of imprisonment, but they do not show that crime is caused by mental illness. Both high crime rates and high mental illness rates may be caused by a third variable, such as the stress of poverty (remember that most prisoners, but not necessarily most criminals, are drawn from the ranks of the poor).

Recent statistics on mental illness in prisoners tend to show higher rates than earlier studies. For example, a recent estimate by the Medical Director in Michigan's Department of Corrections estimates that 20 percent of Michigan's prisoners have a serious mental disorder.[113] This does not mean that they are all psychotic. Only eight percent of the prisoners in the Lewisburg sample were judged to be psychotic. The common diagnoses in that study were personality disorders (31 percent), alcoholism (29 percent), and drug abuse (25 percent).[92] A Japanese evaluation of the mental condition of all prisoners in national prisons showed that the rate of psychopathy and neurosis was 24.6 times the rate in the general Japanese population, while the rate of psychosis was only twice the normal rate. One in every twelve Japanese prisoners was estimated to have a mental disorder.[50] Many prisoners who have mental illnesses that are not clinically the most severe can nevertheless present extremely serious problems for treatment. Although prisoners described as sociopathic, psychopathic, or disruptive may be less mentally ill in a clinical sense than psychotics, they may also be less amenable to treatment.[9]

Evidence is accumulating on the prevalence of mental illness in jail populations, and the results to date suggest that jail populations may have higher rates of mental illness than prison populations. A study of five county jails in California estimated that 37 percent of the prisoners were experiencing a treatable mental disorder.[84] Another study estimated that one-quarter of the prisoners in the Los Angeles County Jail could be classified as mentally ill. Finally, a small random sample of prisoners from a jail in New York State was found to contain over 60 percent mentally disordered prisoners. That is to say, these prisoners suffered from disorders that psychiatrists would normally treat in their offices and that are included in the diagnostic manual used by American psychiatrists.[43]

If mental illness is so common in correctional populations, why aren't these prisoners transferred to mental hospitals? This question is more complicated than it seems. Transfers between prisons and mental hospitals are limited by policies of state agencies, court decisions, enacted law, and the attitudes of institutional administrators. In some jurisdictions, prisoners cannot even voluntarily transfer to a mental hospital with the approval of prison authorities. Involuntary commitment procedures are the only procedures available in those states. At the same time, involuntary removal procedures are complicated by the necessity of protecting the rights of prisoners who may find themselves serving longer sentences in mental institutions than they would have served had they stayed in correctional facilities. Unfortunately, the lack of psychological and psychiatric staff members in correctional facilities means that staying where they are practically guarantees that mentally ill prisoners will not receive adequate treatment.[110]

Some of these complications are illustrated by the situation of mentally ill prisoners in Iowa, which has recently been studied by James Boudouris.[9] A psychiatric unit was instituted at the Men's Reformatory at Anamosa in 1958. Four years later, the unit contained 114 prisoners, of which 15 were received as transfers from mental health institutions, 36 were committed on criminal charges but ruled incompetent to stand trial, and 63 were received as transfers from the general prison population at Anamosa and Fort Madison. In 1965, a committee studying the adult offender in Iowa concluded that between 10 and 15 percent of Iowa prisoners were "blatantly psychotic." At that time, Iowa began to build a secure medical facility at Oakdale to house dangerous mental patients. Despite the existence of an adequate psychiatric facility, there are still mentally ill prisoners in the Iowa State Penitentiary at Fort Madison. Staff at this facility estimated that there were currently approximately 25 psychotics and 50–100 behavioral problems or sociopaths incarcerated at Fort Madison. These prisoners were mostly suitable for transfer to the Iowa Security Medical Facility, but the transfers had not occurred. In addition, the Men's Reformatory at Anamosa was estimated to contain approximately 15 psychotics and sociopaths who might be transferred. Anamosa currently has a treatment unit for psychotic inmates that has a maximum capacity of five prisoners. Among the recommendations made by Boudouris were that (1) mental health and correctional staff members need special training in the area of psychiatric problems among criminals; (2) some of the less dangerous mentally ill prisoners currently at Oakdale could be transferred to less secure mental illness treatment facilities to make room for the transfer of a number of mentally ill prisoners from Fort Madison; and (3) mental health and corrections professionals in the state of Iowa need to communicate more frequently about the mental health needs of prisoners.

The special needs of these prisoners are those directly concerned with their mental health problems. They vary according to the clinical nature of the problem and the correctional environment in which prisoners are currently living. The American Medical Association[4] has adopted revised guidelines for health services in jails which set 69 separate standards, a number of which apply to psychiatric care. The most important of these standards are summarized below.

1. Correctional staff need to be trained to recognize signs and symptoms of emotional disturbance, developmental disability, and chemical dependency.
2. All new prisoners should be interviewed by a qualified psychologist and referred for psychiatric evaluation within 14 days if this is judged appropriate.
3. Psychiatric problems require immediate follow-up, especially where suicidal and psychotic patients are involved.
4. Emergency psychiatric care should be rendered within 12 hours, and prisoners wanting this care should be specially housed and supervised.
5. Housing assignments, program assignments, disciplinary actions, and transfers contemplated with psychiatric patients should not be made without receiving consultation from psychiatric staff members.
6. Prisoners with mental illnesses beyond the capacity of staff and facilities in correctional institutions should be transferred to other facilities where such care is available.
7. All prisoners are to be informed orally and in writing of procedures for access to medical treatment.
8. Special programs must be developed for those prisoners requiring close medical supervision, including psychotics and suicidal prisoners. These programs must be developed by qualified physicians and inplemented by health-trained correctional staff.

Mentally Retarded Prisoners

It has been estimated that approximately 10 percent of American prisoners are developmentally disabled,[12] which is three to ten times the rate found in the nation as a whole.[94] This overrepresentation may be partially due to the incarceration of offenders who really did not understand what they were doing, and who therefore would be better served in an institution for the developmentally disabled.[88] There is evidence that the percentage of mentally retarded offenders can be reduced, for only 3 percent of Danish prisoners[66] and 5 percent of Japanese prisoners[50] are retarded. Even with this lower rate, the proportion of Japanese prisoners who are mentally retarded is 13 times the proportion in the normal Japanese population. Additional evidence about the possibility of reducing the proportion of mentally retarded offenders comes from a doctoral dissertation by Edward Rockoff.[89] He found that approximately 13 percent of the men imprisoned in Iowa state correctional facilities were mentally retarded in 1965, but that by 1972 this had been reduced to only two percent. Rockoff believes that the decline in mentally retarded prisoners in Iowa may have been due to the greater use of community corrections, probation, and parole for these offenders.

The special program needs of mentally retarded offenders are summarized in a recent Prescriptive Package issued by the Law Enforcement Assistance Administration.[94] The most important of these programming needs are listed below.

1. Developing the diagnostic and classification capability necessary to identify different levels of mental retardation so that individuals can be placed in appropriate programs.
2. Creating special institutional environments that are oriented towards the needs of the mentally retarded and are physically safe (from other prisoners as well as from environmental hazards).
3. Developing individualized treatment programs for retarded offenders so that they can increase their understanding of human behavior, acquire the skills, resources, and opportunities necessary to survive in society, and master institutional regulations well enough to avoid excessive rule infractions.
4. Providing for specialized needs of retarded prisoners such as those associated with speech pathology, audiology, and language development.
5. Developing a system of supportive services designed to ease the return of the retarded prisoner into society.
6. Developing training and qualification standards for correctional system personnel who will be working with retarded offenders.

Medically Ill Prisoners

Comprehensive data on the medical condition of prisoners cannot be obtained in more than a handful of states. In fact, one of the recommendations made by the Comptroller General in a report to Congress on medical and dental care in correctional institutions was that correctional administrators must develop information systems capable of documenting the medical needs of prisoners so that they can take steps to develop programs to meet those needs. Medical illnesses found in correctional populations fall into three general categories: (1) illnesses existing at time of admission; (2) illnesses developed naturally while incarcerated; and (3) illnesses caused by the conditions of incarceration. Because prisoners tend to be relatively poor and uneducated, many of them have not had adequate medical care in years prior to imprisonment, so they enter the prison with a high probability of the need for medical attention. It has been estimated that the average prisoner entering the Federal Prison System has a 95 percent probability of needing medical care and a 66 percent probability that he or she will not have received previous medical attention.[70]

Although there is a high probability of the need for medical attention at admission, the natural occurrence of medical problems during incarceration is lowered by the youth of most prisoners. Prisoners have more medical problems than a group of average citizens of the same age, but they have fewer medical problems than the average for the nation as a whole, including people of all ages. Medical conditions caused by incarceration include diseases arising from poor sanitation, crowding, inadequate diet, and victimization by other prisoners. While institution-caused problems can be minimized in well-funded facilities, the majority of state correctional facilities and a very high percentage of local correctional facilities are not well enough funded to minimize the institutional sources of medical problems.

There is considerable overlap between prisoners with medical problems and some of the other groups of prisoners that we have discussed in this chapter. Prisoners with alcohol and illegal drug-related problems always need some sort of medical attention. The same is true of prisoners suffering from mental retardation or senility. In addition to strictly medical needs, groups such as the mentally retarded, the senile, and those with illnesses such as epilepsy tend to suffer high rates of victimization by their fellow prisoners, and need special protection as a result.[39]

Existing fragmentary data on the medical needs of prisoners can be divided into two kinds of information. First, there are medical assessments of groups of prisoners, which yield prevalence rates of various diseases at a given time. The second kind of information consists of medical services utilization data from existing programs in correctional facilities. Medical assessments were carried out by physicians on three groups of prisoners at the Tombs—a jail in New York City. They found that approximately three out of evey ten prisoners had a medical condition requiring immediate treatment.[37] A similar study carried out in a county jail concluded that nearly four out of every ten prisoners required immediate medical care—more than half of them having a medical condition so severe that immediate hospitalization was warranted.[111] Higher rates of medical conditions were reported in a study of selected correctional institutions in Ontario. Forty-five percent of the prisoners at four jails, 44 percent of the prisoners in five adult correctional institutions, and 42 percent of the prisoners in three training schools had identifiable medical conditions requiring treatment.[8]

David Jones[53] asked prisoners about their illnesses rather than using doctors to examine them and give medical judgments of their illnesses. Using this methodology, he found that the rate of acute medical conditions was slightly over 500 per 1000 prisoners per year. The most common problem was physical injury, followed by respiratory infections. The acute medical condition rate was consistent throughout all ages of prisoners, but showed significant variation by length of imprisonment. Medical conditions occurred at a rate of 695 per 1000 prisoners per year for prisoners incarcerated between 6 and 11 months, and then declined unevenly to 389 for prisoners incarcerated 48–59 months. The highest rates of medical conditions were found among prisoners incarcerated for 10 years or more, who had a rate of 788.

Medical facility utilization rates may understate the level of medical problems in correctional populations as compared with self-report or medical evaluation studies because some prisoners do not report their medical conditions to prison authorities, especially if they feel that adequate treatment is not available. On the other hand, it is also true that prisoners may report illnesses that do not exist in order to gain special advantages for themselves. The main way that prisoners receive medical attention in many institutions is the sick call, in which prisoners line up to attend a clinic for a specified complaint that they hope will be judged to merit medical attention. Statistics from the Washington, D.C. Department of

Corrections[81] show that the average male prisoner attended 8.4 sick calls a year and the average female prisoner attended 17.3 sick calls per year. In addition, infirmary admissions provided over 600 person-days of bed care per month, and approximately 100 inpatient days per month were served in hospital facilities outside of the correctional compounds. These statistics were generated with an average population of approximately 1600 prisoners. California Department of Corrections personnel performed 4918 surgical operations, accepted 11,114 patients for hospital stays, and had an average daily sick call line of 2980 with an average population of approximately 19,000 prisons.[33]

Statistics from Great Britain[38] confirm that females utilized medical services more heavily than males, and reveal that a staggering total of nearly 5 million medical treatments were delivered to an average correctional population of approximately 40,000 prisoners during a one-year period. Prisoners in correctional facilities in India[47] were hospitalized an average of 1.24 times per year. Approximately one prisoner in every 28 was on sick call on any given day. Despite this relatively high morbidity rate, the mortality rate was extremely low in Indian prisons. Only 244 deaths were reported in an average daily population of 72,623, for an average annual death rate of 3.4 per 1000 prisoners. In the Tennessee State Penitentiary, Jones[53] found that the average prisoner reported 4.3 consultations per year with a physician. The number of physician visits per illness was 0.82, which means that some prisoners' illnesses were not treated by a physician at all. The number of days spent in hospitals varied from 7.3 per prisoner per year for prisoners age 17–24 to 14.3 days per prisoner per year for prisoners age 45 and over.

Perusal of these statistics indicates that the medical needs of prisoners are both varied and extensive, and their medical services needs must therefore be judged to be substantial. It is clear that relatively few correctional institutions have sufficient staffing capability to meet these medical needs.[11,33] For this reason, the custodial model for health services delivery (in which all services are delivered by medical personnel under the control of correctional officials) is being replaced by two other models of medical services delivery in correctional institutions. These are the health agency model, in which state, local, or federal health agencies control the provision of medical services in prisons; and the contractual model, in which health services are provided by community agencies under contract with correctional systems.[80] The first step in meeting the medical services programming needs of prisoners is to do a comprehensive survey of those needs in order to estimate the proper mix of medical services needed in each institution. It is then possible to decide which model of medical service delivery, or perhaps what combination of models, would be appropriate and to implement a comprehensive health services delivery system. Although the details of health services will differ from institution to institution, it is appropriate to expect that the range and quality of health services available to prisoners should be comparable to health services available in the larger community.

The Aged

The aged, by which we mean offenders aged 60 and over, are greatly underrepresented in prison populations. Using this definition, one percent of the prisoners in Sweden,[103] Canada,[100] and India,[47] and less than one percent of the prisoners in Denmark[66] are aged. The American survey of prisoners in state correctional facilities carried out by the Law Enforcement Assistance Administration did not present data by age in such a way as to identify the aged. The highest category in their data is age 50 and over. The survey showed that 16 percent of the prisoners were age 50 and over at the time of the survey, and 11 percent were age 50 and over at the time of admission. The difference in these two statistics is accounted for by prisoners who pass age 50 while institutionalized. Reports from individual states show that only a very small number of prisoners are age 60 and over.[55] A recent report from Florida,[29] a state with a large number of elderly residents, identified 211 prisoners over the age of 60, most of whom were between 61 and 65. Fifty-three percent of these aged prisoners were incarcerated for murder or manslaughter, 7 percent for sexual battery, and 7 percent for lewd and lascivious behavior. Although the common stereotype of aged prisoners is that they committed violent crimes in their youth and have been incarcerated ever since, the majority of prisoners over age 60 in a New York study were not sentenced until they had passed age 60, and only 10 percent of them had served more than 25 years in prison.[55]

Joseph Ham[41] studied a sample of aged male prisoners, finding that their coping strategies were rather different from those employed by younger prisoners. They attempted to conform totally to institutional rules, and subordinated themselves to correctional officers and other prison staff members. This allowed them to be closer to the staff, and was combined with greater social and physical distance from younger prisoners. The aged prisoners felt that they could gain significant rewards by aligning themselves with the staff, whose protection they needed to guarantee them security and personal safety from victimization by younger prisoners. Some of the older prisoners, who were alcoholics, related so well to prison officers that they were able to convince some of them to smuggle alcohol into the prison for their use. Their withdrawal from younger prisoners meant that they did not make use of most of the recreational facilities available in the prison.

This coping strategy can be interpreted as institutional dependence, which is the focus of a doctoral dissertation by Ronald Aday.[2,3] In this sample, the younger an offender entered the prison, the greater his or her institutional dependency. Those prisoners who had been confined for a long period of time appeared to be somewhat more disoriented toward the outside world, and some of them admitted being afraid of the possibility of returning to the larger society. Respondents in Ham's[41] sample expressed a feeling of loss of strength, vigor, and overall health, which they associated with lack of proper medical care, the effects of long-term imprisonment, and the general effects of the aging process. In contrast, there is a possibility that the protected environment of the total institution preserves some prisoners from the full impact of the aging process. Monika Reed and Francis Glamser conclude that:

Much of what is viewed as part of normal aging does not take place in a prison setting. Many of the losses associated with normal aging take place in young adulthood among prisoners. Retirement and widowhood are not meaningful. Chronological age does not possess much salience for prisoners. Even some of the cosmetic effects of environmental stress appear to mitigated.[87:359]

Reed and Glamser believe that aged prisoners are in much better condition to resist the negative effects of total institutionalization than residents in nursing homes because they are in relatively better health. Some of the negative effects observed in nursing homes may be more due to the vulnerability of aged patients than to institutional procedures and conditions.

Programming designed for aged prisoners must take their special characteristics into account, including degenerative diseases, greater illiteracy, high vulnerability to victimization by other prisoners, and the need for comprehensive and regular monitoring of their medical condition. Aged prisoners may experience greater difficulties in being reintegrated into society than younger prisoners, and correctional administrators need to consider this possibility in structuring reentry services. For those aged prisoners who are also long-term prisoners, the observations in the following section apply.

Long-Term Prisoners

It is difficult to generalize about the length of time served based on length of sentence at admission. Prisoners receiving a 10-year sentence in one state may serve more actual years behind bars than prisoners receiving a 20-year sentence in another state because of differences in parole board procedures, sentencing laws, and so forth. One certainty is that anyone receiving a sentence of life or 98 years and above will be a long-term prisoner. Approximately 12 percent of state prisoners in America fall into this category.[62] There is a great deal of variation between the states as to the average length of sentence served, and there is also much variation between the United States and other nations on this dimension. Only 0.2 percent of Japanese prisoners,[50] 0.9 percent of Indian prisoners,[47] and 9.2 percent of Canadian prisoners are sentenced to life imprisonment.[100]

Empirical studies indicate that there is no intrinsic intellectual deterioration associated with long-term imprisonment. In fact, verbal skills may increase over the years,[7] perhaps as a result of the coping strategies used by prisoners. The balance of the evidence appears to confirm that hostility increases with length of time served,[19,45] although at least one study suggests just the reverse.[7] Long-term prisoners tend to become increasingly introverted over a period of years,[6,95] and they also suffer from flatness of affect, a reduction of motivation, decreased future time-perspective, and increased apathy.[95]

Some studies show a decline in self-evaluation and others show an improvement in self-evaluation associated with an increase in years incarcerated.[27] Perhaps the most negative view of the effects of long-term imprisonment is presented by Willibald Sluga,[97] whose study of long-term prisoners in Austria found that a functional psycho-syndrome often appeared after four to six years of imprisonment. The severity of this syndrome was directly related to the degree of isolation of the prisoner. Sluga believes that the progressive development of regressive behavior, insecurity, obsessional thoughts, and emotional problems making up the functional psycho-syndrome "militate against successful rehabilitation."[97:38] Conversely, Franco Ferracuti and his associates[25] found much less evidence that mental deterioration was likely to be the consequence of long-term imprisonment. Older prisoners and those having fewer "interior resources for confronting the uniform, nonstimulating, and coercive environment of the modern prison"[25:84] were more likely to show signs of mental deterioration than other prisoners.

We have already mentioned the increased verbal skills demonstrated in one study of long-term prisoners. There is other evidence of the successful coping strategies employed by these prisoners. For example, they tend to become increasingly amicable toward prison officers over time.[86,95] Like the aged prisoners discussed above, they appear to be adapting to the prison environment by becoming as close as possible to those in authority. Although they may suffer increased levels of medical illness, they may experience decreased mental illness (as clinically defined) once they adapt successfully to prison life.[44] One of the coping strategies of long-term prisoners is to avoid conflict, not only with fellow-prisoners but also with institutional representatives, so long-termers tend to have a lower rate of disciplinary infractions than other prisoners.[26] However, the participation of long-termers in the Ohio Prisoners' Labor Union shows that they are willing to confront administrators on matters of great importance to them.[46] Since they know that they will be institutionalized for a long period of time, they tend to make decisions about their lives in the institution more carefully than short-term prisoners, and they therefore are a stabilizing factor in institutional affairs. They balance a low level of participation in formal programming with a high level of involvement in self-development activities such as reading, crafts, art, and law studies.[27]

The programming needs associated with long-term prisoners in the United States are usually conceptualized as being internal to the institution. In Europe, it is generally believed that the only way to meet the programming needs of long-term prisoners is by granting them periods of leave from prison as an integral part of their treatment programming.[18] Many European countries have liberal leave policies, such as weekend leaves and supervised leaves.[34] If prisoners are too dangerous to be allowed out on leave, there is always the possibility of conjugal visits,[34] increasing the participation of the prisoners in prison decisions,[18,34] using open prisons which have a high level of interchange between the community and the prisoners,[34] and encouraging work–release and conditional release from confinement.[18] In addition to these specific suggestions for the programming needs of long-term prisoners, it is also true that a different emphasis is applicable to long-termers than to short-termers. All human beings have needs for adequate sensory and cognitive stimulation, a feeling of control over their fate, and meaning in their lives. These considerations are important in programming for prisoners of all sentence lengths, but they are absolutely essential for programming aimed at long-term prisoners.[69]

SUMMARY

It is important to understand the characteristics of correctional clients in order to meet their needs more fully. It must always be remembered that their characteristics are not necessarily the characteristics of criminals in general, for the filtering processes of the criminal justice system introduce many biases into predominantly drawn from the lower classes. They therefore have low status occupations, or none at all; low educational achievement; and low incomes. They tend to be young and are often unmarried. Although it has been demonstrated that personality classifications have some utility for determining appropriate correctional treatment, there is no evidence that there is anything like a "criminal personality." Women, juveniles, racial and cultural minorities, military veterans, the mentally ill, mentally retarded prisoners, those who are medically ill, and the aged all have specialized needs for correctional programming that must be taken into account in developing individualized treatment plans. In addition, certain forms of correctional treatment have the potential to generate needs among correctional clients. Foremost among these is long-term imprisonment, which requires a number of specialized programs designed to maintain adequate physical and mental health, as well as continued involvement with family members and the free community.

REFERENCES

1. Adams, Susan G. *The Female Offender: A Statistical Perspective.* Ottawa: Ministry of the Solicitor General, 1978.
2. Aday, Ronald H. *Institutional Dependency: A Theory of Aging in Prison.* Ph.D. dissertation, Oklahoma State University, 1976.
3. Aday, Ronald H. and Edgar L. Webster. "Aging in Prison: The Development of a Preliminary Model." *Offender Rehabilitation* 3 (1979):271–282.
4. American Medical Association. *Standards for Health Services in Jails.* Chicago, 1979.
5. Arkansas. State Board of Corrections. "Inmate Characteristics, 8–24–79." Montgomery, AR, 1979.
6. Banister, P.A., F.V. Smith, K.J. Heskin, and N. Bolton. "Psychological Correlates of Long-term Imprisonment. I. Cognitive Variables." *British Journal of Criminology* 13(1973):312–323.
7. Bolton, N., F.V. Smith, K.J. Heskin, and P.A. Banister. "Psychological Correlates of Long-term Imprisonment. IV. A Longitudinal Analysis." *British Journal of Criminology* 16(1976):38–47.
8. Botterell, E.H. *Enquiry into the Health Care System in the Ministry of Correctional Services.* Report to the Minister, Toronto, 1972.
9. Boudouris, James. *Mental Health and Correctional Institutions: Issues and Paradoxes.* Des Moines: Iowa Department of Social Services, 1979.
10. Bowker, Lee H. *Women, Crime and the Criminal Justice System.* Lexington, MA: D.C. Heath, 1978.
11. Brecher, Edward M. and Richard D. Della Penna. *Health Care in Correctional Institutions.* Washington, D.C.: Government Printing Office, 1975.
12. Brown, Bertram S. and Thomas F. Courtless. *The Mentally Retarded Offender.* Washington, D.C.: Government Printing Office, 1971.
13. Chesney-Lind, Meda. "Young Women in the Arms of the Law." In Lee H. Bowker: *Women, Crime and the Criminal Justice System.* Lexington, MA: D.C. Heath, 1978, pp. 171–196.

14. Cochrane, Raymond. "The Structure of Value Systems in Male and Female Prisoners." *British Journal of Criminology* 11(1971):73–79.
15. Cocozza, Joseph J., Mary E. Melick, and Henry J. Steadman. "Trends in Violent Crime Among Ex-Mental Patients." *Criminology* 16(1978):317–334.
16. Coleman, James C. *Abnormal Psychology and Modern Life,* 4th ed., Glenview, IL: Scott, Foresman, 1972.
17. Connor, Walter D. *Deviance in Soviet Society.* New York: Columbia University Press, 1972.
18. Council of Europe. European Committee on Crime Problems. *Treatment of Long-term Prisoners.* Strasbourg, France, 1977.
19. Crawford, D.A. "The HDHQ Results of Long-term Prisoners: Relationships with Criminals and Institutional Behavior." *British Journal of Social and Clinical Psychology* 16(1977):391–394.
20. Cripe, Clair. "Religious Freedom in Prisons." *Federal Probation* 41(March, 1977):31–35.
21. Doleschal, Eugene and Anne Newton. "International Rates of Imprisonment." Hackensack, NJ: National Council on Crime and Delinquency, no date.
22. Dunbaugh, Frank M. "Racially Disproportionate Rates of Incarceration in the United States." *Prison Law Monitor* 1(March, 1979):205, 219–222.
23. Echo-Hawk, Walter. "Native Prisoners, Tribal Religion, and the First Amendment." *Prison Law Monitor* 1(March, 1979):205, 219.
24. Ferdinand, Theodore N. "Female Delinquency and Warren's Typology of Personality Patterns: An Evaluation." *Social Work Research and Abstracts* 14(1978):32–41.
25. Ferracuti, Franco, Simon Dinitz, and Aldo Piperno. *Mental Deterioration in Prison.* Columbus, OH: Program for the Study of Crime and Delinquency, Ohio State University, 1978.
26. Flanagan, Timothy J. "The Nature and Distribution of Disciplinary Infractions Among Long-term and Short-term Prisoners." Paper given at the annual meeting of the American Society of Criminology, 1978.
27. Flanagan, Timothy J. "Dealing with Long-term Confinement: Adaptive Strategies and Perspectives Among Long-term Prisoners." Paper presented at the annual meeting of the American Society of Criminology, 1979.
28. Florida. Department of Corrections. *Annual Report, 1977–1978.* Tallahassee, FL, 1978.
29. Florida. Department of Corrections. "Statistical Facts." Tallahassee, FL, March 16, 1979.
30. French, Laurence. "Corrections and the Native American Client." *The Prison Journal* 59(Spring-Summer, 1979):49–60.
31. Furlow, Frances R. *Military Veterans in Georgia Prisons.* Atlanta: Committee on Correctional Facilities and Services, State Bar of Georgia, 1977.
32. Gendreau, Paul, Patrick Madden, and Mary Leipgiger. "Norms and Recidivism for First Incarcerates: Implications for Programming." *Canadian Journal of Criminology* 21(1979):1–26.
33. General Accounting Office. *A Federal Strategy is Needed to Help Improve Medical and Dental Care in Prisons and Jails.* Washington, D.C., 1978.
34. General Accounting Office. *Observations on Correctional Program and the Policies in Selected European Countries.* Washington, D.C., 1978.
35. Gibbs, Carole. "The Effect of the Imprisonment of Women Upon Their Children." *British Journal of Criminology* 11(1971):113–130.

36. Glick, Ruth M. and Virginia V. Neto. *National Study of Women's Correctional Programs*. Washington, D.C.: Government Printing Office, 1977.

37. Goldsmith, S.D. "The Status of Prison Health Care." *Public Health Reports* 89(1974):569–575.

38. Great Britain. Home Office. *Prison Statistics, England and Wales, 1977*. London: Her Majesty's Stationery Office, 1978.

39. Gunn, John. *Epileptics in Prison*. New York: Academic Press, 1977.

40. Halleck, Seymour L. *Psychiatry and the Dilemmas of Crime*. New York: Harper and Row, 1967.

41. Ham, Joseph N. *The Forgotten Minority—an Exploration of Long-term Institutionalized Aged and Aging Male Prison Inmates*. Ph.D. dissertation, University of Michigan, 1976.

42. Handler, Ellen. "Are Prison Inmates Really 'Naked Nomads'?" *American Journal of Correction* 39(November–December, 1977):16–18,31.

43. Harper, Dean and David Barry. "Estimated Prevalence of Psychiatric Disorder in a Prison Population." *Abstracts on Criminology and Penology* 19(1979):237–242.

44. Heather, N. "Personal Illness Among Lifers and the Effects of Long-term Intermediate Sentences." *British Journal of Criminology* 17(1977):378–386.

45. Heskin, K.J. "Psychological Correlates of Long-term Imprisonment. III. Attitudinal Variables." *British Journal of Criminology* 14(1974):150–157.

46. Huff, C. Ronald. *Unionization Behind the Walls: An Analytic Study of the Ohio Prisoners' Labor Union Movement*. Ph.D. dissertation, Ohio State University, 1974.

47. India. Central Bureau of Correctional Services. *Social Defense: A Statistical Handbook*. New Delhi, 1974.

48. Irvine, M.J. *The Native Inmate in Ontario: A Preliminary Study*. Ottawa: Ministry of Correctional Services, 1978.

49. Jacobs, James B. and Lawrence J. Kraft. "Integrating the Keepers: A Comparison of Black and White Prison Guards in Illinois." *Social Problems* 25(1978):304–318.

50. Japan. Ministry of Justice. Correction Bureau. *Correctional Institutions in Japan*. Tokyo, 1973.

51. Japan. Correction Bureau. Ministry of Justice. *Juvenile Institutions*. Tokyo, 1978.

52. Japan. Ministry of Justice. Research and Training Institute. *Summary of the White Paper on Crime, 1978*. Tokyo, 1979.

53. Jones, David A. *The Health Risks of Imprisonment*. Lexington, MA: D.C. Heath, 1976.

54. Joutsen, Matti. *Young Offenders in the Criminal Justice System in Finland*. Helsinki: Research Institute of Legal Policy, 1976.

55. Krajick, Kevin. "Growing Old in Prison." *Corrections Magazine* 5(March, 1979):32–46.

56. Landoffi, Joseph and Daniel P. LeClair. "A Profile of Vietnam Era Veterans Incarcerated in Massachusetts Correctional Institutions." Boston: Massachusetts Department of Correction, 1976.

57. Law Enforcement Assistance Administration. *Prisoners in State and Federal Institutions on December 31, 1971, 1972, and 1973*. Washington, D.C.: Government Printing Office, 1975.

58. Law Enforcement Assistance Administration. *Prisoners in State and Federal Institutions on December 31, 1975*. Washington, D.C.: Government Printing Office, 1977.

59. Law Enforcement Assistance Administration. "Children in Custody: Advance

Report on the 1977 Census of Private Juvenile Facilities." Washington, D.C.: Government Printing Office, 1979.

60. Law Enforcement Assistance Administration. "Children in Custody: Advance Report on the 1977 Census of Public Juvenile Facilities." Washington, D.C.: Government Printing Office, 1979.

61. Law Enforcement Assistance Administration. "Prisoners in State and Federal Institutions on December 31, 1978." Washington, D.C.: Government Printing Office, 1979.

62. Law Enforcement Assistance Administration, *Profile of State Prison Inmates: Sociodemographic Findings from the 1974 Survey of Inmates of State Correctional Facilities.* Washington, D.C.: Government Printing Office, 1979.

63. Lawrence, L.A., *et al.* "Survey of Correctional Institutions." *Quarterly Journal of Corrections* 1(Summer, 1977):35–51.

64. Levy, Sol, R.H. Southcombe, John R. Cranor, and R.A. Freeman, "The Outstanding Personality Factors Among the Population of a State Penitentiary: A Preliminary Report." *Journal of Clinical and Experimental Psychopathology* 13(1952):117–130.

65. Lillyquist, Michael J. *Understanding and Changing Criminal Behavior.* Englewood Cliffs, NJ: Prentice-Hall, 1980.

66. Lønberg, Arne. *The Penal System of Denmark.* Copenhagen: Ministry of Justice, 1975.

67. Massachusetts. Department of Correction. "A Description of the Residents of Massachusetts Correctional Institutions on January 1, 1974 with Indications of Drug Problems." Boston, 1974.

68. May, Edgar. "Inmate Veterans: Hidden Casualities of a Lost War." *Corrections Magazine* 5(March, 1979):3–13.

69. McKay, H. Bryan, C.H.S. Jayewardene, and Penny B. Reedie. *The Effects of Long-term Incarceration.* Ottawa: Ministry of the Solicitor General, 1979.

70. "Medicine Behind Bars: Hostility, Horror and the Hippocratic Oath," *Medical World News* 26(June 11, 1971):27–35.

71. Megargee, E.I. "Undercontrolled and Overcontrolled Personality Types in Extreme Anti-social Aggression." *Psychological Monographs* 80(1966):entire issue.

72. Megargee, E.I., P.E. Cook, and G.A. Mendelsohn. "Development and Validation of an MMPI Scale of Assaultiveness in Overcontrolled Individuals." *Journal of Abnormal Psychology* 72(1967):519–528.

73. Morén, Stefan, Lars Bagge, and Norman Bishop. *Marknadsanpassad Ersättning ÅT Intagna Vid Skogome Kriminalvårdsanstalt—En Uppföljningsstudie.* Norrköping, Sweden: National Prison and Probation Administration, 1978.

74. Nagel, Jack H. "Crime and Incarceration: A Reanalysis." Fels Discussion Paper No. 112, School of Public and Urban Policy, University of Pennsylvania, 1977.

75. New York. Department of Correctional Services. "Characteristics of New Commitments—1978." Albany, 1979.

76. New Zealand. Department of Justice. *Penal Census, 1972.* Wellington, 1975.

77. New Zealand. Department of Justice. *Study of Young Persons Remanded in Custody to a Penal Institution.* Wellington, 1979.

78. New Zealand. Department of Statistics. "Justice Statistics 1977, No. 2, Prisons and Prisoners and Supreme Court (Criminal)." Wellington, 1978.

79. New Zealand. Department of Statistics. "Justice Statistics 1978, Prisons and Prisoners." Wellington, 1979.

80. Novick, Lloyd F. and Mohamed S. Al-Ibrahim. *Health Problems in the Prison Setting: A Clinical and Administrative Approach.* Springfield, IL: Charles C Thomas, 1977.

81. Oakey, Mary H. "Concept Paper. Contracting Out for Medical Services." Washington, D.C.: Department of Corrections, 1979.

82. Oklahoma. Department of Corrections. *Annual Report—Fiscal Year 1978.* Oklahoma City, 1978.

83. Panton, James H. "Personality Differences Between Male and Female Prison Inmates Measured by the MMPI." *Criminal Justice and Behavior* 1(1974):332–339.

84. Petrich, John. "Rate of Psychiatric Morbidity in a Metropolitan Jail Population." *American Journal of Psychiatry* 133(1976):1439–1444.

85. Pope, Patrick J. "Children in Prisons and Remand Centres," *The Howard Journal of Penology and Crime Prevention* 16(1978):134–143.

86. Rasch, W. "Observations in Physio-psychological Changes in Persons Sentenced to Life Imprisonment." In S. Rizkalla, R. Levy and R. Zauberman: *Long-term Imprisonment: An International Seminar.* Montréal: Université de Montréal, 1977.

87. Reed, Monika B. and Francis D. Glamser. "Aging in a Total Institution: The Case of Older Prisoners." *The Gerontologist* 19(1979):354–360.

88. Robitscher, Jonas. "The Retarded Offender." *The Prison Journal* 49(Spring–Summer, 1969):13–23.

89. Rockoff, Edward. *The Retarded Offender in Iowa Correctional Institutions.* Ph.D. dissertation, University of Iowa, 1973.

90. Roffman, Roger A. and Charles Froland, "Drug and Alcohol Dependencies in Prisons." *Crime and Delinquency* 22(1976):359–366.

91. Rogers, Sally and Catherine Carey. *Child-Care Needs of Female Offenders: A Comparison of Incarcerates and Probationers.* Toronto: Ministry of Correctional Services, 1979.

92. Roth, Loren H. and Frank R. Irvine, "Psychiatric Care of Federal Prisoners," *American Journal of Psychiatry* 128(1971):56–62.

93. Sack, William H., Jack Seidler, and Susan Thomas. "The Children of Imprisoned Parents: A Psychosocial Exploration." *American Journal of Orthopsychiatry* 46(1976):618–628.

94. Santamour, Miles and Bernadette West. *The Mentally Retarded Offender and Corrections.* Washington, D.C.: Government Printing Office, 1977.

95. Sapsford, R.J. "Life-sentence Prisoners: Psychological Changes During Sentence." *British Journal of Criminology* 18(April,1978):128–145.

96. Schneller, Donald P. "Prisoners' Families: A Study of Some Social and Psychological Effects of Incarceration on the Families of Negro Prisoners." *Criminology* 12(1975):402–412.

97. Sluga, Willibald. "Treatment of Long-term Prisoners Considered from the Medical and Psychiatric Points of View." In Council of Europe. European Committee on Crime Problems: *Treatment of Long-term Prisoners.* Strasbourg, France, 1977, pp. 35–42.

98. South Africa. *Report of the Commissioner of Prisons of the Republic of South Africa for the Period of 1 July 1978 to 30 June 1979.* Pretoria, 1980.

99. Srivastava, S.P. *The Indian Prison Community.* Lucknow: Pustak Kendra, 1977.

100. Statistics Canada. *Correctional Institutions Statistics 1977.* Ottawa, 1979.

101. Struckhoff, David. "Toward a Model of Involuntary Separation of Families." *Offender Rehabilitation* 3(1979):289–297.
102. Sutker, Patricia B. and Charles E. Moan. "A Psychosocial Description of Penitentiary Inmates." *Archives of General Psychiatry* 29(1973):663–667.
103. Sweden. *The Prison and Probation System 1978.* Norrköping: Official Statistics of Sweden, 1979.
104. Switzerland. Federal Division of Justice. "Informationen der Eidgenoessischen Justizabteilung an die Organe des Straf- und Massnahmenvollzuges." Bern, 1977.
105. Texas. Department of Corrections. *1976 Annual Statistical Report.* Huntsville, 1977.
106. Vinter, Robert D. and Rosemary C. Sarri. *Time Out: A National Study of Juvenile Correctional Programs.* Ann Arbor, MI: University of Michigan, 1976.
107. Virginia. Department of Corrections. *Annual Statisical Report of Felons and Misdemeanants Committed to the Virginia State Penal System During the Year Ended June 30, 1976 and Felons Confined in the Penal System on June 30, 1976 Including Felony Recidivists Committed and Confined.* Richmond, 1976.
108. Waller, Irvin and Janet Chan. "Prison Youth: A Canadian and International Comparison." *Criminal Law Quarterly* 17(1974):47–71.
109. Warren, Marguerite Q. "The Center for Training in Different Treatment," *California Youth Authority Quarterly* 20(Fall, 1969):7–13.
110. Wexler, David B. *Criminal Commitments and Dangerous Mental Patients: Legal Issues of Confinement, Treatment and Release.* Washington, D.C.: Government Printing Office, 1976.
111. Whalen, R.P. and J.J.A. Lyons, "Medical Problems of 500 Prisoners on Admission to a County Jail." *Public Health Reports* 72(1972):497–502.
112. Wilson, Rob. "Juvenile Inmates: The Long-term Trend is Down." *Corrections Magazine* 4(September, 1978):3–11.
113. Wilson, Rob. "Who Will Care for the 'Mad and Bad'?" *Corrections Magazine* 6(February, 1980):5–17.
114. Wisconsin. Division of Corrections. *Drug Abuse Survey.* Madison, 1976.

Chapter 7

Prisoners in Total Institutions

The total institution is "a place of residence and work where a large number of like-situated individuals, cut off from the wider society for an appreciable period of time, together lead an enclosed, formally administered round of life."[23:xii] Prisons, mental hospitals, monasteries, concentration camps, homes for the aged, military boot camps, and long-term-care medical facilities are among the social organizations that fit the definition of a total institution. The concept of the total institution was first elaborated by Erving Goffman,[23] and it is his definition with which we have begun this chapter. Seeing prisons as total institutions alerts us to the similarities between them and other totalistic organizations, and it also directs our attention to the uniquely sociological dimensions of correctional institutions. In the previous chapter, we examined prisoners as individuals. Now we will discuss them as members of prisoner societies, the social organizations that develop among prisoners in correctional institutions. We will begin by explaining the major elements in prisoner societies, such as the convict code, prisoner groups, status within the prison, and the sub rosa prisoner economy. We will then return to total institutions theory to view prisoner societies in a broader light. The chapter concludes with a discussion of prisoner self-help groups and prisoner self-government.

PRISONS AS TOTAL INSTITUTIONS

Erving Goffman[23] describes total institutions as places in which all activities are controlled by the same authority. Inmates of total institutions do everything in concert with their fellow inmates under a schedule imposed by the authority. All of the activities in the institution are rationally and bureaucratically organized to serve the institution's goals and are carried out within a restricted space. The entrance of inmates into the institution is marked by a degradation ceremony which, in the case of the prison, includes fingerprinting, taking "mug shots," exchanging street clothes for institutional clothing, having an intake interview, and giving up most of one's personal possessions to be locked away until release. This is only one of many mortifications to which inmates of total institutions are subjected.

Another mortification is the circulation of embarrassing information about inmates among staff members. These staff members may bring such information up at any time in order to embarrass the inmate in front of other inmates. The inability of individual inmates to protect themselves from undesirable material items, environmental conditions, and other inmates leads to feelings of contamination. When an inmate reacts negatively to some of these mortifications, the reaction becomes the basis for additional mortifications in a retaliatory process that Goffman identifies as "looping."

From Goffman's analysis, we learn that prisoners are not only socialized into the prisoner subculture: they also are socialized into the official life of the prison by being indoctrinated in prison regulations and the many tacit understandings that are enforced by correctional officers and other staff members.

Some prisoners react to this socialization pressure by rebeling. Others withdraw into themselves, convert to the staff's view of life, or colonize the institution. In colonization, inmates make themselves so much at home in the institution that it becomes their only true home, and they often do not want to leave when their release date comes. The various mortifications that occur in total institutions are interpreted by inmates as signs of their stigmatization; indications that they are less valuable than other human beings. In order to counteract this negative threat to their self-images, many of them tell "sad tales." They claim they are innocent of their crimes, really mentally healthy and just sent to a mental institution by accident, and so forth.

Staff members in total institutions are separated from inmates by a caste line that is almost never crossed. There is a tendency for reciprocal negative stereotypes to develop between staff and inmates, and for staff to withdraw and create considerable social distance between their charges and themselves. A counteracting force is that staff members feel the need to normalize their interaction with some of the more desirable inmates, and that tends to draw them together despite the caste line. The structure of total institutions is such that close relations between staff and inmates are difficult to maintain over a long period of time. As staff develop close relations with inmates, they become sympathetic to the needs of the inmates and tend to give them special privileges. The inmates then take advantage of these privileges and embarrass the staff members, which is known as being "burnt." Staff members then withdraw into the safety of the caste system until their normal human tendencies toward close human relations drive them to reach out across the cast barrier again, at which point the cycle begins anew.

Goffman has created an ideal type in his model of the total institution. No real-world institution perfectly matches all of the characteristics of the total institution, and some institutions are closer than the ideal type than others. Goffman himself recognizes that total institutions differ along the dimensions of (1) recruitment, (2) role differentiation, and (3) permeability. Recruitment may be either volunteer or forced; role differentiation refers to the degree of development of the inmates' subculture; and permeability is the degree to which the external world is allowed into the institution. The more fully developed an inmate subculture, the more elaborate subcultural roles become, and the more they are clearly defined as differing from each other. Permeability is not just physical—such as when outsiders come to visit a total institution—but also includes the receipt of printed materials, having access to television and radio, phone calls, and having mail privileges to write and receive letters to friends and relatives.

One implication of total institutions theory is that most of the negative activities occurring in total institutions are seen as being due to the structure of these institutions rather than to the nefarious character of staff or administrators. This insight was experimentally tested by Philip Zimbardo[84,85] and his colleagues at Stanford University. They took a group of normal, emotionally stable college students without criminal records and randomly assigned them to play prisoners or guards in a simulated prison in the basement of a Stanford psychology building. All participants were paid $15 a day for their participation in the project. Three of the prisoners had such acute traumatic reactions to the imprisonment experiment that they had to be released within the first four days. Most of the others were willing to forego all of the money that they had already earned in return for being released from the project. A total institution had grown up so rapidly in the Stanford basement that psychologically normal human beings were transformed in a matter of days into people who acted like long-term prisoners and career correctional officers.

We were horrified because we saw some of the boys (guards) treat others as if they were despicable animals, taking pleasure in cruelty, while other boys (prisoners) became servile, dehumanized robots who thought only of escape, of their own individual survival and of their mounting hatred for the guards.[84:4]

The prisoners initially developed a high degree of social solidarity and resisted the guards actively, but the guards were able to break down the solidarity so that the situation developed into "each man for himself." Approximately one-third of the guards became tyrannical and abused power extensively. They went to great lengths to break the spirit of the prisoners and to convince them that they were utterly worthless. Although the other guards were formally correct in their behavior, none of them ever interfered with the mistreatment of prisoners carried out by the tyrannical guards. In short, both prisoners and guards developed shared norms of behavior very quickly and then were bound by those norms so that they did not feel free to behave as they would have done a few days earlier in the outside world.

The experiment was scheduled to run for two weeks, but Zimbardo had to call it off at the end of six days. The risk of psychological damage was too great. Zimbardo was horrified at what he had created, and felt that it had gotten out of control. "In less than a week the experience of imprisonment undid (temporarily) a lifetime of learning; human values were suspended, self-concepts were challenged and the ugliest, most base pathological side of human nature surfaced."[84:4] Although prisons often claim to be people-changing organizations, they are really people-processing organizations[63] in which change in the prisoners is more of a by-product of the activities of processing rather than anything else. The work of Goffman and Zimbardo, as well as a sizable body of research on prisonization, suggests that these effects are more negative than positive.

Similarities between Prisons and
Other Total Institutions

There is some research evidence indicating that the concept of the total institution has universal application. For example, a comparison of 20 strikes and 20 mutinies showed that the forms, determinants, and outcomes of these conflicts were independent of the institutional setting in which they occurred.[38] In a review of studies of six different types of institutions, Peter Mortimore[48] concluded that differences in the aims, climate, and structure of an institution impacted the inmates of the institution regardless of the type of institution. To put it another way, this means that mental hospitals and homes for the aged seem to work in the same way that prisons do. The following statements were taken from studies of different total institutions. As you read them, try to guess which ones are from prisons.

When [inmates] talk about their day, it is evident that they consider any one day to be much the same as any other. All emphasize, and some are slightly amazed at, how day-to-day life is at the [institution]. This uniformity includes the weekends. As they emphasize over and over again, "no matter when you're talking, each day is the same old routine."[25:162]

A tiny minority held that all trading was undesirable as it engendered an unsavory atmosphere; occasional frauds and sharp practices were cited as proof. Certain forms of trading were more generally condemned; trade with the "staff" was criticized by many...but while certain activities were condemned as antisocial, trade itself was practiced, and its utility appreciated, by almost everyone in the [institution].[54:199]

There was the quite forbidden act of buying or selling liquor, which had been smuggled onto the grounds. [Inmates] claimed that liquor could regularly be had for a price, and while I drank a few times on the grounds, with [staff] and [inmates] I have no personal knowledge of the market and its commodity....A few [inmates] were well known among fellow inmates and staff for lending money to [inmates] and [staff] at relatively high interest, reputed to be twenty-five percent for a short period....[23:267]

To be sure, many of the [staff] would watch their [inmates] for hours waiting to catch them at any small infraction—talking through the windows or heating pipes—and have them condemned to a dark cell or have them deprived of their soup; these [staff] were even in the majority.[74:181]

The most important condition of success in the life struggle of the "inmates" is their *secretiveness*. The character and their intentions are so profoundly hidden that to the experienced novice [staff member] it seems at the onset as if the [inmates] bend like a blade of grass—beneath the wind and the boot. (Only subsequently does he become bitterly convinced of the cunning and insincerity of the [inmates].) Secretiveness is almost the most characteristic trait of the [inmates].[69:517]

The first of the five quotes is from a home for the aged. The second is from a prisoner-of-war camp, and the third is from a mental hospital. The fourth was taken from an account of a concentration camp for women operated by the Nazis during World War II, and the fifth from Aleksander Solzhenitsyn's analysis of the Russian forced labor camps. None of these institutions are prisons as we know them, and yet all of them share many common prison characteristics. These are the common characteristics that Goffman summarized when he created the model of the total institution.

PRISONER SOCIETIES

Whenever human beings are thrown together in a common situation and are simultaneously cut off from extensive communication with the outside world, they begin to develop exceptional ways of relating to each other, common understandings of the rules for behavior, shared definitions of the situation, agreement on the value of certain activities, and many other commonalities. The longer a group is together, and the more it is isolated from outside influences, the stronger and more exceptional its social organization and culture become. This natural process explains why each family has its own special culture, although the uniqueness of individual families is limited by the high degree of interchange that the family members have with the outside world. In the traditional maximum security prison, the isolation of prisoners from external influences is almost complete. Their sentences (at least in nations such as the United States, the Soviet Union, and South Africa) are long, and they face many similar problems of survival and adaptation. It is therefore natural that they would develop prisoner societies.

Theories of Prisoner Societies

Elements of prisoner societies were identified early in the 20th century and were systematically discussed by Donald Clemmer[13] in his classic book *The Prison Community,* written in 1940. However, the first explanatory theory about prisoner societies did not appear until 1958, when Gresham M. Sykes[71] published *The Society of Captives.* His theory, which is referred to as the deprivation theory or the indigenous origin theory of prisoner societies, is that prisoner societies arise as an adaptive social response to the deprivations experienced in imprisonment. These deprivations include the loss of liberty, reduced access to goods and services, lack of heterosexual relationships, loss of autonomy, and seriously diminished security from criminal victimization. Factors such as overcrowding, the isolation of the prison, and the "pressure cooker" atmosphere of the prison life may all be included in the indigenous origin theory of prisoner societies. This theory predicts that the more cohesive the prisoner society, the greater its ability to minimize the discomforts of imprisonment for its members. Although it differs in cultural content from the larger society, it functions to provide many of the same comforts and illusions that we enjoy in the outside world.

The indigenous origin theory of prisoner societies was challenged in 1962 when John Irwin and Donald Cressey[32] published their opposing theory: the importation model. Irwin and Cressey argue that there are really three types of prisoners. The thief subculture refers to norms followed by professional criminals who are loyal to their friends, who share with other thieves, and who avoid seeking leadership positions within the prison. Prisoners following convict subculture norms seek maximum power and status within the prison by manipulating other prisoners and correctional officers for their own gain. The authors point out that the convict code is only a concentrated version of a more general antisocial code that is found in the larger society and that is imported into the prison with the offenders. The manipulative utilitarian "hard core" lower-class criminal element on the streets becomes concentrated and intensified when large numbers of serious criminals are housed together. The third subculture is the conventional subculture. "Square Johns" who have not previously been criminalized practice the legitimate culture of the larger society as much as they can within the limitations imposed by prison regulations.

No other major theory of prison societies has ever been developed. Instead, the two competing theories have been tested in dozens of research studies since the mid-1960s. A survey of these studies shows that—although there are some exceptions—the greater the objective and subjective deprivations in an institution, the more adequate the indigenous origin theory is in explaining the development and maintenance of prisoner societies. This is true from the earliest to the most recent studies, and regardless of the methodology used in the studies. The importation theory assumes greater importance in institutions that are comparatively less depriving, and therefore less totalistic.[8] Even in the most extreme institutions, both theories must be used in order to gain a full understanding of prisoner subcultures.

Basic Elements in Prisoner Societies

Since a prisoner society has the same structure and functions as any other society, its description requires a short course in sociology. The major elements in a society are norms, roles, groups, and the status system in which the roles and groups are hierarchically arranged. Norms are standards for behavior. Some of them are general and apply to all the members of a group; others are specific to a single role. A role is the behavioral aspect of a social position. It is identified by the name of the position (such as "guard") and is defined by the norms which specify appropriate behavior in that position. Roles are not the same as people. An individual may play more than one role (father, son, husband, teacher), switching from role to role according to the situation. At the same time, roles are independent of the individuals who fill them. An individual may withdraw from playing a role (which is what happens when a correctional officer resigns), but the role continues to exist, remaining unplayed until a new occupant becomes available for the social position associated with the role.

The role is the meeting place between the individual who occupies the social position to which the role is attached, the cultural norms which define appropriate behavior in the role, and the structure of the social organization or society. Each role is associated with a social position located in the status hierarchy of a group, just as groups are arranged in a status hierarchy within some larger social body. For example, the role of President of the Inmate Council is associated with a social status position that is above the status of the members of the Inmate Council. All roles have specific status positions associated with them, and groups are made up of at least two role-players who are interacting with each other. In most groups, the social positions are arranged in hierarchical order from the highest to the lowest status. Groups may also be ranked hierarchically by status. Prisoners form small friendship groups, which are the building blocks of the prisoner society. They also form larger groups or associations, which taken together, make up the entire prison society.

Norms. The general set of prisoner norms that is applicable to all roles in the prisoner subculture is called the convict code. The code varies somewhat from institution to institution, but it always has the same basic concepts imbedded in it. These are that one should not interfere with the interests of other prisoners, show any weakness, be a "sucker," exploit "upstanding" prisoners, or lose control of one's behavior.[72] We may say that "the perfect prisoner is strongly proprisoner, antiadministration, tough, cool, dependable, and never uses other prisoners unfairly"[8:15] according to the convict code. Even in the traditional maximum security prison, prisoners do not all follow the convict code, and the code has been weakening for several decades. Prisoner societies are not as monolithic as they once were, and the introduction of large numbers of minority group members, young drug users, and nonprofessional criminals has tended to fragment prison populations so thoroughly that it is no longer accurate to speak of a singular convict code.

Roles. Prisoner societies contain a rich variety of social roles, each of which is defined by a number of specific behavioral norms or their violation. There are "snitches" who write notes ("snitch kites") to administrators telling them about the illegal activities of their fellow prisoners; "wolves," who rape or otherwise force their intentions upon weaker prisoners; "punks," who are the victims of "wolves" and who engage in other forms of "unmanly" behavior; and "fish," first-timers who are insufficiently sophisticated in the ways of prison life to defend themselves against victimization by their peers. In prisons, there are social roles associated with group membership, sentence length, committing offense, degree of dedication to the traditional convict code, specific talents or deficiencies, demographic characteristics, sexual behavior, friendship relationships, and economic activities. To cope successfully with prison life, one must understand who is currently playing what role (for the same prisoner plays different roles at different times or in different social situations), and what the norms are prescribing behavior in that role. It comes as no surprise to learn that "fish" take a long time to understand the social complexity of prison life, and that they are often heavily victimized by more experienced prisoners during this socialization period.

Four general cultural roles have been repeatedly found in studies of prison subcultures. They were first identified by Clarence Schrag[62] in the late 1950s, and have been the subjct of considerable scholarly debate since that time. The four roles identified by Schrag are "square John," "right guy," "politician," and "outlaw." The "square John" is a prosocial prisoner who conforms to the prison rules, is positively oriented toward a law-abiding life, does not get involved with the prisoner society, and is friendly with staff members. The "right guy" is just the opposite, being heavily involved in subcultural activities, oriented negatively toward society, and having little to do with staff members. "Square Johns" tend to have middle-class origins and to have been convicted of either white-collar crimes or crimes of passion, while "right guys" come from the lower class and have been convicted of serious crimes of violence. The third role is the "politician," who attempts to manipulate both staff and prisoners to gain advantages in the struggle for goods and services within the prison. "Politicians" have often been convicted of economic crimes such as fraud, embezzlement, and confidence games, and really have no attachment to either the prisoner subculture or legitimate society as represented by staff members. We have already mentioned that the "square John" is essentially prosocial (in terms of the larger law-abiding society). In comparison, the "right guy" is antisocial, the "politician" is pseudosocial, and the "outlaw" is asocial. That is to say, the prison "outlaw" is severely and violently criminal, uses violence to attain his ends, and victimizes both fellow-prisoners and staff members.

The character of the prisoner society in a given correctional institution will be partially determined by the percentage of prisoners occupying each of these major role types. Prisons having large numbers of "outlaws" are likely to be more violent and less stable than prisons incarcerating mostly "square Johns." Similarly, we can look at prisons over time and learn something about the changes they have experienced from the changes in the roles that prisoners play. The early studies of prisoner roles found that "outlaws" comprised 17–19 percent of the prisoners.[18,20,62] Conversely, a more recent study of prisoner roles in 22 correctional institutions located in five different countries by Werner Gruninger[24] found that approximately half of the prisoners occupied the role of "outlaw." Gruninger believes that diversion and parole have removed many of the less seriously criminal individuals from prison so that the remaining prison populations are dominated by individuals playing the role of "outlaw."

There is a dilemma in a study of prisoner roles: how to go about measuring these roles. Almost all studies have placed prisoners in roles according to their answers to a series of attitude statements. For example, according to Peter Garabedian[19] the "outlaw" role is characterized by statements such as: "'Might is right' and 'every man for himself' are the main rules of living regardless of what people say" and the "politician" role by statements such as "There's a little larceny in everybody, if you're really honest about it." With this kind of methodology, what Garabedian actually found was the percentage of prisoners agreeing with statements that are typical of each role rather than the percentage of prisoners actually occupying that role. A recent criticism of Garabedian's work shows that there is a considerble difference between agreement with these attitude statements and defining oneself (or being defined by others) as playing a social role. There is no doubt that prisoner populations have come to agree more and more with "outlaw" ideas in the past several decades and that the level of violence in correctional institutions has correspondingly increased, but that does not necessarily mean that the number of prisoners who are called "outlaws" has increased as much, nor does it mean that the increase in "outlaw" role players has caused the increase in violence.

Terms such as "outlaw" and "right guy," in the sense used here, cannot be found in the dictionary. They are argot terms which have been developed as part of the prison subculture. The special roles and shared understandings that are developed in that culture are given names unique to that culture. The more isolated the culture, the greater the number of argot terms. In the case of prisoner subcultures, an extensive repertory of argot terminology exists. In one of the earliest studies of prisoner subcultures, James Hargan[26] explained that the argot terminology used at Sing Sing prison helped the prisoners to foster a sense of group solidarity, thus decreasing any negative feelings about themselves that they might have acquired while being processed through the criminal justice system.

Donald Clemmer[13] included a dictionary of 1063 argot terms in *The Prison Community.* He found that 11 percent of the argot terms in use at Menard Penitentiary in Illinois referred to sex, 30 percent to crime, 8 percent to descriptions of individuals, 5 percent to "vagabondage," 32 percent to prison, 6 percent to body parts, 7 percent to alcohol and other drugs, and 1 percent to gambling. The number of argot terms referring to a specific subject may be taken as an indication of the importance of that subject in a subculture. In Menard, there were 64 terms referring to homosexual behavior and only 52 referring to heterosexual behavior. Twenty-two terms described food, while only nine terms described characteristics of clothing. As the extent of illegal drug use has expanded in prisoner subcultures, the number of argot terms has similarly increased so that there are many more argot terms referring to drug use in prisons today than there were in the 1930s.[8] Despite long-term changes such as this one—and also short-term changes in which argot terms are innovated overnight, used for a brief period of time, and then disappear—many of the argot terms commonly used by prisoners today are the same as those of 50 years ago.

Prisoner Groups. When Schrag[62] did his research on prisoner roles, he also examined friendship and leadership in the prisoner subculture. He found that antisocial prisoners tended to be more popular than other prisoners (which is a commentary on the negativity of prison life) and that there was a tendency for prisoners to become friends with those most like themselves in terms of social role and offense history. Recent research on the friendship choices of prisoners add several insights to Schrag's pioneering work. First, between one-fifth[22] and two-fifths[35] of the prisoners are isolationist, and try to keep to themselves as much as possible. Most of the rest try to make a small number of friends among the other prisoners, but are wary of too many social entanglements.[35] The friends they choose are limited by factors other than offense and social role. Proximity and race are also important determinants of friendship choice, with friends tending to live close together within the prison and to be of the same racial or ethnic group.[66]

Until the late 1960s, groups larger than friendship groups of just a few individuals could not exist within a prison without the formal approval of the warden. This limited the number of large groups; it also controlled the activities engaged in by those groups, since any activities displeasing the warden resulted in the withdrawal of permission for continued group meetings. Lifers' groups, athletic clubs, Alcoholics Anonymous groups, community service groups such as the Jaycees, religious groups, and some hobby groups were maintained in this fashion. Political groups were less likely to be authorized, but there were experiments in prisoner self-government that occasionally occurred for brief periods of time.

In addition to holding regular meetings, legitimate prisoner organizations circulate newsletters within the prison, and sometimes to interested individuals in the free community. A special case of these publications is the prison newspaper, which is published in most major correctional institutions. In 1970, there were over 200 prisoner newspapers with a combined circulation of over 300,000 readers,[58] and the number of such newspapers is certainly much higher today.

The tight control exercised in the traditional maximum security prison limited the size of unauthorized prisoner groups. Gangs were not allowed to develop, and the sub rosa activities in the prisoner economy were carried out by isolated individuals and small groups. For example, a prisoner cook in the mess hall might steal food and share it with his friends or trade it for information abstracted from official files by another prisoner who was performing secretarial duties in the administrative offices. As prison regulations become looser and more humane, much more elaborate smuggling operations developed. These operations sometimes involved dozens of prisoners, and also perhaps several staff members and a number of relatives and criminal associates in the free society. Complex smuggling operations, along with protection rackets, gambling and prostitution, were very similar to organized crime syndicate activities in the larger society.

Although large-scale illegitimate prisoner groups have sometimes developed as the result of a single entrepreneur, another development has contributed to the rise of organized crime in prison settings. This is the rise in power of ethnically oriented gangs of prisoners, most of which have their bases outside the prison walls. The two prime examples of this are the California prison system, in which two rival Chicano gangs have been responsible for considerable violence and economic exploitation, and the Illinois prison system, in which whole institutions have been largely taken over by gangs of young men that are offshoots of major gangs on the Chicago streets.[33] Japanese prisons have had similar problems with gang members, and have dealt with these problems by dispersing gang members throughout the national prison system so that they cannot work together to confront prison authorities.[37] The stability and resources that an external base provides for prison gangs makes them formidable components for prison administrators and allows them to completely dominate any prisoners not organized into rival gangs.

Status. If you murdered someone in Europe during medieval times, your penalty was directly related to the status of your victim. The higher the status of your victim, the greater your punishment.[50] The democratic ideals of American society specify that all people are equal before the law, but individuals in prison continue to arrange themselves into status hierarchies. Prisoners who have committed violent crimes against adults and who play the "right guy" role tend to be high in status, while those who have committed sex crimes against minors or who have "snitched" to the administration are low in status. W.E. Mann's[42] study of a Canadian reformatory identified six status levels of prisoners. The highest status prisoners were known as "real wheels," who comprised approximately three percent of the prisoner population. In the standing order of status, the other classes of prisoners were "fifth floor men" (three percent), "wheelers and dealers" (10–15 percent), "solid cons" (15–20 percent), "goofs" (42–45 percent), and "rats" (5–10 percent). The sources of social status differed somewhat between these categories of prisoners. The "real wheels" were large, intelligent, strong, well-connected, and confident. In contrast, the "fifth floor men" gained their status because they worked in the administrative offices of the prison, which allowed them to gain access to valued information. The "wheelers and dealers" produced their status by continuous hustles, and the "solid cons" were respected primarily because of their loyalty to the convict code and their practice of the traditional convict life style. Although the terms differ, the similarities between roles and statuses in Mann's Canadian study and those identified in American studies by Sykes, Schrag, and others are extremely strong.

Social Psychological and Ethological Aspects of Prisoner Subcultures

A prisoner society can be considered to be a sociocultural system, following a definition of a system as discussed in Chapter 2. This system also interfaces with the psychological systems (personalities) of individual prisoners and with the physical environment of the institution. The battle for social status occurs within the boundaries established by the physical environment and also has consequences for the distribution of physical facilities among prisoners. High-status prisoners tend to accumulate more material goods and to have control over a larger amount of territory than low-status prisoners.[3] "Wolves" sometimes establish territories within the prison and only victimize those fellow-prisoners living within their own territory.[60] Interchanges between the physical environment and the prisoner society occur in both directions. Robert Wallace[78] argues that the kinds of living conditions experienced by prisoners determine their behavior to a considerable extent. If this is true, then we might expect that more pleasant and stimulating housing conditions would result in fewer antisocial incidents among prisoners.

What we have been describing in the previous paragraph is the ecology of prisoner societies. This is a subject which is, as yet, poorly understood. In contrast, the social psychology of prisoner subcultures has been extensively studied. Every society has the problem of finding ways to shape individuals so that they fit into the roles that exist in the culture of that society. The general process through which this occurs is called socialization, and the specific term for the process of socialization as it occurs in correctional institutions is *prisonization*. Prisonization does not necessarily imply the deterioration of prisoners. It refers to the taking on and internalizing of the prisoner subculture. Prisoner argot automatically comes to mind when there is something to say. The individual's world becomes defined in terms of the status hierarchy, roles and groups within the prison rather than with respect to these elements in the larger society.

In extremely repressive environments, prisonization may result in emotional apathy and other kinds of deterioration as described by Clemmer.[13] However, most modern prisons are much more humane than the traditional maximum security institution, and permit a greater amount of contact with the outside world, so that the impact of prisonization may no longer be as damaging as it once was. The primary concern with prisonization today is that it tends to be associated with negative views of law-abiding behavior. In fact, prisonization is often measured by the rejection of staff norms or the acception of the convict code.[8] A series of articles by Charles Thomas and his associates have probed the factors associated with prisonization and correctional institutions. Thomas[73] has found that although the influences of prison life are important in producing prisonization, factors over which prison administrators have no control are even more important. The estimates that prisoners make about the chances of their doing well after release from prison are based on conditions in the external society, not on the prison environment, and negative estimates of what will occur after release are more strongly associated with prisonization than with any internal prison factor.

American prisoners appear to be more prisonized than prisoners in other countries, although prisonization occurs to some degree in all nations. The only study completed in a number of different nations using a standard research methodology concludes that prisonization is greater in custodially oriented prisons than in prisons oriented toward treatment. The treatment-custody continuum of institutional orientation was found to be more important than the background of the prisoners in determining the degree of prisonization.[1]

Race Relations in American Prisons

The historical section on prison race relations in Chapter 5 ended in the mid-1960s, when Black Muslims began to win compliance from prison administrators with their religious and dietary customs. Since that time, black and Hispanic prisoners have steadily gained power within prisoner societies at the expense of white prisoners. John Irwin[31] described the changes in the relations between racial and ethnic groups in the California prison system up to 1970. Black prisoners in California began to substitute for their criminal identities those based on racial differences; Chicanos soon emulated this trend. At that time, white prisoners were not always seen as the enemies of minority groups. Irwin observed that "The Blacks and Chicanos, as they focus on the whites as their oppressors, seem to be excluding white prisoners from this category and are, in fact, developing some sympathy for them as a minority group which itself is being oppressed by the white establishment and the white police."[31:82] However, violence between the races soon became so common that California administrators segregated their maximum security "adjustment center" units to reduce prisoner victimization. Some whites responded to the increase in minority group power by forming the neo-Nazi Aryan Brotherhood, which was also built around racial symbolism and ideology.[34]

Black prisoners do not require a numerical majority to dominate white prisoners. If they are as little as a quarter of the prisoner population, their higher degree of social solidarity gives them an advantage over the larger number of white prisoners. Chicano prisoners (in the Southwest) and Latino prisoners (in the East and the Midwest) enjoy the same organizational advantage. Race and ethnicity have greater salience for minority group members than for whites because of the lifelong discrimination that these individuals typically experience in American society. This background of common experience gives minority group prisoners a ready basis for mutual cooperation. When many of them are members of the same ethnic and racial gangs on the streets—as is true in Illinois, New York, California, and other urban states—in-group solidarity reaches an extremely high level.[34]

The most detailed study of race relations in the prison society was carried out in a Northeastern maximum security institution by Leo Carroll[12] in 1970–1971. Black and white prisoners in this facility were forced into a degree of demographic integration by the prison administration, but they expressed mutual mistrust, suspicion, fear, and hatred. There was no unity in the prisoner society. Carroll found different sets of social roles for blacks and whites rather than a single integrated system of roles. Within the work details, in which integration was administratively mandated, social interaction was limited and superficial. In voluntary settings, such as recreational activities, there was much less interracial contact. The gymnasium, movie theater, dining hall, and shop all were divided into racial territories within which meaningful social interaction was largely confined.

Even the sub rosa economic activities of the prisoners were carried out in parallel racial structures. "Neither their rejection by society, nor their proximity within the prison, nor their common subordination to the authority of the custodians, nor the integrationist policies of the Warden, nor the material deprivations they suffer are sufficient to produce a cross-racial solidarity among prisoners."[12:195] Cooperation between black and white prisoner leaders occurred only when it was necessary to achieve a common goal such as obtaining sex and drugs, avoiding a race riot, or dealing with the public. These limited areas of interracial cooperation were continually threatened by strong sentiments of suspicion and hostility.

Variations among Prisons as Total Institutions

Total institutions theory not only allows us to see the parallel between prisons and other types of totalistic organizations; it also calls our attention to variations among prisons. Some prisons are more totalistic than others. How does this affect the characteristics of prisoner societies? Prisons that are high on institutional totality—and that therefore are experienced by prisoners as being highly depriving—tend to be characterized by high levels of violence,[28] punitiveness by correctional officers,[21] strong antisocial sentiments among prisoners,[6,14,64,67,70] tolerance of coercive homosexuality,[51] and relatively poor social relations with both staff members and peers.[22,70,81] A high level of institutional totality may also be associated with increased recidivism[45] and with a weakening of any long-term positive effects that might occur as a result of imprisonment.[59]

This is an impressive array of negative factors associated with institutional totalism, but it would be a mistake to think that these negative effects could be avoided simply by turning maximum security prisons into minimum security prisons. Security level is not the only index of institutional totalism, and there have been a number of studies showing that security level is not associated with many of the negative effects referred to by Goffman in his discussion of total institutions.[2,24,67] Prisoners in a minimum security institution may feel subjectively more deprived than prisoners in a maximum security institution, even though the objective deprivations are greater in the maximum security facility. If the correctional officer subculture is particularly punitive in a minimum security facility, it can produce these negative feelings in the absence of facilities and official policies that are highly depriving.

PRISONER SOCIETIES IN INSTITUTIONS FOR DELINQUENT BOYS

Prisoner societies in institutions for boys are surprisingly similar to prisoner societies in institutions for men. The youth and shorter criminal histories of the boys impact the development of social organization and subcultural norms mainly by producing greater instability. Boys are usually insecure about their sexual identities, and they are even more strongly oriented toward short-term goals than adult prisoners. The result is that victimization rates tend to be higher in youth institutions than in adult institutions. There is also more self-mutilation.[9] Like men, incarcerated boys tend to become prisonized, and prisonization undermines the achievement of institutional goals for positive change among the boys.[86]

The more highly criminal boys tend to have high status and to have a great deal of influence in prisoner societies found in institutions for juveniles[59] just as they do in prisons for men.[62] These negative influences can be replaced with positive influences (or at least with influences that are less negative) in treatment-oriented institutions in which the prosocial staff culture is strong enough to overcome the negative influences of the prisoner subculture.[46,77,83] However, these conditions are rarely found, even in institutions that have the reputation of being treatment-oriented.

The classic study of a treatment institution in which the prisoner subculture completely dominated the staff culture is Howard Polsky's book, *Cottage Six*.[52] This institution employed many professional treatment staff members and it had a high staff–inmate ratio. Despite this, violence-prone boys in the cottges were able to coerce houseparents into allowing them to dictate what would happen to the weaker boys and to impose their own antisocial attitudes upon the operation of the institution. The houseparents were apprehensive of opposing the inmate leaders because they needed their cooperation to keep things quiet in the cottages. The boys at the top of the inmate status structure ruled with an iron hand, forcing the lower-status boys to follow orders and constantly victimizing them verbally and physically. The lower a boy was in the status hierarchy, the more mistreatment he received at the hands of his peers. A rise in status required that the boy defeat a higher-status inmate in a fight. This pattern of exploitative subcultural behavior has been reported again and again from juvenile institutions. The most comprehensive and detailed description of these processes is found in *Juvenile Victimization: The Institutional Paradox*, by Clemens Bartollas, Stuart Miller and Simon Dinitz.[5] A discussion of their findings is presented in Chapter 11.

PRISONER SOCIETIES AMONG WOMEN

The extensive similarities in prisoner societies among men and boys do not always extend to women. There are a number of important differences between male and female prisoner societies. The first is that the importation of social roles from outside of the institution into the prisoner society seems to be more important in institutions for women than for men. Rose Giallombardo[21] argues that women bring values, norms, and beliefs into the prison with them that are consistent with gender stereotypes in the larger society, and that these stereotypes become the building blocks for female prisoner subcultures. A recent study of lesbianism in female institutions lends support for Giallombardo's position. An examination of lesbian behavior in seven institutions for young women revealed that their pre-prison lesbian experiences were seven times as important as the characteristics of the institutions in determining their sexual behavior while incarcerated.[53]

Incarcerated males try to dominate each other, and in the process produce the role of a submissive "punk"—a role construed as female. However, their intent is not in creating a female role per se. Their gratification comes from affirming their own masculinity through dominance rather than by engaging in mutually consensual relationships with female role-players. There are "queens" in male prisons, and these men do play strictly female roles, but they are few in number, particularly in comparison with "punks." The situation in women's prisons is quite different. Dominance is not the major principle of social organization. Male role-players appear in larger numbers than female-role players do in male prisons, and they freely choose these roles rather than being forced into them against their will. Even gender stratification is imported into the prison with the female offenders, for women who play masculine roles within the prison are accorded higher status than women who play feminine roles.[10] In fact, it is probably the relatively high status of male role-players that explains why most female role-players in men's prisons have to be forcibly recruited while male role-players in women's prisons are in good supply without any need of coercion.

The idea of homosexual love appears to be more threatening to male prisoners than to imprisoned women. Male prisoners who rape other men strive vehemently to define homosexual behavior as heterosexual, and they look down upon other men who are involved in consensual homosexual relationships. In contrast, the emphasis in women's prisons is more on affection than on physical sex. Overt homosexual behavior occurs in the context of a loving relationship and is integrated into a total interpersonal experience. It is not isolated from love as it is in homosexual rape and prostitution. Because of the emphasis on love as distinguished from sex, some of the most intense love relationships in women's prisons do not include overt homosexual behavior at all. These lovers may be content to send notes back and forth to each other and to meet briefly over lunch, if that is all that can be arranged within the limitations of institutional regulations. Despite the intensity of lesbian relationships in women's prisons, practitioners generally agree that most women (like men) who participate in prison homosexuality return to a heterosexual life upon release to the free society.[61]

Women in the larger society are generally socialized to look forward to a life that is mainly rewarding because of family relations rather than relations in wider communities of interest. The result of this socialization pattern is that incarcerated women feel the deprivation of family relations more severely than do incarcerated men. A unique social device has been developed by imprisoned women to deal with this deprivation. The pseudo-family is a group of women in which each woman plays the role of a family member: children, parents, grandparents, aunts, and cousins. Family life in these pseudo-families often as intense as normal family life, except that sexual relationships generally occur outside of the pseudo-family structure. Approximately 90 percent of all studies of institutions for women and girls have identified pseudo-family structures. The similarity of form of pseudo-families in such a wide variety of isolated institutions is striking. Women all over the world are responding to a similar set of deprivations with the same social invention in an attempt to ease the pains of imprisonment. It is equally impressive that pseudo-families have not changed between 1929, when the first report appeared in literature,[17] and the present.

Another difference between male and female prisoner subcultures is in the level of development of the sub rosa economic system. Illegal economic transactions among prisoners, such as the smuggling of contraband, trading, gambling, and loansharking, tend to more extensively developed in prisons for men than in prisons for women. Part of the reason for this is that male prisons are much larger than female prisons, requiring more extensive economic socialization in order to keep illegal goods and services flowing. The second reason is that male prisons tend to be more physically depriving than female prisons. The more material items that are prohibited in institutions, the greater the sub rosa economic system that will develop in order to provide these items through black market economic arrangements, and the greater the level of prisoner concern with physical survival needs as compared with more complex sociocultural needs. Finally, many male prisoners have been involved in organized illegal activities outside the prison. These organized crime involvements are almost never found among female prisoners. A key economic role in male prisons is the "merchant," who sells a variety of black market goods to other prisoners.[72] This male social role has no parallel in female prisoner subcultures.

The last gender difference in prisoner societies is with respect to victimization. We have already mentioned that homosexual rape is prevalent in male institutions but almost completely absent from female institutions. Nonsexual assaults are also more common in male institutions, although they are by no means absent from female institutions. A recent survey of all studies and reports on prison victimization has indicated that other types of victimization tend to be more commonly found in male institutions than in female institutions. These include robbery, theft, social discrimination, and a variety of con games that can be summarized under the title "psychological victimization." The two areas in which victimization is least different in male and female institutions are theft and psychological victimization, both of which are almost as common in women's prisons as in prisons for men.[9]

NEW DEVELOPMENTS IN PRISONER SOCIETIES: PRISONER POLITICAL ORGANIZATIONS AND SELF-HELP GROUPS

Most of the discussion in this chapter has implied that prisoner societies have negative effects on individual prisoners and on the prison as a whole. Although this is true in general, it is also true that prisoner societies contain many positive elements. The most obvious of these is that the prisoner society does make prison life more tolerable for many prisoners. It gives them something to be interested in; it explains how best to survive behind bars; it provides them with illegal commodities that soften the deprivations imposed by the prison administration; and it provides an arena in which prisoners can still freely act, compete, and achieve a sense of well-being and self-worth. When we move from the individual level to the level of prisoner groups, we find a number of positive groups operating within the prisoner society. These may be divided into self-help groups and political groups. In this section, we will discuss two examples of each of these kinds of groups.

Self-help groups may be organized on a purely therapeutic basis, such as Alcoholics Anonymous, or they may be organized around skill acquisition (The Speakers Forum), sentence type (lifers' groups), or ethnicity (The Black Prisoners' Union). Lifers are a major stabilizing force in prison life. Lifers know that they will be incarcerated for a long period of time, so they try to keep things calm and to make the prison as livable a place as possible. Many lifers are "square Johns," and regret the crimes of passion they committed. They engage in numerous charitable activities, such as recording books for the blind and repairing toys for disadvantaged children.

A recent lifers' activity that has achieved a national reputation is the Scared Straight Program initiated by the Rahway State Prison Lifers' Group in New Jersey. Lifers participating in this controversial program give talks to potential and actual delinquents about how bad things are in prison in the hope that this will help to deter them from a life of crime. An evaluation of the effects of the Scared Straight Program by James Finckenauer[49] found that the program not only did not result in a decrease in delinquency: it was actually related to an increase in both the frequency and seriousness of delinquency. In contrast to these findings, a recent evaluation of the program by Sidney Langer[39] finds that it has a positive long-term impact on juvenile delinquency. He used a 22-month follow-up period instead of the 10-month follow-up period employed by Finckenauer. The final word in this debate has not yet been heard.

Ethnic Self-Help Groups

Ethnic groups can simultaneously victimize outsiders and be genuinely helpful to group members, as R.T. Davidson[15] showed in his study of Chicanos at San Quentin Prison in California. Other ethnic groups are purely self-help in nature and do not engage in the victimization of outsiders at all. These groups can be an important supplement to therapeutic services provided through the official structure of the prison. They may be successful in attracting the help of volunteer professionals from the free community to add to their own efforts in providing services such as scholastic tutoring, vocational counseling, family counseling, legal aid, literacy and language classes, ethnic studies, and preparation for release. Many prison administrators have come to realize that these ethnic groups are an important resource for institutional control as well as the personal growth and development of individual prisoners. They reduce idleness, increase motivation, and encourage conformity to institutional rules. Cultural identification is a viable alternative to criminal identification.[11]

The most comprehensive study of ethnic self-help groups in prisons is Joan Moore's book *Home Boys*,[47] in which she describes the rise of self-help activities among Chicanos in the California prison system. System administrators have sometimes opposed these self-help groups by declaring them illegal, transferring their leaders to other institutions, and discouraging officers from becoming sponsors. At other times, these groups suffered what Moore labels as an overdose of "cooperation" when administrators attempted to turn the ethnic groups into official therapy groups or to assign officers as honorary group members so that they could control group activities. There were other times, most notably in the mid-1970s, when Chicano self-help groups received general cooperation from administrators in the California prison system.

Ethnic self-help groups may be small and weak or they may be large and well-organized. Moore describes a small ethnic group meeting as follows.

A typical prison meeting might consist of a dozen or two dozen men struggling through parliamentary procedure, hearing committee reports on, for example, how an upcoming Chicano holiday is to be celebrated, or the details on getting a band for some upcoming event. The meeting may be sharpened by an outside visitor, who reports on how an organization is working in the barrios....

But for many of these men such a meeting represents a major change in life style. Barrio gang boys are not trained in public speaking and parliamentary procedure, or in the writing of a report—especially not on their own volition....

Thus the prison self-help groups offered a major self-initiated change in life style, within a legitimate public context invariably turned to altruistic purposes.[47:130–131]

IMPACT: The Natural History of a
Self-Help Group

To illustrate the operation of a self-help therapy group in a prison setting, we will present the natural history of IMPACT, a self-help group that originated in the Washington State Penitentiary in 1967. The group developed around ideas imported from the McNeil Island Federal Penitentiary, where the Self-Improvement Group had been operating as an officially recognized therapy group since 1957. The design for therapy used at McNeil was imported to Walla Walla by prisoners who had previously been incarcerated there, and who wished to start a similar group in their new environment. The early officers of IMPACT were prisoners who were sincerely dedicated to their self-improvement. Some of them were "square Johns," but others were hardened criminals who became more prosocial over a period of years while incarcerated. The group was led by a charismatic black prisoner from its origin up through 1970, when he was released from the prison. He organized group activities around general religious and therapeutic principles rather than specific ethnic topics, and was able to appeal to prisoners of all racial and ethnic heritages.

Participation in the group was structured into five levels according to the degree of therapeutic progress achieved. Staff members were specifically excluded from all of the therapeutic activities of the group. A new prisoner entering the group was oriented to its goals and took an oath confirming these goals. He was then subjected to a series of 10 to 13 group meetings with seven group members who had been fully certified as having completed the therapeutic program of the group. The seven-on-one therapy sessions included attacks on the rationalizations of the candidate to help him face reality, and specific techniques to help him know himself, know how he wished to change, and to identify the barriers that must be surmounted in order to become rehabilitated.

Throughout the early years of its existence, IMPACT steadfastly pursued the goal of personal growth for its members and did not become involved in institutional politics. It achieved an exemplary reputation with prison administrators because its leaders refrained from attempting to gain favors for themselves through their positions. When the initial charismatic head of the group left the institution, it was taken over by more self-serving prisoners. Seeing this process develop, the departing leader warned the membership against trying to make IMPACT something other than a self-help group. In his view, a prisoner who was successfully changed by his participation in the group would not have to seek special privileges, for his rehabilitation would be evident to the Parole Board and to prison administrators, and he would be appropriately rewarded. The charismatic leader had no sooner left the institution than the new leadership of IMPACT begin to change its structure. Decisions were now to be voted on democratically by all members of the group instead of just by members who had reached the highest level of therapeutic achievement. Most of the energy of the leadership was directed toward gaining privileges for themselves and to a lesser extent for group members, instead of toward therapeutic goals. Racism crept into the operation of the group, and the white prisoners began dropping out. Members began to come to meetings to meet attractive street people who were invited as guests and to have fun rather than to improve themselves. The new leader continued to use therapeutic language, proclaiming that "IMPACT has been pointing the way through faith, knowledge and demonstration," but it was empty verbiage.

Prisoners began to distrust the IMPACT leadership. Could they be sure that their inner secrets released in therapy groups would be kept confidential? Attendance at group meetings began to fall off and fewer new members were recruited. Attempts by the IMPACT leaders to gain significant privileges for the group were denied by the Superintendent, and IMPACT disintegrated within a few months.

Prisoners' Unions

The first American prisoners' union was organized at Folsom Prison, a unit of the California Department of Corrections, in 1970. Because of opposition from correction officials, the union established its base of operations outside of the correctional system, largely with the support of ex-offenders.[29] A completely different basis of operation was established by a union at a New York State Prison at Green Haven in 1972. This organization requested affiliation with the Distributive Workers of America, but legal recognition for the prisoners' union was denied by the courts.[16] A third major attempt to establish a prisoners' union occurred in Ohio in early 1973. A wildcat strike by the Southern Ohio Correctional Facility local of the Ohio's Prisoners Labor Union led to strong punitive measures by institution administrators. The outside headquarters of the OPLU was closed in 1974, and has not had any appreciable influence since that time.[30]

Although prisoners' unions can have positive effects on the behavior of prisoners and can also aid administrators in stabilizing institutional life,[82] administrators in American prisons have strongly resisted prisoner attempts to form unions on the grounds that these unions might be a threat to institutional security and order.[41] The trend in legal decisions has been to support prison administrators, culminating in *Jones v. North Carolina Prisoners' Labor Union*, in which the U.S. Supreme Court upheld repressive measures designed to prohibit the organization and operation of prisoners' unions.[75] It appears that decisions in American courts will not permit the development of prisoners' unions in the near future.[16] Unless specific legislation is passed authorizing the formation of unions, it is unlikely that they will be able to survive within correctional institutions. The only alternative model is to locate the organizational base of the union external to correctional institutions and to attempt to negotiate with correctional administrators from outside the system instead of within it.

Prisoner Unions in Scandinavia. The first Scandinavian prisoners' union was formed in 1970, when a national hunger strike involving approximately half of the nation's prisoners occurred. The prisoners demanded among other things to be recognized as a national prisoners' union that had the right to negotiate directly with correctional administrators. The prisoners were initially successful, partially because of the support received from an external reform organization known as KRUM. Talks were held between prisoners and the Swedish National Correctional Administration in January 1971, at which time administrators agreed to make improvements in a number of areas of prison life. When a second conference between administrators and prisoner representatives was held in November 1971, many of the promises still had not been implemented, and the prisoners broke off negotiations.[79]

The various strikes and other conflicts that have occurred since the formation of the Swedish prisoners' union have not been immediately successful, but seem to have had a long-term influence on prison reform. A change of administration in Sweden's Department of Justice has resulted in many prison reforms consistent with the demands of the union leaders.[68] Prisoners' unions in Norway and Denmark have had similar experiences. All three national prisoners' unions have developed the tactic of using brief rather than protracted strikes to alert the external world about what is occurring within the prison system, to focus on specific concrete conditions rather than general goals, and to avoid excessive radicalism that might result in the loss of public support.[43]

Prisoner Self-Government

There have been dozens of experiments with prisoner self-government down through the years, beginning in 1793 at the Walnut Street Jail in Philadelphia.[4] Although self-government can be instituted in relatively small units as a therapeutic program,[27] this is not the same as political self-government in which a single elective body participates with administrative officials in making policy for a large correctional institution. True self-government also should not be confused with the creation of inmate councils that have essentially no input in administrative policy development. These bodies are found in the majority of American prisons,[48] and hardly qualify as prisoner self-government.

Scholars conducting recent examinations of self-government activities in American prisons have concluded that the practice may have positive results for both individual prisoners and the prison as an organization,[7] but that we do not currently know enough about how to implement self-governments in correctional institutions correctly.[36] The failure of the self-government experiment at the Washington State Penitentiary is an instructive example.*

The Resident Government Council at the Washington State Penitentiary was authorized by the Director of the Department of Institutions as part of a package of drastic prison reforms that were essentially forced upon the administration of the Washington State Penitentiary against its will. After drawing up an appropriate constitution, the first RGC was elected in April 1971. The constitution specified that the 11 prisoners receiving the highest number of votes from the total prisoner population of the institution on a ballot containing at least 18 names would constitute the council; that elections would be held twice a year; that vote-counting would be handled by the Civilian Advisory Council rather than by prison staff members; and that the officers of the council would be chosen by a vote among elected Council members.[55] The first President of the RGC was a "square John," who worked well with prison administrators and received considerable support from his fellow-prisoners. The RGC constituted various subcommittees to write reports on different aspects of prison reform, held press conferences with the full cooperation of the prison administration, and participated in regular meetings with the Superintendent of the Washington State Penitentiary. Members of the Civilian Advisory Council were given open access to the institution and were invited to be present at all RGC activities.

*The following discussion is derived from the author's experiences as a member of the Civilian Advisory Council to the Resident Government Council at the Washington State Penitentiary. For a more extensive analysis of the operation of the RGC, see reference 76.

The crucial point at which power passed to the RGC was its series of agenda meetings with the Superintendent of the institution. The agendas were lengthy RGC documents proposing reforms in all areas of prison life. The proposals were discussed one by one at the agenda meetings and either accepted or rejected by the Superintendent, or in some cases referred for further study when legal issues were involved. For example, the first proposal on the agenda of June 25, 1971[56] was a request that prisoners be allowed to keep personal musical instruments in their cells, and this was granted by the Superintendent. The second proposal was that prisoners be allowed to donate coffee and cigarettes to their fellow prisoners in segregation. This was also granted by the Superintendent. Some of the other proposals approved by the Superintendent at this meeting were to permit religious services, including those for the Black Muslim religion, for residents of death row; to allow the RGC to solicit volunteer therapists from local universities and counseling clinics to provide therapy sessions in the mental health unit; to allow prisoners to purchase commercially printed posters and receive them through the mail; and to permit prisoners to receive notices of any unauthorized materials that were delivered to the prison in their name but that could not be delivered to them. The RGC also requested permission to amend its own constitution to include as a Bill of Rights the entire philosophy of corrections written by the Director of the Department of Institutions, and that was also approved by the Superintendent.

Power and prestige in a total institution largely flow from the decisions of the head of the institution. The RGC at Walla Walla initially had a great deal of prestige among the prisoners because of the many concessions made to it by the Superintendent. Another factor was that the proposals put forth to the Superintendent for his consideration were in the best interest of the prisoners as a whole rather than self-serving for the RGC members. The second election of the RGC resulted in the replacement of the "square John" president with a "right guy" President, partially as a result of the use of pressure tactics. Nevertheless, the new President was strongly committed to making the RGC work, and it continued to function efficiently and with the full support of the Superintendent.

One of the visible ways in which the Superintendent supported the RGC was in making paper and duplicating machines available to it so that it could issue voluminous reports every two weeks. These reports abruptly ceased in April 1972 on the pretext that the institution was having budget problems. They never resumed, and the RGC became progressively less successful in extracting concessions from the administration. Part of the explanation is that all of the easily obtainable concessions had been made, and there was strong staff opposition to going any further down the line toward total prisoner self-government. The RGC resigned en masse in November 1972 in an attempt to rectify the situation. It soon reconstituted itself and negotiated a new constitution with the Superintendent.

By this time, the prisoner population felt betrayed by both the RGC and the Superintendent. The early promises of drastic prison reform had given way to a slow retreat toward traditional prison practices. At the same time, the RGC was being used by its own officers to benefit themselves, rather than the entire prisoner population. One of them used the RGC as a shield to run a drug smuggling operation, and eventually he died of a drug overdose. Another ran on the platform that he would not do anything for anyone except himself if elected, and was promptly voted into office. In March 1975, the ninth RGC slate came up for election, and few prisoners bothered to cast a vote. Shortly thereafter, the Superintendent issued a memo stating that "The Resident Government Council is no longer an effective and viable tool for communication between the administration and the resident population of the Washington State Penitentiary. Therefore as of this date the RGC, as presently constituted, is abolished."[57] The memo also provided for a substitute group to be developed by a committee of staff, residents, and Prison Legal Services Representatives, and to continue the Civilian Advisory Council as an input mechanism for the general public into prison affairs.

The cycle of pure motivation followed by the cynical misuse of a prison organization for the self-advantage of its officers that was described in the natural history of IMPACT seems to have been repeated in the history of the RGC. In addition to the takeover of leadership positions by antisocial prisoners, both organizations were also undermined by the unwillingness of the prison administration to make concessions, perhaps because of the realization that the organizations had become a negative force rather than a positive force in prison life. Therapy groups such as IMPACT are not very threatening to prison administrators. They do not challenge the political control of the institution, so they are easily implemented. True self-government programs, on the other hand, require a major restructuring of the distribution of power in the prison, and as a result are rarely seen. The RGC in Walla Walla would never have been implemented by the Superintendent alone. It was ordered from the level of the Director of the Department of Institutions, whose background was in mental health rather than in corrections. His early resignation from this post was probably the factor that began the withdrawal of the Superintendents's support from the RGC, which consigned it to its eventual fate.

SUMMARY

Prisons, like mental hospitals, homes for the aged and many other institutions can be characterized as total institutions. Within these relatively isolated institutions, prisoner societies develop. Isolation, sensory deprivation, and rigidity of scheduling are among the characteristics of total institutions that lead to the development of identifiable behavior syndromes among both prisoners and their captors. The deprivation or indigenous origin theory of prisoner societies tells us that prisoner societies arise as an adaptive social response to the deprivations experienced in imprisonment. A competing theory, the importation model, argues that much of what we take to be unique to prisoner societies is really a concentrated form of lower-class criminal norms, values, social structures, and beliefs that have been imported into the prison with the offenders. Both of these theories have considerable value in understanding prison life.

Prisoner societies have the same elements as free societies, including norms, roles, groups, and hierarchical status systems. They differ from free societies only in the content of these social forms. For example, prisoner roles such as "wolves" and "punks" are very different from the roles of teacher and student in university life, although they are much less different from some of the predatory roles that are found in lower-class street gangs. Prisoner societies seem to have been rather static up through the 1960s, at which point racial and cultural minority groups began to dominate the prisoners in many of the larger states. Other recent developments in prisoner societies include the rise of prisoner political organizations, such as prisoners' unions and prisoner self-government, and the organization of a number of effective prisoner self-help groups. Prisoner societies develop in institutions for juveniles and women in much the same way as they develop in institutions for men. Juvenile institutions tend to be more violent and unstable than adult institutions. Institutions for women are less violent, if not less unstable, and prisoner societies in these institutions are characterized by the unique social development of the pseudo-family in which each of the participating women plays the role of a family member such as mother, father, aunt, or uncle.

REFERENCES

1. Akers, Ronald L., Norman S. Hayner, and Werner Gruninger. "Prisonization in Five Countries: Type of Prison and Inmate Characteristics." *Criminology* 14 (1977):527–554.
2. Alpert, Geoffrey P. "Prisons as Formal Organizations: Compliance Theory in Action." *Sociology and Social Research* 63 (1979):112–130.
3. Austin, W.T. and Frederick L. Bates. "Ethological Indicators of Dominance and Territory in a Human Captive Population." *Social Forces* 52 (1974):447–455.
4. Baker, J.E. *The Right To Participate: Inmate Involvement in Prison Administration*. Metchun, NJ: Scarecrow Press, 1974.
5. Bartollas, Clemmens, Stuart J. Miller, and Simmon Dinitz. *Juvenile Victimization: The Institutional Paradox*. New York: Wiley, 1976.
6. Berk, Bernard B. "Organizational Goals and Inmate Organization." *American Journal of Sociology* 71 (1966):522–534.
7. Bloomberg, Seth A. "Participatory Management: Toward a Science of Correctional Management." *Criminology* 15 (1977):149–164.
8. Bowker, Lee H. *Prisoner Subcultures*. Lexington, MA: D.C. Heath, 1977.
9. Bowker, Lee H. *Prison Victimization*. New York: Elsevier, 1980.
10. Bowker, Lee H. "Gender Differences in Prisoner Subcultures." *In* Lee H. Bowker: *Women and Crime in America*. New York: Macmillan, 1981, pp. 409–419.
11. Burdman, Milton. "Ethnic Self-Help Groups in Prison and on Parole." *Crime and Delinquency* 20 (1974):107–118.
12. Carroll, Leo. *Hacks, Blacks, and Cons: Race Relations in a Maximum Security Prison*. Lexington, MA: D.C. Heath, 1974.
13. Clemmer, Donald. *The Prison Community*. New York: Holt, Rinehart and Winston, 1940.
14. Cline, Hugh F. "The Determinants of Normative Patterns in Correctional Institutions." *In* N. Christie: *Scandanavian Studies in Criminology*, Vol. II. Oslo, Norway: Scandinavian Books, 1968, pp. 173–184.

15. Davidson, R. Theodore. *Chicano Prisoners: The Key to San Quentin.* New York: Holt, Rinehart and Winston, 1974.
16. Fishman, Richard G. "The Prison Union Movement and Related Issues: An Overview of the Legal Aspects Involved." *Prison Law Monitor* 1 (1979):237, 249–254.
17. Ford, Charles A. "Homosexual Practices of Institutionalized Females." *Journal of Abnormal and Social Psychology* 23 (1929):442–448.
18. Garabedian, Peter. "Social Roles and Processes of Socialization in the Prison Community." *Social Problems* 11 (1963):139–152.
19. Garabedian, Peter. "Social Roles in a Correctional Community." *Journal of Criminal Law, Criminology and Police Science* 55 (1964):338–347.
20. Garrity, Donald L. *Effect of Length of Incarceration Upon Parole Adjustment and Estimation of Optimum Sentence.* Ph.D. Dissertation, University of Washington, 1958.
21. Giallombardo, Rose. *Society of Women: A Study of a Women's Prison.* New York: Wiley, 1966.
22. Glaser, Daniel. *The Effectiveness of a Prison and Parole System.* Indianapolis: Bobbs-Merrill,1964.
23. Goffman, Erving. *Asylums.* Garden City, NY: Doubleday, 1961.
24. Gruninger, Werner. *Criminalization, Prison Roles, and Normative Alienation: A Cross-Cultural Study.* Ph.D. Dissertation, University of Washington, 1974.
25. Gubrium, Jaber F. *Living and Dying at Murray Manor.* New York: St. Martin's Press, 1975.
26. Hargan, James. "Psychology of Prison Language." *Journal of Abnormal and Social Psychology* 30 (1935):359–365.
27. Hickey, Joseph E. and Peter L. Scharf. *Toward a Just Correctional System.* San Francisco, CA: Jossey Bass, 1980.
28. Hillery, G.A., Jr. "Freedom, Love and Community: An Outline of a Theory." *Society* 15 (May–June 1978) 24–31.
29. Huff, C. Ronald. "Unionization Behind the Walls." *Criminology* 12 (1974):175–194.
30. Huff, C. Ronald. "Prisoner Militancy and Politicization: The Ohio Prisoner's Union Movement." *In* David F. Greenberg: *Corrections and Punishment.* Beverly Hills, CA: Sage, 1977, pp. 247–264.
31. Irwin, John. *The Felon.* Englewood Cliffs, NJ: Prentice-Hall, 1970.
32. Irwin, John, and Donald R. Cressey. "Thieves, Convicts and the Inmate Culture." *Social Problems* 10 (1962):142–155.
33. Jacobs, James B. "Street Gangs Behind Bars." *Social Problems* 21 (1974):395–411.
34. Jacobs, James B. "Race Relations and the Prisoner Subculture." *In* Norval Morris and Michael Tonry: *Crime and Justice: An Annual Review of Research,* Vol. I. Chicago: University of Chicago Press, 1979.
35. James, Lois. *Influence in the Prison Environment.* Toronto: Centre of Criminology, University of Toronto, 1974.
36. Johnson, Elmer H. "Commentary: Potential of Inmate Self-Government." *Criminology* 15 (1977):165–178.
37. Kuno, Nobuyuki. "Treatment of Gangster Convicts in Prison." *Summarized in* Wing Lee Pi: "Summary Report of the Rapporteur, Workshop III: The Problem of Gangsters." *In* United Nations Asia and Far East Institute for the Prevention of Crime and the Treatment of Offenders: *Report for 1974 and Resource Material Series No. 9.* Tokyo, 1975, pp. 122–123.
38. Lammers, Cornelis J. "Strikes and Mutinies: A Comparative Study of Organizational

Conflicts Between Rulers and Ruled." *Administrative Science Quarterly* 14 (1969):558–572.

39. Langer, Sidney. *Fear in the Deterrence of Delinquency: A Critical Analysis of the Rahway State Prison Lifers' Group.* New York: University Press of America, 1980.

40. Leger, Robert G. "Socialization Patterns and Social Roles: A Replication." *Journal of Criminal Law and Criminology* 69 (1978):627–634.

41. Mann, Jenevra and Lawrence G. Cummings. "The Courts and Prisoner Unions: Conflict and Resolution." Paper presented at the annual meeting of Academy of Criminal Justice Sciences, 1978.

42. Mann, William E. "Socialization in a Medium-Security Reformatory." *Canadian Review of Sociology and Anthropology* 1 (1964):138–155.

43. Mathiesen, Thomas, and Wiggo Røine. "The Prison Movement in Scandinavia." *In* Herman Bianchi, Mario Simondi, and Ian Taylor: *Deviance and Control in Europe.* London: Wiley, 1975, pp. 85–96.

44. McArthur, Virginia. "Inmate Grievance Mechanisms: A Survey of American Prisons." *Federal Probation* 38 (December 1974):41–47.

45. McCord, William and McCord, Joan. "Two Approaches to the Cure of Delinquents." *Journal of Criminal Law, Criminology and Police Science* 44 (1944):442–467.

46. McEwen, Craig A. *Designing Correctional Institutions for Youth: Dilemmas of Subcultural Development.* Cambridge, MA: Ballinger, 1978.

47. Moore, Joan W. *Homeboys: Gangs, Drugs, and Prison in the Barrios of Los Angeles.* Philadelphia: Temple University Press, 1978.

48. Mortimore, Peter. "The Study of Institutions." *Human Relations* 31 (1978):985–999.

49. National Center on Institutions and Alternatives. "Scared Straight: A Second Look." Washington, D.C., 1979.

50. Newman, Graeme. *The Punishment Response.* Philadelphia: J.B. Lippincott, 1978.

51. Parker, Jack B. and Robert A. Perkins. "The Influence of Type of Institution on Attitudes Toward the Handling of the Homosexual Among Inmates." *Offender Rehabilitation* 2 (1978):245–254.

52. Polsky, Howard W. *Cottage Six.* New York: Wiley, 1962.

53. Propper, Alice. *Prison Homosexuality: Myth and Reality.* Lexington, MA: D.C. Heath, 1981.

54. Radford, R.A. "The Economic Organization of a P.O.W. Camp." *Economica* 12 (1945):189–201.

55. Resident Government Council. "Constitution for Self-Government." Walla Walla, WA: Washington State Penitentiary, April 29, 1971.

56. Resident Government Council. "Agenda of the Last Two Weeks of June, 1971." Walla Walla, WA: Washington State Penitentiary, 1971.

57. Rhay, B.J. "Superintendent's Memo." Walla Walla, WA: Washington State Penitentiary, April 1, 1975.

58. Rogers, Joseph W. and Elizabeth S. Alexander. "Penal Press: Opportunities for Correctional Research." *Journal of Research in Crime and Delinquency* 7 (1970):1–10.

59. Rose, Arnold M. and George H. Weber. "Changes in Attitudes Among Delinquent Boys Committed to Open and Closed Institutions." *Journal of Criminal Law, Criminology and Police Science* 52 (1961):166–177.

60. Roth, Loren H. "Territoriality and Homosexuality in a Male Prison Population." *American Journal of Orthopsychiatry* 41 (1971):510–513.

61. Roy, Nirmalendu. "Summary of the Rapporteur. Workshop II: New Programs in

Correctional Institutions." *In* United Nations Asia and Far East Institute for the Prevention of Crime and the Treatment of Offender: *Report for 1974 and Resource Material Series No. 9.* Tokyo, 1975, p. 113.

62. Schrag, Clarence. "A Preliminary Criminal Typology." *Pacific Sociological Review* 4 (1961):11–16.

63. Shichor, David. "To People Changing vs. People Processing Organizational Perspective: The Case of Correctional Institutions." *LAE Journal* 41 (Fall 1978):37–44.

64. Sieverdes, Christopher M. and Clemmens R. Bartollas, "Adherence to an Inmate Code in Minimum, Medium, and Maximum Security Juvenile Institutions." Paper presented at the annual meeting of the Society for Social Problems, 1979.

65. Sigler, Robert T. *Influence and Gang Membership in Three Juvenile Correctional Institutions.* Ph.D. Dissertation, University of Missouri–Columbia, 1974.

66. Slosar, John A., Jr. *Prisonization, Friendship, and Leadership.* Lexington, MA: D.C. Heath, 1978.

67. Smith, Carol F.W. and John R. Hepburn. "Alienation in Prison Organizations: A Comparative Analysis." *Criminology* 19 (1979):251–262.

68. Smith, Polly D. "An Update: Development of KRUM Since 1974." *The Prison Journal* 57 (1977):55–57.

69. Solzhenitsyn, Aleksander I. *The Gulag Archipelago Two.* New York: Harper and Row, 1975.

70. Street, David. "The Inmate Group in Custodial and Treatment Settings." *American Sociological Review* 1965 (30):40–55.

71. Sykes, Gresham M. *The Society of Captives.* New York: Atheneum, 1966. Originally published in 1958.

72. Sykes, Gresham M. and Sheldon L. Messinger. "The Inmate Social System." *In* Richard M. Cloward: *Theoretical Studies in the Social Organization of a Prison.* New York: Social Science Research Council, 1960, pp. 1–19.

73. Thomas, Charles W. "Theoretical Perspectives on Prisonization: A Comparison of the Importation and Deprivation Models." *The Journal of Criminal Law and Criminology* 68 (1977):135–145.

74. Tillion, Germaine. *Ravensbrück: An Eye Witness Account of a Women's Concentration Camp.* Garden City, NY: Doubleday, 1965.

75. Traub, Lois M. "Jones v. North Carolina Prison's Labor Union: A Threat to Unionization in Prisons." *New England Journal on Prison Law* 4 (1977):157–171.

76. Tyrner-Stastny, Gabrielle and Charles I. Stastny. "The Changing Political Culture of a Total Institution: The Case of Walla Walla." *The Prison Journal* 57 (Autumn-Winter 1977):43–53.

77. Vinter, Robert D. and Morris Janowitz. "The Comparative Study of Juvenile Correctional Institutions, A Research Report." Ann Arbor, MI: School of Social Work, University of Michigan, 1961.

78. Wallace, Robert, "Ecological Implications of a Custody Institution." *Issues in Criminology* 2 (1966):47–60.

79. Ward, David A. "Inmate Rights and Prison Reform in Sweden and Denmark." *Journal of Criminal Law, Criminology and Police Science* 63 (1972):240–255.

80. Williams, Virgil L. and Mary Fish. *Convicts, Codes, and Contraband: The Prison Life of Men and Women.* Cambridge, MA: Ballinger, 1974.

81. Wilson, Thomas P. "Patterns of Management and Adaptations to Organizational Roles: A Study of Prison Inmates." *American Journal of Sociology* 74 (1968):146–157.

82. Woolpert, Stephen. "Prisoner's Unions, Inmate Militancy, and Correctional Policy-making." *Federal Probation* 42 (June 1978):40–45.
83. Zald, Mayer N. and David Street. "Custody and Treatment in Juvenile Institutions: An Organizational Analysis." *Crime and Delinquency* 10 (1964):249–256.
84. Zimbardo, Phillip G. "Pathology of Imprisonment." *Society* 90676 (1972):4–8.
85. Zimbardo, Phillip G. "The Psychological Power and Pathology of Imprisonment." *In* John R. Snortum and Ilana Hadar: *Criminal Justice: Allies and Adversaries.* Pacific Palisades, CA: Palisades, 1978, pp. 202–210.
86. Zingraff, Matthew T. "Prisonization as an Inhibitor of Affective Socialization." *Criminology* 13 (1975):366–388.

Chapter 8

Correctional Officers

The primary deliverers of services in prisons are correctional officers. Their characteristics and qualifications are of the utmost importance in determining the success of any correctional institution; yet there has been little research on correctional officers until recent years.

Most corrections employees do not enter the field of corrections directly from high school. They are more likely to have begun their careers in another government job, perhaps in law enforcement, or to have been employed in business and industry. Another source of correctional personnel is the military. Once correctional employees enter the system, many of them make corrections a permanent career. The average longevity of correctional officers is approximately 10 years.[84]

Approximately two-thirds of all correctional officers are male, and this rises to over 99 percent in institutions for men. Slightly more than three-quarters of the officers are white, one-sixth are black, and there are small percentages of Hispanic, American Indian, and Oriental officers.[63] Although blacks appear somewhat more commonly among correctional officers than in the general population, they are much more heavily represented among prisoners, so that correctional institutions tend to have a staff–prisoner racial imbalance. Hispanics are even less well-represented among correctional officers than blacks, whether compared with their percentage in the general population or their percentage in the population of prisoners.

Correctional officers are paid less than probation and parole officers, deputy sheriffs, and police officers.[62] The starting salary for a paid correctional officer varied from $7608 per month in Vermont to $18,288 in Alaska in 1979. By region, correctional officer salaries were highest in the Northeast and lowest in the South,[6] and that is only partially offset by regional differences in the cost of living. With salaries in this range, it is difficult to recruit applicants with college education. In 1974, approximately one out of every five American correctional officers had not completed high school, and only one out of every 20 had completed college. The proportion of adult corrections supervisors having completed a college degree was only slightly higher than the proportion of correctional officers.[62]

RECRUITMENT

Given the relatively low salaries paid to correctional officers, as well as the fact that many individuals do not want to work with offenders, active recruiting becomes an essential operation in correctional systems. Institutional superintendents have traditionally hired practically anyone they could get. There were often fewer candidates than openings, so it was rare when a candidate was turned away. This situation is still true in some states, but conditions in most states have changed due to relatively high unemployment rates, improving working conditions and rewards, more effective recruitment strategies that were made possible when institutions were placed under the centralized control of state departments of corrections, and the passing of federal legislation impacting recruitment. The Equal Opportunity Employment Act of 1972, the 1973 Amendment to the Omnibus Crime Control and Safe Street Act, Executive Orders 11246 and 11375 (and Revised Orders 4 and 14), the Equal Pay Act of 1963, the Age Discrimination in Employment Act of 1967 and its Revision of 1977, the Rehabilitation Act of 1973 as amended, the Vietnam Era Veteran's Readjustment Assistance Act of 1974, and the Crime Control Act of 1976 all provide guidelines for equal opportunity in recruitment or compensation for job performance. Recruitment standards were rised when corrections became more centralized, and recruitment strategies were extended to minorities, women, veterans, and the handicapped as a result of the federal laws mentioned above.

The National Manpower Survey conducted by the Law Enforcement Assistance Administration[62] found that correctional administrators in institutions for adults were more likely to experience difficulties in recruiting than administrators in institutions for juveniles, and that correctional officers were more difficult to recruit than treatment or training personnel. Forty-two percent of all correctional administrators surveyed indicated difficulties in recruiting correctional officers. Minority recruitment is made particularly difficult by the negative image that many minority group members have of correctional systems and by the rural location of many correctional institutions, which puts them far away from the centers of minority populations. Some departments of corrections have gone so far as to hire advertising firms to aid in a state-wide minority recruitment campaign. Other departments seem to have made ony minimal efforts to comply with federal equal opportunity legislation. The data collected by the Equal Employment Opportunity Commission[62] in 1974 show that 41 percent of the correctional officers in South Carolina and 43 percent from Maryland were black, as compared with only 7 percent of the officers in Georgia and 5 percent of the officers in Texas, states that both have sizable populations of blacks.

As a result of the upgrading of standards for hiring, a high school diploma is now required for the position of correctional officer in 86 percent of American correctional institutions. Other common requirements are a physical examination (80 percent), one or more verified personal references (74 percent), no arrest record (61 percent), and a special correctional training certificate (26 percent).[63]

Are these standards adequate for the corrections profession? There is some evidence that the psychological characteristics of correctional personnel impact program outcomes, at least among juvenile delinquents.[38,77] There is also limited evidence to suggest that some correctional officers have personality problems that might predispose them to mistreat prisoners.[48,73] Only one in every five American correctional institutions attempts to weed out such individuals through psychological screening as part of the hiring process.[63] Even if all institutions began psychological screening before hiring, there is still the problem (discussed in Chapter 7) that one of the effects of being employed in a total institution may be an increased tendency to mistreat prisoners.

The Washington, D.C. Department of Corrections recently confronted this question, and decided not to use paper and pencil personality tests or clinical interviews as part of the screening process. Among the problems in using psychological screening tests that were identified in their examination of the issue were: (1) the tests do not take into account the nature of a correctional officer's job, which may interact with personality factors to provoke violence under certain conditions not revealed in the test; (2) there is some question as to the validity of paper and pencil personality tests; (3) there is considerable question about the cultural biases that have been written into these tests that might discriminate against minority applicants. The Department took the position that psychological support services for staff and implementing procedures for minimizing job stress would be more effective in reducing correctional officer misbehavior than psychological screening at the point of hiring. It was also recommended, however, that trained personnel psychologists be involved in the panel interviews in which applicants for correctional positions are evaluated.[95]

A great deal of money is spent to recruit prison officers in the British Prison Service. Approximately $700,000 was paid out for advertising in newspapers and other publications in 1978 alone.[44] The Prison Service also publishes an attractive color brochure entitled "Your Career in Today's Prison Service."[43] This illustrated booklet explains what a prison officer does on the job, what an active social life officers have with their peers, and the many generous fringe benefits associated with prison service work. The brochure explains also how to make application for the position, even going so far as to include examples of the questions that are in the 45-minute written admissions test. If the cost of traveling to the interview and testing site is more than $2.00, the Prison Service refunds the total cost of travel. The application form for the position of prison officer is bound with the booklet so that potential candidates who have become interested by reading the material can complete their application and mail it before they lose their curiosity.

The British recruitment effort produced 28,354 inquiries from men and 10,130 from women in 1978. Twenty-nine percent of the men who made inquiries completed applications and 10 percent of the men who completed applications actually joined the prison service for training. This was not the end of the attrition, for only 47 percent of those who joined for training actually began

Figure 8.1 Correctional officers at a Washington D.C. jail take part in a mock disciplinary hearing as part of their legal training. (Law Enforcement Assistance Administration.)

work in the Prison Service at the completion of training. This means that only 1 out of every 20 applications received by the Prison Service in 1978 resulted in a working prison officer, and even this figure is inflated because it includes former prison officers who returned to the service. Women making inquiries were less likely than men to complete applications, but male and female applicants were equally likely to join for training, and women who joined for training were much more likely than men to stay with the Prison Service upon the completion of training. Despite the extensive recruiting effort of the Prison Service, the 691 positions that were vacated through retirement, resignation, and promotion in 1978 could not be completely filled with the 550 individuals who began work after completing training.[44]

THE TRAINING OF PRISON OFFICERS

The most common type of training provided to correctional officers in American prisons is a short program of on-the-job training, which is found in less than three-quarters of all prisons. Periodic training workshops are held in two-thirds of the prisons, and a pre-work structured training program is found in six out of every ten institutions. Academy training is used to train officers in only one out of every eight institutions[63] despite the fact that correctional academies exist in more than 20 states.[21] Correctional officers in Canadian institutions are as likely as American officers to receive on-the-job training, less likely to be part of a structured training program, and more likely to participate in periodic training workshops.[63]

Pre-work training for correctional officers consists largely of practical rather than theoretical topics. Subjects such as first aid, riot control, disciplinary report writing, the legal rights of officers, weapons maintenance, and tactics for performing shakedowns take up most of the time in the training curriculum.[28] Officers are also warned against being easily manipulated by prisoners. The training guide used at the Colorado State Penitentiary gives the following advice:

One must always be alert for attempts to put something over. Prisonwise inmates have a great many tricks at their disposal for this purpose. It is the officer's duty, for instance, to stop a fight among inmates. Therefore, when they want to put something over, which requires that the officer be some place other than where he is, a phony fight is started to draw the officer away from what is really going on. He must be continually on the lookout for these "phony" occurrences.[23:24]

While officers are being instructed in the practical matters of the guarding profession, they are also learning the norms of the profession. They receive instruction in the formal official standards of professional behavior in their classes and in printed documents. At the same time, they are exposed to the staff code in informal relationships and verbal remarks. Official standards for behavior tend to be unrealistically rigid and demanding, although sometimes morally uplifting. The Correctional Officer Code of Ethics of the Alaska Division of Corrections says in part:

I will keep my private life and personal affairs above reproach as an example for all; maintain courageous calm in the face of danger, scorn, or ridicule; display self-constraint; and show concern for the welfare of others. Honest in thought and deed in both my personal and official life, I will be exemplary in obeying the laws of the land and the regulations of my department. Whatever I see or hear of a confidential nature or that is confided to me in my official capacity will be kept ever secret unless revelation is necessary in the performance of my duty.[2]

The content of correctional officer training in Alaska has a rather different tone. In the 119-hour training course, 46 hours are devoted to the procedures of the Division of Corrections, 12 hours to physical fitness and defense tactics, and 17 hours are used to inform candidates about basic field procedures such as firearms use and prison transportation. First aid is given 8 hours, criminal law 7 hours, and the remaining 29 hours contain all of the training materials earmarked for the subjects of supervision, human relations, and treatment. Methods of communication are covered in 2 hours, officer–prisoner relationships in 1 hour, deviant or abnormal behavior in 4 hours, and cross-cultural awareness in 4 hours. Subjects such as conflict intervention, prisoner violence, institutional counseling techniques, and transactional analysis, which were included in an earlier training format, were eliminated when the six-week training sequence was reduced to three weeks in 1979.[1]

When the Virginia Department of Corrections[93] decided to upgrade its personnel training programs, it set up a steering committee which looked at the possible outcomes of training as well as the content of the training. Major outcomes identified were: (1) changes in attitudes; (2) changes in knowledge about the job; and (3) the impact of training on job performance. A summary of research on these topics indicates that correctional officer training programs tend to have small but positive effects on attitudes toward self, prisoners, and the role of the correctional officer, large and significant impacts on knowledge, and virtually unknown impacts on job performance. It is therefore difficult to evaluate the training efforts that exist in American corrections, since the most important index of training success—job performance—is almost never used in training evaluation studies.

A typical training sequence for correctional officers includes some sort of formal classwork followed by on-the-job supervised experience. In addition, special courses may be offered from time to time by training officers in larger institutions or by consultants brought in from the state corrections office. Recent experiments with specialized courses include a pilot practical law course[32] and a three-day therapy marathon in transactional analysis.[37] Regional and national conferences—such as the "First International Training Conference to Meet the Needs of Female Offenders," which was offered in 1980—are usually attended by correctional administrators rather than officers and their supervisors.

Information on training activities in other nations indicates that both Third World[50,91] and industrialized nations[43,44,66] combine the use of a pre-work training academy with on-the-job training. India's *Model Prison Manual*[50] specifies that correctional officers should receive a basic training course for six months after hiring, and should receive refresher courses for two months out of every five years. The British system involves a four-week preparatory phase at a local institution followed by an eight-week course at an officer training school and then additional institutional training.[44]

The Danish training system is one of the most extensive in the world. A candidate who has passed the appropriate tests and been interviewed by a selection board begins a two-year probationary period by serving two months in a closed prison, one month in an open prison, and one month in a local prison. Considerable in-service training is conducted during these four months. The next part of the training is a five-month session at the training academy, which includes material in both practical and theoretical subjects. Students pay careful attention to the lectures, because if they fail to pass the written and oral tests that come at the conclusion of the five-month curriculum, they are dismissed from the position. Additional in-service training completes the two-year probationary period, after which the candidate is certified as a fully competent prison officer.[66]

THE STAFF CULTURE

When prison officers begin work, they are likely to be assigned to one of seven types of positions. According to Lucien Lombardo,[65] these are:

1. Block officers, who supervise major housing units.
2. Work detail officers, who cover areas such as the clothing room, commisary, hobby shop, and storeroom.
3. Industrial shop and school officers, who maintain order and security, but do not teach prisoners in vocational and educational program areas.
4. Yard officers, who are responsible for keeping order and maintaining security in the prison yard, a large open space in which prisoners congregate during free time or exercise periods depending on the institution.
5. Administration building officers, who have little contact with prisoners, and a great deal of contact with visitors from outside the prison.
6. Wall officers, whose function is to maintain outer perimeter security, and who carry out their responsibility in guard towers and similar structures.
7. Relief officers, who fill in for officers in the other six types of jobs, never staying in one position for very long.

While new officers are learning formal job performance standards for these positions, they are also being informally socialized into the staff culture.

The Socialization of Prison Officers

Newly recruited prison officers enter a world of extreme danger in which the slightest mistake can lead either to victimization by prisoners or to a reprimand from one's own supervisor. This makes new recruits extremely receptive to advice offered by veterans officers. In fact, their orientation toward formal training activities is determined more by their relationships with experienced officers than by their background characteristics.[4] Solidarity among officers is promoted by recounting anecdotes about prisoners and job conditions, some of which may be called atrocity stories. Atrocity stories warn new recruits about the viciousness and deviousness of prisoners, helping them to understand that the only support that they can count on will come from their fellow officers.[28] At the same time, veteran officers are assessing the capability of new recruits to support them unflinchingly when a crisis arises.[46] It is expected that new recruits will be manipulated by prisoners despite their formal and informal training experiences. With increasing experience, the rookie guards are expected to become more skeptical. Otherwise, they will be defined by veterans as being pro-prisoner, and their reputations in the staff culture will be ruined.[96]

The degree of effort that veteran officers put into the socialization of new recruits depends upon their definitions of the situation. If they believe that most new recruits will not stay more than a year or two, they may refrain from putting much energy into developing friendships with the recruits until this period has passed.[56] Another aspect of the situation having negative implications for new recruits is the viewpoint that recruits may take desirable job assignments away from veterans. This was a common outlook at Auburn Prison in New York State prior to 1970. Prior to that year new recruits were negatively received by veteran officers, and were given little help in adjusting to their new jobs. The only advice they received from experienced officers was very general, such as "do what your told," and "learn for yourself, the way I did."[65:121] Rookie officers quickly learned to be cautious around experienced officers because those officers were quick to report even the slightest infraction to a supervisor. The informal socialization experiences of new recruits at Auburn improved considerably after competition for desirable job assignments was reduced in 1970. Previous to that time, job assignments were made by supervisors without consideration of seniority. Experienced officers became more willing to give helpful advice when they were assured that the new recruits would not use the advice to wrest their desired job assignments away from them.[65]

There are many forces tending to mold correctional officers into a group characterized by a high degree of social solidarity. Their job may be somewhat stigmatized in the larger community; their changing shifts make normal socializing with nonofficers difficult; and the isolation of many correctional institutions often leads to the housing of correctional officers in close proximity to each other. In some cases, prisons may own apartments, trailers, and houses that are rented out to correctional officers.[56] The need for cooperation in order to reduce dangers on the job also leads to social ramifications in the lives of correctional officers.

These centripetal social forces among officers are counteracted in the modern prison by centrifugal forces that reduce solidarity to a point at which perhaps only half of the officers retain a positive orientation toward their co-workers.[4] In addition to the split between new recruits and experienced officers, there are also cleavages between whites and racial or cultural minorities; treatment-oriented and custody-oriented officers; and urban and rural officers. Just as a unified prisoner population heavily endorsing the convict code has become a thing of the past in most correctional institutions, staff solidarity has similarly withered away in many of these institutions. Lombardo[65] found that group solidarity among officers at Auburn Prison occurrred only in the face of threats from either prisoners or correctional administrators. At other times, prison officers constituted a highly fragmented collectivity rather than a cohesive group. Although 80 percent indicated a limited loyalty among officers based on their working relationships, few of them carried this loyalty beyond specifics of situations on the job. Most officers avoided involvement with co-workers outside of working hours, and there was a belief that officers who socialized extensively with other officers tended to become gamblers, heavy drinkers, and to suffer marital problems.

The Staff Code

Since the influence of colleagues is more important in determining the role conceptions and job orientations of correctional officers than their formal training experiences,[4] we cannot fully understand correctional officer behavior without examining the standards for behavior common in the staff culture. However, in institutions in which there is little consensus on appropriate job behavior among officers, the image of a monolithic staff subculture is misleading. This was the case at Auburn Prison, where no more than three out of every ten officers agreed on any given standard of behavior.[65]

Ben Crouch and James Marquart[28] believe that there are four fundamental tenets of work as a correctional officer. The first of these is that security and control are the most important aspects of an officer's job. In applying this standard to new activities that are introduced into prison life, any suggestion that these activities might reduce the ability of correctional officers to enforce security and control results in a negative judgment about these activities by the officers. The second tenet is that correctional officers must maintain social distance from prisoners. If they do not, they are likely to be "burned" when prisoners take advantage of them in moments of weakness. The third tenet is that officers must be tough and knowledgeable enough to dominate the prisoners in their care. Finally, officers must by savvy enough to avoid being duped by prisoners, and that requires that they know the formal and informal rules of institutional life so well that they will instantly recognize any deviation from those rules no matter how well it is disguised.

An even more detailed staff code was found by Clemmens Bartollas and his associates[3] at an Ohio institution for juvenile delinquents. The 12 general tenets of this code are listed below.

1. Only blacks "make it" here.
2. Unless you've been there, you don't know what it's like.
3. Be secure.
4. There is a certain way to inform on staff.
5. Don't take no shit.
6. Be suspicious.
7. Be loyal to the team.
8. Take care of yourself.
9. Stay cool, man.
10. The administration will screw you.
11. Don't listen to social workers.
12. Don't do more than you get paid for.

Common understandings among the staff at ths institution also included certain ways of treating the juvenile delinquents in their care. Some forms of neglect of duty were acceptable, while others were not. Under certain circumstances, it was appropriate to engage in exchanges of favors with the boys, even though these exchanges were technically against the regulations of the institution. The final area of general understandings about relationships with prisoners was the area of exploitation. It was acceptable to deceive the prisoners under certain conditions, but not to needlessly brutalize them, to facilitate their victimization by other prisoners, to aid them in making escapes from the institution, or to sexually exploit them.

Perceptions of Prisoners

There is a general tendency for correctional officers to view prisoners as having freely chosen crime as a way of life rather than as having been forced into it by environmental conditions. Officers who accept this view of prisoners are likely to see them as being lazy, adverse to work, and morally deficient.[28] This general negativism is qualified by the specific experiences that officers have with prisoners in their daily lives. On the basis of those experiences, they tend to develop a working typology of prisoners according to their perceived dangerousness, cooperativeness, decency, and so forth.[28,96] Approximately half of a sample of the staff in the Norwegian prison system believe that prisoners are generally the same as ordinary people, and nearly three-fourths of the staff members feel that prisoners are fairly reasonable on the whole.[5] This is remarkably similar to results from the Stateville and Joliet prisons in Illinois, in which slightly more than half of the officers held the opinion that prisoners were similar to guards, and nearly three-quarters of the officers agreed that most prisoners were decent people and that only a few of them were troublemakers.[55]

The relatively positive opinion that many correctional officers have of the majority of prisoners is balanced against the dangers caused by extremely antisocial prisoners and by the general structure of prison life. Assaults, riots, and other forms of prison violence are almost impossible to predict with any accuracy, so that correctional officers must be careful to be on guard at every moment.[65] No matter how well officers perform their jobs, dangerous incidents occur from time to time. The unpredictability of these incidents has many sources. There may be breakdowns of the physical plant of the institution. Illness or the resignation of staff members can leave crucial positions untended without warning. Unreliable rookie officers can be even worse than absent officers in that they may panic and fail to provide the expected support at the last minute in a crisis situation. Lack of communication between shifts often means that the signs of an impending explosion among the prisoners are not communicated from one shift to another. Prisoners may suddenly change their behavior patterns because of information that they have received from outside the prison—such as that their children are sick or that a contraband shipment of drugs has been intercepted by the police.[45] To all these catalysts of prison life unpredictability, we must add the mental illness present in some prisoners and the conflicts between prisoner groups that may not be apparent to correctional officers until it is too late to prevent a violent incident.

Almost all officers contend that even though most prisoners are basically decent people, they will take advantage of the guards if they get the chance.[55] This, combined with the unpredictability of trouble in prison life, leads to a compelling concern with maintaining complete control over the prisoners. The strategies used in controlling prisoners include: (1) the maintenance of social distance; (2) using profanity and "bluster"; (3) always saying "no" no matter what the request; and (4) keeping the prisoners off balance. New recruits are constantly warned to avoid becoming too friendly with prisoners. If they want an order to be obeyed, they should deliver it loudly and profanely so as to convey no irresolution to the prisoners. Rookies are told that since prisoners cannot be trusted, it is better to refuse all requests—except those that are incontestably legitimate—than to take chances. Prolonged staring, unexpected responses, inappropriate demeanor, and the use of words that prisoners do not understand are all techniques for keeping prisoners off balance. When these are used judiciously, they will keep the prisoners on the defensive and make them more wary of offending correctional officers.[28]

In judging prisoners, many correctional officers use racial or ethnic characteristics as an indicator of menace. The Spanish-language communication of Hispanic prisoners is particularly threatening to correctional officers since very few of them speak Spanish. Not understanding what is being said, these officers fear that dangerous or antisocial acts are being plotted. The tendency for black and Hispanic prisoners to develop tightly knit gangs and other subcultural organizations is also perceived as threatening by prison officers. In some correctional institutions, racial slurs—such as "niggers" and "spics"—are still commonly used among white officers when there are no blacks present.[28] There is also some evidence of discrimination against minority prisoners in job assignments,[41] disciplinary hearings,[103] and other officer–prisoner functions.[11,51] Racial discrimination practiced toward prisoners on a continuing—if often subtle—basis can easily carry over into the treatment of visitors[13] and other staff members.[8]

Correctional institutions vary considerably in the amount of racism that is expressed. At Stateville, correctional officers no longer use racial slurs, even in private discussions.[56] However, there is still evidence of institutional racism having its roots in the history of the prison. Because almost all recruitment of minority officers has occurred in recent years, very few of the top staff positions are occupied by those with a minority heritage. The result is that when white officers report racial problems, these tend to be with prisoners; but when black officers report racial problems, these are usually with their white supervisors. Interviews with a sample of officers who had terminated their employment at Stateville showed that 41 percent of the white officers and 57 percent of the black officers felt that they had experienced racial difficulties while employed at the prison.[54]

Relations with Supervisors and Administrators

Correctional officers are the foremen of institutional work. They are caught between the expectations of their supervisors and the behavior of the prisoners, just as foreman in industrial work occupy an intermediate position between the workers on the line and the managers.[85] Being closer to the prisoners, correctional officers may have a more accurate view of the severity of the problems of prison life than their supervisors, and consequently a more negative impression of prison atmosphere.[31] Officers may simultaneously feel that more attention should be given to the maintenance of security and institutional safety[61] and that their supervisors are stifling their creativity and initiative.[99] Relations between officers and supervisors are largely determined by institutional policy. If officers are treated little better than prisoners[12] or if administrators are political appointees who show little concern for the welfare of the officers,[97] relations between correctional officers and higher-level positions are negative. In institutions where administrators and supervisors show more concern for the welfare of officers, relations are more positive.[5]

A more recent element in prisoner–supervisor relationships is the entrance of the courts into correctional settings. When court decisions result in the transfer of power from officers to prisoners—at least in the eyes of the officers–they may become extremely negative toward administrators whom they perceive as having been too headlong in cooperating with the courts. They may react by exaggerating the severity of offenses by prisoners that they bring to the attention of the disciplinary board; by work stoppages; or by increased union activity in a number of other areas.[13]

However, recent studies of American correctional officers suggest that slightly more than half of them have a positive attitude toward supervision.[4,55] Researchers in one of these studies asked questions about relations between officers and both supervisors and administrators. Approximately 50 percent of the officers in this study felt that "...lieutenants are more sympathetic to the problems of inmates than to the problems of officers," but slightly more than 60 percent believed that "When a problem arises between an officer and inmate, the warden and other administrators usually support the officer."[55]

Job Attitudes

What attitudes do prison officers have toward their jobs? This varies with the type of institution, expectations of the individual officer, length of service as an officer, and a number of other factors. There is some evidence that correctional officers in treatment-oriented institutions have more positive attitudes toward their jobs than do officers in custody-oriented institutions. However, this does not apply equally to all officers. Those officers who have a strong custody orientation—perhaps because they have been employed for a long period of time in corrections and because they have limited formal education—will be happier in custody jobs than in jobs requiring treatment skills and the greater amount of collaboration with fellow-officers.[61] Officers who have a positive self-concept are also more likely than average to have positive job attitudes.[83] A study of prison guards in India found that job attitudes were more likely to be positive among older guards, those with longer service in prison work, higher rank, and those who had been exposed to in-service training.[85]

Prison work may be more rewarding than is commonly thought to be the case. A comparison of the job attitudes of samples of institutional officers and community corrections workers drawn from the states of Ohio and Kentucky found that institutional workers were significantly more satisfied with their jobs then community corrections workers.[83] Prison officers at two Midwestern maximum security prisons rated themselves above businessmen, politicians, and police officers.[16] In another study, prison guards at two Illinois institutions indicated that they preferred being a correctional officer to being a construction worker, a policeman, garbage collector, factory worker, auto mechanic, or security guard in a bank or store. Two-thirds of the officers thought that they would still be working in a correctional institution five years hence. Almost half of the officers felt very proud of their profession, and fewer than one in ten were embarrassed by it. The only negative feature in this scenario is that only a fourth of the officers said they would like to see their sons follow in the footsteps.[55]

The most common source of job dissatisfaction spontaneously mentioned by officers at Auburn Prison in New York was lack of support from the administration, supervisors, and other officers. This was mentioned by 54 percent of the sample. Other disgruntling factors spontaneously mentioned by the officers were physical danger and mental strain (mentioned by 50 percent), poor treatment by prisoners (28 percent), inconsistencies and communication problems in the general policies of the prison (28 percent), and difficulties in treating prisoners fairly (22 percent). A rather different pattern or dissatisfaction emerged when the officers were directly asked whether they experienced any discontent with specific areas of concern. These direct questions about job dissatisfaction found that 90 percent of the officers expressed some dissatisfaction with departmental policy, 72 percent with administrative policy toward prisoners, 68 percent with administrative policy toward officers, 50 percent with the expectations that others have of officers, 36 percent with boredom, 34 percent with routine, 30 percent with relations with supervisors, and 30 percent with the conflict between counseling and the enforcement of prison regulations.[65] This sounds like a rather extensive list of gripes at first reading, but it is not an unusually long list when compared with other occupational groups. Consider, for example, the percentage of students who squawk about their professors, and the even higher percentage of students and professors who grumble about the administration of the university.

Outcomes of Correctional Officer Socialization

Ben Crouch and James Marquart[28] have identified five end results of prison officer socialization. These are the abject failure, the limited failure, the ritualist, the successful officer, and the insider.

The abject failure leaves the prison service within the first year or two. Recruits who become abject failures may have had job aspirations or attitudes that were so far removed from the realities of correctional work that they felt compelled to resign, or did so poorly on the job that they were terminated.

The limited failure, by contrast, continues to work within the prison; but he is unable to attain the respect of fellow officers, superiors, and prisoners. Some of these individuals do not have the physical characteristics necessary to become successful as a prison officer, while others may be too limited in intelligence or lacking in self-confidence to project a successful image. These officers will receive minimally acceptable job ratings and be assigned to areas where they can do little damage. The difficulty in filling officer positions found in most correctional systems guarantees that these limited failures can keep their jobs as long as they want them.

Ritualists enter correctional work because of its security. Once they learn how to meet minimal job expectations, they can be sure they will have a paycheck until they retire. They maintain a low profile while on the job, and avoid taking responsibility whenever possible. They prefer to be assigned to positions in which they can mechanically perform their duties with a minimum of effort.

Successful officers quickly pass the ritualists by in promotional examinations. These officers master the staff subculture as well as institutional regulations, and move toward positions of increasing responsibility. Success requires that officers develop a formidable reputation that is then communicated from prisoner to prisoner so that new prisonrs are forewarned about them even before a personal encounter.

The distinction between successful officers and insiders is that in addition to performing their job functions well, insiders have personal and political attitudes that are similar to those of their superiors. Prison managers want to promote individuals who will not only perform well in their positions but also carry on the traditions of the prison. A young officer who does things well but who has personal or political attitudes perceived as too liberal may be considered a threat to the stability of the organization. Such individuals often find themselves passed by when promotions are made.

Changing the Staff Culture

The study of prison officers is still in its infancy. Descriptions of the attitudes, characteristics, and activities of prison officers are accumulating, and simple typologies have been constructed in a number of areas. The next step is to use these data to influence the prison officer culture in positive directions. For example, a study of correctional officers in a Southern medium security prison showed that officers who saw their jobs as being more complex had a tendency to be more professionally oriented, while those who saw their jobs as being more routine tended to be oriented toward personal gain rather than toward social service. Armed with this information, we may recommend to correctional administrators that if they wish to professionalize their staffs, they may want to emphasize the complexity of correctional work in training, job assignments, and other institutional activities. Other findings from this same study suggest that professionalism can also be promoted among correctional officers by emphasizing behavior modification (in a general sense) and humanitarian attitudes over simple custody and punitive perspectives in training correctional employees.[100]

Many of the behavior change techniques that have been applied to prisoners might also be applied to correctional officers in an attempt to improve their job performance. David Duffee[31] suggests that discussion groups meeting with the same set of officers over an extended period of time can develop attitudes and skills that are extremely useful in correctional settings. Officers in a project under his direction developed the ability to identify problems in institutional regulations and to formulate solutions for those problems. They also developed sufficient self-confidence to be willing to openly propose the solutions to prison administrators. As Duffee's group continued, it became clear that the major problem in the development of the officers was not their relations with the prisoners but rather their relations with their superiors in the correctional hierarchy.

ROLE CONFLICTS

To the extent that custody and treatment goals require different kinds of behavior by correctional officers, they may experience role conflict when these contradictory demands are placed upon them. About 1960, when rehabilitation was beginning to challenge custody as the major philosophy of incarceration, a comparative study of a number of institutions for delinquent boys found that institutions emphasizing treatment or placing equal stress on custody and treatment had higher levels of staff conflict than institutions emphasizing only custody.[106,107] Although these conflicts were between staff members, they probably reflected internal conflicts that were going on within each individual staff member. This combined with the already difficult problem of dealing simultaneously with administrators and prisoners[18] to produce severe role conflict.

In an institution that had adopted rehabilitative goals, officers were expected to continue to be disciplinarians and somehow also to be therapeutic in their relations with prisoners.[14] This dilemma might have been overcome had correctional administrators been able to define goals and performance standards that could encompass both roles,[70] but they were unable to do so.[24] Many officers in this situation feel that it is impossible to enforce institutional regulations adequately.[36] They continue to see themselves as guards rather than therapists, and to define the primary purpose of the prison as retribution. As the institution moves further and further away from a pure custody orientation, these officers begin to experience severe anomie.[14] Anomic correctional officers are disoriented, feel isolated from the prison administration, and suffer a great deal of anxiety. They are no longer sure of what to do in a given situation. If they treat prisoners as individuals on the basis of their psychological needs, they will be open to charges of bias and discrimination. They are forced to fall back on their custody role because it is the only certain thing in their occupational lives. If they perform their custody tasks adequately, they will not be punished by their supervisors. Treatment-oriented behavior toward prisoners is much more hazardous; in any case, failure to evince such attitudes will not result in a reprimand.[56]

A recent study of correctional officers in a large Midwestern maximum security prison found that the higher the role stress reported by the officers, the higher their custody orientation. Since a high custody orientation was associated with a high level of disciplinary reports filed against prisoners, one indirect consequence of officer role stress may be increased disciplinary activity.[80] Correctional officers tend to have more positive opinions about the police than about lawyers, presumably because the social control function of the police is closer to their own disciplinary role than is the lawyers' emphasis on the rights of the accused.[27]

More recently, correctional officers have experienced role conflicts when they wished to behave in a more treatment-relevant fashion, but were prohibited from doing so by institutional regulations.[79] One correctional officer says: "There's been times I could have done something for a guy but I couldn't because of the rules." Another points out "If I'd adhere to security in [my area] I couldn't leave to call to see if a guy's commissary account was straight. Lots of times in my job I've breached security."[65:270] The additional role conflict experienced by prison officers who have a concern for helping prisoners but who are charged with exclusively custodial tasks[25] may decrease over time as officers modify their expectations and develop a working personality.[28] Role conflict is a problem that should be attended to by prison administrators, for it is associated with a number of negative outcomes, including cynicism,[28,33] low job satisfaction, and punitive attitudes towards prisoners.[47]

Staff Conflicts

We mentioned at the beginning of this section that the grafting of treatment goals onto custody goals has resulted in increased conflicts among staff members as well as role conflicts for individual staff members. Some treatment staff members may have attitudes consistent with those of correctional officers, and they may get along well with these officers.[60] Except for this situation, the hiring of new treatment staff members in what was previously a custody-oriented institution is bound to result in conflict between staff members. This conflict begins in training sessions before new recruits have even begun work,[81] and occurs in juvenile institutions[97] as well as adult institutions.[52,96] Conflicts developing in an institution can become generalized to the level of state governments, where they continue between heads of major departments.[87]

When counselors were first introduced into Stateville in 1970, correctional officers feared that the counselors would undermine their control of the organization. The behavior of the counselors in defending prisoners soon led to correctional officers thinking of them as a fifth column within the walls.[52] The same pattern was repeated in the mid-1970s when staff psychologists were introduced into Australian prisons. The psychologists were seen as breaching security regulations, criticizing correctional officers, supporting the positions taken by the prisoners, and failing to have adequate allegiance to the institution and its regulations.[59] Correctional officers in one prison responded to these challenges to their authority by failing to send prisoners to counselors for interviews at the stipulated times. They also circulated stereotyped stories about the inadequacies of the counselors, much as they had always done about prisoners, and they lobbied through their union to have no new counselors hired until additional guards were hired.[96]

The Prospects for Continued Role And Staff Conflicts

Irving Piliavin and Arlene Vadum[78] proposed in 1968 that staff conflicts could be reduced by increasing the overlap in their roles. They found that prison officers who volunteered to counsel prisoner groups were slightly more positive toward treatment personnel than other officers. This solution has been proposed for houseparents[82] and correctional officers in a variety of settings.[57,58,90,94] Hans Toch[90] and Robert Johnson[57,58] have identified the treatment activities currently engaged in by a minority of correctional officers. These activities are effective in reducing prisoner stress and self-destructive behavior. Here are two examples of treatment-oriented behavior by correctional officers:

I talked to him several times in the yard. He said "what about this peer pressure thing, explain that to me." So I tried to sit down and tell him the term and just what it meant to him and everybody else and he said "gee, that's very interesting, I never looked at it that way." So then we got talking, and we'd sit down and talk about marriage and the problems he had with his children and that type of thing. We got along pretty good.[90:28]

When his grandmother died, he wasn't able to go to the funeral. Now I knew that he couldn't go and he was quite sure that he couldn't, yet he wanted somebody to check. So I got ahold of his counselor and we discussed this and I kept the inmate in the office when I did this so he would at least know that someone was trying to do something. Then when it was over and he discovered that he couldn't go, the man goes and broke down into tears.

And he sat there and he was crying. And of course the other inmates were going by the office and some of them, you know, had the tendency to snicker a little bit. And just in general conversation with the inmates, I made it plain to them that in my eyes it required some degree of a man to care that much about his family. And I made sure that this particular inmate was there when I said it to kind of reassure him that at least someone in authority didn't consider that crying and concern over a member of the family was childish, was babyish. It was the type of action that one would expect from a sensitive man...[58:65]

These recommendations promise improved services to prisoners and decreased conflicts between custody and treatment staff members. There is no doubt that both of these expectations are accurate. The problem is that they may purchase these accomplishments at the cost of increased role conflict toward correctional officers. At a time when many correctional institutions are beginning to deemphasize rehabilitation, thus perhaps decreasing role conflict, recent arguments about humanizing the role of the correctional officer point to a continued source of role conflict.

LIVING WITHIN THE REGULATIONS

One of the difficulties in attempting to upgrade professionalism in correctional officers is that performance criteria used to evaluate officers in their jobs are limited.[45] Although correctional standards have been established for almost every area of correctional practice, there are not, as yet, any standards for minimum levels of correctional officer job performance.[40] A 69-item scale measuring officer performance in the areas of routine job tasks, responsibility, leadership, emotional reactivity, resident relationships, and staff relationships has been tested in Canada,[101,102] and may eventually receive wide use in evaluating the job performance of correctional officers. In the meantime, the regulations printed in employee handbooks continue to be the main standard against which correctional officer job performance is measured. The implementation of these job standards is handled very legalistically, with employees receiving handbooks that often read like the state laws they are based on, and having to sign a receipt verifying that they have received a copy of the handbook.

It is generally agreed that correctional officers must ignore many minor violations of the regulations in order to do their jobs; yet they are subject to regulations that make the ignoring of any violation adequate grounds for immediate dismissal. Although dismissals almost never occur for ignoring violations of minor institutional regulations, this is a structured source of strain in the role of the correctional officer that can result in a number of management problems.

Michigan[74] has developed a comprehensive Employee Handbook listing five levels of corrective action to be applied to a correctonal employee who has broken a regulation: verbal reprimand, written reprimand, suspension without pay, demotion, and dismissal. This handbook concentrates on the punishments for forbidden activities much more than on the rewards for desired activities. Forbidden activities include criminal acts; improper relationships with employees, visitors, clients, or their families; the use of one's position for personal gain; personal involvements with clients; the excessive use of force; involvement with contraband; the use of illegal drugs; inattention to duty; failure to take proper security precautions; failure to make required reports; insubordination; excessive absenteeism; and absence without leave.

An employee who has been accused of violating any of these regulations is subjected to an investigation by his or her immediate supervisor, which results in a written report that may recommend that formal charges be lodged against the employee. Only if the offense is judged to be serious and well documented will the employee receive a written notice of the formal charges. Otherwise, the matter will be dropped or resolved by an oral or written reprimand. When the notice of charges has been received, the employee may request a fact-finding hearing or file a written response to the charges without a hearing. Should a hearing be requested, the employee may have a representative present, call supportive witnesses, question adverse witnesses, be given a written summary of the hearing, and be allowed to respond to the summary in writing before a final decision is made. These extensive procedural safeguards give employees some assurance that they will not be disciplined on the basis of a false accusation, misinterpretation, or personal prejudice by a supervisor. Nevertheless, it is clear that the job of the correctional officer has become much more difficult in recent years due to the introduction of an increasingly complex set of legal requirements. This parallels the development of legal requirements in the work of the police officer over the past decade.

Distribution of Offenses by Officers and Their Punishments

Hong Kong,[39] which has adopted the British system of prison organization, has published an exact list of the offenses committed by staff members in 1978 and the punishments they received. There were 987 offenses committed during the year in a total staff of 3990. The most common offense was arriving late for work (249 incidents), followed by absenting oneself from work without permission (245 incidents), neglect of duty (225), failing to carry out an order (168), acting in such a way as to bring discredit to the prison service while off duty (41), and making false, misleading, or inaccurate statements in connection with one's duty (12). There were eight incidents in which an officer was found to have used undue force in dealing with prisoners, two incidents in which an officer used his or her position for personal advantage, and two incidents of smuggling contraband.

The first impression one has of these offenses is that they are rather minor in character. To be sure, there were very few instances of severe misbehavior. However, such minor derelictions of duty as arriving late on the job or failing to carry out an order can result in the escape of dangerous prisoners, the victimization of prisoners or staff, and other dire consequences. This is one reason why prisons are administered so tightly.

The most common punishment meted out to offending officers in Hong Kong was to be assigned extra duty, which occurred in 194 cases. Other common punishments were to be fined between one and 50 dollars (159 cases), to be reprimanded (144 cases), to be fined between one and 50 dollars and also severely reprimanded (108 cases), or to be cautioned (106 cases). Only eight officers suffered forfeiture of pay, and 36 were dismissed from the prison service.

OFFICER–PRISONER RELATIONS

Two of the most important determinants of officer–prisoner relations in correctional institutions are (1) whether the institution is treatment-oriented or custody-oriented and (2) the officer–prisoner ratio. We have discussed the differences between treatment and custody institutions earlier in this chapter and in Chapter 7. In general, the relations between prisoners and staff in treatment-oriented institutions are closer and more positive than prisoner–staff relations in custody-oriented institutions.

Officer–prisoner ratios are important in that they indicate how much time staff members will have for interacting with prisoners. Where the ratio is high, the performance of institutional maintenance tasks will completely occupy officers so that there is very little time remaining for interaction with prisoners. In comparison, a low officer–prisoner ratio permits officers to get to know prisoners on an individual basis and to give them personal attention based on their individual needs. A high officer–prisoner ratio also allows staff members to feel more secure from the possibility of victimization by prisoners, which encourages a wider range of officer–prisoner contacts.

Table 8.1 presents officer–prisoner ratios in ten nations. They range from 1:1.61 in Denmark to 1:23 in the Ivory Coast. The United States has the least favorable officer–prisoner ratio of any industrialized country. In interpreting these ratios, it is important to remember that officers generally work three shifts, take vacations and weekends off, receive holidays, are too ill to work on occasion, and may resign without warning. All of this means that the average officer–prisoner ratio in practice is between four and five times the ratio stated in Table 8.1. The American ratio of 1:4.3 means that approximately 20 prisoners will be supervised by a single officer at any given time. Correctional administrators increase the effective officer–prisoner ratio by scheduling more officers on day shifts than the night shift and by assigning more officers to work in dangerous areas than in safe areas within the prison.

There is less variation in officer–prisoner ratios within the United States than there is among nations. As we see in Table 8.2, female institutions have a much higher officer–prisoner ratio than male institutions or co-correctional institutions. This is primarily because of the small average number of prisoners in a female institution. There are many positions in a correctional institution that must be filled by officers regardless of the number of prisoners. Thus, as prison populations drop, the officer–prisoner ratio becomes more favorable. The South is the region of the United States that has the fewest number of officers per prisoner, while the East has the most officers per prisoner. The officer–prisoner ratio in Puerto Rico is more typical of that of Third World countries than that of the rest of the United States.

Table 8.1. Correctional Officer–Prisoner Ratios, International

Nation	Year	Ratio
Canada	1976	1:2
Denmark	1973	1:1.61
Finland	1977	1:2.53
Great Britain	1979	1:2.83
Hong Kong	1978	1:1.92
Ivory Coast	1974	1:23
Japan	1979	1:2.87
Sweden	1978	1:1.88
Thailand	1978	1:8.39
United States	1976	1:4.3

Sources: Lawrence L.A. *et al.* "Survey of Correctional Institutions," *Quarterly Journal of Corrections* 1 (Summer 1977):35–51; Arne Lønberg. *The Penal System of Denmark,* Copenhagen: Ministry of Justice, 1975; Inkeri Antilla. "Corrections in Finland." *In* Robert J. Wicks and H.H.A. Cooper: *International Corrections.* Lexington, MA: D.C. Heath, 1979, pp. 130–122; Great Britain. Home Office. *Report on the Work of the Prison Department 1978,* London: Her Majesty's Stationery Office, 1979; T.G. Garner. *A Summary of the Work of the Prisons Department by the Commissioner of Prisons,* Hong Kong: Prisons Department, 1979; Michel Amiot, "A Brief Glance at the Penitentiary Situation in the Ivory Coast." *In* International Centre for Comparative Criminology and Abidjan Institute of Criminology. *Crime Prevention and Planning.* Abidjan, Ivory Coast: 1974, pp. 55–87; Japan. Ministry of Justice. Correction Bureau. *Correctional Institutions in Japan 1973,* Tokyo, 1974 (updated by hand to 1979); Sweden. National Prison and Probation Administration. *Kriminalvården, 1978.* Norrköping, 1979; Thailand. Ministry of Interior. Department of Corrections. *Annual Report 1978,* Bangkok, 1979.

Styles of Relating to Prisoners

Correctional officers differ in the way they interact with prisoners.[49] Part of the difference is due to personal preferences and characteristics, and part is due to structural factors such as the orientation of the institution and the specific nature of an officer's job. As an example of this last point, Ben Crouch[26] found substantial differences in staff–prisoner interaction between building settings and field settings in a Southern plantation prison. Building officers were able to maintain dominance over prisoners through organizational routines and by having a greater knowledge of what was going on within the institution, so that they did not have to confront the prisoners directly on a continuous basis. The field officer, on the other hand, had to use a much greater amount of personal dominance, physically and emotionally bullying the prisoners to keep them working. Both of these interactional styles are sharply different from officer--prisoner interaction in Japan, where there is a great amount of mutual respect based on an appreciation of each person's role obligations.[20]

Establishing Relationships

The initial experiences of rookie officers with prisoners tend to be negative ones as they are repeatedly tested to find out how easily they can be

Table 8.2. Correctional Officer–Prisoner Ratios, United States, 1976

Category	Ratio
Gender Classification	
Male	1:5.0
Female	1:3.2
Co-correctional	1:4.8
Geographical area (male prisons only)	
South	1:6.2
North	1:4.7
East	1:3.7
Midwest	1:4.8
California	1:6.0
Hawaii	1:4.6
Puerto Rico	1:16.0

Source: Lawrence, L.A. *et al.* "Survey of Correctional Institutions." *Quarterly Journal of Corrections* 1 (Summer 1977):35–51.

manipulated. The more indecisive, weak, or apprehensive new recruits appear to be, the more extensive the process becomes. They will continue to be pushed around and manipulated until they lay down the limits of prisoner misbehavior that they will tolerate.[28]

Not all prisoners participate in testing new recruits. Others are openly and genuinely friendly, particularly in treatment-oriented institutions. Another problem then arises: forming and maintaining normal friendly relationships with prisoners is against the regulations and the informal understandings of appropriate officer behavior in most correctional institutions.[75] Correctional officers who have become friendly with prisoners may feel the need to conceal the extent of that friendliness from both fellow-officers and other prisoners. Correctional workers are less likely to develop relationships with those prisoners who are perceived as dangerous than with other prisoners.[89]

Power and Control

As officers become more experienced, they learn when to enforce the rules and when to ignore violations. Violations of rules defined by officers as unnecessary are more likely to be ignored than violations of other rules. Even serious incidents are not always reported. Lombardo's[65] study at Auburn Prison found that reports were written on 48 percent of the incidents in which prisoners refused an order, 46 percent of the contraband incidents, 36 percent of the violence incidents, and less a quarter of all other kinds of rule violations. Negative sanctions are only one of three sources of authority than can be used by correctional officers to keep order. Prisoners can be rewarded for good behavior instead of being punished for breaking the rules, or officers can gain authority without the use of either punishments or rewards if they are respected on the basis of their position, personality, and how well they perform in their jobs.[29] Officers at Auburn felt that personal authority was more important in controlling prisoners than the use of rewards and punishments.[65] It is possible to achieve personal dominance even in the negative climate of maximum security institutions where correctional officers rarely discuss personal topics with prisoners or talk to them about any topic at all for more than a brief moment.[64]

Prisoners use a variety of techniques to reduce the power exercised over them by prison officers. In a classic article, Gresham Sykes[88] identified three of these techniques as corruption by friendship, reciprocity, and default. More recently, Leo Carroll[15] has added the techniques of confrontation and censoriousness. In corruption through friendship, prisoners work hard at becoming good friends with officers and then ask them for illegitimate favors. The officers feel the need for friendship during their working hours, so they are constrained to go along with the favors. Officers who are lazy often permit prisoners to do part of their jobs for them. Once this becomes institutionalized, they have suffered corruption through default, and the prisoners take on some of the authority previously vested in the officers.

Corruption through reciprocity is a more complicated process. It is extremely difficult for officers to maintain positive job evaluations without some degree of cooperation from prisoners. If there is too much disorder in an officer's area, or if the institutional count comes out wrong too often, the officer suffers reduced chances for promotion. The solution to this problem is to dispense favors to certain prisoners in return for their cooperation in keeping the operation running smoothly. If officers attempt to keep order by filing disciplinary reports instead of through reciprocity, prisoners may press them to file so many reports that administrators may decide that they are unable to cope adequately with their jobs.[68]

As respect for prison officers by prisoners has decreased,[55] two other power techniques have come to be more commonly used by prisoners. In censoriousness, white prisoners continually invoke the regulations in an attempt to convert the personal authority of the officers into rule by law. This limits the authority of the officers to the specific topics covered by the prison regulations. White prisoners are likely to use this technique in those institutions in which they are not strong enough to make direct demands upon prison officers. Confrontation is much more likely to be used by black or Hispanic prisoners. It is a technique in which prison officers are directly threatened into giving up some of their authority. It requires not only individual aggressiveness, but social organization into gangs and other groups large enough to confront individual officers on a 10-to-1 or 20-to-1 basis.[15] At Stateville after 1969, an officer desiring to take a prisoner to isolation often had to confront 10 or 12 gang members who surrounded the pair and verbally challenged his authority with great energy.[52] There is not enough room in isolation to lock up all gang members who behave in this way, so officers may have to back down from at least some of the confrontations that occur. Even worse, they may feel that they have to avoid enforcing institutional regulations in certain situations in order to minimize the chance of a confrontation that would be damaging to their authority, or because their families have been threatened by outside criminal associates of the prisoners in their custody.

THE DANGERS OF LIFE AS A
CORRECTIONAL OFFICER

The rate of assaults on prison officers was relatively low in the traditional maximum security institution. The main danger of assault in that setting came from prison riots that may have occurred in a given institution as infrequently as once in a decade. Although assaults on staff members are still much less common than assaults on prisoners, they have drastically increased in recent years. Riots are no longer the most important source of assaults on officers. They have been replaced by two forms of attacks by individuals or small groups: patterned spontaneous attacks and unexpected attacks.[8]

Patterned spontaneous attacks can be predicted by prison officers. They are associated with certain high-risk activities such as breaking up fights between prisoners, escorting prisoners to punitive segregation, and dealing with prisoners who are "high" on stimulant drugs such as amphetamines. From the individual viewpoint, these attacks on officers are spontaneous, but officers and administrators are aware of their patterned nature. In contrast, unexpected attacks cannot be predicted by any known technique. A bar of soap bristling with razor blades is hurled at the head of an officer who is walking down a tier in a housing unit. Unpopular officers are more likely to suffer unexpected attacks than officers who get along well with prisoners, but many attacks occur at random so that the characteristics of the officer are irrelevant at the time.[8]

In an institution where assaults on officers occur with regularity, officers will become extremely fearful of having contact with prisoners. Some of them will become increasingly repressive, hoping that tight controls will ward off violence. Others make special attempts to become friendly with prisoners in the hope that this will protect them from assaults. A third group retreat from involvement in prison life as much as possible and try to maintain a low profile.[56] A major concern of correctional officer unions is personal safety while on the job, and some unions have been willing to go out on strike or to engage in a "sick-out" when administrators seem unresponsive to union concerns about the victimization of officers. All of these reactions to anticipated victimization have negative effects on prison management, and none of them is particularly successful at avoiding victimization in the long run.

Job Stress

Approximately four out of every ten respondents in a sample of 231 correctional officers in Illinois rated correctional work as extremely dangerous. Most of the other officers rated correctional work as of greater than average dangerousness and only one in every 25 officers believed that correctional work was not dangerous at all.[55] The perception of dangerousness produces job stress, which in turn produces deterioration in mental and physical health and in job performance.

In an Australian study, the higher stress in maximum security institutions as compared with minimum security institutions was found to produce higher absence rates due to sickness.[10] High turnover is another possible result of severe job stress. The National Manpower Survey found an average quit rate of 19 percent per year among correctional officers in state institutions. By mid-1976, the turnover rate in most state institutions had risen beyond that figure. Five states were turning over more than half of their correctional officers each year, and 21 more turned over at least a quarter of their correctional officers per year.[71]

A study of stress among 143 correctional officers in New Jersey by Frances Cheek and Marie Miller[18,19] showed that the most stressful situations faced by correctional officers are those involving violence with prisoners, such as stabbings and prisoner disturbances. Those situations—such as work on the housing tiers and in the dining room and corridors, which require continuous surveillence of prisoners—are more stressful than job assignments in other areas of correctional facilities. Overall, however, the officers in the New Jersey study experienced more stess from administrative matters, including relations with supervisors, than with prisoners. Role conflict and role ambiguity, along with lack of job autonomy, produced a considerable amount of stress. This suggests that the way in which the prison itself is organized is a major source of stress for correctional officers—not just their interactions with prisoners—and that it is possible for correctional administrators to adopt managerial styles that will result in greatly reduced correctional officer stress.

The correctional officers in the New Jersey study denied feeling a great many negative stress symptoms, although they perceived them in their fellow-officers. They reported being lively and energetic as a result of job stress, and they reported behavioral reactions to stress that were aggressive and acting-out rather than passive and unassertive. Cheek and Miller characterized this as "macho denial," because they found much higher indications of job stress in direct reports of physical health, job performance, and marital relations than one would expect by chance. For example, the correctional officer rates of serious physical illnesses such as ulcers, heart disease, and hypertension were higher than the rates of these diseases among police officers. To the extent that job stress causes negative feelings towards prisoners, letting out tension in inappropriate situations, and tightening of discipline where that is not needed, it impairs job performance. It appears that excessive job stress is one of the ways in which correctional institutions produce a working personality among correctional officers.

PRISON OFFICER UNIONS

The emphasis on the rights of offenders and prisoners that began in the 1960s was eventually answered with some concerns for the rights of correctional personnel. Russell Oswald,[76] who was then the Commissioner of Correctional Services in New York, wrote in 1972 that correctional officers had the right to receive full public support. Several years later, Stanley Brodsky[9] codified the rights of correctional officers into six main areas. In his conception, correctional officers had the right to:

1. Participate in decision-making on institutional matters.
2. Be given clearly defined roles and receive appropriate loyalties from correctional administrators.
3. Receive education and training for career development.
4. Be given assignments related to their skills and abilities.
5. Be given behavioral science consulting to develop their ability to manage people.
6. Be allowed to develop specialized sets of knowledge and skills necessary to develop a sense of professionalism.

Correctional officers did not wait for administrators and scholars to proclaim their rights. They followed the example of organized labor in other settings and formed officer unions to demand their rights. Officers in the District of Columbia organized in 1956, and several other states followed suit in the 1960s. Officers in the Federal Prison System became unionized in 1968. By 1980, nearly half of the correctional systems in the United States were unionized. The major motivations for unionization were to improve wages, conditions, and hours, followed by problems of inadequate staffing and equipment, seniority, security hazards, and anxiety over the rising tide of prisoners' rights. In the absence of mutually acceptable agreements on issues such as these, officer unions have gone on strike on a number of occasions. There were six strikes in 1977, two in 1978, and nine in 1979. When a strike was called in Wisconsin during the summer of 1977, it was necessary to call in the National Guard in order to keep correctional institutions functioning.[67]

Although the strike is the activity most closely associated with unions, officer unions also participate in other types of activities to increase their bargaining power. These include lobbying, the use of publicity to sway public opinion, legal actions, "sick-outs," and slowdowns. Lobbyists hired by officer's unions work with both the executive and legislative branches of government. They present arguments and data to support actions and programs designed to benefit correctional officers. When unions can provide campaign workers, funds and favorable publicity for legislators, these public officials are unlikely to ignore their lobbyists.[104]

Officer unions publish their own brochures and also use the public media to develop support for their positions. Lawyers hired by officer unions can fight management actions in the courts. A "sick-out" occurs when a number of officers call in sick instead of formally going on strike.[104] When 100 correctional officers call in sick—as they did at the New Jersey State Prison on January 4, 1976[53]—the effect is not much different that of from a strike. The management of the institution is unable to carry on business as usual, but when "sick" officers can prove that they have visited their physicians, no legal action can be taken against them, even in jurisdiction where strikes by public employees have been declared illegal. Work slowdowns and temporary work stoppages are even milder substitutes for strikes. All of these techniques allow officer unions to select tactics at a level that is appropriate for the problem at hand, whether that problem is relatively minor or critical to the welfare of prison officers.

In an analysis of correctional officer unionism in New York, James Jacobs and Norma Crotty[53] argue that the rise of officer unionism has had effects on both prison administration and penal policy. Through the union, correctional officers have increased job security, control over work assignments, and participation in institutional decision-making. The participation of union stewards and other union officials in institutional decision-making has undermined the paramilitary hierarchical structure of the prison. Statewide collective bargaining has forced state correctional systems to become more specialized and more professionalized, which has limited the autonomy of individual correctional institutions and their administrators. Union activities in New York State appear to have blunted the traditional opposition of correctional officers to prison reform rather than to have enhanced it. Union officials realize that improving the prison for prisoners also means improving it for correctional officers. At least in New York State, the union has played a major role in a number of prison reforms during the 1970s.

FEMALE CORRECTIONAL OFFICERS

Throughout most of the 20th century, all officers having direct contact with female prisoners in their living areas were women and all officers having direct contact with male prisoners in their living area were men. This is appropriate in order to respect the privacy of prisoners. Unfortunately, social myths about the limitations of women kept them from being employed in male institutions even in positions that did not infringe on the privacy of the prisoners.[22] Since correctional institutions for women are small and few in number, this meant that the opportunity for females to become correctional workers was much smaller than the corresponding opportunity for males.

This all changed in 1972 when the Equal Employment Opportunity Commission published new guidelines on discrimination because of gender.[34] Since that time, female correctional officers have been employed in male institutions in almost all states, and they are being integrated in a number of Canadian institutions.[105] Even institutions for the most hardened criminals, such as San Quentin in California, now employ female correctional officers.[22] In a parallel development, male correctional officers have also begun to be employed in female correctional institutions. Approximately half of the states responding to a survey conducted by the New York Department of Correctional Services reported that male officers were also excluded from any assignment in female living quarters.[35] A more recent survey conducted by *Corrections Compendium* in 1979 identified only two women's prisons that totally excluded the use of male correctional officers.[69] Although there are no studies of female officers in male institutions or vice versa, there is no reason to expect that these arrangements will be any less satisfactory than the use of women as police officers,[22] which has rapidly increased in recent years.

VOLUNTEERS AS STAFF MEMBERS

The involvement of volunteers in the criminal justice system began in the early 1800s, but did not begin to rapidly expand until the early 1960s.[42] By 1971, at least 60–70 percent of all criminal justice agencies were utilizing the services of volunteers.[86] A 1975 study of 86 California corrections programs found an average of 72 volunteers in each program, each of whom provided nine hours of free service to the criminal justice agency per month.[42] The national volunteer movement has progressed to the point at which training materials have been nationally distributed for use in any criminal justice agency[92] and there is a national newsletter, *The VIP Examiner,* which functions to keep volunteers in local areas informed about programs and other developments in other parts of the country.

In America, volunteers are normally thought of as having no power in the prison setting; but in Great Britain, there are 113 Boards of Visitors with an average membership of 13 members who visit prisons and jails and who have extensive formal powers. Members of these boards are free to enter any part of a correctional institution at any time of the day or night, to interview any prisoner in confidence, to inspect all prison records, and to issue orders suspending prison officers, allowing prisoners special privileges, and to increase or remove disciplinary action against prisoners. The boards are made up largely of upper-middle-class men aged 50 and over, many of whom have had previous experience in the criminal justice system.[72] Volunteers in American corrections occasionally have some input into decisions about the state of prisoners, but they never have any authority over decisions about correctional officers, and their influence is extremely limited. They never have unilateral decision-making authority as do the British Boards of Visitors. American correctional institutions tend to make heavy use of college students as volunteers,[30,98] and other relatively powerless individuals. When professionals become involved in volunteer programs, they are usually therapists and educators rather than criminal justice professionals.

There are many reasons why administrators might want to make use of volunteers in prisons.

1. Correctional facilities are traditionally understaffed, and need any additional personnel that they can obtain.
2. Volunteers often have specialized skills, such as counseling skills or legal skills, that are not available in correctional institutions.
3. The introduction of volunteers into total institutions tends to break down the isolation of these institutions. This is extremely important in the case of prisoners who will be shortly released.
4. Volunteers can aid correctional institutions in community relations, both formally, which occurs when volunteers prepare news releases, and informally, as they promote the institution in the community.
5. Because volunteers often are trusted by prisoners, they may succeed in

mediating conflicts between prisoners and staff members, bringing both sides together by functioning as a trusted channel of communication.

6. When adequate funds are not available for certain programs, the only way to provide these programs in a correctional setting is to recruit volunteers as staff members.

7. Because volunteers are not in a position to use what prisoners say against them, they can sometimes be more useful than staff members as aids to personal growth among prisoners.

8. Volunteer work in corrections is growth-enhancing for the volunteers, so correctional institutions perform a service to the community when they involve volunteers. This can lead to a source of future corrections workers and can be helpful in institution–community relations.

9. Correctional administrators are always in the position of balancing community opinion against the needs of the institution as they make decisions. Volunteers can act as a barometer of community opinion and give administrators advice as to how certain policies might be seen in the community.[7]

The major problems in the use of volunteers include a high turnover rate, inadequate record-keeping and management, low volunteer dependability, staff opposition, and lack of full-time paid leadership.[86] It is not true that volunteer progams are entirely without cost. It is expensive to recruit, screen, train, and supervise volunteers. It is entirely possible that in some cases, these costs might be greater than the benefits to be obtained from using volunteers. One of the difficult hurdles of administering volunteer programs is to convince volunteers to see themselves as being essentially the same as paid staff members. They must be screened as carefully as staff members, and they cannot be expected to perform complex or sensitive tasks without extensive training. Even the small percentage of volunteers who have professional backgrounds require considerable reorientation to the institutional setting before they can be useful. Volunteers must follow institutional regulations as closely as paid staff members, and they must be supervised by full-time volunteer coordinators. In addition to all of these costs, there are costs associated with providing recognition to volunteers, such as banquets, identification cards, plaques, and newsletters, and there are also hidden costs such as the need to maintain adequate records of volunteer activities and to write appropriate recommendation letters for volunteers just as one does for paid staff members.

SUMMARY

Correctional officers are the largest and most important category of staff members in correctional institutions. They tend to be relatively poorly paid and under-trained for the complex interpersonal tasks to which they are assigned. Much of their learning about job performance comes after they have begun work, as they are socialized into the staff culture. Like the corrections industry as a whole, correctional officers have many conflicting demands made on them, and these result in role frictions. A major clash inherent in the role of the correctional officer is between the treatment needs of the prisoners and the custody requirements of the position. Correctional officers must juggle the interpersonal complexities of their jobs with conformity to detailed sets of institutional rules. Failure to follow these rules can result in instant dismissal. Relations between officers and prisoners conform to a caste model, with limited interaction across the caste line and reciprocal negative stereotypes between the officers and the prisoners. Correctional officers must establish control in their relations with the prisoners and must watch out for the corruption of their authority that can occur when they become too affable with prisoners. There is always the danger of assaults, and there is a high level of verbal abuse in most correctional institutions. Job stress is a major problem for many correctional officers. Recent developments in the role of correctional officers include the rise of correctional officer unions, which have improved working conditions in a number of states; the use of female officers in male prisons and vice versa; and the introduction of volunteers into correctional institutions to supplement the efforts of paid staff members.

REFERENCES

1. Alaska. Division of Corrections. Memo: "Entry Correctional Officer Course." Juneau, Alaska, September 27, 1979.
2. Alaska. Division of Corrections. "The Correctional Officer Code of Ethics." Juneau, Alaska, no date.
3. Bartollas, Clemens, Stewart J. Miller, and Simon Dinitz. *Juvenile Victimization: The Institutional Paradox*. New York: Halsted, 1976.
4. Blum, Lawrence N. *Sources of Influence in the Socialization of Corrections Workers*. Ph.D. dissertation, University of Michigan, 1976.
5. Bødal, Kåre. *Fengselstjenestemannen Har Ordet*. Oslo, Norway: Department of Justice, 1979.
6. Bodner, Harriet and Douglas Hanz. *1980 Pocket Guide: Instant Answers to Key Questions in Corrections*. New York: Criminal Justice Institute, 1980.
7. Bowker, Lee H. "Volunteers in Correctional Settings: Benefits, Problems, and Solutions." In *Proceedings, 103rd Congress of Corrections*. Washington D.C.: American Correctional Association, 1973, pp. 298–303.
8. Bowker, Lee H. *Prison Victimization*. New York: Elsevier, 1980.
9. Brodsky, Stanley L. "A Bill of Rights for the Correctional Officer." *Federal Probation* 38 (June, 1974):38–40.
10. Bullard, C. *A Sociological Study of Prison Officers in New South Wales: A Stressful Occupation*. Ph.D dissertation, University of New South Wales, Australia, 1977.
11. Burns, Haywood. "The Black Prisoner as Victim." *In* Michele T. Herman and Marilyn G. Haft: *Prisoner's Rights Sourcebook*. New York: Clark Boardman, 1973, pp. 25–31.
12. Burns, Henry, Jr. "A Miniature Totalitarian State: Maximum Security Prison." *Canadian Journal of Criminology and Corrections* 9 (1969):153–164.

13. Carroll, Leo. *Hacks, Blacks, and Cons.* Lexington, MA: D.C. Heath, 1974.

14. Carroll, Leo. "Humanitarian Reform and Biracial Sexual Assault in a Maximum Security Prison." *Urban Life* 5 (1977):417–437.

15. Carroll, Leo. "Race and Three Forms of Prisoner Power: Confrontation, Censoriousness and the Corruption of Authority." *In* C. Ronald Huff: *Contemporary Corrections: Social Control and Conflict.* Beverly Hills, CA: Sage, 1977, pp. 40–53.

16. Chang, Dae H. and Charles H. Zastrow. "Inmates' and Security Guards' Perceptions of Themselves and of Each Other: A Comparative Study." *International Journal of Criminology and Penology* 4 (1976):89–98.

17. Cheatwood, A. Derral. "The Staff in Correctional Settings: An Empirical Investigation of Frying Pans and Fires." *Journal of Research in Crime and Delinquency* 11 (1974):173–179.

18. Cheek, Frances E. and Marie D. Miller. "The Experience of Stress for Correctional Officers." Paper presented at the annual meeting of the American Academy of Criminal Justice Sciences, 1979.

19. Cheek, Frances E. and Marie D. Miller. "Managerial Styles and Correction Officer Stress." Paper presented at the annual meeting of the American Society of Criminology, 1979.

20. Clifford, William. *Crime Control in Japan.* Lexington, MA: D.C. Heath, 1976.

21. Cohen, Jay. "The Correction Academy: The Emergence of a New Institution in the Criminal Justice System." *Crime and Delinquency* 25 (1979):177–199.

22. Coles, Frances S. "Women in Corrections: Issues and Concerns." Paper presented at the annual meeting of the American Society of Criminology, 1979.

23. Colorado. State Penitentiary. *Correction Officers Training Guide, In-Service Training.* Cannon City, CO: no date.

24. Cressey, Donald R. "Contradictory Directives in Complex Organizations: The Case of the Prison." *Administrative Science Quarterly* 4 (1959):1–19.

25. Crouch, Ben M. "Role Conflict Among Correctional Officers." Paper presented at the annual meeting of the Midwest Sociological Association, 1976.

26. Crouch, Ben M. "The Book vs. The Boot: Two Styles of Guarding in a Southern Prison." *In* Ben M. Crouch: *The Keepers: Prison Guards and Contemporary Corrections.* Springfield, IL: Charles C Thomas, 1980, pp. 207–224.

27. Crouch, Ben M. and Goeffrey P. Alpert. "Prison Guards' Attitudes Toward Components of the Criminal Justice System." *Criminology* 18 (1980):227–236.

28. Crouch, Ben M. and James Marquart. "On Becoming a Prison Guard." *In* Ben M. Crouch: *The Keepers: Prison Guards and Contemporary Corrections.* Springfield, IL: Charles C Thomas, 1980, pp. 63–109.

29. Dawson, Sandra. "Power and Influence in Prison Workshops." *In* Peter Abell: *Organizations as Bargaining and Influence Systems.* London: Heineman, 1975, pp. 151–186.

30. Denfeld, D. "The Role of Student Volunteers in Corrections Today." Paper presented at the annual meeting of the American Correctional Association, 1973.

31. Duffee, David. "The Correction Officer Subculture and Organizational Change." *Journal of Research in Crime and Delinquency* 11 (1974):155–172.

32. Ellis, Anne M. and David Fulghun. "Correctional Officers Participate in Pilot Practical Law Course." *American Journal of Correction* 40 (March–April 1978):26–27.

33. Farmer, Richard E. "Cynicism: A Factor in Corrections Work." *Journal of Criminal Justice* 5 (1977):237–246.

34. Fitzmaurice, Patricia. "Employment and Assignment of Male and Female Correction Officers." Albany, NY: New York Department of Correctional Services, 1978.
35. Fitzmaurice, Patricia. "Utilization of Male Correction Officers in Female Facilities." Albany, NY: New York Department of Correctional Services, 1978.
36. Francois, J. "Function of Supervisors, Their Difficulties and Their Training." *Notes on Criminology and Sociopathology* 14 (1977):1–21.
37. Frazier, Thomas L. "Transactional Analysis Training and Treatment of Staff in a Correctional School." *Federal Probation* 36 (September 1972):41–46.
38. Furse, G.A. *Whitehorn-Betz A-B' Variable and Personality Correlates of Correctional Personnel as They Affect Helper Success Rate with Juvenile Offenders*. Ph.D dissertation, Temple University, 1975.
39. Garner, T.G. *The Summary of the Work of the Prisons Department by the Commissioner of Prisons*. Hong Kong, 1978.
40. Gilbert, Michael J. "Developing Performance Standards for Correctional Officers." *Corrections Today* 42 (May–June 1980):8–9, 42–43, 52–53.
41. Goldfarb, Ronald. *Jails, the Ultimate Ghetto of the Criminal Justice System*. Garden City, NY: Doubleday, 1976.
42. Goodwin, Robert W. "Citizens in Corrections: An Evaluation of 13 Correctional Volunteer Programs." Sacramento, CA: California Youth Authority, 1976.
43. Great Britain. Home Office. "Your Career in Today's Prison Service." London: Her Majesty's Stationery Office, 1976.
44. Great Britain. Home Office. *Report on the Work of the Prison Department 1978.* London: Her Majesty's Stationery Office, 1979.
45. Guenther, Anthony L. "On Prisoner Processing—Some Occupational Dimensions of Correctional Work." *In* Marc Riedel and Pedro A. Valis: *Treating the Offender— Problems and Issues*. Beverly Hill, CA: Sage, 1977, pp. 75–85.
46. Guenther, Anthony L. and Mary Guenther. "Coping with Uncertainty: Role Dilemmas Among Penitentiary Correctional Officers." *Georgia Journal of Corrections* 1 (1972):55–63.
47. Hepburn, John R. and Celesta Albonetti. "Role Conflict in Correctional Institutions: An Empirical Examination of the Treatment—Custody Dilemma Among Correctional Staff." *Criminology* 17 (1980):445–459.
48. Holland, T.R. "Personality Patterns Among Correctional Officer Applicants." *Journal of Clinical Psychology* 32 (1976):786–791.
49. Hommant R.J. "Correlates of Satisfactory Relations Between Correctional Officers and Prisoners." *Journal of Offender Counseling Services and Rehabilitation* 4 (1979):53–62.
50. India. *Model Prison Manual. Faridabad: Government of India Press, 1970.*
51. Jackson, George. *Soledad Brother: The Prison Letters of George Jackson*. New York: Bantam, 1970.
52. Jacobs, James B. *Stateville: The Penitentiary in Mass Society*. Chicago: University of Chicago Press, 1977.
53. Jacobs, James B. and Crotty, Norma M. *Guard Unions and The Future of the Prisons*. Institute of Public Employment, Cornell University: IPE Monograph No. 9, 1978.
54. Jacobs, James B. and Mary Greer. "Drop-Outs and Rejects: Analysis of the Prison Guard's Revolving Door." *Criminal Justice Review* 2 (1977):57–70.
55. Jacobs, James B. and Lawrence J. Kraft. "Integrating the Keepers: A Comparison of Black and White Prison Guards in Illinois." *Social Problems* 25 (1978):304–318.

56. Jacobs, James B. and Harold G. Retsky. "Prison Guard." *Urban Life* 4 1975:5–27.
57. Johnson, Robert, "Ameliorating Prison Stress: Some Helping Roles for Custodial Personnel." *International Journal of Criminology and Penology* 5 (1977):263–273.
58. Johnson, Robert, "Informal Helping Networks in Prison: The Shape of Grass-Roots Correctional Intervention." *Journal of Criminal Justice* 7 (1979):53–70.
59. Knight, I.A. "Prison Officer's View of Prison Psychologist—Australia." Research and Information Series No. 12, Perth, Western Australia, Department of Corrections. 1976.
60. Lacy, Alice B. *Staff Interaction in a Women's Prison: A Sociological Drama.* Ph.D. dissertation, University of Maryland, 1973.
61. Lane, M.D. *Relationship of Position Institution and Selected Variables to Role Expectations of Correctional Officers and Perceptions of Their Institutional Environment.* Ph.D. dissertation, University of Virginia, 1977.
62. Law Enforcement Assistance Administration. *The National Manpower Survey of the Criminal Justice System, Vol. 3, Corrections.* Washington, D.C.: Government Printing Office, 1978.
63. Lawrence, L.A. *et al.* "Survey of Correctional Institutions." *Quarterly Journal of Corrections* 1 (Summer 1977):35–51.
64. Leonard, Rebecca. *Communication in the Total Institution: An Investigation of Prisoner–Guard Interaction in a State Penitentiary.* Ph.D. dissertation, Purdue University, 1976.
65. Lombardo, Lucien X. *The Correction Officer: A Study of the Criminal Justice in His Work Place. Ph.D dissertation, State University of New York at Albany, 1978.*
66. Lønberg, Arne. *The Penal System of Denmark.* Copenhagen: Department of Prison and Probation, Ministry of Justice, 1975.
67. "Look for the Union Label." *Corrections Compendium.* 4 (February 1980):1–6.
68. Mann, William E. *Society Behind Bars; A Sociological Scrutiny of Guelph Reformatory.* Toronto: Social Science Publishers, 1967.
69. "Man on the Floor." *Corrections Compendium.* 3 (October 1979):1–2.
70. Maxim, Paul. "Treatment—Custody Staff Conflicts in Correctional Institutions—A Re-Analysis." *Canadian Journal of Criminology and Corrections* 18 (1976):379–386.
71. May, Edgar. "Prison Guards in America—The Inside Story." *In* Ben Crouch: *The Keepers: Prison Guards and Contemporary Corrections.* Springfield, IL: Charles C Thomas, pp. 111–137.
72. McConville, Sean, "Boards of Visitors of Penal Institutions." *British Journal of Criminology* 15 (1975):391–394.
73. McGurk, D.J. "Personality Types Among Prisoners and Prison Officers—an Investigation of Megargee's Theory of Control." *British Journal of Criminology* 19 (1979):31–49.
74. Michigan. Department of Corrections. *Employee Handbook.* Lansing, MI, 1979.
75. Millham, Spencer, Roger Bullock, and Kenneth Hosie. *Locking Up Children: Secure Provision within the Child-Care System.* London: Saxon House, 1978.
76. Oswald, Russell G. "Rights of Correctional Personnel." *American Journal of Correction* 34 (November–December 1972):18,20.
77. Palmer, Ted. "The Youth Authority's Community Treatment Project." *Federal Probation* 38 (March 1974):3–14.
78. Piliavin, Erving M.and Arlene C. Vadum. "Reducing Discrepancies in Professional and Custodial Perspectives." *Journal of Research in Crime and Delinquency* 5 (1968):35–43.

79. Pogrebin, Mark. "Role Conflict Among Correctional Officers in Treatment Oriented Correctional Institutions." *International Journal of Offender Therapy and Comparative Criminology*. 22 (1978):149–155.

80. Poole, Eric D. and Robert M. Regoli. "Role Stress, Custody Orientation, and Disciplinary Actions: A Study of Prison Guards." *Criminology* 18 (1980):215–226.

81. Prather, Jerry R. *Congruence Among Measures of Attitudes and Valued Judgments of Training Needs, within Job Classification, Working for the Federal Prison System.* Ph.D. dissertation, University of Oklahoma, 1975.

82. Rettig, Richard G. "A Modest Proposal: Houseparents as Agents of Change in the Juvenile Justice System." Unpublished manuscript, Oral Roberts University, 1979.

83. Richardson, John G. *A Comparison of Professional Institutional Corrections Workers and Professional Community Corrections Workers on Job Satisfaction and Self Concept.* Ph.D. dissertation, University of Cincinnati, 1975.

84. Robel, Don. "A Survey of Correctional Manpower, Montana." Boulder, CO: Western Interstate Commission for Higher Education, 1969.

85. Sandhu, Harjit S. and Donald E. Allen. "The Prison Guard: Job Perceptions and In-Service Training in India." *Indian Journal of Social Work* 32 (1971):115–120.

86. Scheier, Ivan H. *et al. Guidelines and Standards for the Use of Volunteers in Correctional Progams.* Washington, D.C.,: Government Printing Office, 1972.

87. Sebring, Robert H. and David Duffee. "Who are the Real Prisoners? A Case of Win–Lose Conflict in a State Correctional Institution." *Journal of Applied Behavioral Science* 13 (1977):23–41.

88. Sykes, Gresham M. "The Corruption of Authority and Rehabilitation." *Social Forces* 34 (1956):257–262.

89. Tennenbaum, David J. "'Dangerousness' within a Juvenile Institution." *Journal of Criminal Justice* 6 (1978):329–345.

90. Toch, Hans. "Is a 'Correctional Officer,' By Any Other Name, A 'Screw'?" *Criminal Justice Review* 3 (1978):19–35.

91. United Nations. Social Defense Research Institute. *Social Defense in Uganda: A Survey for Research.* Rome, 1971.

92. VIP—National Council on Crime and Delinquency. *National Education—Training Program for Colleges—Professionals—Citizens.* Royal Oak, MI, no date.

93. Virginia. Department of Corrections and Division of Justice and Crime Prevention. *The Development of a Training Evaluation Methodology for the Virginia Department of Corrections.* Richmond, 1977.

94. Ward, R.J. "Correctional Officers with Case Loads." *Offender Rehabilitation* 2 (1977):31–38.

95. Washington, D.C. Department of Corrections. "Concept Paper on Psychological Training and Support Services for Institutional Staff," no date.

96. Webb, G.L. and David G. Morris. *Prison Guards: The Culture and Perspective of an Occupational Group.* Austin, TX: Coker Books, 1978.

97. Weber, George H. "Conflicts Between Professional and Non-Professional Personnel in Institutional Delinquency Treatment." *Journal of Criminal Law, Criminology and Police Science* 48 (1957):26–43.

98. Welch, William. "College Students as Volunteer Correctional Counselors." *Quarterly Journal of Corrections* 1 (Winter 1977):31–33.

99. Wicks, R.J. *Guard: Society's Professional Prisoner.* Houston, TX: Gulf Publishing, 1980.

100. Williams, J. Sherwood and Charles W.Thomas. "Attitudinal Correlates of Profes-
     sionalism: The Correctional Worker." *Criminal Justice Review* 1 (1976):120–125.
101. Willis, J. "Preliminary Data on the Correctional Personnel Rating Scale." *Canadian
     Journal of Criminology* 21 (1979):71–80.
102. Willis, J. and P. Savage. "Correctional Personnel Rating Scale." *Corrective and
     Social Psychiatry and the Journal of Behavior Technology Methods and Therapy.* 25
     (1979):6–14.
103. Wright, Eric O. *The Politics of Punishment: A Critical Analysis of Prisons in
     America.* New York: Harper and Row, 1973.
104. Winne, John M., Jr. *Prison Employee Unionism: The Impact on Correctional
     Administration and Programs.* Washington, D.C.: Government Printing Office,
     1978.
105. "You've Come a Long Way, Baby" *Corrections Compendium* 3 (July 1979):1–3.
106. Zald, Mayer N. "Power Balance and Staff Conflict in Correctional Institutions."
     Administrative Science Quarterly 6 (1962):22–49.
107. Zald, Mayer N. and David Street. "Custody and Treatment in Juvenile Institutions:
     An Organizational Analysis." *Crime and Delinquency* 10 (1964):249–256.

Chapter 9

Administrators and Administration

There are three main groups of administrators in state correctional systems. First, there are those charged with the operation of the state systems as a whole. Second, there are the wardens and superintendents, who head the institutions, and major department heads such as associate superintendents for treatment and associate superintendents for custody. Finally, there are middle-level correctional managers such as educational administrators, custody officers at the level of lieutenant and higher, and hospital administrators. The following sections briefly describe each of these types of administrators.

SYSTEMWIDE ADMINISTRATORS

There are also centralized state departments of corrections. Many of these departments go beyond providing training and other support services and general guidance for wardens and supervisors. So many decisions about individual institutions are now made in these state corrections departments that institutional administrators have had to develop a new leadership style to replace the total authoritarian local control that characterized traditional prisons. Unfortunately, many of them have been slow to move in this direction.

The most common title for the head of a state department of corrections is Director of Corrections. Like the wardens and superintendents of institutions, the directors of state correctional agencies are usually appointed by the Governor. Because the Director of Corrections is the head of a major state governmental unit, confirmation by the state legislature is often required to ratify an appointment.

State central offices are usually legislatively mandated to assure that statewide programs are properly administered in keeping with the intent of enabling legislation, and that they meet local needs. Although institution heads often see state central office activities as interfering in their own spheres of influence, a number of important services are provided to local institutions by some state central offices. These include facilitating the exchange of knowledge among institution heads and between the university research community and correctional practitioners, sponsoring programs for staff development, providing technical support for fiscal and program accountability and evaluation, increasing the amount of decision-making information available to administrators through a uniform data-reporting system, and providing specialized services such as legal advice, collective bargaining expertise, and psychiatric consultations.

There are many administrative positions available in state departments of corrections. For example, the Nebraska Department of Correctional Services has four division heads who report directly to the Director. They are responsible for juvenile services, adult services, community-centered services, and administrative services. There are various units under each new division head. The division of administrative services contains units for physical operations, personnel, engineering, and research and statistics; and the other divisions are also composed of three or four units. Nebraska has a relatively small correctional system. Other states have proportionately larger and more complex central offices.[49]

THE WARDEN

In answer to questions from members of a legislative subcommittee, the superintendent of a Wisconsin correctional institution made the following statement:

There are always gripes and problems—no one is happy to be locked up. Residents should try constructive means, e.g., ICRS memos, request slips, etc. instead of riots. There are always rumors of riots. The visiting policy was reviewed with the Division of Corrections and considered ample. More work/employment has been requested. There are always budget problems. YO Legislation is hard to administer. I have a good staff, everyone has problems and weaknesses. There is a need to develop an orderly plan to get things done.[26:8]

Wardens tend to take a pragmatic view of prison administration. If their employees seem to be making a reasonable effort, then they are "doing the best they can." If things are not going quite right, it is because the prisoners are not being reasonable, there are not sufficient resources to accomplish established goals, there is too much interference from the state corrections office, etc. Wardens will argue that they have made a "good faith' showing in doing their best to carry out their assigned responsibilities with the information and resources at hand.

Some wardens stay outside their institutions almost all the time and have little idea of what occurs within the walls, especially if they are political appointees (as was common in the past) who have not had a career in correctional work. In contrast, other wardens walk freely anywhere that they want within their institutions and are available for conferences with prisoners and staff alike on daily basis. Most institutional administrators fall between these two extremes.

Walter Lunden[32] found that wardens historically have had a short tenure in office. The main reason cited for the high turnover was a change of administration and politics. The Oregon State Prison at Salem had 17 different wardens between 1900 and 1953. With turnover rates such as this, it is easy to understand why correctional administration was a sorry field in most states until the 1960s. By 1975, 63 percent of all adult corrections administrators had college degrees, as did 90 percent of juvenile corrections administrators. Nearly three-quarters of these executives had attended special courses in personnel management, and more than half of them had special training in budget management, facility management, criminal and correctional law, classification, and riot prevention and control.[29]

Although correctional administrators have certain problems in common, and there are certainly specific principles of administration applicable to all institutions, there are also significant differences between institutions, so that each administrator must modify the general principles with respect to the specific institutional situation. This is one of the reasons why corrections is an art as well as a science.

Even such basic statistics as the number of administrators per institution within a single correctional system show considerable variation. In the Federal Bureau of Prisons, the number of administrators per institution in 1973 varied from 1 to 14. This was partially a function of size, but not entirely. The second smallest institution in terms of population had 14 administrators, and the largest institution had only nine. Institutions holding between 500 and 1000 prisoners varied between three and eight administrators. The ratio of correctional officers to prisoners also varied, as did the ratio of case management personnel to prisoners. Differences in the cost per prisoner per year ranged from $2593 to $11,805.[60] These variations in basic statistics only begin to suggest the profound differences in architecture, quality of staffing, local community conditions, and other factors that result in differences between correctional institutions.

A survey of correctional administrators conducted by the Correctional Economics Center of the American Bar Association[2] found that the problems rated as extremely serious or major by most administrators were obtaining sufficient funds, offering competitive salaries to attract qualified personnel, providing continuity between institutional and community programs, gaining access to an adequate amount of evaluation research, receiving feedback on ex-offenders' progress, relating the cost to the effectiveness of programs, and having an information system that provides the data needed for decision-making. The administrators surveyed were less concerned about problems having to do with learning modern budgeting techniques, staff turnover, developing opportunities for advancement for employees, controlling the intake of offenders, having adequate enabling legislation for correctional planning, and the geographic isolation of correctional institutions. When asked how they would like to see physical resources reallocated in the future, their top priorities were community-based services, treatment programs in general, and alternatives to services provided by departments of corrections. They felt that federal subsidies could be most appropriately used to finance new or experimental programs and services rather than for new construction, the general operating budget, or upgrading and improvement of the coordination of local correctional services.

The Double-Bind Dilemma and Administrative Decision-Making

Perhaps the most outstanding characteristic of the role of warden is its double-bind nature. Correctional administrators are often put in the position of making decisions in which there are unresolvable dilemmas. These are sometimes the result of cross-pressures in which there are conflicting interest groups, only one of which can possibly be satisfied by any decision that might be made. An attempt to make a middle-ground decision is more likely to displease all groups than to satisfy any one of them. At other times, dilemmas are created by the incapatibility of the conflicting goals of imprisonment—e.g., the old treatment versus custody dilemma.

The implementation of most kinds of treatment programs involves weakening the degree of social control exerted over prisoners. If they are released on furloughs or allowed to govern themselves in therapeutic communities, there is an enhanced danger of the commission of new crimes or the development of potentially scandalizing institutional conditions. Rehabilitative programs also tend to be associated with greater institutional permeability and a loss of information control by prison administrators, which may lead to negative publicity and a public outcry about conditions at the prison. Tight institutional control up to the point of release mnimizes institutional problems for administrators, but makes the least possible contribution to prisoner rehabilitation. The number of escapes from a minimum security unit or a community corrections program will invariably be much higher than the number of escapes from a maximum security prison.

Another dimension of the custody–treatment dilemma is the problem of centralized versus decentralized authority. Treatment-oriented institutions tend to be decentralized, which makes the administrator's job more complex and difficult and lessens administrative control over the institution. Paradoxically, the implementation of treatment programs may also result in increased instability among the prisoners as they are forced to confront their personal problems instead of ignoring them. This can lead to increased victimization rates, escapes, and riots.

Another dilemma faced by prison administrators is whether to push for the release of prisoners based on their improvement in the institution or to be content with parole board policies that release prisoners largely on the basis of public opinion and sentence structure. Administrators can use the rewarding of prisoners for good behavior in the institution as a social control device, thus making their jobs easier, but this may lead to higher recidivism rates or at least to greater community opposition when exemplary prisoners who had committed serious crimes are released earlier than poorly behaved prisoners who had committed less serious crimes.

Liberal community groups and prisoner groups generally press for prison reform and the liberalization of prison regulations. Other community groups and staff members tend to lobby for increased institutional control and an emphasis on the punishment of either all prisoners (in the case of conservative community groups) or "uncooperative" prisoners (in the case of staff members). There are also professional demands placed on the warden by state departments of corrections, the courts, accreditation procedures, federal regulations, and state and local laws. Cross-pressuring from all of these sources means that correctional administrators can never relax and feel assured that things will go smoothly for a while. The problem of cross-pressuring is exacerbated by the inadequate information available to correctional decision-makers on most topics. Part of this is due to a real deficit in existing research on correctional administration and related topics, and part is due to problems of knowledge dissemination, lack of time or ability to assimilate knowledge that has been properly disseminated, or lack of interest in using research findings as one of the bases for prison decision-making.[10]

The researchers involved in the Comparative Study of Juvenile Correctional Institutions Project at the University of Michigan have observed that executive decision-making among correctional administrors is hampered by a critical lack of information, which results in a considerable discrepancy between fact and belief. The executives that they worked with seemed to have limited time perspectives and were aware of few alternatives for institutional programming.[63] A study of perceptions about the usefulness of research held by correctional administrators found that in-house research units were the main source of research material. However, 24 of the 74 agencies surveyed had no full-time researchers on their staffs, and most of the rest had fewer than five research employees. Only eleven agencies had six or more full-time research employees. In addition, most of the agencies used less than one-tenth of one percent of their budgets for research *and* statistics.[1] These findings suggest that the utilization of in-house research by most correctional administrators is extremely limited.

The result of these double-binds and problems in the utilization of research is that many correctional administrators suffer from what John Meyer[35] refers to as "inverted decision-making." By inverted decision-making, Meyer means decisions based on values instead of facts, incomplete or otherwise inadequate information, goal statements derived from the same values used to make the decision, an emphasis on tradition, and a feeling of isolation from the other elements of the criminal justice system. Managers who make inverted decisions assess programs by comparing them with the values and norms used to formulate them, and this cycle persists indefinitely with little prospect for change or improvement in the efficiency or effectiveness of correctional programs. Although the prevalence of inverted decisions in correctional management has decreased since Meyer made his comments in 1972, this is still a major problem in the less professionalized correctional systems.

MIDDLE-LEVEL CORRECTIONAL MANAGERS

Middle-level managers are correctional employees such as clinical supervisors, hospital administrators, prison industries supervisors, business managers, educational administrators, and custody officers at the level of lieutenant and higher. They are only one or two steps removed from the warden or superintendent of the institution. They supervise correctional officers, teachers, counselors, and a variety of other civilian employees, supplementd by inmate workers. Relationships between administrators and middle managers are crucial in assuring that institutional policies are carried out. Administrators may be committed to a policy of equal opportunity and affirmative action, but if there is a lack of consensus and communication between them and middle-level managers, the institution may fall short of affirmative action goals in the final analysis. Poor relations between administrators and middle managers also impede the flow of information to administrators about what is going on within the institution. If this continues over an extended period of time, a degree of unreality will creep into institutional decison-making.

According to the National Manpower Survey of the Criminal Justice System,[29] there are six main tasks performed by correctional supervisors. These are:

1. Talking with and listening to inmates and staff, concerning decisions regarding custody, discipline, treatment, or parole.
2. Completion of oral or written reports and other routine administrative duties in order to provide inputs regarding institutional needs.
3. Scheduling, assigning, and monitoring personnel under his or her supervision to assure the safety and security of the institution.
4. Conducting formal and informal training of personnel.
5. Accepting custody of suspects or offenders in order to develop the formal record of the agency.
6. Conducting and attending meetings of key personnel to give and receive information.

These are fairly technical tasks which require considerable human relations skills as well as specialized training. It is therefore disappointing to note that newly appointed supervisory personnel are required to have specialized training for their new positions in only 8 percent of the adult corrections agencies and 13 percent of the juvenile corrections agencies.[30]

MANAGEMENT APPROACHES

Vincent O'Leary, David Duffee, and Ernest Wenk[56] have developed a typology of models of correctional policy. According to this typology, there are four basic models of correctional policy: rehabilitation, reintegration, restraint, and reform. The rehabilitation model is the model usually associated with the treatment approach to corrections. It emphasizes concern for the individual and minimizes concern for the community as a whole. The reintegration model also places a high emphasis on the offender, but it combines this with an equivalently high level of concern for the community. This model emphasizes the return of the offender to the community, and requires a complex of traditional institu-

Figure 9.1 A counselor's meeting at a work release prerelease center. (Law Enforcement Assistance Administration.)

tional and community corrections placements under the direction of a centralized correctional system for its full implementation.

The restraint model exhibits relatively little concern for either the offender or the community. The major concern of correctional administrators under this model is the smooth operation of the correctional facility. Institutional maintenance is more important than rehabilitation. The fourth model is the reform model, in which there is a high level of concern for the community and a relatively low level of concern for offenders. The key term in describing this model is compliance, in that inmates are induced to comply with institutional regulations through a series of rewards and punishments. Administrators following this model direct staff members to behave in an exemplary manner so as to serve as role models for the prisoners. Because of the high moral tone with which administrators view law-abiding and conforming behavior, prisoners who do not follow the rules in reform-oriented institutions are subjected to relatively severe levels of punishment.

No one model of correctional policy is right in all institutional settings. Institutions differ in their architecture, staffing, community support, and many other dimensions. A state in which there is strong feeling about punishing criminals would not be the easiest place in which to implement a correctional policy based on rehabilitation or reintegration. The restraint and reform models would prove more useful in such a state, unless correctional administrators could employ a publicity campaign to change public opinion. Regardless of the policy model used in correctional administration, there are some general administrative principles that apply. These principles are associated with the difference between the military approach to administration and the participative approach. The military approach has traditionally been used in maximum security correctional institutions. It involves the issuing of orders by wardens with no input from correctional officers, middle managers, or prisoners, and often very little input from top-level administrators other than the warden. Once issued, regulations become law within the institution, and staff members are pressured to enforce all regulations to the letter of the law. Failure to enforce minor as well as major regulations constitutes grounds for automatic dismissal. These authoritarian hierarchical organizations tend to brutalize not only the prisoners but also the correctional officers.[11] Individuals in both groups may become severely alienated from the prison administration, and may develop negative attitudes that are antithetical to their personal growth and development.[9]

The alternative to the military style of management is known as participative management. In this form of management, employees (and perhaps prisoners) are allowed to have input into the development of correctional policy. They feel as if they are a part of the decision-making process, and they tend to feel that the policies produced through the participative process are their own, not policies that have been thrust upon them by a remote and unresponsive administration. Participative management makes allowances for human growth, and usually produces a much higher level of morale than the military style of management. In general, the restraint and reform models of correctional policy involve the use of the military approach to management, while the rehabilitation and reintegration models are more consistent with participative management.

Clemens Bartollas and Stuart J. Miller[6] offer three alternative forms of participative management. These are the formal plan, the leadership model, and management by objectives. Participative management using the formal plan involves the appointment of joint committees of workers and managers who work together to evaluate new ideas and to solve organizational problems. The committees are attached to different areas of the institution and serve as an adjunct to existing administrative positions. Only workers who are assigned to the committees (and who accept these assignments) participate in any meaningful way in the development of correctional policy.

The leadership model is somewhat more difficult to implement in a traditional correctional institution than participative management because it departs more extensively from the hierarchical relationships to which staff members in traditional institutions are likely to be accustomed. The supervisor is the crucial position in this plan. Supervisors communicate relevant organizational information to correctional officers and other line staff and encourage them to assume greater individual responsibility in their work. The taking of initiative in solving problems is promoted rather than discouraged. New ideas are welcomed, and supervisors are charged with developing communication patterns between workers so that they operate as a team rather than as isolated units. Many minor decisions can be made within the work groups, so that individual workers can feel they have considerable freedom in solving the day-to-day problems of correctional life.

The third mode of participative management is management by objectives (MBO). This approach emphasizes a general planning process. The National Advisory Commission on Criminal Justice Standards and Goals[47] recommends the implementation of MBO management in correctional organizations, and suggests that there are seven steps that must be followed in putting an MBO system into effect.

1. An ongoing system capable of accurately identifying and predicting changes in the environment in which the organization functions.
2. Administrative capability through a management information system to

provide data quickly to appropriate organizational members, work groups, or organizational units for their consideration and possible utilization.

3. Clearly established and articulated organizational and individual goals, mutually accepted through a process of continuous interaction between management and workers and between various levels of management. Unilateral imposition of correctional goals on lower echelon participants will not result in an MBO system but another bureaucracy.
4. An ongoing evaluation of the organizational and individual goals in light of feedback of the system. Such feedback and evaluation may result in the resetting of goals.
5. A properly designed and functioning organizational system for effective and efficient service delivery. In such a system, goal-oriented collaboration and cooperation are organizationally facilitated, and administrative services fully support efforts at goal accomplishment.
6. A managerial and work climate highly conducive to employee motivation and self-actualization toward organizational goal accomplishments. Such a climate should be developed and nurtured through the application of a participative style of management.
7. A properly functioning system for appraising organizational, work group, and individual progress toward goal attainment.[47:446]

A correctional organization having these elements in place can then begin to define its mission (a very general statement of purpose), goals (which specify desired end results, also in relatively general terms), and objectives (which are stated in terms of specific outcomes that can be measured to show either success or failure). These are used in the development of planning statements through which the objectives and goals will be achieved, thus validating the mission of the correctional organization. Periodic progress reviews ensure that adequate progress is being made toward the goals and objectives of the organization.[6] This process can be monitored by using a goal-setting guideline chart containing information on the following topics: (1) the area of managerial responsibility; (2) the name of the manager accountable for goal achievement; (3) a definition of the basic area; (4) the goal, objective, or end result; (5) the methods of communicating the goal, objective, or end result to employees; (6) the dates of interim evaluation conference managers and subordinates at which progress toward goals are reviewed; (7) the target completion date; (8) measures that can be used to evaluate progress toward goal achievement; (9) the maximum cost allowable; (10) the standard used to quantify goal achievement; and as a checkpoint, (11) a statement affirming that the goal relates to overall agency goals.[34]

THE SOCIAL CLIMATE OF CORRECTIONAL INSTITUTIONS

One of the most significant dimensions of correctional management is its use to affect the social climate of correctional organizations. There is considerable evidence that the social climate of an institution is a major factor in determining the behavior of the offenders in the institution,[41] and it may also affect their behavior after release. Unitl the 1960s, discussions about the social climate of correctional institutions were largely anecdotal. Since that time, there have been a number of attempts to quantify and objectify the estimation of institutional climates. The most successful of these measurement devices is a standardized questionnaire known as the Correctional Institutions Environment Scale, which was developed by Rudolph Moos on the Basis of his research on social climates in other settings.[41] This scale consists of nine subscales, each of which measures a single dimension of the institutional climate. These subscales are briefly described below.

1. *Involvement:* measures the level of activity of residents in participating in the daily functioning of the program.
2. *Support:* measures the level of support that residents are encouraged to express toward each other and that staff express toward residents.
3. *Expressiveness:* measures the encouragement of the open expression of feelings by staff and residents.
4. *Autonomy:* measures the encouragement of residents' initiative in planning and leadership in the program.
5. *Practical orientation:* measures the preparation of residents for release from the program.
6. *Personal problem orientation:* measures encouragement for residents to seek understanding for their own personal problems and feelings.
7. *Order and organization:* measures the importance of order and organization in the program.
8. *Clarity:* measures how well residents know what is expected of them and how explicit rules and procedures are.
9. *Staff control:* measures staff members' use of regulations to control residents.

Although the Correctional Institutions Environment Scale has been successfully reduced from nine to four dimensions in a factor analytic study of six community corrections centers,[66] the nine-dimension scale is more useful in pointing out troublesome areas for special attention by correctional administrators. One of the problems in using the Correctional Institutions Environment Scale is that prisoners do not rate institutions exactly in the same way as other members of the prison community. In general, prisoners live in a social environment that is less positive and healthy than that of administrators and supervisors, with correctional officers falling in between. This is one reason why correctional administrators do not always understand why it is that prisoners are dissatisfied with institutional conditions.[21] Regardless of whether officers, administrators, or prisoners are used as the raters of the social climate of the institution, institutions implementing a policy of rehabilitation are characterized by more positive, healthy social climates than institutions emphasizing a correctional policy of restraint.[56]

The Correctional Institution Environment Scale can also be used as an evaluation device. It was administered in all the facilities of the Oklahoma prison system in 1979 at the request of the Oklahoma Board of Corrections. Using the prisoners' responses as estimates of institutional social climates, the study found that Oklahoma's institutions for men were below the national norms on all but two of the nine subscales. The institutions were found to emphasize the control of the prisoners and to place little emphasis in assisting them with personal problems or preparing them for release. In comparison, the community treatment centers for men approximated the national norms for correctional social climates. Female facilities were generally well below the national norms, but the Residential Substance Abuse Program at the McAlester Community Treatment Center displayed an extremely positive social climate. In addition to comparisons among institutions in the Oklahoma system, and to comparisons between these institutions and national norms, it was possible to compare 1979 scores with a 1978 set of scores, which showed that there was a general decline in the positiveness of social climate in the community treatment centers, except that the Positive Reinforcement Program was associated with improved social climate at some centers. On the basis of these and other results, it was recommended that the Oklahoma Department of Corrections make a number of changes in management procedures, and it was predicted that the decision to expand the population of three community treatment centers would be accompanied by declines in the quality of the social climates of those institutions and probably by potentially dangerous outbreaks of violence by offenders.[44]

REGULATIONS AND DISCIPLINE

One of the important tasks that prison administrators must perform is to codify the rules of the institution and to distribute them to all incoming prisoners, along with other information about the institution which will hopefully ease the transition to institutional life as well as serving as a reference for later use. There are a number of ways in which this can be done. Wisconsin and Washington, D.C. have general inmate handbooks with a separate publication outlining the rules and regulations in detail. New Hampshire and South Carolina combine the general handbook and the rules into one document. Many prisoner handbooks are written like legal documents, but the handbook for residents in the detention facilities of the Washington, D.C. Department of Corrections,[64] "Taking Care of Business," includes photographs, drawings, and poems written by prisoners to diversify the prose. Another useful addition to the listing of rules and disciplinary procedures is the indexing of the entire booklet, as the South Carolina Department of Corrections has done, which is helpful to prisoners wishing to look up a specific topic without having to read through the entire manual.

The number of specific rules the violation of which leads to possible disciplinary action varies from system to system. The Oklahoma Department of Corrections lists 17 rules, the New Hampshire State Prison lists 46, the Taycheedah Correctional Institution for Wisconsin Women and the Minnesota Department of Corrections list 50, and the United States Disciplinary Barracks at Fort Leavenworth, Kansas publishes 25 pages of rules plus an additional four pages of explanatory diagrams. The Fort Leavenworth Manual contains so many rules and regulations because the prisoners there are subject to regular army discipline in addition to special regulations relating to incarceration. The

Oklahoma rules for prisoners constitute a basic set of institutional regulations. Each rule is stated in the form of a prohibition:

1. **Riot**—The public advocation, encouragement, promotion, or participation in a group disturbance at the correctional facility.
2. **Disruptive behavior**—Any action which has a serious adverse effect upon the discipline or programs of the facility.
3. **Present in Unauthorized Area**—Being in or at any location not designated by job assignment, scheduled activity, or staff directive.
4. **Battery**—Fighting, or the intentional physical injury of another person or persons.
5. **Menancing**—Placing another person or persons in fear of injury or death.
6. **Coercion**—The compelling or inducing of another person to engage in conduct from which he has a right to abstain, or to abstain from conduct in which he has a right to engage, by instilling fear in him.
7. **Theft**—The taking of property from another with intent to deprive the owner thereof or to appropriate property for oneself or for a third person.
8. **Destruction of Property**—Unauthorized and willful destruction or defacing of property that belongs to the State of Oklahoma or persons other than the prisoner involved.
9. **Possession or Manufacture of Contraband**—Items which are not authorized are Contraband. Authorized and/or unauthorized items must be specified in a field memorandum which is distributed to the inmate population.
10. **Sexual Activity**—Sexually stimulating activity by or between inmates, including sexual intercourse, kissing, fondling, and manipulation of the person's private parts.
11. **Disrespect to Staff**—Action and communications directed by inmates to institutional personnel which indicate hostility or personal animosity.
12. **Disobedience of a Direct Order**—Failure to comply with direct order from any staff member in a prompt manner.
13. **False Statements to Staff Members**—Willful false statements to institutional personnel in regard to material matters.
14. **Gambling**—Staking and risking something of value upon the outcome of a contest, game of chance, or a future contingent event.
15. **Violation of Contractually Agreed Program Regulation**—Failure to abide by regulations specified in a signed contract to participate in a program.
16. **Escape or Walkaway**—A successful or unsuccessful effort to evade the lawful custody of the Department of Corrections.
17. **Bartering**—The trading or selling of services, possessions, or assignments by inmates, or the arrangement of compensation in return for certain action.[55]

There are several things to notice about these regulations. In the first place, many of them do no more than to ban the criminal victimization of other prisoners and correctional officers. The full implications of prison victimization are discussed in Chapter 11. The second point is that the regulations enforce the hierarchical structure of prison life when they require punishment for behavior such as the disobedience of a direct order or for failure to abide by a regulation agreed to in an individual contract for programming. Third, there are regulations that are at least partially designed to enforce the punitive aspects of prison life, such as including masturbation in the ban on sexual activity, outlawing bartering, and forbiding the possession or manufacture of contraband (most prison contraband items being perfectly legal in a free society). The exact definitions of bartering and of the types of contraband are not created entirely for punishment. They also consider the contribution that certain material items and practices make to victimization among the prisoners. It is sometimes necessary to forbid something in prison life that would be permitted in the free society simply to protect the less resourceful prisoners from victimization. Finally, rules regarding disobedience of a direct order and disrespect shown to staff are general catch-all regulations that permit correctional officers to increase their control over prisoners as much as is necessary in a given situation. Many other correctional rule books have many more regulations than the Oklahoma manual because they attempt to specify the details of disobedient behavior in separate items, such as "Failing to stand count or interfering with the taking of a count" and "Possessing money or currency except as authorized for telephone calls."[50]

Prisoner handbooks also state the punishments that may legitimately be meted out by disciplinary committees. There are three ways that this is done in existing manuals. Wisconsin provides prisoners with a general list of penalties that is not directly connected to any of the disciplinary infractions listed in the rules and regulations. With this system, disciplinary committees have maximum flexibility in assigning punishments for infractions. The second model is to list the range of punishments permitted under each regulation. Minnesota's[37] "Inmate Discipline Regulations" pamphlet informs prisoners that creating a fire hazard is punishable by loss of privileges of 30–180 days, 3–10 days in isolation;and obstructing the cell bars or one's door is punishable by the loss of privileges for 14–30 days. Oklahoma's[55] rule book is an example of the third model. It lists four punishments for major infractions and four punishments for minor infractions, and indicates which of the rules are automatically major infractions when they are broken and which may be either major or minor infractions depending upon the situation and the history of the individual. Major punishments in the Oklahoma system are disciplinary segregation of up to 90 days, loss of earned time credit of up to 180 days, or disciplinary transfer to another facility. Minor punishments are the loss of no more than 60 days of good time credit, modification of custody classification, restricted privileges, and restitution from the violator's account, which is called a trust fund.

The Disciplinary Process

Discipline is a problem in all correctional systems. American prison systems have moved in recent years to the application of a specific list of sanctions to a set of offenses that have been codified so that they resemble criminal laws rather than administrative regulations. These changes in American penal practice have been largely brought about by the prisoners themselves, who have filed numerous suits leading to court decisions requiring the formalization of disciplinary regulations and the extending of due process protections to prisoners accused of breaking the rules. Indian prisons continue to operate on the traditional prison model, in which the warden or some other institutional official holds brief hearings at which the prisoner is almost always considered to be guilty rgardless of what is said, and the punishment is often brutal. Punishments in India include fettering to a bar, handcuffing, and corporal punishment such as the "merciless caning of the so-called hotheaded and defiant inmates."[58]

Disciplinary procedures at Ramle Prison in Israel also fail to include the extensive procedural safeguards that have become widespread in American corrections. Prisoners at Ramle are not given a copy of the prison rules, nor are they given a written statement of the alleged violation before the disciplinary hearing occurs. In the Rhode Island Adult Correctional Institution, all of the appropriate procedural safeguards are followed, but prisoners often feel that decisions in their cases are predetermined before they make their appearances and that the process is basically biased. Conversely, despite the absence of many procedural safeguards, the Israeli prisoners generally believe that the decisions made in disciplinary cases are fair, and they do not complain that their rights have been violated by the relative informality of the proceedings.[19] It is apparent from these examples that the institution of due process regulations cannot, ipso facto, bring about an acknowledgment of the disciplinary system as fair by all parties involved. The highly due process-oriented procedures used in Rhode Island apparently are unable to prevent feelings of alienation, negativity, and injustice similar to those evoked by the brutal Indian system of punishment; while the Ramle disciplinary procedures—which are intermediate between those of India and Rhode Island with regard to the degree of respect shown for prisoner rights—produces the highest level of respect shown for prisoner rights and the highest level of respect for the institution and acceptance of the justice of the decisions made.

Disciplinary procedures vary from state to state. We will present the procedures implemented in the Federal Prison System[62] on April 15, 1979 as an example of American correctional disciplinary regulations. Staff members are encouraged to reach an informal resolution of incidents with the parties involved in minor cases; but where that is inappropriate or impossible, an Incident Report is completed and forwarded to the appropriate correctional supervisor, who may also dispose of the report informally and expunge the report from the prisoner's file. The next stage of the disciplinary process is an investigation of the incident, at which time the prisoner is given a copy of the Incident Report. The prisoner is advised of his right to remain silent at all stages of the disciplinary process. A record of the investigation is added to the Incident Report and taken to the initial hearing, at which time minor punishments may be decided upon or the case may be forwarded to the Institution Discipline Committee for a formal hearing.

Prisoners have the right to select their own staff representative to accompany them to the hearing conducted by the Institution Discipline Committee. They must receive a written notice of the charges no less than 24 hours before the hearing. Prisoners are entitled to present evidence, call witnesses, and to make statements on their own behalf. The chairman of the Institution Discipline Committee may refuse to hear certain witnesses, but must document reasons for this refusal. Prisoners have the right to be present throughout the entire hearing, except during the private deliberations of the Committee or when this would violate institutional security. If the Committee decides that a prisoner is not guilty, the entire record of the case is expunged from the prisoner's file. The Committee must give prisoners written notice of all decisions, and these decisions can then be appealed to the warden within 30 days of the receipt of the notice of the Committee's decision and disposition.

The Use of Segregation in Disciplinary Cases

Since American prisons do not permit the use of corporal punishment as an official disposition in disciplinary hearings, segregating prisoners in an isolation facility is a major form of institutional social control. Segregation is used for two reasons other than punishment. The first is administrative segregation, under which the warden removes a predatory prisoner from the population in order to prevent an incident of violence, or for a short time before a hearing can be scheduled, or for some other reason that does not fit the definition of punitive segregation. In practice, administrative segregation can be used in a manner that is punitive in nature. The other use of segregation is for protection. In this case, the prisoners request to be placed in segregation so that they will not be subjected to homosexual attacks, nonsexual assaults, and other forms of intimidation at the hands of their fellow-prisoners.

The guidelines for the use of segregation sometimes differ according to whether it is punitive, administrative, or protective. There are considerable variations between states in the limitations on the length of the use of segregation. Alaska has a limit of 90 days for major infractions and 30 days for minor infractions; Delaware imposes limits of 15 and 5 days respectively; and Indiana allows a maximum of 3 years in isolation, with reviews occurring every 30 days. States such as Oregon and South Carolina have no maximum limit for administrative segregation. Washington limits disciplinary segregation to 10 consecutive days, and requires 72 consecutive hours between the expiration of one isolation sentence and the imposition of another unless the total time of the two sentences is less than 10 days.[16]

Until recent years, a segregation unit with a maximum capacity of five percent of the prisoner population was more than sufficient in any American correctional institution. Relatively few prisoners were placed in administrative segregation, and an even smaller number requested protective segregation. At the Washington State Penitentiary, the percentage of the total population in segregation varied between two and five percent until 1974, and then mushroomed rapidly to eight percent in 1975 and 12 percent in 1976. To meet this need for increased segregation space, institutional administrators had to convert other facilities for segregation use. It was possible to devote an entire tier of 128 cells to protection cases because they did not require the same level of security as the administrative segregation and punitive segregation cases.[14] Between 1964 and 1975, the use of punitive segregation by Washington State Penitentiary officials actually declined, and the increase in the use of administrative segregation was modest, averaging four percent per year. In contrast, there was an increase of over 700 percent in the granting of protective custody at inmate request.[5] We can see from this example that institutional administrators are not always free to use punitive segregation as much as they might like. Limited facilities combined with increases in requests for protective segregation (due to increased victimization among prisoners) may force decision-makers to limit their use of segregation as a sanction with the purpose of maintaining institutional control. At the Washington State Penitentiary, officials adapted to this problem by increasing their use of suspended sentences for the less severe punitive segregation cases.[5]

GRIEVANCE MECHANISMS

A 1973 survey by Virginia McArthur[33] found that 77 percent of 218 institutions responding had some sort of grievance procedure in place. In addition, 31 percent of the institutions were served by an ombudsman, most of them in the states of Georgia, Hawaii, Minnesota, New Jersey, Ohio, Oregon, and South Carolina. The earliest date given for the implementation of a grievance procedure was 1949, at the West Virginia State Prison for Women. A number of other institutions were unable to specify a starting date for the implementation of a grievance procedure, so some institutions may have begun to use grievance procedures even earlier than 1949. Most procedures allowed for either an oral or written complaint to initiate action in a case. Some institutions required that all complaints be submitted to one particular staff member, while others allowed them to be submitted to any staff member or to other individuals or committees. Almost all procedures permitted appeals, generally to the state director of corrections. Most institutions had a time limit on the initial response to the grievance, and many had time limits specified for additional steps in the grievance procedure. Correctional institutions may also make use of inmate councils in an ombudsman role. The Resident Government Council at the Washington State Penitentiary included a People's Action Committee with the specific responsibility of responding to the grievances of individual prisoners.[27] Although the lack of records makes it impossible to evaluate the work of the People's Action Committee, the group was successful in preventing a major race riot in one incident.

Topics that prisoners typically submit to a grievance procedure are those concerning discipline, classification, administrative record-keeping, and medical treatment. Classification is important to many prisoners because it affects access to desired treatment programs as well as living conditions. Prison discipline is probably responsible for more grievances than any other area of concern. Disciplinary grievances either challenge the content of institutional rules and the way in which the rules are created or changed, or they challenge the enforcement of the rules and the way by which it is determined that the rules have been violated.[31] When combined with an adequate management information system, grievance procedures can contribute to the planning and evaluation processes in correctional institutions by serving as an index of whether progress is being made toward the achievement of goals adopted by institutional administrators.

The Ward Grievance Procedure in the California Youth Authority

The Ward Grievance Procedure was developed to deal with grievances brought by wards (offenders) under the jurisdiction of the California Youth Authority. The Ward Grievance Procedure allows for the possibility of informal resolution or resolution at a hearing of the ward–staff grievance committee in each institution. The offenders on the committee are elected by popular vote of their peers and have equal voice with staff members in committee decisions. If the decision of the committee is unsatisfactory to the grievant, there is provision for appeals to higher administrative levels. Ultimately, a grievance can be appealed to an external arbitrator who recommends a final resolution of the case. An evaluation of the use of the Ward Grievance Procedure by David Dillingham[20] found that 15,000 ward grievances were filed in a 28-month period ending in December, 1976. In an intensive nine-month study, one ward in every nine used the Ward Grievance Procedure. Approximately half of the grievances resulted either in a judgment in favor of the offender or in a compromise. Less than one out of 150 cases reached the final level of outside arbitration. Approximately half the offenders interviewed who had filed a grievance indicated satisfaction with the case, and only a quarter of them maintained that a grievance would not be worked out fairly. Most staff members spent less than an hour per week on grievance matters, but administrative staff members carried the heaviest burden of work in processing grievances.

REGIONALIZATION AND STATISTICAL INFORMATION SYSTEMS

Two aspects of state correctional systems having major implications for correctional practice are the trend toward regionalization and the implementation of extensive statistical information systems. A number of state departments of corrections are moving toward or have already instituted a regionalized administrative structure. Florida has been divided into five regions, each of which has its own regional office and takes full responsibility for administering and coordinating employee activities ranging from community corrections to maximum security facilities.[22] South Carolina has determined that three regions are enough for its needs. Each of these regions is planned to be a microcosm of the total correctional system, with a full complement of security levels, programs, and functions.[59] The current configuration of institutions in South Carolina places almost all maximum and medium security prisoners in the Midlands region of the state, has insufficient housing for prisoners in the Appalachian region, and has facilities only for minimum security and work release prisoners in the Coastal region. In order to fully regionalize the system, the South Carolina Department of Corrections is planning to close 12 existing facilities and to build 15 new regionalized facilities by 1989. At that time, maximum, medium, and minimum security facilities—as well as specialized pre-release and work release facilities—will be available in all three districts.[57]

The Michigan Department of Corrections[36] has developed an elaborate plan for regionalizing corrections. Through the 1970s, its system was like other centralized penal systems. All male offenders were sent to a central reception facility for evaluation and then transferred to other state institutions according to their classifications. Throughout their incarcerations, they were subject to multiple transfers as their classifications and treatment exigencies fluctuated. As a result, there was no guarantee that they would be within easy driving distance of their families. Under the regional prison plan, most prisoners serve out their entire sentences in a single institution located close to their home communities. Each of the regional prisons contain all levels of security, so it is not necessary to transfer prisoners to another institution when they move from maximum to medium security classification. Michigan proposes that regional prisons have a design capacity of 350 medium security prisoners plus a close custody unit of 100, a minimum security work release unit of 50, and an additional 5 beds for reception, infirmary, and segregation use. The regional prisons should ideally be located within half an hour's drive from the communities being served. In addition to facilitating family visiting, this will also allow the regional prisons to integrate their correctional services more fully with services available in the community than has been possible in the past.

The Michigan Department of Corrections[36] projects that even when they have regionalized their system as fully as possible, 35 percent of prisoners under their jurisdiction will still be in nonregionalized facilities. Because of the small number of women, they will continue to be housed in a few centralized facilities. Other nonregionalized offenders will be housed in special institutions for high-risk offenders or for those who are management problems, and in community corrections facilities and forest camps. Several units will specialize in the care of geriatric prisoners and those with severe medical problems. The other 65 percent of the population will be housed in 21 regional prisons distributed all over the state. Ten of these regional prisons will be concentrated in the greater Detroit area, and the other prisons will be scattered throughout regions 2 through 9 of the Michigan system.

Statistical Information Systems

Information systems in traditional maximum security prisons were limited to an intake book which listed all prisoners at the time of admission, their offenses, and only as much additional information as would fit on one line of the intake book. There was also some sort of internal disciplinary record, perhaps kept on file cards in the office of the associate warden for custody. Other records relating to the prisoners were placed in central files and could be examined only by leafing through the files individually, a process so time-consuming that institutions almost never assembled any detailed statistics on their prisoners. In addition to being unable to compile general statistics on prisoners, this information system made it difficult to know where a prisoner was at any given time in a state correctional system. The development of modern computer technology has revolutionized information systems in corrections. It is now possible to track individuals throughout their entire incarcerations and to know exactly where they are at any given time, their background characteristics, their institutional behavior, and their projected release dates.

The Bureau of Correctional Information Systems of the New Jersey Department of Corrections[51] has three data-processing systems in use: an admissions and movement system; a parole caseload transaction system; and a parole eligibility determination system. The admissions and movement system records 64 data elements on each offender and is updated daily as to the offender's location and status. This system permits the issuing of reports containing aggregate data as well as printouts on individual prisoners. Besides management reports such as the number of admissions, the average daily population, and the offense distribution, there are operational reports, such as an alphabetic listing of offenders in custody, those having escaped, and a summary of known aliases used by current convicts. The system also furnishes data for specialized research reports, including grant proposals and population projections, and permits the exchange of data with other governmental units.

The parole caseload transaction system tracks parolees in the community and is updated monthly. The parole eligibility determination system calculates parole eligibility dates for all prisoners on a monthly basis according to their accumulated work credits. This monthly record allows the State Parole Board to schedule prisoners accurately for hearings. The Bureau of Correctional Information Systems plans to implement an offender-based state correctional information system (OBSCIS) by late 1981. This would combine the three existing information systems into one unified system from which all information can be made available to any criminal justice agency employee who has clearance to access the information. Some states, such as Minnesota,[38] are at the same stage as New Jersey, with separate correctional information systems for different purposes, while other states, including New York,[52] have already established an OBSCIS system.

Computerized information systems can also be used for specialized purposes. In Kentucky, a computerized system was developed to aid in the initial classification of incoming felons. The screening system was based on an examination of all existing social science data about the relationships between predictor variables and antisocial behavior, which led to the development or modification of existing rating scales. These scales were then extensively pretested on existing offender populations. The result of the development process was a classification summary containing 25 scales summarized under nine predictor categories. The categories presently in use in the Kentucky classification system are: (1) potential for aggressive behavior; (2) depression and suicide potential; (3) intellectual status; (4) vocational skills of interest and educational achievement; (5) criminal sophistication; (6) level of socialization; (7) physical health; (8) mental health; and (9) major functional problems. Inmates are given a 20-minute interview and five test booklets that take approximately two-and-one hours to complete. Prisoners unable to read are administered these tests verbally using a tape-recording of the questions. Many checkpoint items are built into the tests in order to assure prisoner honesty. All results are computerized and the results are available within 24 hours of the completion of testing. The results of the tests are displayed in a detailed printout, which also compares each prisoner with the total population of prisoners previously classified. This case history report constitutes an objective basis for the classification of prisoners, and can also be updated for use as a diagnostic tool in parole decision-making.[4]

Another innovative use of information systems is the "Disciplinary Hearing Data Sheet" developed by the Wisconsin Division of Corrections.[65] This form reports rule infractions committed, attempted, and aided or abetted, as well as the disciplinary committee finding of guilty or not guilty for every incident processed by institutional disciplinary committees. A minimum amount of background information on the incident is provided, as is the punishment applied if the offender was found guilty. The Disciplinary Hearing Data Sheets are forwarded to the state central office for computer analysis, which permits correctional officials to monitor the level of disciplinary infractions. Trends in the level of disciplinary infractions can be discerned, and changes in correctional policies developed in response to fluctuations in the disciplinary infraction rate. Printouts summarizing disciplinary infractions specify each type of infraction, and are produced for individual institutions and for the state as a whole. One of the uses of these statistics is to estimate the total incidence of officially recorded victimization occurring in the system. Are correctional officers reporting increasing rates of disrespect directed toward them by prisoners? Are assaults, sexual assaults, and threats increasing in a system? Are more weapons being found in shakedowns? Thefts, homosexuality, self-mutilation, and many other categories of disciplinary infractions can be used to index changes in the social climate and other conditions in individual institutions, and perhaps to cope with major problems before they become uncontrollable and lead to a prison riot. Alternatively, they may be used as the basis for policy changes designed to increase the protection given to prisoner and correctional officer victims of crimes committed within the institutions.

PRISON EMPLOYEE UNIONISM

The unionization of prison employees is part of the general movement toward unionization of all state employees that began in the 1940s, but that did not accelerate until the late 1960s. Correctional employee unions are affiliated with various larger union organizations. The most prevalent of these unions is the American Federation of State, County, and Municipal Employees, which is an affiliate of AFL–CIO (American Federation of Labor–Congress of Industrial Organizations). Because other groups of public employees began to engage in collective bargaining with the state at earlier dates than corrections employees, state collective bargaining procedures were standardized without reference to the needs of correctional organizations. When correctional employees entered the arena of collective bargaining, existing procedures were used without being adapted to the unique requirements of correctional work. As a result, the quality of correctional programming has sometimes been seriously damaged by the effects of new contract provisions that were not provided for in the budget.[39]

Correctional labor relations are exceptional in a number of different respects. First, custodial and program staff in most institutions have an intense disagreement not only about the methods of achieving correctional objectives but about the objectives themselves. Second, almost all correctional staff members have supervisory responsibilities. They are responsible for the behavior of prisoners in addition to their own work. Third, the continual threat of violence sets all correctional employees on edge, and sometimes makes them unusually resistant to compromise on issues that they perceive to be related to potential violence. A fourth factor is the military model on which most correctional institutions are administered. This model tends to alienate correctional employees from administrators and to minimize communication between the two groups. Finally, the high profile that corrections has in the public eye gives correctional employee unions more political power than might otherwise by the case.[67] The combined effect of these factors is to make bargaining more difficult in correctional organizations than in most other settings involving public employees.

There is practically no limit to the issues that may become the subject of collective bargaining between correctional system administrators and union officials. Many of the issues discussed have to do with the nature of bargaining itself, while others are general issues such as management rights and contract renegotiation. Two other major groups of issues are those relating to employee benefits and to the involvement of the union in state correctional administration. Discussions about employee benefits include salaries, grievance procedures, overtime and sick leave, job security, seniority, training, uniform allowances, pay differentials, and retirement benefits. Some of the most important issues relating to the involvement of the union in state correctional administration are the conditions of work and employee safety, methods and procedures for disciplining employees who have allegedly misbehaved, and fitness for duty standards.[39] Negotiations on these issues have tended to reduce the freedom of correctional management to carry out its own policies over the years.

Correctional employee unions use a number of different tactics to influence correctional administrators into making decisions in their favor. Lobbying is carried out with both the executive and legislative branches of government. The unions publicize their definitions of the situation through newsletters, newspapers, press conferences, marches, and picketing. Correctional unions may take legal action to support their positions, and may also use strikes, sick-outs, lock-ins, slow-downs, and speed-ups to disturb orderly institutional life and bring attention to their causes.[67] *The New York Times* reported 31 strikes and other job actions by correctional officers between 1968 and 1977, mostly in New York and New Jersey, and that was a small proportion of all the job actions by correctional officers that occurred in the nation during that period. Union agreements produced through these job actions (and without them) may, in the long run, undermine the military approach to correctional management and strengthen the power of state centralized corrections departments at the expense of institutional administrators.[25]

CORRECTIONAL PLANNING

Planning is not an esoteric activity engaged in by only a few specialists. All correctional administrators regularly engage in planning activities whether or not they are aware of it. They are compelled to do so by the budgeting process.

Annual or biennial budgets are prepared by both institutional administrators and system-level administrators. Specified in the budget are the projected costs for all continuing programs and new programs proposed for implementation in the coming year. In making decisions about the allocation of resources among programs–as well as between programs and nonprogram areas of financial expenditure (such as building maintenance, staff benefits, and staff development activities)–correctional administrators are making planning decisions. If these decisions are made without an adequate planning process, then the administrators are not properly carrying out their responsibilities.

Planning is not just a matter of the internal allocation of funds. The planning process also compels administrators to be in contact with community elements outside their own correctional systems. This occurs at a minimal level when administrators contract with private agencies to provide treatment and other correctional services to prisoners, staff, or the organization as a whole. The second point of contact with the larger community occurs in that it is unwise to plan correctional matters in isolation from other parts of the criminal justice system. Projected changes in court procedures will have an impact on the correctional system that can be estimated in advance. Correctional officials need to be aware of these other systemic changes and to accommodate the predicted effects of these changes. A third level of contact with the larger community occurs when community elites seek to influence correctional policy. Different coalitions of community influentials interested in correctional matters exist in each state, with elected governmental officials and lawyers having a particularly strong impact on routine correctional decision-making.[7]

The interdependence of correctional matters and general social policy is also something that cannot be completely ignored by correctional administrators. At the highest levels of correctional decision-making—the governor's office and the legislatures in state correctional systems—correctional plans must compete with plans for other social programs. The building of a new mental hospital or the implementation of a new support system for nursing homes may signify the abandonment or postponement of plans for an innovative series of community corrections programs. It is at this general level of budgeting and planning that the linkages between corrections and other parts of society may be minutely scrutinized by legislators and officials in the executive branch of government.

In the late 1970s, M. Robert Montilla[40] argued that if the State of California were to put the 39 million dollars necessary to build facilities for the projected increase in prisoners during the coming four years into programs designed to reduce the unemployment of young nonwhite males, it would result in a greater decrease in crime, plus increases in business revenues, employment, sales and income taxes, and a decrease in welfare payments. As planning and evaluation techniques become more precise, governmental officials will increasingly be making decisions on the basis of a comparison of benefits between corrections and noncorrectional social programs instead of dealing only with the question of allocation of resources within the correctional establishment. In addition to planning activities that are thrust upon administrators by the normal budgeting process, there are also special situations requiring planning expertise. The rise in gang violence in the California Prison System forced administrators to engage in a planning design to control that violence. The need for continued planning to control gang violence in California and a number of other states will continue for some time in the future.[15]

Florida had to engage in short-term planning to accommodate an increase of 4294 prisoners in 1975, which was approximately seven times the annual increase that they had encountered in earlier years. The magnitude of Florida's problem can be visualized when we consider that this one-year increase was larger than the total prison population of more than half the states. The search for alternatives resulted in the identification of approximately 70 existing facilities that could be converted for correctional use, of which seven met all the necessary planning criteria and were incorporated into the Florida system. One of these facilities had formerly been an Air Force radar base; a second had been a migrant labor camp; another had been a state tuberculosis hospital; and a fourth had previously been part of a state mental hospital. In addition, mobile homes, tents, and other temporary accommodations were made available for prisoner use, and seven existing facilities were expanded. It was found that facility expansion was quicker, less expensive, and created less community opposition than the building of new facilities.

Vermont had just the opposite problem than Florida had. When it was decided that the Windsor State Prison—the oldest operating maximum security prison in the United States—was to be closed, it became necessary to engage in extensive planning as how to relocate prisoners and staff members with minimum disruption and expense. The planning method used by the Vermont Department of Corrections is called the Critical Path Method (CPM). CPM identifies all of the activities to be carried out in the proposed change, and associates a specified amount of time with each activity. The activities are charted to show the sequence in which they have to be performed. The critical path is the sequence of activities that takes the longest period of time. It is critical because the only way to shorten the total amount of time to complete the project is to shorten the critical path, which can also be accomplished indirectly by freeing critical path activities from dependence on peripheral activities that may delay the project. The Vermont Department of Corrections had to shift prisoners from Windsor to its medium security prison at St. Albans or to other settings with minimum disruption, cost, and risk of escape. In order to save money, much of the security equipment at Windsor had to be removed to other facilities while the project was in process. Staff members had to be trained for eight weeks as part of their reassignment to new facilities. The CPM technique was computerized to allow correctional planners to calculate time estimates and coordination strategies for a variety of different planning possibilities before selecting the final sequence in which the activities would be carried out.[24]

The Basic Planning Paradigm

Planning consists of three basic steps. The first is policy planning, in which there is an analysis of the problems to be solved in the planning process and the setting of objectives for the correctional system or unit. In short, policy planning establishes what we should do and why we should do it. The second basic step in planning is program planning. In this step, the planners define the strategies, policies, and plans with which they expect to achieve the objectives formulated earlier in the policy planning stage. The third and final stage of planning is operational planning, in which planning decisions are implemented and resources are allocated among competing activities and organizational units.[46]

Although this ends the policy planning process proper, there is still another stage in any comprehensive planning system. This consists of monitoring program performance and conducting formal evaluations of program outcomes in order to assure that planning objectives are being achieved. These evaluative activities provide feedback for the modification of future program plans.

Planning activities are too complex and time-consuming to be conducted by administrators alone. In all but the smallest operations, they require specialized planning units containing professional planners to carry out these activities, and they evaluate the planning and evaluation activities of these planners in the same way that they evaluate the operation of any other units under their control. Evaluation and planning units are most fully developed at the state and national levels. Even at local levels, planning units have greatly increased in size and number. A 1978 survey of local criminal justice planning offices identified 382 planning units with an average size of approximately three professionals per unit. Many of the smaller jurisdictions were limited to one professional, sometimes on a part-time basis. At the other end of the scale, there were 22 jurisdictions employing ten or more planning professionals.[18] These professionals typically distribute their time between law enforcement, judicial and correctional planning activities, and supplement full-time correctional planners attached to correctional agencies.

Population Projections

Population projections are important in any planning process, but they are even more important in corrections than in most other settings. The cost per bed for correctional facility construction and the cost per person for institutional programming are both so high that relatively small increases in correctional populations are almost impossible to accommodate within existing budgets. There are also related problems, such as that institutional overcrowding is related to increased prisoner and officer victimization, and it may also increase the risk of escape.[11] For these reasons, there has been a great deal of attention given to the projection of future correctional populations in the past decade.

Correctional population projections need to take into account a series of general factors, including social conditions and social policies, as well as the operation of the other elements in the criminal justice system that process offenders and pass them on to the corrections system. For example, a population projection made by the Colorado Department of Corrections in 1980 assumed that the Colorado unemployment rate would increase to five percent by the end of 1981 and made four key assumptions about the criminal justice system. These were that the average length of incarceration for offenders would be 28.5 months, that sentences under the new presumptive sentencing law would be three percent higher than the average of earlier sentences, and that there would be no significant changes in criminal law and criminal policy in the near future. Using these assumptions, it was projected that the number of commitments would rise from 1239 in 1980 to 1353 in 1984, and that the total correctional population would rise from 2704 to 3214 during these years.[17]

The Washington, D.C. Department of Corrections also used the unemployment rate, and added 25 criminal justice system processing variables to form a pool from which the most important statistical predictors were selected on the basis of past experience and then used to project the detention population, the sentenced incarcerated population, and the parole population for the coming three years. Each population projection used a different subset of the 25 variables. For the detention population, the model included the number of guilty misdemeanant dispositions, the delay for misdemeanants between arrests and final disposition, the number of sentences imposed, the number of new commitments, and the number of misdemeanor bonds.[54]

Alfred Blumstein and his associates[8] developed a highly sophisticated model for the projection of the Pennsylvania prison population through the year 2000. They were able to show that demographic factors, particularly age and race, were important in the projection of future prison populations. They made projections of future arrests and prison commitments based on demographic changes, and they went on to project the state prison population. They estimated that arrests would peak in 1980 and prison commitments would peak in 1985. Prison populations were projected to peak in 1990, after which there would be a modest decline. They also projected that the percentage of nonwhites in the total prison population would rise from 48 percent in 1975 to 55 percent in the year 2000, and that the prison population would age considerably during this period. Blumstein *et al.* did not allow for feedback adjustments in the criminal justice system. These are likely to occur, and would tend to reduce the total prison population below the levels that were projected using constant values for criminal justice activities derived from current activity levels.

Architectural Considerations in Planning

Assuming that the correctional planning process has been adequately carried out and it has been decided that there is a need for additional bed space in a correctional system, correctional architecture comes into play. Modern correctional architecture is user-oriented. Contemporary correctional architects consider the effects of architecture upon the prisoners as well as the contributions made by structural arrangements to the efficiency of job performance by employees, the security needs of the institution, limitations inherent in the construction site, treatment and accreditation standards, and cost factors.[28] In general, there has been a shift from architectural designs consistent with an authoritarian regime to humanized campus-like designs such as the one used in building the Illinois State Penitentiary at Vienna, the Liberty Institute in Hickman County, Tennessee, and the St. Albans correctional facility in Vermont. William Nagel's[45] survey of modern American prisons found many magnificent new architectural structures that unfortunately were not always accompanied by correspondingly advanced programs and administrative practices.

The human engineering aspects of correctional architecture require social science studies of the effects of different architectural arrangements. Two of the many architectural topics that have been studied in recent years are the effects of high noise levels and of the use of closed-circuit television surveillance. There is an existing body of research on the effects of high noise levels, and the courts have specified that noise level is one of the conditions of incarceration that must be kept to reasonable levels.[23] Social science surveys of prisoners, correctional officers and administrators have determined that despite the obvious usefulness of television surveillance in reducing prison victimization, its use is associated with a number of negative impacts on prisoner attitudes and behavior. It also has a number of negative impacts on the attitudes of correctional officers.[48] This study demonstrates that physical efficiency and architectural safety are sometimes procured at the expense of exacerbated human problems.

There is much competition between manufacturers to supply architectural materials for correctional construction. A mobile home manufacturer has created a brochure showing that its products can be used as dormitories, infirmaries, classrooms, guardhouses, counseling offices, and mess halls in minimum security institutions.[13] The program booklets of the Annual Con gresses of Corrections are full of architectural advertisements, as are the issues of *Corrections Today*, the official publication of the American Correctional Association. Matters that must be considered by architects and criminal justice planners include electronic communications and security monitoring systems, computer systems, locking and other security mechanisms, tamperproof lighting systems, security glass, fencing, barbed wire, and relatively durable furniture bolted to the walls and floor. The public rarely hears anything about these matters until a specific architectural failure precipitates a major security problem. This occurred when the structural failure of recently installed security glass facilitated a major prison riot in New Mexico in February 1980.[61] There is a continuous public relations effort by manufacturers to assure the public and correctional administrators (who might become customers in the future) that their products may be safely used in correctional institutions.

Comprehensive Correctional Planning

Correctional planning takes many factors into account other than population projections and the architectural requirements of new or remodeled institutions. Many state and national prison systems rationalize their planning activities by issuing regular master plans that reach five or more years into the future. We will briefly describe three of these master plans: for North Carolina, Alaska, and Canada.

No planning process can take place without adequate information to begin with, so the North Carolina[53] plan includes both a sophisticated projection of prison populations through the year 1987 and an analysis of what tasks prison unit staff members actually perform while on duty. It was found that custody staff members spent 68 percent of their time in security activities, 12 percent of their time in administrative or clerical tasks, and 8 percent of their time in program related tasks. Program staff devoted only 36 percent of their time to program activities, as compared with 39 percent to administrative and clerical tasks, and 16 percent to security tasks. Assuming steady admissions and increasing sentence length, it was projected that the total correctional population would rise from 14,885 in 1980 to 17,093 in 1989. Taking this into account, strategies examined in the planning process were grouped around four objectives: (1) to decrease the flow of offenders into the corrections system; (2) to increase the flow of offenders out of the corrections system; (3) to increase the capacity of the corrections system; and (4) to increase the capacity of the system to cope with pressures generated by a surplus of offenders and a shortage of resources.

Each major category was then broken down into subcategories, which were, in turn, broken down into specific strategies. For example, increasing the flow of offenders out of the corrections system was divided into shortening prison sentences, shortening probation judgments, increasing parole, and increasing probation/parole terminations. There were 18 specific strategies associated with shortening prison sentences, of which three were analyzed and recommended for implementation. These were recommending judicial sentencing workshops to judges, establishing sentencing guidelines, and increasing public education about the destructive effects of long-term imprisonment. Among the alternatives to be analyzed in later years are reducing maximum sentences, establishing sentencing panels, raising the dollar threshold for felony property crimes, restricting minimum sentences to half the maximum sentence or less, and making sentence length dependent upon restitution.

The Alaska master plan was developed by Moyer Associates,[43] along with the American Foundation and the National Center for Juvenile Justice. Alaska has unique correctional problems in that its small resident population is spread over a vast territory, the cost of operating correctional institutions in Alaska is unusually high, and there are specialized needs for correctional treatment among the American Indians, Eskimos, and Aleuts who make up a significant proportion of the Alaska correctional population. The Alaska plan recommends that a number of correctional institutions be phased out, since they are too old and poorly constructed to be useful in a modern correctional system. Rejecting the full regionalization of correctional facilities because of excessive cost, the Alaska plan recommends ten service areas, six of which are rural. Alcoholism detoxification centers, community corrections, diversion from incarceration, and other nonprison solutions to deviant behavior should be emphasized in these rural areas in order to minimize the need for institutionalization. The extensive high-quality data developed in state plans in support of the planning process constitutes a major contribution to our understanding of correctional systems, one which has not as yet been used with any frequency by academic researchers.

The Canadian five-year plan is issued in two volumes, one for issues and goal statements and the other for operational plans. Issues, goals, and operational plans are developed in each of nine correctional areas: (1) technical services; (2) offender programs; (3) security; (4) personnel; (5) medical; (6) inmate employment; (7) finance; (8) communications; and (9) management. These nine fundamental areas are then broken down into issue statements, each of which is associated with an operational goal statement, and most of which are developed into detailed operational plans.[12]

We will take one of the operational goal statements under the heading of offender programs as an example of the Canadian planning system. This operational goal is "To implement the Inmate's Rights Concept that allows the inmates to exercise all the rights of ordinary citizens except those taken away by law or which cannot be exercised by reason of his incarceration"(reference 12, Vol. 1, Ser. No. OPO 978:1). The plan describes the present situation and the future situation of inmate's rights in Canada, and specifies two alternatives for action. The first alternative consists of 16 separate steps and the second alternative contains 15, each of which has a specific completion date. The operational goals statement has an issue manager, whose name and telephone number are part of the plan, and the plan also contains his recommendation to follow the first alternative, which is more gradual than the second alternative. All of the action steps necessary to achieve the goal are assigned to specific persons, and have a limited period of time in which they are to be accomplished. There is also a cost summary attached which estimates that the implementation of the inmate's rights plan will cost $67,000 in 1979/80, and somewhat less in each succeeding year. The operational plan concludes with a specification of the means to be used to follow-up the implementation of the inmate's rights goal.[12] The Canadian planning system is admirable, both for its detailed specification of goals and activities, and because the assignment of individual staff members to be responsible for the achievement of each goal assures that none of the elements of the plan will be disregarded in the crush of day-to-day affairs.

SUMMARY

Correctional administrators include those in state central offices, institution heads, major department heads, and middle-level correctional managers such as educational administrators, custody officers at the level of lieutenant and higher, and prison hospital administrators. The position of the warden or superintendent is perhaps the most stressful of all correctional administrative positions because of its double-bind nature. Correctional administrators are often put into the position of making decisions in which there are unresolvable dilemmas and pressure groups strongly advocating opposing positions. This means that a relatively high proportion of the decisions made by wardens are of a "no-win" nature. The four basic models of correctional policy are rehabilitation, reintegration, restraint, and reform. The restraint and reform models of correctional policy generally involve the use of the military approach to management, while the rehabilitation and reintegration models are more consistent with participative management. Correctional managers are responsible for the social climates of their institutions, for the determination of regulations and the administering of discipline to both prisoners and staff members, for correctional planning and policy development, and for the protection of the civil rights of all prisoners. They are also held accountable for minimizing escapes, maintaining institutional order, and a wide variety of other responsibilities defined by law or administrative regulation. Some of the most recent developments affecting administrative performance in correctional systems are the regionalization of state corrections, the development and implementation of statistical information systems, and prison employee unionization.

REFERENCES

1. Adams, Stuart. "Correctional Agency Perceptions of the Usefulness of Research." *American Journal of Corrections* 37(July–August 1975):24–30.
2. American Bar Association. Correctional Economics Center. "Resource Needs of Correctional Administrators: A Survey Report." Washington, D.C., 1974.

3. Bachman, David D. "Florida's Success/Failure in Prison Planning." *In* M.Robert Montilla and Nora Harlow: *Correctional Facilities Planning.* Lexington, MA: D.C. Heath, 1979, pp. 169–179.

4. Baker, Robert A. *et al.* "A Computerized Screening System for Correctional Classification." *Criminal Justice and Behavior* 6 (1979):251–273.

5. Barak (Glantz), Israel L. *Punishment to Protection: Solitary Confinement in the Washington State Penitentiary, 1966–1975.* Ph.D. dissertation, Ohio State University, 1978.

6. Bartollas, Clemens and Stuart J. Miller. *Correctional Administration: Theory and Practice.* New York: McGraw-Hill, 1978.

7. Berk, Richard A. and Peter H. Rossi. *Prison Reform and State Elites.* Cambridge, MA: Ballinger, 1977.

8. Blumstein, Alfred, Jacqueline Cohen, and Harold D. Miller. "Demographically Disaggregated Projection of Prison Populations." *Journal of Criminal Justice* 8 (1980):1–26.

9. Bowker, Lee H. *Prisoner Subcultures.* Lexington, MA: D.C. Heath, 1977.

10. Bowker, Lee H. "The Warden: A Classic Case of the Double-Bind Dilemma." *International Journal of Offender Therapy and Comparative Criminology* 23 (1979):159–163.

11. Bowker, Lee H. *Prison Victimization.* New York: Elsevier, 1980.

12. Canada. Correctional Service. *Five-Year Operational Plan for the Correctional Service of Canada,* 2 volumes. Ottawa, 1979.

13. Cliff Industries. "Cliff Mobile Housing: Serving a Variety of Housing Needs of Minimum Security Institutions." Elkhart, IN, no date.

14. Conrad, John P. and Simon Dinitz. *In Fear of Each Other: Studies of Dangerousness in America.* Lexington, MA: D.C. Heath, 1977.

15. Conrad, Joseph P. "Who's in Charge? The Control of Gang Violence in California Prisons." *In* M. Robert Montilla and Nora Harlow: *Correctional Facilities Planning.* Lexington, MA: D.C. Heath, 1979, pp. 135–147.

16. CONtact. *Corrections Compendium Survey Book.* Lincoln, NB, 1979.

17. Crago, Tom G. and C. Hromans. "Inmate Population Projections 1980–1985." Denver: Colorado Department of Corrections, 1980.

18. Cushman, Robert C. *Criminal Justice Planning for Local Governments.* Washington, D.C.: Government Printing Office, 1980.

19. Dauber, Edward and David Schichor. "A Comparative Exploration of Prison Discipline." *Journal of Criminal Justice* 7 (1979):21–36.

20. Dillingham, David D. *Right to be Heard: Evaluation of the Ward Grievance Procedure in the California Youth Authority.* Sacramento: California Youth Authority, 1978.

21. Duffee, David. *Correctional Management: Change and Control in Correctional Organizations.* Englewood Cliffs, NJ: Prentice-Hall, 1980.

22. Florida. Department of Corrections. "Annual Report 1977–1978." Tallahassee, FL, 1978.

23. Gersten, Raymond. "Noise in Jails: A Constitutional Issue." *Clearinghouse Transfer* 19 (no date):1–4.

24. Hogan, Cornelius D. and William R. Steinhurst. "Managing Change in Corrections." *Federal Probation* 40 (June 1976):55–59.

25. Jacobs, James B. and Norma M. Crotty. *Guard Unions and the Future of the Prisons.* Ithaca, NY: Institute of Public Employment, Cornell University, 1978.

26. Kahn, B. and A. McClendon. "Report of the Wisconsin Legislation Joint Sen-

ate–Assembly Subcommittee on Problems in Wisconsin's Adult Correctional Institutions." Madison, WI, 1979.

27. Keating, J. Michael, Jr. *et al. Grievance Mechanisms in Correctional Institutions.* Washington, D.C.: Government Printing Office, 1975.

28. Law Enforcement Assistance Administration. *Planning and Designing for Juvenile Justice.* Washington, D.C.: Government Printing Office, 1972.

29. Law Enforcement Assistance Administration. *The National Manpower Survey of the Criminal Justice System, Volume 1, Summary Report.* Washington, D.C.: Government Printing Office, 1978.

30. Law Enforcement Assistance Administration. *The National Manpower Survey of the Criminal Justice System, Volume 3, Corrections.* Washington, D.C.: Government Printing Office, 1978.

31. Lindquist, Charles A. "Inmate Participation in Correctional Institution Governance: An Analysis of Inmate of Grievance Mechanisms." Paper presented at the annual meeting of the Academy of Criminal Justice Sciences, 1978.

32. Lunden, Walter A. *The Prison Warden and the Custodial Staff.* Springfield, IL: Charles C Thomas, 1965.

33. McArthur, Virginia. "Inmate Grievance Mechanisms: A Survey of 209 American Prisons." *Federal Probation* 38 (December 1974):41–47.

34. McConkie, Mark L. *Management by Objectives: A Corrections Perspective.* Washington, D.C.: Government Printing Office, 1975.

35. Meyer, John C. "Change and Obstacles to Change in Prison Management." *Federal Probation* 36 (June 1972):39–46.

36. Michigan. Department of Corrections. "State-Wide Implementation of a Regionalized Corrections System." Lansing, MI, 1979.

37. Minnesota. Department of Corrections. "Inmate Discipline Regulations." St. Paul, MN, 1979.

38. Minnesota, Department of Corrections. "Research and Information Systems Activity Report." St. Paul, MN,1979.

39. Montilla, M. Robert. *Prison Employee Unionism: Management Guide for Correctional Administrators.* Washington, D.C.: Government Printing Office, 1978.

40. Montilla, M. Robert. "Economic, Fiscal, and Manpower Issues in Planning for Prison Population Growth." *In* M. Robert Montilla and Nora Harlow: *Correctional Facilities Planning.* Lexington, MA: D.C. Heath, 1979, pp. 181–190.

41. Moos, Rudolph H. *Evaluating Correctional and Community Settings.* New York: Wiley, 1975.

42. Moyer, Frederic D. and Edith E. Flynn. *Correctional Environment.* Washington, D.C.: Government Printing Office, 1973.

43. Moyer Associates. *Alaska Corrections Master Plan: Executive Summary.* Chicago, 1979.

44. Myers, Kevin and Henry Clark. "Social Climates at Facilities within the Oklahoma Department of Corrections as Measured by the Correctional Institution's Environment Scale." Oklahoma City: Department of Corrections, 1979.

45. Nagel, William G. *The New Red Barn: A Critical Look at the Modern American Prison.* New York: Walker, 1973.

46. Nanus, Bert. "A General Model for Criminal Justice Planning." *Journal of Criminal Justice* 2 (1974):345–356.

47. National Advisory Commission on Criminal Justice Standards and Goals. *Corrections.* Washington, D.C.: Government Printing Office, 1973.

48. National Clearinghouse for Criminal Justice Planning and Architecture. "A Summary of Potential Impact Associated with Closed Circuit Television Surveillance in Correctional Environments." Urbana, IL, 1974.
49. Nebraska. Department of Correctional Services. "Annual Report 1974–1975." Lincoln, NB, 1975.
50. New Hampshire State Prison. "Manual for the Guidance of Inmates." Concord, NH, 1978.
51. New Jersey. Department of Corrections. "The Bureau of Correctional Information Systems." Trenton, NJ, 1979.
52. New York. Department of Correctional Services. "Toward a Safer Society: Report of Operations and Development for 1978." Albany, NY, 1978.
53. North Carolina. Department of Correction. "1978–1987 Strategies." Raleigh, NC, 1979.
54. Ojalvo, Phil. "Population Projections for the Department of Corrections 1980–1982." Washington, D.C.: D.C. Department of Corrections, 1980.
55. Oklahoma. Department of Corrections. "Inmate Manual of Rules and Regulations." Oklahoma City, 1978.
56. O'Leary, Vincent, David Duffee, and Ernest Wenk. "Developing Relevant Data for a Prison Organizational Development Program." *Journal of Criminal Justice* 5 (1977):85–104.
57. South Carolina. Department of Corrections. "Ten Year Capital Improvement Plan for Fiscal years 1979–80 through 1988–89." Columbia, SC, 1979.
58. Srivastava, S.P. "The Exercise of Authority in Prison (an Analysis of the Problems of Discipline in a Central Prison of Uttar Pradesh)." *Indian Journal of Criminology* 4 (1976):50–61.
59. Stephen Carter and Associates. "Comprehensive Growth and Capital Improvements Plan: Executive Summary." Columbia, SC: South Carolina Department of Corrections, 1979.
60. Tabasz, Thomas F. *Toward an Economics of Prisons.* Lexington, MA: D.C. Heath, 1975.
61. Travisono, Anthony P. "Security Glass: A Fragile Issue." *Corrections Today* 42 (July–August 1980):34.
62. United States. Federal Prison System. "A Program Statement: Inmate Discipline." Washington, D.C., March 21, 1979.
63. Vinter, Robert D. and Morris Janowitz. "The Comparative Study of Juvenile Correctional Institutions: A Research report." Ann Arbor, MI: School of Social Work, University of Michigan, 1961.
64. Washington, D.C. Department of Corrections. "Taking Care of Business." Washington, D.C., 1979.
65. Wisconsin. "Disciplinary Hearing Data Sheet." Madison, WI, 1975.
66. Wright, Kevin N. "The Conceptualization and Measurement of the Social Climate of Correctional Organizations." *Journal of Offender Counseling, Services and Rehabilitation* 4 (1979):137–152.
67. Wynne, John M. *Prison Employee Unionism: The Impact on Correctional Administration and Programs.* Washington, D.C.: Government Printing Office, 1978.

Chapter 10

Prison Programs and Services

The application of the medical model to correctional institutions has left us with a vocabulary for describing correctional services that is not entirely accurate. We tend to see correctional institutions as having a specific number of treatment programs operating on the medical model of sickness and health, plus various services which have few implications for human development. This distinction between treatment programs and service is an artificial one, for many services are run like treatment programs, and have similar effects on the prisoners involved in them. For example, working on a maintenance crew may have extremely positive (and unrecognized) effects on a prisoner. Some of the basic services in prisons are medical services, recreational services, institutional maintenance, and food services. All of these services have therapeutic aspects for some prisoners that go beyond the services themselves, such as improvements in self-image, the acquisition of needed job skills, and the formation of meaningful relationships with staff members.

FOUR BASIC PRISON SERVICES

Medical Services

Medical care in prison is of primary importance since the prisoners are not free to seek their own medical services elsewhere. Moreover, there is the factor of the penury of most prisoners lowering the level of their medical care prior to admission. Consequently, their medical needs during the early months of imprisonment are often extensive. Where medical care is inadequate, as it is many American prisons, the courts have shown a willingness to support prisoner lawsuits related to health care. In one case, Henry Tucker was awarded $518,000 by a federal judge because he was permanently paralyzed by the injection of excessive amounts of antipsychotic drugs by untrained inmate nurses while he was at the Virginia State Penitentiary in Richmond.[32]

Prisoner health care is probably even more problematic in institutions for women than in institutions for men. The most recent survey of medical services to incarcerated women notes numerous deficiencies in health care services.[74] Despite these problems, the interest of the American Medical Association in correctional matters, the continuous pressure of legal action against correctional administrators, and the movement toward a national set of standards for prison conditions have resulted in a number of significant improvements in prison health care during the past decade. One sign of the professionalization of prison health care was the appearance of the publication *Journal of Prison Health*[42] in 1980. Addressed to the needs of physicians, legal authorities, and correctional professionals, this bi-annual publication is the first scholarly journal to be entirely devoted to the health care of incarcerated individuals.

When prisoners accidentally injure themselves, the medical treatment they receive is clearly a prison service. On the other hand, an unknown number of prisoners have medical conditions that contribute to their criminal habits, and the medical correction of these conditions can have a rehabilitative effect on their lives. In this case, the medical services become treatment. The use of plastic surgery to correct skin tumors, traumatic hand disabilities, scars, and self-inflicted or professionally applied tattoos among the prisoners at the State Industrial Farm for Women in Goochland, Virginia is an example of the provision of a medical service that has treatment implications.[19] Other forms of medical service having potential psychosocial implications include the correction of poor eyesight or poor hearing and the treatment for metabolic abnormalities or brain tumors, either of which might interfere with normal brain function if left untreated. In a general sense, any medical condition impinging on individual capacity to engage in legitimate economic activity can also aggravate an inherent propensity to indulge activities. The cure or reversal of such bodily malfunctions have promising long-term rehabilitative implications. (See Chapter 6 for more information on prison health care.)

Recreational Services

Recreational services in correctional institutions tend to command a rather low priority with administrators. Few prisoners have access to adequate recreational programs. Those that exist are usually limited to athletic programs, arts and crafts, and watching television. Arts and crafts objects produced by prisoners are sold to visitors and staff members through the prison store, and the sales are credited to the prisoners' individual accounts—often minus deductions for a prisoner welfare fund. The Law Enforcement Assistance Administration began awarding arts and crafts grants to specific institutions under Project CULTURE in 1977, and had awarded nearly $2 million to 54 programs in 35 states by mid-1980.[82]

Like medical services, recreational activities can also have rehabilitative implications. Participating in a weight-lifting program can improve the self-image of a prisoner, and can also reduce the probability of victimization by other prisoners. Arts and crafts activities can have positive psychological effects on prisoners. The money earned through these programs allows prisoners to be financially independent of prison rackets, and can assist prisoners to occupy their time productively so that they do not become immersed in antisocial activities of the prisoner subculture. Even if participation in art programs does not substantialy diminish the risk of recidivism after release, it can still be a satisfying experience for prisoners, promoting positive attitudes and stimulate them to improve themselves in a number of skill areas.[66]

Institutional Maintenance

Correctional institutions almost never have sufficient funding to pay civilian employees to perform all institutional maintenance tasks. Prisoners are heavily used on maintenance crews, ranging from basic cleaning to heavy construction, electrical engineering, and plumbing. The more technical maintenance tasks are directly supervised by civilians who have considerable expertise in maintenance activities. In many cases, prisoners taking part in these activities receive extensive vocational training in what amounts to an apprenticeship. For some prisoners, these apprenticeships are the first normal long-term work experiences in which they have ever participated

One of the most salient aspects of institutional maintenance is sanitation. North Carolina monitors sanitation in its correctional institutions by using a rating scale scored by an inspector. The North Carolina scale contains 162 possible demerits for sanitation inadequacies in lighting and ventilation, vermin control, the handling and storage of food, and waste disposal. The demerit scores permit comparisons between the various prisons in the North Carolina system as well as an absolute rating of the adequacy of sanitation at the specific institutions.[8] In states without an objective rating scale and regular inspections, there may be a great discrepancies in sanitation between institutions, except on those aspects of sanitation that are enforced by public health inspectors.

Food Services

Food is the most essential commodity in a prison setting. For many prisoners, there is little to look forward to in their daily round of activities except meals, which may afford an opportunity for enjoyable social interaction as well as the pleasure of eating. Correctional institutions vary greatly in the quality of food served to prisoners, with some institutions providing food that is barely adequate nutritionally and substantially inadequate in terms of esthetics and sanitation, while other institutions prepare food that is superior to the food served in many college cafeterias. The food service is always administered by civilian employees, generally supplemented by a sizable number of prisoners. Many institutions offer a number of different vocational education courses in food preparation, butchering, and related skills as part of the food service operations.

CORRECTIONAL CLASSIFICATION

Classification refers to the process by which prisoners are assigned to institutions, housing units, and treatment programs based on their needs and characteristics. The National Advisory Commission on Criminal Justice Standards and Goals has stated that classification systems "are more useful for assessing risk and facilitating the efficient management of offenders than for diagnosis of causation and prescriptions for remedial treatment...".[63:210] It also recommends that classifications should occur in specific institutions rather than in central state reception centers serving entire correctional systems, and that institutional classification may be accomplished in a specialized reception unit, or by a classification committee or team. Institutional classification may be carried out using a sophisticated computerized screening system such as the Kentucky system discussed in Chapter 9,[4] or it can be done through the examination of an assortment of materials in the prisoners' central files.

The primary use of classification in most correctional systems is to assign prisoners to different risk categories. This is a management rather than a treatment task, but it is included in this chapter because of the important treatment implications of classification decisions. The Federal Bureau of Prisons has six security levels into which prisoners must be classified. The higher the security level, the more likely a facility is to have extensive perimeter security, such as a double fence or wall, manned towers, external controls, electronic detection devices, secure housing in single cells, and a high staff–prisoner ratio.[48] As carried out within individual institutions, classification determines housing assignments. Most institutions have a variety of housing assignments, including single cells, double cells, dormitories, and cell blocks varying in staffing and provisions for physical security.

At the New Hampshire State Prison,[64] the Classification Board makes decisions in nine separate areas: (1) custody grades; (2) housing assignment; (3) special statuses; (4) legal conditions; (5) work training assignments; (6) educational opportunities; (7) post-release plans; (8) special programs; and (9) transfers. There are five different custody classifications, beginning with minimum "A" (in which prisoners live outside the walls of the institution and can come and go from work with few restraints) to maximum custody (in which prisoners are housed in the most physically secure part of the institution and receive special custodial controls and handling because of their threat of violence, risk of escape, and generally disruptive behavior).Special statuses used at the New Hampshire State Prison include administrative segregation, medical segregation, disciplinary segregation, and protective custody. In this type of an institution, the Classification Board assumes a major decision-making role.

The variables used in making classification decisions vary from system to system. Edith Flynn[22] has provided us with a list of critical predictor variables most commonly used in classifying prisoners. These are (1) age; (2) prior institutional committment; (3) institutional adjustment; (4) marital status; (5) type of current offense; (6) prior record; (7) employment record; (8) family ties; (9) community ties; and (10) personality traits and characteristics. By institutional adjustment, she means the number of disciplinary citations or the amount of time spent in disciplinary segregation by prisoners. Some of these factors are more important for institutional behavior than for risk of recidivism in the community. However, community risks must always be taken into account because of the possibility of escape.

Of the psychological tests that have been used in classification procedures, the Minnesota Multiphasic Personality Inventory (MMPI) has been the greatest potential to aid in classification for both treatment and risk. The MMPI classification system developed by Edwin Megargee and his associates[57] at the Federal Correctional Institution at Tallahassee classifies prisoners into ten groups. An extensive program of experimentation has allowed these researchers to develop separate profiles for each group, with specific recommendations for treatment. In a recent application of this classification system, the number of assaults at FCI–Tallahassee was reduced by 46 percent when the assaultive potential of prisoners was estimated using the MMPI typology and the more aggressive prisoners were housed in dormitories separate from those reserved for the prisoners most likely to be victimized.

TREATMENT PROGRAMS

Correctional institutions contain four basic types of treatment programs. These are educational programs, vocational programs, individual treatment, and group treatment. Institutions also offer an assortment of specialized programs such as drug rehabilitation programs, alcoholism programs, conjugal visits, and co-correctional programs. These programs combine elements of individual and group therapy techniques, and perhaps also education or vocational programs, but they often modify the content of these programs to meet the special needs of their own clients. A reanalysis of data collected in the 1974 survey of state prisoners by Joan Petersilia[68] showed that 40 percent of all state prisoners participated in some sort of treatment program while incarcerated. She estimated that 68 percent of all prisoners needed educational treatment, 31 percent needed job training, 23 percent needed a drug rehabilitation program, and 22 percent needed an alcohol rehabilitation program. Only 25 percent of the prisoners in need of job training were actually enrolled in a job training program or had completed such a program prior to the time of the survey. Even smaller proportions of prisoners with vocational, drug, and alcohol treatment needs had previously participated or were currently participating in relevant programs. At the time of the survey, only one prisoner in every eight was engaged in an educational program, and only one in every 14 was receiving psychological counseling.

The staff of the National Study of Juvenile Correctional Programs found that individual counseling and group counseling were used in more than three-quarters of the 34 juvenile correctional programs they studied. Remedial education classes were used in 59 percent of the programs, and vocational training was used in 44 percent of the programs. The most common therapeutic techniques used were reality therapy (71 percent of all programs), behavior modification (68 percent), family therapy (59 percent), psychotherapy (56 percent), and guided group interaction (44 percent). Chemotherapy was used in 26 percent of the programs.[83]

These statistics demonstrate that, although there are many significant treatment programs in existence in American correctional institutions, total treatment utilization rates still leave much to be desired. Individual and group therapy is used more extensively in juvenile institutions than in adult institutions, and the medical model of treatment is correspondingly stronger in the juvenile institutions. Even where the medical model has been largely abandoned, educational and vocational programs are still seen as essential to prepare most prisoners for successful community reintegration.

Educational Programs

Educational programs in correctional institutions begin at the most basic level, since many prisoners are functionally illiterate, and progress at least to the completion of a high school degree or its equivalent. Nearly all correctional institutions permit prisoners to take correspondence courses at the college level, and most of the larger correctional institutions offer at least a few college courses for high school graduates taught by professors from local colleges.[60] Few correctional systems require participation in educational programs, as Texas does for prisoners reading below the fifth-grade level,[69] but the general belief that parole boards reward prisoners for education achievement has the same effect. Few correctional educational administrators have any difficulty in filling their programs.

A recent national survey of correctional education programs sponsored by the Law Enforcement Assistance Administration found some improvements over earlier years. At the same time, it was recommended that correctional education programs be substantially expanded to meet the needs of prisoners currently excluded from participation. Prison education programs appear to be underfunded and to depend too heavily on a diversity of funding sources, many of which supply funds for only a short period of time. These funding problems lead to difficulties in the planning, continuity, and staffing of correctional educational programs in many institutions. Although most correctional educators are certified, many of them feel the need for specialized training in the needs of correctional clients. Resources available for educational programming at the college level are generally less adequate than resources available for adult basic education, secondary education, GED programs, and vocational education.[6]

These problems are illustrated by a recent evaluation of academic and vocational education programs in Florida's Department of Offender Rehabilitation.[21] This project found that all Florida correctional facilities were in full compliance with only 13 of 70 educational standards developed as part of the evaluation process. Less than half of the institutions were in compliance with 21 of the standards. The lack of compliance with many of these standards was related to difficulties in budgeting, lack of standard entrance criteria and progress measures, and the absence of a standardized curriculum. Educational offerings differed from institution to institution according to the preferences of local administrators and teachers. A standard appropriation per student was used to develop the education program budget in only 35 percent of the institutions, and adequate funds for necessary expenditures were available in 25 percent of the institutions. Auditing and budget controls were used in 30 percent of the institutions. The strong points of Florida educational programs included adequate space facilities in most institutions, a sensitivity to the need for ethnic studies in the curriculum, availability of library materials and college extension courses, and the provision of individual counseling for all students requesting it. Questions not answered by this evaluation are: (1) Did the educational programs affect the cognitive development of the prisoners they served? (2) Did participation in these programs help the prisoners obtain and keep jobs after release? and (3) Did participation reduce recidivism?

Work Programs

As a mode of treatment, work in prison industry and prison farms suffers from a confusion of goals. Prison administrators are concerned about the profitability of prison industries and farms, so prisoners are often assigned where they are needed rather than to the positions that best relate to their requirements. Many work programs are irrelevant to the goal of developing job skills, partly because there are no comparable positions available in the larger society and partly because the job skills learned are so rudimentary that any outside position involving the use of these skills would prove unattractive to many prisoners as an alternative to a continued life of crime. Even when irrelevant, work programs may be beneficial in that regular work for as little as a year may be the longest continuous work experience that most of the prisoners have ever had.[27]

Vocational training programs aim at the goal of improving the work skills of the prisoners in meaningful trades. Operating in the mode of educational programs rather than correctional industries, they are more likely to be tailored to meet the vocational needs of the prisoners. A 1972 survey of vocational training programs in correctional institutions found that the most common programs were auto mechanics, welding, machine shop, masonry, radio and television repair, auto body repair, carpentry, barbering, baking and cooking, architectural and mechanical drafting, air conditioning and refrigeration, and small engine repair. Some of these courses were tied to prison maintenance needs, and where that was true, confusion crept in as to the real purpose of the program.[56] The question of the usefulness of the training looms large with vocational education, just as it does with prison work programs. The answer appears to be the same. Vocational programs that do not enable prisoners to look forward to higher earnings upon release are not likely to be associated with a decrease in recidivism. An evaluation of vocational programs in Michigan by Sandra Gleason[29] found that programs teaching clerical, operative, craftsman, and service worker skills did not have favorable impact on the post-prison earnings and recidivism of the prisoners. By comparison, professional vocational training programs such as computer programming, data-processing, electronics, machine drafting, and vocational music were associated with an increase in average post-prison earnings and a decrease in the probability of recidivism. Gleason concludes that a reduction in recidivism is ony partially explained by gains in legitimate earnings. Other factors, such job satisfaction and career potential, are also relevant to ex-offender decisions about indulging in criminal activities.

A recent examination of employment-related programs in the federal prison system and four state systems by the Comptroller General[16] concluded that the institutions did not provide enough work for all their prisoners. Too many of the programs entailed no usable training at all. Furthermore, there was little effort to match the job skills and experiences of offenders with the available work programs, except in the Texas system. A similar report on prison industries in Canada also found a discrepancy between prisoners and available work. There are too many prisoners in Canadian institutions for the available employment opportunities; this results in overstaffing, underemployment, and low productivity per capita. Prisoners tend to have fewer usable job skills than citizens in the free population, and many of them serve sentences that are too short for the development of job skills to be efficient. Other institutional programs and needs take priority over work programs, and most programs are operated at the lowest common denominator in order to make use of whatever prisoners are available after other institutional needs have been met.[49]

The vocational training situation for female prisoners is considerably worse than it is for male prisoners. Institutional maintenance takes precedence over vocational training values in work programs. The small size of most female institutions, combined with their geographical isolation (which is also a problem for many male institutions), places severe limits on the variety and quality of programs available. The kinds of job training generally provided tend to conform to sexist stereotypes of female roles, and are usually limited to occupations such as secretary, cosmotologist, nurse's aide, waitress, and cashier. Many women find these programs so boring or irrelevant that they do not participate. When innovative programs are occasionally offered, utilization is limited by the small number of slots available.[26]

The Free Venture Model. The Free Venture model of prison industries specifies a full 40-hour work week, prisoner wages that are tied to work output, productivity standards comparable to those of the outside world, hiring and firing procedures that also approximate outside practices, and transferable training and job skills. This model allows prisoners to earn enough money to partially reimburse the state for the cost of their own confinement and to make restitution payments to victims.[62] Additional aspects of the Free Venture model are the integration of institutional work with job placements upon release, financial incentives to prison industries, and self-supporting or profit-making operations.[70] Unlike traditional prison industries, which are a poor approximation of work in the outside world,[47] Free Venture industries represent a serious attempt to bring competitive capitalism within the walls of correctional institutions.

The first three Free Venture programs were begun in Minnesota, Connecticut, and Illinois in 1977. A preliminary assessment of these programs shows that paying of higher wages to inmate workers results in a rapid alteration in the pattern of institutional programming. Applications for reassignment to industry programs rise sharply, while institutional maintenance crews have difficulty in recruiting enough prisoners to keep the institution functioning. Prisons in these states, as well as in other states that have received federal grants to develop Free Venture programs, are just beginning to become acquainted with capitalism in the outside world. The requirement of high productivity has implications for designing and implementing production scheduling systems and efficient equipment. Profitability cannot be calculated unless there is an adequate accounting system, something rarely seen in contemporary American correctional industries. Sales markets must be investigated and expanded, which requires considerable interaction between institutional staff members and the outside community.[62] These comments suggest that the long-range effects of Free Venture programs may not be limited to changes in correctional industries.

Prison Therapists

Psychological treatment programs in correctional institutions are staffed by individuals from a variety of professional backgrounds. For example, the Mental Health Satellite Unit at Attica in New York contains an administrator, a full-time and a part-time psychiatrist, two full-time psychologists, a psychiatric social worker, two psychiatric registered nurses, and twelve correctional officers.[20] The use of psychiatrists, psychologists, and social workers has been supplemented by peer counselors in some settings.[14] Community mental health resources can be obtained on a contract basis to supplement in-house resources. This is an essential practice in states such as Vermont, where the small number of prisoners makes in-house staffing for psychological services inefficient.[15] Another variation in the use of mental health professionals is to bring psychological consultants into the institution to affect in-house staff and programs rather than to provide direct services to prisoners.[24] A crucial dimension for the provision of therapy to prisoners is the ratio of prisoners to treatment personnel, which is very high in most correctional institutions.

What are the ethics of professional performance for human services professionals working in correctional agencies? The Task force on the Role of Psychology in the Criminal Justice System[73] of the American Psychological Association has attempted to sort out the conflicting responsibilities of these professionals, and has made a number of recommendations on the matter. It is recommended that confidentiality be maintained at the same level in correctional institutions as in the free society, and that any deviation from this standard should be made known to clients in advance of counseling contacts, preferably in writing. Another recommendation states that psychologists should be exceedingly cautious in making predictions about criminal behavior that might be used in criminal justice system decisions about the freedom of offenders. The Task Force on the Role of Psychology in the Criminal Justice System argues that there is ". . . . no incompatability between abandoning rehabilitation as the *purpose* of imprisonment and maintaining vigorous rehabilitation programs in prison."[73:1110]

Individual Therapies: Counseling Modalities

A large number of counseling modalities are used in prison treatment programs. These include Transactional Analysis, Reality Therapy, Transcendental Meditation, psychedelic therapy, traditional psychoanalysis, and social casework. We will discuss two of these therapeutic modalities in this section: Transcendental Meditation and Reality Therapy. The first of these is an example of the new wave of prison counseling modalities, while the second is an example of the more traditional therapeutic techniques that have been used in prisons for decades.

Transcendental Meditation. Transcendental Meditation involves repeating a nonsense phrase to oneself as a technique of achieving relaxation and mental alertness.[7] The use of meaningless thought to transcend all thought is said to reduce physiological stress by removing negative thoughts from consciousness. Although there has been some criticism on the quality of research on Transcendental Meditation, much of which has been performed by movement members, the reports of positive findings associated with the use of the technique are intriguing. At least 25 correctional institutions are currently using Transcendental Meditation, and evaluations have been conducted at five of these institutions. Most of these studies are limited to the evaluation of psychological changes reported by the participants in the programs, but two studies suggest that program participation is associated with a decrease in institutional rule violations.[18] A study of the effect of Transcendental Meditation on recidivism has yet to be conducted.

Reality Therapy. Like Transcendental Meditation, Reality Therapy utilizes a simple methodology that can be practiced with a minimum of training. Clients begin by forming an honest personal relationship with their therapist in which there is a rejection of antisocial behavior rather than of the individuals themselves. Treatment plans detailing small increments of progress toward mutually agreed-upon goals are worked out between the clients and counselors, and these plans are adjusted in future treatment sessions. The emphasis in the therapy is on confronting reality as it exists in the external world rather than on internal problems, on the future rather than on the past, and on human potential instead of personal problems. There is no punishment associated with Reality Therapy. However, clients who do not show sufficient effort may be dropped by therapists, who will claim that they are wasting their time.[28] Although Reality Therapy has been widely accepted in corrections, and although there are many general descriptions and testimonies of program successes using the technique,[5] there is a surprising lack of scientific studies on the effects of Reality Therapy on prisoner behavior and recidivism.

Behavior Modification

Behavior modification offers a precise technology for changing the behavior of prisoners. Like Reality Therapy, behavior modification is not concerned with the past. It attempts to change clearly defined, measurable behavior by the application of positive and negative reinforcements. An example of behavior modification is aversion therapy, which is often used in programs for sex offenders. In one such program, offenders were shown slides of socially unacceptable sex objects that were accompanied by shocks. Sexual arousal was measured by penis volume, and shocks were administered at half-second intervals until sexual response was inhibited. Once sexual response to inappropriate sex objects had been extinguished, it was possible to expose the sex offenders to repeated slides of the deviant sexual activity in which they had previously engaged without their now showing any physical evidence of sexual arousal.[46]

Therapies such as this one bring the ethical question of the informed consent of prisoners into sharp focus. The problem exists for all prison treatment programs, but is less visible when the program does not involve a great deal of obvious unpleasantness or danger. To comply with the ethical principle of informed consent, therapists need to fully inform prospective clients of the nature and potential dangers of the proposed therapy so that they can *freely* decide whether they want to participate in the program. Even if therapists are careful to fully explain their techniques to prospective prisoner clients, there is some question as to whether they are really free to decline to participate. When prison release dates are partly determined by participation in treatment programs, the prisoners are being coerced to participate. The new justice model of corrections solves this ethical predicament by setting release dates independently of program participation, so that prisoners are truly free to refuse to participate in treatment programs if they so desire.

Technologies involving the devotion of expensive professional time and equipment to individual prisoners cannot be implemented in most correctional institutions. In these institutions, positive and negative reinforcement becomes a general problem of social engineering. Once outside of the psychologist's office, prisoners must deal with the negativism of the prisoner subculture. Social values become so twisted that it is no longer possible to make commonplace assumptions about the nature of positive and negative reinforcements. There is some evidence that prison officers are not able to accurately estimate the effects of reinforcements and punishments that are applied to recalcitrant prisoners.[54] The social system in many correctional institutions tends to punish prosocial behavior and to reward antisocial behavior, which is particularly difficult for staff members to deal with because much of the positive reinforcement for antisocial behavior occurs on nonverbal levels of communication.[12] One way to gain control over the prison environment is to institute a token economy. Although this is more properly a group treatment technique than an individual technique, we will discuss it here because of its affinity with individual behavior modifications.

Cottage Seven is a unit in a larger treatment institution for delinquent boys. The cottage uses an aggressive behavior modification program in which the behavior of the boys, including language behavior, is monitored using an array of charts, plans, status reports, and a daily log book. Each boy has an individualized behavior plan which emphasizes three or four of the most problematic of his behaviors. Performance on these behaviors is rated four times daily, along with conformity to the general rules of the cottage. Rewards are doled out to the boys based on their accumulated points for conformity and treatment progress. Margaret Gold[30] reports that the use of this behavior control technology has been successful in suppressing the prisoner subculture in Cottage Seven, but it also has involved a number of inconsistencies in application that resulted in the introduction of a considerable amount of unfairness into the system.

Difficulties in implementing a behavior modification program that is seen as fair by prisoners and staff alike have plagued a number of other correctional experiments, including the token economy of the Patuxent Institution in Maryland and the START Program at the Medical Center for Federal Prisoners in Springfield, Missouri. These two programs also produced a high level of coerciveness and harsh conditions for entering prisoners, for these prisoners were forced to live in dehumanizing surroundings, and to earn their way into more humane settings by conforming to the rules and the expectations of institutional personnel. Prisoners in both programs exerted what specialists in behavior modification refer to as counter-control, which means that they engaged in prison disturbances and filed lawsuits against program administrators.[72]

Another implementation of a token economy is the project developed at the Draper Correctional Center in Elmore, Alabama. Experimenters at Draper found that while the use of punishment procedures produced increased conformity, there was no generalization to nontargeted areas. This means that the prisoners showed no general improvement; only improvement in those specific negative behaviors for which they were punished. The effects of the punishment did not extend beyond the period of the punishment, and the days on which negative behavioral incidents occurred increased from 12 to 48 percent.[58] Since the effects of a punishment model did not appear to be sufficiently positive to be worth continuing experiments in this direction, it was decided to implement an alternative management system using positive reinforcement.

In one experiment, a token economy was used to motivate prisoners to keep the area and themselves in good condition and also to motivate participation and performance in a remedial education program. Points earned through conforming behavior were recorded in bank accounts for each prisoner, and the prisoners could then write checks on these bank accounts to purchase commissary items and to gain special privileges. The program had strongly positive effects on prisoner behavior without the negative side effect of increased disciplinary problems. The improvements in prisoner behavior also lasted longer after the end of the experimental program than they had in the case of the punishment program, although prisoner behavior did eventually decline to the baseline levels that had existed before the beginning of the experiment. This experiment worked out so well that the positive reinforcement technique was extended to all areas of prisoner life.[59] Since the program did not target behaviors that would be likely to reduce recidivism, it is no surprise that a 15-month follow-up study found no differences in recidivism between the token economy graduates and other prisoners.[76] It has yet to be demonstrated that behavior modification in the form of a token economy can reduce adult recidivism over an extended period of time.

Physical Control Techniques

For prisoners who do not respond well to counseling or behavior modification, there are more coercive techniques available. These include chemotherapy, shock treatments, castration, and frontal lobotomies. These techniques sometimes overlap with behavior modification, as when drugs are used to induce intense suffering as part of a plan to extinguish antisocial behavior. The most notorious examples of this approach to the task of reducing criminal behavior have occurred in California, where succinylcholine chloride has been used to produce a paralysis of the diaphram and suppression of breathing. The prisoners were subjected to this form of "therapy" at Atascadero State Hospital and Vacaville Rehabilitation Center, often without the consent of the prisoners or their relatives.[65] The public outcry over these programs resulted in their being terminated without an adequate evaluation of their effect on recidivism or any other outcome measure.

There is no record of the recent use of castration, frontal lobotomies, and shock treatments as punishment in American correctional institutions. Instead, psychoactive drugs such as tranquilizers and depressants continue to be widely used in some prison systems. Richard Speigleman[80] has recently observed the use of psychoactive drugs in the California prison system as a quasi-punishment for having socially unacceptable ideas. He also suggests that drugs are used in California as chemical pacifiers to keep prisoners from challenging the inadequacies of the system.

Women are apparently more likely than men to receive psychotropic medication while incarcerated. The summary of criticisms of the use of psychotropic drugs in female institutions by Judith Resnik and Nancy Shaw[74] also applies to the use of these drugs in male institutions. They point out that the proportion of severely mentally ill prisoners is rather small, and that psychotropic medications in correctional institutions tend to be given for minor complaints or as a "cure" for "behavior problems." Psychotropic medications are sometimes given without carrying out a comprehensive evaluation of the patient, and drug administration is rarely accompanied by psychotherapy (as it should be according to current psychiatric opinion). These comments indicate that there are serious questions to be answered about the use of psychotropic drugs in correctional institutions.

The misuses of drugs in correctional settings have given organic therapies a negative image in the mind of the public. This is unfortunate, in that there are also positive possibilities for the biological intervention in criminal behavior. A number of genetic problems may be related to criminal behavior in specific instances, and the resolving of these problems can facilitate the transition to a law-abiding life for prisoners so afflicted. Pioneering research on the biochemistry of the brain shows promise of making contributions to our understanding of criminal behavior in the coming decade.[36]

Group Treatment Modalities

There are two main types of group treatment in correctional institutions. The first type is group therapy, in which groups of prisoners meet with a therapist or counselor for limited periods of time to discuss their problems. The second type of group treatment is the restructuring of the social milieu through institutional management to produce a social climate in which positive personal changes can occur. It is also possible to combine both of these group treatment techniques into one comprehensive program.

Group Counseling. Group counseling may be defined as "...a plan of activity in which three or more people are present for the purpose of solving personal and social problems by applying the theories and methods of counseling in a group. It can be either structured or relatively unstructured in regard to purpose or leadership. It can be an intensive emotional experience or a superficial 'bull session'."[33:152] Group therapy and group psychotherapy refer to the same type of activity, except that psychotherapy is more likely to be led by a human services professional such as a social worker or a psychologist. In some cases, counseling groups may be led by experienced prisoners rather than trained human services personnel.

The main reason for using group counseling instead of individual counseling in correctional institutions is that of limitations on staffing. There are not enough trained counselors in correctional institutions to offer individual counseling to all prisoners requesting it. Group counseling reduces costs without necessarily decreasing therapeutic effectiveness except when the group becomes very large. Increased efficiency in the use of staff time is not the only advantage of group counseling. A second strength of the modality is that prisoners are able to test their ideas against their fellow-prisoners as well as a counselor from the free society. When the group contains a number of prisoners who are committed to the ideals of therapeutic growth, they can have a much greater influence on new group members than even the most skilled group leader.

There are many variations in the use of group counseling in correctional settings. Four commonly seen are encounter groups, psychodrama, marathon therapy groups, and guided group interaction. Encounter groups differ from other counseling groups in that they are more confrontive. The public presentation of self is stripped away to reveal the inner personality, and no superficialities are acceptable. When carried to its ultimate, the encounter group becomes attack therapy.

Psychodrama concentrates on role-playing as a way of encouraging prisoners to act out their personal problems. It is also useful in training prisoners in acceptable techniques of social interaction. Marathon therapy groups are distinguished primarily by their length. They may last an entire day or perhaps a weekend, during which sleep is generally prohibited. Marathon groups are usually developed on the encounter model, and they may also use psychodrama or other psychological counseling techniques. They are designed to use exhaustion and intense personal relationships to break down barriers that might survive in a series of brief counseling sessions.

Another form of group conseling is guided group interaction, which is discussed in Chapter 16. This technique combines a form of encounter group therapy with the manipulation of the total social milieu to create an unusual alternative to traditional juvenile delinquency programs. Guided group interaction is effective in day programs as well as institutional programs, and evaluations of a number of these programs during the 1960s generally found that they reduced recidivism as compared with juvenile reformatories.[81]

In one of the finest evaluation projects ever conducted, Gene Kassebaum, David Ward, and Daniel Wilmer[43] studied the effects of participation in group counseling on the prisoners at the California Men's Colony-East, a medium security facility that was added to the California Department of Corrections in 1961. These researchers were unable to find positive results from prisoner participation in group counseling. They did not identify attitude shifts in a law-abiding direction. Instead, they "found shifts toward greater dissatisfaction with treatment and much shifting and changing of views in both directions over a six-month period."[43:176] In addition, there were no statistically significant differences in parole outcomes over a 36-month period between either mandatory or voluntary group counseling participants and two control groups of prisoners who did not participate in group counseling. One way to interpret these findings is to say that the negativism of the prison environment overwhelms the positive potential of group counseling and similar therapy programs. A more hopeful interpretation is that it takes a higher level of resources than were committed to the counseling program at California Men's Colony-East to make significant modifications in the criminal identifications and post-prison success of prisoners.

Milieu Therapy. We will discuss two types of milieu therapy in this section: traditional therapeutic communities and the Just Community model of correctional treatment. Both of these treatment modalities seek to manipulate the entire correctional environment and to have an effect upon the behavior of individual prisoners through environmental control and the modification of interaction among prisoners.

Therapeutic communities are relatively small groups of individuals who consistently engage in intimate interaction in the service of rehabilitative progress. In the prison setting, these communities must be at least semi-isolated from the negative influences of the prisoner subculture, or they will not be able to develop a prosocial culture. Decisions in these communities are made by prisoners and staff members together, operating as a group. Group members participate in a common work project or projects and join together in community meetings on a regular (usually daily) basis. An experimental therapeutic community for young violent offenders in the California Institution for Men at Chino significantly reduced the recidivism of program graduates as compared with a control group participating in the normal program at Chino. It was found that nine months was the optimum time for an offender to spend in the program in order to have the most positive effect on parole survival.[11]

The Just Community formalizes the therapeutic community's commitment to shared rule-making. Just Community programs involve a very high degree of inmate self-government. Rules are democratically adopted at regular community meetings. The system is based on Kohlberg's theory of six moral stages, which were adapted to form six stages of legal perspectives for use in correctional institutions. In the first two stages, "Moral value resides in external, quasi-physical happenings, in bad acts, or in quasi-physical needs rather than in persons or standards," while, in the next two stages, it "resides in performing good or right roles, in maintaining the conventional order and the expectancies of others."[44:376] For individuals at the two highest stages of moral development, "Moral value resides in conformity by the self to shared or shareable standards, rights, or duties."[44:376] Kohlberg's basic point is that the ethical primitiveness of correctional institutions cannot possibly serve to raise the level of ethical decision-making of prisoners. Since he views this as the primary problem of criminal behavior, it follows that prisons must be restructured to give prisoners experiences in living at a higher ethical level than exists in prisons at present.[77]

The implementation of a Just Community at the Niantic State Farm for

Women in Connecticut resulted in a significant increase in the level of moral reasoning used by the prisoners. Furthermore, the recidivism rate for women released from the program was approximately half of the recidivism rate for other Niantic releasees.[77] Evaluation results in other settings have also been positive.[35,45] This suggests that the organization of correctional programming may be more important than its content. That is to say, Just Community results are not based on the use of a specific therapeutic technique or the discussion of particular problems. They appear to derive from the use of democratic principles to organize life in therapeutic communities.[45] If this is true, then the principle of the Just Community can be combined with many other therapeutic techniques to maximize their effectiveness. We need to observe Just Community programs over an extended period of time before we can be sure of this, for many programs lose their positive impact on prisoners when they move from being new and innovative to being part of the normal institutional environment.

PROGRAMS FOR SPECIAL OFFENDERS

In addition to general programs made available to the entire institutional population, most institutions also provide specialized programs for specific groups of offenders. Alcoholics and drug addicts have special programs in most correctional facilities, and there are programs for violent offenders and sex offenders in a number of states. We have already mentioned the use of aversion therapy with sex offenders. The Fort Steilacoom program offers an alternative form of therapy for sex offenders in its therapeutic community. Members of this program participate in formal group meetings for approximately 25 hours a week, and are in close contact during their other waking hours. They practice attack therapy to force each other to confront their personal problems and to construct positive solutions to these problems. Offenders who are accepted into the Fort Steilacoom program after three months of observation usually serve 15–20 months, which is shorter than sex offenders could expect to serve in a penal institution. The intensity of the program, which makes conning almost impossible, packs many years of therapy into this relatively brief period of institutionalization. Other elements of the Fort Steilacoom include couples therapy with the wives of the sex offenders, work assignments within the institution, psychodrama, and work release at the end of the inpatient phase of treatment. Outpatient treatment generally continues for 18 months after release. An offender who does not make adequate progress in the program is returned to the court to serve a normal criminal sentence.[10]

Where there are no specialized programs for sex offenders, these prisoners receive little more in the way of treatment than the average prisoner. A New York report on 121 prisoners under custody for sex offenses found that most of the sex offenders for whom reports were available had not become involved in vocational programs, and only 22 percent had been consistently involved in academic programs. More than half the prisoners were to receive individual counseling according to the recommendations made at the point of classification, but only 15 percent of the prisoners were receiving individual counseling on a regular basis. An additional 10 percent were regularly participating in group counseling sessions. A review of the case folders of these offenders led to the conclusion that "...the Department is not providing adequate treatment for a large number of sexual offenders who appear to be desperately in need of it: over half of the inmates in the sample received no form of psychological help whatsoever."[56:6]

A common method of dealing with violent offenders who continue to engage in antisocial behavior within the institution is to segregate them in an adjustment center. These centers consist mainly of single cells, shower rooms, and limited facilities for dining, recreation, and work. There are also special "quiet cells," in which anything that might be used as a weapon or for self-mutilation has been removed. Within this setting of extraordinary physical control, prisoners may be exposed to various therapy programs.[17] Unfortunately, many institutions use adjustment centers for punishment rather than for treatment, and confine prisoners in these facilities for institutional misconduct rather than because they have been judged to require specialized treatment in a confined setting before they can be considered safe enough to be released to the free community.

Alcohol treatment programs in correctional institutions have suffered from the general acquiescence to alcohol abuse by American society. There are many Alcoholics Anonymous groups, which usually receive only minimum institutional support, but few institutions have dedicated substantial funds to programs for alcohol abusers. The explosion of other forms of drug abuse in American society has led to the rapid proliferation of drug abuse programs in many correctional institutions. The most common programs for drug abusers are therapeutic communities and behavior modification programs. All of the other therapeutic techniques that have been described earlier in this chapter are also used with drug abusers. One unusual technique that has not been mentioned above is biofeedback. In this technique, drug abusers are connected to machines which feed back information on their basic physiological states. This feedback permits them to learn to relax consciously and otherwise alter their physiological states at will. This is particularly important for drug abusers (and alcoholics) because one of the functions of drug use is to reduce stress.[78] If prisoners can learn to recognize and fulfill a need in socially acceptable ways—a need that they previously fulfilled through illegal activities—they have made an important step toward a future free of trouble with the law.

MANAGEMENT ALTERNATIVES THAT HAVE TREATMENT IMPLICATIONS

We began this chapter by pointing out that the distinction between treatment programs and basic institutional services is an artificial one. In this section, we will discuss a number of management options not necessarily considered to be formal treatment programs but which clearly offer possibilities for offender rehabilitation. We will discuss unit management, mutual agreement programming, coeducational programming, conjugal visits and other family unification programs, and the Morris model of correctional organization.

Unit Management

The unit management strategy consists of dividing an institutional population into living groups of approximately 100 prisoners, each of which has its own staff members. The staff in each unit consists of a unit manager, a psychologist, two or three correctional counselors, one or two case managers, and as many correctional officers as are necessary for supervision. This breaks up prison populations, thus forestalling mass antisocial behavior, and it also assures that prisoners will be treated as individuals. There is the additional advantage that the availability of a large number of relatively small units permits classification committees to refine their housing assignments so that individuals with similar problems can be housed together and can be exposed to staff members who have developed a degree of expertise in helping individuals with their particular problems. The Federal Bureau of Prisons has been the major innovator in the use of unit management and the implementation of a unit management system at Lewisburg Penitentiary is credited with having reduced tensions and physical aggression between the prisoners.[79]

Mutual Agreement Programming

Mutual agreement programming is used in institutional corrections as well as in community corrections programs. It involves the signing of a contract between the individual prisoner and representatives of the state. In a Wisconsin program, these negotiations include the project coordinator, a representative of the institution, and a member or representative of the parole board. The institution agrees to give the prisoner access to the programs and services necessary to complete the contract, and the parole board agrees that the inmate will be paroled when the contract is completed. The contract is a legally binding document, and can only be changed through renegotiation. Renegotiation involves all the parties and procedures from the initial contract negotiation, and the original contract remains in force until the renegotiation is completed.[1]

A recent evaluation report of the MAP program in Wisconsin shows that its use had risen to 42 percent of all prisoners released from incarceration in the Wisconsin system by 1977. Participation in the MAP program only slightly shortened the institutional stay of prisoners. On the average, MAP releasees in 1976 served sentences that were two months shorter than non-MAP releasees, and the differential in 1977 was three months. Twelve-month follow-up statistics for 1975 releasees show that 91 percent of the MAP releasees were successful, as compared with 87 percent of the non-MAP releasees. Both MAP and non-MAP releasees in 1976 had a one-year follow-up success rate of 91 percent. Differences between MAP and non-MAP releasees on employment status, reasons for unemployment, or education status were not statistically significant.[71] The general import of this evaluation is that MAP programming has saved the state a considerable amount of money by releasing prisoners to the community without any increased risk of recidivism, but that it has not had substantial effects on the experiences or behavior of prisoners after release from correctional institutions.

Co-Corrections

Co-correctional institutions allow men and women to have regular social contacts in supervised situations. Housing areas are sexually segregated, and sexual relations are strictly forbidden. The amount of contact that is allowed between the sexes differs from institution to institution. Fort Worth allows couples to hold hands or put their arms around each other, while Lexington limits contact to holding hands; yet both are units in the Federal Bureau of Prisons.[2] A study of prisoner interaction at the Fort Worth institution concluded that the co-correctional program was associated with a positive behavior pattern, better grooming habits, more positive attitudes toward incarceration, reduced incidents of homosexuality, and reduced monotony.[40] The Federal Bureau of Prisons has been a leader in co-correctional programs, and initiated the first co-correctional program at the Kennedy Youth Center in Morgantown, West Virginia in 1971. A comprehensive examination of co-correctional institutions financed by the Law Enforcement Assistance Administration concluded that co-corrections does have the potential for reducing adjustment problems within the institution, and it does appear to be associated with reduced recidivism after release. However, the reduced recidivism may be due to aspects of correctional programming other than co-corrections, since co-correctional institutions are often model institutions in aspects other than their co-correctional facets.[75]

Conjugal Visits and Other Family Visiting Programs

Conjugal visits are now permitted in at least three American prison systems, and informally tolerated in many others. They have long been acceptable in many other nations, including Mexico, Bolivia, Brazil, Ecuador, El Salvador, Guatemala, Honduras, and Canada.[34] Conjugal visits have traditionally been made available to men in the Mississippi Penitentiary at Parchman,[38] and they were begun in California in 1968[37] and in New York in 1976.[23] New York uses mobile homes to provide three visiting cycles per unit per week, and has made the program available to women as well as men. The only married individuals not eligible to participate in this program are those who are eligible for furloughs, who have been found guilty of unusually serious crimes, or who engage in repeated disruptive behavior within the institution. A preliminary evaluation of the New York Family Reunion Program indicates that it contributes to the maintenance of family ties and seems to be associated with low recidivism rates, but it has not resulted in a reduction of assaults within the institutions in which it has been implemented. Perhaps any reduction of violence by conjugal participants is countered by increased violence by unmarried and homosexual prisoners who feel frustrated because of their exclusion from the program. Methodological difficulties in the evaluation make it impossible to be sure that the apparent reduction in recidivism associated with program participation is not due to the way in which prisoners are selected to participate in the program.[23] An evaluation of the California conjugal visiting program at Soledad prison came to the same conclusion. Program participants appear to greatly increase their chances of maintaining their families intact and also seem to experience reduced recidivism, but difficulties in the evaluation design make it impossible to be sure that these effects are really due to the characteristics of the program itself.[13]

The Morris Model and the Butner Program

In *The Future of Imprisonment,* Norval Morris[61] argues that prisons should be restructured so as to allow prisoners to freely choose to participate in available treatment programs without coercion. Since the parole date is set upon entry into prison, there is no way that "programming" by prisoners can affect their sentence length. This program was implemented in the Federal Correctional Institution at Butner, North Carolina. The population exposed to the Morris programming model at Butner consists of approximately 150 chronic and violent offenders. All of them are given the right to transfer from Butner back to their previous prison after a 90-day trial without any penalty, and those who stay participate only in those programs that they personally select. Mandatory requirements are limited to working half a day, participating in unit discussion groups, and obeying institutional regulations. A graduated release plan and unit privileges are part of the treatment program, but they are not related to performance in any of the optional programs. They are instead distributed on the basis of seniority, behavior on the mandatory work assignment, and compliance with institutional regulations.[39] A preliminary evaluation of the Butner program suggests that program participation increased the number of program enrollments and completions, generated a high level of prisoner and staff satisfaction, but had no effect on the number of reported disciplinary infractions per prisoner.[9]

A GENERAL EVALUATION OF PRISON TREATMENT PROGRAMS

We have mentioned the effects of numerous treatment programs in this chapter. Since we have tended to discuss the more successful programs and to ignore the less successful ones, these comments present a positive picture of the general success of correctional treatment programs that might be misleading. Two other problems with these evaluations are that they too often emphasize recidivism at the expense of more sensitive measures of prisoner change and that they invariably evaluate the effects of entire programs rather than of specific transferable elements within programs. This last point is crucial, for many treatment programs may succeed because they are new (a Hawthorne effect), because they are temporarily led by charismatic leaders who inspire their members to heights of behavior change that would not be brought about by the therapeutic techniques themselves, or because of the impact of therapeutic elements other than those specified as the major dimensions of the programs. Given these problems, what is needed is a general evaluation of evaluations that brings together an exhaustive list of evaluations meeting certain technical criteria and aggregates their results to show the relative effectiveness of different therapeutic techniques.

A number of social scientists have attempted this task since W.C. Bailey[3] analyzed the results of 100 correctional outcome studies in 1966. Leslie Wilkins[84] concluded that there was no research support for the imposition of harsh measures in correctional programs, and that there is strong evidence to support the idea of interaction effects between types of programs and types of offenders. That is to say, certain programs work better with some types of offenders than with others, and no programs work well with all types of offenders. This sensible finding was replicated in the mammoth study of the effectiveness of correctional treatment conducted by Douglas Lipton, Robert Martinson, and Judith Wilks.[51] They summarized the results of 231 published evaluations of correctional treatment methods such as imprisonment, probation, parole, group methods, milieu therapy, skill development, and individual psychotherapy. To be included in the survey, a study had to have "no more than minimal research shortcomings."[51:6] The main outcome measure used in these evaluations was recidivism. Other outcomes used in a dozen or more studies were institutional adjustment, vocational adjustment, educational achievement, drug and alcohol readdiction, personality and attitude change, and community adjustment. Martinson interpreted and publicized these findings to mean that the research literature has produced "no clear pattern to indicate the efficacy of any particular method of treatment."[53:49]

Ted Palmer[67] takes a more positive view of these findings, suggesting that "a cup half empty is also half full. That is, one should not overlook the fact that many programs *have* reduced recidivism and have provided personal assistance to a sizable portion of the offender population" (p. xxi). As an example of the application of the "half-full" approach, Dale Mann[52] compared the effectiveness of four types of treatment aimed at behavioral change in juvenile offenders: clinical psychology and psychiatry, sociology and social work, schooling, and career education. He found that it was not possible to make finely grained judgments about the relative merit of the different approaches, but he also found that there were limited successes within each of these treatment modalities. Programs that appeared to have positive effects had similar characteristics regardless of the treatment modality utilized. These characteristics were client choice of programming, maximizing the involvement of the youngsters in their own rehabilitation, learning theory features such as clear tasks, behavior models, early and frequent successes, reward structures, and training that was as close as possible to real-world situations, the use of a wide variety of techniques in the same program, and a heuristic management approach in which failures were used as a guide for new program developments.

The evaluators of correctional evaluations continue to disagree on the effects of correctional treatment, recalling the Martinson–Palmer debate of the mid-1970s. A recent survey of the effects of eight types of correctional programs by David Greenberg concludes that "The blanket assertion that 'nothing works' is an exaggeration, but not by very much."[31:141] A contrasting opinion put forth by Paul Gendreau and Bob Ross is that "...the success is reported by the intervention studies included here, and the range of situations in which they were carried out and the variety of services offered, should not be ignored."[25:485] Our position in this text is that no treatment program will have positive results unless it relates directly to the living situation of offenders after their release into the free community. Since individuals and their situations differ, no single treatment modality could possibly be effective with all prisoners, or even with prisoners having a number of characteristics in common. This is why Mann[52] found that successful programs tended to include multiple treatment modalities. More evidence in support of this conclusion is found in Chapter 16, particularly in the discussion of the Community Treatment Project of the California Youth Authority. A final caution is that evaluations of treatment programs in correctional facilities use other groups of prisoners for their comparisons. They do not usually use groups of probationers or other individuals who have not been subjected to institutionalization. Therefore, it would be inappropriate to conclude from these comparisons that any of the institutional programs are more effective or more desirable than alternative programs in the community or radical alternatives that are discussed in Chapter 18.

SUMMARY

Four basic prison services are medical services, recreational services, institutional maintenance, and food services. These services are essentially available to all prisoners regardless of their classification. Prisoner classification refers to the process whereby prisoners are assigned to institutions, housing units, and treatment programs based on their needs and characteristics. Depending upon their classification status, prisoners may not be eligible for certain educational, vocational, and other treatment programs. Although educational and vocational programs are adequately administered in most correctional institutions, there is little quality control in many of these programs. Programs that have been evaluated and found to be effective are the exception rather than the rule. Individual and group treatment modalities have received much more attention. These include individual counseling modalities such as transcendental meditation and reality therapy, behavior modification, and physical control techniques; and group treatment modalities such as group counseling and milieu therapy. In addition to these broad-spectrum programs, there are programs designed for special groups of offenders such as alcoholics, drug addicts, and sex offenders. Unit management, mutual agreement programming, co-corrections, conjugal visits and other family visiting programs, and the Morris model are among the many recently implemented management alternatives that have treatment implications. There is considerable dispute and experts as to the value of many correctional treatment programs. Perhaps the most accurate generalization that can be made at this time is that many accepted correctional programs make few documented contributions to the lives of correctional clients or to the reduction of recidivism. A number of correctional programs appear to be effective with some types of offenders but not with others, so that they are not very useful unless they are combined with a careful program of correctional classification to ensure that their efforts are confined to those offenders who would most benefit from them.

REFERENCES

1. American Correctional Association. *The Mutual Agreement Program: A Planned Change in Correctional Service Delivery.* College Park, MD, 1973.
2. Anderson, David C. "Co-Corrections." *Corrections Magazine* 4 (September 1978):33–41.
3. Bailey, W.C. "Correctional Treatment: An Analysis of One Hundred Correctional Outcome Studies." *Journal of Criminal Law, Criminology and Police Science* 57 (1966):153–160.
4. Baker, Robert A. *et al.* "A Computerized Screening System for Correctional Classification." *Criminal Justice and Behavior* 6 (1979):251–273.
5. Bassin, Alexander, Thomas E. Bratter, and Richard L. Rachin. *The Reality Therapy Reader.* New York: Harper and Row, 1976.
6. Bell, Raymond *et al. Correctional Educational Programs for Inmates.* Washington, D.C.: Government Printing Office, 1979.
7. Blackmore, John. "'Human Potential' Therapies, Behind Bars." *Corrections Magazine* 4 (December 1978):28–38.
8. Blair, Louis H. *et al. Monitoring the Impacts of Prison and Parole Services: An Initial Examination.* Washington, D.C.: The Urban Institute, 1977.
9. Bounds, Lee. "Summary of University of North Carolina Report." Washington, D.C.: Federal Bureau of Prisons, 1979.
10. Brecher, Edward M. *Treatment Programs for Sex Offenders.* Washington, D.C.: Government Printing Office, 1978.
11. Briggs, Dennic L. "A Transitional Therapeutic Community for Young, Violent Offenders." *The Howard Journal of Penology and Crime Prevention* 13 (1972):171–183.
12. Buehler, R.E., G.R. Patterson, and J.M. Furniss. "The Reinforcement of Behavior of Institutional Settings." *Behavioral Research and Therapy* 4 (1966):157–167.
13. Burstein, Jules Q. *Conjugal Visits in Prison.* Lexington, MA: D.C. Heath, 1977.
14. Cahill, Thomas J., John C. Gessell, and Arthur M. Horne. "Peer and Professional Counselors: Prisoners' Preferences and Evaluation." *Criminal Justice and Behavior* 6 (1979):400–415.
15. Cheek, Frances E. "Some Reflections on the State of Forensic Psychiatry, August 1979." Paper presented at the Annual Meeting of the Correctional Association, 1979.
16. Comptroller General. *Correctional Institutions Can Do More to Improve the Employability of Offenders.* Washington, D.C., 1979.
17. Cook, Allen, Norman Fenton, and Robert A. Heinze. "Methods of Handling the Severely Recalcitrant Inmate." *In* Leonard J. Hippchen: *Correctional Classification and Treatment.* Cincinnati: W.H. Anderson, 1975, pp. 267–273.
18. Druker, Stephen M. "Understanding and Controlling Crime Through a Scientific Understanding of Consciousness: A New Perspective Suggested by Recent Research on the Transcendental Meditation and TM-Sidhi Program." Paper presented at the Annual Meeting of the Law and Society Association, 1980.
19. Fisher, Jack C. "Plastic Surgery Emphasized as a Resource for Rehabilitation." *American Journal of Corrections* 40 (September–October 1978):11–12.
20. Fitzmaurice, Patricia and Valerie Willison. "Descriptive Analysis of The Mental

Health Satelite Units: Operations and Clients Characteristics." Albany, NY: New York Department of Correctional Services, 1979.

21. Florida. "Report to the Florida Legislature on the Evaluation of the Academic and Vocational Educational Programs of the Department of Corrections." Tallahassee: Florida Department of Offender Rehabilitation, 1978.

22. Flynn, Edith E. "Classification for Risk and Supervision—A Preliminary Conceptualization." *In* John C. Freeman: *Prisons Past and Future*. London: Heinemann, 1978, pp. 131–149.

23. "Follow-up Survey of Participants in Family Reunion Programs." Albany, NY: New York Department of Correctional Services, 1979.

24. Gendreau, Paul and D.A. Andrews. "Psychological Consultation in Corrections Agencies: Case Studies and General Issues." *In* Jerome J. Platt and Robert J. Wicks: *The Psychological Consultant*. New York: Grune and Stratton, 1979, pp. 177–212.

25. Gendreau, Paul and Bob Ross. "Effective Correctional Treatment: Bibliotherapy for Cynics." *Crime and Delinquency* 25 (1979):463–489.

26. General Accounting Office. *Female Offenders: Who Are They and What Are the Problems Confronting Them?* Washington, D.C., 1979.

27. Glaser, Daniel. *The Effectiveness of a Prison and Parole System*. Indianapolis: Bobbs-Merrill Co., 1964.

28. Glasser, William. *Reality Therapy*. New York: Harper and Row, 1965.

29. Gleason, Sandra E. *A Benefit/Cost Analysis of Institutional Training Programs in Michigan Prisons*. Ph.D. dissertation, Michigan State University, 1978.

30. Gold, Margaret. *Cottage Seven: Intended and Unintended Consequences of a Behavior Modification Program*. Ph.D. dissertation, Case Western Reserve University, 1975.

31. Greenberg, David F. "The Correctional Effects of Corrections: A Survey of Evaluations." *In* David F. Greenberg: *Corrections and Punishment*. Beverly Hills, CA: Sage, 1977, pp.111–148

32. Hart, William. "Warning: Prison Medical Care May Be Hazardous to Your Health." *Corrections Magazine* 5 (September 1979):4–11.

33. Hatcher, Hayes A. *Correctional Casework and Counseling*. Englewood Cliffs, NJ: Prentice-Hall, 1978.

34. Hayner, Norman S. "Attitudes Toward Conjugal Visits for Prisoners." *Federal Probation* 36 (March 1972):43–49.

35. Hickey, Joseph E. and Peter L. Scharf. *Toward a Just Correctional System*. San Francisco: Jossey-Bass, 1980.

36. Hippchen, Leonard J. *The Ecologic–Biochemical Approaches to Treatment of Delinquents and Criminals*. New York: Van Nostrand Reinhold, 1978.

37. Holt, Norman and Donald Miller. "Explorations in Inmate–Family Relationships." Sacramento, CA: California Department of Corrections, 1972.

38. Hopper, Columbus B. *Sex in Prison: The Mississippi Experiment With Conjugal Visiting*. Baton Rouge, LA: Louisiana State University Press, 1969.

39. Ingram, Gilbert L. "Butner: A Reality." *Federal Probation* 42 (March 1978):34–39.

40. Jackson, Dorothy A. *A Study of Residential Socialization and Interpersonal Relationships in the Fort Worth Correctional Institution*. Ph.D. dissertation, Texas Woman's University, 1974.

41. Jeffrey, C.R. "Criminology as An Interdisciplinary Behavioral Science." *Criminology* 16 (1978):149–170.

42. *Journal of Prison Health.* Published by the Human Sciences Press. Volume 1 began in Fall 1980.

43. Kassebaum, Gene, David Ward, and Daniel Wilmer. *Prison Treatment and Parole Survival: An Empirical Assessment.* New York: Wiley, 1971.

44. Kohlberg, L. "Stage and Sequence: The Cognitive Development Approach to Socialization." *In* D. Goslin; *Handbook of Socialization Theory and Research.* Chicago: Rand McNally, 1969.

45. Lanza-Kaduce, Lonn and John R. Stratton. "Organization vs. Content in Correctional Programming: Policy Implications." Paper given at the Annual Meeting of the Midwest Sociological Society, 1980.

46. Laycock, Gloria. "Behavior Modification in Prison." *British Journal of Criminology* 19 (1979):400–415.

47. Legge, Karen. "Work in Prison: The Process of Inversion." *British Journal of Criminology* 18 (1978):6–22.

48. Levinson, Robert D. and J.D. Williams. "Inmate Classification: Security/Custody Considerations." *Federal Probation* 48 (March 1979):37–43.

49. Lightman, Ernie S. "Industrial Work by Inmates in Correctional Institutions." Toronto: Centre for Industrial Relations, University of Toronto, 1979.

50. Lillyquist, Michael J. *Understanding and Changing Criminal Behavior.* Englewood Cliffs, NJ: Prentice-Hall, 1980.

51. Lipton, Douglas, Robert Martinson, and Judith Wilks. *The Effectiveness of Correctional Treatment: A Survey of Treatment Evaluation Studies.* New York: Praeger, 1975.

52. Mann, Dale. *Intervening with Convicted Serious Juvenile Offenders.* Washington, D.C.: Government Printing Office, 1976.

53. Martinson, Robert. "What Works? Questions and Answers About Prison Reform." *Public Interest* 35 (April 1974):22–54.

54. Masters, F.G. and G.R. Wardlaw. "An Analysis of Reinforcers and Punishers in Three New Zealand Prisons." *Australian and New Zealand Journal of Criminology* 11 (1978):19–22.

55. McCarty, Dennis. "Institutional Adjustment and Program Participation of Male Inmates Under Custody for Sex Offenses." Albany, NY: New York Department of Correctional Services, 1979.

56. McCreary, Phyllis G. and John McCreary. *Job Training and Placement for Offenders and Ex-Offenders.* Washington, D.C.: Government Printing Office, 1975.

57. Megargee, Edwin I. and Martin J. Bohn, Jr. *Classifying Criminal Offenders: A New System Based on the MMPI.* Beverly Hills, CA: Sage, 1979.

58. Milan, M.A. and J.M. McKee. "Behavior Modification: Principals and Applications in Corrections." *In* Daniel Glaser: *Handbook of Criminology.* Chicago: Rand McNally, 1974, pp. 745–776.

59. Milan, M.A. *et al.* "Applied Behavior Analysis and the Imprisoned Adult Felon Project I: The Cell Block Token Economy." Montgomery, AL: Experimental Manpower Laboratory for Corrections, 1974.

60. Morris, Edward C. "The National Survey of College Programs in Correction." *Journal of Correctional Education* 24 (Winter 1972):26–28.

61. Morris, Norval. *The Future of Imprisonment.* Chicago: University of Chicago Press, 1975.

62. Nagel, William G. "Implications of 'The New Red Barn' and 'Free Venture' Industries for Prison Planning." *In* M. Robert Montilla and Nora Harlow: *Correctional Facilities Planning.* Lexington, MA: D.C. Heath, 1979, pp. 59–66.

63. National Advisory Commission on Criminal Justice Standards and Goals. *Corrections*. Washington, D.C.: Government Printing Office, 1973.
64. New Hampshire State Prison. "Classification Manual." 2nd Edition. Concord, NH, 1978.
65. Nietzel, Michael C. *Crime and Its Modification: A Social Learning Perspective.* New York, NY: Pergamon, 1979.
66. Oakey, Barry H. "Evaluation, Lorton Art Program Inc." Washington, D.C.: D.C. Department of Corrections, 1980.
67. Palmer, Ted. *Correctional Intervention and Research.* Lexington, MA: D.C. Heath, 1978.
68. Petersila, Joan. "Which Inmates Participate in Prison Treatment Programs?" *Journal of Offender Counseling Services and Rehabilitation* 4 (1979):121–135.
69. Pollack, Ricki. "The ABC's of Prison Education." *Corrections Magazine* 5 (September 1979):60–66.
70. "Prison Industries and the Free Venture Model." *Corrections Compendium* 3 (October 1978):1–3.
71. Puckett, Stephen N. "Mutual Agreement Program: Time Served and Outcome Analysis Report." Madison, WI: Wisconsin Department of Health and Social Services, 1979.
72. Remington, R.E. "Behavior Modification in American Penal Institutions." *British Journal of Criminology* 19 (1979):333–352.
73. "Report of the Task Force on the Role of Psychology in the Criminal Justice System." *American Psychologist* 33 (1978):1099–1113.
74. Resnik, Judith and Nancy Shaw. "Prisoners of Their Sex: Health Problems of the Incarcerated Women." *In* Ira P. Robbins: *Prisoner's Rights Sourcebook.* New York: Clark Boardman, 1980, pp. 319–413.
75. Ross, J.G. *et al. Assessment of Co-educational Corrections.* Washington, D.C.: Government Printing Office, 1978.
76. Saunders, A.G. "Behavior Therapy in Prisons: Walden II or Clockwork Orange." Paper presented at the Annual Meeting of the Association for Advancement of Behavior Therapy, 1974.
77. Scharf, Peter L. and Joseph L. Hickey. "The Prison and the Inmate's Conception of Legal Justice: An Experiment in Democratic Education." *Criminal Justice and Behavior* 3 (1976):107–122.
78. Smith, Roger. *Drug Programs in Correctional Institutions.* Washington, D.C.: Government Printing Office, 1977.
79. Smith, W. Alan and C.E. Fenton. "Unit Management in a Penitentiary: A Practical Experience." *Federal Probation* 42 (September 1978):40–46.
80. Speiglman, Richard. "Prison Drugs, Psychiatry, and the State." *In* David F. Greenberg: *Corrections and Punishment.* Beverly Hills, CA: Sage, 1977, pp. 150–171.
81. Stephenson, Richard M. and Frank Scarpitti. *Group Interaction as Therapy: The Use of the Small Group in Corrections.* Westport, CT: Greenwood Press, 1974.
82. Taft, Philip B., Jr. "The Alchemy of Prison Art." *Corrections Magazine* 5 (September 1979):12–19.
83. Vinter, Robert D., Theodore M. Newcomb, and Rhea Kish. *Time Out, a National Study of Juvenile Correctional Programs.* Ann Arbor, MI: University of Michigan, 1976.
84. Wilkins, Leslie T. *Evaluation of Penal Measures.* New York: Random House, 1969.

Chapter 11

Problems of Prison Life

In this chapter, we will discuss seven of the many problems of prison life that are of concern to prisoners, correctional officers, and administrators. It is not our intention to provide a comprehensive survey of the problems of prison life. That would be the subject of an entire book. Instead, discussions of violent victimization, other forms of victimization, homosexuality, race relations, drug abuse, prisoner militancy, and prison riots are intended to exemplify the severity of the difficulties that confront the actors in the prison drama.

PRISON VIOLENCE

There are two major types of prison violence: rape and nonsexual assaults. Rape is a shorthand term for all forcible sexual encounters, whether heterosexual or homosexual in nature. It includes forced masturbation, oral intercourse, and anal intercourse, all three of which may be endured by homosexual as well as heterosexual victims. Nonsexual assaults range from minor incidents such as slaps and pushes to multiple homicides.

Prison Rape

Institutions differ greatly as to the rape rate that is estimated based on prisoner reports. Interviews with prisoners always produce a much greater number of rape reports than the examination of official records, even when lie detectors are used to insure the honesty of the prisoners.[10] Many prisoners do not report havng been raped or otherwise assaulted because of threats from the aggressors, direct discouragement from correctional officers, or beliefs that it will not do them any good to report the crime because prison officials will not give them adequate protection from future assaults. Sexual assaults are extremely common in some institutions and quite uncommon in others. Even where they rarely occur, there may be such widespread fear of the possibility of sexual assault that it remains a major factor in prison life. Institutions for juvenile delinquents are not free of sexual assaults, which is particularly problematic because the effects of an assault on the developing sexual identity of an adolescent may be much more permanent than they are for an adult. Women's institutions are, as a whole, relatively free from sexual assaults, although there have been a number of reports of lesbian rapes in recent years.[9,11,12,28]

What is a prison rape like? It involves a combination of sexual and nonsexual violence. As an example of this, here is an account given by the victim of a rape who submitted to a lie detector test to substantiate his story.

All of a sudden a coat was thrown over my face and when I tried to pull it off I was viciously punched in the face for around ten minutes. I fell to the floor and they kicked me all over my body, including my head and my privates. They ripped my pants from me and five or six of them held me down and took turns f...ing me.

My insides feel sore and my body hurts, my head hurts, and I feel sick in the stomach. Each time they stopped I tried to call for help, but they put their hands over my mouth so that I couldn't make a sound. While they held me, they burned my legs with a cigarette.[10:12]

Acts such as this are far from the experiences of most college students. In order to understand why prison rapes occur, it is necessary to inquire as to the motivations for homosexual assaults. The most important is the need to achieve dominance. Many male prisoners have been taught that they are not "real men" unless they can dominate others. In the outside world, women are often the victims of this aggressive behavior; but when isolated from that world in prison, the male aggressors seek male surrogates as outlets for their belligerent drives. What we are saying is that the primary aim of homosexual rape is not sexual satisfaction. Dominance is the crucial element of homosexual rape in prison, just as it is in heterosexual rape on the outside.

The second factor in American prison rapes is race relations. Most aggressors are black, and most victims are white.[8,10,27] Alan Davis[10] argues that part of the black motivation in raping whites is revenge for racial discrimination suffered outside the prison where whites have the upper hand; part of it is due, he says, to the need to affirm their own masculinity in a setting in which homosexual rape is the most extreme form of asserting dominance over another human being. Even where blacks are a numerical minority, well-organized black gangs can succeed in raping isolated whites without fear of retribution.[8]

Rape victims are disproportionately found among prisoners who are middle class, slight of build, young, inexperienced in prison life, and who have been convicted only of minor property offenses. These young men appear to be rather feminine when compared with the average prisoner, and so are prime candidates for being dominated and for being "made into a woman." When the rapists redefine their victims as "girls," they succeed in the self-deception that they are "real men" while simultaneously resorting to homosexual activity that they would totally reject as unmanly if it were to be consensual in nature.

Prison rape is sufficiently common that social roles have been developed to identify rapists and their victims. A "wolf" or a "jocker" is an aggressor in a homosexual assault, and a "punk" is a victim. These same roles were found in an Indian prison by S. Srivastava,[45] except that the "wolves" were called "boyhunters" and "barrack hawks."

Prison rapes and other forms of prison victimization are essentially zero sum games. The zero sum game is a situation in which someone must lose in order for someone else to win. When a rapist raises his status through his predatory activities, his victim suffers a corresponding loss of status. Once a newly admitted prisoner has been raped, he is marked for the rest of his prison sentence, and entails a greatly exacerbated risk of future victimizations. Once a rapist has "broken in" a "girl," "she" is immediately redefined as having been female all along. Only "baby rapers"—men who have sexually assaulted young children in the outside world—have lower status in a men's prison than "punks."

Nonsexual Assaults

Vicious assaults, with and without weapons—some resulting in death—are a fact of life in many correctional institutions. It is extremely rare to find a prison in which prisoners are so tightly controlled or so thoroughly influenced in a prosocial direction that violence does not regularly occur. Twenty-two percent of a small sample of ex-prisoners from the Cook County Department of Corrections testified that they had been the victims of beatings while incarcerated.[15] Prisoners at Angola Prison in Louisiana suffered approximately 12 stabbings a month between 1973 and 1975.[3] The assault rate in the California prison system in 1974 was 4.3 per 100 prisoners.[36] A Virginia juvenile correctional institution had an assault rate of 21.7 per 100 prisoners per year between 1974 and 1976.[21] High as these rates are, they greatly understate the true level of violence in these institutions because most violent acts are not reported to prison officials and are not witnessed by correctional officers. Even in prisons that have far lower assault rates than those quoted above, the increased risk of assault when incarcerated as compared with the rate in the free population must be considered to be one of the most frightening aspects of imprisonment.

As with homosexual rapes, nonsexual prison assaults are aimed primarily at achieving dominance for the aggressors. Dominance not only reinforces a relatively positive self-image: it also makes it possible to easily obtain material goods of all kinds that are in short supply behind the walls. Many prisoners work hard at weight-lifting and other body-building activities in order to be able to defend themselves against assaults, while others depend on weapons such as homemade knives, clubs, brass knuckles, fire bombs, and even guns. Some prisoners become so adept at creating weapons that they make a business out of it. One study of prison-made weapons describes items such as a ball-point pen gun capable of firing bullets that can penetrate a one-inch sheet of plywood, a gun made of a glued paper that was capable of shooting ground glass when fired with a compote of crushed match heads, and a hand-cannon capable of shooting two-ounce cubes of brass out of a square pipe.[40] More common weapons include a bar of soap or piece of metal in a sock, a sawed-off baseball bat, and a piece of scrap metal from prison industries fashioned into a knife and taped at one end to form a handle.

Although it is true that most prisoner violence is directed against other prisoners, the availability of weapons to prisoners and the frequency with which assaults erupt means that correctional officers can never feel completely immune to the possibility of assault so long as they are in personal contact with prisoners. The impact of the dangerousness of prison work has been described in Chapter 8.

OTHER FORMS OF PRISON VICTIMIZATION

Most of the victimization incidents that occur in prisons are not physically violent. Table 11.1 displays 16 types of prison victimization. A fundamental characteristic of a victimization incident is the staff–prisoner caste relations between the aggressor and the victim. The direction of the aggression in a given incident may be staff–prisoner, prisoner–staff, prisoner–prisoner or staff–staff. The content of the incident may be physical, economic, psychological, or social. The reality of prison victimization is even more complicated than Table 11.1

Table 11.1. Types of Victimization in Prisons

	Aggressor	Victim	Nature of Victimization
1A	Staff	Prisoner	Physical
1B			Economic
1C			Psychological
1D			Social
2A	Prisoner	Staff	Physical
2B			Economic
2C			Psychological
2D			Social
3A	Prisoner	Prisoner	Physical
3B			Economic
3C			Psychological
3D			Social
4A	Staff	Staff	Physical
4B			Economic
4C			Psychological
4D			Social

Source: Lee H. Bowker. *Prison Victimization.* New York: Elsevier, 1980.

would lead us to believe, for many events combine more than one type of victimization at once and other events are so complex that it is difficult to determine who is the aggressor and who is the victim. For example, Daniel Lockwood[30] identified many incidents in which rapists making advances to potential victims were themselves assaulted by the victims in self-defense. They did not necessarily start the fights: they merely made verbal comments, and that was enough to set off their intended victims.

Economic Victimization

There are eight different types of economic victimization among prisoners. Gambling frauds are often perpetrated on new prisoners or on those who are mentally deficient. Card games and other gambling activities are manipulated so that the victims cannot avoid losing. Once they are far enough in debt, they will then be ready for the second type of economic victimization: loansharking. Loansharking occurs when prisoners charge exorbitantly high rates of interest on loans. In an incident in the semi-fictional novel, *The Riot,*[13] the loanshark charged his victim 50 percent interest per month on a carton of cigarettes. Once prisoners are caught in this cycle, they quickly get so far into debt that they can never get out, and they become virtual slaves of the loanshark. If they cannot convince the loanshark to accept some kind of personal service to pay off the debt, they may be subject to violent victimization as a warning to other debtors that they had better make their payments on time.

Simple theft and robbery occur in prisons in the same variety of forms that are found in the free society. This is also true of a fifth form of economic victimization: protection rackets. These rackets deliver freedom from harassment in return for regular payments of money, goods, or services. If victims in a protection racket resist, violent incidents can be arranged to convince them that they cannot survive without making regular payments.

The final three types of economic victimization are "business violations" rather than street crimes. These are the deliberate misrepresentation of products, nondelivery of products, and pricing violations. Products are misrepresented when they are claimed to be more valuable than they are in fact. As an example of this, a combination of deleterious chemicals may be claimed to be LSD and sold at a high price on the prison market until it becomes generally known that prisoners do not have a psychedelic experience as a result of taking the pill: they just get sick. The nondelivery of products involves taking money from victims and then "burning" them by failing to deliver the promised products. If an aggressor is much tougher than a victim, there is nothing that can be done about nondelivery. Pricing violations occur when one gang of prisoners attempts to create a monopoly within a correctional institution by forcing other prisoners out of business and then raising prices unilaterally. Alternatively, they may scheme with other prison entrepreneurs to fix the prices at an extremely high level. Competing prisoners can be forced out of business by direct physical threats, as was the case when gangs of prisoners took over all illegal economic enterprises at Stateville in Illinois,[26] or it can be done by sending "snitch kites" exposing the activities of rivals to the prison administration.[22]

Psychological Victimization

Psychological victimizations are manipulations, called con games in common terminology. The object of the aggressor is the manipulate the victim into giving up material goods, sex, or something else without having to risk injury by fighting for it. Some games are general, and are intended to keep the victim off balance so that other forms of victimization can be carried out whenever the aggressor wants to do so. Spreading rumors that new prisoners are "punks" or "snitches" may cause them to become so busy defending themselves that they do not notice that they are being set up for robbery until it is too late.[24]

Other manipulations have a short-term goal and are completed in a matter of minutes.

Soon after he arrived, this inmate was approached by two others carrying a jar containing some orange liquid. They told him the liquid was acid and threatened to throw it over him if he did not "come across" for them which he immediately did, only to find out the liquid was orange juice. Hereafter, he was repeatedly coerced into performing sexual activities and eventually placed himself into protective custody.[8:80]

Because this prisoner was inexperienced in the ways of the prisoner subculture, he did not understand what was happening, and was tricked into making a crucial mistake in his relations with other prisoners. Once he had given in and performed an "unmasculine" sexual act, there was no way that he could easily gain respect within the institution.

The victims of psychological aggression may be driven so far as to attempt suicide or to otherwise mutilate themselves. J. Gibbs[20] found that the dominant theme expressed by prisoners who had mutilated themselves was fear. These inexperienced nonviolent young prisoners were prime candidates for victimization by prisoner aggressors. One self-destructive prisoner described what it is like to be psychologically victimized.

Yeah, there were a lot of people riding me, because, like, guys were coming by, guys would say in a crowd, "I would get him myself, but I don't want to get the extra time for it." Because the word was already out that I was a rat; it was put out by the two guys that came up to prison with me.[47:67]

Social Victimization

Social victimization occurs when a prisoner is victimized because he or she is a member an identifiable social group. Social victims may be members of racial or religious minority groups, have unusual ideological or political beliefs, or have committed crimes (such as sexual offenses against children) that are detested by other prisoners. Their personal characteristics matter little in the selection process because it is their group membership that identifies them as potential and appropriate victims. Thorsten Sellin[42] points out that imprisonment was once reserved for slaves. At that time in history, social victimization probably occurred relatively infrequently among prisoners because they were all members of oppressed groups. When the mix of prisoners changed to include a large number of disadvantaged dominant group members, then social victimization began to gain prominence in prison life. Beginning with the early 1960s, the racial balance in American prisons shifted sufficiently away from white prisoners so that blacks began to dominate most of the urban prisons in the East and Midwest, and Chicanos did the same in the Southwest. The new victims of social victimization among prisoners became the whites, and that is the situation in most American prisons today.

We have already mentioned that prison rapes are predominantly committed by blacks against whites. This is also true for other forms of violence. A North Carolina prison system study found that blacks had a victimization rate that was approximately 45 percent lower than whites. In those incidents that were interracial, 82 percent involved black aggressors and white victims, while only 50 percent of the aggressors would have been black by chance.[19]

Social victimization is not a mutually exlusive category. It overlaps with physical, psychological, and economic victimization. In fact, the only forms of social victimization that do not overlap with one of the other three major types of victimization are those that we would call discrimination in the free society. When members of one racial or ethnic group systematically exclude members of other groups from desired job assignments, housing areas, or activities, this is discriminatory social victimization. In highly controlled prisons, the amount of social discrimination that occurs among prisoners can be sharply curtailed by administrative policies, so that it rarely occurs without some degree of cooperation from prison staff members.

Victimization Involving Correctional Officers

Only 4 of the 16 categories listed in Table 11.1 refer to victimization among prisoners. The other 12 categories are divided among staff–prisoner victimization, prisoner–staff victimization, and staff–staff victimization. Relatively little is known about victimization among staff members. Cases that become public usually involve prison administrators who have gone out of their way to harass or otherwise victimize staff members who have displeased them.[7] Since we have already discussed the victimization of correctional officers in Chapter 8, we will not review it here. The remaining possibility, staff–prisoner victimization, has always been a major concern of prison reformers, and so has been fairly well documented.

Physical victimization of prisoners by staff members is called brutality. It was once extremely common in American prisons, but this is no longer the case. Brutality by correctional officers has been almost completely eliminated from the more progressive correctional systems. Those prison systems that are less professionalized and a number of institutions for juvenile delinquents continue to be cited in legal testimony and investigators' reports for brutality against prisoners. Hans Toch[48] argues that one of the factors favoring correctional officer brutality is the presence of norms in correctional officer subcultures that promote violence against prisoners. These norms probably developed partly as a reaction to the pervasive fear of being victimized by prisoner violence. There was also more of a need to use force to subdue mentally ill prisoners in the days before the introduction of psychotropic drugs than there is today.

Except for incidents of extreme brutality and obvious reprisals carried out after prison riots, it is often difficult to decide whether or not a given action by a correctional officer constitutes brutality. If a prisoner resists an order and three officers use force to enforce the order, it is not always clear where the necessary and appropriate use of force ends and brutality begins. It is not easy to accuse an officer of personal brutality if that officer is acting within the public regulations of the institution. For that reason, there is a degree of cultural relativity in the definition of brutality; and what constitutes brutality in a progressive correctional system may be quite acceptable under the regulations of a system in an adjacent state. Once the order of the day, correctional officer brutality is no longer much of an issue in most prison systems.

Psychological victimization by correctional officers has come to replace brutality as a major means of punishing prisoners who are "uncooperative." For example, an officer can deliberately agitate a prisoner by refusing legitimate requests until the prisoner blows up, receives a disciplinary citation, and is punished by a stretch of time in segregation. Staff members who really want to upset prisoners can mention things about their families, their release date, and their health to make them feel helpless and abandoned, or they can mention intimate secrets from their files in front of other prisoners as a way of embarrassing the victims. These events do not constitute victimization in a legal sense, and so they rarely come to the attention of the public.

Victimization in Institutions for Women and Juveniles

The discussion of victimization thus far has been limited to adult males, so it is appropriate to say something about variations in victimization patterns found in institutions for juveniles and women. The stereotype that young people are less vicious than adults does not apply when it comes to correctional institutions. A number of research projects carried out over a 20-year period have substantiated extensive and extremely brutal forms of victimization in juvenile institutions. Psychological victimization is not as refined among juveniles as it is among adults, but the incidence of rape and other assaults is high in many juvenile institutions. This is particularly true where professional staff members do not have direct control over the day-to-day activities of the prisoners.

Howard Polsky's study, *Cottage Six*,[37] showed that juvenile delinquents were quite capable of dominating cottage parents, neutralizing the effects of the professional personnel who were housed separately from the juvenile living areas, and producing a cottage subculture dominated by aggression, deviant skills and activities, threat–gestures, ranking, and scapegoating. Deviant skills and activities were the only nonvictimizing activities in the cottage. The aggression, including kicking, punching, and pushing, constituted physical victimization; and threat–gestures, ranking, and scapegoating constituted psychological victimization. In a threat–gesture, the aggressor pretended to hit the victim when he had no intention of doing so and the victim jumped back and looked frightened, to the amusement of all present. Ranking was the use of verbal insults, such as "your mother is a subway and you can get in for fifteen cents." Scapegoating consisted of blaming everything that went wrong on the powerless, in this case the lowest-status boys in the cottage. Once identified as a scapegoat, a boy suffered victimization for the rest of his cottage sentence. It no longer mattered what he did, for he was automatically victimized because of his social role.

Houseparents were unable to stop these victimizing incidents from occurring because they were, in essence, blackmailed by the aggressors. Houseparents were rated on how well they kept order in their cottage, not on the therapeutic progress of the boys. To keep things quiet, they had to have the cooperation of the aggressive boys who dominated the prisoner subculture in the cottage. In return for their cooperation, they allowed these boys to victimize the lower-class boys in the cottage on a continuous basis. Without realizing it, the administration of the institution was consistently rewarding the houseparents for turning their back on lower-status boys who were cryng out for help.

In a study of victimization in an Ohio institution for boys, Clemmens Bartollas, Stuart Miller, and Simon Dinitz[5] painted a frightening picture of violence and degradation. As soon as they knew a boy was admitted into the institution, he was subjected to a testing process by the older prisoners who wanted to find out how well he could defend himself from exploitation. Staff members were of no help to the new boys in this process. There was an exploitation matrix in the institution, and each new boy was pushed as far into it as possible. The least severe exploitation was to take the victim's dessert at meals, followed by stealing his favorite food, his canteen pop and candy, pop and candy given to him by his parents, institutional clothing, toilet articles, cigarettes, personal clothing and radio, and then a series of increasingly severe acts of physical victimization. The least severe level of physical victimization was a physical beating. After that, there was submission to the passive role in anal sodomy, being forced to masturbate others, and, finally, being forced to commit oral sodomy. The latter was perceived as the ultimate degradation in the institution. Because all these victimizing activities are more humiliating than those preceding, they arrange themselves in strata: any boy permitting himself to be victimized at one level is certain to be victimized at all of the less severe levels in the scale. Thus, a boy who is able to draw the line at the passive role in anal sodomy will be able to evade masturbating others and committing oral sodomy, but he will be physically beaten and will suffer the economic victimizations in the matrix.

Bartollas et al. found that 19 percent of the boys exploited others and were never themselves exploited; 34 percent exploited others and were sometimes exploited themselves; 21 percent were occasionally exploited; 17 percent were commonly exploited; and 10 percent remained completely immune to the exploitation matrix. The victims were better adjusted than the aggressors on the streets, but were poorly suited for institutional survival. One might argue that most of them should never have been institutionalized in the first place. Here is how one victim describes his experiences in the institution.

I'm weak, I'm kind-hearted. Take, for instance, my cigarettes. People keep coming up and asking for one and I would say "yeah, take one." But they would take the whole pack. And then I began to give up sex. I'm always tense and anxious. I've always been degraded. I'd rather be dead then continue to suffer in this hellhole.[5:173]

Female Prison Victimization. The general impression gained from reading the literature on victimization in women's prisons is that physical, economic, and social victimization are less common than they are in male institutions, but that psychological victimization is extremely high. When violence does occur in a female institution, it can be just as vicious as violence in male institutions. For example:

A quiet girl was severely kicked in the stomach and the breast by five other inmates, evidently because, after first encouraging them, she would not submit to homosexual threats. None of the officers [guards] saw what happened as it occurred in a bedroom, but when she told the officer in the next shift, they attemped to beat her again—right in the presence of the officer.[28:39]

Fear of victimization does not permeate most women's institutions to the extent that it does men's institutions, but it is evident that there are many individuals who suffer severely victimizing experiences. A unique characteristic of physical victimization in women's prisons is the use of cutting weapons to permanently disfigure the victim's face. Homosexual rapes are perhaps only a tenth as common in women's institutions as in men's.

Another characteristic of violence in women's institutions is that it is concentrated in one group of prisoners. At Frontera, a women's facility in the California prison system, four times as many homosexuals had three or more disciplinary reports each as did nonhomosexuals.[49] More than half of the disciplinary offenses committed in the Florida Correctional Institution for Women were carried out by only 5 percent of the prisoners.[29] At Occoquan, a Washington, D.C. women's facility, violence was concentrated in the "life" subculture, one of the three dominant subcultures in the institution. It was found that 61 percent of the women in this subculture had officially recorded disciplinary infractions for fighting on their records. In contrast, only 22 percent of the women in the "cool" subculture and 9 percent in the "square" subculture had similar disciplinary infractions on their records.[23] Except for the activities of a few violence-prone individuals, it appears that questions of status and dominance in women's institutions are not settled by the use of violence unless all other measures fail.

The use of rumors, particularly about husbands or lovers in the outside world, is a major technique for psychological victimization in female institutions. In one women's prison, women who show signs of paranoid thinking are victimized by having their cells altered just enough to confuse them, and comments are made to them about things that never happened to keep them wondering about how sane they really are.[12] It is entirely possible for a victim to become severely disturbed as a result of continuous psychological victimization. In some cases, aggressors may desire to economically or sexually victimize the target of psychological manipulations, but in others it is done just to pass the time in institutions where there is not enough to do to relieve the boredom.

HOMOSEXUALITY

In addition to the forcible sexual activity that was discussed previously, there is also a great deal of consensual homosexual activity in correctional institutions. This is a problem for correctional administrators for two main reasons. First, even consensual homosexuality is illegal in most states, and prison administrators are charged with enforcing state laws within their institutions. Even in states where homosexuality between consenting adults is legal, it may be forbidden by the regulations of state departments of corrections. The second reason why homosexuality in a prison setting is problematic is that it causes a great many fights between lovers, particularly when lovers' triangles develop.

The first careful study of prison subcultures in maximum security institutions is about homosexuality. This is Joseph Fishman's book *Sex in Prison,* which was published in 1934.[16] Fishman had the advantage of being able to visit most of America's correctional institutions in his position as a prison examiner for the United States Department of Justice. It was his impression that homosexuality was practiced by between 30 and 40 percent of all male prisoners, a percentage which is probably just as accurate today. His description of both forced and consensual homosexual behavior is little different from descriptions published four decades later. Homosexual behavior takes on many guises in a closed environment. W.E. Mann[31] identified an unusual process for recruiting homosexual partners at the Guelph reformatory in Ontario. Called "lugging," this process involved the development of intense friendships between older prisoners and younger men who had recently entered the institution. The young attractive "fish" would be given tobacco and other gifts as part of the deepening relationship, and then would be persuaded to engage in sexual behavior. The junior partners in these relationships were not brutalized. They appreciated the many favors that their older companions gave to them, and were probably only dimly aware that they had been manipulated into relationships that were not in their best interests in the long run. A successful "lugger" describes the process as follows.

> It all sounds very easy to him, and he's going to make something on it—new clothes and more tobacco, etc. So he never thinks of what it's going to cost him. The brighter the picture you paint him, the better he likes it. That's just the start. After he's in it for a while, it lowers his dignity to a certain level and then it doesn't really matter. (Here he is referring to homosexual acts.)[31:146]

A study of the psychological characteristics of homosexuals and nonhomosexuals at the State Prison of Southern Michigan failed to find any differences between these two groups. Significant differences were also lacking between homosexuals assuming active roles and those assuming passive roles.[38] This suggests that psychological characteristics may not be the major determinant of the choice as to whether or not to practice homosexual behavior while incarcerated. The institutional setting may be much more important. A comparison of 25 prisons from six countries found that the more custodial the institution, the higher the incidence of known homosexual behavior. Prisons serving younger felons had higher rates of known homosexual behavior than prisons serving older felons, but this was not as important as the degree of custodial orientation of the prison.[1] Taken together, these findings support Gresham Sykes'[46] deprivation theory of the origin of prisoner subcultures. In this case, the more depriving the institution, the higher the degree of subcultural adaptation (homosexuality) developing in response to the deprivation.

Homosexuality in women's institutions is very common, and strongly consensual. It is sometimes difficult to determine whether or not a given relationship is overtly homosexual, because many intense love relationships develop among incarcerated women which involve the sending of love letters and the use of terms of endearment and caresses, but no overt sexual activity.

The book *Women's Prison: Sex and Social Structure,* by David Ward and Gene Kassebaum,[49] portrays lesbian relationships among women in a California prison during the mid-1960s. A number of social roles were elaborated around homosexual behavior, the two most important of which were the "butch" and the "femme." The butch took a masculine aggressive role, not only in overt sexual behavior but also in her ("his") daily behavior. In contrast, the femme played a very coy role reminiscent of the stereotype of feminine behavior in traditional American society. Most of the love affairs found by Ward and Kassebaum were short-lived, unstable, and explosive. They were also rigid, in that the butch and the femme were expected to conform exactly to their roles and to refrain from ever mixing or switching roles. It appeared that the need for social support and relationships of great emotional depth were more important in the formation of lesbian relationships than their purely sexual aspects.

Participation in lesbian activities may not be determined by institutional type to the same extent as homosexuality in institutions for men. A study of seven institutions incarcerating female juvenile delinquents (three of which were coeducational) by Alice Propper[39] revealed that previous homosexual experience was much more important than institutional characteristics in determining whether or not a young woman engaged in lesbian activity while incarcerated. Only 12 percent of the young women who were homosexually inexperienced at entry into the institution admitted engaging in lesbianism while incarcerated, but this was true for 71 percent of the young women who had previously engaged in homosexual behavior. It may be that in women's institutions, the general level of deprivation drives women into intense, supportive love-relationships, but does not necessarily result in their engaging in overt lesbian activities.

Imogene Moyer[34,35] did a careful study of the relationship between homosexuality, leadership, and interaction between prisoners at the State Industrial Farm for Women in Goochland, Virginia during 1973. She found that the percentage of women engaging in overt homosexual behavior increased directly with the number of previous prison sentences that they had served. It was also true that the longer their current sentence, the more likely they were to engage in overt lesbian behavior. The homosexual participants who played masculine roles were likely to be leaders in this female prisoner subculture, but the homosexual participants playing feminine roles were not. Staff members were very upset at the incidence of homosexual behavior at Goochland, and they constantly tried to break up affairs by separating the participants. When this occurred, one of them invariably found a new lover, creating a lovers' triangle that tended to be resolved through violence. In this situation, we can see that staff attempts to enforce the rules unintentionally led to more violence than probably would have occurred had they allowed the lovers to continue to live together.

RACE RELATIONS

We have already pointed out the role that race relations play in victimization among prisoners. Racism and intergroup conflict are facts of life in all correctional institutions. Prison administrators have to work hard to keep situations from getting out of hand (such as happened in the California prison system when a war erupted between the Mexican Mafia and Nuestra Familia, or in Stateville Prison, where the ethnic gangs literally took control of the institution away from the administration). Race relations, along with prisoner militancy and politicization, has transformed prisons from places in which individual prisoners act on the basis of their own motivations to conflicts which have distinct political overtones between large groups of prisoners. Individuals must be associated with a power bloc in order to protect themselves from victimization. The individual competition to achieve dominance has, to some degree, been replaced by competition among groups organized into power blocs and sustained by racial, political, and religious symbols.[26]

It is much easier for prison administrators to control their institutions when they are dealing with diverse individual prisoners, each of them carrying out personal agendas for dominance, growth, survival, and other goals. The control of power blocs is a much more difficult proposition. At one time, racism was useful to prison administrators as a control technique. If the population could be divided so that blacks and whites and other racial and ethnic groups worried more about each other than about escaping, confronting the administration, or other more disruptive possibilities, then the prison could be kept quiet.[33]

Racism has also been used in women's prisons as a control strategy. A study of a women's prison in the Midwest found that nonracial incidents were often redefined by staff members as having racial overtones so that the level of racial tension in the institution would rise. The process of playing blacks and whites off against each other was dampened if racial tension became so high that there was a danger of a race riot. Then favors would be given to appropriate leaders and incidents would temporarily be defined as having no racial implications.[44]

The first prison race relations riot in the United States did not occur until 1962.[18] Racial conflict has become a major source of prison riots since that time. It appears that racial conflict is limited so long as white prisoners control the prisoner subculture without question. As more minority group members enter institutions, they begin to challenge that control, and mass violence breaks out between the groups. The percentage of minority prisoners continues to grow, and this, combined with a higher degree of social organization than is found among white prisoners, allows them eventually to wrest control of the prison from whites. Once this occurs, group violence decreases, although violence between individuals because of racial animosity continues. During the time of the racial takeover—which may last as long as a decade in some cases—the task of prison administrators is to reduce racial tension sufficiently to avoid major riots, rather than stimulating racial antagonisms as a way of keeping prisoners from rioting against the administration.

DRUG ABUSE

One way to avoid the boredom of institutional life is to become intoxicated on drugs. In the traditional prison, alcohol was the drug of choice. Produced by the prisoners from whatever substances were available, the crudely fermented "pruno" was a sickening brew. Nevertheless, it was highly prized as a diversion. Alcohol continues to be manufactured by prisoners in modern correctional institutions, but alcohol use has been overshadowed by the wholesale importing of a wide variety of illegal drugs. It is relatively easy to discover a hidden gallon jar of fermenting fruit juice, but an ounce of marijuana or a few pills require an almost superhuman level of custodial vigilance to suppress.

What has happened is that the drug revolution that has occurred in the outside world has been imported into the prison. In a related process, there has been a change in the characteristics of prisoners. They are younger and much more drug-oriented than was the case in the past. Relatively few prisoners today are professional criminals exhibiting a perverse pride in their "workmanship." Young drug users are difficult to control in a correctional institution because their behavior is unpredictable. They do not even have a strong allegiance to the convict code, so that it is hazardous to predict what they will do in any given situation.

The use of illegal drugs leads to violence in prisons in two ways. The first is through the psychopharmacology of the drugs. Amphetamines and other strong stimulant drugs are taken in runs until the user becomes extremely agitated and paranoid. In this state, the danger of violent episodes is greatly increased. However, this psychopharmacological effect does not extend to depressants and hallucinogens, both of which probably diminish the chances of violence. Hallucinogens tend to produce a contemplative mood, and depressants lower aggressive impulses at the same time as they lower the general activity level of the user. The only drug that surpasses amphetamines in its potential for violence is alcohol, which releases inhibitions in such a way as to enhance the probability of a violent episode in individuals who have a predisposition toward violence.

The other way in which drug use leads to prison violence is when irregularities occur in the economic and political transactions making up the sub rosa economic system. Some users buy drugs they can't afford because they are unable to forego the pleasure of the drug use even temporarily, and thus incur a debt that may end up being settled through violence. Another prisoner sells drugs that are not what he advertises them to be; when his victims realize that they have been "burned," they may decide to administer a vicious beating as a warning to other drug dealers. Irregularities such as these are a constant occurrence in the prison drug trade, and each of them has the potential for violence.

Drug distribution systems are less well developed in institutions for juveniles than in institutions for men. Drug use is therefore somewhat lower in these institutions. It is still lower in institutions for women, where very few of the prisoners have the connections necessary to operate a fully developed drug racket. Most prison administrators are content to keep drug use down to a moderate level rather than expend the huge resoures necessary to wipe it out completely. For those who are insistent on eradicating illegal drug use, Raymond Irizarry[25] has proposed a solution. He believes that the correctional institution of the future will use forced doses of drug antagonists to block the action of any recreational drugs that prisoners might want to use. In addition, medical monitoring such as urine tests will be routinely used as a backup system to identify any prisoners who are using drugs. It is unlikely that Irizarry's proposals are constitutional, but even if they are, no prison could afford them.

PRISONER POLITICIZATION
AND MILITANCY

Political prisoners have always been part of the American prison scene. Some of the heroes of the American Revolution were incarcerated in British detention facilities. After the nation had attained independence, 17 political prisoners from the Whiskey Rebellion were incarcerated in 1794–1795. The modern era of the American political prisoner began when Ms. Rosa Parks was incarcerated at the beginning of the Montgomery Bus Boycott in 1955. In addition to the imprisonment of civil rights activists, the development of the Black Muslim religion and organized resistance to the Vietnam War all added political prisoners to the nations's correctional institutions. Mixing with the other prisoners, these politicals gave them a theoretical education in the "evils" of the system. This spread the idea of the prisoner as a political hostage far beyond the specifics of civil rights workers, war resisters, and the Black Muslims to embrace many other prison groups, particularly those containing minority group members. While traditional prisoners "knew" that they were wrong and acknowledged the legitimacy of the system that had incarcerated them, the new way of thinking proclaimed the legitimacy of street crime and the oppressiveness of the system.

Ethnogenisis is the creation of a culture. Prisons, because they force many different kinds of people into close contact with each other, provide the opportunty for ethnogenisis to occur. The mixing of radicals from different movements has resulted in a generalized culture of radicalism in many correctional institutions. College students who are well versed in theories of oppression and revolution learn about what it is like to live in abject poverty from hearing the tales of street criminals from the ghettos, and vice versa. One commentator on the prison scene has gone so far as to say that prisons may have replaced college campuses as the major developing-ground for radicalism.[4]

A study of a medium security correctional facility in Kentucky found that prisoners brought a great amount of radicalism to the institution with them, but they became even more radical the longer they spent behind the walls. Older felons and those who had stable heterosexual relationships outside the prison and no criminal friends were the least likely to increase their radicalism, but no category of prisoners decreased its radicalism between the initial testing and a post-testing nine months later. Denying the legitimacy of the system, perceiving class oppression as a major evil, and advocating revolution were all common among these prisoners.[14]

Prison administrators often find it extremely difficult to work with political prisoners. The political prisoner role interprets imprisonment in a way that requires no changes in the criminal. There is no need to change oneself because one is the victim of oppression rather than deficient in any way. Ronald Berkman,[6] after studying prisoner political activity in a group of institutions, concluded that today's prisoners usually see administrators as lawless, unwilling to follow the law any more than they have to, and opposed to sharing any power with the prisoners or the public. The prisoners believe (and there is much evidence in their favor) that administrators deliberately conceal institutional procedures and conditions from both the courts and the public in order to maximize their own freedom to do as they please. Because there is no moral or legal compulsion to obey administrators who are defined as amoral and lawless, the only way to obtain compliance is through threats, intimidation, and other social control techniques based on the exercise of raw power.

Sophisticated radicals cannot easily be co-opted into the system. They are leery about any friendly overtures from the prison administration. When other tactics have failed to produce acceptable results, some prison administrators have resorted to locking radical leaders in segregation or transferring them to other institutions.

PRISON RIOTS

The fundamental characteristic of a prison riot is that the correctional officers and administrators lose control of the prison. Several dire consequences flow from this loss of control. There is a greater chance of prisoner escape, and there may be much destruction of property in the area controlled by the rioters. Correctional officers may be taken hostage during the takeover and injured or killed as the riot progresses. The victimization of prisoners also increases during a riot. Prisoners who are known to be "snitches" are likely to be assaulted or murdered. Homosexuals and effeminate prisoners may suffer gang rapes. Additional injuries may occur when correctional officers—usually reinforced with state police or National Guardsmen—retake the facility. A final affront occurs if correctional officers take revenge on the rioters—as they did at Attica, New York in 1971, where prisoners were beaten, burned, and otherwise mistreated in retaliation for their participation in the riot of that year.[33]

A particularly disturbing aspect of recent prison riots has been their increasing viciousness. Correctional officers taken hostage in a prison riot can no longer be sure that they will be released unharmed. Even worse, there are a growing number of reports of hostages being tortured, maimed, raped, and murdered. For example, during a riot at the Maryland Penitentiary, the prisoners had a meeting at which they intended to decide whether to incinerate, hang, or behead one of the officers that they were holding hostage. They finally decided to burn him, but could not find any lighter fluid. They then decided to hang him. The officer's life was saved by a friendly prisoner just as he was on the verge of death.[32] It is not uncommon for friendly prisoners to help hostages in these situations, but they do not usually have sufficient power to challenge the pro-violence prisoner leaders directly.

The most destructive riot since the Attica riot of 1971 occurred in New Mexico's State Penitentiary in February 1980, when 14 correctional officers were held hostage, half of whom were beaten and some of whom were raped by their captors. As many as 200 prisoners were also beaten or raped. The prisoner death toll of 33 included individuals who had been brutally tortured and mutilated before they were murdered. Only 13 of the 33 had been labeled as "snitches" who passed prisoner secrets on to the administration. The reasons for most of the other murders are still unknown. The acts committed by the rioters included hanging, burning their victims to death, gouging out their eyes, and torturing them with blowtorches. One National Guardsman who had been in action in Vietnam said that he had never seen such savage carnage, not even in battle.[43] The brutality of the violence in the New Mexico riot easily outdistanced the Attica riot and other major prison disturbances that have occurred in this century.

Riots seem to be spontaneous events, and it is true that they are generally set off by an apparently inconsequential spark. However, this does not mean that they cannot be predicted. For example, race riots at the Deuel Vocational Institution in California during the early 1960s were essentially "scheduled" by white prisoner leaders who felt that blacks were becoming too influential. The actual spark setting off an incident might be an interracial boxing match or a news report of a racial incident; at Deuel this was just an ideological smokescreen for the political conflict beween racial groups in the prisoner subculture.[41]

Various opinions have been advanced as to the causes of prison riots. The American Correctional Association[2] has determined that there are two general causes, five institution-related causes and five causes not related to the institution. The general causes are the unnatural institutional environment and the antisocial characteristics of the prisoners. The institution-related causes are inept management; inadequate personnel practices; insufficient constructive and meaningful activity for the prisoners; insufficient and legitimate rewards; and inadequate facilities. Basic social attitudes, unrest in the larger community, inadequate finances, lack of meaningful rewards, and problems in the criminal justice system are causes unrelated to the specific correctional institution.

Edith Flynn[17] has developed a rather different list of causes of recent prison riots. Her list includes disturbances of the prisoner social structure; racial and political tensions originating in the larger society; facilitation of the political prisoner ethic as a justification for violence; the perpetuating of proviolent ecological conditions; limited communications that allow problems to get out of hand before reaching the ears of the administration; the faulty classification and treatment of military-type revolutionaries; and the practice of causing hopes to rise too high by promising more reforms than can possibly be delivered.

These scholary opinions have been supplemented by a research study of the causes of prison riots occurring between January 1971 and June 1972. There was no specific factor that always resulted in a prison disturbance during this 18-month period. However, there were a number of frequency differences between those prisons that experienced riots, those that experienced nonriot prison disturbances, and those that experienced neither form of resistance to authority. Both rioting and nonriot resistance were associated with overcrowded conditions and lack of adequate activities. Social disorganization among the prisoners tended to lead to riots, as did focussing a considerable amount of attention on the prison in the popular press. Other factors that earlier scholars have cited as possible causes of prison riots were not found to be associated with riots in this investigation.[50] The most interesting thing about this study is what it does not tell us. Some institutions in which most of the factors related to riots were found did not have riots. Why not? What actions were taken by prison administrators in those institutions to avoid riots? If social science can contribute to the elimination of prison riots, it will have the answer to this question.

SUMMARY

Homosexuality, race relations, drug abuse, prisoner militancy, prison riots and other disturbances, and prison victimization are major social problems that are found in most correctional institutions. Prison violence includes both sexual (homosexual rape) and nonsexual assaults. In addition to these forms of physical victimization, prisoners also suffer economic victimization, psychological victimization, and social victimization. High levels of victimization are found among prisoners in institutions for juveniles and women as well as those for men. Prisoners are sometimes victimized by correctional officers who are themselves the victims of prisoner violence from time to time. Consensual homosexuality should not be confused with homosexual rape, but it may cause just as much violence because of the jealousies that develop among homosexual couples and triangles. Racial conflict is severe in many institutions and has moved from the individual level to the group level, with large power blocs of prisoners competing for institutional dominance. Drug abuse and prisoner militancy have become major problems in the past decade. Prison riots are not necessarily more common today than they were in the past. However, they differ from past riots in that they have become more savage, with torture, mutilation, and murder being increasingly feared by both prisoners and correctional officers as the potential consequence of a prison riot.

REFERENCES

1. Akers, Ronald L., Norman S. Hayner, and Werner Gruninger. "Homosexual and Drug Behavior in Prison: A Test of the Functional and Importation Models of the Inmate System." *Social Problems* 21 (1974):410–422.
2. American Correctional Association. *Causes, Preventive Measures, and Methods of*

Controlling Riots and Disturbances in Correctional Institutions. Washington, D.C.: American Correctional Association, 1970.

3. Astrachan, A. "Profile/Louisiana." *Corrections Magazine* 2 (September–October 1975):9–14.

4. Baker, Ross K. "Politics Goes to Prison." *In* J. Susman: *Crime and Justice, 1971–1974.* New York: A.M.S. Press, 1974, pp. 84–89.

5. Bartollas, Clemens, Stuart J. Miller, and Simon Dinitz. *Juvenile Victimization: The Institutional Paradox.* New York: Wiley, 1976.

6. Berkman, Ronald. *Opening the Gates: The Rise of the Prisoners' Movement.* Lexington, MA: D.C. Heath, 1979.

7. Bowker, Lee H. *Prison Victimization.* New York: Elsevier, 1980.

8. Carroll, Leo. *Hacks, Blacks, and Cons.* Lexington, MA: D.C. Heath, 1974.

9. Cottle, Thomas J. "Children in Jail." *Crime and Delinquency* 25 (1979):318–334.

10. Davis, Alan J. "Sexual Assaults in a Philadelphia Prison System and Sheriff's Vans." *Transaction* 6 (December 1968):8–16.

11. Deckert, D. "Criminal Law—Prisons—Necessity a Defense to Escape When Avoiding Homosexual Attacks—People v. Lovercamp, 33 Cal App. 3d 823, 118 Cal Rptr.110 (1974)." *Western State University Law Review,* 3 (1975):164–175.

12. Dimick, Kenneth. *Ladies in Waiting Behind Prison Walls.* Muncie, IN: Accelerated Development Inc., 1979.

13. Elli, Frank. *The Riot.* New York: Coward-McCann, 1976.

14. Faine, John R. and Edward Bohlander, Jr. "The Genesis of Disorder: Oppression, Confinement, and Prisoner Politicization." *In* C. Huff: *Contemporary Corrections: Social Control and Conflict.* Beverly Hills, CA: Sage, 1977, pp. 54–77.

15. Felton, Charles A. "Violence in Prison." Paper presented at the annual meeting of the Academy of Criminal Justice Sciences, 1979.

16. Fishman, Joseph F. *Sex in Prison.* New York: National Library Press, 1934.

17. Flynn, Edith E. "Sources of Collective Violence in Correctional Institutions." *In* National Council on Crime and Delinquency: *Prevention of Violence in Correctional Institutions.* Washington, D.C.: Government Printing Office, 1973, pp. 15–32.

18. Fox, Vernon. "Analysis of Prison Disciplinary Problems." *Journal of Criminal Law, Criminology and Police Science* 49 (November–December 1972):321–326.

19. Fuller, Dan A., Thomas Orsagh, and David Raber. "Violence and Victimization Within the North Carolina Prison System." Paper presented at the annual meeting of the Academy of Criminal Justice Sciences, 1977.

20. Gibbs, J.J. *Stress and Self-Injury in Jail.* Ph.D. dissertation, State University of New York at Albany, 1978.

21. Grasewicz, Linda. "A Study of Inmate Assaults in Major Institutions." Unpublished paper, Virginia Department of Corrections, 1977.

22. Guenther, Anthony L. "Compensations in a Total Institution: The Forms and Functions of Contraband." *Crime and Delinquency* 21 (1975):243–254.

23. Heffernan, Esther. *Making it in Prison: The Square, the Cool and the Life.* New York: Wiley, 1972.

24. Heise, Robert E. *Prison Games.* Fort Worth: Privately published, 1976.

25. Irizarry, Raymond. "Drugs, Institutions and Mental Health: A Prophetic View." *American Journal of Corrections* 33 (November–December 1971):26–27.

26. Jacobs, James B. *Stateville.* Chicago: University of Chicago Press, 1977.

27. Jones, David A. *The Health Risks of Imprisonment.* Lexington, MA: D.C. Heath, 1976.

28. Kassebaum, Gene. "Sex in Prison, Violence, Homosexuality, and Intimidation are Everyday Occurrences." *Sexual Behavior* 2 (January 1972):39–45.

29. Lindquist, Charles A. "Female Violators of Prison Discipline: Backgrounds and Sanctions." Paper presented at the annual meeting of the American Society of Criminology, 1978.

30. Lockwood, Daniel. *Prison Sexual Violence.* New York: Elsevier, 1980.

31. Mann, W.E. *Society Behind Bars: A Sociological Scrutiny of Guelph Reformatory.* Toronto: Social Science Publishers, 1967.

32. "Maryland Inmates Hang Two Guards." *The Free World Times* 2 (April 1973):1, 3.

33. Mitford, Jessica. *Kind and Usual Punishment.* New York: Random House, 1971.

34. Moyer, Imogene L. *Interaction and Leadership Among Female Prisoners.* Ph.D. dissertation, University of Missouri–Columbia, 1975.

35. Moyer, Imogene L. "Leadership in a Women's Prison." *Journal of Criminal Justice* 8 (1980):233–241.

36. Park, J. "The Organization of Prison Violence." *In* A. Cohen, G. Cole and R. Bailey: *Prison Violence.* Lexington, MA: D.C. Heath, 1976, pp. 89–96.

37. Polsky, Howard. *Cottage Six.* New York: Wiley, 1962.

38. Porter, Howard K. *Prison Homosexuality: Locus of Control and Femininity.* Unpublished Ph.D. dissertation, Michigan State University, 1969.

39. Propper, Alice M.L. *Importation and Deprivation Perspective on Homosexuality in Correctional Institutions: An Empirical Test of Their Relative Efficacy.* Ph.D. dissertation, University of Washington, 1976.

40. Rees, C. "Arsenals Behind Prison Walls." *Guns and Ammo* (January 1970):29–33.

41. Rudoff, Alvin. *Prison Inmates: An Involuntary Association.* Ph.D. dissertation, University of California, Berkeley, 1964.

42. Sellin, Thorsten. *Slavery and the Penal System.* New York: Elsevier, 1976.

43. Serrill, Michael S. and Peter Katel. "The Anatomy of a Riot: The Facts Behind New Mexico's Bloody Ordeal." *Corrections Magazine* 6 (April 1980):6–24.

44. Spencer, Elouise J. *The Social System of a Medium Security Women's Prison.* Ph.D. dissertation, University of Kansas, 1977.

45. Srivastava, S. *The Indian Prison Community.* Lucknow: Pustak Kendra, 1977.

46. Sykes, Gresham M. *The Society of Captives.* New York: Atheneum, 1966.

47. Toch, Hans. *Men in Crisis, Human Breakdowns in Prison.* Chicago: Aldine, 1975.

48. Toch, Hans. *Police, Prisons, and the Problem of Violence.* Washington, D.C.: Government Printing Office, 1977.

49. Ward, David and Gene Kassebaum. *Women's Prison: Sex and Social Structure.* Chicago: Aldine, 1965.

50. Wilsnack, Richard W. "Explaining Collective Violence in Prisons: Problems and Possibilities." *In* A. Cohen, G. Cole, and R. Bailey. *Prison Violence.* Lexington, MA: D.C. Heath, 1976, pp. 61–78.

Chapter 12

Administrative Problems Caused by Social Change

One of the intriguing aspects of prison administration is that administrative problems are caused by any kind of change that occurs in the institutional environment. It does not matter whether the social change is negative or positive in nature: it still endangers orderly institutional life. Desirable prison reforms may create even greater administrative problems than drug abuse and gang violence within the institution. The gravity of the administrative problem is determined more by the amount of social dislocation caused by social change than it is by the nature of the change, everything else being equal.

This chapter begins with an examination of some of the changes in correctional practice that have been brought about by court decisions in recent years. The courts are probably the major source of change in contemporary American correctional institutions. They are also the main avenue through which other elements of the criminal justice system have input into the operation of the corrections system.

A second source of change in correctional practices is the appearance of standards for corrections. In the past, the publication of standards for corrections has rarely had the degree of impact on the correctional system intended by the authors of these standards. However, it is likely that these standards will become a more important force in correctional change in the coming decade. This trend is accentuated by the appearance of the accreditation movement in corrections.

The third and final major topic discussed in this chapter is a general survey of the impact of the change of administration from one program orientation to another. Both the effects of the process of change and of the new treatment arrangements implemented in the change are examined.

COURT-MANDATED CHANGES IN PRISONS

The traditional position of the courts on prison matters was summarized in the "Hands Off Doctrine," under which it was assumed that prisoners lost their constitutional rights when incarcerated and might receive these back only as privileges. Although the first challenge to this position was made in a federal court in 1944 (*Coffin v. Reichard,* 143 F. 2d 443 [6th Cir. 1944]), this doctrine was not strongly opposed until the 1971–1972 term of the United States Supreme Court, in which the court decided eight correctional cases, all in favor of the prisoners. Then, in the case of *Wolff v. McDonnell* (418 U.S. 539 [1974]), the Supreme Court proclaimed the substitute doctrine that there was to be no iron curtain drawn between the American Constitution and the nation's prisons.[38]

The courts still reject becoming involved in correctional administration much more than they accept it, and a recent statement of the Supreme Court said that "the federal courts do not sit to supervise state prisons, the administration of which is of acute interest to the States." (*Meachum v. Fano,* 19 CrL 3167, U.S. Supreme Court, June 25, 1976). These facts notwithstanding, there has been a clear trend toward increasing involvement of the courts in correctional matters extending back over the past several decades. Court involvement in corrections is most likely to occur when judges feel that the actions of correctional administrators are in direct conflict with constitutional principles or that they threaten the stature and authority of the courts.[14] No matter what a court may think of correctional practices, no intervention can occur unless a case is brought before the court.

Until recent years, the main legal device through which cases were brought to the attention of the courts was the writ of habeas corpus. Prisoners using this approach generally sought release from prison on the basis of what they alleged to be an error of the handling of their cases by the courts. More recently, writs of habeas corpus have been used to challenge the legality of conditions of imprisonment. The number of writs filed by prisoners in federal courts rose from 814 in 1957 to 4845 in 1965,[9] and then to 9063 in 1970. At that point, they began to decline, reaching 7033 in 1978.[2]

Correctional officials are also subject to suits for damages on the basis of tort liability. The most important recent decisions on correctional matters have been based on a form of tort liability authorized under Title 42, U.S.Code §1983, the Federal Civil Rights Acts of 1871. This act allows prisoners to file class actions requesting that certain policies be prohibited as well as legal actions requesting that correctional officials be assessed penalties for acts that they have already committed.[9] Only 218 cases were filed under section 1983 in 1966, but this ballooned to 9730 cases filed in 1978.[42] The rapid rise in these cases was of such great concern to correctional administrators that the American Correctional Association issued a handbook outlining defenses that correctional officials and state attorneys acting on their behalf could utilize against section 1983 actions.[45]

An Analysis of 1983 Suits in the Federal Courts

Many texts[4,10,21,34] approach the subject of court intervention in prison affairs in terms of prisoner's rights, citing specific cases in support of each right as they go along. We will not do so here. Our interest is in how the legal process works and in what ways it impacts the correctional establishment. William Turner's[42] study of section 1983 suits is the most important source of information about recent prisoner legal action.

Turner studied statistics on prisoner 1983 cases in all 95 federal district courts, and made an intensive analysis of case-processing in five federal districts. He found that there was little relationship between the number of prisoner cases filed and the number of prisoner cases going to trial. Many districts that were high in filings actually tried only a handful of cases. Other districts had relatively few filings, but tried a much higher proportion of the cases that were filed.

Fifty-six percent of all 1983 prisoner filings in 1976 were made in the South. The two highest states, Florida and Virginia, accounted for nearly a quarter of all 1983 prisoner filings in the entire nation. A high number of filings may indicate particularly poor prison conditions, or it may be indicative of other factors. If a prison has no grievance procedure for inmates, then prisoners have no recourse except to the courts. On the other hand, a prison with a fully developed grievance procedure may siphon off a high percentage of cases before they get to the courts. Another factor is the policy of the judges on prison cases. The district trying the highest number of cases in Turner's study was the Southern District of Alabama, which tried 52 cases in four years. This was partially because the judges in that district preferred to try any case in which there was the slightest possibility of a factual question in order to avoid later appeals.

Turner also conducted an in-depth study of the 664 prison cases filed in five districts under Section 1983 and terminating between January 1975 and June 1977. Approximately nine out of every ten cases were disposed of by the court without any response by the defendants, and only a small number of cases actually came to trial. Most of the prisoners could not afford the $15 filing fee, and so filed *in forma pauperas*. Relatively few prisoners were able to afford an attorney either. The screening process through which the courts decided whether or not to go ahead with a case was based on tacit rules, and often carried out by a law clerk rather than a judge.

Cases were much more likely to be filed from maximum security prisons than from other correctional institutions. The subjects most commonly found in the 1983 cases were medical care, property loss or damage, and interference with access to the courts. Claims of discrimination because of race or ethnicity, censorship of reading material, grooming regulations, religious discrimination, failure to protect the plaintiff from other prisoners, sexual discrimination, and illegal searches and shakedowns were infrequently seen. Claims of guard brutality fell in between these two extremes, and consistently made up between 7 and 10 percent of all prisoner suits. Approximately 20 percent of all cases did not relate to the conditions of confinement, but instead involved detainers, parole denial, improper arrests, and other topics beyond the control of correctional administrators.

Since so few cases (three percent, to be exact) went to an evidentiary hearing or trial, it would not be accurate to say that the trials involved a great burden on the court. The main burden was on the law clerks who had to work up a recommendation on each action. Even when a case went to court, relief was unlikely to be obtained by the prisoner. Only three injunctions were granted in 664 cases and there were but two cases that resulted in the rewarding of minimal damages. Preliminary (not permanent) injunctions were obtained in five cases. Successful cases invariably involved the services of lawyers on behalf of the prisoners, which suggests that although prisoners technically have access to the courts, justice is not fully available to them unless they are wealthy or unless their cases are sufficiently interesting to attract legal counsel.

Having reviewed Turner's research on 1983 suits, we gain an entirely different view of court actions on behalf of prisoners in recent years from the impression given by reading long lists of successful prison suits and their impact on correctional practice. It is true that correctional practice has been significantly affected by court actions, but it is not true that the courts are quick to jump to the aid of prisoners. It is evident that prisoner access to the courts is still restricted in ways that are not immediately apparent to the public and that the likelihood of a prisoner's being successful in a suit against a correctional administrator is extremely remote. Cases in which correctional practices altered

Figure 12.1 A jail cell badly in need of repair but still in service, 1968. (Law Enforcement Assistance Administration.)

as a result of court decisions are statistically rare, and it is only their accumulation over an extended period of time, along with the high volume of cases now being filed, that results in the significant impact that the courts have had on correctional affairs.

On May 23, 1980, the "Civil Rights of Institutionalized Persons Act"[44] became law in the United States. Under this act, the Attorney General is charged with promulgating "minimum standards for the development and implementation of a plain, speedy, and effective system for the resolution of grievances of adults confined in any jail, prison, or other correctional facility." In institutions that have grievance systems in compliance with these standards, prisoners must exhaust the administrative remedies available locally before involving the Attorney General in their cases. In other institutions, prisoners may contact the Attorney General directly. Where the Attorney General judges that the civil rights of a prisoner have been violated as part of "a pattern or practice of resistance to the full enjoyment of such rights, privileges, or immunities," a civil action may be instituted in any appropriate United States district court to ensure that minimum corrective measures are carried out. This law is certain to increase the involvement of the courts in correctional matters beyond the involvement that occurred in the 1970s.

Examples of Court Intervention in Corrections

In August 1977, a U.S. District Court Judge ruled that the State of Rhode Island was practicing cruel and unusual punishment in its prisons. A considerable number of changes were ordered in the daily operations of the prisons, and the judge gave the state 12 months to close down its maximum security facility. It was ruled that minimum public health standards had to be practiced in all facilities, that prison services and programs had to be greatly expanded, that every prisoner had to have a job, and that the system of prisoner classification had to be redesigned. When the reclassification of prisoners by a February 1978 deadline was not completed, Judge Raymond J. Pettine held the state in contempt and threatened fines of $1000 per day if the classification was not fully implemented by May 1st, a deadline which *was* met (at least on paper).[28]

Conditions at the Mississippi State Penitentiary at Parchman were declared unconstitutional in 1972 by District Court Judge William C. Keaday, following which significant changes were made in Mississippi's correctional system. The number of prisoners at Parchman declined, the number of civilian employees mushroomed, and the state corrections budget increased from $3 million to $18 million by 1979. These changes were not eagerly assented to by the state. It was necessary for Judge Keaday to issue a number of increasingly strict court orders to ensure that the required reforms were carried out. For example, he ordered in January 1975 that each prisoner must be given 50 square feet of living space, and he mandated the closing of six camps over a period of two years in August of that year. The closing of four additional camps was not accomplished until he threatened the state with contempt of court and fines of $10,000 per day.[17]

What are the limits of the court's intervention in correctional matters? We have seen in the two examples above that federal judges are willing and able to take on entire state correctional systems when necessary. When their own court resources are not adequate to the task, they have the power to appoint special masters to aid them in designing decisions, collecting data on compliance, and, if required, actually making the essential arrangements for compliance to occur.[30] The cost of mandated reforms is not an impediment to change. Recent cases make clear that female prisoners must be given the same services and programs as male prisoners, despite the fact that it is much more expensive to do so on a per capita basis because of the small proportion of women in the correctional system.[33] Where prison conditions and prison treatment do not meet minimal constitutional standards, the courts have recently been willing to support prisoner behavior that would be considered illegal under normal conditions. Thus, it may, under certain conditions, be legal to escape from a correctional institution in order to protect oneself from sexual assault[16] and it may be permissible for prisoners to use force against guards in order to protect fellow-prisoners from being beaten inappropriately.[18] These examples show that where correctional officials permit unconstitutional situations to exist, they are inviting the involvement of the courts.

Why do Prisons Lose Cases?

Students may think that, given the array of legal talent and other resources available to prison administrators, it is surprising that prisoners win as many suits as they did win during the 1970s. A commentary by Lawrence Bershad[7] helps us to understand this situation. In the first place, the legal advice available to correctional administrators is not always of high quality. Superintendents often have their questions answered by assistant attorneys general who are recent graduates of law schools and have not yet had much practical legal experience. Without a substantial working knowledge of the field, these young lawyers could not possibly give correctional administrators the best advice on how to handle difficult legal situations.

Even worse, legal advice is often unavailable on short notice. Because many correctional decisions must be made quickly, they run the risk of being made incorrectly. Another problem is that many prisoner suits are based on accepted institutional practices that never normally come to the attention of the legal counsel for the administrator. To deal with this problem, it is necessary for counsel to systematically review all institutional procedures in order to ensure that they are in comformity with the latest court decisions. Given the fact that extremely few correctional administrators are trained in the law themselves, these problems in the legal support services provided by state central offices to administrators may cause them to fail to adequately protect themselves against legal action.

Implementation and Resistance

The issuing of a court decision does not necessarily mean that it will be as fully implemented in the correctional system as was intended by the issuing judge. It is often possible to carry out the letter of the law without adhering to the spirit of the law so that the fundamental intent of a decision is subverted. The major result of many court decisions may be no more than the increased bureaucratization of correctional institutions. This occurs as administrators move to document and control every action more minutely so that it can be defended in future cases or so that it can be shown that there has been technical compliance with past decisions.[42] Alternatively, administrators may go beyond the intent of the court in a reform direction, hoping to obviate what they regard as intrusion into their own affairs by anticipating any possible legal action that might occur in the future.[14] Correctional systems in which full due process rights are not accorded to correctional officers and other employees are less likely to fully implement court decisions about the rights of prisoners than systems in which employees are also accorded a full range of constitutional rights. Employees find it difficult to understand why it is necessary to give prisoners rights that staff members do not have themselves.[40]

The Texas Department of Corrections. In *Johnson v. Avery* (393 U.S. 483 [1969]), the court forced the Texas Department of Corrections to hire two attorneys to administer a small legal assistance program limited to habeas corpus* proceedings rather than to rescind the TDC's rule against prisoner mutual assistance in writ writing. This rather feeble attempt to undermine the intent of the court was held insufficient in the case of *Novak v. Beto* (453 F.2d 661 [5th Cir. 1971]). As a result of that decision, the TDC increased the number of attorneys in its legal assistance program from two to twelve, but it still did not provide legal assistance for civil rights suits. Furthermore, the TDC paid the attorneys salaries so low that it was difficult to keep the twelve positions filled. When the U.S. Supreme Court ordered the establishment of a legal assistance program for civil rights suits in addition to habeas corpus proceedings in *Wolff v. McDonnell* (418 U.S. 539 [1974]), the TDC failed to act until mid-1975, at which time it finally rescinded its rule against inmate mutual assistance in legal cases. It also cooperated with the State Bar of Texas in implementing a new attorney-staffed legal aid program in 1976.[8]

Despite dragging its feet, the Texas Department of Corrections is now technically in compliance with court decisions. The problem is that prisoners continue to allege that they are being covertly punished for writ-writing. This can be accomplished by false accusations that they have broken regulations unrelated to writ-writing. Writ-writers also have claimed harrassment, parole denials, and the confiscation of property related to writ-writing, such as typewriters. Many of these claims remain unsubstantiated, but corroborating evidence has been introduced in enough cases to make clear that there is some substance to these allegations.[8]

State Correctional Institutions in Arkansas. *Holt v. Sarver* includes six decisions made by the United States District Court for the Eastern District of Arkansas, all dealing with the mistreatment of prisoners in Arkansas correctional institutions. The court issued approximately 40 separate orders in this case, not all of which made specific demands for compliance. Those orders including compliance demands requested changes such as dismantling the trusty system under which prisoners had control over other prisoners, expanding the employment of outside world personnel to compensate for the decreased responsibilities of the prison trusties, improving security from personal attacks for prisoners, improving working conditions in agricultural programs, increasing the number and quality of rehabilitation programs, tightening controls against

*A writ intended to bring an accused party before the court without delay.

the introduction of contraband into the prison, and raising the level of basic services in the prison (including clothing, diet, and medical and dental care). Prisoners were to be guaranteed access to the courts and to legal counsel, and threats and other reprisals against them for legal actions were to be terminated. Segregation and other forms of racial discrimination were to be eliminated, and an evidentiary hearing was ordered to examine prisoner complaints about brutality, homosexual assaults, and other unconstitutional conditions in the Arkansas prison.[20]

Substantial compliance to these various directives was achieved in Arkansas, although compliance was by no means complete. The trusty system of prisoner guards was completely dismantled. Prisoner safety from attack was increased due to the hiring of additional outside world personnel and a more vigorous program of shakedowns of the prisoners and their cells on a regular basis. A maximum security building was constructed and used to isolate extremely violent prisoners from the rest of the prisoner population. Prison brutality was no longer an official policy, but it persisted on an individual basis, and the court attributed this to lack of employee professionalism. Overcrowding in the Arkansas prisons was not eliminated, and there continued to be serious problems in the area of racial discrimination. Although greatly improved, medical care—particularly for mental health problems—continued to have deficiencies. Conditions in isolation cells were unacceptable, improvements in sanitation were uneven, and there were still reports of filth and infestations. Despite these problems in achieving total compliance with the court orders, the Arkansas Prison System made immense changes in a short period of time, raising their budget from $1 million to $6 million, adding nearly 500 civilian employees, and moving from isolated independent prisons to a unified state department of corrections.[20]

The problems with court-mandated change in correctional institutions have not been due to lack of understanding of correctional matters on the part of judges. Court orders have generally been realistic and carefully framed. Instead, the problems arise at the point of compliance. No matter how well an order is drawn up, it is impossible to enforce it in such a way as to produce compliance with not only the letter but also the spirit of the law. There are many situations in which prison administrators can contrive the appearance of compliance without any intention of fully implementing the provisions of the court orders. It is no easier to produce compliance by prison administrators than it is to enforce speed limits on the highways. Some individuals follow both the letter and the spirit of the law, others habitually break the law, but minimize their deviations from legal standards, and a small proportion of them make no attempt to follow accepted standards of behavior except when under the direct observation of law enforcement authorities.

CORRECTIONAL STANDARDS AND ACCREDITATION

The writing of standards for correctional treatment is a significant force in American corrections. Rather than having no standards for correctional practice, the primary problem confronting most correctional administrators is to decide which of the many standards to follow. As an example, the National Advisory Commission on Criminal Justice Standards and Goals[31] recommended 80 square feet per prisoner sleeping area as a minimum standard. The standard published by the Federal Bureau of Prisons is 75 square feet, and the standard published by the National Clearinghouse for Criminal Justice Planning and Architecture is 70 square feet. The Standard Minimum Rules for the Treatment of Prisoners issued by the United Nations requires 65 square feet of sleeping area per prisoner, and the American Correctional Association has adopted a 60 square foot standard (80 square feet if the prisoner is locked in the cell more than 10 hours per day).[35] Which of these standards is the most appropriate one for use in a given institution? Is there one standard that should be universally applied regardless of the institution? If so, is this a moral question, a technological/scientific question, or a political question? At the moment, it is fair to say that none of these questions have been answered in a way that is universally acceptable across the different constituencies having vested interests in corrections.

The United Nations Standard Minimum Rules for the Treatment of Prisoners

The Economic and Social Council of the United Nations approved the Standard Minimum Rules in 1957. There are 55 rules applying to the treatment of prisoners in general, and 39 rules applicable only to special categories of prisoners, such as prisoners under sentence, insane and mentally abnormal prisoners, prisoners under arrest or awaiting trial, and civil prisoners. The full text of the United Nations document also includes sections on the selection and training of correctional personnel and open penal and correctional institutions. The general rules define the minimum acceptable standards for the treatment of prisoners from the viewpoint of basic human rights. For example, every prisoner should be served "at the usual hours with food of nutritional value adequate for health and strength, of wholesome quality and well prepared and served."[43:179] No prisoner shall be allowed to discipline another prisoner, although self-government is to be encouraged. "Corporal punishment, punishment by placing in a dark cell, and all cruel, inhuman, or degrading punishments shall be completely prohibited as punishments for disciplinary offenses."[43:181] Although these standards embody the medical model of treatment now being discarded in many correctional systems, the Standard Minimum Rules constitute a major international contribution to correctional practice.

Given that the Standard Minimum Rules have the full endorsement and continuing support of the United Nations, one might expect them to have had considerable influence on international corrections. This possibility has been examined in a handful of surveys conducted between 1967 and 1974. The 1974 survey conducted by the United Nations obtained data from 58 nations; according to the reported data, the rules on accommodation and living conditions were implemented in 50 percent of those nations completing the questionnaire, the separation of categories in 62 percent, medical services in 65 percent, discipline and punishment in 65 percent, treatment standards in 69 percent, classification and individualization standards in 59 percent, and work standards in 52 percent. Most of the countries indicated that prison law and administrative regulations had been influenced by the Standard Minimum Rules, an improvement over the one-third of the countries making that statement in the 1967 United Nations survey. Unfortunately, the documentation provided for these statements did not always substantiate the claim of influence.[39] Examples of decisive influence include Zambia, which wrote a new Prison's Act and Prison Rules to be consistent with the Standard Minimum Rules,[23] and Israel, which reported that parts of its prison regulations were directly translated from the Standard Minimum Rules.[39]

A further analysis of the implementation of the Standard Minimum Rules in nine selected nations was made in 1969 by Bad-El-Din Ali.[3] Using reports from expert investigators rather than questionnaires completed by correctional officials, he found that the implementation of the United Nations standards had increased between 1955 and 1968 in all of the countries surveyed. The nations achieving the highest percentage of rule implementation were Israel (90 percent), Hungary (87 percent), and Italy (84 percent), and the nations with the lowest levels of implementation were Costa Rica (34 percent), the United States (68 pecent), and Australia (72 percent). There was a tendency in these nine nations to implement the general rules more fully than the rules for specific groups of prisoners that are found in part two of the standards. Third World nations showed a greater improvement between 1955 and 1968 than the fully industrialized nations included in the study. Although the absolute level of implementation of the rules was higher in the fully industrialized countries than in Third World countries in 1968, it was higher still in those nations which were intermediate between the two extremes of industrial development. For the Third World nations, financial and technical obstacles were much more important reasons for nonimplementation than in the fully industrialzed nations.

Correctional Standards in the United States

The American Prison Association, which preceded the American Correctional Association, first published a manual of standards for correctional practice in 1946. Revisions were issued in 1954, 1959, and 1966, but they were never more than suggestions for self-evaluation.[36] They were directed primarily toward the concerns of prison administrators.[5] In contrast, the correctional standards issued by the National Advisory Commission on Criminal Justice Standards and Goals,[31] which were issued in 1973, contain a much greater emphasis on human rights in general and the rights of prisoners in particular.

Standards have continued to proliferate, so that there are now 15 or 20 sets of partial or complete standards in existence, written by groups such as the American Bar Association, American Public Health Association, National Sheriff's Association, International Halfway House Association, American Institute of Architects, and the American Medical Association. These standards are generally high. The problem with them is that each set of standards is written with the vested interests of the sponsoring association in mind. They do not entirely represent the interests of the public. One reason why selected standards developed by the National Advisory Commission on Criminal Justice Standards and Goals were chosen to be emphasized in this text over other sets of standards is that this set of standards more closely approximates the interests of the public than any of the other available standards.

The Accreditation Strategy of the American
Correctional Association

With the publication of the comprehensive set of standards on correctional practices by the National Advisory Commission on Criminal Justice Standards and Goals in 1973, there was, for the first time, a major challenge to the interpretation of correctional standards made by the American Correctional Association. The ACA had been content to allow correctional institutions to evaluate themselves or to do nothing at all in reference to ACA standards up through the early 1970s. The Association did not adopt a code of ethics until 1975.[6] When comprehensive standards were issued by the National Commission, this undercut the ACA strategy and threatened to put teeth into correctional standards for the first time. With comprehensive standards in existence, it would not be unreasonable for federal agencies to require compliance with these standards as a condition for continued financial aid to state and local correctional units.

Although the Law Enforcement Assistance Administration backed away from using the standards in this fashion, the ACA moved quickly to strengthen its position. The Commission on Accreditation for Corrections was created in 1974 with grant funds secured by the ACA from the Law Enforcement Assistance Administration. The self-evaluation emphasis of earlier ACA standards was dropped and replaced by an emphasis on accreditation by professionals external to the local corrections agency. While accreditation substantially strengthens the standards program of the ACA, it does not change its basic character. Unlike standards determined by interdisciplinary commissions charged specifically with protecting the public interest, the ACA standards are "...*standards which have been determined by corrections professionals...to be required as optimum levels of practice in the operation of correctional institutions and community programs and services.*"[37:23]

The ACA-sponsored Commission on Accreditation for Corrections issued its first manual of standards, for adult parole authorities, in July 1976. By April 1979, the full set of ten manuals was complete. The areas covered by these manuals include prisons, jails, probation, parole, community corrections, and general administrative standards for adults and juveniles.[13] Invitations to participate in the accreditation process were extended to approximately 5000 correctional agencies and programs.[5] By 1980, 440 agencies had accepted the invitation and were involved in the accreditation process. Fifty-eight of these agencies had completed the process and received accreditation for a three-year period. The other agencies were currently in process.[1]

The accreditation process begins when an administrator sends a letter of intent to the commission indicating the willingness of the agency to become accredited. Upon processing by the Commission, the agency enters Correspondent Status. It then begins applying the commission's standards to its own activities in a process of self-evaluation with consultation and technical assistance from the Commission. Six months later, a report based on the self-evaluation activity is submitted to the commission, along with a plan of action for correcting deficiencies. The agency then enters Candidate Status for a period of one year, during which the deficiencies are to be corrected. Accreditation Status is requested at the end of the year, and a committee of three or more corrections professionals make a site visit to confirm that the agency is in compliance with the standards. When the visiting committee's report is accepted by the Commission, Accreditation Status is awarded.[12]

All of the standards developed by the Commission are not considered to be equally important. Some of them are rated as essential, others as important, and the remaining standards as merely desirable. To be successfully awarded Accreditation Status, an agency must be in compliance with 90 percent of the essential standards, 80 percent of the important standards, and 70 percent of the desirable standards. This means that an institution can be fully accredited for 3–5 years even though it has not met 10 percent of the essential standards, 20 percent of the important standards, and 30 percent of the other standards applicable to its institutional type. When combined with the fact that the standards were originally developed by correctional administrators without input from the general public or from correctional clients, this shows that there are still a number of problems to be worked out in the accreditation process before it can achieve its full potential as a stimulant for correctional reform.[41]

If all American correctional agencies were to become accredited, this would result in a significant improvement in the level and quality of services to correctional clients. There can be no doubt that the effect of the Commission on Accreditation for Corrections on the corrections industry is a positive one, and that its impact will increase in coming years. At the same time, the awarding of accreditation when standards are not fully met can be misleading to the general public. Another problem is that since the accreditation process is entirely voluntary, it is unlikely to impact those correctional systems most in need of upgrading. There is no provision in the procedures of the Commission to request that an agency subject itself to an evaluation. Without such a mechanism, the corrections industry is unable to effectively police itself. Historically, this tends to lead to increased federal regulation, which is what the American Correctional Association seeks to obviate through the strategy of the creation of the commission on Accreditation for Corrections. Whether or not this strategy will be successful in the long run remains to be be seen.

THE IMPACT OF CHANGES IN ADMINISTRATIVE ORIENTATION ON INSTITUTIONAL STABILITY

To someone who is unfamiliar with organizational matters, it may seem relatively easy to come into an institution that has languished in traditional correctional practices and then rapidly make a series of changes to bring it to the forefront of progressive correctional administration and programming. A growing body of research literature indicates that this is far from the truth. Correctional institutions contain many vested-interest groups, and these groups have worked out stable patterns of accommodation over extended periods of time. Any rapid social changes that upset these patterns of accommodation may produce anomie, a state of normlessness in which all accepted standards of behavior vanish. Stability is essential in correctional institutions. A high level of anomie implies a breakdown of institutional stability, which is associated with increased conflict among staff members, riots, prisoner victimization, and other indices of social disorganization.

In addition to the general anomic effects of institutional change, there is also a reallocation of power that systematically undercuts the previously accepted prerogatives of certain groups and transfers their prerogatives to newly created or existing groups. In some cases, their prerogatives may simply be eliminated rather than being reallocated to other groups. It is a delicate task to reallocate power without producing strong reactions from those who have been disadvantaged by the reallocation. Disadvantaged groups may deliberately foment prison disturbances, decrease work efficiency, and engage in other organized designs calculated to undermine the new social order in expectation of reversion to the previous state of affairs.

What is meant by "the previously accepted prerogatives of certain groups" in the prison? Richard Cloward[11] points out that prison administrators accommodate to the prisoner society by permitting the creation of illegitimate opportunity structures. Through these arrangements, high-status prisoners are permitted to dominate (and, to some extent, to victimize) low-status prisoners in return for their cooperation with the administration in preventing major prison disturbances and other events that might disturb the status quo of the institution. These high-status prisoners ". . . develop a vested interest in maintaining the higher positions they have gained. Seeking to entrench their relative advantage over other inmates, they are anxious to suppress any behavior that might disturb the present arrangements."[11:33]

It appears that it is the structure of events that matters in producing these negative reactions to social change rather than the content of the events. An institution changing from a custody orientation to a treatment orientation may experience just as many disruptions as an institution changing from a treatment orientation to a custody orientation. Conversely, an institution may maintain the same basic orientation on the custody–treatment continuum, but make enough changes in the structure of the institution to have the same result. It also matters little whether the change is generated within the administration of the institution or whether it is thrust upon the institution by the state correctional agency or some other external body. These generalizations about change in correctional institutions are illustrated in the examples which follow.

Changes Induced by External Forces

One of England's newest prisons, Albany, was opened in 1967 as a medium security institution. It rapidly became an example of the finest development of British institutional programming. When the British penal system implemented the dispersal policy under which serious offenders were spread throughout the prison system, the character of the prison population at Albany began to change.

The violent prisoners transferred into Albany were, in a sense, wolves among the sheep. The amount of violence soared, fear permeated the prisoner subculture, and there was a sharp increase in requests for protective custody. Prison officials were powerless to maintain the positive social climate that had existed prior to the arrival of the violent prisoners.[22]

A parallel situation arose in a Midwestern state prison that had been built to relieve the population pressure in the state's maximum security facility. According to the original plan, only selected prisoners were to be transferred to the new facility. When the institution opened for occupancy, this plan was followed, and the new prison began to operate under a progressive administration. Then, only six months later, the superintendent of the institution died and was replaced by a more custody-oriented administrator. Security was rapidly tightened up, and the prisoners reacted with an increase in escape attempts. The state hired a new director of corrections who supported architectural modifications in the new prison to make it more secure. This, in turn, led to the assigning of a more serious group of offenders to the institution. The destruction of property and prisoner–staff conflict increased. The transition from a remarkably humane (although not treatment-oriented) prison to the negative environment of a total institution was complete. Although the new superintendent was not necessarily opposed to the change, the change was entirely imposed on the institution from the State Central Office of Corrections.[15]

Internally Controlled Shifts in Institutional Orientation

Many of the shifts in institutional orientation reported in the literature were accomplished by local administrators rather than forced upon the institution from the state or national levels. Oscar Grusky[19] describes what happened in a prison camp when a treatment-oriented administrator was replaced by a custody-oriented administrator. Formal rules were quickly substituted for informal understandings as a basis of social control in the institution. Security increased, and line staff were instructed to keep the prisoners under closer supervision than they had before. The prisoners reacted with hostility, damaged institutional property, and escaped or transferred out of the institution in increasing numbers. Correctional officers who were treatment-oriented were offended by the change in policy and became alienated and isolated from the remainder of the staff. They often refrained from enforcing the new authoritarian rules. Communication channels from prisoners to officers to administrators broke down, so that administrators no longer had full knowledge of what was going on within the institution. All these negative developments occurred without the added impetus of an influx of violent prisoners such as took place in the two examples given above.

The shift from a custody to a treatment orientation is more common than the shift from treatment to custody in the institutions described above. Since these changes generally result in increased privileges for the prison population taken as a whole, one might expect that they would be given wholehearted support by the prisoners. Quite to the contrary, the social disorganization is just as great, and sometimes greater, than the problems caused by shifts from a treatment to a custody orientation. This occurs in juvenile institutions[25] and agricultural plantation prisons[29] just as it does in maximum security institutions for adults.

The classic description of the effects of a custody-treatment shift in institutional orientation is the narration of events at Oahu Prison in Hawaii from 1946 through 1955. In this description, Richard McCleery[26,27] explains how liberal policies came to be implemented at the prison between 1946 and 1950, describes the social disorganization that occurred as a result of the liberalization and reached its peak in 1953, and the subsequent tightening up of the organization in 1954 and 1955.

The new warden of Oahu Prison shortly became aware of a number of abuses and improprieties within the institution, and responded to this by calling in outside investigators and dismissing a number of correctional officers. The institutional disciplinary committee received input from treatment staff members, and began to adjudicate cases on the basis of principles of justice rather than exemplary punishment. Treatment staff members began to accumulate information about prisoners, and opened channels of communication with them in order to become aware of their needs. Their information base increased their importance in institutional decision-making. It also made it impossible for correctional officers to suppress prisoner requests and applications that they did not wish to be passed on to higher authorities.

A manual outlining democratic rather than authoritarian methods of administration set forth the theory of the new regime. As long as the change of philosophy did not directly impact daily affairs, the level of conflict was manageable. Conditions in the institution began to deteriorate as the new philosophy was translated into operational details. The old cons, who avoided direct contact with prison staff, withdrew gradually from positions of power and were replaced by violence-prone prisoners as the dominant group in the prisoner subculture. As treatment staff moved into more of the areas of prison life, they continually disregarded the unwritten agreements between correctional officers and the old cons in these areas. The total effect of a large number of individual incidents and changes in procedures was the breakdown of both the staff and prisoner social systems. In the first stage of the reform movement, the inmate council was dominated by treatment-oriented prisoners, and had a positive effect on the prisoner subculture. By 1952, the prisoners could no longer exercise social controls over disruptive elements in the prisoner population, and there was a sharp rise in institutional violence. The influence of the old cons was now limited to protecting themselves and their friends from assaults by the reform school graduates who were now dominating the prisoner subculture. Calling themselves a syndicate, these individuals took over the inmate council and the inmate craft shop. Statistics from the disciplinary committee show that the number of major disciplinary violations in 1953 was four times as high as it had been before the beginning of the reform movement.

Syndicate members misused their control of the inmate council to make excessive profits from the craft shop while they drove the rest of the prisoners close to economic collapse. They rapidly lost the degree of support that they had achieved in the prisoner subculture, and began to break up themselves as the responsible members of the group cut all ties to their more antisocial acquaintances in disgust. Those who were left in the syndicate organized for gang warfare in an attempt to regain control, but the administration mounted machine guns on the cell block roof and was able to avert a crisis.

The prisoners were so shaken up by the events of 1953 that they were ready to compromise with the administration. Correctional officers, who had pubicly challenged the administration in 1953 and lost (with the resignation of some of their leaders), were also ready to compromise. The result was that it was possible for the administration to work out a procedure for carrying out both treatment and custody functions under the same roof. One innovative technique was to stage a series of warden's nights in which the warden met with the entire prisoner population to discuss institutional problems one by one. It was possible to forge a new working coalition between prisoners, correctional officers, treatment staff, and administrators, so that by 1954 things had returned to normal.

Institutional changes need not always be as extreme as they were at Oahu. An experiment carried out at a small Swedish prison between 1971 and 1974 disrupted institutional relations to a much lesser extent, and resulted in reactions from prisoners and correctional officers that were similar to the reactions reported in the Oahu example, but much less extreme. In the Swedish experiment, institutional regulations were amended to allow prisoners to have a much greater amount of contact with the free community than they had had in the past. These changes included provisions for leave, work release, group activities in the community, and the use of the telephone. Correctional officers were much less in favor of the changes than were treatment staff. They came to feel uncertain and insecure in their work. Some of them became more nervous and two reported that they had become ill because of the new arrangements. Although the officers privately held positive opinions about the value of the program for the prisoners, they did not share these opinions with each other. The result was pluralistic ignorance, in which each officer thought that the other officers were more negative toward the experimental program than they were in fact.[24]

This study points out one of the reasons why it is so difficult to engineer social change in a correctional institution. The prison officers were not consulted during the time that most of the changes were designed and implemented. This was why they felt left out, though it was certainly not the only reason why they opposed the experimental program. Nevertheless, had they been included from the beginning, much of their opposition to the program might have been undercut. When the prison administrator realized the error, the officers were included in decision-making meetings. Unfortunately, most of the crucial decisions had already been made, so it was not possible to completely negate the negative effects of the error.[24] This suggests that correctional administrators implementing social change in authoritarian institutions should be careful to change to a fully participative model of program development before they implement the program changes rather than afterwards. It is customary in authoritarian organizations to develop programs in secret and then announce them fully formed in order to avoid excessive opposition. The problem is that this technique also ensures that the new program will not receive the full cooperation of everyone involved. It might be better to have more conflict in the planning stage if that would lead to a higher level of acceptance of the program as finally implemented.

Not all prison administrators are equally suited for this type of work. A study by Elmer Nelson and Catherine Lovell[32] identified six administrator characteristics affecting the readiness of an administrator to implement institutional change and additional six characteristics associated with carrying out the change. The most important of these characteristics are an adequate scientific knowledge base, having concern for the welfare of the employees as well as prisoners, a high level of planning skills, the willingness to take risks in order to achieve goals, dissatisfaction with the status quo, and a sensitivity to the need to fully institutionalize new procedures so that they will become a permanent part of the life of the institution. This is a profile that is rarely seen among prison administrators, which is one of the reasons why prisons have so much trouble when significant changes occur in programming.

SUMMARY

The courts are probably the major source of change in contemporary American correctional institutions. They are also the main avenue through which other elements of the criminal justice system have input into the operation of the corrections system. Court-mandated changes in American prisons in the 1970s fundamentally redefined the rights of prisoners. A second source of changing correctional practices is the appearance of standards for corrections, one version of which is contained in Appendix 2 of this text. The accreditation strategy of the American Correctional Association represents an attempt to gain public support for the self-regulation of the correctional industry. One problem with the accreditation process as it presently exists is that institutions can become accredited without complying fully with all of the standards in the accreditation document, thus potentially misleading the public about the quality of correctional programming offered. A third category of changes in correctional institutions is a major alteration in the pattern of accommodation which has developed among the multiple vested-interest groups that exist in each institution. Rapid social changes such as a switch from a custody orientation to a treatment orientation can undermine the stable patterns of accommodation and can lead to chaos, increased victimization, and prison riots. Prison administrators who wish to implement major institutional reforms can avoid these negative consequences of social change by studying the social structure, both formal and informal, of the institution before changing institutional arrangements and by carefully examining the potential for social disruption in each step of the change process before it is implemented.

REFERENCES

1. "Accreditation Update." *On the Line* 3 (July 1980):1.
2. Administrative Office of the United States Courts. *1978 Annual Report of the Director.* Washington, D.C., 1978.

3. Ali, Badr-El-Din. "Treatment of Prisoners in Nine Nations: A Pilot Study on Standard Minimum Rules." *Criminologica* 7 (1969):2–18.

4. Allen, Harry E. and Clifford E. Simonson. *Corrections in America: An Introduction.* Encino, CA: Glencoe, 1978.

5. Allinson, Richard S. "The Politics of Prison Standards." *Corrections Magazine* 5 (March 1979):54–62

6. American Correctional Association. "Code of Ethics." *American Journal of Correction* 37 (November–December 1975):15.

7. Bershad, Lawrence. "Law and Corrections: A Management Perspective." *New England Journal on Prison Law* 4 (Fall 1977):49–82.

8. Boettner, Janet C.N. *Prisoners' Rights of Access to the Courts: The Impact of the Federal Judiciary on the Texas Department of Corrections.* Ph.D. dissertation, University of Texas, Austin, 1976.

9. Carter, Robert M., Richard A. McGee, and E. Kim Nelson. *Corrections in America.* Philadelphia: J.P. Lippincott, 1975.

10. Clare, Paul K. and John H. Kramer. *Introduction to American Corrections.* Boston: Holbrook, 1976.

11. Cloward, Richard A. "Social Control in the Prison." *In* Richard A. Cloward: *Theoretical Studies in the Social Organization of the Prison.* New York: Social Science Research Council, 1970, pp. 20–48.

12. Commission on Accreditation for Corrections. "A Progress Report." Rockville, MD, 1977.

13. Commission on Accreditation for Corrections. "Accreditation: Blueprint for Corrections." Rockville, MD, 1979.

14. Duffee, David. *Correctional Management: Change and Control in Correctional Organizations.* Englewood Cliffs, NJ: Prentice-Hall, 1980.

15. Galliher, John F. "Change in a Correctional Institution: A Case Study of the Tightening-up Process." *Crime and Delinquency* 18 (July 1972):263–270.

16. Gardner, Martin R. "The Defense of Necessity and the Right to Escape from Prison—A Step Towards Incarceration Free from Sexual Assault." *Southern California Law Review* 49 (1975):110–152.

17. Gettinger, Stephen. "Profile/Mississippi." *Corrections Magazine* 5 (June 1979):4–19.

18. Gilman, David. "Did the Highest Court in Massachusetts Give Inmates the *Right* to Use Force Against Guards?" *Corrections Magazine* 2 (June 1976):13–16.

19. Grusky, Oscar. "Role Conflict in Organization: A Study of Prison Camp Officials." *Administrative Science Quarterly* 3 (1959):452–472.

20. Harris, M. Kay and Dudley P. Spiller, Jr. *At the Decision: Implementation of Judicial Degrees in Correctional Settings.* Washington, D.C.: Government Printing Office, 1977.

21. Kerper, Hazel B. and Janeen Kerper. *Legal Rights of the Convicted.* St. Paul, MN: West, 1974.

22. King, Roy E. and Kenneth W. Elliott. *Albany: Birth of a Prison—End of an Era.* London: Routledge and Kegan Paul, 1977.

23. Kraien, Rubin. "Prisoners' Rights and the Standard Minimum Rules for the Treatment of Offenders." *Journal of Offender Therapy and Comparative Criminology* 22 (1978):156–163.

24. Landerholm-Ek, Ann-Charlotte. "On Change in Prison—Shortened Version of the Final Report on an Experiment." Report Number 17. Stockholm, Sweden: National Prison and Probation Administration, 1976.

25. Lubeck, Steven G. and LaMar T. Empey. "Mediatory vs. Total Institution: The Case of the Runaway." *Social Problems* 16 (1968):242–260.
26. McCleery, Richard H. "Policy Change in Prison Management." Governmental Research Bureau, Michigan State University, 1957.
27. McCleery, Richard H. "The Governmental Process and Informal Social Control." *In* Donald R. Cressey: *The Prison: Studies in Institutional Organization and Change.* New York: Holt, Rinehart, and Winston, 1961, pp. 149–1188.
28. Morin, Stephen P. "Rhode Island Rebounds." *Corrections Magazine* 4 (December 1979):32–35.
29. Mouledous, Joseph C. "Organizational Goals and Structural Change: A Study of the Organization of a Prison Social System." *Social Forces* 41 (March 1963):283–290.
30. Nathan, Vincent M. "The Use of Masters in Institutional Reform Litigation." *The University of Toledo Law Review* 10 (Winter 1979):419–464.
31. National Advisory Commission on Criminal Justice Standards and Goals. *Corrections.* Washington, D.C.: Government Printing Office, 1973.
32. Nelson, Elmer K., Jr. and Catherine H. Lovell. *Developing Correctional Administrators.* Washington, D.C.: Joint Commission on Correctional Manpower and Training, 1969.
33. "Prisons Must Provide Women, Men Equal Access to Programs." *The Criminal Law Reporter* 26 (November 21, 1979):1031.
34. Reid, Sue T. *Crime and Criminology.* Hinsdale, IL: Dryden, 1976.
35. Rutherford, Andrew *et al. Prison Population and Policy Choices. Volume 1, Preliminary Report to Congress.* Washington, D.C.: Government Printing Office, 1977.
36. Sechrest, Dale K. "The Accreditation Movement in Corrections." *Federal Probation* 40 (December 1976):15–19.
37. Sechrest, Dale K. "The Legal Basis for Commission Standards." *American Journal of Correction* 40 (November–December 1978):14–17, 23.
38. Shover, Neal. *A Sociology of American Corrections.* Homewood, IL: Dorsey, 1979.
39. Skoler, Daniel L. "World Implementation of the United Nations Standard Minimum Rules for Treatment of Prisoners." Washington, D.C.: American Bar Association, Commission on Correctional Facilities and Services, 1975.
40. Sullivan, Dennis C. and Larry L. Tifft. "Court Intervention in Corrections: Roots of Resistance and Problems of Compliance." *Crime and Delinquency* 21 (1975):213–222.
41. "The Business of Correctional Standards." *Prison Law Monitor* 1 (September 1978):74, 96.
42. Turner, William B. "A Study of Prisoner Section 1983 Suits in the Federal Courts." *Harvard Law Review* 92 (1979):610"63.
43. United Nations. "Standard Minimum Rules for the Treatment of Prisoners and Related Recommendations." *In* Benedict S. Alper and Jerry F. Boren: *Crime: International Agenda.* Lexington, MA: D.C. Heath, 1972, pp. 175–202.
44. United States. 96th Congress. "Public Law 96-247, Civil Rights of Institutionalized Persons Act." May 23, 1980.
45. Weisz, M. "Defenses to Civil Rights Actions Against Correctional Employees." College Park, MD: American Correctional Association, 1977.

Local Correctional Institutions—Jails and Misdemeanants

Jails are not usually thought of as alternatives to prisons—but they are. When an offender plea-bargains an admission of guilt in return for a reduction of the charge from a felony to a misdemeanor, a jail sentence is substituted for a prison sentence. When federal courts limit the population of state prisons to a reasonable level because of overcrowding, convicted felons may be kept in local jails for much longer than a year until the overcrowding in the state facilities is relieved. Chapter 13 discusses the characteristics of jail residents and jail facilities, prisoner subcultures, staff members in jails, jail administration, major problems of jail administration, characteristics of jails, and jail programs.

Except for a few small states, jails are administered on the city or county level. The correctional system at these levels is not generally separated from law enforcement to the extent that it is at the state and federal levels. Instead of answering to a separate correctional authority, jailers are usually under the supervision of the county sheriff or the chief of police.[19] The number of jails in the United States has been gradually declining. There were 4037 jails in 1970, 3921 jails in 1972, and 3493 jails in 1978.[13,14] The South has more jails than any other region in the country: 1678 in 1978. The states with the highest jail incarceration rates are Georgia, Nevada, Alabama, and Louisiana. Nevada's presence in this list is misleading, since the state has a very small population but a large number of tourists. This tends to inflate the jail incarceration rate since none of the tourists are counted in the population base to which the number of jail inmates is compared. California has the highest total of jail inmates, 26,206 in 1978. In terms of region of the country, the West and the South incarcerate people at approximately twice the rate of the Northeast and North Central regions. One hundred out of every 100,000 residents in the West are in jail at any given point in time, and the comparable figure for the South is 98 per 100,000.[14]

Because a full analysis of the 1978 census of jails and survey of jail inmates has not been published, the following figures are from an earlier LEAA report, *The*

Nations Jails.[13] Most jails are located in law enforcement or judicial facilities such as a county courthouse, police station, or sheriff's office. More than half of the facilities do not have even one cell designed to be occupied by a single prisoner. The smaller the facility, the less likely it is to have at least one single occupant cell. Slightly less than half the jails have a drunk tank, a dormitory-like room in which drunks are incarcerated while they sober up. Half of the drunk tanks have no seats, 40 percent have no beds, 26 percent have no windows, 20 percent have no water source, and 14 percent have no toilets. The smaller the jail, the less likely it is to have adequate accommodations in its drunk tank.

Despite decades of the acceptance of the principle that juvenile and adult prisoners must be separated, there are still many jails in which this is not done. Mentally ill prisoners are generally separated from other jail occupants, but first offenders are unlikely to be detained separately from repeat offenders, and pre-trial prisoners are unlikely to be separated from sentenced prisoners. It is understandable that very small jails would have difficulty in separating different types of offenders, but it is surprising that many of the nation's largest jails also fail to separate pre-trial from sentenced prisoners. This means that one of the penalties of being accused of a crime—even though one has not yet been judged guilty—is contamination. That is to say, many legally innocent individuals who are imprisoned awaiting trial are exposed to hardened criminals, often under conditions of minimum supervision. The potential for victimization in such situations is extremely high.

Relatively few jails have any kind of in-house medical facility. Only one out of every eight jails has any space set aside for medical use, generally an infirmary. Most jails have a very small amount of recreational opportunity or entertainment, but almost 40 percent lack any at all. Even where recreation facilities are available, they are usually minimal. For example, sports equipment is available in approximately three-quarters of the large jails, a quarter of the medium-sized jails, and in almost none of the small jails. Exercise yards, even without equipment, exist in only 10 percent of the small jails and 30 percent of the medium-sized jails, as compared with three-quarters of the large jails.

PRISONERS IN JAILS

The preliminary report of the 1978 census shows that more than 158,000 individuals are incarcerated in the nation's jails, which is 12 percent above the 1972 level of jail incarceration. Table 13.1 summarizes the characteristics of these inmates, and also presents data from the province of Ontario in Canada as a point of comparison. We see that somewhat more than half of the American inmates and just under half of the Ontario inmates have been found guilty and have been sentenced for the current charge. Most jail inmates have not committed—nor have they been accused of having committed—a violent crime on a current charge. Only 30 percent of the American inmates and 17 percent of the Ontario inmates have been incarcerated in connection with an alleged or proven violent offense. Property crimes are much more common, and the use of illegal drugs is responsible for the incarceration of one out of every eleven American jail inmates and one out of every eight Ontario jail inmates.

Table 13.1. Characteristics of Jail Inmates in the United States and Ontario, Canada

Characteristics	USA, 1978	Ontario, 1977
Sentenced on the current charge	58%	47%
Sentenced/accused of offenses against persons (violent)[1]	30%	17%
Sentenced/accused of offenses against property[1]	41%	54%
Sentenced/accused of drug offenses[1]	9%	13%
Male	94%	96%
Under 30 years old	70%	73%
White	57%	87%
Married	—	23%
One or more previous convictions	—	76%
Prearrest annual income under $3000	46%	—
Less than 12 years of education	61%	—
Less than 11 years of education	—	73%
Unemployed before arrest	43%	—
Number of inmates	158,394	2430

[1]Offense figures are not strictly comparable because the United States counts a prisoner only once, under the most serious offense, while Ontario lists them separately for each type of offense charged. *Sources:* Law Enforcement Assistance Administration. "Census of Jails and Survey of Jail Inmates, 1978, Preliminary Report." Washington, D.C., 1979; Patrick G. Madden. *A Description of Ontario's Jail Population.* Toronto: Ontario Ministry of Correctional Services, 1978.

The average jail inmate is male, white, and less than 30 years old. He is not married, and has at least one previous conviction on a criminal offense. Whether one uses income, employment, or education as an index of social status, it is evident that jail inmates tend to be from the lower classes of society.

The social class, education, age, employment, and marital characteristics of jail prisoners are roughly the same as the characteristics of prison inmates, which suggests that they have approximately the same programming needs. Unfortunately, these needs are even less well met in jails than they are in prisons, due to differences in funding levels, prisoner turnover, size, and staffing. One way in which jail inmates do differ from prison inmates is that they are less likely to be incarcerated in connection with a crime of violence. This means that a large number of minor property and public order offenders who may be not terribly good at defending themselves are thrown into contact with a small number of violence-prone prisoners in situations of minimum supervision. That is a recipe for high prisoner victimization rates.

Medical Problems Among Jail Residents

Since so many jail prisoners come from destitute backgrounds, it is understandable that their medical needs have not been met prior to institutionalization. In addition to the prevalence of conditions such as tuberculosis, venereal disease, diabetes, and dental problems, there are the inmates who are afflicted with alcoholism, drug addiction, and mental illness.[8] Jails are used as temporary holding tanks for citizens who have behaved strangely enough to convince their families or others around them that they are mentally deranged. In most jurisdictions, police officers do not take such individuals to a mental hospital. They instead deposit them at the city or county jail where they remain until their futures have been decided for them by legal authorities, mental health experts, and family members. In all but the best of these facilities, the most that these prisoners can hope for is to be given tranquilizers so that they do not injure themselves, and to be kept segregated from the other prisoners so that they are not victimized. Mentally ill individuals who are poor and homeless are more likely to end up in jails than those who are middle-class and well provided with a home and family. An individual behaving strangely on the street whose identification indicates residence in a middle-class area may simply be taken home. It is taken up to family members to decide what to do in this situation. On the other hand, if the individual seems to be without these trappings of conventionality, a direct route to jail is more likely to be the outcome of the incident.[8]

These are not the only mentally ill individuals in jail. Some who have been sentenced and some who are awaiting trial are also mentally ill. They share the same lack of mental health services as the others, and are, in addition, less likely to be segregated in a separate section of the facility to protect them from victimization.

Alcoholism is a major problem in America's jails. Arrests for drunkenness are more common than arrests for any other criminal offense. Drunks may be charged for drunkenness, or perhaps for disorderly conduct or vagrancy. It is public drunkenness—typically by individuals living in poverty—that is particularly likely to result in incarceration. Private drunkenness, especialy in middle-class areas, is much less likely to come to the attention of police officers, and therefore less likely to lead to incarceration. When middle-class individuals are picked up by officers, they are usually permitted to obtain their release on bail rather than spending time in jail. Public drunks, particularly those who have a tendency to become disorderly when intoxicated, do not have the resources at their disposal with which to obtain bail. Many of them are in and out of jail dozens of times. Withdrawal from alcohol can be fatal if it is not done under medical supervision, and the repeated partial withdrawal that many public drunks experience in jails is extremely detrimental to their health.[8] This is why states such as Washington have rewritten their laws to prohibit the use of jails as the detoxification facilities.

The criminal processing of drunks is cursory, and only minimal attempts are made to accord them their full legal rights. After all, who would believe the testimony of a drunk? James Spradley[27] obtained so many reports of the mistreatment of drunks by Seattle police officers and jailers that he decided to try and find out why this was so. He finally ascertained that officers who had been found guilty of misconduct in the performance of their jobs were routinely reassigned to jail duty. Many of these officers had drinking problems themselves.

One out of every six American jail inmates is a regular heroin user, and one out of every four uses the drug at least occasionally.[14] These proportions do not describe the upper limits of drug-related problems in jail inmates, for many of them are involved in the use or sale of other kinds of illegal drugs. A sample of jail prisoners in eight Washington counties found that 31 percent of the prisoners had committed a crime while under the influence of drugs, 29 percent had been convicted for the possession or sale of drugs in the past, and 11 percent had committed crimes to obtain drugs or to get money with which to buy drugs.[29] Although withdrawal from narcotic drugs is less likely to be fatal than withdrawal from alcohol, it is still dangerous to allow prisoners to undergo withdrawal without medical supervision. It is difficult for all but the largest jails to provide extensive drug treatment services in-house, and many do not even have sufficient funding to contract with community agencies to provide a minimal level of drug treatment services.

The picture that emerges from this brief discussion of the medical needs of jail inmates is one in which there are extremely high levels of needs for assorted medical services (as well related psychological and social services) among these prisoners. As we will see later in this chapter, the staffing, facilities, and funding levels under which jails operate make it impossible to adequately meet these needs.

Women in Jails

Women may comprise more than the 4–6 percent of jail inmates shown in Table 13.1. A study of jails in Minnesota found that one out of every ten jail inmates was a woman, but because they generally stayed for shorter periods of time than the men, they accounted for only four percent of the statewide average population. Many of the rural jails held women infrequently, in some cases as few as two or three per year.[18] An even higher proportion of individuals booked at the San Francisco city prison was female, with 3363 women in 22,594 bookings, a rate of 15 percent.[1]

A San Francisco study by Laura Bresler and Donald Leonard[1] tells us much about characteristics of the jailed women and their crimes. A scant majority of the women jailed in San Francisco are white, and less than a quarter are age 30 or more. Although less than a quarter of the women are living alone at the time of their arrests, only one in every 11 is legally married. More than a third of them have children under 18 years of age, and a similar percentage are living with a common-law husband or boyfriend. Most of the women are unemployed when they are arrested, with the average length of employment being between one and two years. Those who had worked recently were employed in unskilled, sales, semi-skilled, or personal service work.

More than two-thirds of the women felt that the use of drugs and/or alcohol had contributed to their arrest, and more than a one-third reported being addicted. Most women had previously been arrested more than six times, and the average age of their first arrest was 16.7. The key to understanding what appears to be a heavily criminal background on the part of these women is to look at the offenses for which they are booked. Fully three-quarters of them are booked either for prostitution or for an alcohol-related offense. Even among the more select population of women who have been found guilty and sentenced to the county jail, only 10 percent are guilty of offenses against persons, and an additional 27 percent of offenses against property. What we see in San Francisco is that the jail functions as a revolving door for many minor female offenders, particularly those associated with prostitution. Public funds are expended to warehouse these deviants rather than to help them, and the time that they spend in jail is so brief that they return to being public nuisances almost before the police have finished with the paperwork.

Racial and Cultural Minorities

Everything that was said about racial and cultural minorities in prisons applies to them in the jail setting. Those minority groups that are overrepresented among the poor are also overrepresented in jail populations. These include blacks, Hispanics, and American Indians.[14,15] The line of analysis we have been pursuing in our discussion of jails suggests that the standards of treatment and legal safeguards accorded to jail inmates tend to be less adequate than those experienced by prison inmates. This is likely to result in grave problems for many jail inmates of minority heritage.

One advantage that jails do have over prisons is that, because they are local facilities, the minority prisoners they incarcerate are close enough to be easily visited by their families and friends, if jail regulations permit it. The isolated placement of many state and federal correctional facilities poses a particular hardship for minority group individuals who wish to keep in regular contact with their imprisoned family members and friends. Where poverty is a factor, round trips of as much as 500 miles to state facilities are an impossibility. Minority-oriented community programs can also be awarded contracts to provide services more easily in jails than in most state correctional facilities. These potential benefits do not matter unless they are taken advantage of. Enhanced visiting possibilities are irrelevent if a jail's visiting facilities and policies do not permit frequent visiting, and the availability of community services means nothing if funding is not available to pay for services requested from these agencies.

Juveniles

Testifying before the House Committee on Education and Labor's Subcommittee on Human Resources, former Deputy Attorney General Charles B. Renfrew estimated that as many as 500,000 juveniles are admitted to adult jails and lock-ups each year in the United States. These juveniles are often the victims of physical and sexual abuse, and have a suicide rate seven times higher than the rate for those incarcerated in secure juvenile detention institutions. Renfrew labeled this situation "a national catastrophe."[12]

What are the facts about juveniles in jails during the 1970's? A Wisconsin study[31] found that 10,688 juveniles were placed in county jails during 1974. Of these, only 5 percent had committed offenses against persons and 16 percent had committed offenses against property. The majority of the youngsters had not committed any crimes at all. Many of the youngsters were quite young, with 49 being age 11 and under, and 657 being age 12 or 13. It is hard to believe that more than a handful of these juveniles were incarcerated because of their menace to society.

A Minnesota study[18] adds to our knowledge of juveniles in jails. Seventeen percent of all the individuals held in Minnesota jails during 1975 were juveniles.

The average length of stay for these young people was 1.9 days, but half of them stayed only 14 hours. This is why the average number of juveniles in jail populations can be very low even though the total number of juveniles processed through a jail in a year can be quite high. Another interesting finding of the Minnesota study was that there was a great deal of variation between counties in the mean length of stay, ranging from 8 hours to 6.9 days. Once again, this suggests that factors other than the delinquency of the young people are operative in determining policies about their incarceration.

When the Children's Defense Fund sponsored a survey of children in jails in nine states, they found that nearly half of the facilities incarcerated children at least occasionally, and 38 percent held them regularly as a matter of policy. Only one of every eight of these youngsters was charged with a crime of violence. The proportion of females among the juveniles was four times as high as the proportion of females among adult jail prisoners. Although proportionately fewer minority children were jailed than minority adults, it was still far above the proportion of minorities in the general population. The campaign to remove juveniles from jails has not made the progress that the similar campaign to remove status offenders from all institutional facilities has made in the past few years. The situation is still serious enough that the removal of juveniles from jails is considered to be a national priority.[2]

PRISONER SOCIETIES

Jails meet all of the prerequisites for the development of prisoner societies except one. The length of time that most individuals spend in jails is too short for a subculture to develop beyond the common criminal subculture that they import into the institution with them. For example, the mean pretrial stay in Minnesota jails was 2.4 days in 1975, and the mean length of stay for sentenced offenders was 21.7 days.[18] Turnover in most jails is so high that it is impossible for a stable prisoner society to develop. (See Chapter 12 for a discussion of the negative effects of an unstable prisoner society.)

Jail populations change rapidly, and staff members must be constantly vigilant for cliques and alliances among the prisoners that might lead to violence, escape attempts, and other management problems. Victimization is carried out on an individual rather than on a group level, except where a number of members of the same gang happen to be incarcerated together. It is likely that the higher the proportion of jail inmates at any given time who have had prior experience in prisons, the more the prisoner subculture in that jail will tend to develop prison-like charactistics. It is still possible in most jails to relate to prisoners as individuals rather than as members of power blocs.

JAILERS

Data from the 1972 LEAA jail survey[13] show that there are approximately three prisoners for every employee in America's jails. Approximately one-quarter of the jail employees are administrative workers, and slightly less than half are correctional officers of one sort or another. Few jails are able to employ staff members with advanced degrees in the behavioral sciences or medicine.

Despite a favorable staff–prisoner ratio, the small number of staff members in jails outside of large cities means that coverage is minimal and there is no time for anything except custody considerations. In many jails, custodial staff members not only have no time to provide rehabilitative services themselves: they also do not have time to work with treatment staff members who might be hired or volunteer to provide services in the prison. They often cannot provide the necessary supervision for activities conducted by volunteers and may find it difficult to even to move prisoners to and from program areas. Conflicts between custody and treatment staff members in these facilities are common, and are based on structural features such as lack of adequate staffing as well as differing attitudes toward prisoners.[5]

Because the need of jailers for professionalized training programs is so great, the National Institute of Corrections[21] selected jailer training as one of four major programs of the agency in 1977. It created a Jail Center which aids jailers through training, technical assistance, and information services. These programs are aimed at operational rather than theoretical issues. Special issue seminars are used to upgrade the skills of in-service jailers. The Jail Center provides assistance to local jails on subjects such as jail policy and procedure, conducting analyses of manpower and staffing, improving classification and intake services, training line officers, improving security and control, and so forth. Along with training and assistance programs for jailers sponsored by other national groups such as the National Sheriff's Association, the National Institute of Corrections has already had a positive impact on the quality of services in America's jails.

JAIL ADMINISTRATION

Jail management differs from prison management in a number of ways. Although most jails are small, jails in large urban areas are often larger than maximum security prisons in rural states. Prisoners tend to be less violent in jails than in prisons, but this advantage is compromised by the constant turnover of prisoners, so that administrators are bound to have extremely explosive situations from time to time. Because jails are located in local communities, they need not have as full a range of in-house services as prisons, and can make a correspondingly greater use of services provided by community agencies. Jails must simultaneously house pretrail detainees and sentenced prisoners. Finally, jail administrators are more likely to be sheriffs or police chiefs than to be extensively trained in corrections.

Law enforcement officers who take on responsibilities as jail administrators often have continuing law enforcement duties in addition to their jail work. The more rural the county, the more this is likely to be true. In South Dakota, for example, only 30 percent of the jails had a full-time jailer in 1970.[6] These facilities not only had an administrator whose major responsibilities were elsewhere: they also did not have a full-time deputy to concentrate on jail management. Some counties hire their jail employees as a matter of political patronage rather than with consideration of their qualifications.[17]

Jail administrators suffer from severe isolation from their peers. There is no state corrections system to provide the administrator with a constant flow of information about how best to manage the institution. There may be no other professional correctional colleagues in the immediate area with whom to exchange observations and advice. This is why the outreach activities of the National Institute of Corrections and other national organizations is so important. This outreach effort is not limited to programs and staffing. Even the design of new facilities is a problem in isolated areas, and requires sophisticated consulting in order to get the best structure for the available money.[7]

The task facing jail administrators is enormous. They must have a knowledge of total system planning, adult intake services, pretrial detention, the admission process, staffing patterns, internal policies, programming, release programs, and the evaluation–planning cycle. In addition to these subjects, there are also standards relating to the state inspection of local facilities up until such time as states can actually absorb jails into the state correctional system. The extremely high level of professionalism and technical competence demanded to administer jails contrasts with the limited training and correctional professionalism of the average contemporary jail administrator. This technical competence exists only in the larger jails and in a scattering of unusually progressive and well-funded smaller local correctional facilities.

Jail Classification

As an example of the complexity of jail administration, we will look at the problem of the classification of jail prisoners. Jail standards require that diverse categories of incarcerated persons be identified and segregated from each other. The mentally ill, drug addicted, and alcoholic inmates are unlikely to receive adequate treatment due to limitations of staffing, funding and facilities, so they should be moved to appropriate facilities outside of the jail proper. Prisoners who have other disabilities need to be segregated from their fellow-prisoners in order to avoid excessive victimization. Potential suicides must be identified and receive special care if they are to survive. Pretrial prisoners must be separated from post-trial prisoners, and first-timers or those with minor offenses should be separated from serious or multiple offenders. Jailers in many facilities would have to be magicians to approximate these standards, since these facilities do not permit the segregation of so many different types of prisoners from each other. Should their facilities be instantly transformed into adequate correctional structures, they would be left with the problem of how to become adequately trained themselves or to hire sufficiently well-trained staff to carry out comprehensive classification procedures.

Recognizing this problem, the U.S. Bureau of Prisons published a pamphlet on the classification of jail prisoners in 1971 that describes a prisoner inventory designed to highlight various prisoner problems and also to estimate the degree of required supervision for each prisoner. This system was successful in classifying jail prisoners into three custody grades. However, in a 60-day test period conducted in six jails, it is noteworthy that only six percent of the prisoners were classified as minimum custody.[25] A classification system for jail inmates that finds so few prisoners able to be adequately housed in a minimum security building is far too conservative to be realistic.

In a more recent discussion of the classification process, E. Eugene Miller[17] has specified the major sources of information that shoud be taken into account by the classification officer or classification committee in a jail. These are summarized as follows:

1. The charge.
2. The amount of the bond set by the court.
3. The commitment paper (which may contain remarks by the judge or other court officers relevant to classification).
4. Any available information on prior commitments.
5. The results of a medical examination.
6. The FBI "rap sheet."
7. Detainers.
8. Subjective knowledge about the offender obtained from the classification interview.
9. Any records on the individual existing in the State Department of Corrections.
10. The results of a psychological inventory, such as the Minnesota Multi-Phasic Personality Inventory.
11. Results of educational achievement and nonverbal intelligence tests.
12. Results of a vocational aptitude test.
13. Information from other agencies, including the probation, police department, and welfare department.
14. Any information contributed by community sources such as family members and employers.
15. Observations made by security staff from the point of intake until the classification hearing occurs.

Miller realizes that staff in most local correctional facilities do not have the time or the expertise to develop all of these sources of information fully. He therefore suggests that paid staff members be supplemented by community volunteers, such as an educator who might do some of the psychological testing for the facility.

PROBLEMS OF JAIL ADMINISTRATION

Problems such as homosexuality, drug abuse, and victimization that were discussed with reference to prisons are also problems in jails, so they will not be repeated here. Instead, our discussion will focus on those problems which are at least partially unique to jails.

High Prisoner Turnover*

Extensive training and therapy programs are impossible for most jail prisoners because their sentences are too short. Having a large number of prisoners for a brief period of time also places a much greater strain on record-keeping, classification, and other functions that must be performed for each prisoner regardless of length of incarceration. When prisoners are incarcerated for such a short time, they are unlikely to perceive the facility as "theirs" in any sense, and may be more prone to destroy property than prisoners with long sentences.

As the front line institution of the correctional system, the jail often receives prisoners without the extensive case workups that are made available to state prison authorities. There is also no correctional diagnostic center to which jail inmates are sent for classification before being assigned to the most appropriate correctional institution. The result is that there is considerable pressure on jail staff members to classify prisoners immediately at intake on the basis of information that may be inadequate. Except for the small proportion of prisoners who are sentenced for more than six months and those who consistently return to the institution on minor offenses in a revolving-door sequence, staff members do not have the opportunity to get to know individual prisoners well enough to be particularly helpful to them. In the case of the revolving-door prisoners, the extremely high level of recidivism is likely to discourage staff from providing any meaningful help at all. In their view, the jail has simply become an alternative housing facility for these prisoners.

The Variety of Offense Categories

Imagine a correctional facility that must simultaneously house someone who failed to pay a parking ticket, an accused murderer, a sentenced thief, and a divorced spouse who has failed to pay child support. The diversity among jail inmates is far greater than the diversity among prison inmates, and the need for segregating the different groups of inmates from each other is correspondingly greater. Any weakness in vigilance can potentially be the cause of extensive victimization of the weak by the strong. The different types of prisoners also require different levels of security classification. In practice, this often means that everyone has to be housed at a maximum security level even though comparably few jail inmates require this level of security. Many of the programs possible in state correctional facilities are not feasible given the variety of inmates found in city and county jails.

Idleness

Most state correctional facilities are able to provide work for nearly all prisoners. This is true in only a small proportion of jails. Educational programs

---

*Problems 1 through 4 are derived from Mark A. Schneider. "Problems in Short Term Correctional Settings." *International Journal of Offender Therapy and Comparative Criminology* 23 (1979):164–171.

cannot pack enough material into the short time for which most jail residents are incarcerated to do any good. Furthermore, the inmates differ so much in their educational needs that staffing and programming would be prohibitively complex and expensive.

There are legal limitations on imposing correctional programs on prisoners awaiting trial. If they have not been convicted, they cannot be forced to engage in work programs against their will. For that reason, inmate participation in institutional maintenance jobs is usually limited to sentenced offenders and those who volunteer out of boredom. Any work assignments that require extra supervision are unlikely to be made available in jails. The instability of the inmate population also affects work participation. If someone expects release on bond or an early dismissal of the charges, it is unlikely that that person will participate in work or education programs.

Psychological Stress

Jail inmates experience a more rapid series of psychological stresses because of legal matters and family arrangements than do prisoners in state facilities. A great many decisions and arrangements are made within a short period of time. In addition, the jail experience is the first institutional experience for many first-timers, and these individuals sometimes have such an acute reaction to their first incarceration that they attempt suicide. The withdrawal from alcohol or illegal drugs exacerbates the psychological distresses in many jail prisoners.

Some prisoners react to these stresses by increased resentment and un-cooperativeness, while others become severely depressed and suicidal. By the time an offender reaches a state correctional facility, most of these problems have been solved. An occasional crisis may arise, and there is always the problem of victimization, but these problems are less severe and less continuous than the problems that prisoners confront in their jail stays. Both pretrial and post-trial anxiety occurs frequently in jail inmates. The lack of in-house psychological counseling and monitoring in most jails makes it impossible for jail managers to successfully identify and treat these problems on a systematic basis.

Difficulties Associated with Medical Treatment

In view of the fact that the United States Supreme Court has ruled that basic health care services must be provided to jail inmates, and that the lack of such services constitutes cruel and unusual punishment under the Constitution,[11] jail administrators cannot afford to ignore the issue of health care. Even basic health screening is extremely expensive, and jail budgets do not have sufficient funds to pay for these medical services. Very large jails may be able to afford to have physicians on their staff and urban jails can draw on external resources if funds are available to contract for community health care services. For the under-funded jail in a rural county, and this is the typical American jail, neither of these solutions can be easily implemented. In addition to severe funding shortages, there also may be shortages of qualified medical personnel. A solution for this problem that has been pioneered by the American Medical Association is to attempt to train jailers in health care screening.[9]

Holding State Prisoners

According to a survey conducted by *Corrections Magazine,* more than 8000 state prisoners were being held in local jails in early 1979. These included 1750 state prisoners in Alabama jails, 1190 in Louisiana jails, 1214 in Tennessee jails, and 971 in Mississippi jails. This situation has developed because inadequacies in these state corrections systems have led to court orders requiring that newly sentenced state prisoners be kept in jails until room is made available for them in the overcrowded state facilities. The result is that overcrowding in the prisons has been changed in these states to overcrowding in the jails under conditions that are generally even worse than those of the prisons.[28] This is an example of a reform that has engendered quite unintended negative results.

Jailers may be happy to take state prisoners if they are paid more than their cost for housing these prisoners; but in states such as Alabama, where the reimbursement rate was only $1.75 per day for holding state prisoners, the sheriffs were losing a considerable amount of money by consenting to house the prisoners. In Richmond, Virginia, the sheriff fought back in the courts and was able to have 200 state prisoners transferred from his jail to a state facility. Overcrowding the jails with prisoners increases the proportion of violent prisoners in the jails, overtaxes facilities and staffing, and leads to the abuses associated with overcrowding.[28]

Overcrowding

Although many rural jails stand half-empty most of the time, occasions arise in which they do not have sufficient capacity for all their prisoners. Urban jails are more typically overcrowded on a continuous basis. This problem is enhanced by the use of jails for many different purposes.[17] Jails are even less able to absorb excess inmates than prisons. Staffing is more limited and less flexible. The facilities have often been designed in such a way that adequate supervision cannot be provided when the resident population passes a certain point. After that, the possibilities for escape, prisoner disturbances, and victimization among prisoners rise sharply. Like prison administrators, jailers often can do nothing but take however many prisoners are delivered to them. In the long run, this problem can only be solved by an extensive support network of diversionary programs and other alternatives to jail incarceration.

Physical Facilities

Physical facilities impact all aspects of jail life. If a facility does not allow supervision except under restrictive confinement, it has implications for the implementation of treatment programs in the institution.[23] Jail facilities tend to be outdated and in a poor state of repair. A number of jails currently in use were opened before the Civil War, and at least one was in service during the American Revolution.[17] A detailed study of South Dakota's jails reveals that 36 percent were built before 1920—some as early as 1880—and that only 25 percent have been constructed since 1950. A few of these jails have never had any renovations since the day they were built. More than half of the jails have a rated capacity of between one and five prisoners, generally in two-man cells. Facilities are so limited that even men and women cannot be fully separated in many of these jails. Men and women have separate cells, but they are housed in the same area. Even more South Dakota jails are unable to separate juveniles from adults, drunks from sober prisoners, sexual deviants from sexually normal prisoners, misdemeanants from felons, and pretrial from sentenced prisoners. Some of the facilities do not have flush toilets available to the prisoners.[6] With facilities such as these scattered throughout the rural areas of America, it is pointless to talk about advanced rehabilitative programs. The primary problem in these facilities is the basic human need for decent housing.

THE JAIL REFORM MOVEMENT

The social reform movements in America during the 19th century had little or no impact upon local correctional facilties. The first national survey of jails and lockups was not released until 1931, and was accompanied by eight recommendations for jail reform.[20] Hastings Hart's recommendations were as follows.

1. Provide for desegregation of men and women, old and young, sick and well, and the dangerous and harmless classes.
2. Provide a single cell for each prisoner.
3. Facilities should be completely fireproof.
4. Communication between male and female prisoners should be impossible.
5. The use of the "third degree" by policemen and detectives should be abolished.
6. A responsible state commission should inspect facilities and have the power to condemn them if unfit for use.
7. The professional quality of jailers, guards, and matrons should be radically improved.
8. Local correctional structures should be planned by competent architects according to the reqirements of such facilities.[10]

It is interesting that while recommendations 5, 6, and 8 have become standard practice in most jurisdictions, the other recommendations made in 1931 have yet to become the norm in American local correctional facilities.

There has been considerable pressure for reform placed on state and federal correctional agencies by forces outside of the criminal justice system. This has not generally been the case for local correctional institutions. The major sources of jail reform in the 1970s were the courts, national criminal justice associations, state criminal justice planning agencies, and the National Coalition for Jail Reform. By issuing sets of standards relating to jail conditions and services, a number of national organizations have greatly increased the pressure to upgrade jails. Almost all state governments have now issued standards for local correctional facilities that have the same effect.[30] State planning agencies often commission surveys of jails to use as a basis or proposals for reform. This strategy was the origin of the South Dakota survey that we have mentioned several times in this chapter.[6]

The National Coalition for Jail Reform was formed at the 1978 Wingspread Conference in Racine, Wisconsin. Thirty-one national organizations were represented at this conference, and 28 were still part of this Coalition in 1980. These include the American Correctional Association, American Public Health Association, John Howard Association, National Association of Blacks in Criminal Justice, National Association of Counties, National Institute of Corrections, National Jail Association, National Jail Managers Association, National Sheriff's Association, National Council on Crime and Delinquency, and National Urban League.[4,30] The mission statement discussed by this group included alleviating the lamentable conditions in jails, providing just and effective sanctions against criminal behavior, removing inappropriately confined individuals from jails, reducing the tax burden of jails, and providing for public safety. These are goals that would have been completely acceptable in the early 1900s, which is an indication of how long jail reform has been neglected. The interesting thing about the National Coalition for Jail Reform is that it includes both conservative and liberal organizations. At the level of jail reform currently needed in the United States, liberals and conservatives have no difficulty in agreeing on basic strategies. Only after minimum standards had been implemented would the members of the Coalition begin to argue among themselves as to what to do next. A recent national symposium co-sponsored by the Coalition emphasized the position that no child should be held in an adult jail.[4]

The major source of jail reform is the same as the major souce of prison reform—the courts. For example, 22 local jails in Louisiana were under suit in 1979, and six of them had already been ordered to improve living conditions and relieve overcrowding. In January, 1979, the Lafourche Parish jail was ordered by a state court judge to refrain from holding state prisoners for more than 15 days. This forced the state to do something about the prisoners that it was backing up into the local jail.[28] In general, the rights of prisoners specified in court decisions, discussed in Chapter 12, apply as fully in jails as they do in prisons. The courts have handed down decisions in such diverse areas as discipline, methods of punishment, exercise and recreation, medical care, clothing and attire, grooming and personal hygiene, environmental conditions, mail censorship, visiting, access to legal materials, the use of jailhouse lawyers, and the right to safety from victimization.[17] Despite these indications of change, most jails will continue to suffer from multiple deficiencies so long as they are administered by law enforcement authorities. When jails must compete with law enforcement priorities for funds, they are bound to continue to be underfunded.

SELECTED PROGRAMS IN LOCAL CORRECTIONAL FACILITIES

The 1972 survey of American jails[13] included questions about rehabilitative programs and services offered in each facility. Table 13.2 summarizes the results of this survey. Of 3921 local correctional facilities, nearly 1300 had no programs

Table 13.2. Number of American Jails with Selected Rehabilitative Programs, 1972

Program Type	Number of Jails
Non-federally funded programs or services of any kind	2646
Non-federally funded programs operated from outside the jail	2365
Weekend sentence programs	1821
Work-release programs	1665
Jails operating their own rehabilitative programs or services	825
Referrals to federally funded programs or services at release	635
Federally sponsored vocational training programs	542
Non-federally funded programs or services provided during incarceration	475
Total facilities surveyed	3921

Source: Law Enforcement Assistance Administration. *The Nation's Jails.* Washington, D.C.: Government Printing Office, 1975.

or services of any kind made available to the prisoners. Somewhat less than half of the facilities offered weekend sentence programs and work-release programs. Federally sponsored vocational training programs offered during incarceration and federally funded programs made available to inmates at release were utilized by less than one jail in every six. Just slightly more than one jail in every five operated their own rehabilitative programs. These statistics demonstrate the dependence the jails have on external sources for the provision of programs and services.

Table 13.3 breaks down non-federally funded programs and services into

Table 13.3. Non-federally Sponsored American Jail Programs and Services, by Size of Jail

Program/ Service	Number of Jails	Proportion of Jails		
		1–20 Inmates	21–249 Inmates	250 + Inmates
Group counseling	678	11%	33%	62%
Vocational counseling	348	5%	17%	39%
Remedial education	419	5%	23%	66%
Vocational training	542	10%	23%	43%
Prevocational training	266	3%	14%	34%
Job development and placement	491	8%	23%	46%
Alcoholic treatment	1385	30%	49%	66%
Drug treatment	1028	20%	40%	68%
Religious services	2294	49%	85%	89%
Number of jails	3921	2901	907	113

Source: Law Enforcement Assistance Administration. *The Nation's Jails.* Washington, D.C.: Government Printing Office, 1975.

program categories. The most commonly offered program is religious services, followed by alcohol treatment, drug treatment, group counseling, and vocational training. Religious services are the only activity offered by more than half of the jails. Table 13.3 also shows the proportion of jails of various sizes having these services. In every case, the larger the jail, the more likely it is to offer a program of service. The small jails, which comprise approximately three-quarters of all American jails, offer very few programs, if any. The medium-sized jails are two to four times as likely to offer each program as the small jails, and the large jails often have a wide assortment of programs available. Indeed, some large urban jails have a wider range of programs than many state prisons. Most jail programs are not staffed with paid personnel. Nearly two-thirds of the jails reporting the type of staff members used in programs indicated that their programs were staffed entirely by volunteers.[13] This is sharply in contrast with programs and services offered in other American prisons.

Four Service Delivery Models for Jails

Charles Newman and Barbara Price[22] have developed four delivery models that describe the ways in which jails should ideally go about delivering services to inmates. The first model is an *internal model,* in which all services are provided to inmates by staff members employed by the jails. This allows maximum control over the programs by administrators and minimizes security risks. It is also very expensive, and is recommended for use only in those large jails that are relatively inaccessible to the needed range of community service agencies.

In the *intersection service delivery model,* the jail interacts with community agencies to provide inmate services. Specialists can be utilized as needed without high commitment of limited resources. Security risks increase with this type of operation and it is difficult for the jail to retain programmatic control, but jails that are fairly small and have good accessibility to all of the needed community services are perfect for this service delivery model.

The intersection model is particularly useful in jails where sentences are very short, while the internal model has an edge where sentences tend to be long and inmate turnover is reduced.

In the *linkage model,* the jail develops a close relationship with one agency that takes over the responsibility of dealing with other community agencies in brokering services for jail inmates. This linkage agency screens prisoners and refers them to the outside service providers. The outside service providers can then continue to work with the inmates after they have been released to the free community. Like the intersection model, the linkage model is very efficient in that it provides maximum services for a minimum commitment of jail resources. Newman and Price recommend that a linkage agency be used only in jails with populations of 250 and up, as this system is not cost-efficient in small jails.

In very large jails, those containing 1000 or more prisoners, there are so many competing needs for services that it may be useful for the jail to utilize two or all three of the models described above. There is always the danger that this will result in an inefficient duplication of services, and the *combination service delivery model* is bound to be more expensive than either the intersection or the linkage model. Only relatively well-funded jails in large urban areas should make use of this model.

Examples of Jail Programs

The Sheriff's County Jail Appointed Program. This San Francisco program began helping recently released jail prisoners to find jobs in late 1977. The program was initially funded with CETA money, and employs four job counselors. Jail prisoners accepted into the program are interviewed before their release to determine appropriate jobs for each individual and his or her motivation for work. The program allows up to $315 for each client to be used for job-seeking expenses. Staff members act as advocates for clients in obtaining job-training services for them from other community agencies. The job counselors are evaluated using quantitative as well as qualitative standards. Each counselor is required to place 15 clients on jobs every month.[1]

Bucks County Citizens Committee for Rehabilitation and Corrections. This volunteer citizens group was formed in 1962 to aid correctional clients in Bucks County, Pennsylvania. Citizens volunteers in this group, which had grown to 400 by the early 1970s, work in a wide variety of positions in three Bucks County correctional facilities, including typists and file clerks, counselor aids, canteen cashiers, visitors for socially isolated inmates, tutors, courthouse messengers, education counselors, employment counselor aids, transportation aids, recreation specialists, child care aids, and handicraft aids. An LEAA grant allowed the volunteer program to be supplemented in 1971 with a volunteer coordinator, assistant coordinator, and secretary. In the 13 months following the establishment of the volunteer office, a total of 13,912 hours of volunteer services were contributed by community residents. A unique facet of this program is that the volunteers not only work directly with the prisoners: they also do some of the routine paperwork and service delivery tasks normally left to correctional employees. By doing this, they free the paid employees to put more time into treatment activities with the prisoners.[3]

Offender Aid and Restoration of Virginia, Inc. OAR is administered by an 18-member board of directors. It receives money from both governmental and private agencies, and hires a skeleton paid staff to administer its service activities. Each community volunteer joining OAR is assigned to one jail inmate. The volunteers visit the prisoners in jail and continue to work with them after release. The volunteer–prisoner relationships are formed around planning for the future and carrying out these plans after release. In addition to the direct service delivery to the inmates, OAR hopes to change the nature of jails by bringing many citizens into contact with jail conditions.[16]

The Spokane County–City Jail Programs. When the new county–city jail in Spokane, Washington was opened, it was staffed with two-and-one-half positions for rehabilitative programming. These individuals recruited community volunteers to provide approximately four-fifths of the service delivery capacity of the expanded programs, and proceeded to develop a classification system for evaluating new prisoners and deciding which programs they should be exposed to. The two programs previously existing in the jail were expanded sevenfold, and property destruction and violence in the facility decreased considerably. In addition to programs staffed by volunteers, it was possible to obtain services from the Spokane County and City libraries, the YMCA, five local churches, and the Washington State Employment Security Department. Both college students and adults from the free community were utilized as volunteers in these programs. This example demonstrates how efficient use of programming must be linked to a classification system, and also shows that a complex service delivery system can be elaborated with minimum paid staffing levels.[19]

SUMMARY

Jails are generally administered at the local level of government and supervised by a law enforcement administrator rather than a corrections administrator. Chronic underfunding, high prisoner turnover, the impossibility of any meaningful form of classification in the smaller jails, and the differences in the legal status and the needs of jail residents who are waiting trial and those who have been judged guilty and are serving sentences are among the factors that make it difficult for jail administrators to conform to modern standards of humane and productive correctional practice. Many prisoners spend too short a period of time in jail to be fully evaluated, to say nothing of receiving an appropriate package of correctional services. In all but the largest facilities, it is difficult to separate offenders having drastically different offense histories from each other. Idleness, overcrowding, deteriorating physical facilities, inadequate medical and psychiatric treatment, and the psychological stress associated with rapid changes in status all contribute to the instability and negative social climate existing in many jails. The jail reform movement has made only slight progress through 1981 and there have been few scholarly investigations designed to improve the efficiency of humanity of the nation's jails.

REFERENCES

1. Bresler, Laura and Donald Leonard. *Women's Jail: Pretrial and Post-Conviction Alternatives.* San Francisco: Unitarian Universalist Service Committee, 1978.
2. Brown, James and Doyle Wood. "National Priority: Removing Juveniles from Adult Jails and Lockups." *Corrections Today* 41 (May–June 1979):21–33.
3. Case, John D. and James F. Henderson. "Correctional Volunteers in Bucks County." *American Journal of Corrections* 35 (January–February 1973):44–45.
4. "Children in Jails." Brochure issued by the Community Research Forum in cooperation with the National Coalition for Jail Reform. Champaign, IL: University of Illinois at Urbana–Champaign, 1980.

5. Culbertson, Robert G. "Personnel Conflicts in Jail Management." *American Journal of Corrections* 39 (March–April 1977):28–29, 35.

6. Dahlin, Donald C. *South Dakota Jails: Current Conditions and Proposed Directions.* Vermillion, SD: Governmental Research Bureau, University of South Dakota, 1971.

7. Folse, Sidney, J. "Issues and Problems in Jail Design." *Corrections Today* 41 (March–April 1979):20–22.

8. Goldfarb, Ronald. *Jails: The Ultimate Ghetto of the Criminal Justice System.* Garden City, NY: Doubleday, 1976.

9. Guzzardi, Lawrence J., G. Richard Braen and K. David Jones. "Health Care in Jails: A New Approach to an Old Problem." *Corrections Today* 42 (March–April, 1980):40–41, 46.

10. Hart, Hastings, H. "Police Jails and Village Lockups." In *Report on Penal Institutions, Probation and Parole* 9. Washington, D.C.: National Commission on Law Observance and Enforcement, 1931, pp.327–344.

11. Isele, W.P. *Constitutional Issues of the Prisoner's Right to Medical Care.* Chicago, IL: American Medical Association, 1976.

12. "Jailing Youths With Adults 'A National Catastrophe'." *Justice Assistance News* 1 (May 1980):3.

13. Law Enforcement Assistance Administration. *The Nation's Jails.* Washington, D.C.: Government Printing Office, 1975.

14. Law Enforcement Assistance Administration. "Census of Jails and Survey of Jail Inmates, 1978, Preliminary Report." Washington, D.C.: Government Printing Office, 1979.

15. Madden, Patrick G. *A Description of Ontario's Jail Population.* Toronto: Ontario Ministry of Correctional Services, 1978.

16. McCrea, Tully L. and Don M. Gottfredson. *A Guide to Improving the Handling of Misdemeanant Offenders.* Washington, D.C.: Government Printing Office, 1974.

17. Miller, E. Eugene. *Jail Management.* Lexington, MA: D.C. Heath, 1978.

18. Minnesota. Governor's Commission on Crime, Prevention and Control. "A Study of the Local Secure Facilities in Minnesota." St. Paul, 1977.

19. Moynahan, J.M. "Volunteer Aides: A Necessity for Corrections in Spokane County, Washington." *Volunteers in Corrections Newsletter* 2 (May 1975):3–11.

20. Moynahan, J.M. and Earle K. Stewart. "The Origin of the American Jail." *Federal Probation* 42 (December 1978):41–50.

21. National Institute of Corrections. "NIC's Jail Training Programs are Geared to Addressing Major Operational Issues." *Corrections Today* 41 (March–April 1979):6–12.

22. Newman, Charles L. and Barbara L. Price. *Jails and Drug Treatment.* Beverly Hills, CA: Sage, 1977.

23. Newman, Charles L. and Barbara L. Price. "Jails and Services for Inmates: A Perspective on Some Critical Issues." *Criminology* 14 (1977):501–511.

24. Pollier, Justine W. and Donald Rademacher. *Children in Adult Jails.* Washington, D.C.: Children's Defense Fund, 1976.

25. Richmond, Mark S. *Classification of Jail Prisoners.* Washington, D.C.: U.S. Bureau of Prisons, 1971.

26. Schneider, Marc A. "Problems in Short Term Correctional Settings." *International Journal of Offender Therapy and Comparative Criminology* 23 (1979):164–171.

27. Spradley, James. *You Owe Yourself a Drunk.* Boston: Little, Brown, 1970.

28. Taft, Phillip B., Jr. "Back Up In Jail: County Lockups Overflow as Courts Clamp Down On State Prisons." *Corrections Magazine* 5 (June 1979):27–33.
29. Washington.Department of Social and Health Services. *A Study of Drug/Alcohol Use Among Jail Residents and Treatment Clients in Eight Washington Counties.* Olympia, 1977.
30. "Wingspread Brief: The Formation of a National Coalition for Jail Reform." Racine, WI: The Johnson Foundation, 1978.
31. Wisconsin. Department of Health and Social Services. "Juvenile Detention in Wisconsin, 1976, Final Report." Madison, 1976.

Chapter 14

Probation

Probation is the assignment of an offender to community supervision as an alternative to incarceration in a jail or prison. A sentence to probation is pronounced after the offender has been found guilty of a crime, and so it falls into the province of corrections even though probation functions are administered by the courts. At a minimum, the nature of the community supervision experienced by probationers consists of regularly scheduled meetings with a probation officer and/or written reports to the officer. There are generally conditions written into the probation agreement that require compliance by the probationer as a condition of continued freedom in the community. Any significant deviation from the stipulations of the probation, including the commission of a new crime, is likely to result in revocation and remandment to jail. If an offender maintains a "clean" record for a reasonable period of time, a discharge from probation may be granted.

We stated in Chapter 3 that probation began with the work of John Augustus, which led to the first United States law authorizing a probation officer in 1878. Like most other innovative behaviors, the path-breaking work of Augustus builds on earlier practices. Augustus might not have started his private probation program in Boston had it not been for the earlier policy of Judge Peter Thacher, who began to allow convicted offenders to go free on what was essentially unsupervised probation shortly after he took office. The first recorded case of unsupervised probation is that of Jerusha Chase, whom Thacher allowed to be at large on her own recognizance in January 1830 instead of being jailed after she was convicted of burglary.[27] Earlier European practices related to the development of probation included the benefit of clergy, the recognizance, and judicial reprieve. The benefit of clergy was used primarily to obviate capital punishment for the clergy, and later, for anyone who could read a passage from the Bible.[23] Recognizance originated as a method for assuring that individuals who were expected to commit crimes in the future would refrain

322

from doing so. These individuals were asked to make a public statement that they would not engage in the anticipated misbehavior. Recognizance also came to be used for suspects in crimes that had already occurred, with the intent of assuring that they would remain available for trial at a later date. Judicial reprieve was initially a temporary suspension of sentence while the offender applied for a pardon, or because the judge had serious questions about the guilt of the offender. In some cases, it led to the abandonment of prosecution, so the offender went free.[47]

In the United States, individual states enacted probation laws one by one, and 30 such laws were in force by 1925. It was not until that time that the federal court system was authorized to implement its own national probation program. Civil service examinations were conducted, and the first salaried federal probation officers were appointed in 1927. By 1931, there were 62 paid probation officers who served average caseloads of 400. There were ten volunteer probation officers for every paid officer in 1933. Caseloads gradually decreased as the number of paid officers increased over the years. In 1950, 303 federal probation officers supervised 30,087 offenders, the first time that the average caseload had decreased to 100 clients per officer.[17]

The number of offenders under supervision expanded to 59,534 by 1974, but the number of officers increased to 1148, so the average caseload declined to 52 offenders per officer. In addition to their caseload supervision task, the probation officers had responsibilities for pre-sentence, pre-parole, and other investigative reports, so the amount of time devoted to supervising each client was still extremely small.[35] In 1976, there were 1929 agencies performing adult probation functions and 2126 agencies performing juvenile probation functions in the United States. Eighty-six percent of 923,064 clients being supervised in the adult probation agencies were men. Approximately half were felons and half were misdemeanants. Nearly half of all the offenders on probation were located in five states: California, Texas, Massachusetts, New York, and Michigan. This is not just due to the size of these states. It reflects policies favoring the use of probation much more than is true in many other states.

There were 328,854 juvenile delinquents on probation, of whom 77 percent were male. Seventy-six percent of the males and 59 percent of the females in the juvenile probation system were delinquents. Nearly twice the proportion of juvenile females on probation (40 percent) were status offenders as was true for males (24 percent).[30]

The total number of probation agency employees doing counseling and supervision was 33,248, with an additional 5307 employees serving as administrators in the agencies. Most agencies had fewer than ten employees, including clerical staff as well as administrators and parole officers. Most adult probation agencies were administered by states, but most juvenile probation agencies were administered by counties. There were 20,263 volunteers involved in agencies serving probation and/or parole clients, most of them working at the county level. Almost all of the volunteers were involved in client counseling. The average caseload for full-time employees in agencies serving only juvenile probation clients was 27. For agencies serving only adult probation clients, it was 107, and for agencies offering probation services to both adults and juveniles, it was 39. Agencies serving juvenile probation and parole clients together had about the same caseload as agencies serving only juvenile probation clients, but agencies serving adult probation and parole clients had a caseload (68) that was much lower than the caseload for agencies serving only adult probation clients. For all probation and parole agencies, the national caseload average in 1976 was 48 clients per full-time employee. This does not take into account any of the other functions of the probation officers, including intake screening, conducting pre-sentence investigations, and performing various administrative duties.[30]

PROBATION AND PAROLE OFFICERS

Because the roles played by probation and parole officers are somewhat similar, and because many agencies perform probation and parole functions with the same personnel, we will treat probation and parole officers at the same time. However, there are distinctions in the tasks performed by probation and parole officers, so we will begin this section with a discussion of the tasks performed by each of them.

Parole officers begin their contact with cases when they perform field investigations to verify conditions and arrangements for parole plans developed by parole workers in correctional institutions. Newly released offenders have an initial interview with their parole officer, and then continue on with routine contacts throughout the period of active parole supervison. These contacts may be face-to-face, in writing, or by telephone. If a parolee commits a felony or breaks major conditions of the parole agreement, the parole officer will start revocation procedures to return the parolee to the institution. If there are no significant violations, the parolee is discharged upon the recommendation of the parole officer,[49] except in those states that have recently converted to a more rigid system of parole discharge.

As an example of the work of a probation officer, we will look at the operation of the probation system in Des Moines, Iowa, which was cited as an Exemplary Project by the National Institute of Law Enforcement and Criminal Justice in 1973. Probation officers in Des Moines have their first contact with cases while offenders are still under the jurisdiction of the judicial system. This is for the purpose of preparing a pre-sentence report. Probation officers gather background information, some of it by investigations carried out in the field, and assemble this information in the pre-sentence report, together with a recommendation for a disposition of the case. The Des Moines officer preparing the pre-sentence report is not the same person who supervises offenders if they are placed on probation. In other jurisdictions, this might be the same person, or perhaps two different individuals working out of the same office. Offenders in Iowa may be placed on probation as a result of either a deferred or suspended sentence. In the case of a deferred sentence, the period of probation is usually set by the judge at one or two years. An offender receiving a suspended sentence normally is subject to an indeterminant period of probation that is terminated when the probation officer and the judge agree that a discharge is appropriate.[6]

The probation supervision process begins with intake, which consists of an interview in which the court order and the terms and conditions of probation are explained in detail, and during which the probationer signs the probation contract. The case is then assigned to a specific probation agent for supervision and the probation officer meets with the probationer for the initial interview. Iowa probationers who have committed crimes involving victims must agree on a plan for restitution. The restitution payment plan is worked out between the probation officer and the probationer and then submitted to the court for approval. (This would not necessarily be true in other states.) In addition to supervising the probationer, the probation officer counsels, makes referrals to appropriate sources of help in the community, investigates possible new offenses or violations of the conditions of probation by the probationer, and, finally, recommends the probationer for discharge. Probation officers who wish to avoid revocation may use other punitive measures such as incarceration in the county jail. This allows the probationer to be coerced into conformity without being subjected to the stringent negative sanction of the revocation proceeding.[6]

The average probation officer may have a large and demanding caseload in addition to preparing pre-sentence reports, documents for revocation, and other paperwork. The result of this is that many pre-sentence reports are not fully researched. A report to the Congress by the Comptroller General of the United States[10] showed that pre-sentence investigations were not made in 46 percent of the cases sampled. Few of the pre-sentence reports contained recommendations relating to the offender's menace to the community or the type of probation supervision needed. Professional diagnoses of the probationers' problems were made in only 15 percent of the cases. Judges were therefore forced to make dispositions based on inadequate information in most of the cases before them.

Probation/Parole Officer Roles

A number of typologies of the roles of probation and parole officers have been developed by sociologists. These generally include the punitive/law enforcement officer, the welfare/therapeutic officer, the protective/synthetic officer, and the passive/time server officer. The punitive/law enforcement officer focuses on protecting the community by controlling the probationer. The welfare/therapeutic officer is primarily interested in improving the welfare of the probationer, which is just the opposite orientation from the role of the punitive/law enforcement officer. The protective/synthetic officer tries to balance the need for community protection and the welfare of the probationer. The passive/time server officer is on a completely different dimension. This individual has little concern for either the community or the probationer, but instead is interested in putting out a minimum of effort on the job.[2] These typologies imply that probationers and parolees receive substantially different supervision according to whom they happen to be assigned to. Since it is rare to systematically assign correctional clients officers on the basis of client needs and officer characteristics, it is likely that there are many cases in which the officer to whom an individual client is assigned has just the opposite characteristics from those that would be optimum for the client's benefit.

Cutting across these officer role typologies are several other models of probation/parole officer performance that have been only recently developed and are not yet widely accepted in the field. The first of these is the officer as a broker for community services. Probation and parole officers are generalists, and cannot possibly provide for the specific needs of most of their clients. If client needs are to be fully met, the officer in charge must serve as a service broker, referring the client to the most appropriate community services and monitoring service provision to ensure that it fully meets the client's needs. To play this role adequately, the officer needs to have a knowledge of the services available in the community and the need profile of the client.[36] The officer should also have some diagnostic skills in order to be sensitive to emerging client needs, but the initial diagnosis and specialized evaluations performed as needed during the period of supervision can be contracted out to trained diagnosticians.

Shelle Dietrich[13] argues that probation officers are poorly trained to be adequate change agents. In addition to limitations of training, there is also a tradition in the literature that simplistic advice and humanistic intentions are sufficient to help correctional clients readjust to the community. In actuality, this kind of advice given by inadequately trained officers can often do more harm than good. In her words, "Shouldn't the probationer be protected from being the nonvolunteer patient of an unlicensed and untrained person, even if the person's intentions are the most purely humanistic?"[13:18] Dietrich proposes the model of the case manager as more appropriate to the training and capabilities of probation officers. This model, which differs little from the model of the agent as service broker, sees intervention by agents as no more than a "bandage job," and recommends frequent consultations with qualified psychologists and other social science professionals for the officers as well as for the purpose of diagnostic workups on the clients. In this way, officers can continually upgrade their therapeutic skills and can also obtain advice on specific cases.

The scientific classifications of the roles played by individuals are not necessarily the same as the perceptions of those roles that the individuals would give to you if you asked them what they were doing on their jobs. Probation and parole officers generally view themselves as being professionals who have the needs of their clients uppermost in their minds. The law enforcement aspects of their jobs tend to be played down in their own self-images.[33] In a Canadian study, it was found that the probation officers saw themselves primarily as social workers, with only a small percentage of the officers seeing themselves as primarily law enforcers or office administrators. In contrast, they believed that the primary view of their position by the Canadian public was that of a law enforcer.[11]

American studies have generally shown that probation and parole officers spend a great deal of time performing tasks other than direct contact with their clients. In the case of probation officers, the average amount of time spent on pre-sentence investigations is approximately one third of their entire workload, with somewhat less than half of their workload being devoted to the supervision of active cases.[2] In Ontario, probation and parole officers spend approximately one-third of their time counseling clients. Those concerned specifically with probation and parole supervision are in their offices nearly two-thirds of the time and in the field one-quarter of the time. They also spend some time in court, and additional time is lost waiting around for court appearances.[11] A Swedish study found that officers devoted a higher proportion of their time to direct services to clients than in the United States or Canada. More than half of the officers' working hours were devoted to direct service delivery to clients. However, the probationers received less time than the parolees and the other types of cases handled by the officers. One reason that the ratio of direct service to paperwork was higher in the Swedish study than in Canadian and American studies is that the Swedish officers had much lower caseloads, averaging 33 cases each, 24 of which were probationers.[15]

The Quasi-Judicial Function of the Probation/Parole Officer

The quasi-judicial role of the probation officer was first pointed out by Eugene Czajkoski[12] in an article in *Federal Probation*. In his conception, the probation officer has "awesome authority" over the probationer. By claiming that rehabilitation is the goal of supervision, the probation officer can greatly restrict the freedom of the probationer, thus inflicting considerable punishment. Herbert Roll[42] has suggested nine areas in which probation officers have discretionary power over their charges. These are:

1. The power to influence the sentencing disposition of criminal cases.
2. The authority to make an arrest, with or without a warrant.
3. The authority to issue warrants.
4. The authority to search and seize evidence without a warrant.
5. The power to detain clients in custody and to influence bail and release decisions.
6. The power to influence charges that are brought by the prosecutor's office.
7. The power to determine charges in cases of probation violations.
8. The power to institutionalize clients through revocation procedures and other mechanisms.
9. The power to modify or terminate the conditions of probation.

Roll sees the discretionary power of probation officers as being so great that it has impact on the entire criminal justice system as well as on the probationers.

The view of the power of the probation/parole agent may be somewhat exaggerated. A study of parole agents in California by Richard McCleary[33] showed that there were considerable constraints on the exercise of discretion by parole officers. Although McCleary focused on parole agents, his results can be taken to apply equally to probation agents. The occasional exercise of discretion in extreme cases gave the appearance of omnipotence, obscuring the fact that the discretionary power of the officers in day-to-day activities was much more restricted. Informal norms for case supervision were established in each local office and were enforced by other officers as well as by supervisors. The more promising the offender, the greater the freedom of the officer to decide what to do in the case. The more serious the misbehavior of the offender, the clearer the norms specifying what must be done.

To be labeled as fair, the parole officer had to be willing to stand behind parolees who were thought to be innocent of an alleged crime while on supervision, but to turn against those parolees who were judged guilty. To be competent, an officer had to avoid excessive emotional involvement with clients and, in particular, to avoid being caught lying on behalf of clients. Officers careful to follow the norms were able to build up impressive reputations that permitted them greater discretion in helping carefully chosen parolees whose cases were borderline. If they did not carefully protect their reputations, they soon lost all credibility with other criminal justice personnel, and then had little ability to help any of their clients.

McCleary[32,33] noted that parole officers were not quick to file written reports about the misbehavior of their parolees. Such reports made a great deal of extra work for the agents, and an excessive number of these reports might be seen by supervisors as indicating that the agents were not doing their jobs properly. Many incidents were never recorded by the parole officers. When an incident was recorded, it was usually done for one of three reasons: to intimidate or coerce a parolee; to remove a troublesome parolee; or to protect the officer and the entire parole unit from external criticism. If a parolee is not performing up to expectations, written reports can be used as a threat to increase parolee conformity. The threat often works, because parolees have no way of knowing whether or not the records are being accumulated as a prelude to revocation. If threats are not successful, and any other strategies utilized by the parole officer also do not bear fruit, the reports will then be used to support the revocation warrant.

Because it is embarrassing to lose a revocation hearing, the parole agent is very careful to build an extensive case against those parolees who are likely to be revoked. When there is the possibility of adverse publicity on cases, parole officers can protect themselves and their units by carefully documenting each violation, no matter how minor. In this way, there is no possibility that a later investigation by newspaper reporters will reveal any deviation from literal compliance with the rules.

These manipulations of parole records sound rather cynical, and contrast with the rather idealistic intentions of many students in training to become probation and parole officers. The process of moving from youthful idealism to what might be called realistic cynicism is not an easy one. Officers who are too lenient with their clients will be badly "burned" and their reputations will suffer as a result. On the other hand, they may become similarly disenchanted with the system when they confront the conflict of goals between service provision and social control. A study of juvenile probation workers in Denver, Colorado found that compliance with the norms of the criminal justice system often resulted in having to abandon individual delinquent children to the system instead of continuing to help them as much as possible. The rehabilitative goals of their work were not consistent with the realities of the cases or with the operation of the criminal justice system. In the end, the officers were forced to put the protection of the public above the welfare of the individual clients, which many of them found to be morally acceptable.[38]

MANAGING PROBATION SERVICES

A major management problem in probation and parole officers is how to assign cases to individual officers. They may be assigned randomly, with regard to administrative considerations such as balancing caseloads, with regard to geography such as by giving all clients in one area to the same officer, or by assigning clients to officers on the basis of client needs. In some cases, all clients having one specific characteristic (such as a problem with alcohol) are assigned to the same officer. In other cases, a number of different client characteristics are considered in making assignments to officers.[2] While the consideration of client needs is presumably superior to random assignment of clients to officers, there is no standard model currently in existence that is well supported by scientific evidence. In the absence of a clear system for assigning clients to officers based on client needs, it may be better to adopt a team model than to assign cases to individual officers. By working as teams, officers with different skills may be able to meet the needs of clients in shared caseloads better than these needs could be met in individual caseloads.[40]

A second management problem is how to evaluate the work of individual probation and parole officers. More than 90 percent of the respondents to a survey of state probation/parole administrators reported that they use a standardized evaluation form. The most important factor used in the evaluation of probation and parole officers was the ability to develop and maintain counseling relationships, followed by skill in caseload management and client evaluation. Ability to use diagnostic information, to work with other profession-als, to find jobs for clients, and to be successful in public relations were also important in job evaluation.[35] Although these categories are appropriate ones to use in the evaluation of probation and parole officers, their use in standard evaluation forms suggests that supervisors may not be communicating very much information to higher-level administrators. These forms typically take only a few minutes to complete, and are subject to norms specifying that all but the worst officers are to be given ratings that are at least "good," if not "excellent." Within local offices, supervisors almost certainly make judgments about the value of officers on the basis of much more refined criteria, some of which have to do with institutional maintenance and survival rather than with client welfare.[33]

A third concern of probation and parole managers is training. The first level of training is the educational achievement required of newly hired officers. Most states require a bachelor's degree, a few require only a high school education,[24] and several require a master's degree.[2] Once hired, there is probably some sort of orientation to the position, and there may also be a limited amount of in-service training from time to time. A major problem with in-service training is that training sequences tend to be offered on a one-time basis so that there is not a continuous reinforcement of training objectives in the officers.[37] In-service or orientation training can be implemented on a local level or on a state level. It can be oriented toward individuals in a university model or toward entire units in an organization development model.

In the state of Texas, state criminal justice planners and government officials decided that the best way to implement in-service training, given the rural nature of the state, was to develop a training plan for the entire state. Texas has 254 counties, most of which are served by probation departments of one to four members. The state was divided into five geographic areas and a workshop was planned for all the probation officers in each area. Planning for the workshops began with preliminary contacts with judicial administrators, and also involved site visits to local judges and probation departments. There were also formal planning meetings in which chief probation officers and judges participated in the fine-tuning of the workshop plans. The workshops were organized on the basis of small groups of six to eight officers, with urban officers separated from rural officers and adult officers separated from juvenile officers. The workshops followed the participant–involvement model and avoided lectures as much as possible. Professional group facilitators were used to ensure that everyone was involved in the sessions and that a feeling of being part of a team was developed through the sessions. The final phase of the project was to appoint an advisory board—made up of judges and chief probation officers who had been through one of the initial workshops—to plan and monitor future workshop series.[5]

The university model sees orientation and in-service training to be a matter of communicating knowledge to individual probation or parole officers.[46] This training can be provided by agency personnel with the help of consultants drawn in from the surrounding community, or a department can fund its staff members to go directly to universities for training. In Philadelphia, probation officers were given full financial support while they were full-time students at Temple University's School of Social Service Administration.[45] The danger with this approach is that the educational orientation of the university may not adequately meet the training needs of the department.

The organization development approach takes the entire department as the unit for training rather than individual officers. The goal is more to build team cooperation than to impart specific academic knowledge. An organization development plan was used in the Maricopa County, Arizona, Adult Probation Department in 1978. It began with a two-day seminar for top administrative staff and first line supervisors. Problems were identified in two separate working groups, and then unified as the basis for the planning of a three-day team-building seminar conducting in a conference retreat away from the pressures of office work. This session acted as a catalyst for department staff members to begin operating on a team basis instead of as individuals. Technical services for the organization development program were provided by an outside agency through a contract, and the contract was written to fund 12 months of consulting after the second seminar in order to reinforce the team process in the department.[22]

VOLUNTEERS IN PROBATION

Probation services started as a volunteer effort, and volunteers were prominent in the early years of service delivery to federal probationers. Professionalizing probation left volunteers behind, and it was only after 1960 that volunteer services to probationers began to come into their own. There may be as many as 300,000–500,000 volunteers serving probation clients in the United States today. There are four models of volunteer involvement in probation work. These are the one-to-one model, the supervision model, the professional model, and the administrative model. In the one-to-one model, a volunteer works with a single probationer with a goal of developing trust and confidence in that relationship so that there can be openness in seeking out sources of help for current needs in the community and in planning for the future. Volunteers working under the supervision model function as case aides to probation officers, and volunteers working under the administrative model provide assistance to administrators rather than interacting directly with probationers. Under the professional model, volunteers who have professional skills serve only those probationers who have needs in their particular areas of expertise. One volunteer may give legal consultations, another may do psychological testing, and a third may teach financial management skills.[16]

Probation organizations that utilize volunteers face problems of recruitment, screening and selection, training, matching, and supervising. Special recruitment techniques may be necessary to ensure that racial minorities are adequately represented in the cadre of volunteers. Application forms, interviews, letters of reference, police checks, performance during training, and encouragement for the volunteers to screen themselves are all part of a comprehensive screening and selection process. Training is essential to an efficient volunteer operation, but the lack of funding for volunteer programs in many jurisdictions makes the provision of adequate training a difficult proposition. The matching of probationers to volunteers is particularly important in one-to-one programs. In addition to demographic characteristics, such elements as community contacts, interests, and counseling skills should be considered in the matching process.[16] The need for the supervision of volunteers is continuous, which illustrates the point that no volunteer program is without cost.

The appointment of volunteers is generally done on a local basis, and is authorized by administrative regulations. However, the federal government and seven states provide for the appointment of volunteer probation officers by statute. These statutes generally say something about the types of activities to be engaged in by the volunteers and the nature of their supervision, but they make no provision for financing the selection and training of volunteer probation officers. This probably reflects the general impression that volunteer programs are free, which is far from the truth. The closest that any statute comes to funding volunteer programs is in Wyoming, where there is a statutory provision for the reimbursement of volunteers who incur expenses in the performance of their duties.[2]

There has been some impressive theoretical work accomplished on the helping process and on the advantages that volunteers may enjoy over paid professionals as change agents.[8] It is probably fair to say that volunteers will be more effective than paid staff members with certain clients and in certain situations, but less effective with other clients and in other situations. Research on the general effectiveness of volunteer programs in probation has produced mixed results. Some studies indicate a positive impact achieved through the use of volunteers, and others do not. Available research indicates that the indirect savings achieved through volunteer programs (in the reduction of future crime, etc.) are much greater than the cost of the programs.[2]

The Volunteer Probation Counselor Program
of Lincoln, Nebraska

Lincoln, Nebraska's Probation Counselor Program is one of the outstanding probation volunteer programs in the nation. It has been designated as an Exemplary Project by the National Institute of Law Enforcement and Criminal

Justice. This program focuses on high-risk misdemeanants between the ages of 16 and 25. Each probationer is assigned to a volunteer on a one-to-one basis. Additional volunteers provide other support services, including educational classes, tutoring, writing and editing a monthly newsletter, and performing clerical and public relations work for the Probation Office. All volunteer activities are unreimbursed, even for expenses incurred in the performance of their duties. A paid staff member in the Probation Office provides coordination and supervision for the volunteers. The screening of volunteers includes psychological testing and personal interviews. Eight hours of training, packaged in three evening sessions, is a prerequisite for acceptance into the program. Volunteers are supervised professionally, and also participate in monthly in-service training seminars and small self-help volunteer groups.[29]

A comparison of high-risk probationers participating in the volunteer program and those placed on regular probation showed that 70 percent of the regular probationers committed an additional offense during a one-year period while they were on probation, but that only 56 percent of the probationers in the volunteer program did so. This small improvement is misleading, because most of the offenses committed by probationers in the volunteer program were traffic offenses, while the regular probationers committed a large number of personal and property offenses. When compared with their offense records during the year prior to entrance into the probation programs, the regular probationers showed a reduction of 11 percent in their total offenses, but an increase of 70 percent in their property and personal offenses. In comparison, the volunteer probationers recorded a 62 percent decline in total offenses and an outstanding 81 percent decline in property and personal offenses.[29]

CLIENT CHARACTERISTICS

The Comptroller General's study[10] of state and county probation systems found that only 42 percent of a sample of probationers in three counties were employed at the time of their arrest. At the termination of probation, this proportion had risen to only 46 percent, so there is little evidence that the conditions and services associated with probation were helpful in improving the employment status of the probationers. Twenty-eight percent of the closed cases and 37 percent of the active cases sampled by the Comptroller General were judged to be in need of vocational training. Twenty-five percent of the closed cases and 31 percent of the active cases were judged to be in need of academic training. More than a quarter of the probationers were in need of drug treatment services; one in every seven needed alcohol treatment services; and one in every six needed services for a mental health problem. These statistics indicate a rather high level of needs for specific professional programming on the part of probationers—needs that were not met in most of the cases studied by the Comptroller General.

From the viewpoint of the probation or parole officer, clients may also be categorized by their attitudes toward supervision. Richard McCleary[33] found that parole officers in Los Angeles used a working classification of parolees as a guide to the type of supervision required. This classification probably applies to probationers just as well as it does to parolees. The first category is "dangerous men." These are individuals who do not respond rationally to threats or promises. (In the future, this type will have to be expanded to include dangerous women.) The dangerous man is publicized to supervisors as a potential troublemaker, so that any sanctions recommended against him will be quickly approved all the way up the line. An intensive supervision schedule is developed so that parole can be revoked as soon as there is any sign of criminal behavior.

The second type of parolee is the "criminal"—by which parole officers mean that the individual is committed to criminal norms. Criminals are not particularly dangerous, because they exercise rational control over their behavior. An important use of the criminal type is its obverse, the "noncriminal"—referring to someone who has needs for specialized treatment programs or who has severe psychological problems. "Sincere clients" differ from dangerous men, criminals, and noncriminals in that they honestly intend to stay out of trouble with the law. Operationally, the sincere client is someone who can be placed in the most helpful programs, and who can be depended upon to be a good client in therapy.

THE CONDITIONS OF PROBATION

Probationers are not free to do whatever they would like in the community. Their freedom is contingent upon fulfilling a number of obligations that are a written part of the probation agreement. Probation conditions have the force of law, and violation of these conditions can return an offender to jail or prison just as quickly (in fact, even more quickly) than the commission of a new criminal offense. Probation conditions are of two types: standard conditions written into every contract, which may be stipulated in state statutes; and optional conditions, which are added to the contract by the judge, often with the recommendation of a probation officer. Standard conditions in Pennsylvania consist of the following nine points.

1. Report to the probation officer.
2. Obtain the officer's written permission to change residence.
3. Be law-abiding and conform to administrative regulations governing the probation.
4. Notify the probation officer of any arrests or criminal investigation involving oneself.
5. Make every effort to become employed and to support one's dependents.
6. Obtain written permission for all changes of employment.
7. Refrain from traveling outside of the community without written permission.
8. Refrain from the use or sale of illegal drugs and deadly weapons.
9. Comply with any special conditions subsequently imposed by the probation officer or stipulated in the original sentence.[26]

Common conditions included in other states include obtaining written permission from the probation officer before marrying, applying for a motor vehicle license, or borrowing money.[1]

The many general conditions and special conditions that are written into a probation agreement create the possibility of abuse by the probation officer. There are often so many conditions for probation that the probationer is bound to be in violation of at least one of them. As it happens, probation officers are not quick to revoke probation on the basis of minor breaches of the probation contract. In one District Court, there were only 12 revocations in 700 cases over a period of three months, and ten of those revocations were for new crimes rather than for technical violations of the probation agreement.[44] Special probation conditions are not limited to prohibitions and requests for reports. They can also demand positive behavior by the probationer. A program initiated in the Western District of Tennessee in 1976 involved the writing of unpaid public service into probation contracts. A list of charitable agencies was drawn up, and appropriate probationers were assigned to these agencies at the time they were placed on probation. The agencies naturally retained the right to refuse any probationer who did not meet their needs. The amount of work required in the probation condition is the equivalent of one day per week, and usually extends over a two-year period in this program. Agencies participating in the program include the Boy's Club of Memphis, the Memphis Public Library, The Salvation Army, the Veteran's Hospital, a local hospital, and a Head Start agency.[7]

EXAMPLES OF PROBATION PROGRAMS

The National Advisory Commission on Criminal Justice Standards and Goals[39] recommends that probation systems be organized to deliver a wide variety of services to probationers by a range of staff members. This is obviously impossible to accomplish in most probation agencies without contracting for services external to the agency because there are too few staff members involved in the operation of the agency to provide a wide range of services in-house. Larger agencies located in urban areas have more flexibility in meeting client needs, although even these agencies usually contract for certain services with other community organizations. As illustrations of the creative programming that can be done in the area of probation, some descriptions of probation programs follow.

Shock Probation

Shock probation is an attempt to impress offenders with the gravity of their crimes and the severity of institutional punishment by shocking them with a brief period of incarceration followed by probation. The Ohio shock probation law, which was passed in 1965, allows the courts to release offenders from state correctional institutions after 30–130 days of imprisonment for continued supervision on probation. Ohio courts were slow to make use of the new law. Only 85 offenders received shock probation in 1966, but the number grew steadily to 907 cases in 1971[41] and 1454 cases in 1975. The proportion of offenders subjected to shock probation who were recommitted to an institution following failure on probation averaged 10 percent over the first ten years of the shock probation program in Ohio,[1] which was better than national recidivism figures for parolees,[21] but may not have been better than recidivism in a control group of Ohio probationers not subjected to shock institutionalization.

Shock probation is a good example of the pitfalls of common sense. To most people, the idea that frightening offenders through a short term in prison will keep them from a life of crime makes good sense. Although social scientists found out many years ago that permanent behavior change comes through the use of rewards rather than punishments, this has not yet been fully assimilated into the popular consciousness. In Ohio, the success of shock probation was partially defined in terms of convincing more judges to use the program than in terms of the recidivism rate or other outcome criteria applied to the proba-tioners. The Ohio Adult Parole Authority was so pleased with the "success" of shock probation that it was successful in lobbying to have shock parole also written into law. This differs from shock probation primarily in that it is administered by the parole board instead of the courts.

The National Advisory Commission on Criminal Justice Standards and Goals[39] recommends that shock probation be discontinued because it "defeats the purpose of probation, which is the earliest possible reintegration of the offender into the community. Short-term commitment subjects the probationer to the destructive effects of institutionalization, disrupts his life in the commu-nity, and stigmatizes him for having been in jail."[39:321] Aside from this philosophical disagreement with shock probation, a recent evaluation of shock probation shows that the probability of reincarceration is greater for those having experienced shock probation than those subjected only to regular probation. When background characteristics of regular probationers and shock probationers were held constant, it was found that the regular probationers had a 42 percent lower probability of reincarceration than shock probationers.[48] These results testify to the wisdom of the National Advisory Commission's position on shock probation. It would seem that Ohio residents are paying a considerable amount of extra money (since institutionalization is much more expensive than probation) for a program that has the effect of increasing rather than reducing crime. Paradoxically, the practice of shock parole, which developed as an offshoot of shock probation, actually saves public money by reducing institutionalization.[43] Whether or not it does so without having any negative effect on recidivism remains to be seen.

The Job Bank Project

The Job Bank Project is an employment service operated by the Bergen County, New Jersey, Probation Department. Probationers who are accepted into the project receive vocational counseling, job interview training, and direct job referrals. In addition, probationers can be referred to community agencies for remedial education programs, job training programs, and other employ-ment-related help-sources. The project operates on the assumption that concentrated employment services reduce recidivism. Although probationers were not assigned to the Job Bank Project randomly, there was no skimming involved. That is to say, the program did not admit only those offenders having characteristics associated with success on probation, thus ensuring that the program would have successful graduates.[34]

An evaluation of the Job Bank Project was performed using all of the probationers terminated during 1973 in Bergen County, which included 342 Job Bank clients and 1307 regular probationers. It was found that there were no differences between the Job Bank clients and the regular probationers on level of job skills or total number of previous convictions. However, the Job Bank clients were younger, had somewhat more education, and tended to have more problems with drugs than the regular probationers. Analyzing the two groups together, it was found that the most important factor associated with success on probation was having a job. The next step in the examination of the success of the Job Bank Project is to see to what extent participation in the program was associated with holding onto a job. It was found that participation in the program was much more important than any other factor in continued probationer employment.[34] It appears that the scientific evidence confirms the value of the employment approach to probation just as much as it leaves us with questions about the value of shock probation.

The Complex Offender Project

The Complex Offender Project began in Madison, Wisconsin in 1974. It operates on a therapeutic model, and is sponsored by the Mendota Mental Health Institute. The agency employs a psychologist, a social worker, two psychological services associates, two psychiatric nurses, a vocational rehabilitation counselor, and numerous lower-level personnel. Clients accepted into the program negotiate treatment goals with staff members, and receive intensive support in their efforts to achieve those goals. Contacts with clients average three per week, plus six weekly phone calls and five weekly contacts with other community agencies. During crisis periods, individual clients receive as many as 20 hours of service per week from staff members. In addition to traditional counseling techniques, the program emphasizes social learning theory. Efforts are made to increase the adaptive skills of all clients so that they can improve their performance in areas such as work and education. In addition to their problems wih the law, most clients have received mental health services for emotional disturbances at some time in the past.[28]

The Complex Offender Project is an example of the application of the medical model to probation supervision. Because of the combination of mental health, social adaptation, and legal problems in the specialized sample of probationers admitted to the project, the medical model is more appropriate in this program than it might be for programs with most probationers.

A comprehensive evaluation of the effects of the program was carried out using a rigorous experimental design. Volunteers were randomly assigned both to the program and to a control group that received regular probation supervision. Both groups showed some improvements, with initial improvements occurring more frequently than lasting improvements. The Complex Offender Project was most effective in those areas of social adjustment that it dealt with directly, such as enrollment in educational programs and job placement.[28] Overall, however, the improvements were modest, and it is hard to justify the high cost of such an intensive program of services on the basis of relatively meager results. Comparing the three probation programs described in this section, it appears that the pure employment program was the most successful and shock probation was the least successful, with the program based on the medical model of intervention (but including an employment component) falling in between.

REVOCATION

Because of the similarities between revocation in probation and revocation in parole, they will be treated together in this section. An offender who commits a serious crime can be sure that community supervision will be terminated. In addition, the offender may be violated for failing to follow the conditions of supervision, even though law-abiding behavior has been maintained throughout. In this case, the officer has probably terminated the community supervision of the offender because there is a strong possibility that a serious crime will be committed if the offender remains at large. The nature of revocation procedures changed in 1972 when the United States Supreme Court ruled in *Morrissey v. Brewer,* 408 U.S. 471 (1972) that parole (and by implication probation) revocation proceedings must fully comply with due process standards. Along with *Gagnon v. Scarpelli,* 411 U.S. 718 (1973) and other Supreme Court decisions, *Morrissey* rewrote the book on revocation procedures. Community supervision is no longer considered to be a state of grace revokable at any time on no more than a whim of the granting authority.[1]

The most important difference between parole and probation revocation hearings is that the probation revocation hearing is a judicial process, while the parole revocation hearing is an administrative process. Both procedures involve a notice of violation, a preliminary hearing, a revocation hearing, and the three possible decision outcomes that: (1) no violation occurred, (2) a violation occurred but a reprimand is sufficient punishment, and (3) a violation occurred and the offender is to be imprisoned as punishment.

As examples of revocation procedures, we will examine the probation and parole revocation sequences used for federal offenders. Federal probationers have a preliminary hearing before a federal judge or magistrate as soon as possible after the accusation of a violation has been made by a probation officer. The probationer receives a petition listing the alleged violations, and is entitled to appear personally at the preliminary hearing to present evidence and witnesses. Any witnesses who have supplied information supporting a revocation decision may be cross-examined by the probationer unless the hearing officer makes a determination that this might endanger the witness. A written report of the preliminary hearing reviews the evidence and makes a determination as to whether or not there is probable cause to hold a full revocation hearing. Probationers who are without funds have legal counsel made available to them by court appointment. Even if the probationer fails to quash a case at the point of the preliminary hearing, it is still possible to remain free on bail until the final revocation hearing is held. The final hearing includes all of the rights mentioned in connection with the preliminary hearing. The federal judge must issue a written statement including the evidence examined as well as the decision for or against revoking probation.[18]

In the case of parolees, only the United States Parole Commission may issue a warrant (based on the recommendation of a parole officer) to bring the parolee into custody and to start the revocation process. The preliminary interview is conducted by an officer other than the offender's regular parole officer, or may be held before a U.S. magistrate. A report summarizing the evidence and making a recommendation is submitted to the Parole Commission, and leads to the full revocation hearing. A parolee who has not been convicted of a new offense is granted a local revocation hearing rather than a hearing at the correctional institution. The local revocation hearing is conducted with the rights of cross-examination of adverse witnesses, personal testimony, and the presentation of evidence in self-defense.[18]

PROBATION RISK SCALES

Probation risk scales predict how successful a group of probationers will be based on the experiences of earlier groups of probationers. This is useful to probation agencies in that it allows them to select individuals with a very high probability of success and to grant them greater freedom (lower levels of supervision) than would be granted to the average probationer. Probation risk scales rate each probationer on a variety of background factors and then total the scores on these factors to get a summary risk score that is equated with a given probability of probation success.

Two problems with probation risk scales are that scales applicable to one population of probationers may not be applicable to a different population located elsewhere in the country, and that probation risk calculations based on earlier groups of offenders may not be applicable to the current group of offenders because of changing conditions. As an illustration of this, probation success in Washington, D.C. was strongly determined by opiate use in 1972, when only 28 percent of the opiate users succeeded on probation. By 1975, the proportion of opiate users succeeding on probation had risen to 55 percent. Changes such as this in probation success rates may signal that social conditions for opiate users have changed. For example, discrimination against opiate users in the job market might have declined. Another possibility is that the meaning of opiate use for the users may have changed. In the case of the Washington, D.C. sample, the proportion of probationers on opiates nearly doubled over a three-year period. When a deviant act becomes much more common, its association with other forms of deviance and social problems may change drastically.[25] Alternatively, the increased probation success rate may reflect changes in the tolerance level for drug offenses, or that the law enforcement system's capacity to detect drug violations may be overwhelmed by the volume of offenses and limitations on available enforcement personnel.

The Comptroller General's study[10] of state and county probation in the United States identified eight risk scales that could be used with probationers and tested these scales in three counties. It was found that all eight scales were capable of differentiating between probation successes and failures. There was also considerable evidence that scales that worked in one area would also work in other areas. The use of scales predicted the success of probationers more accurately than the probation officers and judges. The joint prediction of success using both the clinical judgment of local personnel and statistical prediction using a risk scale was more accurate than either local judgment or the risk scale used separately. It is therefore reasonable to assume that the widespread adoption of risk scales by probation departments would result in increases of operating efficiency and perhaps also decreases in crime.

The Base Expectancy Scoring Form used in Newark, New Jersey is a good example of a probation prediction device. It consists of 12 background characteristics that are assigned between four and 12 points. The points for the 12 items are then summed, and the sum for each probationer is taken as a prediction of the probability of success on supervision. The items and the points associated with them are given in Table 14.1. Items that are assigned a high number of points have greater predictive strength than items assigned a low number of points. The Comptroller General[10] found that this scale accurately differentiated successes from failures in populations of probationers selected from counties in Oregon, Pennsylvania, and California. In the Oregon sample, probationers with a total score of 69 or higher were successful 82 percent of the time. In contrast, probationers with scores between 44 and 50 were successful 71 percent of the time, and probationers with scores of 43 or below were successful only 39 percent of the time.

Table 14.1. The Base Expectancy Scoring Form, Newark, N.J.

Characteristic	Points
1. Arrest-free period of five or more years.	12
2. No history of any opiate use.	9
3. Not more than two jail commitments.	8
4. No checks, forgery, or burglary on the most recent court commitment.	7
5. No family criminal record.	6
6. No alcohol involvement.	6
7. First arrest was not for auto theft.	5
8. Worked 12 or more consecutive months for one employer prior to the present offense.	6
9. Worked 4–11 months with one employer. (Is automatically given if characteristic 8 is present)	4
10. No aliases.	5
11. A favorable living arrangement.	4
12. Not more than two prior arrests.	4

Source: Comptroller General of the United States. *Report to Congress. State and County Probation: Systems in Crisis.* Washington, D.C., 1976.

THE EVALUATION OF
PROBATION SERVICES

Probation administrators want to know how well their units are doing in comparison with other units. The public has an interest in seeing to it that funds expended for probation supervision yield better results than might have been obtained if there had been no supervision. Adequate answers to questions on these topics can only be obtained through the use of social science evaluation techniques. Not all "evaluations" are evaluations in the fullest sense of the term. Many constitute no more than a monitoring of an agency's activities, which allows no possibility for the evaluation of the quality of those activities. Even when an outcome measure such as the proportion of probationers violated is employed, it may not be used in such a way as to permit evaluative conclusions to be drawn. An in-house evaluation of Florida's juvenile probation and aftercare services presented the percentage of cases resulting in violations for different kinds of caseloads, but because there was no attempt to evaluate the characteristics of the individuals in the different caseloads, there is no way that this comparison can tell us anything about the success of the services delivered in different settings. One type of caseload might have shown a lower violation rate than another type of caseload simply because it contained a much lower proportion of high-risk offenders.[19]

Violation is the most common measure of probation failure, but there are other possibilities that might be used, some of which are actually superior to the violation rate as a measure of agency effectiveness. The behavior of clients can be monitored directly to show improvements in social adaptation. Changes in the attitudes of clients might also be assessed. In addition to measures of client change, there are various measures of agency performance that do not depend on client attitudes and behavior. In a sense, it is not entirely fair to evaluate someone's job performance on the basis of the behavior of someone else. It may be more appropriate to rate the quality of service delivery directly rather than indirectly through the estimation of client changes or revocation rates.

A model proposed for evaluating operations in adult probation and parole offices in Virginia includes six quantitative and four qualitative measures of program performance, but there is no mention of client recidivism or revocation rates. The qualitative criteria, which cannot be analyzed statistically, are the level of services provided to clients, the scope of the record-keeping systems, the quality of the records, and the validity of the reported data. The quantitative measures, which could be used in evaluation studies with great precision, are cost per client-year, the staff–client ratio, the probation/parole officer–client ratio, the rate of staff turnover, the proportion of parole/pardon cases in compliance with minimum standards of treatment, and the proportion of probation cases in compliance with minimum standards of treatment.[14] Using these criteria, it is possible to carry out comparisons of different units without making any mention of revocation rates, provided that the effects of differences in client character-istics and environmental conditions (such as rural vs. urban service areas) are taken into account.

The Influence of Size of Caseload on
Probation Success

Another common sense idea in the area of probation is the notion that the lower the caseload, the higher the success of community supervision. Should we not expect that the more time a probation officer can give to each client, the more likely these clients will be to avoid future entanglements with the criminal justice system? Numerous projects have been implemented on this theory, and surveys of these studies are unanimous in concluding that there is no support for the argument that a simple decrease in caseload size will result in decreased recidivism.[3,4,9] As a matter of fact, a survey of international research on probation outcomes concludes that the less the supervision and control of the probationer, the more positive the outcome.[20] Ironically, decreased caseloads may contribute to increased recidivism because there is a higher level of surveillance of the activities of the probationers.[3] Through this mechanism, projects that are actually having a beneficial effect on probationers may appear to be less effective than regular probation supervision.

This generally negative evaluation of reduced caseloads must be qualified in three ways. There is some evidence that decreased caseloads are successful with juvenile probationers. A second positive point is that projects specializing in serving narrowly defined client groups are more likely to be successful than projects serving probationers in general.[3,9] Finally, intensive probation programs can be successful because of the increase in the quality and variety of specialized services offered rather than because of a decrease in the average caseload.[4] It may be that studies that focus on the quality and quantity of contact time between probationers and probation officers will show more positive results than have been shown with the rather crude factor of caseload size.

Another major evaluation question is whether probation is more effective than alternative forms of criminal sanctions. Studies invariably show that the more severe the sanctions, the higher the recidivism. There is some evidence that providing probation supervision for misdemeanants is no more effective than providing no supervision at all. It is impossible to draw any conclusions with regard to other comparisons between different forms of criminal sanctions because of lack of comparability in offender populations. It is natural that offenders who are subjected to imprisonment will do poorly when compared with offenders given probation because of the selection process involved. Judges understandably send the more serious offenders to prison and the less serious offenders are placed on probation. No direct comparisons can be made unless the characteristics of the offender subjected to the different levels of criminal sanctions are held constant. For reasons of Constitutional safeguards and public safety, the possibilities for experiments along these lines are extremely limited.[2]

Macro Evaluations

Evaluations are not limited to single agencies or specialized experimental treatment programs. Because state correctional systems implement probation policies and programs simultaneously for all units in their jurisdictions, it is appropriate to evaluate the effects of these programs at the state rather than at the local level. Such evaluations can be of greater importance than local evaluations because of the impact they may have on state correctional policies. The California Probation Subsidy Law, which was passed in 1965, is an example of a state probation program that has received a macro evaluation. This law authorized the payment of county governments for reducing their commitments of first offenders to state correctional facilities. In addition to the decreased rate of commitment, a county had to show that it had organized special probation units offering intensive supervision in order to qualify for the funds.

Touted as a major correctional reform, probation subsidy did succeed in decreasing commitments to state facilities, but when Paul Lerman[31] performed a macro analysis of the effects of probation subsidy on juvenile incarceration, he found that county incarceration rates went up as state incarceration rates went down, and that the average length of time spent in a state facility by each juvenile increased between 1965 and 1970. Both the California Youth Authority and the county correctional systems experienced significant expansions during the first five years of probation subsidy, so that California taxpayers actually suffered additional costs through the program instead of the savings that had been promised. Lerman argues that instead of decreased formal social controls, probation subsidy ended up increasing social controls in California. If Lerman is correct, any taxpayers desiring to adopt the probation subsidy system in other states on the basis of projected fiscal savings or because they believe that it is a "liberal" correctional reform are going to be disappointed.

SUMMARY

Probation is the assignment of offenders to community supervision as an alternative to incarceration in a jail or prison. Probation supervision is carried out by probation officers who often combine probation and parole functions. These officers are charged with seeing to it that their clients comply with the conditions of their probation or parole and with helping them to establish a law-abiding style of life. The role conflict between the supervision and helping (or therapeutic) functions of the officers has not yet been resolved.

Probation services are managed in local offices so that offenders can continue to live in their own communities. This means that many probation departments contain only 1–4 members and are rather isolated from the probation field as a whole. Probation services started as a volunteer effort, and volunteers have recently begun to return to the field. There may be as many as 300,000–500,000 volunteers working with probation clients in the United States today.

Probationers who fail to conform to the conditions of their probation are subject to revocation. This is most likely to happen when a serious crime has been committed, but it may also occur when the violation of a number of less serious conditions over a period of time leads the supervising officer to conclude that a crime is likely to be committed in the future if the client is not revoked. Until 1972, community supervision was considered to be a state of grace revokable at any time on no more than the whim of the granting authority. A revocation proceeding must now fully comply with due process standards as defined by the United States Supreme Court.

Evaluations of correctional programs tend to show that the more severe the sanctions, the higher the recidivism. Attempts to substitute community supervision for institutionalization may end up increasing rather than decreasing costs and may also increase the span of social control exerted on the community by the correctional system. Although there is evidence that there are many successful probation programs in the nation, it appears that many of the intuitive understandings that we have had about probation in the past must be subjected to statistical scrutiny in order to put probation practices on a more rational basis in the future.

REFERENCES

1. Abadinsky, Howard. *Probation and Parole: Theory and Practice.* Englewood Cliffs, NJ: Prentice-Hall, 1977.
2. Allen, Harry E., Eric W. Carlson, and Evalyn C. Parks. *Critical Issues in Adult Probation: Summary.* Washington, D.C.: Government Printing Office, 1979.
3. Banks, Jerry *et al. Evaluation of Intensive Special Probation Projects: Phase 1 Report.* Washington, D.C.: Government Printing Office, 1977.
4. Banks, Jerry, Terry R. Siler, and Ronald L. Rardin. "Past and Present Findings in Intensive Adult Probation." *Federal Probation* 41 (June 1977):20–25.
5. Bertinot, Libby and Jack E. Taylor. "A Basic Plan for Statewide Probation Training." *Federal Probation* 38 (June 1974):29–31.
6. Boorkman, David *et al. Community-Based Corrections in Des Moines.* Washington, D.C.: Government Printing Office, 1976.
7. Brown, Bailey. "Community Service as a Condition of Probation." *Federal Probation* 41 (December 1977):7–9.
8. Carkhuff, Robert R. *Helping and Human Relations,* Volumes I and II. New York: Holt, Rinehart and Winston, 1969.
9. Carney, Robert J. "Research on Probation Effectiveness." Paper presented at the annual meeting of the American Society of Criminology, 1979.
10. Comptroller General of the United States. *Report to the Congress. State and County Probation: Systems in Crisis.* Washington, D.C., 1976.
11. Crispino, Leonard, Nancy Mulvihill, and Sally Rogers. *The Concerns and Attitudes of Probation Officers: A Study of Perceptions.* Toronto: Ontario Ministry of Correctional Services, 1977.
12. Czajkoski, Eugene H. "Exposing the Quasi-Judicial Role of the Probation Officer." *Federal Probation* 37 (September 1973):9–13.
13. Dietrich, Shelle G. "The Probation Officer as Therapist: Examination of Three Major Problem Areas." *Federal Probation* 43 (June 1979):14–19.
14. Duke, James. "A Proposed Model for Evaluating District Operations in Adult Probation and Parole Services." Richmond, VA: Virginia Department of Corrections, 1978.
15. Ericsson, Stig. *Assistenternas Arbetsuppgifter Vid Skyddskonsulenten I Sundsvall.* Norrköping, Sweden: Kriminalvårdsstyrelfen, 1978.

16. Eskridge, Chris W. "Issues in VIP Management: A National Synthesis." Unpublished manuscript, University of Nebraska–Omaha.

17. Evjen, Victor H. "The Federal Probation System: The Struggle to Achieve It and Its First 25 Years." *Federal Probation* 39 (June 1975):3–15.

18. Fisher, H. Richmond. "Probation and Parole Revocation: The Anomaly of Divergent Procedures." *Federal Probation* 38 (September 1974):23–29.

19. Florida. Department of Health and Rehabilitative Services. "Evaluation of Florida's Juvenile Probation and Aftercare Services." Tallahassee, 1977.

20. Friday, Paul C. *Critical Issues in Adult Probation: International Assessment of Adult Probation.* Washington, D.C.: Government Printing Office, 1979.

21. Galvin, James L. *et al. Characteristics of the Parole Population, 1977.* San Francisco: Research Center West, National Council on Crime and Delinquency, 1979.

22. Graham, Gary and Herbert R. Sigurdson. "An Organization Development Experience in Probation: 'Old Dogs' Can Learn New Tricks!" *Federal Probation* 44 (March 1980):3–12.

23. Grinnell, Frank. "The Common Law History of Probation." *Criminal Law* 32 (May–June 1941):15–34.

24. Hecker, Benson, Timothy F. Field, and Gleam Powell. "Survey of Probation/Parole Supervisors and Counselors." *American Journal of Correction* 38 (March–April 1976):31–32,44.

25. Hemple, William E., William H. Webb, Jr., and Steven W. Reynolds. "Researching Prediction Scales for Probation." *Federal Probation* 40 (June 1976):33–37.

26. Hussey, Frederick A. and David E. Duffee. *Probation, Parole and Community Field Services: Policy, Structure and Process.* New York: Harper and Row, 1980.

27. Keve, Paul W. "Some Random Reflections on the Occasion of a Barely Noticed Anniversary." *Crime and Delinquency* 24 (1978):453–457.

28. Kloss, James D. "The Impact of Comprehensive Community Treatment: An Assessment of the Complex Offender Project." *Offender Rehabilitation* 3 (1978):81–108.

29. Ku, Richard Moore, and Keith Griffiths. *The Volunteer Probation Counselor Program.* Washington, D.C.: Government Printing Office, 1975.

30. Law Enforcement Assistance Administration. *State and Local Probation and Parole Systems.* Washington, D.C.: Government Printing Office, 1978.

31. Lerman, Paul. *Community Treatment and Social Control: A Critical Analysis of Juvenile Correctional Policy.* Chicago: University of Chicago Press, 1975.

32. McCleary, Richard. "How Parole Officers Use Records." *Social Problems* 24 (1977):576–589.

33. McCleary, Richard. *Dangerous Men: The Sociology of Parole.* Beverly Hills, CA: Sage, 1978.

34. McGinnis, Robert D., Kenneth L. Klocksiem, and Carl Wiedman. "Probation and Employment: A Report of the Bergen County, N.J. Probation Department." *Offender Rehabilitation* 1 (1977):323–333.

35. Meeker, Ben S. "The Federal Probation System: The Second 25 Years." *Federal Probation* 39 (June 1975):16–25.

36. Miller, E. Eugene. "The Probation Officer as Broker." *In* E. Eugene Miller and M. Robert Montilla: *Corrections in the Community: Success Models in Correctional Reform.* Reston, VA: Reston Publishing Co., 1977, pp. 75–82.

37. Miller, E. Eugene and M. Robert Montilla. *Corrections in the Community: Success Models in Correctional Reform.* Reston, VA: Reston Publishing Co., 1977.

38. Moynihan, Michael H. *Getting Burned: A Study of the Socialization of Correctional Workers.* Ph.D. dissertation, University of Colorado, 1976.
39. National Advisory Commission on Criminal Justice Standards and Goals. *Corrections.* Washington, D.C.: Government Printing Office, 1973.
40. Nelson, E. Kim, Howard Ohmart, and Nora Harlow. *Promising Strategies in Probation and Parole.* Washington, D.C.: Government Printing Office, 1978.
41. Ohio. Shock Probation Task Force. "Evaluation." Columbus, 1972.
42. Roll, Herbert W. "Discretionary Decision-Making in Probation Agencies." Paper presented at the annual meeting of the American Society of Criminology, 1979.
43. Scott, Joseph E., Simon Dinitz, and David Shichor. "Pioneering Innovations in Corrections: Shock Probation and Shock Parole." *Offender Rehabilitation* 3 (1978):113–122.
44. Solomon, Hassim M. *Community Corrections.* Boston: Holbrook, 1976.
45. Sternbach, J.C. "Philadelphia Probation Department In-service and Graduate Training Project—Project Evaluation. Summary." Harrisburg, PA: Governor's Justice Commission, 1975
46. Stratton, John. "A Training Approach for Probation Departments." *American Journal of Correction* 38 (January–February 1976):28–30.
47. United Nations. Department of Social Affairs. *Probation and Related Measures.* New York, 1951.
48. Vito, Gennaro F. and Harry E. Allen. "Shock Probation in Ohio: A Comparison of Outcomes." Unpublished paper, California State University, Long Beach and California State University, San Jose, no date.
49. Weller, Charles D. and John L. Flood. *An Operational Analysis of the Parole Task.* Boulder, CO: Western Interstate Commission for Higher Education, 1969.

Chapter 15

Parole

Parole is the administrative process through which imprisoned offenders are released to community supervision before the expiration of their maximum sentences. The release is decided by an administrative body known as the parole board, and it is the board which makes the final decision to reinstitutionalize a parolee who has either committed a new crime or failed to comply with the stated conditions of his or her parole. Community supervision is provided by parole officers operating out of units that often combine probation and parole functions.

THE DEVELOPMENT OF PAROLE

The two most important innovators in the area of parole are Alexander Maconochie and Sir Walter Crofton. Beginning in 1842, Maconochie used a ticket-of-leave system to release men on Norfolk Island, a penal colony five miles long off the coast of Australia. Prisoners granted tickets-of-leave were given group farms on which four to six prisoners cultivated six to ten acres of land. Prisoners worked for the privilege of receiving tickets-of-leave, and were also assigned marks for good behavior and work on the island. When 5000 marks were accumulated in a prisoner's account on Norfolk Island, the prisoner was released to freedom in Australia. Although a precursor of parole in a general sense, Maconochie's system lacked an essential element of parole: the freedom of the parolee to live in a normal community. Norfolk Island was not only an environment of limited size: it also containd no free society.[51] It must therefore be considered to have been a prison colony, albeit a humane one.

In 1854, Sir Walter Crofton developed a penal system in Ireland based on the principle of the ticket-of-leave. Prisoners released on tickets-of-leave were supervised either by the police (in rural districts) or by the Inspector of Released Prisoners (in Dublin). The offenders reported to the Inspector regularly, and in addition were visited in their homes twice a month. The Inspector also verified their employment. The system began in 1854, and then expanded after 1864 when prisoners aid societies were established. These societies were partially funded by the government, and employed what were in essence parole agents to supervise released offenders.[1] Because offenders in Crofton's system lived in the free community and were supervised by a government official, he is generally credited with having developed the first true parole system.

As we mentioned in Chapter 3, the first American use of parole occurred at Elmira Reformatory in 1876 under the direction of Z.E. Brockway. Like Crofton's system, the Elmira system required good behavior while incarcerated in order to earn conditional release to community supervision. There were regular reports to what were called guardians, and the reports were also monitored by Brockway. After six months of supervision, parolees were discharged; it was felt that a longer period of time would be discouraging to them.[23]

The Washington State Board of Prison Terms and Paroles

Parole is now used in every state and also for federal prisoners. As an illustration of the development of parole in these many jurisdictions, we will examine the case of the Washington State Board of Prison Terms and Paroles. A technical paper prepared for the Governor's Task Force on Decision-Making in Corrections[19] gathered together material on the Board from its conception through 1970.

Parole in the state of Washington began in 1899 when the governor was given the authority to authorize and regulate the paroling of prisoners, as well as to revoke paroles at any time. A Prison Board was created under the Indeterminate Sentencing Law of 1907. This Board dealt with the parole of prisoners from the state penitentiary, while parole at the reformatory was still administered directly by the governor. A full-time Board was not created until 1935. This Board consisted of three members appointed by the governor with the advice and consent of the Senate. The Board was empowered to set minimum terms, grant parole, hold disciplinary hearings, and make revocation decisions. All parole decisions in the state were to be under the control of this single Board.

The maximum sentence in each case was set by the judge or by statute, but the Board met with each prisoner within six months after admission to a correctional institution to set the minimum term of incarceration. Disciplinary hearings conducted by the Board were of a limited nature, and consisted of hearings at which the accused prisoners were allowed to present evidence and witnesses in their own behalf. Following each hearing, there was a determination as to whether or not the existing minimum term should be modified. "Good time" earned by prisoners for keeping their behavior within the regulations of the institution could be forfieted by the Board. The Board also had control over the setting of conditions of parole and the issuing of warrants for the taking of parole violators into custody.

The size of the Board was changed from three to five members in 1959, and the Board was authorized to transact business in panels of as few as two members. If the members of these panels did not agree on a decision, then the matter would go to the full Board. Until 1967, the Board had its own field staff that was in charge of the supervision of parolees, but Chapter 134 of the Laws of 1967 transferred that admnistrative responsibility to the newly créated Division of Probation and Parole within the Department of Institutions.

The continuing increase in the workload of the Board led to its increase from five to seven members in 1969. In 1971, these seven members held a total of 1641 admission hearings, 1726 progress hearings, 163 disciplinary hearings, 789 parole hearings, and 272 on-site revocation hearings. The average time per hearing was 30 minutes, except for the revocation hearings which were each scheduled for an entire day. The 30-minute average hearing length is misleading, for this included discussions before the prisoner was admitted to the hearing as well as decision-making after the hearing proper had been concluded. The average amount of time spent with each prisoner was probably no more than 15 minutes per hearing.[19]

A revised parole system in Washington was legislated in 1974. The Board of Prison Terms and Paroles was continued as it had been in the past. There were seven members appointed by the governor, who also selected one of these members to chair the Board. The Board was authorized to see only adult prisoners, with juveniles appearing before the Juvenile Review Board. The actual supervision of parolees in the community continued to be lodged in a separate administrative unit from the Board itself. That unit was now designated as the Department of Social and Health Services. Adult parolees were supervised through the Office of Adult Probation and Parole, and juveniles were supervised through the Bureau of Juvenile Rehabilitation.[29]

The most recent change in Washington parole practices has been the implementation of a set of guidelines that substantially reduces the decision-making authority of the Board of Prison Terms and Paroles. The Board continues to set minimum terms and to approve final release dates, but its actions are now governed by guidelines based on 13 offense categories. There are also specified allowances for either aggravated or mitigating circumstances.[28] These allowances are so specific and detailed that one wonders how long it will be before Washington legislators decide that discretion has been so extensively limited that there is no longer a need for a Board composed of seven full-time members whose salaries were set at a time when the Board's discretionary power was immense.

A NATIONAL PICTURE OF CONTEMPORARY PAROLE

Contemporary information on the status of parole nationally is found in the 1978 survey performed by the Uniform Parole Report project of the National Council on Crime and Delinquency. In this report, James Galvin[14] and his associates analyzed aggregate national parole statistics. They estimate that approximately 200,000 parolees (actually 185,000 parolees and 15,000 individuals on mandatory release under the jurisdiction of parole authorities) were active cases in the United States at the end of 1978. Somewhat more than half of these individuals entered parole during the year, with the remainder being carryovers from previous years. The South was the region having the highest rate of persons on parole, 90 per 100,000 residents. The North Central region had the lowest parole rate, 51 per 100,000. In between, the Northeast had a parole rate of 70 and the West had a parole rate of 87 per 100,000 individuals. Three jurisdictions had parole rates of more than 200 per 100,000 residents: Washington, 358; the District of Columbia, 246; and Kentucky, 232. Other states had extremely low parole rates, led by North Dakota at 21 and Iowa, Nebraska, and Rhode Island at 22.

A low parole rate may reflect a low crime rate, or it may reflect a tendency for felons to serve a relatively high proportion of their sentences in prison, the implementation of a new flat time sentencing law with no provision for parole, a policy of dealing with many felons by giving them a jail term followed by probation instead of a prison term followed by parole, or any one of a number of other policy possibilities. It is impossible to make any generalizations about the degree of social control exercised by the criminal justice system in a given jurisdiction based on a single statistic such as the parole rate. It is necessary to have several dozen indices of criminal justice system activities in order to have an overall view of the total social control pressure exerted by the system.

In reaction to the trend toward the abolition of parole, or at least of discretion exercised by the parole authority, which had become law in seven states by the end of 1978, many parole boards have moved to adopt guidelines limiting their own discretion. In some cases, legislatures have required parole boards to do so. A total of 23 jurisdictions had experienced some degree of reduction in their discretion by the end of 1978, and these jurisdictions accounted for 61 percent of all parole cases in the country.[15] There was a slowdown of legislative action to limit parole board discretion in 1979,[27] but it is not clear whether or not this is the beginning of a new trend.

An earlier report by Galvin and his associates[15] contains data on the characteristics of offenders admitted to parole in 1976. Ninety-four percent of the parolees were male, 48 percent were white, and their average age was 25.6 years. The median time served in prison on the current charge was 15.9 months, and only 26 percent of the parolees had been committed to prison prior to the current sentence. Most individuals released from prison were paroled, with a national average of 69 percent. The West had the highest percentage of parolees among prison releases (83 percent) and the South had the lowest percentage (58 percent).

DECISION-MAKING BY PAROLE BOARDS

The prisoner enters the hearing chamber and is seated. He does not know what the observer has already heard, which is that the Parole Board members have already decided to release him. Due to institutional infractions, his period of incarceration had been lengthened far beyond the minimum originally allowed in the sentence, and is now only a year or two from its maximum term permissable under the law. The prisoner's counselor has made some positive comments about his progress before his entrance, and repeats several of them now for his benefit. The two Parole Board members, one black, and one white, both men, gently ask him a few questions about what he is going to do upon release and how he has been doing in the institution. He is under tremendous emotional pressure, and fears that they will again fail to grant him his release as they have so many times in the past. He misinterprets several of their questions and, as he becomes increasingly agitated, gives socially inappropriate answers. He begins to appear as if he is "mentally ill," and perhaps even "dangerous." After he has left the hearing room, the Parole Board members change their minds, and decide they cannot release him into the free community. However, they indicate a willingness to transfer him to a mental institution or other appropriate non-penal facility in his home state, where he still has relatives, if an appropriate institution can be located.*

As a human drama, the parole board hearing rivals the operating room and the courtroom in intensity. A prisoner's freedom may be won or lost in a few minutes. How does the decision-making process actually work in parole boards? Before statistics began to be used in an attempt to predict parole outcomes, parole board members were completely on their own in making decisions. They looked at such factors as institutional behavior, the nature of the crime, community reaction to the crime, and the behavior of the offender during the hearing in making their decision. It is from these early practices that the myth continues among prisoners that it is possible, through an outstanding performance in a hearing, to obtain an underserved early release. Parole board members in most states still make decisions with some degree of discretion, but the magnitude of the discretion has been diminished by statistical prediction studies which have influence administrative practices in many states.

Federal Parole Decision-Making Guidelines

The Unites States Parole Commission has moved further than most other jurisdictions in the direction of limited discretion through the use of objective rating scales. Leslie Wilkins and Don Gottfredson directed a study of recent parole decisions of the Board, and used these data to construct a set of guidelines for decision-making.[17] Three variables were found to be outstanding in explaining previous Board decisions: (1) the seriousness of the offense; (2) the Board's estimate of the probability of recidivism; and (3) the institutional behavior of the prisoner. Institutional behavior was much less important than the first two variables, so it was dropped from the analysis, and a table of guidelines for parole decisions was constructed on the basis of the interaction of offense characteristics and offender characteristics, the latter making up a scale used to estimate the probability of recidivism.[49]

Three sets of guidelines were constructed, for adults, youth, and individuals committed under the Narcotic Addict Rehabilitation Act. The development of these aids to decision-making followed the recommendations of the National

---

*This hearing was observed by the author as part of his fact-finding activities as a member of the Governor's Task Force on Decision-Making in Corrections, State of Washington, 1973.

Advisory Commission on Criminal Justice Standards and Goals,[36] and it also made it possible to implement another recommendation made by the Commission, which was that "case-by-case decisionmaking should be done by hearing examiners responsible to the board who are familiar with its policies and knowledgeable about correctional programs."[36:418]

The estimate of the probability of recidivism in the decision-making matrix is based on nine characteristics: (1) number of prior convictions, (2) number of prior incarcerations, (3) age at first commitment, (4) commitment offense did not involve auto theft, (5) never having had parole revoked or committed a new offense while on parole, (6) no history of heroin, cocaine, or barbiturate dependence, (7) completed 12th grade or received GED, (8) worked or attended school for at least six months during the last two years in the Community, and (9) has a release plan to live with spouse and/or children. Scores on each of these factors range from zero to two, and are summed to create a total score ranging from zero to eleven. Prisoners having a score of zero to three are rated as poor risks; those having a score of four or five are rated as fair risks; those scoring six to eight are rated as good risks; and anyone receiving a score of more than eight is rated as a very good risk.

The dimension of severity of offense is broken down to six levels: low, low moderate, moderate, high, very high, and greatest. An immigration law violation is an example of an offense with low severity. The theft of a motor vehicle not for resale is an example of a moderately serious offense, while kidnapping is an example of a crime of the greatest severity. Once a hearing examiner has calculated the risk score and the offense severity score, the recommended period of total time served (including jail time) can be found in the decision-making matrix. In this matrix, adults with a very good prognosis who committed a moderate crime have a recommended sentence length of 12–16 months, but if their risk score is poor, the guideline is 24–30 months. The lowest guideline is 6–10 months (for someone who is a very good risk and who committed an offense of low severity) and the highest guideline is 55–66 months (for someone with a poor prognosis who committed a very serious crime). Values are not given in the matrix for those few offenders who committed crimes of the most extreme gravity, so those decisions are made on an individual basis.[21]

A study of the use of the guidelines by hearing examiners in the Northeast between October 1973 and March 1974 showed that examiners were making decisions above or below the guidelines in only eight percent of the cases, four percent above the guidelines and four percent below the guidelines. In addition, cases which had minimum sentences greater than the guideline range and those which had maximum sentences or mandatory release dates below the guideline range forced release times that were not consistent with the guidelines. This occurred in 28 percent of the cases, but it was not due to the decisions of the hearing examiners. When hearing examiners kept prisoners longer than specified by the guidelines, it was generally so that they could complete a specific training program or because of poor institutional conduct. When they released prisoners earlier than specified in the guidelines, it was usually because of outstanding institutional progress or because of the amount of time already served or to be served in state custody.[21]

The federal decision-making guidelines are admirable in that they bring order into a situation of confusion and inconsistency. The use of a formula sounds dehumanizing, but this effect is lessened when the parolling authority is allowed to deviate from the formula provided written reasons are given. Furthermore, the alternative to a formula is often the intrusion of conscious and subconscious prejudices and biases into the decision-making process. There is evidence from a study of two prisons in a Midwestern state that the parole board allowed its release decisions to be influenced by the reputation of the institution in which an offender was incarcerated.[43] In this same study, it was also found that the parole board gave the legal seriousness of the crime tremendous weight in making its decision and ignored information about the offender's adjustment and improvement while incarcerated.[41]

A study of 243 prisoners who appeared before the parole board in an Eastern correctional institution also found that biases crept into parole decision-making processes. Participation in treatment programs was not related to parole decisions for white prisoners, but it was the most important factor in parole decision for black prisoners. The nature of the offense had a moderate impact on black paroles, but no relationship with white paroles. Age was directly related to parole for whites, but inversely related to parole for blacks. These findings indicate a clear racial bias, which was probably based on the parole board members' reactions to what they perceived as the militancy of the prisoners before them. Blacks who were older or who had participated in treatment programs were seen as nonmilitant, and therefore were more likely to be granted paroles.[10]

An examination of the criteria for parole deferral use in New York State parole hearings during 1968, by Keith Hawkins,[20] revealed that there was a considerable difference between the criteria that the parole board members said they were using to decide cases in general and the criteria that they reported actually using in individual cases. They rated selling narcotics as the most important factor in deferring parole, but it was only fifth in influence in actual practice. The second most significant factor they named was committing a grave offense to support a drug habit; however, it was actually number nine in practice. The third was committing a grave offense against property: that was actually number eight in practice. The factors that actually had the greatest influence on parole deferrals were poor behavior at the parole hearing, and the opinion of the board members that release would have a negative effect on prison morale. Hawkins showed that there was great confusion between the criteria that board members said they were using in general and what they actually used in practice. In addition, the character of the factors actually used was so diverse and the factors so unsystematically organized that there was no consistency in the application of these factors from case to case.

The Gottfredson–Wilkins technique for clarifying parole decision-making criteria used in the development of the federal decision-making matrix was applied to seven states in the mid-1970s. Since this technique consists of gathering data on current decision-making criteria and using these data to formalize a decision-making plan for the guidance of future decisions, the exercises revealed the factors currently in use as decision-making criteria. There was no single factor that had significant influence in the parole decision of more than five out of the seven states. The most important factors, listed in order of decreasing significance, were as follows: (1) prior criminal record, (2) institutional discipline, (3) institutional program participation, (4) assaultive potential, (5) seriousness of offense, (6) social stability, (7) presence of a parole plan, (8) amount of time served to date, (9) community attitude toward the offender, and (10) number of prior parole hearings held. The last two of these factors were significant in only a single state, and factors seven and eight were significant in only two states.[18] These data convincingly show that factors likely to be used in judging the parole application of a prisoner will substantially differ from state to state. There is no national unanimity of opinion on the philosophy of parole.

THE SUBJECTIVE EXPERIENCES
OF THE PAROLEE

From the viewpoint of the prisoner, it is not always easy to guide one's behavior in order to maximize the possibility of a postive parole decision. To test out prisoner opinions of factors related to release, prisoners in two sociology classes taught by the author developed a list of 101 items that they thought might be related to either a positive or a negative decision by Parole Board members. The 26 items most commonly mentioned were then submitted to 240 prisoners, the entire prisoner population of one cell block at the Washington State Penitentiary. The 225 questionnaires that were returned are summarized in Table 15.1. In prison argot, a reduction of the minimum sentence to be served by the parole board is a "cut," and increase in the minimum sentence is a "flop." If a hearing results in neither an increase nor a decrease in the minimum sentence, it is a "no action" decision. The only two actions that prisoners felt were guaranteed to produce an increase in the minimum sentence at the next parole board hearing were assaulting an officer and attempting to escape from the institution. There were no activities that prisoners felt were sure to produce a reduction in the minimum sentence.

For many parole boards, the only decision is whether or not to parole, but the Board of Prison Terms and Paroles in Washington State has the power to set, increase, or decrease the minimum sentences served by prisoners, and may make these adjustments at any of the annual hearings conducted with each prisoner. Prisoners believed that a large number of items could possibly lead to an increase in the minimum sentence: the use of narcotics, selling items on the black market, cursing officers and engaging in other kinds of insubordination, and participating in homosexual activity. More items were associated with a possible decrease in the minimum sentence than with the possible increase in the minimum sentence. Some of the prisoners rather cynically believed that being a stool-pigeon and having influential friends outside the institution were important but all of the other factors were related to behavior within the institution. In 1970, the Washington State Penitentiary was strongly treatment-oriented, and had one of the most productive educational programs in the nation. Prisoners believed that the Parole Board supported participation in educational activities very strongly, and it gave the four highest ratings in the scale to doing well in high school, grade school, vocational training, and college. Each of these programs involved hundreds of prisoners in a total prisoner population of approximately 1000.

The prisoners in this study were generally dissatisfied with the operation of the

Table 15.1. Prisoner Ratings of 26 Items Relevant to Parole Board Action

Item	Rating[1]
1. Assaulting an officer.	1.4
2. Attempted escape.	1.5
3. Use of narcotics.	2.0
4. Wheeling and dealing (black market, etc.).	2.3
5. Cursing officers, insubordination.	2.4
6. Homosexuality.	2.5
7. Fighting in general.	2.6
8. Spending time in the hole (in segregation from the inmate population).	2.6
9. Having bad work reports.	2.7
10. Wearing hair too long.	3.0
11. Being unhealthy, often on the pill line.	3.1
12. Appealing your case, writing writs.	3.2
13. Having just a couple of tags (official reports of bad behavior).	3.3
14. Being a stool pigeon.	3.5
15. Being clean, no tags at all.	3.6
16. Being in Alcoholics Anonymous.	3.6
17. Being in group therapy.	3.6
18. Having a good attitude.	3.6
19. Having a good job (nurse, clerk, etc.).	3.7
20. Involved in club activities (Gavel Club, etc.).	3.7
21. Playing sports (football team, boxing, etc.).	3.7
22. Pressure from outside (influential friends).	3.7
23. Doing well in high school.	3.8
24. Doing well in grade school.	4.0
25. Doing well in vocational training.	4.0
26. Doing well in college.	4.1

[1]The ratings were scored 1.0 for a "sure flop," 2.0 for a "possible flop," 3.0 for a "no action," 4.0 for a "possible cut," and 5.0 for a "sure cut."
Source: Lee H. Bowker. "Prisoner Perceptions of Activities Relevant to Parole Board Action." *Volunteers in Corrections Newsletter* 2 (May 1975):11–18.

Board of Prison Terms and Paroles, and felt that many Parole Board decisions were unfairly made. When an institution is strongly treatment-oriented, it is natural for prisoners to expect that the parole board will strongly reward prisoners for progress made in rehabilitative programs. When they do not perceive this to be the case, they will judge the board to be unfair. We do not know exactly how the Parole board made its decisions in Washington during 1970, but data from 1975 show that the two most important factors were the seriousness of the offense and the prior criminal record of the offender. Institutional behavior in general, and program participation in particular, were not important factors in Parole Board decisions.[18] This was probably also true in 1970 and so it is likely that there was considerable confusion between the treatment-oriented ideology of the institution and the criminal record/offense seriousness orientation of the parole board.

James Beck[3] has recently compared the perceptions of prisoners participating in parole hearings in the Pennsylvania correctional system and the Federal

Bureau of Prisons. The Pennsylvania system is officially characterized as treatment-oriented, while the federal system has adopted a justice model of incarceration. Prisoners in Pennsylvania felt that they had more influence over the parole decision because there was a greater emphasis on behavioral improvements made while incarcerated. One might expect that the clear criteria used in the federal system would allow prisoners to predict the outcomes of parole hearings with greater accuracy than the outcomes of Pennsylvania hearings. This was not the case. As a matter of fact, the Pennsylvania prisoners predicted their hearing outcomes with slightly higher accuracy than federal prisoners (76 percent to 72 percent).

Another claim for the justice model is that prisoners are much more likely to perceive it as being fair than they would under the treatment model. This also was found to be untrue in Beck's study. Forty-eight percent of the Pennsylvania prisoners agreed that the parole process was "basically fair," as compared with only 20 percent of the federal prisoners sampled. Many of the federal prisoners complained about the use of the decision-making matrix because it did not make allowances for their institutional behavior and personal growth. It may be that parole decisions in Pennsylvania are sufficiently strongly based on institutional performance that many prisoners find them to be consistent with the treatment ethos, which reduces the amount of potential prisoner negativity about the fairness of parole decisions. Alternatively, they may prefer mercy to justice because they feel it will result in shorter periods of incarceration.

Release on Parole

As a prisoner's time for parole approaches, there is usually a substantial increase in anxiety. "Thoughts of getting out dominate the inmate's thinking, and time drags by in what sounds like an interminable and excruciating limbo."[33:28] A number of prisoners fear that they will be provoked into misbehavior that will delay their release. The tension is so great that it is often impossible to focus on making plans for life in the free community.[33] When asked what was the most important thing they did on their first day out of the institution, a sample of Canadian offenders mentioned such factors as being with family and relatives, enjoying freedom, and indulging in pleasures after the extended period of deprivation. Forty-six percent of the offenders said that they felt relieved and dazed, and depression, fear, or anxiety were mentioned by 31 percent as their main feelings. Between a third and a half of the parolees experienced difficulty in talking to people, loneliness, sleeplessness, feelings of looking like an ex-con, and having a hard time becoming accustomed to free life.[50] Young men in an American study often reported feeling left out because life had gone on without them and they were now excluded from it. Their friends had changed and they no longer fitted in. The lack of social involvement often led to feelings of boredom and meaninglessness as the novelty and excitement of the initial release wore off. Employment, family, and friends were strangely lacking as sources of positive experiences in the lives of these offenders.[33]

There is evidence from Canada,[26] England,[34] and the United States[7] that parolees have relatively positive attitudes towards their parole officers. They may be critical of many of the conditions of parole, but they do not necessarily view those conditions as having been caused by their parole officers. A California study showed that most parole conditions were almost never used by officers to violate parolees.[47] Black offenders in a second American study were more negative toward the police and the courts than white offenders, but they were equally supportive of the activities of parole officers.[7] Only 16 percent of the parolees in a British sample reported being annoyed because of the power of the supervising agents to recall them to prison should they fail to observe the conditions of parole.[34] Canadian parolees felt that guidance, support, and material aid provided through the supervising agent were important contributions to staying out of prison. Three-quarters of the offenders sampled felt that parole supervision made a difference in their "going straight."[26]

COMMUNITY SURVIVAL: THE EMPLOYMENT EXPERIENCE

No matter how good the preparation for parole in the correctional institution, and no matter how competent and helpful the parole officer, few parolees can hope to remain at liberty for long unless they can find a job. When Irvin Waller[50] asked 91 parolees how prospective employers reacted when they were told about the parolees' records, 29 of them said that they were turned down immediately; 39 were not immediately turned down, but no further information was requested; and 23 reported that their employers reacted by requesting further information about their criminal records. A number of prisoners tried to cover their time in prison in some job applications by fabricating jobs to explain the missing years in their employment histories. One useful technique was to claim that they worked for their fathers or were self-employed, so that the prospective employer could not track down their employment records. Other techniques used were inventing jobs in remote areas and claiming that they had been hospitalized.

Parolees applying for jobs are caught in a dilemma. If they admit to their criminal records at once, they may not be hired. There is always the hope that they can establish a good work record and then reveal their background at a later date when the company will no longer be concerned about it. Meanwhile, there is the danger that they will be fired for falsifying their application if something occurs to "blow their cover."[25] In addition to employer discrimination against ex-offenders, the parolee may be subject to legal barriers in connection with licensing and bonding.[46] A comprehensive study by the American Bar Association concluded in 1973 found an average of 39 statutory provisions per state that affected the licensing of anyone with a criminal record.[24] Bonding is required for many jobs, and there are cases in which employers require bonds for ex-offenders in positions for which individuals having no criminal record would not have to be bonded.

By 1979, approximately half of the states had changed legislation that was keeping ex-prisoners from working in certain jobs.[16] For example, Wisconsin placed individuals with criminal records under the protection of the State's Fair Employment Law in 1977. Since that time, it has no longer been possible for any

Wisconsin employer to discriminate arbitrarily againt ex-prisoners.[12] The federal government attempted to deal with the bonding problem by funding a bonding assistance program. The program was successful in that the loss ratio was lower than the ratios for comparable activities in the bonding industry in general, but the program resulted in only 6555 bonds over an eight-year period, a mere drop in the bucket of the need for ex-prisoner bonding.[46]

Despite these improvements, a recent study of the post-release employment of federal releases still found that the unemployment rate was between 25 and 30 percent. The average earnings of the parolees were around $7000 for the first year after release. Minority offenders had higher unemployment rates than whites, and earned salaries that were more than $3000 below the white employees' salaries. In addition to minority offenders, females, young offenders, and offenders with extensive criminal records were those encountering the most severe employment problems.[4] These ex-prisoner employment difficulties are not necessarily the product of their pre-prison problems. A recent analysis of a Baltimore parolee support program found that post-prison experiences had more impact on employment success than any other factors.[35]

In the late 1970s, there were more than 250 programs serving the employment needs of ex-prisoners in the United States. These programs differed widely in the training, support, and job placement services offered to the parolees. It is not known which services or what modes of service provision are the most effective in promoting ex-offender employment at this time. Most projects report that the majority of their clients have been successfully placed in a job, and comparisons generally indicate reduced recidivism in program clients as compared with nonprogram clients. Because the impact measures are usually quite limited, and the comparison groups are rarely perfectly matched with the client groups, these results must be considered to be tentative.[48]

One of the most innovative approaches is also the simplest: to give the ex-offender a certain amount of money per week for a limited period of time while job-hunting is occurring. A Washington program paying up to $55 per week for a maximum of 26 weeks was unable to show a significant decrease in recidivism rates,[13] although recidivists receiving the weekly stipends managed to maintain themselves longer in the community before recidivating than recidivists who did not receive stipends.[2] A California study providing up to $80 a week for 12 weeks was somewhat more successful, but the difference was too small to be statistically significant.[40] A third support study, LIFE, provided a group of Maryland releases with up to $60 per week for 13 weeks, producing a theft rate among these prisoners was 27 percent lower than the rate in a comparison group.[31]

A recent study published in the *American Sociological Review* evaluates the Transitional Aid Research Project (TARP) that was implemented in Texas and Georgia. Releases in the TARP program received $63 (in Texas) or $70 (in Georgia) per week and were divided into groups on the basis of length of payments (13 or 26 weeks) and employment tax (100% or 25% on all earnings over $8 per week in Texas and $13.75 per week in Georgia). The employment tax reduced the TARP payments over the $8 or $13.75 minimum level by either one dollar for every dollar earned (100% tax rate) or one dollar for every four dollars earned (a 25% tax rate). It was found that, in both Georgia and Texas, TARP payments tended to reduce the number of weeks worked by the releases, but also reduced the number of arrests for property and nonproperty crimes. Since employment also reduced arrests for property and nonproperty crimes, the TARP payments had a negative effect by reducing employment at the same time that they had a positive effect by reducing arrests for property and nonproperty crimes. For future experiments, the negative effect could be eliminated by completely removing the employment tax from the program or by actually increasing payments as an incentive for releases who become employed.[6] The TARP experiment provides convincing evidence that economic need is a factor in failure on parole, and that reducing economic need can result in increased parole success rates (and therefore a reduction in crimes committed in the community).

EX-OFFENDERS AS PAROLE WORKERS

We have already discussed the roles, training, and management of parole officers in Chapter 14. This section adds to that material by outlining the use of paraprofessionals in parole services, particularly paraprofessionasls who are ex-prisoners. The social services have been experiencing a trend toward the hiring—or at least the recruitment as volunteers—of indigenous paraprofessionals. These are individuals drawn from the group of successful clients—or if not ex-clients, then people from the same social class background and geographical area—as current clients. The major manifestation of this trend in correctional work has been the hiring of ex-prisoners by state and federal agencies.[5]

A survey of state and federal jurisdictions conducted under the sponsorship of the Experimental Manpower Laboratory for Corrections identified 240 ex-prisoners working in correctional agencies in 1974. The most common position was maintenance and service (68 ex-prisoners), followed by counseling (51 ex-prisoners) and line staff correctional officers (40 ex-prisoners). A few states, such as Illinois and West Virginia, have never probibited the employment of ex-prisoners in state agencies. The recent movement toward ex-prisoner paraprofessionals began in 1960, when California and Rhode Island implemented a policy of hiring prison released prisoners. At least another 18 states began to hire ex-prisoners between 1961 and 1969, and an additional eight states did so between 1970 and 1972.[44] By 1977, 315 ex-offenders were employed by state and federal correctional systems.[45] The move to employ ex-prisoners as paraprofessionals has not always been easy. When the officials of one California county proposed to hire paraprofessionals in the probation office, the regular probation officers filed suit to block the move and were supported by the state's professional probation organization in doing so.[37]

Two Models of the Use of Ex-Offenders in Community Supervision

One model for the involvement of ex-offenders in community supervision is based on the part-time concept of paraprofessional work, while the other more fully integrates the paraprofessionals in the supervising units as full-time workers. The part-time model was pioneered by the Probation Officer–Case Aide Program in Chicago, which began in 1971. In this project, ex-offenders were hired to supervise up to three probationers under the supervision of a regular probation officer. The project employed a total of 53 case aids who provided supervision to 161 probationers. The aides were matched to the probationers on the basis of race, class, drug and alcohol abuse, and other variables.[5]

Applicants for an aide position were interviewed by a selection committee and, if accepted, were given ten hours of training spread over four evening sessions. The exact number of hours worked by each aide varied according to the needs of the caseload, so salaries also varied from aide to aide. In contrast to the usual correctional problem of too small a number of minority employees, the Probation Officer–Case Aide Program received a large number of minority applicants, and experienced some difficulty in identifying white applicants for the program. The response of black probationers to black aides was particularly impressive. An subjective evaluation of the program included the statement that "the level of mutual support and client identification appeared to be unusually high."[5:14]

The full-time model of paraprofessional employment has been extensively publicized by the Ohio Parole Officer Aide Program. This program was implemented in 1972 by the Adult Parole Authority of the Ohio Department of Rehabilitation and Corrections. Each parole aide works full-time and is assigned a caseload of 30 parolees. It is expected that fully professional community supervision services will be delivered to these 30 clients by the aides. The only limitations on the aides are that they may not own or carry firearms, arrest parolees, transport arrested offenders, or assume responsibility for the sole supervision of parolees. The aides meet weekly with their senior parole officers and unit supervisors. In addition, the supervising officers visit the homes of parolees who are under the supervision of parole aides every month to validate information provided by the aides.[38]

The selection process for the Ohio aides is much more detailed than the process used to hire part-timers in the Chicago program. The initial interview is conducted by the ex-offender's former parole officer, and this is followed by interviews with the unit supervisor, the regional supervisor, and the project director.[8] Applicants who survive the interviewing process are involved in a training seminar that lasts two weeks. In addition to providing academic and practical materials relating to job performance, the seminars are used to break down barriers between the aides and their supervisors, to promote communication within the organization, and to develop a feeling of team membership.[38] Once they begin working, the aides are paid a modest salary approximately 15 percent below the regular parole officers.[8]

By 1974, there were 29 aides employed by the Ohio Adult Authority. Their caseloads were increased to 50 clients per aide.[42] Only 11 percent of the aides hired under the program were asked to resign because of inadequate job performance. By 1976, almost half of the aide positions had been converted to civil service positions permitting promotion to regular parole officer status. Two of the aides had already become officers, and others were motivated to move in that direction by the career ladder that had been created for them.[8]

Evaluations conducted of the Ohio Parole Officer Aide Program suggest the following conclusions.

1. Aides supervise more difficult clients than the regular officers.[42]
2. Aides terminate a higher percentage of cases than regular parole officers.[37]
3. Parolees under the supervision of aides are more likely to spend time in jail than parolees under the supervision of regular officers.[42]
4. Neither the recommendatons of aides, nor the way in which they gather data for the making of recommendations, differ from the job performance of regular parole officers.[38]
5. Unit supervisors have rated the effectiveness of parole officers and parole officer aides to be equal.[38]
6. Overall, parolees under the supervision of an aide are no more of a risk to the community than a similar group of parolees under the supervision of regular parole officers.[37]

It is rare that any correctional program receives as strong a level of support in careful evaluations as has been demonstrated for the use of ex-offenders in community supervision.

RECIDIVISM

It is common to hear people talk about recidivism rates of 30–50 percent for offenders processed by the criminal justice system. This is inaccurate, for figures developed by the Uniform Parole Report Project of the National Council on Crime and Delinquency show that only one out of every six offenders on parole has a negative outcome in the first year after release, and just over one out of every four has a negative outcome after three years in the free community. Negative outcomes include absconding for two months or more, being recommitted to prison for a new major conviction, and being returned to prison for a technical violation or a new minor conviction. Only one out of every eight offenders on parole is known to have committed a new crime in the first year after release. Only one out of every 33 is known to have committed a new violent crime—i.e.homicide, involuntary manslaughter, forcible rape, armed or unarmed robbery, or assault.[14] As a general impression of the operation of the criminal justice system, these statistics imply success much more than they do failure. One reason why people often overestimate the recidivism rate is that they focus on offenders released from the maximum security institutions and ignore all other offenders processed by the criminal justice system. Since the maximum security prisons stand at the end of a long series of filters—each one of which sends the worst risks on to the next stage of criminal justice system processing—it is natural that their recidivism rates will be much higher than the recidivism rates for offenders in general.

A second reason for the confusion about recidivism rates is that no one agrees on what recidivism means. Does it mean any return to prison, or only those returns based on the commission of a new crime? Should minor misdemeanors be included in the definition of recidivism, or only FBI index offenses? How do we differentiate between a "purely technical" violation of parole conditions and a violation that is actually a substitute for an unprosecuted crime committed in the community? How do we control for differences in parole officer, unit supervisor, and state policies on revocation when comparing different programs? There are literally dozens of technical problems associated with constructing an exact definition of recidivism that would permit fair comparisons between programs in different jurisdictions.

Another issue is the length of follow-up time that is used in the calculation of the recidivism rate. In general, the risk of rearrest is highest in the first year after release from a correctional institution, and declines steadily until it levels out after the fourth year. Even then, small percentages of offenders continue to be rearrested in each subsequent year.[22] A perfectly accurate estimate of total offender recidivism cannot be calculated until the entire cohort of offenders has died. Only then can we be sure that some of them will not commit additional crimes. The pressure to produce evaluation results usually means that a 12-month follow-up is taken as a sufficient measure of recidivism. It is entirely possible that some programs that appear to be only modestly successful at the end of the 12-month follow-up will have a more significant long-term effect, so that if the evaluation were extended to three or four years, they would be found to be outstandingly successful. Other programs may appear to be successful at the end of 12 months and might experience a ballooning of recidivism after that time, but this information is also lost when follow-up studies are limited to 12 months. Politicians are often unwilling to wait even 12 months to see if a program that "looks good" is actually lowering recidivism. They refund the program, perhaps with a considerable expansion of scope, before the initial evaluation results have been submitted.

Factors Associated with Recidivism

The myriad studies of recidivism that have been done in the last 50 years make it unfeasible to cite single examples here. There are a number of "studies of studies" available in which all known research studies meeting certain technical criteria are summarized in order to obtain an overall estimate of the relative impact of various offender characteristics or correctional treatment experiences upon recidivism. Douglas Lipton, Robert Martinson, and Judith Wilks[32] created a storm of controversy when they published *The Effectiveness of Correctional Treatment: A Survey of Treatment Evaluation Studies* in 1975 (See Chapter 10).

A survey of offender characteristics related to recidivism was published by David Pritchard[39] in 1979. He summarized the findings of studies of the recidivism of 177 independent samples of offenders, 138 being composed of parolees and 39 being probationers. The factor most commonly found to be related to recidivism in these samples was stability of employment, which was found to be significantly related to recidivism in 93 percent of the samples in which it was tested. The next two most important factors were a history of opiate use and the number of prior arrests, both of which were related to recidivism in 90 percent of the samples in which they were tested. Other factors of major importance were the number of prior adult convictions (85 percent), living arrangements (85 percent), a history of alcohol abuse (82 percent), the nature of the current offense (81 percent), and age at first arrest (81 percent). Those factors least likely to be associated with recidivism in the samples were the number of associates in a current offense (33 percent), a history of alcohol, but not abuse (38 percent), educational achievement (46 percent), and the number of dependents (47 percent). The reader should be cautioned that none of these factors was found in every study, so it should not be expected that any local sample of probationers or parolees will yield recidivism results exactly matching this general pattern.

There is a danger in approaching recidivism from the viewpoint of individual characteristics. When we do this, we are ignoring not only the differential impact of rehabilitative programs to which offenders may have been exposed but also the organization characteristics of the correctional agencies through which the offenders were processed.[51] Just as studies focusing on the background characteristics of individual offenders may miss the impact of rehabilitative programs on recidivism, studies which focus only on specific programs may miss the impact of more general organizational characteristics and broad trends in criminal justice processing.

An example of a more general (and a more policy-relevant) approach to recidivism is Daniel LeClair's[30] analysis of recidivism data in Massachusetts during the 1970s. His studies and investigations sponsored by the Massachusetts Department of Correction compared the effects of participation and various forms of community reintegration on recidivism. In order to avoid biases due to the selection of more promising offenders for community reintegration programs, the statistical analysis controlled for risk of recidivism using the Massachusetts Base–Expectancy tables. It was consistently found that prisoners participating in community reintegration programs, such as furloughs (while incarcerated), pre-release centers (after release from the institution), and the graduated movement of offenders from institution to institution within the Massachusetts system (which is discussed in Chapter 18) had lower rates of recidivism than prisoners who did not participate in community reintegration programs. Furthermore, as the proportion of offenders participating in community reintegration programs rose in the Massachusetts system, the overall recidivism rate systematically decreased. The decrease in recidivism was directly proportional to the number of individuals participating in these programs. The percentage of released offenders utilizing pre-release centers rose from none in 1971 to 42 percent in 1977, and the total state recidivism rate decreased from 25 percent to 15 percent during this period.

By juxtaposing various recidivism studies, LeClair shows us how to use recidivism data to develop and evaluate correctional policies on a macro level. He theorizes that the reintegration model undermines the negative effects of prisonization. At the same time, it fosters the development of community linkages that enhance the probability of successful adjustment when offenders are released into the free society. The strength of positive external influences peaks in the pre-release centers, and changes the post-release expectations of the offenders by locating them in work, education, and community-based treatment programs before they are completely released into the community. The transition to normal levels of freedom and responsibility is a gradual one which facilitates community reentry with minimum risk of recidivism.

SUMMARY

Parole is the administrative process through which imprisoned offenders are released to community supervision before the expiration of their maximum sentences. The release is decided by an administrative body known as the parole board, and it is the board that makes the final decision to reinstitutionalize a parolee who has either committed a new crime or failed to comply with the stated conditions of parole. Community supervision is provided by parole officers operating out of units that often combine probation and parole functions. Parole decision-making has, in the past, been subject to many subjective biases. In an attempt to rectify this situation, parole decision-making guidelines have been adopted in a number of correctional systems. Parolees often need a great deal of help in readjusting to free life, particularly in the area of employment. Unfortunately, high caseloads, funding limitations, and the law enforcement responsibilities of parole officers make it unlikely that they will be able to provide the employment support needed by their correctional clients. There is some evidence that the direct payment of unemployment benefits to prisoners for a period of time after their release would ease their transition to a normal employment pattern.

An examination of national recidivism statistics collected by the Uniform Parole Report Project of the National Council on Crime and Delinquency shows that successful outcomes occur for three out of every four prisoners released. People often overestimate the recidivism rate because they focus on offenders released from a small number of maximum security institutions rather than from all correctional institutions taken together. These institutions understandably have lower success rates because they house only the worst risks. Many research studies have been carried out using recidivism as the dependent variable, and these studies show that a number of background characteristics of offenders are related to the probability of success on parole. The evidence that specific institutional arrangements and treatment modalities can significantly affect success rates is less convincing. Unfortunately, differing definitions of recidivism are used in these studies, so it is difficult to make any general statements about them.

REFERENCES

1. Abadinsky, Howard. *Probation and Parole: Theory and Practice*. Englewood Cliffs, NJ: Prentice-Hall, 1977.
2. Ballard, Kelly B., Jr. "Adult Corrections Release Stipend Program: An Evaluation." Olympia, WA: Washington Department of Social Health Services, 1976.
3. Beck, James L. "Offender Perceptions of Parole Decision-Making." Unpublished paper, United States Bureau of Prisons, 1979.

4. Beck, James L. "Vocational Training Evaluation–Interim Report—'Finding a Job: The Post-Release Employment of Federal Parolees'." Unpublished paper, Federal Bureau of Prisons, 1979.

5. Beless, Donald W., William S. Pilcher, and Ellen J. Ryan. "Use of Indigenous Nonprofessionals in Probation and Parole." *Federal Probation* 36 (March 1972):10–15.

6. Berk, Richard A., Kenneth J. Lenihan, and Peter H. Rossi. "Crime and Poverty: Some Experimental Evidence From Ex-Offenders." *American Sociological Review* 45 (1980):766–786.

7. Berman, John J. "Parolees' Perception of the Justice System: Black–White Differences." *Criminology* 13 (1976):507–520.

8. Blew, Carol H. and Kenneth Carlson. *Only Ex-Offenders Need Apply: The Ohio Parole Officer Aide Program.* Washington, D.C. Government Printing Office, 1976.

9. Bowker, Lee H. "Prisoner Perceptions of Activities Relevant to Parole Board Action." *Volunteers in Corrections Newsletter* 2 (May 1975):11–18.

10. Carroll, Leo. "Racial Bias in the Decision to Grant Parole." *Law and Society Review* 11 (1976):93–107.

11. Carter, Robert M., Richard M. McGee, and E. Kim Nelson. *Corrections in America.* Philadelphia: J.B. Lippincott, 1975.

12. Center for Public Representation. "Employment Discrimination and the Ex-Offender." Madison, WI, no date.

13. Dightman, Cameron R. and Donald R. Johns. "The Adult Correction Release Stipend Program in Washington." *State Government* 47 (Winter 1974):32–36.

14. Galvin, James L. *et al. Characteristics of the Parole Population, 1977.* San Francisco: Research Center West, National Council on Crime and Delinquency, 1979.

15. Galvin, James L. *et al. Parole in the United States: 1978.* San Francisco: Research Center West, National Council on Crime and Delinquency, 1979.

16. Gilman, Andrew D. "Legal Barriers to Jobs are Slowly Disappearing." *Corrections Magazine* 5 (December 1979):68–72.

17. Gottfredson, Donald M. *et al. The Utilization of Experience in Parole Decision-Making: Summary Report.* Washington, D.C.: Government Printing Office, 1974.

18. Gottfredson, Donald M. *et al. Classification for Parole Decision Policy.* Washington, D.C.: Government Printing Office, 1978.

19. Governors Task Force on Decision-Making in Corrections. "A Brief Statutory History of the Washington State Board of Prison Terms and Parole." Seattle, WA, 1972.

20. Hawkins, Keith O. *Parole Selection: The American Experience.* Ph.D. Dissertation, University of Cambridge, Cambridge, England, 1971.

21. Hoffman, Peter B. and Lucille K. DeGrostin. "Parole Decision-Making: Structuring Discretion." *Federal Probation* 38 (December 1974):7–15.

22. Hoffman, Peter B. and Barbara Stone-Meierhoefer. "Post Release Arrest Experiences of Federal Prisoners: A Six-Year Follow-Up." *Journal of Criminal Justice* 7 (1979):193–216.

23. Hussey, Frederick A. and David Duffee. *Probation, Parole, and Community Field Services: Policy, Structure, and Process.* New York: Harper and Row, 1980.

24. Hunt, James W., James E. Bowers, and Neal Miller. *Law, Licenses, and the Offender's Right to Work.* Washington, D.C.: American Bar Association, National Clearinghouse on Offender Employment Restrictions, 1973.

25. Irwin, John. *The Felon.* Englewood Cliffs, NJ: Prentice-Hall, 1970.

26. James, Lois. *Prisoner's Perceptions of Parole: A Survey of the National Parole System Conducted in the Penitentiaries of Ontario, Canada.* Toronto: Centre of Criminology, University of Toronto, 1971.

27. Kannensohn, Michael. "A National Survey of Parole-Related Legislation Enacted During the 1979 Legislative Session." Washington, D.C.: Bureau of Justice Statistics, U.S. Department of Justice, 1979.

28. Krajick, Kevin. "Parole: Discretion is Out, Guidelines are In." *Corrections Magazine* 4 (December 1978):39–45.

29. Law Enforcement Assistance Administration. *State and Local Probation and Parole Systems.* Washington, D.C.: Government Printing Office, 1978.

30. LeClair, Daniel P. "Community-Base Reintegration: Some Theoretical Implications of Positive Research Findings." Unpublished paper, Massachusetts Department of Correction, 1979.

31. Lenihan, Kenneth J. *Unlocking the Second Gate: The Role of Financial Assistance in Reducing Recidivism Among Ex-Prisoners.* Washington, D.C.: U.S. Department of Labor, 1977.

32. Lipton, Douglas, Robert Martinson, and Judith Wilks. *The Effectiveness of Correctional Treatment: A Survey of Treatment Evaluation Studies.* New York: Praeger, 1975.

33. McArthur, A*. Verne. *Coming Out Cold.* Lexington, MA: D.C. Heath, 1974.

34. Morris, Pauline and Farida Beverly. *On License: A Study of Parole.* London: John Wiley and Sons, 1975.

35. Myers, Samuel L., Jr. "Work Experience, Criminal History, and Post-Prison Performance." Discussion paper No. 595–80, Institute for Research on Poverty, University of Wisconsin–Madison, 1980.

36. National Advisory Commission on Criminal Justice Standards and Goals. *Corrections.* Washington, D.C.: Government Printing Office, 1973.

37. Nelson, E. Kim, Howard Homart, and Nora Harlow. *Promising Strategies in Probation and Parole.* Washington, D.C.: Government Printing Office, 1978.

38. Priestino, Ramon R. *A Comparative Analysis of the Functioning of Ex-Offenders and Parole Officers as Parole Agents.* Ph.D. Dissertation, Ohio State University, 1976.

39. Pritchard, David A. "Stable Predictors of Recidivism: A Summary." *Criminology* 17 (1979):15–21.

40. Reinarman, Craig and Donald Miller. "Direct Financial Assistance to Parolees: A Promising Alternative in Correctional Programming." Research Report#55. Sacramento, CA: California Department of Corrections, 1975.

41. Scott, Joseph E. "The Use of Discretion in Determining the Severity of Punishment for Incarcerated Offenders." *Journal of Criminal Law and Criminology* 65 (1974):214–224.

42. Scott, Joseph E. *Ex-Offenders as Parole Officers.* Lexington, MA: D.C. Heath, 1975.

43. Scott, Joseph E. and Patricia J. Snider. "Effects of Different Perceptions of Penal Institutions on the Severity of Punishment." *In* I. Drapkin and E. Viano: *Victimology: A New Focus,* Vol. V. Lexington, MA: D.C. Heath, 1975, pp. 169–178.

44. Smith, Robert R., Larry F. Wood, and Michael A. Milan. *A Survey of Ex-Offender Employment Policies in American Correctional Agencies.* Montgomery, AL: Experimental Manpower Laboratory for Corrections, Rehabilitation Research Foundation, 1974.

45. Smith, Robert R. and Charles M. Petko. "An Updated Survey of Four Policies and

Practices in American Adult Corrections." *Journal of Criminal Justice* 8 (1980):123–128.

46. Stanley, David T. *Prisoners Among Us: The Problem of Parole.* Washington, D.C.: The Brookings Institution, 1976.

47. Star, Deborah and John E. Berecochea. "Rationalizing the Conditions of Parole: Some Recommended Changes." Research Report #58. Sacramento, CA: Department of Corrections, 1977.

48. Toborg, Mary A. *et al. The Transition From Prison to Employment: An Assessment of Community-Based Assistance Programs.* Washington, D.C.: Government Printing Office, 1978.

49. Travis, Lawrence F., III and Vincent O'Leary. *Changes in Sentencing and Parole Decision Making, 1976–78.* Albany, NY: National Parole Institutes, 1979.

50. Waller, Irvin. *Men Released From Prison.* Toronto: Centre of Criminology, University of Toronto, 1974.

51. White, Stephen. "Alexander Maconochie and the Development of Parole." *Journal of Criminal Law and Criminology* 67 (1976):72–88.

52. Wright, Kevin N. "An Examination of Recidivism Trends in Relation to Organizational Rather Than Program Differences." *Journal of Offender Counseling, Services and Rehabilitation* 4 (1979):63–80.

Chapter 16

Contemporary Community Corrections

Community corrections institutions are alternatives to traditional prisons in that they are located in local communities instead of remote areas, they are generally smaller in size, and they permit greater permeability between the community and institutional settings. Noninstitutional—or day—programs have the additional difference of having no residential requirements. Another distinction between community corrections and prisons is that community corrections programs are much more likely to be privately operated. This is not part of the technical definition of community corrections, but it is an important aspect. The private nature of many community corrections programs is probably the major reason why there is such wide diversity in community corrections, and it also has implications for correctional staffing.

PLANNING FOR COMMUNITY CORRECTIONS

Many community corrections agencies may be operated under private auspices, but most of the funding for the operation of these agencies comes from federal, state, and local governments. To bring order into the chaos of community corrections programming, it is necessary for government agencies to develop comprehensive detailed plans for service delivery. The *Unified Correctional Master Plan* developed by Ohio[52] in 1979 includes an extensive section on community corrections. The plan recognizes five categories of community placement: probation, shock probation, parole, shock parole, and furloughs. The plan proposes the diversion of 15 percent of the institutional placements into community corrections in addition to the use of community corrections for offenders who would not normally be placed in state correctional institutions. It also favors what it calls "judicial (probation-based) diversion" over the use of parole and furloughs wherever possible. The Ohio probation caseload is projected to rise from between 26,400 and 27,200 in 1980 to between 29,100 and 35,400 in 1995. In the same time period, the parole caseload is projected to decrease from 8000 to 6200.

A 1978 survey of community corrections in Ohio found that 90 persons were residing in four small state community corrections facilities and 370 persons were in private halfway houses. These individuals comprised less than 1.5 percent of all current community placements. Because of the reported success of these programs, Ohio's Unified Correctional Master Plan recommends increasing the halfway house client load to two percent of the community supervision population as quickly as possible. It also recommends a decrease in community supervision caseloads to 60 by 1985 and to 50 by 1990. The Ohio plan assumes that one-quarter of all diversions from institutional placement will spend an average of three months in a structured residence in the community.

These recommendations and projections require a considerable increase in the quality and quantity of existing community corrections programs in Ohio. The plan proposes to accomplish this through community corrections subsidies. In addition to the probation subsidy already existing in Ohio, the plan recommends a diversion subsidy and a service enrichment subsidy. The diversion subsidy program would pay local jurisdictions with state money for services such as intensive probation and halfway house placement for offenders diverted from state institutions, and the service enrichment subsidy would transfer funds to probation departments for reducing caseloads and to halfway houses and other community corrections programs for services approved by the state. The amount of the diversion subsidy money paid to each county would be dependent upon the decrease in commitments to state institutions coming from that county. The plan includes an estimate of the cost of the proposed diversion program as compared with the cost of building new institutions and operating them to house the expected increase in offenders in Ohio between 1980 and 1995. These calculations show that the implementation of the diversion program, even with subsidy payments taken into account, would save Ohio taxpayers between 70.6 and 80.4 million dollars, standardized to the 1979 value of the dollar.

As a point of comparison, we should look at a plan from a rural state with a small population. The Montana Department of Institutions,[49] following the directive of House Bill 483, developed a Correctional Alternatives Plan in early 1980 designed to provide alternative placements for prisoners in excess of the capacity of the Montana State Prison. The absolute capacity of the institution is 820 beds, and it is projected that this number will be surpassed sometime in 1983. The actual capacity of the institution is 672, but double bunking, the use of counselors' rooms, and other devices can raise this to 770, plus 50 additional beds at the Swan River Youth Forest Camp.

The Montana plan recommends that the Community Services Bureau, which was created in 1976, be expanded and allotted funds to contract for bed space with private community corrections programs. These programs cost approximately 30 percent less than the cost of incarceration at the Montana State Prison, and there is the additional savings that no further construction costs will be incurred by the state. The plan focuses on post-institutional community placement, assuming that probationers rarely need residential placement. The plan includes the recommendation that up to 100 residents per year be funded in community corrections agencies. There should be three regional pre-release centers in operation by 1985, and the Community Services Bureau should have sufficient funds to stimulate the private community-based corrections network in the state through purchase of service agreements. The Women's Life Skills Home in Billings should be expanded from 12 to 40 beds, and should be relocated to a more central location in the state. The work furlough program should be expanded, and should make extensive use of trained and properly supervised citizen volunteers.

Community Corrections in Minnesota

Correctional plans are useless unless they can be successfully implemented. Minnesota is an appropriate example of the implementation of a community corrections plan, because it was the first state to pass a community corrections act. Since 1973, single counties or adjacent counties working together to provide a full range of local correctional services can receive substantial subsidy grants from the state. Local correctional programs offered under the Community Corrections Act include probation, parole, prevention, pretrial, residential, detention, alcoholism treatment, and school drug-abuse programs. The subsidy level is determined by the crime level and economic affluence of the participating counties, with funds being subtracted for prisoners sent to state facilities on sentences of less than five years. Participation in the Minnesota program is optional, and the counties have only gradually initiated participation.[45] Twenty-seven of 87 counties were participating in early 1979,[14] and it was projected that 49 counties, containing 82 percent of the state's population, would be participating by the end of 1980.[60] By 1981, the number of participating counties was expected to rise to 53, and state payments under the program were projected to total 12 million dollars.[7]

One of the goals of the Minnesota plan was to decrease correctional costs. That goal had not been realized by 1980. The level of funding for the Department of Corrections and for payments under the Community Corrections Act increased every year through 1979. However, this could be expected as part of the changeover to local corrections. State institutions were still being maintained at former levels, and many counties were not yet participating in the program. The cost of funding parallel systems is bound to be higher than the cost of funding a single system. In the long run, since per diem costs for community corrections are much lower than per diem costs for institutional corrections in Minnesota as elsewhere, the program is expected to show a savings to the taxpayers of Minnesota.[45]

ADULT COMMUNITY CORRECTIONS

Adult community corrections can be divided into noninstitutional programs, partly institutional programs, and institutional settings. Noninstitutional programs include pretrial release programs and the use of sentencing alternatives

Figure 16.1 New Mexico prisoners rappel down cliffs of the Grand Canyon in a Wilderness Experience program aimed at turning around behavior that leads to crime. (Law Enforcement Assistance Administration.)

such as fines, restitution, and community service. Partly institutional programs are community programs for offenders presently housed in correctional facilities. Work-release, study-release, furloughs, and the Huber Law are partly institutional forms of community corrections. Institutional community corrections settings are facilities such as halfway houses, community treatment centers, and therapeutic communities. These facilities often house work- and study-release programs in which offenders spend most of the day in the community and return to the facility to spend the night; so they overlap with partly institutional programs. There is such a high degree of variation in these programs that any attempt at categorizing them results in a great many exceptions. Students should therefore be wary of applying these categories too strictly.

Pretrial Release Programs

Pretrial release programs are not technically a correctional matter, since they occur before a finding of guilty has been made by the court. We mention them only because they often involve the use of correctional facilities and programs. Bail and "release on own recognizance" are two common forms of pretrial release. There is also the possibility of supervised release, which is essentially supervison under probation that occurs before rather than after trial. The diversion of individuals away from the criminal justice system to employment, drug, alcohol, and mental illness projects may also occur at this point in the criminal justice processing sequence.

Fines, Restitution and Community Service

A fine is a payment of money to the state by an offender as a penalty for having broken the law. Fines as punishment for committed crimes discriminate strongly against the poor unless they are linked directly to the average daily earnings of offenders—as they are in Sweden. Offenders who are imprisoned for the nonpayment of fines are almost always too poor to have any choice in the matter. Permitting fines to be paid on an installment plan can greatly decrease the proportion of fined offenders who serve jail terms in lieu of payment. When installment payments for fines were legalized in England, the annual total of offenders imprisoned for nonpayment decreased from 79,583 in 1913 to 15,261 in 1923. Additional legislation requiring that the courts take the offenders' ability to pay into account resulted in the further reduction of imprisonment for the nonpayment of fines to 2646 in 1946.[64] Fines continue to be extensively used as punishment for minor crimes in the United States, but exact statistics on the prevalence of the practice are not available.

Restitution is the literal carrying out of the dictum of an eye for an eye and a tooth for a tooth. It is particularly applicable to economic offenses, in which the victim (which is often a business or the government) receives payment from the offender, perhaps routed through the courts so that there is no direct contact between aggressor and victim. Restitution is increasingly used in the United States, but is mandatory in only a few jurisdictions, such as Iowa.[9] In countries such as Sweden, Norway, Argentina, and Colombia, there is mandatory restitution for all offenders.[3] Restitution is normally built into the conditions of probation, but it may also be part of the programming in halfway houses and other community corrections facilities, and it has been used in pretrial diversion programs in several cities.[22]

The offender restitution program in Orleans Parish, Louisiana, began operation in 1977. This program provides for the possibility of monetary restitution, symbolic restitution, and community service by convicted criminals. Before being admitted to the program, offenders must be evaluated by the program's diagnostic unit. Once admitted to the program, they receive occupational counseling, are provided with a job, participate in educational programs, and have psychological services made available to them as needed. An individual participation plan is developed for each offender, and this is incorporated in an agreement signed by the offender and the sheriff. The amount and type of restitution to be made is part of the contract.[1]

The program initially developed in the local correctional institution, and then attempted to relocate in the larger community. When relocation became an issue, the support the program had received from community residents turned into opposition. After a number of false starts, the Orleans Parish Criminal

Sheriff's Office submitted a bid on an abandoned school. Although the bid was $10,000 above the minimum bid announced, and there were no other bidders, the school board decided to reject the offer because of "public policy." A suit was then filed against the school board, and it was eventually ruled that the property could not be disposed of except by sale to the bidder. The program moved into its new facility amid considerable local opposition from citizens, who did not want offenders living in their neighborhood.[1] Further information on this project is not yet available, so we cannot say whether the project will be able to overcome the community opposition in the long run.

Community service differs from restitution mainly in that services are provided to the state or nonprofit community service agencies rather than to an individual and that the services are rendered in-kind rather than through a monetary payment. As currently used in the United States, community service orders are for part-time work by offenders. It is assumed that these offenders will hold regular jobs and support themselves and their families in addition to doing the community service work in their spare time. We have yet to develop the full-time community service alternative that is recommended by G. Thomas Gitchoff.[23] He proposes the development of an Urban Ecology Corps that would plant trees in every open space throughout cities and the surrounding areas. The offenders in the Urban Ecology Corps would be supervised by volunteers and probation assistants, and student interns from universities would also provide volunteer supervision in the program. Such a program could save enough money, by sentencing offenders to the Urban Ecology Corps instead of to prison, to pay them a minimum wage.

One of the earliest community service programs was developed in West Germany in the late 1950s. This program required vandals to spend their leisure time working on projects of value to the community.[3] American community service programs date from 1966, when the Volunteer Bureau of Alameda County, California, established its Court Referral Program. This program concentrated on minor traffic offenders, and assigned more than half of its referrals to 40 or fewer hours of community work. England began experimenting with community service orders in 1972, and found them to be so successful in six experimental areas that they were extended to the entire nation in 1975.[5]

One of the most outstanding community service programs began in Multnomah County, Oregon, in 1972. The Alternative Community Service Program is administered by a supervisor working within the local courts. By 1976, the program was making 180 referrals per month and had placed offenders in 150 different community agencies. Any nonprofit agency supplying services to the general public is eligible to receive offenders from the program. Approximately 80 percent of the offenders sentenced to community service complete their work successfully, and the others are returned to the court to serve a traditional sentence (not necessarily incarceration) without any additional penalty for having failed in the Alternative Community Service Program. In its first four-and-one-half years of operation, the project provided 107 person-years of community service to community agencies by 8661 misdemeanants. Typical community service orders were 24 hours for a minor in possession of liquor or for possession of less than one ounce of marijuana, and 24–40 hours for the first offense of petty theft.[5]

The British system is also limited to part-time community service. Offenders working on community projects are supervised either by employees of the agency receiving the labor or by part-time supervisors attached to the probation unit. The emphasis in the program is in establishing a relationship between the offender and community members. The supervisor does not attend court for the breach action that occurs when offenders fail to complete their service order. In this case, offenders are reassigned to a work party supervised directly by someone out of the probation office, and it is only when this second alternative results in failure that there is a full presentation in court leading to reassignment through a traditional form of punishment. This keeps the supervisors at arms length from the criminal justice system in the eyes of the offenders. At the same time that the offenders are kept separate from the criminal justice system proper, the system is integrated more fully with the nonpunitive service community through the mechanism of community service. Close cooperation between criminal justice units and other community agencies is encouraged.[27]

Offenders accepted into the British program have not necessarily committed only minor or innocuous crimes. The average number of previous criminal offenses among offenders is four, and 42 percent of the cases evaluated in the early years had been imprisoned on a previous sentence. These individuals contributed an average of 120 hours of work to the community in their spare time, while also holding down regular jobs and supporting themselves and their families. Community service orders of more than 200 hours have been discouraged in this program because of the difficulty that offenders sometimes have in working through orders of greater length. Offenders involved in community service projects perform genuinely needed services for the poor, the elderly, young people, and other groups in need. A study of a run of 100 cases found that many of the offenders gained pride and satisfaction from their work. A quarter of them enjoyed their community service so much that they wished to carry on as volunteers after the completion of their sentence. A few obtained paid employment in social work programs, youth clubs, day centers, and criminal justice agencies as a result of their community service experiences.[27]

The community service program in the province of Saskatchewan, Canada is called the Fine Option Program. This program permits offenders who would otherwise spend time in jail because of inability to pay their fines to substitute community service that is credited against their fines at the current minimum wage rate. This program began in 1975, at which time two Fine Option agencies were opened within the province. These agencies were charged with developing work placements in suitable nonprofit organizations. By 1979, there were 160 Fine Option agencies in operation, and offenders were placed in an additional 150 agencies to carry out their community service work. After March 1977, offenders were given a brief description of the Fine Option program as part of their Notice of Fine. Any offender allowed to pay a fine on time rather than be required to pay it immediately had the option of choosing community service instead of a schedule of cash payments. In 1977–1978, 3.5 percent of all fine money assessed in Saskatchewan was paid through the Fine Option Program. A preliminary assessment of the impact of the program suggests that it has resulted in declines in the number of admissions to provincial correctional centers and in the total days of incarceration served.[29]

Community Corrections Programs Involving
Partial Institutionalization

Community corrections programs involving partial institutionalization often release offenders to work or study in the community during the day, but require that they return to a correctional institution to spend the night. Work release and training release are the most important types of these programs. An alternative form of partial institutional community corrections is the furlough, in which prisoners are given their freedom for specific periods of time, after which they must return to their home institution. Furloughs range in length from a day to a month or more, although few American offenders receive furloughs of longer than a weekend.

The Huber Law. The Huber Law was passed in Wisconsin[72] in 1913, and has been amended many times since that date. This early community corrections program is a prototype for the work release programs that later developed in the United States and abroad. In its current form, anyone who is sentenced to the county jail for a crime, nonpayment of a fine, or contempt of court may be released to work a normal 40-hour week, returning to the jail in the evenings and on weekends. The law no longer discriminates against women, and recognizes homemaking as a legitimate employment for which an offender should be released from the jail. Earnings accumulated by offenders are kept until release, and then given to them less a deduction for room and board at the jail.

Unlike many other programs that have been discussed in this text, the Huber Law is utilized for a significant portion of Wisconsin offenders. Fifty-seven percent of all persons sentenced to county jails in Wisconsin in 1976 were sentenced under the Huber Law or a related work-release statute. The total number of offenders working under these programs in 1976 was 4770, and an additional 437 offenders were released for participation in educational programs. The net income earned by these individuals was $1.7 million, approximately one-third of which was kept by the counties for room and board. Only 129 offenders had their privileges revoked by the courts during the year, which indicates that most offenders handle responsibilities of work combined with living in a correctional institution rather well.[72]

Work-Release. Offenders in work-release programs may be housed in the prisons in which they serve sentences or they may be moved to special community corrections facilities located close to the location of their jobs. A survey of prisoners on work-release during 1971 found that some states had not placed any prisoners on work-release, while others had placed as many as 20 percent of all male prisoners on work-release. The jurisdictions showing the highest use of work-release in 1971 were Delaware (20 percent of all prisoners), the District of Columbia (19 percent), Vermont (19 percent), South Carolina (18 percent), and Alaska (12 percent).[40]

Work-release is generally used in the final 6 or 12 months before release.[58] It therefore cannot constitute a grave risk to the community. Even if offenders abscond, it usually amounts to no more than a shortening of their sentences by a few months. There is also the additional risk to community that offenders on work-release may commit new offenses a few months earlier than they would have done had they served their full sentences behind bars. These risks are both extremely small. A study of work- and study-release placements in Wisconsin during 1973 and 1974 found that only 2.2 percent of the work-release placements ended in escape and 0.3 percent resulted in a new offense.[71] If the total impact of work-release on the 1140 offenders served in the program during 1973 and 1974 was to reduce the number of new crimes committed after release by three incidents, the program would have a net increase in community risk of zero; and if the projected crime reduction was more than three incidents, the net effect of the program would be to reduce the total community risk of suffering new criminal offenses.

Despite the relative safety of work-release programs, there are many states which exclude offenders thought to be dangerous from participating in work-release. A survey conducted in the early 1970s identified 20 states that excluded violent offenders from work-release programs, 18 that excluded sexual offenders, and smaller numbers of states excluding offenders who have been guilty of the sale or use of narcotics, notorious crimes, and being a participant in organized crime.[57] Community opposition to work-release programs has been so strong that many states with large penal populations place only a few offenders on work-release. A small number of violent incidents involving prisoners on work-release in California and New York resulted in severe reductions of work-release assignments in those states. There are many reports of resistance to work-release because of citizen fears of the potential menace of the releasees. There has also been resistance to the idea of permitting prisoners to hold jobs that might otherwise be available to free community members. Female prisoners in the Goree Unit located at Huntsville, Texas worked in a nearby plywood factory at one time, but the community resistance to this program forced its termination. The main point of opposition was not the dangerousness of the women but rather that their employment in the plywood factory was thought to be taking jobs away from local citizens.[54]

There is evidence from a number of different sources that work release is in trouble. A study of 188 Florida offenders on work-release and 93 offenders in a control group that was not exposed to work-release found that work-release was not associated with reductions in recidivism no matter how it was measured. Furthermore, there were no specific subgroups of prisoners for which work-release was effective.[67] Work-release programs operating out of isolated fortress prisons are limited because there are relatively few jobs available in surrounding communities. Jobs are easier to find in urban areas, but wages are low and the positions made available for offenders may offer little in the way of challenge or skill development.[57] Community opposition often limits the relocation of work-release programs from the releasing institution to community correctional institutions located in urban areas.[54] Finally, there is some evidence that the self-esteem of prisoners may be significantly lowered by experience on work-release. It may be that their experiences in the community reinforce their feelings of rejection by law-abiding citizens by exposing them to hostility and distrust.[66] These problems suggest that an intensive evaluation of work release and its effects on criminals and crime needs to be undertaken to provide guidance for the future use of this program.

Study-Release. Study-release—or training release, as it is sometimes called—is the same as work-release, except that offenders on study-release are exposed to educational experiences instead of work experiences. A 1974 survey of study-release programs by David Shichor and Harry Allen[62] found that 41 states, the Federal Bureau of Prisons, the District of Columbia, Guam, and Puerto Rico had study-release programs in operation. Almost all of these programs were implemented after 1965. One-third of the participants in study-release were in college programs, and nearly half were in vocational education programs. High school students and participants in adult basic education were few in number. As with work-release, many states prohibited certain types of offenders from participating in the program, most notably sex offenders and offenders who had committed notorious crimes or other crimes against persons. The national rate of absconding was approximately four offenders in every 100 placed on study release.

Furloughs. A furlough is a temporary release from confinement, generally considered to be overnight or longer. In the traditional maximum security prison, furloughs were granted only for extreme family emergencies such as the death of close relatives. Even in these cases, prisoners had to be accompanied by correctional officers for their entire time away from the correctional facility. Some states did not even make provision for furloughs under these exceptional conditions. The most recent survey of American furloughs identified 39 states with home furlough programs. States such as California use furloughs only at the end of institutional sentences, while states such as Washington allow furloughs to all minimum security residents who do not have pending detainers and who have served at least six months (90 days if their sentences are 12 months or less). Offenders in Washington may receive an unlimited number of furloughs, except that the total number of days on furlough in any given year may not exceed 60. The first and second furloughs will ordinarily be five days or less, and no single furlough may exceed 30 days.[32] Furloughs are used extensively in many foreign countries, including England, Scotland, Denmark, Switzerland, West Germany, and Greece.[13] Sweden has the most liberal furlough policy, with the first furlough being given after six months of imprisonment and a heavy use of furloughs throughout a prisoner's stay in order to counteract the negative effects of institutionalization.[28]

Recent research on furloughs suggests that they are rather successful in terms of low absconding rates and reduced recidivism. A survey of absconding rates in 28 states found that the highest rate of furlough violations in a large prison system was 2.5 percent in Ohio. Florida reported a violation rate of only two cases per thousand. Smaller prison systems experienced a greater amount of variation in the furlough violation rate, but this was related to the extremely small number of individuals placed on furlough in some of these jurisdictions.[19] E. Eugene Miller[46] has noted that if the violation rate is under 1.5 per 100, the screening process is probably too severe, and many appropriate applicants are being rejected. On the other hand, if the violation rate rises to 5 per 100, the screening process is not rejecting enough poor risks. From his viewpoint, the goal of screening for furloughs is to allow as many good risks to have the experience as possible rather than to minimize the use of furloughs so that only excellent risks are released.

Several recent studies[39,58] have shown that offenders who have experienced furloughs before being released are less likely to recidivate than offenders who have not experienced furloughs. Most correctional studies showing results such as these may be attacked because of the confounding effect of the selection process for program participation, but studies carried out in Massachusetts[39] and Washington, D.C.[58] were standardized for offender characteristics and were still able to show that furlough participation was associated with reduced recidivism. These hopeful results imply that furloughs could be more widely used than they are at present with a net benefit to the community.

COMMUNITY CORRECTIONS FACILITIES

Some community corrections programs provide housing in local communities and permit varying amounts of contact with the free society. Many of these programs are little more than urban bedroom communities out of which offenders attend work and educational activities. Others, such as some therapeutic communities, are as isolated from the free society as maximum security prisons. They differ from those prisons in the nature of their programs and in their heavier use of the community resources. The basic form of institutional community corrections is the halfway house, which accepts prisoners near the end of their sentences to help them be slowly reintegrated into the free community. Halfway houses may also be used in the place of sentences to penitentiaries and jails. In this case, offenders are halfway into the criminal justice system instead of halfway out of it. Another variation is the development of specialized community corrections facilities for drug addicts, alcoholics, women, and other groups with specific needs that might not be met in a general halfway house.

The development of the idea of the halfway house and the first attempts at opening halfway house facilities occurred in England and Ireland in the early 1800s.[12] The first documented American halfway house opened in 1864. This Boston residence was called the "Temporary Asylum for Discharged Female Prisoners."[61] The early halfway houses operated independently of the remainder of the correctional system. By the end of the 19th century, the halfway house movement had become large enough to make significant contributions to the welfare of ex-prisoners.[44] They then began a long period of decline that was accelerated by the Depression, the expansion of parole, and the adoption of a requirement that offenders have a job in the community before they could be released from a correctional facility. It was not until the 1950s that the halfway house movement began to recover.[61]

The new wave of halfway houses was similar to the earlier development of halfway houses in many ways. Both made heavy use of volunteers and many were sponsored by religious organizations. Their general concern with the reintegration of the ex-prisoner into the community was not bolstered by specific treatment programs. They operated as a buffer between the rigidities of correctional institutions and the freedom of life on the streets. Few halfway houses were closely associated with the correctional institutions from which they received prisoners.[44]

A survey of American halfway houses conducted in the mid-1970s identified approximately 400 facilities with a total bed capacity of 10,000 offenders. Since the average stay in these facilities was close to three months, this means that the capacity of the halfway house system was approximately 40,000 offenders per year. The largest halfway house identified in this survey contained 140 beds, and the smallest contained six beds.[61]

The halfway house movement has made significant strides internationally as well as in the United States. The International Halfway House Association was formed in 1964 to bring together practitioners working in halfway houses around the world. Canada introduced halfway houses for its federal prisoners in 1968. Halfway houses are widely used in Scandinavian correctional systems. Japan established its first halfway houses in the 1880s, and now has more than 200 halfway houses for adults and juveniles. These houses are operated by volunteer groups and officially recognized by the Minister of Justice. The average Japanese halfway house accommodates 23 offenders who generally work in the community during the day and return to the facility in the evening. Some of these halfway houses have sheltered workshops and are designed to meet the needs of individuals who are not yet able to work in the free community.[15]

Planning Halfway Houses

Individuals or community groups who are interested in starting halfway houses should begin by assessing the needs of offenders in their area in light of existing services. They need to locate funding sources and to understand funding mechanisms. Many groups will find it necessary to write formal grant proposals. A site for the facility must be selected, and community support courted. If community opposition to the proposed location of a new halfway house is strong enough, it may be necessary to consider the selection of an alternative site. Administrative and management patterns must be developed, including record-keeping systems. Programming should be developed on the basis of the need assessment performed at the beginning of the process, and must take existing services into account so that the halfway houses do not duplicate services that are already available to offenders in the community. Finally, an evaluation design should be built into the initial proposal for the halfway house. Evaluations are required for most forms of funding, and a superior design is a definite asset in the competition to secure scarce funds.[2]

Gaining public support is probably the most difficult problem that most halfway houses face in the early stages of their development. It is important to keep the number of residents small so that the local community does not fear being overwhelmed. Zoning laws, the availability of public transportation, and appropriate architecture are among the factors that must be investigated prior to the selection of a site. Architecture and appliances must be consistent with building codes and standards for health and public safety. One way that community opposition manifests itself is when the halfway house requires a zoning variance from the zoning regulations. Local community opposition at the hearing on the variance often pressures authorities to refuse to grant the variance, thus blocking the establishment of the halfway house at the selected site. A great deal of public relations work is necessary with community leaders and with residents in the neighborhood o the projected site of the halfway house. A steering committee of influential citizens should be formed to facilitate communication between the program and the community and also to reassure community members that community interests are being taken into account.[55]

One of the reasons why halfway houses often receive considerable community opposition may be pluralistic ignorance on the part of the citizens. A study of residents in the Spokane, Washington area found that only 39 percent of the citizens personally disapproved or strongly disapproved of the location of a halfway house or other community corrections facility in their own neighborhood, but 58 percent believed that their neighbors disapproved or strongly disapproved of the establishment of a halfway house or other community corrections facility in their neighborhood. The overestimation of the degree of opposition on the part of your neighbors may tend to increase your own opposition to community correction facilities in practice even if your general attitude toward community corrections is strongly positive. Respondents in the Spokane survey gave strong approval to four major community corrections programs: work-release (approved by 83 percent of the sample), training release (approved by 80 percent), halfway houses (approved by 70 percent), and pre-release centers (approved by 68 percent). The programs given the least support by the sample were furloughs (51 percent), diversion programs (41 percent), and probation subsidy (40 percent).[56] The strategy of convincing influential community leaders to make positive statements about a planned halfway house may be successful because it directly undermines the multiple ignorance of the citizens in which they selectively overestimate each other's opposition to halfway houses.

Patterns in the Utilization of Community Corrections Facilities

There is no single mechanism by which state or other public correctional agencies fund community corrections programs. The Federal Bureau of Prisons placed offenders in 400 private agencies in 1978. More than 60 percent of these agencies are private community corrections programs that receive funds on a per diem basis under a contract with the Federal Bureau of Prisons. Approximately 85 percent of the offenders sent to these community corrections programs have already served time in a federal prison. The others have either been committed directly from a federal court or are individuals who experienced difficulty on probation or parole and were placed in a residential community facility to avoid being incarcerated in a prison. The Federal Bureau of Prisons also operates its own chain of halfway houses, called Community Treatment Centers, in a number of major American cities.[50]

The Pennsylvania correctional system was operating 15 halfway houses in 1979, 12 for men and three for women. This was the maximum number allowable under state law. When additional community settings were needed, the Pennsylvania Bureau of Corrections contracted with community corrections facilities in the private sector. There were 18 such facilities complementing the 15 state community corrections facilities in 1979. The private sector facilities concentrated on serving offenders with drug or alcohol problems, a pattern also found in some other states.[50]

Nearly all Maryland releasees spend some time in community corrections centers at the end of their prison terms. The usual length of stay in the community facility is 90 days or less. Many Maryland prisoners are on the MAP (Mutual Agreement Programming) program, and these prisoners have their halfway house placements written into their MAP agreements. Maryland judges have the power to place offenders directly into halfway houses as an alternative to a prison term. Due to limited available facilities, the state Community Corrections Division tries to discourage this practice so that beds will be available for reintegrating felons who are approaching the end of their prison terms.[50]

Evaluations of Halfway Houses

A survey of halfway evaluations by Richard Seiter and his associates[61] comes to the following conclusions about the effectiveness of halfway houses:

1. Halfway houses are as effective in preventing criminal behavior as alternatives involving community release.
2. The opening of a halfway house in a community has no effect on property values.
3. Halfway houses are effective in assisting ex-prisoners in locating employment, but not necessarily in maintaining that employment.
4. Halfway houses are as successful at meeting the basic needs of their clients as other forms of release from incarceration.
5. When utilized at full capacity, halfway houses cost no more, and probably less than imprisonment. However, they cost more than parole or outright release.
6. Current per diem costs are inflated because the available capacity of halfway houses is only partially utilized. That is to say, many halfway houses are unable to fill all of their beds on a continuing basis.
7. By and large, evaluations that have been performed of halfway houses have not produced changes in the operation of those houses.

One other point should be added to these seven conclusions. This is that recidivism studies on the effects of halfway houses have been uneven to date, so that it is not possible to make a clear-cut statement that halfway houses reduce criminal recidivism. A recent evaluation of the federal community treatment centers shows that the centers are effective in finding employment for offenders, but there is no difference in recidivism. Offenders processed through the community treatment centers are as likely to be rearrested as offenders who have not been referred to community treatment centers.[4]

An evaluation of community corrections programs in Minnesota has produced rather positive results. This study found no significant differences in the recidivism rates of halfway house clients and comparison group members at the end of a six-month follow-up period, but the halfway house clients had a significantly lower rate of recidivism at the 12-month follow-up period. The effect of reduced recidivism also held at the 24-month follow-up period. One would expect that the short-term effects of the halfway houses would be greater than the long-term effects, so these results are rather puzzling. It may be that the long-term superior performance of offenders who have been processed through halfway houses is at least partially due to some factor other than the halfway houses themselves.[48]

Halfway Houses as Alternatives to Imprisonment

The Fort Des Moines community corrections facility in Iowa is an example of a halfway house that primarily serves offenders as an alternative to imprisonment. Only a small proportion of its clients are pre-release transfers. The others come to the program directly from the court. The program is located in a two-story army barracks on a military reservation. It uses an individualized approach for problem-solving, and provides one staff member for every two clients. An intensive evaluation is performed during the first two weeks of a client's stay in the program to determine educational, vocational, and psychiatric needs, following which a treatment plan is agreed upon and written up as a contract. The program makes extensive use of existing community agencies, and so has avoided having to make capital investments in its own facilities. All of the residents at Fort Des Moines hold regular jobs in the community and attend remedial education or vocational training programs.[36]

Security at the Fort Des Moines facility is minimal. There are no bars or fences, but there is close coordination with local law enforcement officials to monitor the behavior of program residents in the community. During 1972, there were ten escapes from the facility out of 148 resident admissions. As a result of the implementation of the Fort Des Moines program and other community corrections programs in Des Moines, the average daily population of the Polk County Jail decreased from 135 in 1970 to 75 in 1972 and 65 at the beginning of 1973.[36]

Community Corrections Programs for Women

The National Study of Correctional Programs for Women conducted by Ruth Glick and Virginia Neto[24] found that there was one woman in a community corrections program for every two imprisoned or jailed in the states they studied. Three types of programs were identified: halfway houses, treatment programs for drug abusers or alcoholics, and work-release centers. The main approach used in these programs was a realistic emphasis on jobs and survival skills. The heaviest use of psychotherapeutic techniques was in therapeutic communities for drug offenders.

Evaluations of community corrections programs for women in Washington[34] and Minnesota[59] suggest that community corrections has considerable potential for female offenders. Newgate for Women, a residential community corrections program in Minnesota, was successful in involving many of its clients in educational and vocational programs, and was associated with reduced recidivism, particularly among those women who completed the program.[59] The Women's Community Center in Washington was found to be more cost-effective than the Purdy Treatment Center (the state women's prison), and appeared to pose no greater risk to the community. None of the graduates of the center between April 1975 and December 1976 recidivated within six months of their release, as compared with a two percent recidivism rate six months after release for Purdy (which is itself an outstanding recidivism rate). Like Newgate for Women, the Women's Community Center concentrated on the employment and educational needs of its clients. It was very successful at maintaining family ties, and permitted women with minor-aged children to bring the youngsters into the center for day or overnight visits.[34]

Drug and Alcohol Treatment Programs

Community-based alcohol and drug treatment programs may be residential, or they may be day programs that provide services to correctional clients on an "outpatient" basis. A comparison of inpatient and outpatient treatment programs for alcoholics in Washington State found that there was no difference in outcome. Clients served by both inpatient and outpatient programs maintained total abstinence for a period of a year and a half in approximately one case out of five, and they engaged in frequent drinking in a slightly higher proportion of cases. Most clients fell in between these two extremes, being neither total successes nor total failures.[33]

A 1973 survey identified 597 community residential facilities for alcoholics in the United States and found that they were currently serving more than 10,000 clients.[51] People with alcohol problems who have not committed serious criminal offenses are increasingly being diverted away from the criminal justice system. Many individuals with alcohol problems may voluntarily consent to enter a community facility in return for an agreement to drop prosecution. Others are sent to these facilities by the court after being found guilty of an alcohol-related offense. Recent years have also seen a sharply increased use of detoxification facilities as an alternative to minor misdemeanor arrests for behavior related to drunkeness.

A treatment modality for drug addicts that has been increasingly used in the past decade is methadone maintenance. Methadone maintenance programs may include a brief period of intensive treatment during which the clients are stabilized at the appropriate dosage of methadone, and then they are released into the community. They initially report back to the methadone program on a daily basis to receive their prescribed amount of methadone and then are permitted to take methadone home with them so they don't have to report in as often. The more successful programs provide a wide range of economic and psychological support services in addition to the administration of the methadone.[10]

The classic community corrections drug treatment modality is the therapeutic community, in which ex-addicts serve as paraprofessional staff members who help current addicts to give up their drug dependence and to began to construct a new life for themselves. The most important milestone in the development of the therapeutic community for drug addicts occurred when Synanon House was opened in 1958. The model developed at Synanon House has been used in more recent treatment programs such as Daytop Village, Marathon House, and

Gaudenzia House.[21] Synanon's ex-addict staff members practice attack therapy to force newly admitted addicts to confront their problems squarely and to encourage them to put forth the immense effort that it takes to throw off addiction. The Synanon therapeutic community is essentially communal, with a pooling of funds and resources that are then distributed according to the needs of the program and its members. Having been addicts themselves, and having joined the program and shaken off their addictions, the leaders working with newly admitted addicts know all of the deceptions and manipulations used by addicts to perpetuate their dependence on drugs. They tolerate none of them, and new recruits who think they can manipulate the program by taking a few days off for a spree and then coming back to dry out find the door locked. One of the reasons that Synanon-type programs seem to work as well as they do is that the only addicts who stay with the program for an extended period of time are those who are strongly motivated to give up drugs and find new lives for themselves.[73] It is entirely possible that their success rates would fall to the level of government-sponsored prison drug programs if they had no control over intake and could not release program members who refuse to follow the rules.

COMMUNITY CORRECTIONS PROGRAMS FOR JUVENILES

Like community corrections programs for adults, juvenile community correctional programs vary in their degree of social control. Many of them make only minor alterations in the lives of juveniles, perhaps requiring them to attend a counseling session for an hour or two a day. Other programs provide full-day services, but permit the juveniles to return to their homes in the evening. There are also a number of different types of institutional community corrections programs for juveniles.

Home Detention and Group Homes

Home detention programs allow juveniles to live at home with their parents while they receive intensive counseling and supervision from youth workers. Some jurisdictions emphasize service delivery and others emphasize supervision. Some programs focus on providing services to the juveniles, and others try to provide services to the parents as well as to the youngsters themselves. These programs have the advantage of maintaining and strengthening family ties at the same time that they minimize expenses and avoid any negative effects that might occur from institutionalization.

The home detention program of the Metropolitan Social Services Department of Louisville and Jefferson County, Kentucky is designed to serve juveniles whose offenses are serious, but who have stable homes as well as those having committed less serious offenses. Home detention caseworkers have caseloads of five juveniles. This permits sufficient time for intensive supervision and counseling to be given to each juvenile. The program is estimated to have reduced the average juvenile population of the Louisville Detention Center by 12 youngsters per day, and the cost per child of home detention is only one-third of the cost of placement in the Detention Center.[43] The program was found to have a recidivism rate of 15 percent in a 1977 evaluation study.[30]

Slightly removed from home detention is the use of foster homes for youngsters who are capable of living in home situations but whose parents are not able to properly care for them. Foster home placements do not generally involve as high a level of support services from professional staff members as home detention programs. Foster parents who work with social agencies over an extended period of time develop considerable practical expertise in parenting youngsters who are in trouble. A foster home placement can become almost a permanent living situation for some youngsters, but other foster homes operate as holding facilities for youngsters while long-term placements are being arranged.

Group homes are an extension of foster homes in which parents become houseparents and operate their own mini-juvenile shelter facilities. The size of the group home varies according to the amount of space available in the homes of parents who agree to accept juveniles under the program. The Family Group Home Program in Florida began by adding five juveniles to existing families living in their own homes. It later modified the model to permit from one to nine children to be placed with each family. Since subsidies for expenses were minimal, Group Home parents were partly volunteers and partly paid staff members of the Florida Department of Health and Rehabilitative Services. All of the juveniles in each group home are assigned to the same counselor, who is also the liaison person between the parents and the Family Group Home Program. An evaluation report published in 1977 found that only 16 percent of the juveniles committed a new offense while living in a family group home, and the recidivism rate for youngsters 10–16 months after leaving the group homes was 28 percent. Placement in a group home had significant effects on most types of behavior problems. Truancy was reduced from 87 percent to 50 percent of the youngsters; the use of illegal drugs was reduced from 43 percent to 29 percent; the destruction of property was reduced from 36 percent to 15 percent; and abusive actions toward others were reduced from 54 percent to 39 percent of the juveniles.[20]

Attention Homes are group homes that are slightly more institutionalized than the homes in the Florida Family Group Home Program. They provide somewhat more structured activities for the youngsters, occupy residences that have been modified to accommodate somewhat larger groups of youngsters, and have live-in houseparents rather than being established in the homes of existing families. The first Attention Home was established in Boulder, Colorado in 1966. Other Attention Homes have been developed in small cities such as Helena and Anaconda, Montana.[74]

Juvenile Programs Requiring Less than Full-Day Attendance

These programs attempt to influence juveniles away from a continued career in delinquency without requiring them to be involved in some sort of program away from home and community for the entire day. The Big Brothers of Sussex

County, Delaware matches juveniles with volunteer Big Brothers and Big Sisters on a one-to-one basis. The volunteers engage the youngsters in informal activities and act as substitutes for missing or inadequate fathers and mothers in the juveniles' families.[68] The Community Arbitration Project of Anne Arundel County, Maryland, utilizes an arbitration hearing in a courtroom-like setting at which victims are present to work out constructive sentences such as community service, restitution, counseling, and special education programs. This program handles juvenile delinquents in a more humanistic way than traditional juvenile justice system processing, reduces the amount of criminal justice system resources expended per juvenile delinquent, increases the integration of the delinquents with the community, and was found to reduce the number of rearrests per client by 37 percent.[8]

Project New Pride in Denver, Colorado, uses somewhat higher levels of social control than the programs described above. Juveniles in Project New Pride receive intensive services including education in an alternative school or a learning disability center, job skills, counseling, and cultural education. Daily to weekly contact is maintained during the nine-month follow up.[37] Intensive supervision is carried out by counselors with caseloads of 10–15, and their services are supplemented by the extensive use of volunteers. Project New Pride attempts to place juveniles in new jobs, and pays their salaries in these jobs for the first three months of employment.[38] Taking all clients together, Project New Pride graduates had a rearrest rate that was 16 percent lower than the rearrest rate of a control group during a 12-month follow-up period. New Pride was successful in placing 70 percent of all clients in jobs, and the rearrest rate for these clients was only one-third of the rate for unemployed clients.[37] This indicates the centrality of employment in discouraging juvenile delinquents from continued antisocial behavior.

Full-Day Programs

A full-day program requires the presence of juvenile delinquents at a community facility or participation in work and education activities at specified community locations. A pioneer program of this nature was conducted at Provo, Utah in 1956. It required either gainful community employment or participation in school, plus daily group meetings utilizing the technique of guided group interaction. All group members as well as staff members were responsible for defining problems, finding solutions, and making release decisions for all of the juvenile delinquents in the program. The basic assumption of the Provo Project was to treat the delinquent group rather than to treat individual delinquents on a clinical basis. It was felt that peer influences were so important in the lives of juvenile delinquents that it would be impossible to modify their antisocial behavior successfully if they were treated only as individuals.[17]

The Provo Project was unusually successful, reducing the six-month recidivism rate from the 45–50 percent level that existed before implementation of the program to 27 percent of all delinquents assigned to the program and 16 percent of all the delinquents completing the program. Delinquents assigned to regular probation also improved their recidivism rate during this period, perhaps due to a sense of competition with the program or to changes in organizational procedures. In comparison, a second control group composed of incarcerated juveniles had a six-month recidivism rate of 58 percent.[16]

The Community Treatment Project of the California Youth Authority. The Community Treatment Project refers to a differential treatment experiment conducted between 1961 and 1969 and a differential setting experiment conducted between 1969 and 1974 with youngsters assigned to the California Youth Authority. The randomized assignment of juveniles either to experimental or control groups permits careful comparisons of the effects of the experimental programs tested. The basic plan of the differential treatment experiment involved classifying youths according to their level of maturity and matching them with parole officers thought to be particularly successful at meeting their needs. The officer–juvenile relationship was expected to extend over the entire length of time that the juvenile was associated with the project.[53] Caseloads were restricted to eight to ten juveniles per officer,[16] so that officers could have flexibility in meeting client needs, especially whenever emergencies arose. In addition to intensive supervision, youngsters in the experimental group could be placed in group homes or foster homes, a special education program administered by the project, and various recreational and social activities.[53]

It was found that neurotic delinquents performed much better in the experimental program than in the control group, the members of which received an institutional sentence followed by standard parole. In contrast, power-oriented youths did much better with traditional programing than the experimental program. Female juvenile delinquents appeared to perform equally well in both programs. This showed that no treatment modality could be expected to be equally successful with all kinds of juvenile delinquents. The experimental program was more expensive than the traditional program in the early 1960s, but the relative cost began to equalize in the late 1960s. If capital costs are included, institutional treatment is clearly more expensive than the intensive community supervision provided in the Community Treatment Project.[53]

The differential setting experiment attempted to identify youngsters who did not do well in the first experimental group and assigned them to an intensive residential program, following which they were released to the intensive Community Treatment Program. The same parole agent worked with the youngsters regardless of whether they were institutionalized or in the community. This experiment found that the initial period of intensive institutionalization was more successful with what the Youth Authority identified as troubled, troublesome, or resistant youth than direct placement in intensive community supervision. Once again, the challenge for the juvenile justice system is shown to be not merely providing the best program, but classifying juveniles appropriately so that they can be placed only in those programs in which they have the highest probability of success.[53]

Outward Bound-Type Programs. Programs specializing in the provision of wilderness experiences to challenge delinquent youth and develop their self-esteem first appeared in the United States in 1962, when the Colorado Outward Bound Program School was opened. The major elements of this program are mountaineering, backpacking, high-altitude camping, solo survival, and technical rock climbing.[3] Anecdotal evidence suggests that Outward Bound programs do result in positive attitudinal changes, but a limited evaluation of an Outward Bound course offered for the Colorado Department of Corrections found that participation in the program was not associated with increased success on parole.[70]

A water-based version of Outward Bound is the Jacksonville Marine Institute, which serves a maximum population of 36 boys and girls between the ages of 14½ and 17. The youngsters participating in the program live at home most of the time, including during the initial 30-day evaluation period. Youngsters remaining in the program after the evaluation take an average of two out-of-town trips per month, most of which are integrated with classes offered at the institute. These include taking sailing trips from Florida to the Bahamas, skin diving, and collecting marine specimens. The recidivism rate for youngsters completing the 30-day evaluation in the program was 20 percent, which was reduced to only 13 percent for those graduating from the program or terminating early to return to school or some other prosocial activity.[6]

Residential Community Corrections Programs for Juveniles

An early experiment in institutional community corrections for juveniles that has had an immense impact on the field is the Highfields Project, which was begun in New Jersey during 1950. Like the Provo program described earlier in this chapter, Highfields used guided group interaction in an attempt to treat the delinquent as a group member rather than as an individual. It differs from Provo in that it housed the boys overnight instead of returning them to their homes at the end of the day. Highfields appeared to be more successful with juvenile delinquents than the state reformatory at Annandale, but the experimental and control groups were not completely equivalent, so these results are open to some question. The second interesting finding is that Highfields was more successful with blacks than with whites. H. Ashley Weeks[69] attributes this to the impact of the acceptance of the black delinquents in the predominantly white guided interaction group. An alternative possibility is that the blacks may have been subcultural delinquents whose antisocial behavior was more fully a group phenomenon and less of an indication of psychosocial maladjustment than the behavior of the white delinquents.

Modern community corrections programs for juveniles vary in their characteristics and their client populations. Some operate much like halfway houses for adults, accepting only clients who are referred from juvenile reformatories and other secure facilities. Others exist more as an alternative to juvenile incarceration in a traditional correctional facility. Houses for runaways are residential facilities that deal as much with prevention as with corrections. Many facilities accept different types of youngsters and mix them together, so that character of client population changes from week to week.

One of the most unusual residential programs for juveniles is Elan, a therapeutic community for troubled hard-core delinquent youth. Elan grew rapidly from 13 juveniles and two staff members in 1971 to a six-unit national operation housing 250 residents and employing 100 staff members in 1979. It utilizes attack therapy on the Synanon model and bizarre punishments to curb impulsive and self-destructive behavior. Personalities are subjected to intense pressures from peers and staff members, and are virtually torn down and rebuilt within the program. There is some informal evidence that Elan is successful with those youngsters that stay with the program until they are released, but there has not been a full evaluation by researchers outside of the organization.[63]

COMMUNITY CORRECTIONS AS A WIDENING OF THE NET

There is considerable evidence that the implementation of a wide range of corrections programs (which are considered to be more humane than traditional institutionalization) has resulted in a widening of the social control net cast by the criminal justice system. Because the community programs are considered to be less damaging than traditional institutional programs, judges are more willing to use them in borderline cases. Instead of serving as a direct alternative to institutionalization, these community programs tend to be used for offenders who would otherwise not have been sentenced to any type of a formal intervention in their lives. In the meantime, institutional populations rarely diminish as a result of the expansion of community corrections programs. They more typically continue to rise at the same time that the number of offenders committed to community corrections programs is rapidly multiplying.[11,25,35,41,47]

Although programs described in this chapter have generally been shown to have positive results, it is also possible for the rapid expansion of community corrections programs to greatly increase the social control span of the criminal justice system *without* decreasing recidivism.[18] Although rates of institutionalization can be shown to have declined in certain types of institutions between 1950 and 1975, Paul Lerman[42] points out that shifts away from certain kinds of institutions have been accompanied by increases in the use of other types of institutions. He believes that the net result of these shifts has been that the total rate of commitment per 100,000 youth was probably higher in 1975 than in 1950.

The association of community corrections with a widening social control net is not unique to the United States. It appears to be true in Australia[65] and in Canada.[26,31] John Hylton[31] found that the development of community corrections programs in Saskatchewan was associated with an increase in the proportion of the total population coming under some form of state supervision. The caseload in Saskatchewan's probation units rose from 277 in 1962 to 2283 in 1977. Community treatment residences opened in 1974 and had an average caseload of 63 residents by 1977. The average daily institutional population was only 506 in 1962, and rose slowly and unevenly to 643 in 1969, when the major expansion in community corrections began. Although it temporarily decreased, it rose to 743 in 1977. Total admissions to the Saskatchewan correctional system rose from 4396 in 1962 to 11,232 in 1977. One might argue (without evidence) that the expansion of the institutional population would have been far greater had it not been for the development of community corrections during this period, but it is clear that a vast increase in community corrections supervision was not associated with a decrease in the institutionalized population.

SUMMARY

Community corrections institutions are alternatives to traditional prisons in that they are located in local communities instead of remote areas, they are generally smaller in size, and they permit greater permeability between the community and institutional settings. In addition, community corrections includes noninstitutional—or day—programs that have the additional difference of having no residential requirements. The diversity of community corrections programs requires a level of planning and coordination for maximum efficiency that has not yet been attained in most states. Adult community corrections programs include pretrial release programs, fines, restitution, and community service; community corrections institutions such as halfway houses and Synanon-type therapeutic communities for drug users; and programs that grant temporary release to prisoners, such as work-release, study-release, and furloughs. There are a large number of specialized community corrections programs for juveniles, but relatively few programs for women and racial or cultural minorities. Programs for juveniles include home detention, group homes, foster homes, attention homes, day programs, and Outward Bound-type programs.

A major concern in community corrections is that many programs that were intended to divert offenders from institutional treatment have instead served to widen the net of the criminal justice system. That is to say, many more offenders are now being subjected to correctional processing than was the case when the only alternatives were imprisonment or no supervision at all. Judges who previously felt that the extreme control of a correctional institution was not merited in a case and so released the offender can now select from a variety of community corrections alternatives that subject offenders to less rigorous conditions while maintaining some degree of criminal justice system control.

REFERENCES

1. Alarcon, Terry Q. "The Orleans Parish Offender Restitution Program: A Case Study." Unpublished paper, Orleans Parish District Attorney's Office, 1979.
2. Allen, Harry E. *et al. Halfway Houses.* Washington, D.C.: Government Printing Office, 1978.
3. Alper, Benedict S. *Prisons Inside-Out: Alternatives in Correctional Reform.* Cambridge, MA: Ballinger, 1974.
4. Beck, James L. "An Evaluation of Federal Community Treatment Centers." *Federal Probation* 43 (September 1979):36–39.
5. Beha, James, Kenneth Carlson, and Robert H. Rosenblum. *Sentencing to Community Service.* Washington, D.C.: Government Printing Office, 1977.
6. Berry, R. Stephen and Allan N. Learch. "Victory at Sea: A Marine Approach to Rehabilitation." *Federal Probation* 43 (March 1979):44–47.
7. Blackmore, John. "Minnesota Community Corrections Act Takes Hold." *Corrections Magazine* 4 (March 1978):46–54.

8. Blew, Carol H. and Robert Rosenblum. *The Community Arbitration Project, Anne Arundel County Maryland.* Washington, D.C.: Government Printing Office, 1979.

9. Boorkman, David, *et al. Community-Based Corrections in Des Moines.* Washington, D.C.: Government Printing Office, 1976.

10. Brecher, Edward M. *Methadone Treatment Manual.* Washington, D.C.: Government Printing Office, 1973.

11. Bullington, Bruce *et al.* "A Critique of Diversionary Justice." *Crime and Delinquency* 4 (1978):59–71.

12. Carlson, Eric W. and Richard P. Seiter. "Residential Inmate Aftercare: The State of the Art." *Offender Rehabilitation* 1 (1977):381–394.

13. Cavan, Ruth S. and Eugene S. Zemans. "Marital Relationships of Prisoners in Twenty-Eight Countries." *Journal of Criminal, Criminology and Police Science* 49 (1958):133–139.

14. "Community Corrections: Where They Belong." *Jericho* 18 (Fall 1979):4–5.

15. Dodge, Calvert R. *A World Without Prisons.* Lexington, MA: D.C. Heath, 1979.

16. Empey, LaMar T. *Alternatives to Incarceration.* Washington, D.C.: Government Printing Office, 1967.

17. Empey, LaMar T. and Jerome Rabow. "The Provo Experiment in Delinquency Rehabilitation." *American Sociological Review* 26 (1961):679–696.

18. Fishman, Robert. "An Evaluation of Criminal Recidivism in Projects Providing Rehabilitation and Diversion Services in New York City." *Journal of Criminal Law and Criminology* 68 (1977):283–305.

19. Florida. Division of Corrections. "Furlough Programs—National Survey." Tallahasee, 1973.

20. Florida. Department of Health and Rehabilitation Services. "Evaluation of Florida's Family Group Home Program, 1975–76." Tallahassee, 1977.

21. Fox, Vernon. *Community-Based Corrections.* Englewood Cliffs, NJ: Prentice-Hall, 1977.

22. Galaway, Burt. "The Use of Restitution." *Crime and Delinquency* 23 (1977):57–67.

23. Gitchoff, G. Thomas. "Socio-Economic Sentencing Alternatives." *Criminal Justice Columns* 4 (2)(1980):3–7.

24. Glick, Ruth M. and Virginia Neto. *National Study of Women's Correctional Programs.* Washington, D.C.: Government Printing Office, 1977.

25. Greenberg, David. "Problems in Community Corrections." *Issues in Criminology* 10 (1975):1–33.

26. Hackler, James C. *The Prevention of Youthful Crime: The Great Stumble Forward.* Toronto: Methuen, 1978.

27. Harding, John. "The Development of Community Service: Its Application and Relevance to the Criminal Justice System." *In* Norman Tutt: *Alternative Strategies for Coping with Crime.* Oxford, England: Basil Blackwell, 1978, pp. 164–185.

28. Hassin, Yael. "Prisoners' Furlough: A Reassessment." *International Journal of Criminology and Penology* 5 (1977):171–178.

29. Heath, Margery. "The Fine Option Program: An Alternative to Prisons for Fine Defaulters." *Federal Probation* 43 (September 1979):22–27.

30. Hildenbrand, T.A. "Louisville/Jefferson County (KY)—Metropolitan Social Services Department—An Evaluation of Home Detention, May, 1977." Louisville, KY: Kentucky Metropolitan Social Services Department, 1977.

31. Hylton, John H. *Reintegrating the Offender: Assessing the Impact of Community Corrections.* D.S.W. Dissertation, University of California, Berkley, 1978.

32. "I'll Be Home for Christmas." *Corrections Compendium* 4 (December 1979):1–7.
33. Johnson, Gary W. and Renia Dagadakis. "Follow-up Drinking Status of Persons Treated in Inpatient and Outpatient Treatment Programs in Washington State." Olympia, WA: Department of Social and Health Services, 1978.
34. Johnson, Robyn L. "Project Evaluation: Women's Community Center." Olympia, WA: Department of Social and Health Services, 1977.
35. Klein, Malcolm W. "Deinstitutionalization and Diversion of Juvenile Offenders: A Litany of Impediments." *In* Norval Morris and Michael Tonry: *Crime and Justice: An Annual Review of Research,* Vol. 1. Chicago: University of Chicago Press, 1979, pp. 145–201.
36. Law Enforcement Assistance Administration. "Community Based Corrections in Des Moines." Washington, D.C.: Government Printing Office, 1973.
37. Law Enforcement Assistance Administration. "Project New Pride, Denver, Colorado." Washington, D.C.: Government Printing Office, 1977.
38. Law Enforcement Assistance Administration. *Project New Pride: Replication.* Washington, D.C.: Government Printing Office, 1979.
39. LeClair, Daniel P. "Community-based Reintegration: Some Theoretical Implications of Positive Research Findings." Unpublished paper, Massachusetts Department of Corrections, 1979.
40. Lenihan, Kenneth J. "The Financial Condition of Released Prisoners." *Crime and Delinquency* 21 (1975):266–281.
41. Lerman, Paul. *Community Treatment and Social Control: A Critical Analysis of Juvenile Correctional Policy.* Chicago: University of Chicago Press, 1975.
42. Lerman, Paul. "Trends and Issues in the Deinstitutionalization of Youths in Trouble." *Crime and Delinquency* 26 (1980):281–298.
43. Louisville/Jefferson Counties Metropolitan Social Services Department. "Louisville-/Jefferson (KY)—Metropolitan Social Services Department—Home Detention—A Preliminary Evaluation." Louisville, KY, 1976.
44. McCartt, John M. and Thomas J. Mangogna. *Guidelines and Standards for Halfway Houses and Community Treatment Centers.* Washington, D.C.: Government Printing Office, 1973.
45. McSparron, James. "Community Correction and Diversion." *Crime and Delinquency* 26 (1980):226–247.
46. Miller, E. Eugene. "Furloughs as a Technique of Reintegration." *In* E. Eugene Miller and M. Robert Montilla: *Corrections in the Community: Success Models in Correctional Reform.* Reston, VA: Reston Publishing Co., 1977, pp. 201–209.
47. Minnesota. Department of Corrections. "The Effect of the Availability of Community Residential Alternatives to State Incarceration on Sentencing Practices: The Social Control Issue." St. Paul, 1977.
48. Minnesota. Governor's Commission on Crime Prevention and Control. *Residential Community Corrections Programs in Minnesota: Summary and Recommendations.* St. Paul, MN, 1977.
49. Montana. Department of Institutions. "Correctional Alternatives." Helena, 1980.
50. Morgenbesser, Lenard I. "Utilization of Private-Sector Community Correctional Organizations by State Correctional Agencies." Albany, NY: Department of Correctional Services, 1979.
51. Noble, Ernest P. "The Role of Halfway Houses in the Rehabilitation of Alcoholics." Statement submitted to the Subcommittee on Alcoholism and Drug Abuse, Committee on Human Resources, United States Senate, July 27, 1977.

52. Ohio. Department of Rehabilitation and Correction. *Unified Correctional Master Plan*. Columbus, 1979.

53. Palmer, Ted. "The Youth Authority's Treatment Project." *Federal Probation* 38 (March 1974):3–14.

54. Potter, Joan. "Will Work-Release Ever Fulfill Its Promise?" *Corrections Magazine* 5 (June 1979):61–65.

55. Rachin, Richard L. "So You Want to Open a Halfway House." *Federal Probation* 36 (March 1972):30–37.

56. Roll, Herbert W. "Social Correlates of Public Attitudes Toward Community Based Corrections Programs." Paper presented at the annual meeting of the Western Society of Criminology, 1977.

57. Root, Lawrence S. "State Work Release Programs: An Analysis of Operational Policies." *Federal Probation* 37 (December 1973):52–58.

58. Ross, Debbie and Phil Ojalvo. "The Impact of Furloughs on Recidivism." Washington, D.C.: D.C. Department of Corrections, 1979.

59. Sadacca, Mark. *Newgate for Women: An Evaluation of a Community Corrections Program for Women Offenders*. St. Paul, MN: Minnesota Crime Control Planning Board, 1977.

60. Schoen, Kenneth F. "The Community Corrections Act." *Crime and Delinquency* 24 (1978):458–464.

61. Seiter, Richard P. *et al. Halfway Houses*. Washington, D.C.: Government Printing Office, 1977.

62. Shichor, David and Harry E. Allen. "Study-Release: A Correctional Alternative." *Offender Rehabilitation* 2 (1977):7–17.

63. Taft, Philip B., Jr. "Elan." *Corrections Magazine* 5 (1979):18–28.

64. Tappan, Paul W. *Crime, Justice and Correction*. New York: McGraw-Hill, 1960.

65. Tomasic, Roman and Ian Dobinson. *The Failure of Imprisonment: An Australian Perspective*. Sydney, Australia: George Allen and Unwin, 1979.

66. Waldo, Gordon P., Theodore G. Chiricos, and Leonard E. Dobrin. "Community Contact and Inmate Attitudes: An Experimental Assessment of Work Release." *Criminology* 11 (1973):345–381.

67. Waldo, Gordon P. and Theodore G. Chiricos. "Work Release and Recidivism: An Empirical Evaluation of a Social Policy." *Evaluation Quarterly* 1 (1977):87–107.

68. Webb, W. "Big Brothers of Sussex County—Big Brothers of Delaware—A Project Evaluation." Wilmington, DE: Delaware Criminal Justice Planning Commission, 1976.

69. Weeks, H. Ashley. *Youthful Offenders at Highfields: An Evaluation of the Effects of the Short-Term Treatment of Delinquent Boys*. Ann Arbor, MI: University of Michigan Press, 1958.

70. Winterfield, Laura. "Evaluation of Outward Bound." Denver, CO: Colorado Department of Corrections, 1979.

71. Wisconsin. Department of Health and Social Services. "Work Release Study Release Program, Calendar Years 1973 and 1974." Madison, 1977.

72. Wisconsin. Department of Health and Social Services. "Huber Law and Work Release Programs, 1976." Madison, 1978.

73. Yablonski, Lewis. *The Tunnel Back: Synanon*. New York: Macmillan, 1965.

74. Young, Thomas M. and Donnel M. Pappenfort. *Secure Detention of Juveniles and Alternatives to Its Use*. Washington, D.C.: Government Printing Office, 1977.

Chapter 17

Comparative Corrections: The International Scene

We have included international material where appropriate in many earlier chapters. References to programs and practices in other countries occur in these chapters only where the material is germane to the general topic under discussion. These references were not intended to give students a general impression of correction in any nation other than the United States. The purpose of this chapter is to provide an overview of world corrections so that students will have multiple points of comparison from which to review the American correctional experience. It would be presumptuous to think that international corrections could be adequately summarized in a single chapter. It would take a dozen volumes to examine the subject in as much depth as our discussion of American corrections in this text. Chapter 17 therefore has a more limited scope. We will discuss some of the highlights of corrections in a few selected countries (Canada, Sweden, England, South Africa, New Zealand, Japan, and India), with additional background material on other Scandinavian countries, and a special section on Third World countries other than India.

THE POVERTY OF CROSS-CULTURAL RESEARCH ON CORRECTIONS

Considering the advances in communications technology that the United States has made in the past several decades, it is surprising to note how remarkably insular most Americans continue to be concerning international affairs. Many American newspapers rarely report anything at all about international affairs. Few Americans have more than a superficial idea of what goes on in Canada and Mexico, to say nothing of nations that are further afield.

Correctional research suffers from the same cultural parochialism. No more than one out of every 50 journal articles and technical reports on correctional matters make any reference at all to international comparisons. A study is referred to as "comparative" if it compares two different institutions in the same state, and even that degree of comparison is infrequently seen in the correctional literature. There are at least four reasons why this is so.

The first is that relatively few American correctional scholars have the ability to read reports of correctional research written in foreign languages. The mass of material that appears in Italian, Spanish, German, French, Japanese, and other languages is simply unavailable to these scholars, and these reports from international sources are rarely translated into English.

A second reason for the paucity of American research on international corrections is that most sources of research funding either follow a policy of funding only American research or else manage to convey the impression to researchers that international projects will not be given the same consideration for funding as American projects will.

A third problem is that researchers who are trained to focus only on American problems are unlikely to think about developing proposals for international research. Their insulated educations have failed to widen their horizons to the international level.

Finally, there are technical difficulties in international research that have discouraged many investigators who have an interest in international matters. For example, there is the problem of translating questionnaires into multiple languages so that they can be given in different countries. Another problem is establishing contacts in these countries, given the dissuasion to international travel that is built into American university and government travel policies.

As a result of these problems, the student of international corrections is forced to seek government reports and other official documents from those countries publishing documents in English, and to use outdated material on most non-English-speaking countries. Many of these reports read like travelogues rather than technical scientific studies of international corrections. Europe (except for Scandinavia) is poorly represented in the English-language literature, and Third World nations other than India are almost unknown. Perhaps the greatest challenge for correctional scholarship in the 1980s is to develop an international community of scholars within which information can be shared on a regular basis. At the moment, the only sign of movement in that direction is the beginning of a series of *International Summaries* published by the National Criminal Justice Reference Service. These volumes translate outstanding articles from diverse foreign languages into English to make them available to practitioners and scholars in the American criminal justice community.

An Example of Cross-Cultural Correctional Research

Ronald Akers, Norman Hayner, and Werner Gruninger[3,4] have conducted a study of prisoner attitudes and roles in 22 prisons distributed over five nations: The United States, Great Britain, West Germany, Spain, and Mexico. The institutions were rated on a treatment–custody continuum based on interviews

Figure 17.1 A lounge area in a modern correctional facility. (Law Enforcement Assistance Administration.)

with top administrators and the observations of an investigator at each institution. Written questionnaires translated into the local language were then administered to samples of prisoners drawn from the institutions. This research is unusual in that it provides us with information on both the institutions and the prisoners, and also that it standardizes the information collected from different nations.

It was found that American prisoners were more fully assimilated into the prisoner society and therefore more opposed to staff than prisoners in the European countries. In Mexico, the prisoners generally were in conformity with prosocial staff norms. The characteristics of a nonconformist prisoner subculture were discernible in every country, and these prisoner subcultures were similar to subcultures described in American prisons since the 1930s. Another cross-cultural similarity was that prisoners in all institutions were affected by pluralistic ignorance, which caused them to overestimate the degree to which their fellow-prisoners agreed with the antisocial attitudes of the prison subculture. It was also true that the more antisocial individuals exhibited higher degrees of pluralistic ignorance than the less antisocial individuals.[4]

The researchers found that there were no clear relationships between institutional characteristics and prisoner attitudes. The institutions were rated on a continuum running from a high treatment orientation to a high custodial orientation. First-time prisoners were more likely to play an antisocial role in a treatment-oriented institution than in a custody-oriented institution. There was a slight tendency for just the reverse to occur among experienced criminals, with their being more likely to take on prosocial roles in treatment-oriented institutions than in custody-oriented institutions. A very interesting finding was that, except in England, the relationship between criminal background and occupying antisocial roles was stronger in custody-oriented prisons than in treatment-oriented prisons. This might indicate that the treatment activities in the latter institutions are able to partially suppress the effects of having a criminal background. More important than these differences, the researchers found that—with the exception of Mexico—the generally high level of antisocial attitudes among the prisoners prevailed regardless of the strength of the treatment orientation of the institution. This suggests either that there are common elements in the criminal backgrounds of the prisoners predisposing them to antisocial attitudes while incarcerated or that the general negative conditions of imprisonment are so strong that they overcome differences on the treatment–custody orientation continuum.[3]

CANADA

The Canadian system of correctional institutions is divided into federal penitentiaries for offenders sentenced to more than two years imprisonment and provincial prisons for offenders sentenced to less than two years. This differs from the American system, in which state prisons incarcerate felons with sentences of all lengths, while the federal prison system accepts only offenders who have broken federal criminal laws. Offenders in Canadian prisons and penitentiaries are generally lodged in individual cells and are not forced to work.[67] The Canadian Penitentiary Service administers 59 correctional institutions spread from Victoria, British Columbia to Halifax, Nova Scotia. None of these institutions is large by American standards, the largest having a rated capacity of only 650 prisoners.[14]

Canada is divided into five regions, with a Regional Reception Centre in each region. When a prisoner is sentenced to more than two years of incarceration, the initial assignment is to the nearest Regional Reception Centre, in which classification occurs during a seven- to eight-week period.[12] At the end of the classification period, approximately 35 percent of the prisoners are transferred to a maximum security institution, 50 percent to a medium or minimum security institution, and 15 percent to a special institution. Special institutions include psychiatric facilities, women's prisons, and facilities for the aged.[67] Offenders who are not given a sentence to a correctional institution may be placed on probation. Fines are heavily used in Canada, and a more recent alternative to incarceration is the community service order. All of these alternatives are under the jurisdiction of the provinces rather than the federal system.

Community service orders were introduced as an intermediate sanction between imprisonment and regular probation. Community service orders came into use in British Columbia in 1975 and in Ontario in 1978. Offenders in the Ontario program contribute a median of 30 hours of work through community service assignments, generally completing the work in less than three months. Services are delivered to needy individuals as well as to community organizations. The nature of the services provided varies according to the capabilities of the offenders, the most common services being maintenance activities, helping the handicapped, and working on parks and recreation projects. In the first 12 months of Ontario's use of community service orders, probationers delivered 12,798 hours of unpaid community service, with 93 percent of the offenders successfully completing their assignments.[69]

An international comparison of imprisonment rates using data from the early 1970s found that Canada had lower rates than the United States, Poland, Australia, Finland, and New Zealand, but higher rates than England and Wales, Denmark, Sweden, France, Italy, Japan, Spain, Norway, and the Netherlands.[99] This places a heavy burden on the institutions of the Canadian Penitentiary Service. For both humane and budgetary reasons, Canada has been working to find alternatives to traditional correctional institutionalization since the mid-1970s. One alternative that has been tried is the intermittent sentence. Intermittent sentences are imposed where the total time to be served is 90 days or less, so its use is limited to the provincial institutions. Most intermittent sentences are served from Friday evening until Monday morning, with the offenders being allowed to spend the rest of the week at work or at school, and their weekday evenings at home. An evaluation of the use of the intermittent sentence in Ontario found that the option was being used for individuals who were unemployed and who had no family responsibilities as well as for those who needed to work (including housewives) to keep their families together. It was found that the program caused serious overcrowding and staffing problems in the correctional institutions on weekends when all of the intermittent sentence offenders were present. There were also problems with offenders being drunk on readmission and with the presence of contraband. The evaluators recommended that intermittent sentences not be imposed unless the defense counsel offers proof of gainful employment or educational involvement, and that the cessation of either of these activities while serving an intermittent sentence should automatically convert the sentence to a traditional continuous sentence. It was also recommended that as many intermittent sentence prisoners as possible serve their time in community resource centers rather than in other provincial institutions, as that would reduce cost and would have less "institutionalizing effects."[19]

Another Canadian innovation is the temporary absence program, under which prisoners are released to the community on a daily basis for work or education. The program also permits longer periods of community stay that are useful in locating and applying for employment.[56] A survey of agencies and businessses accepting offenders under the plan found that educational institutions were much more positive about the program than employers. Some of the employers apparently had bad experiences with workers in the temporary absence program, while educators were uniformly supportive of the progarm and felt that inmate students had as much ability and performed as well as noninmates. Employers, educators, institutional staff, and prisoners all agreed that the temporary absence program had a positive effect on prisoners and that it was more humane than traditional institutional programs.[32]

Canada has moved to increase the quality and quantity of vocational experiences made available to prisoners in the federal penitentiary system. By 1970, it had been decided that correctional industries were a failure in Canadian institutions, and that they needed to be reorganized on a self-supporting basis, with reasonable wages paid to participating prisoners. By having industries within prisons approximate the conditions of industries in the outside world, this would also help to accustom prisoners to the working conditions that they would encounter after release. In 1974, the Canadian government agreed to purchase $5 million worth of penitentiary products per year, effective immediately, and to gradually increase the level of purchases to $25 million by 1985. Industrial marketing activities such as formal market penetration, research, and product identification were begun in 1976, at which time the first industries program under the new model was implemented at Joyceville. Hourly wages began at $1.25 and rose to $2.80, with the payment of an additional group bonus incentive to work groups exceeding production standards.[13] It will take approximately a decade to implement the new industries program in all of the major Canadian penitentiaries.[15]

An alternative approach to the development of state industries within correctional institutions is to invite private industries to occupy prison facilities and to employ prisoners under what are, in essence, outside world conditions. This approach was used in the Guelph Abattoir Programme. This factory provides 40–50 prisoners with regular jobs and a starting wage of $3.15 per hour. Because the factory is technically outside of the security perimeter of the institution, the prisoners employed are formally released under the temporary absence program. Prisoners pay part of their wages to the institution for room and board. After August 1977, they were represented by the Canadian Food and Allied Workers (AFL-CIO). An evaluation of the progam found that both prisoners and staff had extremely positive attitudes towards Guelph Abattoir. Employment in the industrial program was shown to have positive effects on post-release employment, but had no measurable effect on recidivism.[36]

We cannot leave the topic of institutional corrections in Canada without mentioning a remarkable arrangement begun in 1973, when the position of Correctional Investigator was created. This official has the status of a Commissioner under the Canadian Inquiries Act, and has the power to investigate problems of prisoners on all subjects for which the Canadian Solicitor General is responsible. A kind of ombudsman, the Correctional Investigator travels among the Canadian federal institutions, hearing and investigating prisoner complaints, and making announced and unannounced inspections. In 1976, the Correctional Investigator was supported by a staff of eight individuals. An annual report summarizes the inspections, complaint investigations, and other activities of the Correctional Investigator and his staff. The cases summarized in the annual reports are written with remarkable objectivity, and make no attempt to present the prison administration in a positive light where that is not supported by the facts of the case. The following example, Case No. 1840, is typical of the way in which cases are reported.

The inmate complained that there was a letter from him in his file requesting permission to marry another inmate, also a male. He first learned of this when he was told that his request for permission to marry was refused. The inmate explained to the administration that the letter was a joke and that he had never written any such letter. The inmate did not know the information was left in his file.

Some two years later, during an interview, it was suggested by a counselor that he might have a problem of homosexuality. The complainant denied any such orientation and made several unsuccessful requests to have the letter removed from his file.

The inmate was advised by our office to use the grievance procedure. This he did. On review by the first level, the grievance was accepted and it was ordered that the information be removed from his file and destroyed. However, an inquiries officer, on checking the file on a subsequent occasion, found that the information had not yet been removed. It was brought to the attention of authorities and the letter was finally removed and destroyed.[31:51]

Canada has an extensive parole system, federal applications being judged by the National Parole Board. Once released on parole, the parolee is under the spervision of an officer of the National Parole Service or a member of a private after-care agency.[60] Beginning in 1968, the Canadian Penitentiary Service has made halfway houses, called community correctional centers, available for the use of parolees in need of intensive supervision. Residents in these facilities are allowed to work and participate in recreational activities in the free community, but they must return to the residence at the stated time marked on their parole pass.[12] There were 15 federal halfway houses in Canada in 1978, and additional community-based residential centers were provided by provincial correctional systems. For example, there were 24 community resources centers in Ontario in 1978.[105] A one-year follow-up study of these Ontario community corrections facilities found that recidivism rates for community corrections graduates were 10 percent lower than recidivism rates for prisoners who had participated in temporary absence programs before being released directly to the community from traditional correctional institutions in the province.[10]

SWEDEN

Sweden's correctional system has received more positive publicity in the United States than corrections in any other country. Although it does not have the lowest incarceration rate in the world, nor the shortest sentences, it is among the leaders on both dimensions, and its accomplishments have been evaluated and publicized in the English language to a much greater extent than the accomplishments of other outstanding correctional systems, such as those in Japan and The Netherlands. The approbation of the Swedish system increased even further as it began to implement the reforms mandated under the 1974 "Act on Correctional Treatment in Institutions." This document stipulates that offenders should be kept out of institutions wherever possible and also increases the possibilities for prisoners to leave institutions on a temporary basis for work, study, and recreation.[74]

The primary criminal sanction used in Sweden is the fine. Approximately 20 offenders receive fines for every offender who is admitted to a correctional institution. Of those admitted to institutions in 1978, 72 percent were sentenced to less than four months' imprisonment, 17 percent to between four and twelve months, and only 11 percent to imprisonment for a year or more.[90] Approximately one-third of all prison inmates are serving time for driving while intoxicated, generally a sentence of one months' imprisonment. Property crimes constitute approximately a quarter of all prison admittees, and violent crimes, a mere 14 percent.[89] Probation is used as an alternative to imprisonment rather than as a general punishment device, and is applied in a relatively small proportion of cases. Prisons for young people are practically nonexistent, with only 63 new admittees in 1978. A small number of incorrigible adult recidivists are sentenced to prison each year under an internment scheme that provides for longer sentences where necessary to protect the public.[90]

Institutional corrections in Sweden consists of a large number of very small institutions. In 1979, there were 21 remand prisons for those awaiting trial, 51 local institutions intended for individuals serving prison sentences of a year or less and generally having a capacity of 20–60 prisoners, and 20 national institutions for prisoners with longer sentences. The average capacity of the national institutions is 38 prisoners,[90] and the largest Swedish prison, Kumla, has a capacity of 390.[100] A number of these institutions have achieved an international reputation for their treatment programs. These include Gavle, which is a modified therapeutic community; the Gruvberge Village, an open forestry camp;[24] Studiegarden, an open prison for students near the University of Uppsala; and the industrial prison at Tillberga.[74] Furloughs are extensively used for prisoners, with 41,974 being approved in 1978 alone. Prisoners fail to return on time in six percent of the furloughs granted, and engage in misconduct in the community in three percent of the furloughs.[89]

One of the disadvantages of incarcerating an extremely small percentage of offenders is that recidivism rates for the few who are incarcerated tend to be much higher than they would be if the incarceration net were more inclusive. A calculation of recidivism rates for those released from Swedish prisons during 1973 showed that 71 percent of those up to age 30 and 56 percent of those over 30 recidivated within the 30-month follow-up period. First-timers were less likely to recidivate (46 percent) than multiple offenders (75 percent), and violent criminals were less likely to recidivate (53 percent) than property criminals (70 percent).[47] Another disadvantage of the Swedish system is that, since so many Swedish prisons are open rather than closed, it is easy for prisoners to escape. There were 1726 escapes from Swedish institutions in 1978, a year during which the average national institutional population was 4278 prisoners.[90]

OTHER SCANDINAVIAN COUNTRIES AND THE NETHERLANDS

The rate of imprisonment in The Netherlands is between 20 and 21 per 100,000 population,[24] which is probably the lowest imprisonment rate in the world. Imprisonment rates in Denmark and Norway are also extremely low. Finland incarcerates a higher proportion of its citizens than the other Scandinavian countries,[9] but its rate is still one of the lowest in the world.[33]

Imprisonment in The Netherlands is used only if the public safety is in danger. In other cases, restitution, fines, and other alternatives to imprisonment are used. The implementation of a set of social sanctions relying so little on imprisonment is made easier by the Dutch low rate of violent crime, but even when this is taken into account, their imprisonment rate is still remarkably low.[8] An important key to the understanding of low imprisonment rates in The Netherlands is the extremely short average sentence length, which decreased from somewhat over three months in the 1950s to a month and a half in 1972.[24] In 1975, 56 percent of all sentences to correctional institutions in The Netherlands were for less than one month. The staff–prisoner ratio is perhaps the highest in the world, with 1.3 staff members per prisoner. Rather than permitting overcrowding, the Dutch correctional system asks offenders to wait to serve their sentences until room is available for them. When the backlog became hopelessly large in 1975, the government announced a general amnesty for all sentences of 14 days or less.[33]

The situation in Denmark is similar to that in The Netherlands. No prison holds more than 200 inmates, and the average sentence is just over three months. Until 1973, all probation and parole supervision in Denmark was carried out by the Danish Welfare Society, a private organization that was heavily funded by the federal government. When this organization was absorbed into the national correctional system, the period of supervision for most offenders was reduced to one year, which helped to decrease the number of Danes on probation and parole to about 4000 in 1977. At that time, there were approximately 800 inmates incarcerated in closed prisons and 1400 inmates in open prisons in Denmark.[73] Most of these institutions look more like college campuses than prisons. In addition to liberal regulations for institutional life, there is also a heavy use of leaves of absence and other devices for keeping prisoners in contact with the outside world. Of 14,728 leaves of absence granted in 1973, eight percent were abused in some way, such as late return to the institution, and criminal offenses were committed on one percent of the leaves.[52]

Correctional practices in Finland are, in many ways, similar to correctional practices in the other Scandinavian countries.[9] Finland has decriminalized public drunkenness, abortion, pornography, sex crimes, and petty traffic offenses. Minor property crimes such as passing bad checks and social security frauds have been depenalized, perhaps in anticipation of a future decriminalization of some of these offenses.[104] However, there are also indications that Finland has less liberal policies than the other Scandinavian countries, including the use of closed institutions that are much like maximum security prisons in Great Britain or the United States,[58] a higher percentage of prisoners in closed as opposed to open prisons, and a heavier use of institutionalization for juvenile offenders.[9] One of the most interesting aspects of corrections in Finland is the existence of eleven labor colonies and four prison colonies which function as alternatives to traditional incarceration. The prison colonies receive long-term prisoners with 4–6 months remaining before release, while labor colonies receive offenders with sentences of no more than two years and other types of less serious offenders. In both types of institutions, there are no detailed rules, surveillance procedures, or extensive custody staffs. All prisoners are paid the same wages as they would receive for comparable work in the free community, from which approximately 25 percent is deducted for services provided by the state.[44] A careful comparison of the recidivism of prison/labor colony groups and other inmates matched on the degree of risk to the community showed that work in the camps has as great a deterrent effect on criminality as traditional institutionalization.[98]

GREAT BRITAIN

The incarceration rate in Great Britain is higher than Scandinavian rates but lower than the rate in the United States. Correctional programs in Great Britain are similar to American and Canadian programs. The British prison system incarcerated an average of 41,796 offenders in 1978, the highest ever in its history. Due to the overcrowding, more than a third of the prisoners were housed in double and triple cells. There was also overcrowding in many juvenile institutions and in institutions for women. A major problem faced by the British correctional system is its heritage of ancient and outmoded facilties. The British system contains 56 correctional institutions opened before 1930, only ten of which are in good physical condition.[30] When the psychiatric facility at Grendon was opened in 1962, it was the first facility built for special types of offenders in Great Britain since Victorian times.[25]

Great Britain also contains a number of open institutions in which social control is exercised through individual responsibility rather than walls and towers. The first of these institutions was opened in 1933, and there were 13 such institutions by 1975. Fifteen percent of all British prisoners were housed in institutions in 1965, but that proportion declined to 11 percent by 1975, partially due to the adoption of a parole system in Britain in the late 1960s. These institutions are similar to the Finnish labor and prison camps described above.[45]

An unusual aspect of the British system is the use of Boards of Visitors to inspect correctional institutions, adjudicate in certain disciplinary cases, and to act as ombudsmen on prisoner complaints.[55] The 113 Boards in existence in 1974 contained approximately 1400 members, most of whom were citizens of some importance who were over 50 years of age. Each Board meets at the institution at least once a month, and some Boards are responsible for more than one institution.[42] In addition to their routine work, Board members may be called to the institution on short notice in emergencies. When participants in the Hull riot were dispersed to other institutions, the Hull Board of Visitors formed a touring panel which visited previous Hull inmates housed in other facilities around the country to conduct 185 adjudications relating to alleged misbehavior in the riot.[54] Although the use of Boards of Visitors has great potential for community oversight of the correctional establishment, in practice, the British Boards of Visitors have often been accused of being insufficiently independent of prison authorities to exercise that function adequately.[18]

Despite the increase in the number of prisoners in the British correctional system, the courts have been imprisoning a decreasing proportion of offenders for some time. The courts imprisoned 59 percent of the adult offenders that they sentenced in 1948, as compared with 34 percent in 1975. The increase in the British population base and the rise in the crime rate account for an increasing prison population in the face of a decreasing tendency for judges to sentence offenders to prison terms.[87] The probation system has always been extensive in

Great Britain, and other alternatives to incarceration include the use of absolute and conditional discharge, binding over (a form of bail), fines, suspended sentences, and community service orders.[24]

The British Parole Board did not come into existence until 1967. Prior to that time, released prisoners had received help from units of the National Association of Discharged Prisoner's Aid Societies. When these functions were transferred to the Probation Service, a new organization, NACRO, was formed to improve and increase the range of noninstitutional facilities and programs for offenders and ex-offenders. NACRO-sponsored programs in recent years include the Talbot Road House, which offers special accommodations for female offenders (including women with babies); Onward Industries to create jobs for unemployed offenders; and the Hammersmith Teenage Project, which provides community support for juveniles at risk.[59]

Every British prisoner is automatically considered for parole. The first stage of the process is an interview of the prisoner by a member of the Local Review Committee. The report of this interview, along with written representations by the prisoner, is considered by the entire Local Review Committee, which normally consists of five members, including the administrator of the institution or a designate and a member of the institution's Board of Visitors. The decision of the Local Review Committee is sent to the Home Office Parole Unit, where the dossier is scrutinized and a decision is made as to whether or not the case should be forwarded to the Parole Board for consideration of a full panel of four or five members. Unanimous recommendations on sentences of up to four years (with certain exclusions) by the Local Review Committees can be implemented without being referred to the Parole Board at all. If the case is forwarded to the Parole Board, the dossier is discussed in committee, and a decision is rendered. Prisoners are not allowed to have personal interviews with either the Parole Board or the Local Review Committee.[102]

British institutions specifically designed for juvenile offenders fall into four separate classifications: borstals, remand homes, approved schools, and detention centers. Borstals are relatively treatment-oriented institutions that accept young offenders between the ages of 15 and 21. In contrast, the detention centers provide a strenuous experience based on the military model. Approved schools concentrate on vocational training and basic education and are used for youngsters who are in need of care, protection and control as well for those who have been found guilty of an offense. Remand homes are short-term holding and observation facilities through which juveniles pass on their way to one of the other three types of institutions.[37] Of 25,301 juvenile offenders received into custody under sentence in 1977, most were sent to detention centers (10,863) or borstals (7,250).[29]

SOUTH AFRICA

South Africa represents as extreme a correctional policy as The Netherlands, except that it is an unusually conservative policy instead of an unusually liberal one. The incarceration rate in South Africa is probably the highest in the entire world. This is because imprisonment is used as a major device for maintaining the racial separation system of *apartheid* in South African society. Nonwhites who break any of the minor segregation regulations are subject to imprisonment for short stretches of time; anyone—white or nonwhite—seriously challenging the system of *apartheid* is subject to a lengthy term of imprisonment. They are also in danger of being tortured while in detention. Although the international attention brought by Steve Biko's death under interrogation in 1977 reduced the death rate, Amnesty International[7] reports that torture is still being systematically used against political detainees.

Table 17.1 shows the results of this policy. White South Africans are incarcerated at a rate which is roughly similar to incarceration rates in other nations, but Black Africans and Coloureds (an official South African classification for individuals whose racial ancestry is both Caucasian and non-Caucasian) are incarcerated at rates between four and five times the white rate. The difference between the incarceration rate and the prison admission rate in Table 17.1 is a reflection of the length of sentence imposed. Since the relatively small portion of whites who are incarcerated have committed relatively serious crimes, their prison admission rate is not much higher than their incarceration rate. Asians, who comprise a rather small group in South Africa, have a very low incarceration rate, but show some evidence of short sentences. For Black Africans and Coloureds, the prison admission rate is roughly three to four times the incarceration rate. This indexes the extent to which these nonwhite South Africans are being imprisoned on sentences of only a few months' length as a result of the violation of *apartheid* laws.

Once admitted to the prison system, nonwhite Africans suffer from continued discrimination. They serve their time in segregated facilities in which the amenities are not equal to those provided to white prisoners. Whereas white prisoners are given training in a wide variety of trades, ranging from electricians and welders to sheetmetal workers and cabinet makers, nonwhite prisoners are restricted to less prestigious and profitable occupations, such as bricklaying, painting, plumbing, plastering, and carpentry. Only one black prisoner was permitted to take an occupational test in a field outside of these five trades during 1978–1979, and he failed the test.[80] Whipping and execution continue to

Table 17.1. Prison Admission Rates[1] and Incarceration Rates,[2] South Africa, 1975, by Racial Groups

Racial Group	Prison Admission Rate	Incarceration Rate
African	1280	402
Coloured	1580	384
Asian	161	69
White	134	91
TOTAL	1083	376

Source: Adapted from South African Institute of Race Relations. *A Survey of Race Relations in South Africa: 1977.* Johannesburg, S.A., 1978.

[1]Prison admissions per 100,000 of each racial group as officially classified by the South African government.

[2]Total incarcerated population per 100,000 of each racial group as officially classified by the South African government.

be used in South African prisons, with Black and Coloured Africans receiving 98 percent of the beatings meted out to juveniles and 99 percent of the beatings meted out to adults.[81]

Nonwhite women share the burden of the use of the correctional system to enforce *apartheid*, for 154 of them bore children in incarceration in 1978–1979, and 2093 had their infants admitted to correctional institutions with them.[80] Another aspect of life in South African prisons is the possibility of maltreatment and torture beyond the corporal punishment allowed under the law. In 1974, five correctional officers were convicted of having beaten a prisoner to death, and the presiding judge indicated that he did not believe that this was an isolated incident.[57] The Prisons Department upheld 226 of 373 charges of assault on prisoners made in the 12-month period between mid-1978 and mid-1979, and an additional six staff members were found guilty and sentenced in magistrate's courts after investigations by the South African police.[80] The Special Committee on *Apartheid* of the United Nations,[96] after hearing endless testimony of the torture and general mistreatment of offenders in the South Africa criminal justice system, compared the South Africa situation to Nazi Germany, and concluded that "while some effort is made to apply the principles of modern penal administration with respect to common law crimes in South Africa, political prisoners are treated vindictively and are deliberately subjected to humiliating conditions, designed to lower their morale and to intimidate the oppressed people."[96:119]

In keeping with an emphasis on punishment rather than treatment, community corrections has had an exceedingly limited development in South Africa.[86] The aftercare of prisoners is the primary mission of the South African National Institute for Crime Prevention and Rehabilitation of Offenders (NICRO).[82] NICRO operates a number of aftercare hostels designed to aid prisoners in making the transition to community life. NICRO also sponsors a bus service making monthly trips to major prisons so that prisoners can be visited by their relatives, and is active in crime prevention. Unfortunately, limitations on resources force NICRO to limit its offerings to a relatively small number of released offenders per year.

NEW ZEALAND

New Zealand has developed its correctional system on the British model, and has generally incarcerated citizens at a somewhat higher rate than most European nations, although at a much lower rate than the United States.[99] However, there has been a recent decline in the use of correctional institutions for the imprisonment of both adults and juveniles in recent years.[62,64] A unique aspect of New Zealand corrections is the presence of a high proportion of Maori offenders. In 1977, 40 percent of all adults sentenced to imprisonment were of a Maori heritage, as were 40 percent of the juveniles committed to detention centers and 56 percent of the juveniles committed for borstal training.[63]

Juvenile corrections in New Zealand uses the same distinction between borstal and detention institutions that is found in England. The borstals accept young people on indeterminant sentences and emphasize treatment, while detention institutions accept less serious offenders, and subject them to a three-month period of hard labor and tight discipline.[92] Periodic detention was introduced in New Zealand in 1963. In this program, juvenile offenders spend their weekends and some evenings at an attendance center, and are free to live normally during the week. The number of weeknights spent at the center can be varied to reward good behavior by the juveniles.[75] A more recent version of periodic detention involves no overnight stays at all. A comparison with overnight and noninstitutional periodic detention programs in Wellington found no statistically significant differences in outcomes, but some indication that a continuation of the study with a larger sample might show a significantly lower reconviction rate among noninstitutional program graduates than those subjected to overnight stays.[53]

Adult corrections in New Zealand involves the classification of offenders sentenced to imprisonment into maximum, medium, and minimum security settings. The courts have extensive powers to enforce restitution orders on offenders, and the national government has taken the responsibility for providing compensation to the victims of violent crimes, including those committed by escaping prisoners.[79] New Zealand follows just the opposite policy from South Africa on sentence length. Since 1967, the courts have been instructed not to use prison sentences of less than six-months duration. If the offense is relatively minor, it does not justify using imprisonment, and if imprisonment is necessary, it is likely to be necessary for more than six months.[71]

Probation has a long history of extensive use in New Zealand. Recidivism rates for probationers are unusually high. Fifty-nine percent of a sample of probationers sentenced in 1974 recidivated during a 30-month follow-up period. Juveniles, men who had no job or an unskilled job, and probationers with a previous criminal justice history had the highest rates of recidivism. In addition to recidivating more frequently, offenders with a previous cirminal justice history were more likely than first-timers to commit serious offenses.[66] New Zealand has an extensive program of prison visitors, who are also urged to provide help to the prisoners after discharge. These volunteer visitors are trained and supervised by the 18 groups that make up the New Zealand Prisoner's Aid and Rehabilitation Society. The Society also operates three post-release hostels and overnight facilities close to several major penitentiaries for the convenience of visiting relatives.[65]

JAPAN

Japan has a criminal justice system that had been progressively Westernized for some decades before World War II, and was further influenced by Western corrections after that war. At the same time, corrections in Japan has continued to retain unique aspects which are not found anywhere in Western nations. The number of offenses against the penal code rose rapidly as a result of the social disruption that followed the Japanese defeat in World War II. Instead of contiuing to rise as economic growth mushroomed, these offenses declined as social control was reasserted, and the number of nontraffic crimes known to the police declined from 1,436,000 in 1955 to 1,246,000 in 1976. Yoshio Suzuki[88] suggests a number of reasons for this decline in crime. Social control could be effectively reasserted after the war because of the power that family members and lifetime work tenure have over behavior. Japan is a very homogeneous society, so few minority–majority group conflicts disturb this placid scene. The distribution of benefits from economic growth has been relatively even and well above the expectations of the public. Approximately 90 percent of the Japanese people consider themselves to be members of the middle-class. Finally, a reasonable level of efficiency in the criminal justice system and effective gun control policies may also have contributed to the declining crime rate.

Public prosecutors offices in Japan received 841,926 offenders who were accused of breaking the penal code in 1978, while they had received 1,005,473 penal code violators in 1971.[38,41] This has allowed the correctional system to operate without the constant pressure for expansion that was typical of many Western nations during the 1970s. As a result, Japan has worked on improving its correctional services instead of expanding them, and has made particularly strong advances in the area of community corrections.

Only 21 percent of the offenders entering the criminal justice system in 1978 were arrested. The others appeared voluntarily before public prosecutors. Since the acquittal rate was close to zero, nearly everyone entering the criminal justice system was found guilty and passed on to the correctional system. Ninety-seven percent of all judgments imposed fines on offenders, and three percent were sentenced to imprisonment, in most cases with forced labor. Because of the relatively low crime rate and the heavy use of fines as an alternative to incarceration, the average daily population of Japanese penal institutions in 1978 was only 49,887 (of whom 40,796 were sentenced prisoners and the others were awaiting a judicial disposition), and the incarceration rate was approximately 44 per 100,000—one of the lowest incarceration rates in the world.[41]

Once admitted to the system of correctional institutions, all prisoners are classified according to demographic characteristics—foreigners receiving different treatment from Japanese nationals, length of sentence, mental and physical disorders, and treatment needs. As might be expected in a system that incarcerates so few of its criminals, the majority of the prisoners in Japanese institutions have advanced criminal tendencies. There are detailed treatment standards for each classification type, and these are used as the basis for individual treatment plans.[41] Life in Japanese prisons is often hard, but always fair. Escapes are rare, and extensive maximum security devices are unnecessary. The courts were heavily involved in assuring the maintenance of justice in Japanese correctional institutions long before America experienced its sudden rise in judicial intervention in corrections. Prison industries are well developed, and Japan also has special vocational training institutions. The centralization of control over Japanese prisons not only permits the national standardization of prison conditions, but also allows the Ministry of Justice to provide special services to all of the prisoners in the country. These services include radio programs specifically aimed at the needs of prisoners that are broadcast to all correctional institutions, and three periodicals especially edited for prisoners.[103] Another aspect of the Japanese correctional system is the large number of prison labor camps, many of which are open prisons and allow reasonably normal living. There were 55 prison labor camps in Japan in 1972, of which 15 were open prisons.[38]

In some cases, offenders sentenced to a fine or institutional confinement may be given probation instead. This is another way of keeping prison populations down to manageable dimensions. In 1978, 8501 adults and 44,934 juveniles were placed on probation.[41] Since there are 50,000 volunteer probation officers in the country, probationers can receive a reasonable level of supervision and help without great cost to the state. The volunteer probation officers participate in special training courses and also receive a monthly magazine published by the Japan Rehabilitation Aid Association. The volunteer probation officers apparently find their positions to be valuable experiences, for nearly half of the officers in 1972 had already amassed more than 10 years of service to probationers.[40]

Approximately half of the releasees from Japanese correctional institutions are paroled, with most parole supervision periods being three months or less. A follow-up study of recidivism in 1976 found that 25 percent of those released on parole and 50 percent of those released directly to the community without supervision recidivated within three years. Japan also provides aftercare assistance to all released prisoners requesting it. This assistance includes travel expenses, clothing, medical treatment, and room and board. There are 106 rehabilitation aid hostels in Japan, all of them operated by voluntary associations with financial support from the Ministry of Justice.[41]

Only three percent of the juvenile cases heard in family courts in Japan result in commitments to correctional institutions. Most cases are dismissed without a hearing, and the majority of cases that go to a hearing are dismissed after the hearing. Probation is the preferred disposition for the remaining youngsters, and less than one percent of the cases are considered to be serious enough to merit referral to a public prosecutor. Juveniles adjusted in courts other than the family courts are committed to juvenile prisons, where they are incarcerated until they are 26 years old. The extremely small proportion of Japanese juvenile delinquents who are violent enough to merit this disposition is reflected in the total juvenile prison population at the end of 1978, which was only 104 individuals. Juveniles incarcerated by order of the family court are sent to juvenile training schools, which concentrate on inmate discipline, academic and vocational training, and medical care. There were 61 juvenile training schools operating in Japan at the end of 1978, with a total population of 3779.[41]

INDIA

With an estimated population of 674 million in 1980,[16] India is more populous than the United States and the U.S.S.R. combined. Its correctional system is similarly large and complex. It is estimated that approximately 1,500,000 Indians were admitted to correctional institutions in 1974, many of them to await trial.[28] The capacity of Indian correctional institutions was 171,898 in 1971, but the average daily population in those institutions was 200,535, which indicates the problem of overcrowding that exists in most Indian institutions.[35] The Indian

Supreme Court ruled in 1979 that all prisoners awaiting trial, who had already been incarcerated for more than the maximum term allowed for the crimes of which they were accused, must be released. The state of Bihar responded by releasing half of the 20,000 prisoners awaiting trial.[7] India is one of the developing countries in which industrialization is still in the early stages of expansion. This is reflected in the gross national product per capita (GNP/C). According to statistics compiled by the Central Intelligence Agency[16] at the beginning of 1980, the GNP/C for Sweden was $10,550. GNP/C's for other nations discussed in this chapter include $8,520 for Japan, $6,530 for Finland, $5,520 for the United Kingdom, and $4,250 for New Zealand.

In contrast to these highly industrialized nations, GNP/C's in developing Third World nations are extremely low. The GNP/C in Mexico is $1,340, and it is $1,000 in the Ivory Coast, $510 in Nigeria, $240 in Indonesia, and $200 in Sri Lanka. South Africa is an anomaly in that GNP/C of $1,680 appears to be low, but this is an average figure that subsumes the relatively wealthy whites and the much larger number of nonwhite Africans who are almost entirely excluded from participating in the economy at any level above menial labor. All of these nations are well off when compared with India, where the GNP/C is $140. This severely limits government expenditures for Indian correctional institutions, and it also makes it difficult for correctional institutions to be too humane, lest many of the poor deliberately commit crimes so that they can be incarcerated and raise their standard of living over what they are able to manage in the free society. India's *Model Prison Manual*[34] is an admirable document, but the full implementation of the provisions it contains awaits greatly improved economic conditions. The availability of 40 million rupees in federal grants to the Indian states for the improvement of prison conditions after 1978[6] barely made a dent in this problem.

Judges in India have enormous discretion in sentencing. Many crimes can result in sentences ranging from a day to 20 years, and little is said in the statutes about the factors to be weighed in exercising judicial discretion.[28] Under the Central Probation of Offenders Act of 1958, any offender guilty of an offense punishable by less than life imprisonment is eligible to be released on probation with or without supervision. This act authorizes judges to release offenders upon the payment of compensation or fines.[83] Judges have not been quick to utilize the provision for probation, and only 7829 offenders were on probation caseloads in the entire country at the end of 1971. They were supervised by 368 paid probation officers plus a handful of volunteers.[35] A study of two courts in the state of Rajasthan found that 71 percent of the convicted offenders were sent to prisons, 14 percent were fined, 4 percent received probation without supervision, 2 percent received probation with supervision, and 9 percent received other dispositions. Because the probation officer has so many duties other than supervising probationers, the amount of time actually devoted to supervision and providing aid to probationers is extremely small.[2]

Although the tendency to use correctional institutions is extremely strong in India, the average sentence length is quite short. Approximately 85 percent of Indian prisoners serve sentences of less than six months.[77] Prison conditions are considerably worse than conditions in most industrialized nations, but not necessarily worse than the living conditions experienced by many of the Indians before they were incarcerated. The food is boring and may not be properly prepared, but it is nutritionally adequate. Proper sanitation is not always available, and accommodations in the barracks are minimal. Describing the barracks in one central prison, S.P. Srivastava[84] calls it "....a place where stinking smells suffocate one's nose and throat, and the total atmospheric pollution makes one's life miserable."[84:346] Rehabilitative programs are minimal,[85] and the work programs provided are of little value to the prisoners. They produce goods that are sold to government agencies, as is done in the United States.[93] A study of the work program at the Central Prison, Madras found that the prisoners were capable of performing work tasks and interested in doing so.[46] Unfortunately, four out of every five prisoners were placed in trades not of their choosing, and this had a negative impact on their performance and acquisition of work skills.[97]

A work scheme in which prisoners would be able to earn sufficient money to send part home to their families would be particularly welcome in India, where the imprisonment of the major breadwinner of the family can result in severe consequences, such as incurring personal debts, mortgaging houses, and selling the family plot of land.[1] Perhaps the most interesting aspect of institutional corrections in India from the American viewpoint is the development of a number of open prisons, beginning in Uttar Pradesh in 1952. By 1970, there were 20 open prisons scattered throughout India. Indian open prisons are generally plots of land between 10 and 50 acres in size with fencing added only to mark boundaries, not to act as a deterrent to escape. Most open prisons hold no more than 200 inmates, but the 5800-acre Sampurnanand Agricultural Camp in Uttar Pradesh has a capacity of 3300 prisoners. Prisoners with long sentences who have already served one-third of their time with good records and are healthy are eligible for transfer to open prisons. They are generally paid something for their work, although not at the prevailing rates in the outside world. Some open prisons grant home leave for as much as 21 days a year. Visits from friends and relatives are encouraged; and, in Rajasthan, prisoners can keep their families with them. The recidivism rate for 3855 prisoners released from open prisons in Uttar Pradesh was calculated at only eight percent.[76] Because of differences in legal definitions, criminal justice policies, research methods, and other factors, it is impossible to compare this rate with rates from other nations.

Aftercare for offenders in India is extremely limited. There is no parole system as it is known in Western nations. Parole in India is home leave granted by institutional superintendents to prisoners who have served one-third of their sentences with good behavior. This conditional release is not accompanied by any system of regular supervision.[43]

India's problems with juveniles are perhaps more pressing than those in the industrialized nations. In addition to difficulties associated with juvenile delinquency, there are severe problems associated with destitute and neglected children. To attempt to deal with this problem, India has allocated a considerable amount of resources. Juvenile institutions follow the British model, with borstal schools, remand and observation homes, approved schools, and children's homes in existence.[35] For example, the Union Territory of Delhi has 14 institutions for destitute, neglected, and delinquent juveniles. These have a capacity of 2100 children, and an additional 500 children receive care in foster homes. Staff members receive limited training, and are periodically moved from one position to another, so they are not able to maintain relationships with the juveniles for extended periods of time.[78] A summary of three studies of juvenile justice in India concluded that the main problem was not in the legal provisions for juvenile treatment, but rather in the implementation of these provisions at the practice level. Excessive caseloads, overcrowding, limitations in the quality and availability of services, and insufficient use of community corrections are among the problems which plague the treatment of juvenile delinquency in India.[27]

CORRECTIONS IN OTHER THIRD WORLD COUNTRIES

Like India, most other nations in the Third World were governed by the European colonial powers when their correctional systems were developed. These colonial correctional systems were operated with a greater concern for minimizing expenditures than for basic human rights. When the colonial powers pulled out, the Third World nations were left with decaying facilities, few trained staff members, and very little money with which to continue—to say nothing of improving—their correctional systems. Institutional populations mushroomed beyond the capacity of existing facilities and caused overcrowding in many developing nations, stimulated by the imprisonment of large numbers of accused individuals awaiting trial, which in some cases comprised two-thirds of the total prison population.[68] For example, 88 percent of all Venezuelan prisoners in 1966 were awaiting trial. The median time before trial was four years, and 15 percent of the prisoners had already been waiting for more than 12 years.[50] Governmental efforts to reduce the backlog had succeeded in decreasing the proportion of prisoners awaiting trial to 79 percent by 1971. This is the major cause of overcrowding in Venezuelan correctional institutions, where 26 prisons originally built to hold 10,000 prisoners were holding approximately 15,000 in 1971.[20]

In the following sections, we will present examples of corrections in Latin America, Asia, and Africa. These presentations are necessarily selective because of the limited amount of material available in the English language. In addition, the examples that have been selected for presentation either typify correctional conditions in the region or contain correctional practices that appear to be particularly promising.

Latin America

Manuel López-Rey,[49] who is probably the world's expert on Latin American penology, has declared Latin American prison conditions to be "generally unsatisfactory or really bad."[49:92] Overcrowding, underfunding, and a high proportion of prisoners awaiting trial are endemic to the region. Despite a tendency toward relatively moderate sentences, most of which are less than three years,[51] the large number of pre-trial prisoners pushes the incarceration rate in Latin America to a higher level than is found in the developing countries of Asia and Africa, although the incarceration rate in Latin America is still lower than the incarceration rate in the United States.[101] López-Rey estimates that 25–35 percent of offenders are given suspended sentences in Latin America, but there are no probation services available. Many of those receiving prison sentences—often because they are too poor to pay the fine assessed—spend less than six months behind bars. Comparing the lengthy periods of time spent by many offenders awaiting trial and the comparatively short sentences that many of them ultimately receive, there is some question as to where most of the punishment is meted out in the criminal justice processing sequence in Latin American nations.

In Mexico, the movement to apply the United Nation's minimum standards for the treatment of offenders began in 1966, and was extended to all federal correctional institutions in 1971. Intent is not the same as implementation; and by 1976, only 35 percent of Mexico's prisons were roughly in comformity with the United Nations' standards.[26] Three aspects of the Mexican prison system which have proved interesting to American researchers are conjugal visits, the free market economy practiced in many of the institutions, and the famous open prison on Tres Marias Island. Although the general standard of living in Mexican prisons is quite low in comparison with prison standards in the industrialized nations, the willingness of prison officials to permit normal economic commerce to exist within the walls, and the encouragement of a high degree of contract between prisoners and outsiders (particularly family members) creates less of a disjunction between prison life and life in the outside world after release than exists in the industrialized nations.[70]

Africa

The correctional system in the Ivory Coast illustrates the problems of corrections in Third World societies. At the major prison in Abidjan, a total correctional staff of 41 individuals was in charge of 1100 prisoners in the early 1970s. Since there were three shifts, vacations, and other absences, the number of employees available for supervision during the crucial day shift was only 12. The staff–prisoner ratio at the Bouaké Penal Colony was even worse.[48] In 1974, 20 of the 31 correctional institutions in the Ivory Coast were overcrowded, with some institutions having two or three times the number of prisoners for which they were designed. Nearly four out of every ten prisoners were awaiting trial. More than half of those found guilty were returned to a correctional institution to serve their sentences. Most of the rest received fines. Since more than half of the sentences were six months or less in length, the offenses involved were presumably minor, and it would have been feasible to replace many of these prison sentences with noninstitutional punishments.[5]

The situation is much the same in many other African countries. For example, 73 percent of the Kenyan prisoners in 1967 and 69 percent of the Nigerian prisoners in 1965 were imprisoned on sentences of less than six months.[17] Like the Ivory Coast, Ghana uses imprisonment as the primary form of punishment, limits most sentences to less than six months, and has little funding available for any type of rehabilitative programming.[72] A recent summary of Nigerian correctional practices concludes that medical and mental health care in correctional institutions ranges from minimal to nonexistent. Although educational programs are mandatory for juvenile prisoners, the rapid expansion of educational programs in the free society has made it impossible to recruit enough teachers for correctional programs. Vocational training exists at the level of tailoring, footmat-making, and carpentry, and agricultural experience is provided at the Kakuri Open Prison.[11] Although the prison systems in Uganda, Kenya, and Tanzania are efficiently administered,[17] López-Rey's[49] conclusion that the coming of independence to the African colonies has not improved their correctional systems continues to hold in the 1980s.

Asia

Thailand[91] incarcerated an average of 69,797 prisoners in 499 correctional institutions during 1978. In many ways, the correctional system in Thailand is intermediate between Third World correctional systems and the correctional systems in highly industrialized nations. This is true despite a gross national product per capita of $470,[16] which is well within the definition of a developing nation. The correctional officer–inmate ratio is 1:8.39.[91] Thirty-two percent of the incarcerated population consists of individuals who are awaiting the ajudication of their cases.[94] Education programs are taught at four different levels, and involve more than one out of every eight prisoners. All prisoners are expected to work and are paid fifty percent of the net profits of their labor. In addition, more than one out of every ten prisoners receives specialized vocational training. The educational and vocational programs both lead to examinations, which are generally passed by those taking them, and which result in diplomas or certificates issued by the Thai Ministry of Education.[91]

Although there is a parole system, very few prisoners are released on parole.[94] The introduction of a good-time system in 1977 has made it possible to reduce prison sentences by two months per year served, which may help to reduce the present level of overcrowding in a system which was 72 percent over capacity in 1978.[91] A furlough system for those approaching release is just beginning to take hold, and there is only one halfway house in the Thai correctional system. Recent developments in Thailand indicate that it is possible for developing countries with limited amounts of available funds to move toward correctional systems based on rehabilitation or humane treatment, rather than punishment.

Another developing Asian country which has made considerable strides in its correctional system is Sri Lanka, a large island off the coast of India with a gross national product per capita of $200. This small nation contains approximately 15 million people, and was previously known to the West as Ceylon.[16] The average number of convicted prisoners in Sri Lankan correctional institutions is approximately 6000, and these are distributed among 11 closed prisons, three open prison camps, and numerous lesser open facilities. Only offenders sentenced to more than two years of imprisonment and those who have already recidivated more than twice are sent to the closed prisons. A parole scheme is called "Release on License," and is available to prisoners with sentences of more than four years. Long-termers are also eligible for seven-day home leaves during their final year of incarceration. There are two borstal institutions for juvenile offenders. Probation is used for approximately 1500 offenders per year, and released offenders are supervised by community volunteers.[23]

Sri Lanka has had an open prison at Pallekelle for 25 years. This facility involves hard work, a reasonably normal life style, and a degree of prisoner self-government. In addition to their tasks at Pallekelle, the prisoners often perform volunteer service in the surrounding area. To be selected or transferred to Pallekelle, prisoners must have a good disciplinary record and a low probability of escape. Despite the selectivity inherent in this process, it is amazing that no more than eight of the nearly 3000 men processed through Pallakelle since its opening have escaped, and that only one has recidivated.[21]

Another recent experiment carried out in Sri Lanka under the leadership of Commissioner Delgoda[22] is the opening of a coconut estate in 1976 in which prisoners are completely free of any custodial supervision. In fact, they patrol the perimeter of the estate themselves in order to keep citizens from the surrounding area from stealing the coconuts. Although the prisoners on the estate are paid only a very small wage per month, they receive a large lump sum payment if they stay with the project until they are discharged. Family visits at this facility are encouraged and include conjugal privileges.

A survey of correctional institutions in Asia and the Far East conducted by the United Nations Asia and Far East Institute for the Prevention of Crime and the Treatment of Offenders[95] in 1965 found that many countries possessed open prisons similar to those described for Sri Lanka. In the Philippines, Iwahig Penal Colony was established in 1904 and the Davao Penal Colony was opened in 1932. Other institutions are scattered from Taiwan and Hong Kong to Malaysia and Bangladesh. In general, these institutions are characterized by agricultural labor, simple living conditions, and minimal institutional regulations. At many of the facilities, prisoners are allowed to invite their families to live with them. So closely do some of the institutions match the social amenities available in the outside world that they even include elementary schools for the children of prisoners, community clubs such as the Catholic Women's League, and Parents–Teachers Associations.

SUMMARY

Although correctional systems exist in all of the nations of the world and although many of these correctional systems follow practices and policies from which American correctional administrators could learn a great deal, international corrections is almost completely unknown in the United States. Correctional research published in the United States rarely makes reference to international studies and almost never includes an analysis of data that have been obtained cross-culturally. One of the amazing findings of some of the cross-cultural research that has been carried out in recent years is the great similarity in the prisoner societies that grow up within correctional institutions in nations with unique histories and cultures.

Canada, Great Britain, and New Zealand have correctional systems that are very similar to the American system. The Scandinavian countries and the

Netherlands are remarkable in their low incarceration rates, their short sentences, and their humanistic policies for criminals. South Africa is just as remarkable for its brutal oppression of the non-Europeans who make up the majority of its citizens. Japan has developed a unique blend of Eastern and Western correctional practices. Combined with a decreasing crime rate and seemingly boundless economic prosperity, these correctional practices have contributed to a criminal justice system that is one of the most successful in the world. Corrections in the Third World must take a back seat to more immediate social and economic needs in these developing countries. In many of these countries, the courts are as poorly funded as correctional institutions and agencies, with the result that large numbers of citizens sit in correctional institutions for years awaiting trial. Despite chronic underfunding, many Third World nations have developed correctional practices in specific settings that have much to recommend them. An example of this is the open prison, a relatively humane institutional type in which prisoners live lives that are remarkably free from the trappings of total institutions and therefore from the negative effects of these institutional arrangements. India, Sri Lanka, the Philippines, and Mexico are among the Third World nations to have pioneered in the development of open institutions.

REFERENCES

1. Adwani, Nirmala H. *Perspectives on Adult Crime and Corrections*. New Delhi, India: Abhinov Publications, 1978.
2. Ahuja, Ram. "Probation Act: A Sociological Appraisal." *Indian Journal of Social Work* 43 (1979):201–208.
3. Akers, Ronald L., Werner Gruninger, and Norman Hayner. "Prison Inmate Roles: Inter-Organizational and Cross-Cultural Comparisons." *International Journal of Criminology and Penology* 4 (1976) 365–381.
4. Akers, Ronald L., Norman S. Hayner, and Werner Gruninger. "Prisonization in Five Countries: Type of Prison and Inmate Characteristics." *Criminology* 14 (1977): 527–544.
5. Amiot, Michel. "A Brief Glance at the Penitentiary Situation in the Ivory Coast." *In* International Centre for Comparative Criminology and Abidjan Institute of Criminology: *Crime Prevention and Planning*. Montreal: Université de Montréal, 1974, pp. 55–87.
6. Amnesty International. "Report of an Amnesty International Mission to India, 31 December 1977–18 January 1978." London, England, 1979.
7. Amnesty International. *Amnesty International Report 1979*. London, England, 1979.
8. Anderson, Lauren. "A Cross-Cultural Analysis of the Use of Prison." *Prison Law Monitor* 2 (1979):156–158.
9. Antilla, Inkeri. "Corrections in Finland." *In* R.J. Wicks and H.H.A. Cooper: *International Corrections*. Lexington, MA: D.C. Heath, 1979, pp. 103–122.
10. Ardron, Dale K. "Community Resource Centres: A One Year Follow-up Study." Toronto: Ontario Ministry of Correctional Services, 1978.
11. Asuni, T. "Corrections in Nigeria." *In* R.J. Wicks and H.H.A. Cooper: *International Corrections*. Lexington, MA: D.C. Heath, 1979, pp. 163–182.

12. Canadian Penitentiary and National Parole Services. "Returning to Society: Community Correctional Centres." Ottawa, 1976.
13. Canadian Penitentiary Service. "Joyceville Industrial Pilot Project." Ottawa, 1977.
14. Canadian Penitentiary Service. "List of Penitentiaries." Ottawa, 1977.
15. Canadian Penitentiary Service. "Reorganization of Industries in the Canadian Penitentiary Service." Ottawa, 1977.
16. Central Intelligence Agency. *National Basic Intelligence Fact Book.* Washington, D.C.: Government Printing Office, 1980.
17. Clinard, Marshall B. and Daniel J. Abbott. *Crime in Developing Countries: A Comparative Perspective.* New York: Wiley, 1973.
18. Cohen, Neil P. "The English Board of Visitors: Lay Outsiders as Inspectors and Decisionmakers in Prison." *Federal Probation* 40 (1976):24–27.
19. Crispino, Leonard and Catherine Carey. "Intermittent Sentence: Process and Problems." Toronto: Ontario Ministry of Correctional Services, 1978.
20. De Bray, Leo. "Prisons in Venezuela." *International Journal of Offender Therapy and Comparative Criminology* 17 (1973):193–195.
21. Delgoda, J.P. "A Long Term Open Prison in Sri Lanka." *International Journal of Offender Therapy and Comparative Criminology* 21 (1977):184–192.
22. Delgoda, J.P. "A Prison Without Guards." Sri Lanka: Department of Prisons, 1980.
23. Delgoda, J.P. "The Correctional System of Sri Lanka." Sri Lanka: Department of Prisons, no date.
24. Dodge, Calvert R. *A World Without Prisons.* Lexington, MA: D.C. Heath, 1979.
25. Edwards, Amy. "The Prison System in England and Wales 1878–1978." Edinburgh, Scotland, Her Majesty's Stationery Office, 1978.
26. Galindo, Antonio S. "The Present-day Situation Regarding Prisons in Mexico." *In* R.J. Wicks and H.H.A. Cooper: *International Corrections.* Lexington, MA: D.C. Heath, 1979, pp. 89–102.
27. Gokhale, S.D. and N.K. Sohoni. "The Juvenile Justice System in India: Summary of Findings of the Three Sub-Studies in Bombay, Delhi and Madras." *In* United Nations Social Defense Research Institute: *Juvenile Justice: An International Survey.* Rome, 1976, pp. 15–54.
28. Gokhale, S.D. and N.K. Sohoni. "Wither Correction?" *International Social Work* 22 (1979):9–25.
29. Great Britain. Home Office. *Prison Statistics. England and Wales. 1977.* London: Her Majesty's Stationery Office, 1978.
30. Great Britain. Home Office. *Report on the Work of the Prison Department. 1978.* London: Her Majesty's Stationery Office, 1979.
31. Hansen, Inger. *Annual Report of the Correctional Investigator, 1975–1976.* Ottawa: Supply and Services Canada, 1977.
32. Hug, James J. "A First-Year Examination of Education and Employment Temporary Absence Programs." Toronto: Ontario Department of Correctional Services, no date.
33. Hulsman, L.H.C. "The Evolution of Imprisonment in The Netherlands." *In* National Criminal Justice Reference Service: *International Summaries, Volume 2.* Washington, D.C.: Government Printing Office, 1978, pp. 43–52.
34. India. *Model Prison Manual.* Faridabad: Government of India Press, 1970.
35. India. *Social Defense: A Statistical Handbook.* Coimbatore: Government of India Press, 1976.

36. Irvine, Michael J. "The Guelph Abattoir Programme: An Innovative Approach to Correctional Industries III. A Follow-up." Toronto: Ontario Ministry of Correctional Services, 1978.
37. Jackson, Wayne P. "Treatment of the Offender in the United Kingdom: Observations by an American Probation Officer." *Federal Probation* 35 (June 1971):50–57.
38. Japan. Ministry of Justice. *Criminal Justice in Japan.* Tokyo, 1972.
39. Japan. Ministry of Justice. *Summary of the White Paper on Crime, 1972.* Tokyo, 1973.
40. Japan. Ministry of Justice. *Non-Institutional Treatment of Offenders in Japan.* Tokyo, 1974.
41. Japan, Ministry of Justice. *Summary of the White Paper on Crime, 1979.* Tokyo. 1980.
42. Jellicoe, the Rt. Hon. The Earl. Boards of Visitors of Penal Institutions. *London: Barry Rose Publishers, 1975.*
43. Jeyasingh, J.V. "Parole: A Strategy to Prison Reform." *Indian Journal of Criminology* 6 (1978):101–105.
44. Johnson, Elmer H. "Finland's Penal Colonies: The Forbearant Model and Community-Based Corrections." *Journal of Criminal Justice* 1 (1973):327–338.
45. Jones, Howard and Paul Cornes. *Open Prisons.* London: Routledge and Kegan Paul, 1977.
46. Kahn, M.Z. and N.P. Unnithan. "Capability of Inmates and Their Interest in Work-Programmes at the Central Prison, Madras." *Indian Journal Social Work* 39 (1978):9–26.
47. Krantz, Lars, Lars Bagge, and Norman Bishop. *Recidivism Among Those Conditionally Released from Prison During 1973.* Norrköping, Sweden: National Prison and Probation Administration, 1977.
48. Landreville, Pierre. "Penology in West Africa and in Abidjan in Particular." *In* International Centre for Comparative Criminology and the Abidjan Institute of Criminology: *First West African Conference in Comparative Criminology.* Abidjan, Ivory Coast, 1972, pp. 81–104.
49. López-Rey, Manuel. *Crime: An Analytic Appraisal.* New York: Praeger, 1970.
50. López-Rey, Manuel. "Crime and the Penal System." *Australian and New Zealand Journal of Criminology* 4 (1971):5–20.
51. López-Rey, Manuel. "The Correction of the Criminal Offender in Latin America." *In* R.J. Wicks and H.H.A. Cooper: *International Corrections.* Lexington, MA: D.C. Heath, 1979, pp. 71–88.
52. Lønberg, Arne. *The Penal System of Denmark.* Copenhagen, Denmark: Ministry of Justice, 1975.
53. Markland, F.J. "Periodic Detention: A Comparison of Residential and Non-Residential Centres." Wellington, New Zealand: Department of Justice, 1979.
54. Martin, J.P. "Jellicoe and After—Boards of Visitors Into the Eighties." *The Howard Journal of Penology and Crime Prevention* 19 (1980):85–101.
55. McConville, Sean. "Boards of Visitors of Penal Institutions." *British Journal of Criminology* 15 (1975):391–394.
56. McFarlane, George. "Ontario's Temporary Absence Programs: 'Phantom' or 'Phoenix'-Like Phenomena." *American Journal of Criminology* 20 (1979):310–339.
57. Midgeley, James. "The Prospect of Penal Reform in South Africa." *International Journal of Offender Therapy and Comparative Criminology* 23 (1979):99–108.

58. Moseley, L.G. "Finnish Labour Colonies." *Howard Journal of Penology and Crime Prevention* 14 (1973):317–330.

59. NACRO. "For Care of Offenders and Prevention of Crime." London, 1977.

60. National Parole Service of Canada. "List of Districts and Sub-Offices." Ottawa, 1977.

61. National Prison and Probation Administration. Newman, J. and James Midgeley. "Crime and Penal Statistics in South Africa." *In* J. Midgley, J.H. Steyn and R. Graser: *Crime and Punishment in South Africa.* Johannesburg, South Africa: McGraw-Hill, 1975.

62. New Zealand. Department of Statistics. "Justice Statistics 1977, Prisons and Prisoners." Wellington, 1978.

63. New Zealand. Department of Statistics. "Justice Statistics 1977, No. 2, Prisons and Prisoners and Supreme Court (Criminal)." Wellington, 1978.

64. New Zealand. Department of Statistics. "Justice Statistics 1979, Prisons and Prisoners." Wellington, 1980.

65. New Zealand Prisoner's Aid and Rehabilitation Society. "New Zealand Prisoner's Aid and Rehabilitation Society." Wellington, New Zealand, no date.

66. Oxley, P.C. "Probationers and Their Reoffending." Wellington, New Zealand: Department of Justice, 1979.

67. Parizeau, Alice and Denis Szabo. "The Correctional System in Canada." *In* R.J. Wicks and H.H.A. Cooper: *International Corrections.* Lexington, MA: D.C. Heath, 1979, pp. 21–38.

68. Pillai, D.N. "An Approach to Crime and Corrections and Developing Countries." *In* United Nations Asia and Far East Institute for the Prevention of Crime and the Treatment of Offenders: *Report for 1978 and Resource Material Series No. 16.* Tokyo, 1979.

69. Polonoski, Marian. "The Community Service Order Programme in Ontario. 1. Description of the Initial Cases." Toronto: Ontario Ministry of Correctional Services, 1979.

70. Price, John A. "Private Interprise in a Prison: The Free Market Economy of La Mesa Penitenciaria." *Crime and Delinquency* 19 (1973):218–227.

71. Robson, J.L. "Crime and Penal Policy." *New Zealand Journal of Public Administration* 33 (1971):20–54.

72. Seidman, Robert B. and J.D. Abaka Eyison. "Ghana." *In* Allan Milner: *African Penal Systems.* New York: Praeger, 1969, pp. 59–88.

73. Serrill, Michael S. "Profile/Denmark." *Corrections Magazine* 3 (March 1977): 23–29.

74. Serrill, Michael S. "Profile/Sweden." *Corrections Magazine* 3 (June 1977):11–36.

75. Seymour, J.A. "Periodic Detention in New Zealand." *British Journal of Criminology* 9 (1969):182–187.

76. Shah, J.H. *Open Prisons in India.* New Delhi, India: Central Bureau of Correctional Services, 1970.

77. Shah, J.H. "Probation Services in India." *International Journal of Offender Therapy and Comparative Criminology* 18 (1974):187–191.

78. Shukla, K.B. "Management of Institutions for Children: A Delhi Study." *Indian Journal of Public Administration* 25 (1979):725–733.

79. Sidwani, K.L. "Crime and Penal Institutions in New Zealand." *Criminology* 9 (1971):330–331.

80. South Africa. *Report of the Commissioner of Prisons of the Republic of South Africa. 1 July 1978 to 30 June 1979.* Pretoria: Government Printer, 1980.
81. South African Institute of Race Relations. *A Survey of Race Relations in South Africa: 1977.* Johannesburg, South Africa, 1978.
82. South African Institute for Crime Prevention and Rehabilitation of Offenders. "NICRO, 70 Years of Service." Cape Town, South Africa, 1979.
83. Srivastava, S.P. "The Legal Frame-Work of Probation in India." *Indian Journal of Social Work* 31 (1970):263–269.
84. Srivastava, S.P. "The Quality of Basic Necessities in Prison: An Analysis of Food, Clothes and Shelter." *Indian Journal of Social Work* 33 (1973):337–346.
85. Srivastava, S.P. *The Indian Prison Community.* Lucknow, India: Pustak Kendra, 1977.
86. Steyn, J.H. "The Punishment Scene in South Africa—Developments over the Past Decade and the Prospects of Reform." *In* Roger Hood: *Crime, Criminology and Public Policy: Essays in Honour of Sir Leon Radzinowicz.* New York: Free Press, 1974, pp. 541–570.
87. Stockdale, Eric. "The Correctional System in England and Wales." *In* R.J. Wicks and H.H.A. Cooper: *International Corrections.* Lexington, MA: D.C. Heath, 1979, pp. 5–20.
88. Suzuki, Yoshio. "Corrections in Japan." *In* R.J. Wicks and H.H.A. Cooper: *International Corrections.* Lexington, MA: D.C. Heath, 1979, pp. 141–162.
89. Sweden. National Prison and Probation Administration. Kriminalvården, 1978. Norrköping, 1979.
90. Swedish Institute. "Fact Sheets on Sweden: Correctional Care in Sweden." Stockholm, Sweden, 1979.
91. Thailand. Ministry of Interior. Department of Corrections. *Annual Report 1978.* Bangkok, 1979.
92. Thorsen, D.M. "Waikeria Youth Centre, New Zealand's Borstal Farm." *British Journal of Criminology* 5 (1965):440–441.
93. Trivedi, Vishhal. "Relevance of Work-Programmes in Institutional Correction in India." *Indian Journal of Criminology* 6 (1978):87–89.
94. Vongehaisuwan, Kiertisuckdi. "Solution for Prison's Overcrowding: The Thai Experience." *In* United Nations Asia and Far East Institute for the Prevention of Crime and the Treatment of Offenders: *Resource Material Series No. 17.* Fuchu, Tokyo, Japan, 1980, pp. 159–162.
95. United Nations Asia and Far East Institute for the Prevention of Crime and the Treatment of Offenders. *The Open Correctional Institution in Asia and the Far East.* New York, 1965.
96. United Nations. *Maltreatment and Torture of Prisoners in South Africa: Report of the Special Committee on Apartheid.* New York, 1973.
97. Unnithan, N.P. and M.Z. Kahn. "The Acquisition of Skills by Inmates in Work Programmes at the Central Prison, Madras." *Indian Journal of Social Work* 40 (1979):1–14.
98. Uusitalo. Paavo. "Recidivism After Release from Closed and Open Penal Institutions." *British Journal of Criminology* 12 (1972):211–229.
99. Waller, Irvin and Janet Chan. "Prison Use: A Canadian and International Comparison." *Criminal Law Quarterly* 17 (1974):47–72.
100. Ward, David A. "Sweden: The Middle Way to Prison Reform?" *In* Marvin E. Wolfgang: *Prisons: Present and Possible.* Lexington, MA: D.C. Heath, 1979.

101. Wickwar, Hardy. *The Place of Criminal Justice and Developmental Planning.* New York: New York University Press, 1977.

102. Williams, J.E. Hall. "Parole in England and Wales: A Success Story." *University of Toledo Law Review* 10 (1979):465–492.

103. Yanagimoto, Masajru. "Some Features of the Japanese Prison System." *British Journal of Criminology* 10 (1970):209–224.

104. Zagaris, Bruce. "The Finnish Penal System: Recent Reforms." *The England Journal on Prison Law* 3 (1977):437–486.

105. Zeitoun, Louis. "The Development of Community-Based Residential Centres in Canada." *Offender Rehabilitation* 3 (1978):133–150.

Chapter 18

The Critique of Traditional Corrections

There is a danger in any survey of the field of corrections. This is that by devoting so many pages to an examination of existing correctional practices, we appear to be justifying these practices and accepting them as legitimate. The problems that are exposed seem solvable by merely tinkering with the system rather than requiring its dismantling and replacement with a radically different system, or even a nonsystem. Any introductory course in anthropology contains enough cross-cultural material to demonstrate that the same human problems can be solved in many different ways. What seems to work best in one situation and at one point in time is a matter for debate, not dogma.

It would be a disservice to students to publish a text without attempting to widen students' horizons beyond existing programs and practices. In *Corrections: The Science and the Art,* we have already attempted to do this along three dimensions. We have examined corrections using philosophical, historical, and cross-cultural perspectives. This chapter, by presenting contemporary radical criticisms of the correctional system, broadens our view of corrections in a fourth way.

Radical criminology is characterized by a strident rejection of the existing system, a sensitivity to the role that the historical development of corrections plays in its contemporary institutional arrangements, an emphasis on the ways in which vested interests are served by the existing system, and a preference for the use of social class and economics as explanatory variables instead of behavioral, clinical, and social–psychological variables. Before we try to understand some of the radical critiques of the correctional system, we need to look at another group of critics of the system: those who go further than mere tinkering but do not propose solutions that are as extreme as those of the radical genre.

NON-RADICAL CRITIQUES OF THE
CORRECTIONAL SYSTEM.

Correctional administrators are not safe from criticism in any camp except their own. Criticisms and proposals for change come from every side. Conservatives as well as Liberals are critical of the system. A recent article by Ernest van den Haag,[47] who is generally considered to be quite conservative* on the issue of punishment, stated that current correctional practices are lethally irresponsible. He then goes on to propose that half of all presently confined prisoners should be redeployed in what he calls the no-security prison. With no security precautions or specialized construction being necessary, this would significantly reduce the cost of operating the correctional system.

A second major source of prison reform has been the courts. Once considered by liberals to have abdicated their judicial responsibility by following a hands-off policy with regard to prison conditions,[7] the courts have now waded into the fray, mandated numerous prison reforms, exposed and denounced prison conditions, and outlawed certain traditional prison practices. Together with asserting the rights of prisoners in a variety of areas, these actions have put the courts in the forefront of the critics of American correction. For a more detailed discussion of these issues, see Chapter 12.

Six other sources of nonradical critiques of corrections are journalistic social critics (who might be called gadflies), religious organizations, ex-corrections professionals, clinicians, liberal academics, and cost or cost–benefit analysts. Each of these types is discussed below, with at least one example presented of each type.

Journalistic Gadflies

The journalistic gadfly does not necessarily have a long-term professional interest in corrections. Gadflies typically have a more general concern with injustice in society, and move from topic to topic throughout their careers. When a given institution or practice seems to be appropriate for their attention, they carefully research it and publicize it to the general public in a nontechnical style which ranges from exposés to proposals for reform.

An example of a journalistic gadfly in the area of corrections in Jessica Mitford, who had earlier received national acclaim for her analysis and criticism of American mortuary practices. Her major assault upon the correctional establishment is the book, *Kind and Usual Punishment: The Prison Business*, which was published in 1973.[25] In this book, she argues that "treatment" programs are often no more than the administration of heavy doses of tranquilizers and extensive paperwork. She condemns the use of prisoners for drug experimentation, comparing drug testers to the Nuremberg war criminals and commenting that experimentation on prisoners is cheaper than experimentation on chimpanzees. The quality of her analysis is exemplified in the following

*See, for example, Ernest van den Haag. *Punishing Criminals*. New York: Basic Books, 1975.

quote, which summarizes her evaluation of individualized treatment in correctional institutions:

> The cure will be deemed effective to the degree that the poor/young/brown/black/captive appears to have capitulated to his middle-class/white/middle-aged captor and to have adopted the virtues of subservience to authority, industry, cleanliness, docility. Subtle methods are, of course, preferable if and when they work. If and when they do not, there are cruder ones in the closet: the club, such products of advanced chemistry as tear gas and Mace, and, in the last analysis, the gun.[25:128]

Religious Groups

A number of religious groups have actively supported prison reform. Three relatively small religions have been particularly vocal: the Mennonites, the Quakers, and the Unitarian Universalists. At the very least, Christian critics of corrections argue that prison conditions are inhumane and that they should immediately be drastically altered. Some groups go further, and suggest that few criminals require imprisonment. The Unitarian Universalist Service Committee has formed an organization called the National Moratorium on Prison Construction, which publishes a newsletter entitled *Jericho*. A recent issue of this publication includes articles on the following topics.

1. An analysis of a riot at the New Mexico state penitentiary which points out that the riot would never had occurred had the state followed the recommendation in its own Corrections Master Plan, which was commissioned by the legislature in 1976.
2. A critique of correctional policy in Maryland, where a governor who had appeared to be in favor of deinstitutionalization had made a 180-degree turn and was now pushing for the building of new facilities and the renovation of old facilities to accommodate additional prisoners.
3. A continuation of a long series of articles in opposition to the Olympic Prison, the plan to turn housing facilities used for the Winter Olympics at Lake Placid into a federal correctional institution.
4. A criticism of correctional policy in Texas. This report shows that the increase in the Texas prison population cannot be explained by either the increase in the state's population or the increase in Texas crime rate. Instead, the article favors changes in sentencing and probation policies as the major cause of the prison population increase, showing that judges lengthened sentences by 26 percent between 1973 and 1979, and that the average time served by prisoners increased by more than 80 percent during this period.[13]

Ex-Corrections Professionals

Once a practitioner in the criminal justice system, William Nagel[27] headed a team of correctional officials, sociologists, psychologists, and architects that visited over 100 correctional facilities, all of which were less than ten years old.

He concluded that even these fine facilities could do little about the basic problems of imprisonment, such as dehumanization, family disruption, racism, and lack of privacy. Following the tenets of the total institution view of the prison, he voiced concern about the effects of institutionalization on administrators as well as prisoners. Despite the much-trumpeted emphasis on community corrections, most of the new institutions visited by Nagel and his team were as isolated as the old ones. His conclusion was that there should be a moratorium on the construction of new prisons, jails, and training schools. During this period, there should be a concentrated effort to reduce the jail population, to search for alternatives to incarceration, and to unify the correctional system.

Though hardly positive, Nagel's criticisms are mild compared with those of Thomas Murton,[26] who headed up an Arkansas correctional institution in the late 1960s. Murton generalized his own experiences to a model of reform efforts. In this model, a scandal creates a demand for reform and leads to the hiring or volunteering of a capable reformer. Reforms are quickly instituted and programs innovated. This leads to political pressures that result in the withdrawal of support by governmental agencies from the reformer. The threat to the power structure posed by the reformer is recognized, and although correctional agency heads may pose as reformers themselves, they eventually move from the support of reform to the inhibition of reform, and finally to the repression of reform. They invariably remove the reformer from office along the way. The cycle may end up with some net gain as a result of the process, a net loss, or a return to exactly the same level at which the cycle began. When a new scandal arises, the cycle is then repeated.

Murton is highly critical of the American Correctional Association. He believes that it has survived by such tactics as "purging itself of reform prophets from time to time, and ignoring fundamental issues in penology."[26:258] He cites various quotes from ACA meetings between 1970 and 1973 to show that correctional administrators have little interest in serious rehabilitation and are much more concerned with a meaningless round of institutional maintenance. He scoffs at the 1973 presentation of the E.R. Cass Award to Russell G. Oswald, who was made famous by his role in the Attica Riot in which 43 men died. In making this award, "the 'professional' association for prison workers has bestowed its highest award upon the man who presided over the greatest massacre in American prison history."[26:266]

Clinicians

Clinicians such as psychologists, psychiatrists, and psychiatric social workers have often been critical of the correctional system. Some of these criticisms have reflected the treatment–custody conflicts in the institutions in which these individuals work. Karl Menninger[23] carried the clinical criticism of corrections to a high moral plane when he condemned the correctional establishment for implementing what he referred to as te crime of punishment. Using good psychological strategies throughout, he was always quick to praise advances made in correctional programming so that his words were not automatically dismissed by correctional administrators. He managed to be critical and yet positive at the same time. Asked to deliver a lecture at the Institute of

Contemporary Corrections and the Behavioral Sciences, Sam Houston State University, Menninger summarized his view of contemporary corrections by saying that "Few of us have ever seen anybody whipped to death; but the people of England had a chance to see it. You and I don't have to see what we do; we have people tortured slowly out of sight, so we don't have to see it. I want to tell you that it is torture to be confined anywhere."[23:5]

Liberal Academics

Until recent years, scientific correctional research has been dominated by sociologists, and sociology is the most politically liberal of the social sciences. It is therefore understandable that a great many of the sociologists studying corrections would be exceedingly critical of their subject matter. A recent Canadian example of this is James Hackler's book, *The Prevention of Youthful Crime: The Great Stumble Forward.*[5] With a title like this, no one could be mistaken about the orientation of the author. Hackler is at pains to expose the various fads and foibles of juvenile delinquency prevention in Canada. He points out that we cannot understand juvenile delinquency prevention unless we have an idea about what interest groups benefit when certain acts are defined as delinquent and then subjected to specified social controls. He compares the rising concern with juvenile delinquency to the processes through which we have outlawed recreational drugs and temporarily outlawed and then re-legalized the use of alcoholic beverages. He cautions us that the arrogant recommendations of reform panels appointed by government officials may serve various interest groups and also provide a general rationale that meets the psychological needs of society's members without being helpful to juveniles or reducing the incidence of juvenile delinquency.

An American sociologist, Charles Thomas,[44] has gone so far as to label the correctional institution as an enemy of corrections. He points out that the effects of a hostile prisoner subculture can make it essentially impossible for even the best treatment programs to have positive impacts. When treatment programs are grafted on top of custody-oriented staff organizations, the institution has not made a significant commitment to a change of goals from custody to treatment. A serious commitment to the treatment philosophy requires that the staffing pattern be dramatically altered.

> The autonomy of the treatment staff increases. The highly centralized power structure typical of custodially oriented institutions becomes decentralized. Daily operations become more or less routinized. Authority becomes more heavily invested in professional personnel.[44:12]

When the staffing pattern of the prison changes, the prisoner subculture begans to change in response to it. Only then can treatment programs begin to have positive effects in prisons. Because Thomas believes that "...most of the people now in the field are neither willing or able to see beyond the exceedingly narrow focus provided by psychological and psychiatric models," he concludes that "...the organizational structures of many correctional institutions are the major enemy of effective correctional programs."[44:12]

Cost Analysts

An interesting "back door" approach to correctional reform is to show that the taxpayers can actually save money while being more humane. At the very least, the cost analysts can argue that there will be no significant cost associated with a new program, as Arthur D. Little, Inc.[16] did in an analysis of the impacts of the deinstitutionalization of status offenders in ten states. Cost analysis can make a much stronger case for reform by doing a detailed cost-benefit analysis of alternatives to incarceration or whatever other practice they are attemping to perform, which allows them to show in dollars and cents how much money can be saved by implementing more humane alternatives.

An example of this approach is the cost-benefit analysis of a number of alternatives to incarceration in Maine that was prepared by a committee of the Maine State Bar Association. The committee prepared separate cost–benefit analyses for alternatives to the institutional confinement of adults and alternatives to institutionalization for juveniles. They showed that all of the prisons, the pre-release center, and the halfway house had greater costs than the expected benefits to be derived from these facilities. Benefits included in the analysis ranged from increased governmental tax revenues to reduced welfare payments and criminal justice system expenditures. The least efficient program of all was the women's correctional center, which spent $574 for every $100 of benefit. In contrast, the county jail realized $100 of benefit from every $62 spent (partially because of the underfunding that plagues nearly all jails), and estimates for various community alternatives to adult institutional confinement ranged between $100 for every $50 spent and $100 for every dollar spent.[4]

The figures for juveniles were similar, with the Maine Youth Center spending $533 for every $100 benefit and an assortment of community alternatives spending between $1 and $43 for every $100 of benefits. As in the adult analysis, nonresidential alternatives are shown to be much more cost-effective than the residential alternatives for juveniles, which suggests that conservatives as well as liberals should seriously consider supporting these alternatives unless it can be shown that they are less effective (in terms of recidivism) than institutional treatment.[4] Since research conducted to date does not support the notion that institutional treatment is more effective than community-based alternatives, the cost–benefit analysis strategy is an effective way of supporting correctional reform for those offenders who are not considered to be too dangerous to be at large in the community.

RADICAL CRITIQUES OF TRADITIONAL CORRECTIONS

According to Jock Young,[54] the work of radical criminology is not to support the existing system, but instead, to "...show up the law, in its true colour, as the instrument of a ruling class, and *tactically* to demonstrate that the state will break its own laws, that its legitimacy is a sham, and that the rule-makers are also the greatest of rule-breakers." Furthermore,...."it is precisely the nature of law to conceal particular interests behind universalistic ideology and rhetoric."[54:89] Even where decriminalization occurs, the official rhetoric conceals the fact that it is being done because the system cannot cope with an excessive number of prisoners or social work cases. Decriminalization does not occur unless it serves the interest of the ruling-class. "It is the role of the radical criminologist to demystify control and to join with those movements which seek to provide tangible alternatives in areas of choice."[54:90] In the following sections, we will examine radical theory, radical analysis of historical and contemporary corrections, radical advocacy on behalf of oppressed groups such as minorities, juveniles, and women, and intellectual radicalism in action.

Radical Theory

For Karl Marx, the exploitation of the working class that was the crucial characteristic of capitalist society became equally crucial in the understanding of prison life. The factory came to be recognized as the ideal workhouse, and prisons became ideal factories. Marx thus saw prison punishment as a representation of the dominant capitalist ideology. In his view, the same productive work that could free the working class from the alienating work of the factory could have similar positive effects on criminals.[21]

Because the punishment of criminals in capitalist societies is aimed specifically at the working class, the characteristics of punishment are determined by the condition of the lowest stratum of the working class. Georg Rusche[33] believed that there was no hope for prison reform that went beyond the minimum life standard existing in the lowest part of the working class, since to do so would make prison more attractive than free life. Through long periods of history, the condition of the lowest segment of the working class was starvation, and this is still the condition of many groups of people in Third World societies today. If starvation is the reward of the free, prison life guaranteeing adequate food and shelter could lose its status as a fearsome punishment. How many among the poor would be willing to work for starvation wages in a society in which the prisons were humane? We do not know, for no society has ever experienced this combination of conditions.

Rusche applied this approach to the historical development of punishment in a manuscript that was later altered by Otto Kirchheimer and jointly published as *Punishment and Social Structure*.[34] This is essentially a qualitative rather than a quantitative theory, which attempts to explain the nature and character of punishment rather than its magnitude. Rusche and Kirchheimer argue not only that the upper limit of the conditions of punishment is set by the lower limit of conditions in the working class: they also show how the type of punishment favored in a given historical era is dependent upon the structure of economic relations in that era. A synopsis of their historical analysis will be presented in the following section on history. It is unfortunate that they did not live to extend their theory to modern capitalist relations, in which new means of social control have arisen so that imprisonment is no longer as central to the process of social control as it once was. The radical critique of contemporary capitalism posits that even if the long-term trend in the use of imprisonment is downward, this does not mean that the total pressure of social control is diminishing. It is simply a symptom of the rapid diversification of social control mechanisms beyond the boundaries of criminal justice system.[22]

Richard Quinney[30] discusses this process in a recent treatment of criminal justice in capitalist society. He finds little to distinguish liberal from conservative responses to the problem of social control, both being reduced to what he calls "the utilitarianism of pain." Under this principle, we can only expect people to conform if the penalty is clearly more painful than the reward to be gained from deviant behavior. In Quinney's view, conservative and liberal theorists alike do no more than to "merely justify further repression within the established order."[30:17] He sees the courts in contemporary capitalist society as being less interested in the question of guilt and innocence than in making dispositions that minimize recidivism, and believes that everything that is written about the criminal justice system in America amounts to no more than an apology for punishment.

Quinney believes that the capitalist state is in crisis, and must constantly expand its social control apparatus. What needs controlling is mainly the surplus population. During periods of depression and recession, the surplus population grows through unemployment. Women, blacks, the young, and unskilled workers are thrown out of their jobs at a higher rate than white males over age 21. The greater the economic crisis, the greater the use of prisons to control the surplus population. Quinney shows that the unemployment rate and admissions to the federal prison system rose and fell in concert between 1960 and 1972. (We have already presented additional evidence in support of the linkage between unemployment and imprisonment in Chapter 1.) This social control process does not include criminals of the capitalist class—the owners and managers of businesses who commit crimes of great gravity through illegal business practices but who are rarely subjected to prison sentences. It is interesting that the concept of menace, which is so quickly applied to street criminals, is almost never used in reference to corporate executives.[45]

Quinney[30] does not find prison reform to be necessarily a positive step. To understand prison reform, it must be seen in the light of the total set of changes in the social control mechanisms of capitalist society. Prison reform usually has the effect of controlling a greater number of people with no additional expenditure. The criminal justice system does not have unlimited funding, and it can accommodate to the managerial need for increased social control over the working class by placing a larger number of people under less expensive social control mechanisms (such as community treatment programs) than it could under the extremely expensive alternative of imprisonment.

Another line of attack on imprisonment is to expose a series of latent unrecognized functions that are met by imprisonment. Charles Reasons and Russell Kaplan[32] point out latent functions of American and Canadian prisons that include the provision of jobs for criminal justice system employees, the use of slave labor, the reduction of unemployment rates, a safety valve for racial tensions, a mechanism for birth control in the lower class, and a ready source of guinea pigs for scientific research. As evidence for their claim that prisoners constitute slave labor, Reasons and Kaplan cite the extremely low wages that prisoners are paid for their work, such as 35 cents a day. The State saves a great deal of money by having license plates and other materials for State use manufactured in prisons instead of having to contract to purchase these products on the open market. The labor of these prisoners is expropriated as part of their punishment, and it is extremely rare to find prisoners who share in the profits of their industrial prison labor.

The use of prisoners as guinea pigs for scientific research is an area in which there has recently been a great deal of progress. Until recent years it was possible for pharmaceutical companies to test potentially dangerous drugs on prisoners at a fraction of the cost of drug testing on animals, to say nothing of human beings in the free society. In addition, convict labor could be hired to assist in these projects at convict wages rather than at the level of wages paid in the free society. Social workers and lawyers also developed their skills by practicing on prisoners, and social scientists have often built successful careers by doing studies of captive populations.

The final radical theoretical approach that we will mention in this section is Harold Pepinsky's[29] book *Crime Control Strategies*. Pepinsky agrees with liberal apologists of the criminal justice system that the United States has developed an impressive array of alternatives to institutional treatment. He differs from them in that he argues that the alternatives are really additions to the social control apparatus of society. In fact, he suggests a law of social behavior as follows: "The more society resorts to incarceration, the more it tends to develop and use other forms of official supervision and confinement."[29:180] In his view, if we are to use incarceration to treat criminality, then we are doomed to failure, and incarceration rates may expand beyond all control (which seems to have been happening in the United States in recent years).

Criminality refers to a quality of individuals that is essentially unchangeable, while crime refers to external behavior that presumably is subject to change. Therefore, correctional institutions need to treat crime as they would any other issue of normal human behavior. As soon as we attempt to suggest that criminals are somehow fundamentally different from other members of society, we loose our chance to deal effectively with their behavior. This approach implies that the search for the causes of crime has nothing to do with controlling it. Causes, at least when seen clinically rather than as broad social conditions, lead to the treatment of criminals rather than crime. Once we understand that criminals are just like the rest of us, we can plan more realistically for the control of crime. In Pepinsky's words, "...explanations of criminality, cloaked in value neutrality, can only reinforce the idea that crime is out of control, and worse, is uncontrollable. Explanations of criminality are fatalistic. However, human beings in various societies have demonstrated that crime control *is* possible"[29:191]

The History of Corrections in a Radical Perspective

The first three parts of this section—on theory, history, and contemporary critiques on the correctional system—cannot be satisfactorily separated from each other. All three of these categories of analysis overlap in critical writing. No radical critique of the contemporary corrections system would be complete without at least a summary of historical conditions leading to the contemporary system and a theoretical analysis of both the historical and the current social conditions. The separation of material to these three categories is arbitrary and has been accomplished to make the presentation easier to follow.

Karl Marx showed how the bourgeoisie systematically removed the rights and possessions of the poor, thus creating a class of paupers and beggers. By the 18th century, the transformation in England had been completed, and it was necessary to enact penal laws in order to defend the "rights" of those who had enriched themselves through the process and, at the same time, declare the vagrancy of the poor to be criminal.[21] Marx's concern with the criminalization of the poor did not extend to a detailed examination of penal systems. This was left to Rusche and Kirchheimer in 1939. Their book, *Punishment and Social Structure*,[34] has been called the single most outstanding piece of scholarship on the history of punishment.[43]

Rusche and Kirchheimer went back before the industrial revolution to examine life in the early Middle Ages. During that time, the only common form of punishment was the fine. There were relatively few crimes against property, and population pressure was so low that someone desiring to farm a plot of land could easily select one and do so. It was only in the later Middle Ages, when the population pressure increased and overcrowding occurred, that wages were driven down by an excess of workers who no longer had property of their own on which to grow food to feed their families. Criminality changed from a matter of sexuality or hatred to a preponderance of property crimes and a large number of beggars, thieves, and robbers. The propertyless criminals had no money with which to pay fines, and so new punishments had to be devised that made use of the only thing the criminals had to give, their physical bodies. Whippings, mutilations, and killings were initially redeemable through monetary substitutions because they were intended only to apply to those individuals who had no property.[33]

It was around the year 1600 that the economics of labor began to change again, when trade and new markets increased the size of the economic system quickly and wars and plagues simultaneously decreased the size of the labor force. Labor again became valuable, and it became wasteful to execute a thief who could possibly bring profit to the state or to an entrepreneur if allowed to live. The humanitarian trend in punishment was not long-lived, for the industrial revolution, which was the focus of much of Marx's analysis, altered the relationship between owners and workers in the 1700s by creating a surplus of laborers who were no longer needed in the automated factories. Penal servitude was not so profitable, and prison conditions were deliberately made to be as brutal as possible. Productive work gave way to meaningless work such as carrying stones from one pile to another and then back again.[33] At a time when the poor were being dominated by economic and political forces beyond their control, the reigning ideology was that criminals and paupers had freely chosen their own conditions. It is because of this assumption that the utilitarian response of penal institutions had to be so repressive.[8]

One reason why prisons in the United States pioneered relatively humane practices in the 19th century was that America did not suffer from the population pressures of the European countries. There was concern that prisoners be productive while incarcerated, and this limited the degree of misery that could be forced upon them. The need for agricultural labor in the United States during the 19th century was comparable to the situation in Europe before the industrial revolution.[33]

An example of the way in which this mechanism worked was the population of Chinese immigrants in the West. During the years that Chinese laborers were used to build the railroads and to perform other manual labor in Western states where there were not enough American laborers to accomplish all of the tasks that needed to be done, few Chinese were imprisoned. The percentage of Chinese prisoners at San Quentin in California was 2.6 in 1854, and it stayed in the vicinity of 6 percent for the next decade. After the railway work was completed and there were now sufficient nonChinese laborers to go around,the percentage of Chinese in California's prisons rose sharply to approximately 19 percent in 1879 through 1883. It then gradually declined, reaching 4.1 percent in 1900.[42] In this example, as in the earlier examples drawn from Europe, the imprisonment rate for the poor is proportional to the need for their labor in the economic system. Recent statistical studies by Matthew Yeager[53] and Ivan Jankovic[12] show that unemployment and imprisonment vary together. Although there are some exceptions, high unemployment (which means low demand for labor) is associated with high rates of imprisonment. Yeager concludes that "...it appears that imprisonment functions, at least in part, to contain and regulate the marginal secondary labor force composed of the unemployed and subemployed."[53:588]

A final example of the radical historical analysis of corrections is an amusing application of Parkinson's law to the U.S. Bureau of Prisons by Alfred Villaume.[48] Parkinson's law predicts that the number of workers in a unit will continue to increase regardless of the amount of work to be done, or even if there is any work is to be performed at all. In applying this principle to the U.S. Bureau of Prison, Villaume took the number of employees dealing with federal prisons just before the creation of the Bureau and traced the growth of employees from that time until the present. He also charted the rise in the prisoner population, and showed that the growth of employees was not related to the growth in the number of prisoners. As soon as the Bureau was created in 1930, there was an immediate increase from 650 to 1000 employees to handle approximately 15,000 prisoners. By 1977, the number of prisoners had not quite doubled, but the number of staff members had increased to 8740—more than 800 percent. Looking at just the period from 1970 to 1975, the number of prisoners processed by the Bureau increased 21 percent and the number of employees increased 83 percent. Of course, one criticism of Villaume's analysis is to say that the reason the number of employees increased so greatly is that services to the prisoners increased correspondingly. Villaume has no way of empirically undermining this criticism, but he offers personal experiences as a prisoner in a system to argue that the fourfold increase in employees doing casework with prisoners over the past ten years has had no more effect than to make it more difficult to see a caseworker today than it was a decade ago.

Contemporary Corrections

Radical theorists generally believe that the State is expanding its social control apparatus in response to the contemporary crisis of capitalist society. Janet

Schmidt,[36] writing on parole in California, concludes that "The mechanisms of social control are tightening up, illustrative of the way in which intensification of punishment is a response to deteriorating social and economic conditions.[36:141] In Australia as in the United States, the implementation of alternatives to imprisonment has been associated with an increase in the social control span of the correctional system rather than a substitution of less coercive alternatives for the extreme coercion of imprisonment.[45]

In a "criminal policy paper" issued by the Norwegian Cabinet, it was argued that increased social sanctions were necessary in Norway because of the weakening of nonlegal social controls. Thomas Mathiesen[19] believes that the future holds a continuing expansion of the social control system in Norway. Prisons will continue to be used as a backstop for these less severe controls, and the total sphere of control exercised by criminal justice agencies will continually increase. In a postscript to his article, Mathiesen adds that recent developments in Norway have included a new Minister of Justice who rejected the deinstitutionalization proposed in the "criminal policy paper," and, at the same time, indicated his support for the additional controls proposed in the paper. Thus, it seems that Mathiesen's prediction had begun to materialize even before his article was published.

A fundamental difference between radical theorists and conventional correctional administrators is that radical theorists emphasize the political nature of imprisonment while correctional managers emphasize the individualistic, volitional, and rehabilitative aspects of incarceration.

Political Prisoners. Bettina Aptheker[1] has identified four different types of political prisoners. First are those who have been framed because of their political success in the outside world. Draft resisters and those who have committed other acts of civil disobedience make up the second category of political prisoners. A third group of political prisoners are men and women from the working and poverty classes who were convicted of crimes they did not commit because of inadequate legal counsel. The final group consists of prisoners who actually committed criminal offenses on the streets and then developed a political consciousness after imprisonment. These individuals are political prisoners not only because of their change of consciousness, but because they may be persecuted (e.g., privileges taken away and their sentences lengthened) because of their political activism in the prisoner population.

We might add a fifth category to Aptheker's list. In a sense, any prisoner who has been successfully rehabilitated runs the danger of becoming a political prisoner because successful rehabilitation should lead to an individual who is self-sufficient, socially sensitive, and involved, and willing to make personal sacrifices for the improvement of society. Such individuals might easily come into conflict with the prison administration and be suppressed as a result. It is a weak rehabilitative program that produces only mindless conformity to the rules rather than an active questioning stance towards social arrangements, but this is the only kind of rehabilitation program that does not run the risk of creating political prisoners.[10]

We conclude this section on radical critiques of contemporary corrections with three examples of criticisms of treatment programs. These three examples are the use of drugs by prison psychiatrists in California, the operation of the

Federal Prison Industry, and the installation of a step-system type of behavior modification program in the Massachusetts Department of Corrections. From a liberal treatment viewpoint, this program seems to be exemplary, but the radical critique of the step-system is that it is merely a veneer designed to deceive the public about the basic repressiveness of the correctional system. Any prisoners continuing to protest have been severely repressed and denied their rights. At the same time, prisoners and outsiders interested in liberal reforms have been welcomed into the system and been provided with minimal support services to aid in program development. Outsiders who are sympathetic to the militant prisoners have been denied access to the institution.[18]

Prison Psychiatrists and Drugs. The California Medical Facility at Vacaville is heavily staffed with psychiatrists who prescribe heavy doses of psychoactive drugs for many prisoners. Although the acceptance of psychoactive drugs is technically voluntary, threats of being moved to a more repressive housing facility and of having their paroles delayed are more than sufficient to induce compliance in the prisoners. Similar threats are successful at recruiting prisoners for electroshock treatment and adversive therapy. One recent program of adversive therapy involved the injection of Anectine, a muscle relaxant that produces a severe sensation of suffocation in the prisoner that is sufficiently frightening to cow prisoners into obeying institutional rules. By using medical terminology, the psychiatrists avoid having to answer the question as to whether treatment by electroshock and adversive therapy is sufficiently cruel and unusual as to be unconstitutional.[39]

The Federal Prison Industry. Although Federal Prison Industries Inc. was established by Congress to provide jobs and vocational training for prisoners in the Federal Bureau of Prisons, its managers have concentrated more on making profits than on rehabilitation. Instead of employing all the prisoners, only one prisoner out of every five is employed. The training tends to be for jobs that are nonexistent or unattractive in the outside world. The wages paid to prisoners are as low as $.17 an hour, and yet the 1975 profits of the corporation were over $8.8 million, approximately 12 percent of the year's sales. This is tantamount to slavery, and is in violation of Article 23 of the "Universal Declaration of Rights" of the United Nations, which guarantees the right to work and just and favorable conditions for that work to everyone. Furthermore, Article 23 guarantees equal pay for equal work. Every time the federal prisoners have attempted to secure these rights, they have been repressed in the same ways that state prisoners who have attempted to organize unions have been repressed by state correctional administrators.[24]

The Massachusetts Correctional System. Prisoners in the Massachusetts State System were successful in attracting considerable attention for their cause between 1971 and 1973. It was partially in response to these prisoner protests that the Massachusetts Department of Corrections instituted a new step-system behavior modification program which integrated all of the state prisons together into one massive system. The system consisted of ladder of progressively desirable living conditions up which prisoners could crawl, step by step, by demonstrating responsible behavior at each level. The initial placement of each prisoner on the ladder was through a classification analysis performed at the Reception Diagnostic Center, where all newly sentenced prisoners were interviewed, tested, and observed for approximately four weeks. After the initial assignment was made, each step up the ladder required approval from a classification board made up of correctional officers, administrators, social workers and psychologists.[18]

In all three of these criticisms of existing treatment programs, radical theorists have made clear their distrust of therapeutic programs. Aside from the specific violations of rights that they cite in each program, they have a much more general objection. This is that the implementation of programs treating offenders as individuals who have personal deficiencies obscures the more general social sources of crime and thus makes it impossible to address these sources with solutions that involve basic changes in the social structure. In their view, any program that detracts from fundamental social reforms is misguided. Even worse, these "therapeutic" activities serve to legitimate the system in the eyes of the public, thus removing any pressure that might exist toward more fundamental structural reforms.

Radical Advocacy on Behalf of Oppressed Groups

The radical critic of the correctional system is unlikely to be worried about the rights of the ruling class. It would be almost a contradiction in terms to suggest that the ruling class would take away its own rights. In contrast, radical theorists have always been particularly concerned about the rights of oppressed groups. Three major oppressed groups in American society are women, racial and cultural minorities, and juveniles. We summarize the radical position on the oppression of each of these three groups in the criminal justice system in the following sections.

Racial and Cultural Minorities. Radical theorists are closely associated with the struggle for racial equality in American society. They have indicated the correctional system for racism practiced against prisoners. Haywood Burns says that "...racism can become so pervasive that racists guards and racist white prisoners team up in their attacks upon non-white prisoners."[2:27] Aaron Wald[49] argues that the death of George Jackson, a black prisoner at San Quentin, was a racist murder planned and organized by correctional officials. Erik Wright[52] presents extensive evidence of racism at San Quentin going far beyond the George Jackson killing. At San Quentin, blacks and Chicanos were disproportionately placed in segregation facilities, and both black and white prisoners agreed that prison officials were more lenient with whites than with blacks. The letters of George Jackson provide much evidence of this, and also of a virulent personal racism practiced by some of the correctional officers.[11] The correctional processing of blacks in California in 1970 was so extensive that one out of every eight black men aged 20–24 was in the system during that year.[52]

Women. Women have tended to be ignored in most criminological writings, so much so that Carol Smart[38] recommends developing a separate feminist criminology. She finds that the policies of correctional institutions for women are "geared to supporting the inferior position of women in society and the naive belief that feminity is the antithesis of criminality."[38:182] Women who approximate traditional gender stereotypes are unlikely to be processed by the criminal justice system, but women who are deviant from those stereotypes, even if they have committed no criminal act, run a serious risk of being scooped up by the system. Meda Chesney-Lind[3] points out that the court simultaneously requires female juvenile delinquents to be obedient and chaste while permitting young men to "sow wild oats" without penalty. The noncriminal behavior of female juvenile delinquents (in status offenses) is punished as harshly as the criminal behavior of male juvenile delinquents.

Dorie Klein and June Kress[14] put female imprisonment in perspective by relating it to other methods of social control. In their view, the treatment of women by the criminal justice system "...is not isolated or arbitrary, but rather is rooted in systematic sexist practices and ideologies which can only be fully understood by analyzing the position of women in capitalist society."[14:45] Although it is true that women are less likely to be imprisoned than men, their incarceration as mental patients and subjection to various forms of chemotherapy function as social controls in the same way that imprisonment does for men. Chivalry applies only to women from the ruling class. Third World women, the poor, and radicals are less likely to receive chivalrous treatment. "Documentation of police beatings, court severity and harsh imprisonment for female radicals throughout American history illustrate this..."[14:44]

There is no reason why racism and sexism cannot be practiced at the same time. Elouise Spencer's[41] study of a women's prison in the Midwest demonstrates this. In addition to sexist programs and institutional regulations, the administration at this institution used racism as a social control technique. By encouraging racial antagonisms among the prisoners, it was possible to keep them from working together against the administration. In addition, the myth of white superiority was subtly perpetuated by discriminatory practices in work assignments, living quarters, and pay incentives. White staff members were subtly victimized by other matrons if they dared to become friendly with black prisoners. It is misleading to talk about women in the criminal justice system as a group without acknowledging the high percentage of racial and cultural minorities among female prisoners. Many of the administrative practices in women's institutions that appear to be the result of sexism may actually be due more to the influence of racism.

Juveniles. The same thing can be said about juvenile delinquents, a high percentage of whom are racial and cultural minorities. Barry Krisberg and James Austin put it this way: "The practices and procedures of juvenile justice agents reflect class and racial prejudices that extend to the larger social order and fall disproportionately on Third World and poor people."[15:105] This point is illustrated in Gerald Wheeler's study *Counter-deterrence.*[50] Wheeler found that length of sentence in a juvenile institution was determined much more by the nature of the institution than by the nature of the delinquency committed by the youngster. This has a counter-deterrent effect in that minor law violators who see that they are receiving exactly the same punishment as serious criminals realize that they will have nothing more to lose by becoming serious criminals, while serious delinquents will believe that there is no reason for them to reform when they are being given sentences no longer than those of minor offenders. The major function of the indeterminant sentence for juveniles is that institutions can arrange to assure maximum occupancy by keeping youngsters longer than usual when commitments are down and releasing them early when commitments are up. The therapeutic and deterrent aspects of programming are subverted in favor of institutional maintenance policies. In a general sense, *"the net effect of the therapeutic state is to decriminalize the felony—index offender, while assigning a criminal role to the status violators."*[50:26]

Wheeler[50] examined a three-month cohort of juvenile delinquents coming under the jurisdiction of a youth commission in a Midwestern state. Black women received considerably longer stays than white women regardless of offense, but black men served longer periods of time than white men in only one of four institutions. It turns out that the racism in this system is much more subtle than mere comparisons of time incarcerated can reveal. Treatment-oriented institutions tended to release blacks earlier than whites, while custody-oriented institutions tended to retain them longer than whites. Therefore, the essence of discrimination was not in the length of time served but rather in the amount of money spent in an attempt to help the juvenile delinquents. Less money was expended to treat black than white juvenile delinquents. In a second analysis, Wheeler found that time on parole for juvenile delinquents was also determined more by age, race, and region than by the needs of the individual delinquent.

INTELLECTUAL RADICALS IN ACTION

The radicals whose work we are discussing in this chapter are not bomb-throwers. They are intellectual radicals who attempt to change society through the power of words. However, these men and women do make efforts to help groups and individuals whom they define as being particularly oppressed by the system. For example, radical attorneys and intellectuals rallied to the support of the San Quentin Six, a group of black and Hispanic prisoners who were accused of having joined George Jackson in an attempt to escape from the prison in 1971, the event in which Jackson was killed.[49] Feminists have occasionally joined with radicals in the support of female prisoners, and have sometimes carried out radical activities separate from nonfeminist radical organizations, most of which are dominated by men. For example, a task force from the Dade County Chapter of the National Organization for Women (NOW) pioneered a program among Dade County Jail inmates that was designed to build inmate solidarity instead of separating the prisoners out and treating them as individuals. One of the initial effects of the NOW task force was improved legal services to the incarcerated women, although that improvement vanished as soon as the task force ceased to function in the jail.[28]

Prisoners themselves also may engage in activities in support of radical goals. The leaders of many prison riots proposed radical solutions to prison problems as part of their list of demands. At Attica, one of the prisoner demands was to "stop slave labor" and another was to "allow all New York State prisoners to be politically active, without intimidation of reprisals."[51]

The Marion Political Collective is a group of prisoners at the Federal Penitentiary, Marion, Illinois. Its objectives are the elevation of political consciousness and the liberation of what it deems the oppressed classes in America. The collective meets twice a week together, and also has two study group meetings a week. It holds that the two primary purposes of prisons are to remove those who refuse to submit to economic deprivation from the community and to enforce compulsory labor at slave wages to produce exploitative profits for the State. The view that the collective has of the therapy and social control at Marion is summarized in the following quotation.

By means of behavior modification programs (Transactional Analysis in the extreme), authorities seek to forcibly restructure prisoners' personalities and thought processes, reducing rebellious spirits to pliant automatons (those who succumb) or vegetables (those who resist). Repeat: Truly rebellious and conscious prisoners are often murdered. Long-term segregation, wherein social contact is kept to a minimum and sensory deprivation is dominant, serves to further terrorize prison populations into docility.[17:51]

The contrast to small collectives, whether within the prison or in intellectual circles on the streets, is a large nationally based organization to campaign for radical change. The United States has many hundreds of organizations promoting liberal change in areas from sexism and racism to the prevention to cruelty to animals, but there is not one single national organization of any size dedicated to the promotion of radical social change. By radical social change, we do not mean violent social change, but rather the peaceful implemention of basic changes in the social structure so as to make the distribution of resources in society more just.

To find examples of this alternative form of radical organization, we have to look at international organizations. An example of such an organization that has ties with many countries is Amnesty International. Although not composed of radicals in the usual sense, this organization has as its primary goal the release of political prisoners everywhere, which is a major goal of most radical programs. In the mid-1970s, there were more than 70,000 contributing members of Anmesty International in 65 nations. According to one estimate based on the organization's annual report, a total of 10,439 prisoners have been released and 159 have received amnesties as a result of the activities of the organization between 1961 and 1976.[6]

Organizations favoring radical change have developed in a number of European nations since the mid-1960s, most notably the Scandinavian countries. KRUM, KROM, and KRIM are the radical organizations for prison reform in Sweden, Norway, and Denmark, respectively. These organizations do not provide individual aid to prisoners. They are not interested in liberal reforms or in treatment programs. They do not wish to make minor adjustments in the correctional system; they want to abolish major parts of it. For example, they have supported actions such as the abolition of the youth prison system and a sharp reduction in the use of pretrial detention as well as minor reforms such as the ending of censorship of mail in prisons. Techniques used by these groups include large public meetings, seminars, strikes, teach-ins, plays, films, books, presentations on the academic lecture circuit, and so forth. Four central strategies of KROM in this work have been to always include ex-convicts as participants in protest and educational activities, to rely only on their own resources, to coordinate activities in order to increase the effect of each individual activity, and to unmask the policies and the moves of the penal system by publicizing penal activities as much as possible.[20]

RADICAL ALTERNATIVES TO PRISON REFORM

Radical critics of the correctional system (and an increasing number of liberals) hold that the alternatives to institutionalization discussed in Chapter 17 and other chapters of this text do not constitute meaningful reforms in corrections. They merely extend the sphere of control exercised by the correctional establishment over the citizenry. For this reason, radicals often oppose liberal prison reforms as an attempt to drain off support for more basic structural changes in the correctional process.[39] What reforms do these critics then propose? Examples of truly radical alternatives to correctional processing are radical nonintervention, anmesty, and total deinstitutionalization. Radical nonintervention is the refusal of corrections workers to interfere in the lives of juvenile delinquents. Amnesty is the complete and total nullification of criminal sanctions against a group of individuals. Neither of these two alternatives has been given much attention in the United States. The third radical reform, deinstitutionalization, has not only been examined more carefully in scholarly writing on the subject:[37] it has also been tried out in practice in Vermont and Massachusetts. The maximum security prison was closed in Vermont and turned into a facility for the aged, and Massachusetts completely eliminated its chain of juvenile prisons. We will examine the Massachusets example in some detail.

Deinstitutionalization in Massachusetts. *Dr. Jerome Miller was appointed Commissioner of the Department of Youth Services of the State of Massachusetts on October 28, 1969. He immediately began to make changes designed to humanize the juvenile reformatories in the Massachusetts system. He also spent a great deal of time on television and radio or in giving speeches designed to develop political support for his programs. Conditions in the Bridgewater Correctional Institution, the most oppressive of all the Massachusetts facilities, were so brutal that Miller found it necessary to close it down in September, 1970. In the meantime, his attempts to retrain staff members in the other juvenile institutions met with limited success. Miller finally realized that it would not be possible to remake these institutions in a liberal therapeutic

*This account of deinstitutionalization in Massachusetts relies heavily on Andrew Rutherford. "The Dissolution of Training Schools in Massachusetts." *In* Barry Krisberg and James Austin: *Children of Ishmael: Critical Perspectives on Juvenile Justice.* Palo Alto, CA: Mayfield Publishing Co., 1978, pp. 515–534.

image, so he turned to the radical solution of closing them entirely. Deinstitutionalization went into full swing in January 1972 with the support of the Governor and the unusual device of a one-month National Conference on Juvenile Delinquency Prevention and Treatment Programs at Amherst College.

Deinstitutionalization did not mean that every youngster was allowed to roam free in the community. A small number of youngsters were placed in psychiatric hospitals, a youth center, and two detention facilities. On December 1, 1973, there were only 219 youngsters in detention under the supervision of the Department of Youth Services in the entire state of Massachusetts. Furthermore, only 70 of these youngsters were in secure facilities. Although deinstitutionalization can be accomplished along with decreasing costs in the long run, the Massachusetts experience was that costs increased considerably in the short run. One of the reasons for this was that the agency's caseload increased sharply. Another was that it was necessary to continue to pay institutional staff members who were protected in the civil service system even if they had no youngsters to supervise. Commissioner Miller resigned a year after the deinstitutionalization had been accomplished, but he had laid a sufficiently resilient political groundwork that the consolidation of the radical reform continued in his absence. He has not embodied his approach to corrections in a new organization, the National Center on Institutions and Alternatives. This organization investigates correctional reforms and publicizes them in its newsletter, *Institutions, Etc.*[9] It also publishes pamphlets and bibliographies on subjects such as deinstitutionalization and the juvenile justice system, and provides technical assistance to criminal justice organizations that are interested in implementing more humane systems for offender processing.

THE RELATIONSHIP BETWEEN RADICAL AND NONRADICAL CORRECTIONAL CRITIQUES

Nonradical critiques of corrections are taken seriously in many quarters. They often lead to minor reforms in correctional institutions and practices. In contrast, radical critiques are quickly dismissed by administrators, politicians, and the vast majority of citizens. Since this is the case, what contributions do radical critiques make to the correctional scene? The first is that they alert us to inequities in corrections (and in the larger society) that are systemic rather than occurring only in isolated settings. For example, take the observation that it is not so much the "overcriminalization" of street crimes committed by members of the lower classes, as the "undercriminalization" of white collar and corporate crimes committed by members of the upper classes[39] that highlights the inequities in the enforcement of the law. This observation indicts the entire criminal justice system—not just a few "corrupt administrators" or "brutal guards."

The second contribution of radical critiques is that they widen our horizons and force us to examine our assumptions. In the above example, students who would never question the appropriateness of punishing street crime may be stimulated to ask themselves why corporate executives who commit crimes having a greater cost in dollars than street crimes receive such light punishments (or none at all). Finally, radical critiques extend the boundaries of the changes that are theoretically possible in corrections, thus causing non-radical proposals to appear tame by comparison. It may be that many correctional reforms would not have been implemented in the past decade if more radical proposals had not been made, which redefined these reforms as "reasonable, middle-of-the-road, and workable."

SUMMARY

A great many radical and nonradical critiques of corrections have been published in recent years. The nonradical critiques go further than mere tinkering with the criminal justice system but do not propose solutions that require a major alteration of the social order. In contrast, radical criminologists stridently reject the existing system and call for major systemwide reforms. Nonradical critiques of corrections can come from any direction, including liberals as well as conservatives, and also from other parts of the criminal justice system, most notably the courts. Other sources of nonradical critiques of corrections are journalistc social critics, religious organizations ex-corrections professionals, clinicians, liberal academics, and cost or cost-benefit analysts.

According to radical theorists, the punishment of criminals in capitalist societies is aimed specifically at the working class, and the characteristics of punishment are determined by the condition of the lowest stratum of the working class. Radical theorists believe that the capitalist state is in crisis and must constantly expand its social control apparatus in order to avoid a collapse. Liberal reforms of correctional institutions and practices are not seen as particularly meaningful by radical theorists. Instead, these reforms are seen as drawing off much of the impetus for "true" reforms, which would be much more sweeping in nature. Among the radical alternatives to liberal prison reform are radical nonintervention, amnesty, and total deinstitutionalization. Although these recommendations may seem rather far-fetched to most students, deinstitutionalization has been tried with some degree of success in both Massachusetts and Vermont. Perhaps the greatest impact of the radical criminologists on contemporary corrections has been that they have made correctional administrators more willing to consider the implementation of the less extensive reforms proposed by liberal critics of correctional institutions and practices.

REFERENCES

1. Aptheker, Bettina. "The Social Functions of the Prisons in the United States." *In* Angela Davis: *If They Come in the Morning.* New York: New American Library, 1971, pp.51–59.

2. Burns, Haywood. "Black Prisoner as Victim." *In* Michele G. Hermann and Marilyn G. Haft: *Prisoners' Rights Source Book.* New York: Clark Boardman, 1973, pp. 25–31.

3. Chesney-Lind, Meda. "Judicial Paternalism and the Female Status Offender." *Crime and Delinquency* 29 (1977):121–130.

4. Cole, Ellerbe P., Richard F. Spellman, and Susan P. Tresk. *Cost–Benefit Analysis of Alternatives to Incarceration.* Augusta, ME: Maine State Bar Association, 1977.

5. Hackler, James C. *The Prevention of Youthful Crime: The Great Stumble Forward.* Tornonto: Methuen, 1978.

6. Hassan, Ibne. *Amnesty International as a Human Rights Organization.* Ph.D. dissertation, New York University, 1977.

7. Hirschkop, Phillip J. and Michael A. Millmann. "The Unconstitutionality of Prison Life." *Virginia Law Review* 55 (1969):814–834.

8. Hogg, Russell. "Imprisonment and Society Under Early British Capitalism." *Crime and Social Justice* 12 (1979):4–17.

9. *Institutions Etc.* Published monthly by the National Center on Institutions and Alternatives at 1337 22nd St., N.W., Washington, D.C. 20037.

10. Irwin, John. "The Trouble with Rehabilitation." Paper presented at the annual meeting of the American Sociological Association, 1973.

11. Jackson, George. *Soledad Brother: The Prison Letters of George Jackson.* New York: Bantam, 1970.

12. Jankovic, Ivan. "Labor Market and Imprisonment." *Crime and Social Justice* 8 (1977):17–31.

13. *Jericho* 20 (Spring 1980), entire issue.

14. Klein, Dorie and June Kress. "Any Woman's Blues: A Critical Overview of Women, Crime and the Criminal Justice System." *Crime and Social Justice* 5 (1976):34–49.

15. Krisberg, Barry and James Austin. *Children of Ishmael: Critical Perspectives on Juvenile Justice.* Palo Alto, CA: Mayfield Publishing Co., 1978.

16. Little, Arthur D., Inc., with Counsel of State Governments and Academy for Contemporary Problems. *Cost and Service Impacts of Deinstitutionalization of Status Offenders in Ten States: "Responses to Angry Youth."* Washington, D.C., 1977.

17. Marion Political Collective. "Notes of a Prison Collective." *Crime and Social Justice* 5 (1976):50.–53.

18. Martin, Bob. "The Massachusetts Correctional System: Treatment as an Ideology for Control." *Crime and Social Justice* 6 (1976):49–57.

19. Mathiesen, Thomas. "The Future of Control Systems—The Case of Norway." *International Journal of the Sociology of Law* 8 (1980):149–164.

20. Mathiesen, Thomas and Wiggo Røine. "The Prison Movement in Scandinavia." *In* Herman Bianchi, Mario Simondi, and Ian Taylor: *Deviance and Control in Europe.* London: Wiley, 1975, pp. 85–96.

21. Melossi, Dario. "The Penal Question in *Capital.*" *Crime and Social Justice* 5 (1976):26–33.

22. Melossi, Dario. "Georg Rusche and Otto Kirchimer: *Punishment and Social Structure.*" *Crime and Social Justice* 9 (1978):73–85.

23. Menninger, Karl. "The Crime of Punishment." Lecture delivered at the Institute of Contemporary Corrections of the Behavioral Sciences, Sam Houston State University, Huntsville, TX, April 24, 1970.

24. Mintz, Robert. "Federal Prison Industry–the 'Green Monster' Part One—History and Background." *Crime and Social Justice* 6 (1976):41–48.

25. Mitford, Jessica. *Kind and Usual Punishment: The Prison Business.* New York: Random House, 1974.

26. Murton, Thomas O. *The Dilemma of Prison Reform.* New York: Holt, Rinehart and Winston, 1976.

27. Nagel, William G. *The New Red Barn: A Critical Look at the Modern American Prison.* New York: Walker and Co., 1973.

28. Pendergrass, Virginia E. "Innovative Programs for Women in Jail and Prisons: Trick or Treatment." *In* Annette M. Brodsky: *The Female Offender.* Beverly Hills, CA: Sage, 1975, pp. 67–76.

29. Pepinsky, Harold E. *Crime Control Strategies: An Introduction to the Study of Crime.* New York: Oxford University Press, 1980.

30. Quinney, Richard. *Class, State, and Crime: On the Theory and Practice of Criminal Justice.* New York: David McKay, 1977.

31. Reasons, Charles E. *The Criminologist: Crime and the Criminal.* Pacific Palisades, CA: Goodyear Publishing Co., 1974.

32. Reasons, Charles E. and Russell L. Kaplan. "Tear Down the Walls? Some Functions of Prisons." *Crime and Delinquency* 21 (1975):360–372.

33. Rusche, Georg. "Labor Market and Penal Sanction: Thoughts on the Sociology of Criminal Justice." *Crime and Social Justice* 10 (1978):2–8. Translated by Gerda Dinwiddie. (Originally written in 1933).

34. Rusche, Georg and Otto Kirchheimer. *Punishment and Social Structure.* New York: Columbia University Press, 1939.

35. Rutherford, Andrew. "The Dissolution of the Training Schools in Massachusetts." *In* Barry Krisberg and James Austin: *The Children of Ishmael: The Critical Perspectives on Juvenile Justice.* Palo Alto: Mayfield Publishing Co., 1978, pp. 515–534.

36. Schmidt, Janet. *Demystifying Parole.* Lexington, MA: D.C. Heath, 1977.

37. Scull, Andrew T. *Decarceration: Community Treatment and the Deviant: A Radical View.* Englewood Cliffs, NJ: Prentice-Hall, 1977.

38. Smart, Carol. *Women, Crime and Criminology: A Feminist Critique.* London: Routledge and Kegan Paul, 1977.

39. Smith, Joan and William Fried. *The Use of the American Prison: Political Theory and Penal Practice.* Lexington, MA: D.C. Heath, 1974.

40. Speiglman, Richard. "Prison Psychiatrists and Drugs: A Case Study." *Crime and Social Justice* 7 (1977):23–39.

41. Spencer, Elouise J. *The Social System of a Medium Security Women's Prison.* Ph.D. dissertation, University of Kansas, 1977.

42. Takagi, Paul. "The Correctional System." *Crime and Social Justice* 2 (1974):82–89.

43. Takagi, Paul. "Devising Liberal Conceptions of Penal Reform: A Bibliographic Review." *Crime and Social Justice* 5 (1976):60–64.

44. Thomas, Charles W. "The Correctional Institutional as an Enemy of Corrections." *Federal Probation* 37 (March 1973):8–13.

45. Tomasic, Roman and Ian Dobinson. *The Failure of Imprisonment: An Australian Perspective.* Sydney, Australia: George Allen and Unwin, 1979.

46. Van den Haag, Ernest. *Punishing Criminals.* New York: Basic Books, 1975.

47. Van den Haag, Ernest. "Prisons Cost Too Much Because They Are Too Secure." *Corrections Magazine* 6 (April 1980):39–43.

48. Villaume, Alfred C. "Parkinson's Law and the United States Bureau of Prison." *Contemporary Crises* 2 (1978):209–214.

49. Wald, Karen. "The San Quentin Six Case: Perspectives and Analysis." *Crime and Social Justice* 6 (1976):58–68.

50. Wheeler, Gerald R. *Counter-deterrence: A Report on Juvenile Sentencing and Effects of Prisonization.* Chicago: Nelson-Hall, 1978.

51. Wicker, Tom. "Fifteen Practical Proposals by the Inmates of Attica." *In* John R. Snortum and Ilana Hader: *Criminal Justice: Allies and Adversaries.* Pacific Palisades, CA: Palisades Publishers, 1978, p. 194.

52. Wright, Erik O. *The Politics of Punishment: A Critical Analysis of Prisons in America.* New York: Harper and Row, 1973.

53. Yeager, Matthew G. "Unemployment and Imprisonment." *Journal of Criminal Law and Criminology* 70 (1979):586–588.

54. Young, Jock. "Working-Class Criminology." *In* Ian Taylor, Paul Walton, and Jock Young: *Critical Criminology.* London: Routledge and Kegan Paul, 1975, pp. 63–93.

Part III

The Future of Corrections

Chapter 19

The Future of Corrections and Your Future in Corrections

The readers of this book who choose corrections as a career will never work in the institutions, community programs, and other alternatives that have been described in the earlier chapters. Their contact will be with the correctional system of the future. Social science has proven itself to be excellent at describing the present and moderately good at resurrecting the past, but woefully deficient in predicting the future. Nevertheless, we must make the effort, for it would hardly be fair to ask college students to consider a lifetime of work in corrections (as we do in the second part of this chapter) without giving them a reasonable estimate of what that future is likely to contain. Before we present our predictions for the year 2000, we will look at the predictions that have been made by other correctional scholars.

VIEWS OF THE FUTURE OF CORRECTIONS

Correctional textbooks generally contain a section on the future of corrections, and many other books and articles have been written on that subject in the past few years. The interesting thing about many of these publications is that they do not predict the future: they prescribe what the authors would like to see occur in the future. In many cases, these prescriptions are clearly not what the future holds. The authors may hope that they may have some slight influence on future trends by making these prescriptions, which is an entirely different purpose from trying to accurately predict what will occur.

Robert Sommer[8] tells us that imprisoning men and women for long periods of time has failed as a method of social control. It has proved itself to be expensive, discriminatory, and inhumane. He believes that long-term imprisonment should be replaced by short-term detention with a maximum length of six months. At the end of the six months, there would be a jury trial to determine whether or not the offender still represented a danger to society. Unless the state can convince a jury that this is so, the offender must be released. If it is decided that confinement is to continue, it can only last an additional six months, following which there must be another jury trial, and so on until the offender is finally released. Sommer believes that the threat of six months in jail would be more than sufficient to deter most potential criminals without the negative effects of long-term imprisonment. Anyone who would not be deterred by six months in jail probably would also not be deterred by the possibility of a longer prison sentence.

David Fogel's[3] justice model of corrections also recommends the end of massive maximum security institutions and injustices in the correctional process, but his recommendations are otherwise much more palatable to law and order practitioners than Sommer's liberal prescriptions. Fogel recommends viewing crime as a volitional act and punishing criminals on a utilitarian basis. To avoid continued abuses of the criminal justice system, discretion in all areas of criminal justice processing is to be greatly diminished, but not completely eliminated. Since large maximum security institutions cannot be eliminated overnight, the short-term goal should be to make them safe and sane for prisoners and staff alike. The less severe offenders should be sentenced to community-based programs, so that only the more severe offenders will be sentenced to prison. Prison sentences should consist of flat time rather than being of indeterminant length. Prisoners should know how long they will be incarcerated at the beginning of their terms. Prisoner participation in institutional programs would be entirely voluntary, since it could have no effect upon release dates. When an offender's sentence had been served, release would occur without continued supervision under parole.

The final prescription for the future of corrections that we will mention here is *The Future of Imprisonment* by Norval Morris.[7] Morris argues that rehabilitative programs for prisoners must be expanded and improved, but participation in these programs must be entirely voluntary. A prisoner's release date cannot be made contingent upon program participation without undermining the value of that participation. Prisoners should be informed of sentence length (and therefore parole date) at the beginning rather than at the end of their terms. They should be given increasing amounts of freedom and their continued good behavior under these conditions of increasing freedom should be used as the primary predictor of success on parole rather than the background characteristics currently used in parole prediction tables. The least restrictive correctional sanction should always be used. The prediction of future criminality should not be used as the basis for determining sentence length, and sentences should be no longer than the just desserts for the crime or crimes committed.

"True" Predictions of Future Corrections

Sommer, Fogel, and Morris tell us where they would like to see corrections go in the future. If we want to know where corrections *will* go in the future, we must look elsewhere. Two early sets of predictions for the future of corrections were written in 1969 by Richard McGee[6] and in 1970 by Daniel Glaser.[4] More recently, McGee has joined with Robert Carter and E.K. Nelson[2] to write a comprehensive view of the future of corrections.[5] McGee[6] predicts that there will be a decrease in the number of offenders serving long sentences. Institutions will tend to be smaller, and will place increased emphasis on preparation for release. Probation will come to include a wide range of community-based correctional programs, and parole will follow suit. There will be an increased use of contracting with community agencies for the provision of services as an alternative to in-house service delivery. Information systems utilizing computer technology will be used to assist in decision-making procedures, and these will be buttressed by empirical evaluation research studies.

Glaser's[4] vision of the future of American corrections includes the revision of institutional programs so that they more closely approximate employment in the free community, including appropriate salary levels. Prisons will be located closer to large urban areas than they are at present, which will enable them to have closer links with community organizations ranging from churches and service clubs to offender self-help groups. All correctional staff members will be treatment personnel, and will combine treatment and custody functions. Most interpersonal counseling will be done informally by line staff rather than in separate formalized counseling programs. Future prisons will be much smaller than prisons are at present, and will mix offenders of different age levels in order to stabilize prisoner population. Personal relationships between staff and prisoners will be systematically used for rehabilitative purposes.

The most comprehensive set of predictions for the future of corrections, and the one that is most systematically developed, was written by Carter, McGee, and Nelson.[2] It begins with an examination of three bases for prediction: (1) changes in the crime problem, (2) changes in the offender population, and (3) the development of alternatives to corrections. These authors believe that correctional philosophy will become much more unified by the year 2000 than it is at present. There will be a clear differentiation of correctional goals by type of offender and treatment programs will be linked to offender types. Local governments will increase their operation of correctional programs, but the funds for these programs will continue to be largely supplied by state and federal governments. The confidence and diversity of correctional staff members will increase. The maximum security institutions that remain will continue to be formalistic and authoritarian, but the rehabilitation-oriented institutions that will continue to proliferate will be based on participative management styles.

There will be a mushrooming of the availability of noncorrectional treatment resources, and these resources will be used to implement an extensive strategy of diversion from the criminal justice system. An increased amount of attention will be given to misdemeanants as a way of discouraging them from the possibility of graduating to more serious levels of crime. The correctional system will, to some extent, become involved in the effort to prevent crime as well as continuing its efforts in reforming offenders. The medical model will continue its decline in popularity and offenders will increasingly be regarded as people who have poor habits for problem-solving. Although Carter, McGee, and Nelson made their recommendations in 1975, subsequent events have not outdated them. They continue to be convincing, and have a significant influence on our own view of the future of corrections, which is presented in the following section.

NEW PREDICTIONS FOR THE
FUTURE OF CORRECTIONS

In this section, we present a series of predictions for the future of American corrections. These are based to some extent on a rudimentary model of social change that is described below. In addition, there are inputs from three sources. The first is the existing literature on predictions for the future, particularly predictions made by Carter, McGee, and Nelson.[2] The second input is existing correctional standards, as developed by the American Correctional Association, the American Bar Association, the United Nations, and the National Advisory Commission on Criminal Justice Standards and Goals. The final source of information about the future of American corrections comes from observations of corrections in other nations. Programs that were tried in Sweden in the 1970s may be tried in the United States in the 1980s, and if found to be effective in this setting may become standard practice by the 1990s. Chapter 17 contains international material that is relevant to the future of American corrections.

Before we can predict what is going to happen in American corrections by the year 2000, we need to have some idea of what is going to happen in other areas of American society. Corrections is not a closed system, and so it is greatly influenced by what is happening in society as a whole. Figure 19.1 presents some examples of the types of factors that impact the correctional system. These include demographic factors, "social progress" effects, economic conditions, and social policy on crime. Some of these factors impact the correctional system directly, and others impact it indirectly through effects on crime rates. In Figure 19.2, this simple model is further expanded, with examples given of some of the types of factors, and intervening variables inserted at certain points. This is still an extremely simple system that does not even begin to communicate the complexity of the interaction between the correctional system and society as a whole. The model could be made much more complex by the addition of further variables. The model presented in Figure 19.2 is also oversimplified in that it does not show feedback loops existing between different elements in the model. All of the arrows are shown as going in one direction, but that is never entirely

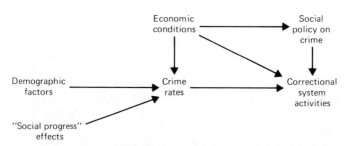

Figure 19.1 Examples of types of factors impacting the correctional system.

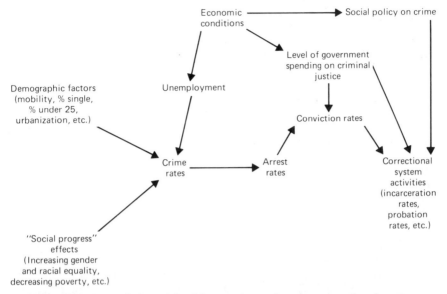

Figure 19.2 Expanded model of factors impacting the correctional system.

true in reality. The problem with this kind of system modeling is that complex social systems contain too many elements and feedback loops to be grasped at one time or to be portrayed in a single figure or chart. The intent of Figure 19.2 is to give the student a feel for the complexities of the system rather than to provide a completely accurate portrayal of the system.

We predict that, all things being equal, the overall impact of changes in demographic factors would be to lower crime rates and to decrease correctional system activities by the year 2000. Geographical mobility is expected to remain constant, the percentage single is expected to rise very slightly, urbanization is expected to hold steadily, and the percentage of the population under age 25 is expected to decrease sharply. "Social progress" effects such as decreasing poverty and increasing gender and racial equality would also tend to increase, all things being equal, and this would tend to depress crime rates and correctional system activities. Economic conditions will fluctuate between now and the year 2000, and are expected to be considerably worse in 2000 than they were in 1980, due to increasing energy costs. This will tend to increase unemployment and crime rates, and may also reverse the projected increase in gender and racial equality and the projected decrease in poverty. The joint action of economic conditions, demographic factors, and "social progress" on crime rates by the year 2000 should produce modestly increased crime rates, which will lead to modestly increased arrest rates and to modestly increased rates of correctional system activities. This assumes that arrests and correctional processing continue to occur in the same ratio to crime as they do at present, even though there will be internal adjustments within the total crime picture, such as decreasing "victimless" crime and increasing white collar crime.

It is possible that the energy crisis will force a greater deterioration in economic conditions than has been suggested above. We have alredy mentioned that increasing gender and racial equality, and decreasing poverty, which depend upon steady economic growth for public support, could slow down or even be reversed if economic conditions worsened. If economic conditions deteriorate even more than predicted, it could lead to the hardening of class and race lines (but probably not gender lines), a sharp rise in street crime, and a similarly sharp increase in criminal justice system activities that will be justified by government officials as necessary to maintain order. On the other hand, should a new technological breakthrough terminate the energy crisis, none of these negative trends would be likely to occur.

Social policy on crime refers to politically debated, legally adopted, and administratively implemented philosophies and guidelines for institutional activities. In general, worsening economic conditions tend to stimulate harsher criminal justice policies, which tend to increase the level of correctional system activities. At the same time that worsening economic conditions are linked to increased correctional system activities through social policy and through the chain of influence beginning with unemployment and then moving through the crime rate and the arrest rate, economic conditions also may have an impact on government spending. While it may be tempting to assume that economic pressure would result in decreased government expenditures for criminal justice activities, history suggests that a government that has begun to worry about the maintenance of the social order in the face of deteriorating economic conditions may choose to increase the percentage of its budget that is allocated to social control organizations, most of which are part of the criminal justice system. This would allow criminal justice expenditures to continue to rise in the face of a gross national product that is declining in purchasing power. These factors, taken together, also suggest an increase in correctional system activities by the year 2000.

This analysis has assumed that everything else will be equal, but that is not entirely true. The population of the United States will continue to grow, and so we can be sure that the correctional system will experience considerable growth between 1980 and the year 2000, even under the conservative assumption that its relative growth will be smaller than the level of population increase. It should also be pointed out that modest increases in total correctional system activities may obscure the fact that certain system elements (such as halfway houses) will be rapidly growing while others may be shrinking. It is likely that most of the increase in correctional system activities will be in community corrections. Because most people think of corrections as being limited to prisons and jails, they will not be aware of the magnitude of the expansion of the criminal justice system.

Having arrived at a general prediction of increased correctional system activities by the year 2000, we will now make specific predictions for the construction of institutions, programming, staffing, and management. These predictions have a more positive tone than the preceding paragraphs, for deteriorating social conditions tend to increase expenditures for criminal justice system activities, which increases funds available for program development, career enhancement, and other processes that are invigorating for the corrections industry.

The Construction of New Facilities

1. A number of the antiquated prison fortresses will be phased out by the year 2000, but many will remain in use due to the excessive cost of building replacement institutions.
2. During periods of increasing crime, or when forced to build new institutions because older institutions have been closed down by court orders, some correctional systems will react by building new fortress prisons to replace the old ones. These institutions will meet the minimum standards set by court orders, but they will often fail to achieve the range and quality of correctional programs that will have become the national standard by the year 2000.
3. Many maximum security prisons will be constructed to replace some of the fortresses that were closed down. There will be an even larger number of medium and minimum security institutions constructed. The majority of these institutions will be mini-prisons housing 500 or fewer prisoners and located in or near urban areas. Most of the community correctional programs will be housed in existing structures that have been renovated for the purpose rather than in newly constructed facilities.

Institutional Programs

4. It is predicted that the movement toward the justice model will have reached its zenith by 1985. At that time, justice model sentencing reforms and the correctional practices will have been implemented in all but a handful of the American states.
5. The movement away from correctional treatment will reverse after 1990, but the new emphasis will be on economic rehabilitation rather than psychological rehabilitation.
6. Due to the increased use of community corrections programs and other correctional innovations, there will be few offenders remaining in large fortress prisons by the year 2000 other than those violent offenders who are judged to be too dangerous to be released into the community. These individuals will be incarcerated for long terms, so the average term served will be longer than in 1980.
7. The level of prisoner violence and other victimizing behavior will decrease due to the elimination of nonviolent prisoners from maximum security institutions. The present levels of violence are not due so much to the presence of violent offenders as to their being mixed with nonviolent offenders who are easy victims. If the weak are removed, violence will decrease because the strong rarely attempt to victimize the strong. The economics of victimization do not make that a rational investment of effort and reputation.
8. One legacy of the justice model of corrections is that prisoners will be treated more like citizens in the year 2000 than they are in 1980. They will work at jobs similar to jobs that exist in the free community, and they will be paid wages that are much closer to the community scale than they are at

present. Their civil rights will be more fully protected, and they will not be systematically subjected to any verifiable forms of abuse or misuse. They will serve their time in boring decency punctuated by hard work.

9. Prisons and jails will buy even more community services in the year 2000 than they did in 1980. As the needs of a given population change, it is easy to change contracts with community agencies, but once the services are being provided in-house, civil service regulations make it almost impossible to make major modifications in existing patterns of service delivery. Utilizing increased levels of services provided by community agencies will increase the permeability of prisons and jails. There will also be other factors increasing permeability, including extensive availability of telephones, much more liberal visiting regulations, social work support systems for the family members of prisoners, and a wide variety of work-release and training-release programs.

10. The classification of prisoners will be much improved, and will combine offense patterns, background characteristics, and psychodynamic assessments of prisoner personalities. Treatment will be more individualized than it is at present, and the impact of treatment programs on prisoners will be carefully monitored and used as one indication of readiness to move to programs and settings with higher levels of freedom. Risk estimation will become increasingly accurate as a greater number of factors are identified and entered into prediction equations used to estimate the risk to the community in releasing offenders or in moving them from one custody level to another.

11. There will be experimentation with new kinds of institutions, many of them specializing in one type of offender and providng only the kinds of programs and services needed by that offender group. Experimentation with new institutions and programs will be aided by a worldwide increase in cross-cultural communication.

Community Corrections Programs

Points 10 and 11 above apply to community corrections programs as well as institutional programs. In addition, there are six predictions that are specific to community corrections.

12. County correctional systems and correctional services provided by private agencies will increase greatly between 1980 and the year 2000. State and federal correctional systems will not wither away, but their increases will be more modest than the increases in local corrections systems.

13. Experimentation with restitution, although widespread, is really just beginning in 1980. By the year 2000, restitution will be a much more significant part of correctional arrangements. Community service activities contributed by offenders are a type of restitution—to the state and community agencies rather than to individual victims. These activities will also increase greatly by the year 2000.

14. The total use of parole will decrease, partially because of the decreasing proportion of offenders who will be sentenced to incarceration, and partially

because of the effects of the justice model of corrections. Those parole functions that will remain will be more service-oriented than they are at present. Parole supervision in a law enforcement sense is likely to be carried out by police officers in order to avoid the contradiction in roles that occurs when a parole officer is asked to be both a counselor and an officer of the law. Probation will increase, and will also become more service-oriented. Because there will be no essential difference between probation and parole services as delivered in the field, the number of jurisdictions retaining separate probation and parole officers will decrease as they merge these functions under one roof.

15. One of the community service functions that will expand steadily between 1980 and the year 2000 is the provision of services to the families of prisoners (a presently neglected area). This effort will be aimed at keeping wives and husbands in contact, and also keeping children in contact with their parents. There will be serious attempts to deal with the psychological and social problems that arise when a family member is incarcerated. Part of this new emphasis on services to the families of prisoners will be due to concern about their welfare, since they are also currently being punished even though they have committed no crime. These services will also be designed to have positive effects upon offenders by keeping them more involved with life outside the prison walls. It will be part of a major emphasis on the reintegration rather than the punishment of institutionalized offenders.

16. Self-help groups of ex-prisoners will continue to grow, and will receive increased financial support from private and public sources. Ex-prisoners will become politically active and forge a new alliance with liberals to campaign not only for prison reform but also for changes in community conditions that currently hamper the reintegration of released offenders.

17. Correctional agencies serving offenders and ex-offenders in the community will also become involved in delivering preventive services to adults and juveniles who are in danger of coming into contact with the criminal justice system proper. This will greatly increase the span of social control exercised by these agencies.

Correctional Staff Members

18. All correctional positions will professionalize between 1980 and the year 2000, and this will increase the quality of services delivered to correctional clients. The educational standards for hiring and the in-service training required of position occupants will be raised. Correctional staff salaries, which have lagged far behind law enforcement salaries in recent years, will begin to close the gap, but will not have reached parity with law enforcement salaries by the year 2000.

19. There will be an increased use of women and minority staff members in all areas of corrections. Paraprofessionals will also be increasingly used, and it will be found that they can provide significant services to correctional clients. Ex-prisoners will be an important group of paraprofessionals, but by no means the only group to be brought into the correctional system by this route.

20. Role distinctions between custody and treatment staff began to merge on an experimental basis in American corrections as early as the 1940s, and there has been a continued but extremely slow trend toward merging custody and treatment functions since that time. By the year 2000, roles will have been substantially merged in all treatment-oriented facilities, and also in many of the remaining maximum security prisons. The merging of treatment functions into the job descriptions of correctional officers will be one of the strategies that enables them to professionalize.

Correctional Management

21. Correctional management will become increasingly systematic. Prison administrators will become executives on a par with the best administrative talent that is available in other human service agencies and systems. They will be well-trained and educated. Only in a few isolated areas will politics have anything at all to do with the appointment of correctional managers in correctional institutions and community corrections agencies.

22. The universities and corrections professionals will coordinate their activities more closely in the future than they have in the past. Correctional managers will be more receptive to university research because of their increased education and sophistication. Academic researchers will produce information that is more useful to correctional administrators. Following the lead of disciplines such as social work and nursing, correctional research will become distinctly practice-oriented at the same time that it will achieve higher levels of scientific rigor.

23. Court decisions and the continued federal funding of state and local correctional programs will have the effect of increasing the standardization of correctional practices by the year 2000.

24. The use of computerized information systems will become common in all but the smallest correctional agencies. These systems will permit the matching of client needs with available spaces in employment and other programs. They will also display risk scores and other decision-making criteria. Computerized correctional information systems will be tied into law enforcement and computerized court information systems so that the entire criminal justice system will be able to share information more effectively.

25. Ongoing evaluation procedures will be a part of most correctional programs by the year 2000. Feedback from these evaluation studies will be used to modify programs in order to make them more effective. Recidivism rates and personality and behavioral changes by correctional clients will be used more for internal monitoring than for external evaluation. External evaluation will be dominated by cost–benefit analysis. When recidivism measures are used, they will be more sensitive than the current yes or no, failure or success measure that is used in most studies. The seriousness of new crimes committed and the length of crime-free time in the community are two of the many refinements of the measurement of recidivism that will be used in recidivism studies.

YOUR FUTURE IN CORRECTIONS

The National Manpower Survey of the Criminal Justice System[5] has projected an increase in correctional employees of 60 percent between 1974 and 1985. The most rapid growth is expected to be in probation and parole agencies, with substantial growth in adult institutions and only very modest growth in juvenile institutions. These projections are only for public employees. They do not include any of the community agencies that are supported by private funds, nor do they include those agencies which, although private, obtain most of their funding from service provision contracts with state corrections units.

Looking at the manpower projections in terms of position types, the greatest increase will be in managerial personnel. This is followed by custodial officers, treatment specialists, and parole and probation officers. All of these groups of workers were projected to increase between 50 and 70 percent between 1974 and 1985. Child care workers were projected to increase only 10 percent. The reason why the number of probation and parole officers is not expected to increase as much as the total staffing of probation and parole offices is because of the projected high rate of growth in supporting positions in these agencies, including paraprofessionals, clericals, and administrative personnel.

The Manpower Survey has also projected a substantial increase in the use of community-based facilities by 1985 (and we predict that this increase will continue through the year 2000). Since community-based facilities such as pre-release centers and halfway houses are much more likely to be privately owned, this means that the expansion in private correctional positions is likely to be even greater than the expansion in public correctional positions in the years to come. These statistics suggest that corrections is a major growth industry in the United States, and an excellent area for young people to head toward as a life's career.

Job Opportunities Available within Corrections

The fact that most corrections officers do not have college degrees may tend to discourage college students from thinking of corrections as a career. Although an increasing number of correctional systems will require at least a two-year junior college degree for recruitment in the future, this still does not make the job appear very attractive to many college students. It is true that college graduates can obtain higher salaries elsewhere. The main reason why a college graduate might wish to become a correctional officer is that he or she desires to gain two or three years of basic experience before moving rapidly up the career ladder into correctional administration. Correctional officers with college degrees tend to be promoted much more rapidly than officers with high school diplomas. Custody staff hierarchies almost always promote from within, so the only way to become an administrator in the hierarchy is to start at the bottom and suffer a few years of modest salaries while gaining the experience that, when combined with the educational background already achieved, will equip the individual to do well on civil service promotion examinations.

Probation and parole officers are already more professionalized than correctional officers. College degrees are generally required for these positions, and the more progressive states will begin to require master's degrees in the next decade. Probation and parole organizations tend to allow individual officers a greater amount of freedom and decision-making authority than prison organizations. Salaries are also higher for probation and parole officers than for correctional officers. The disadvantage of being a probation or parole officer as compared with being a correctional officer is that students with college degrees are less likely to stand out, and therefore less likely to be rapidly promoted than they might be in institutional work.

There are a number of specialized positions within correctional institutions that require college degrees, and, in some cases, master's degrees. These include counseling, teaching, business management, dietary planning, certain positions in the medical facilities of the institution, the heads of therapeutic programs, and middle-level management positions such as information officers and volunteer coordinators. More technical psychological assessments and medical services require a Ph.D. or an M.D.

It is common to find individuals with bachelor's degrees heading up community corrections agencies. Even in the more professionalized and larger agencies, a master's degree is usually the highest degree present among any agency staff members. As with management positions in the correctional hierarchy, it is necessary to gain some job experience at the level of counselor, house manager, or some similar position in order to be able to move into a more responsible position after two or three years. Because of the rapid expansion of community corrections programs, upward mobility can be extremely rapid. State and county programs are subject to civil service regulations, but private corrections programs vary tremendously in their hiring requirements. A persistent college graduate can be certain of finding a challenging and rewarding position if enough effort is devoted to the task of job hunting in the area of community corrections.

Local jails in urban areas are hiring an increasing number of college graduates to perform a variety of tasks ranging from correctional officer to counselor to teacher. Local school districts often hire qualified teachers to offer classes in jails and state prisons. Another local job possibility is to be hired on a project funded for a limited period of time (often three years) under a grant from a government agency or a private foundation. These positions are not as attractive to established career employees because of their temporary nature, but they are an excellent opportunity for a young college graduate who wishes to gain experience and develop a successful job record. Examples of such projects include a special assessment of the educational and vocational needs of jail inmates, a community involvement project for adolescent drug users, and a restitution or community service project for misdemeanants.

There is one remaining area of correctional employment that is available to college graduates. This is employment in correctional administration at the federal, state, or regional level. Aside from general administrative jobs, there are specialized positions in these agencies having to do with computer programming and data analysis, program evaluation and program planning.

These positions are all extremely exciting in that they give recently graduated students a chance to have a major impact on the delivery of correctional services. Salaries are generally higher in these positions than in other entry level correctional system positions for college graduates. The primary disadvantage of these positions is that they provide very limited opportunities to become involved in direct service delivery. College students who wish to work with correctional clients, and who enjoy the personal contact that they have with clients in counseling positions, may not find information processing, evaluating, and planning to be personally fulfilling.

The Preparation Necessary for Correctional Work

What should a student who is interested in going into corrections as a career choose for a major? The American Correctional Association[1] recommends a wide variety of disciplines as appropriate background for a career in corrections. These disciplines include sociology, psychology, psychiatry, medicine, social work, economics, architecture, law, engineering, public administration, data processing, and research. In addition, criminal justice programs often offer an entire sequence of courses on corrections. The exact mix of courses depends on what area of corrections a student leans toward. Students interested in a career in counseling will want to take a great many courses in psychology, sociology, and social work. The makeup of departments varies from university to university, and so does the mix of courses offered in each individual department. In some universities, the criminal justice department offers the corrections courses, but these courses are offered in the sociology department or the social work department of other universities. Some professors have had experiences in corrections that make them particularly valuable as instructors for students interested in a career in corrections. It is usually possible to arrange to take an independent study course with such professors regardless of the department in which they teach.

It is important to find out what the hiring and civil service promotion regulations are in the state in which you intend to work, since this may determine your choice of major. If you wish to become a counselor in a state that requires a social work degree in order to become an institutional counselor, then that dictates your choice of major. Students who are interested in becoming teachers in correctional institutions will probably have to become certified, so they need to work closely with the department of education in their institution.

For the student who is interested in a career in corrections, there is something that is perhaps even more important than the choice of a college curriculum. This is the choice of part-time jobs and volunteer positions that are obtained during the college years. Field placement courses and internships may be available through criminal justice and social work programs, and these are equally important. The careful student can arrange three or four different correctional experiences during the four years of a college career. These experiences are not only helpful in determining a final choice of specialization within corrections: they also produce recommendation letters that will be exceedingly useful in obtaining a job after graduation. There is nothing worse than approaching the job market with a portfolio that contains nothing more than letters that have been written by college professors.

ADVANTAGES OF A CAREER
IN CORRECTIONS

We have already alluded to the personal pleasure that many individuals gain from working closely with people. This is one of the reasons why so many college graduates go into teaching and the human services even though these positions pay rather modest salaries. Meaningfulness and fullness in life come primarily through human relationships. It is entirely possible to gain most of the human contact that one requires from one's family and friends, but many individuals also feel the need to have a job that includes a heavy component of human contact. Others feel the need to lend a helping hand to those who are temporarily in need. Correctional work, like social work, is an ideal occupation for such people. Another benefit of correctional work is the cross-cultural contact that it invariably brings. Experiences with people who have basically different values from oneself promote personal growth and development.

We have already mentioned the advantages of the possibilities for rapid promotion in most areas of correctional work. Promotional possibilities for students with college degrees in public corrections are considerable, and they are probably even higher in private corrections. One factor to consider in choosing between private and public correctional work is that public positions generally have the protection of civil service regulations. They are career positions which, within the limitations of published regulations, become lifetime positions after a brief probationary period. The fringe benefits associated with these positions tend to be considerably higher than the fringe benefits associated with positions in private agencies. These include extensive health care, insurance, support for specialized training and continuing education, and, in some states, early retirement with a very generous pension. It is not unknown for a correctional official to retire after 20 or 30 years of service in one state and then take a similar position in a different state, drawing a double salary for the remainder of his or her career.

SUMMARY

Most of the views of the future of corrections that have been presented by scholars and practitioners do not predict the future: they prescribe what the authors would like to see occur in the future. A small handful of writers have made nonprescriptive predictions of future corrections, and the employment needs of the correctional industry have been projected by the National Manpower Survey of the Criminal Justice System. Our own prediction for the future includes worsening economic conditions and an increase in criminal justice system funding and activities. Correctional institutions, community corrections programs, and other elements of the corrections system will be larger and more complex in the year 2000 than they are at present. This will provide numerous opportunities for jobs and also for the rapid promotion of college students who "get in on the ground floor" and obtain the necessary on-the-job experience that, when combined with their college education, will allow them to make rapid progress in their careers.

Positions available in correctional systems include correctional officers, probation and parole officers, counselors, teachers, business managers, dieticians, a number of medical positions, unit heads, and a variety of other administrative positions in institutions ranging from local agencies to state and federal central correctional offices. There will be significant growth in those administrative positions having to do with computer programming and data analysis, program evaluation, and program planning. Students interested in pursuing careers in corrections may major in a variety of disciplines, including sociology, psychology, psychiatry, medicine, social work, economics, architecture, law, engineering, public administration, data processing, and criminal justice. Careers in corrections offer many opportunities for personal growth, career development, meaningful human interaction, and financial security.

REFERENCES

1. American Correctional Association. "Careers in Corrections." College Park, MD, no date.
2. Carter, Robert M., Richard A. McGee, and E. Kim Nelson. *Corrections in America.* Philadelphia: J.B. Lippincott, 1975.
3. Fogel, David. *". . . We Are The Living Proof. . ." The Justice Model for Corrections.* Cincinnati, OH: W.H. Anderson, 1975.
4. Glaser, Daniel. *Crime in the City.* New York: Harper and Row, 1970.
5. Law Enforcement Assistance Administration. *The National Manpower Survey of the Criminal Justice System. Volume III. Corrections.* Washington, D.C.: Government Printing Office, 1978.
6. McGee, Richard A. "What's Past is Prologue." *The Annals of the American Academy of Political and Social Science,* 381 (January 1969):1–10.
7. Morris, Norval. *The Future of Imprisonment.* Chicago: University of Chicago Press, 1974.
8. Sommer, Robert. *The End of Imprisonment.* New York: Oxford University Press, 1976.

Appendix—Scholarly Periodicals in the Field of Corrections

Abstracts on Criminology and Penology

Abstracts drawn from all major criminology and corrections publications are printed in this journal. In addition to its general usefulness as a reference source, *Abstracts on Criminology and Penology* is uniquely useful in its publication of foreign-language journals and books that are not usually available to American readers.

American Criminal Law Review

This is a general law review that provides commentaries on a wide variety of criminal law subjects. It occasionally contains an article of interest to students of corrections.

American Journal of Correction, *See* Corrections
Today

American Journal of Orthopsychiatry

Articles about correctional treatment and conditions in correctional institutions for juveniles appear in this publication from time to time. It also contains articles about the background and characteristics of various clinical groups of juveniles that have a high probability of becoming involved in the criminal justice system.

American Journal of Sociology

Primarily a journal devoted to sociological theory and research, the *American Journal of Sociology* publishes an article of interest to students in corrections once every few years.

American Sociological Review

Like the *American Journal of Sociology,* this periodical prints an article in the area of corrections only once every several years. Articles are generally related to correctional administration rather than to treatment programs.

Australian and New Zealand Journal of Criminology

A number of articles on corrections in Australia and New Zealand have appeared in this journal in recent years. Articles on Maori offenders provide a basis of comparison for studies of the criminal justice system contacts of American Indian and ethnic Hawaiian offenders.

British Journal of Criminology

Primarily a theoretical criminological journal, the *British Journal of Criminology* publishes numerous articles on corrections in Great Britain. It is the major English-language journal containing information about corrections in Europe.

California Youth Authority Quarterly

Most state correctional organizations publish informal newsletters, but the California Youth Authority sponsors a professional journal that contains correctional articles of general interest as well as descriptions of California programs and evaluations. It is particularly valuable to have a publication concentrating on juveniles in California corrections because the California Youth Authority has been a major innovator in juvenile correctional work.

Canadian Journal of Criminology and Corrections

Much of knowledge about corrections in Canada comes from this journal, which contains many articles of interest to American corrections students.

Corrections Compendium

A monthly newsletter, this publication presents surveys of current conditions in correctional institutions based on questionnaires mailed to all state correctional systems. It therefore provides current data on correctional topics that are often impossible to obtain elsewhere.

Corrections Digest

Another national newsletter. *Corrections Digest* is published bi-weekly by Washington Crime New Services to keep corrections professionals informed of the latest developments in their field.

Corrections Magazine

The field of corrections did not have a general popular magazine until *Corrections Magazine* began publication in 1974. Profusely illustrated, it covers topics of interest to corrections professionals and the general public in nontechnical language.

Corrections Today

This is the official journal of the American Correctional Association, and replaces the *American Journal of Correction,* which began publication in 1920. It contains few reports of social science studies, but a great many general commentaries and practical articles by corrections professionals.

Corrective and Social Psychiatry and Journal of Behavior Technology Methods and Therapy

Though this publication contains articles about the treatment of institutionalized individuals, both criminal and otherwise, a number of these articles describe or evaluate treatment programs in correctional settings.

Crime and Delinquency

The National Council on Crime and Delinquency is a major force in the movement for correctional reform. *Crime and Delinquency* contains many articles on subjects such as capital punishment, deinstitutionalization, sexism and racism in the criminal justice system, and alternatives to institutionalization.

Crime and Delinquency Literature, See Criminal Justice Abstracts

Crime et/and Justice

This Canadian journal publishes articles in both French and English. While it is a general criminology journal, it contains articles on correctional subjects from time to time.

Crime and Social Justice

Crime and Social Justice is the primary periodical for the publication of articles on radical criminology, or the "new criminology," as it is sometimes called. It provides critical interpretations of correctional and other criminal justice system activities that are rarely seen in other journals. It is particularly strong on historical studies.

Crime, Punishment and Corrections

This journal, which is written in English and Afrikaans, includes articles on corrections in South Africa.

Criminal Justice Abstracts

Formerly known as *Crime and Delinquency Literature, Criminal Justice Abstracts* annotates articles, books and reports in corrections and other areas of the criminal justice system. Along with *Abstracts on Criminology and Penology*, this is an appropriate starting place for a student desiring to research any topic in corrections.

Criminal Justice and Behavior

Since 1974, this journal has published articles that take a psychological approach to criminal behavior and its treatment. It is the official publication of the American Association of Correctional Psychologists.

Criminal Justice Review

An experimental publication, the *Georgia Journal of Corrections*, became the *Criminal Justice Review* in 1976. This journal gives particular emphasis to articles dealing with more than one aspect of the criminal justice system at once.

Criminology

Criminology is the official publication of the American Society of Criminology, and contains scientific articles on criminological topics. One or two articles per issue are usually on corrections, and many of the other articles relate to corrections in that they explain some aspect of criminal behavior.

Federal Probation

As its title indicates, this periodical concentrates on probation and other community corrections topics. Institutional corrections and general criminal justice systems articles are also published. It is produced by the Administrative Office of the United States Courts with the intention of stimulating professional growth and development among corrections workers in the United States.

Howard Journal of Penology and Crime Prevention

This British journal was founded in 1921, and is unashamedly dedicated to correctional reform. It is the official journal of the Howard League for Penal Reform, whose name commemorates the great British reformer John Howard.

Indian Journal of Criminology

More social science journals are produced in India than in any other Third World nation and they all appear in English. Correctional subjects are given heavy coverage in this journal, which is the official publication of the Indian Society of Criminology. Juvenile deliquency and its treatment are also well represented among articles in this publication.

International Journal of Criminology and Penology

One of the few journals concentrating on international materials, this periodical produced a number of important contributions to the correctional literature during its short seven-year history. It has now been replaced by the *International Journal of the Sociology of Law.*

International Journal of Offender Therapy and Comparative Criminology

Unlike other journals focusing on the treatment of offenders, the *International Journal of Offender Therapy and Comparative Criminology* regularly publishes articles from Third World nations. It is published in England by the Association for the Psychiatric Treatment of Offenders and includes summaries in English, French, German, and Spanish.

International Journal of the Sociology of Law

Although this journal has a broader focus than the *International Journal of Criminology and Penology,* which it replaced, it is expected to include occasional articles on corrections in the future.

International Review of Criminal Policy

Articles in English, French, and Spanish are published in this journal which appears from time to time under the sponsorship of the United Nations. It is always international in scope and usually contains a number of articles or notes that are relevant to corrections.

Issues in Criminology

Originated in 1965 at the School of Criminology, University of California, Berkeley, *Issues in Criminology* consistently published articles that were critical of the existing criminal justice system until it recently merged with *Crime and Social Justice.*

Jail Administration Digest

One of the newsletters published by Washington Crime News Services, this publication briefly notes numerous developments relevant to jail administrators in each monthly issue.

Jericho

This is the official newsletter of the National Moratorium on Prison Construction, which is a project of the Unitarian Universalist Service Committee. It publicizes victories and campaigns in the movement to stop the construction of additional correctional facilities and to humanize conditions in those facilities already in existence.

Journal of Correctional Education

This journal is an expanded newsletter which contains a few articles in each issue, most of which have practical application for correctional educators.

Journal of Criminal Justice

The Journal of Criminal Justice is the official publication of the Academy of Criminal Justice Sciences, which encompasses all parts of the criminal justice system. There is usually at least one correctional article in each issue of this social science journal.

Journal of Criminal Law and Criminology

Previously known as the *Journal of Criminal Law, Criminology and Police Science,* this quarterly was one of the first criminal justice publications to come into being in the United States. Although the bulk of each issue is used for criminal law, one section is reserved for criminology, and this section often contains correctional articles of the highest quality. Some of the law notes are also on corrections cases.

Journal of Homosexuality

Although this journal is not associated with corrections, criminal justice or criminology, it sometimes contains articles about correctional institutions because of the prevalence of homosexuality in these facilities.

Journal of Psychiatry and Law

Applications of psychiatry to legal debates are featured in this journal. Articles in this publication occasionally touch on corrections.

Journal of Research on Crime and Delinquency

The *Journal of Research on Crime and Delinquency* is issued semi-annually by the National Council on Crime and Delinquency. Unlike its sister publication, *Crime and Delinquency,* this journal concentrates on highly technical scientific studies of crime and delinquency.

Justice Assistance News

The recent reorganization of Justice Services previously located within the Law Enforcement Assistance Administration led to the renaming of the *LEAA Newsletter* as *Justice Assistance News.* This monthly magazine summarizes the results of research projects and programs funded by LEAA and related federal agencies.

Juvenile Justice

Although most of the articles in this journal, which is sponsored by the National Council of Juvenile and Family Court Judges, do not deal with corrections, juvenile correctional programs and legal issues relating to juvenile incarceration are occasionally discussed.

Juvenile Justice Digest

This bi-monthly newsletter is one of the family of newsletters published by Washington Crime News Service. Like the other periodicals in this series, it provides practical rather than theoretical or research-oriented information for professionals in the correctional industry. This particular newsletter concentrates on juveniles who are in contact with the criminal justice system.

LEAA Newsletter, *See*Justice Assistance News

New England Journal on Prison Law

A semi-annual publication of the New England School of Law, this journal gives readers an in-depth understanding of the issues, court decisions, and newly enacted laws that impact correctional practice.

Offender Rehabilitation

This journal presents articles on all aspects of offender rehabilitation and is particularly noteworthy for the attention that it has given to community corrections in recent years.

Prison Journal

The *Prison Journal* was first published by the Pennsylvania Prison Society in 1921. Although it has continued to be modest in size, generally nontechnical in approach, and is issued only semi-annually, it has published a number of important articles on institutional corrections over the years.

Prison Law Monitor

A technical newsletter, the *Prison Law Monitor* allows correctional administrators to keep fully up-to-date on legal developments that are relevant to correctional practice. In addition, feature articles survey correctional issues from a legal viewpoint.

Prison Service Journal

This quarterly has been published for prison service officers and other employees of the Prison Department Home Office, Great Britain, since 1960.

Probation and Parole

Probation and Parole is an annual publication of the New York State Probation and Parole Association. Written primarily for probation and parole officers, its articles are of value to those who are interested in noninstitutional correctional programs nation-wide as well as in New York State.

Probation Journal

This quarterly focuses on probation and other correctional issues in Great Britain. It occupies a place in British correctional literature that is similar to the place occupied by *Federal Probation* in the United States.

Social Defense

Social Defense is a quarterly publication of the National Institute of Social Defense in India. Its primary areas of interest are juvenile delinquency and juvenile corrections.

Social Forces

Social Forces is primarily a sociological journal, but it occasionally includes an article on corrections.

Social Problems

This journal is the official organ of the Society for the Study of Social Problems, which has always had a strong interest in correctional matters. Some of the classic articles in the correctional literature have appeared in *Social Problems* during the past several decades, although there has been a recent trend away from publishing correctional articles.

Victimology

A general social science journal, *Victimology* occasionally publishes articles about victimization in correctional institutions or in other settings relevant to the student of corrections.

Author Index

Subject Index